The Arabic Literary Heritage describes a cultural tradition which is unfamiliar to many, that of literary texts in Arabic from unknown beginnings in about the fifth century AD to the present day. While this is a work of literary history, the organising principle is generic rather than dynastic. After introductory chapters on principles and contexts – physical, linguistic, dynastic and intellectual – there are chapters devoted to the Qur'ān as literature, poetry, bellettristic prose, drama, and criticism. Within each chapter the emphasis is on the texts themselves and on those who created and commented on them, but there is also an awareness of recent theoretical and critical approaches. The volume as a whole, which also includes a guide to further reading, makes a major non-Western literary tradition newly accessible to students and scholars of the West.

THE ARABIC LITERARY HERITAGE

THE ARABIC LITERARY HERITAGE

The development of its genres and criticism

ROGER ALLEN

University of Pennsylvania

CAMBRIDGE
UNIVERSITY PRESS

PUBLISHED BY THE PRESS SYNDICATE OF THE UNIVERSITY OF CAMBRIDGE
The Pitt Building, Trumpington Street, Cambridge CB2 1RP, United Kingdom

CAMBRIDGE UNIVERSITY PRESS
The Edinburgh Building, Cambridge CB2 2RU, United Kingdom
40 West 20th Street, New York, NY 10011-4211, USA
10 Stamford Road, Oakleigh, Melbourne 3166, Australia

First published 1998

Printed in the United Kingdom at the University Press, Cambridge

Typeset in 11/12.5 pt. Baskerville [VN]

A catalogue record for this book is available from the British Library

Library of Congress cataloguing in publication data

Allen, Roger M. A.
The Arabic literary heritage / Roger Allen.
p. cm.
Includes bibliographical references and index.
ISBN 0 521 48066 3 (hardback)
1. Arabic literature–History and criticism. I. Title.
PJ7510. A44 1998 97-27113CIP
892'.709–DC21

ISBN 0 521 48066 3 hardback

Contents

Preface

> The scholar who does not constantly limit himself to a narrow field of specialization and to a world of concepts held in common with a small circle of like-minded colleagues, lives in the midst of a tumult of impressions and claims on him; for the scholar to do justice to these is almost impossible. Still, it is becoming increasingly unsatisfactory to limit oneself to only one field of specialization. . . On the other hand, there are fields of specialization that have become so widely various that their mastery has become the task of a lifetime.
>
> Erich Auerbach, *Centennial Review*, 13 : 1 (Winter 1969), 8–9.

This book may be considered as further confirmation of the fact that two negatives can have positive significance. The beginning of the project can be traced to a letter that I received from Dr Katharina Brett of Cambridge University Press. Pointing out that she had been making inquiries as to the need for a single-volume historical survey of Arabic literature, she wondered if I shared the view of many scholars in the field whom she had consulted to the effect that such an idea was not feasible. My reply was that I did not agree. Many years later, I can look back on that exchange as marking the beginning of the planning stage for this lengthy and complex project.

As a scholar in the field of Arabic literature studies and the teacher of a university-level course on Arabic literary history, I had, of course, long been considering the issues arising from the ways in which the relatively small library of works on the subject that is currently available in English and other European languages is of limited use to students attending universities at the end of the twentieth century and almost inaccessible – in the many senses of that term – to a more general reading public. This seemed especially the case in a period when, within the general academic field of Comparative Literature, an increased emphasis on literary theory and critical approaches had almost inevitably impinged – albeit at a less phrenetic pace – upon the study of non-Western literary traditions as well. Such a process had certainly influenced my own research and teaching. In a desire to encourage incipient scholars to address themselves to the issues involved I had often made use of essay questions in the qualifying examinations for students in my university's post-graduate programme to ask them both to comment on the merits of previous attempts at writing a history of Arabic literature and to prepare an organising matrix for a new work on the topic. I am pleased to acknowledge here that the principles I have applied in preparing this work are a reflection of many classroom debates and essay responses, as well as much profitable discussion with academic colleagues. With its publication my former students are fully entitled to feel a certain *schadenfreude* in that the work involved has obviously been a case of 'the biter' being firmly 'bit'. During the course of preparing this book, some of my colleagues in Arabic literature studies, that 'small circle of like-minded colleagues' perhaps, have communicated to me, with varying degrees of scepticism and anxiety, their continuing belief that the project is intrinsically impossible or, at least, unwise. While this book is clear evidence of the fact that I have not heeded the basic thrust of their advice, I would still like to acknowledge the challenge that their opinions have presented to me and the ways in which their objections have forced me at several stages to clarify general objectives and points of detail. However, I must also express my special gratitude to that set of colleagues who served as readers of the initial and very experimental outline of this project. It was the extremely positive nature of their responses which really provided me with the incentive to start the lengthy planning and writing process.

This work has been written without resorting to footnotes. I have therefore not had the opportunity to acknowledge in a formal way the debt which I owe to numerous colleagues whose critical studies of the Arabic literary tradition are reflected in the pages that follow. I can only express the hope that the citation of major sources in English that are listed in the Guide to Further Reading will give some idea of the extent to which I am grateful for their insights. I might perhaps take a leaf out of the book of the Middle East's primary jokester, Juḥa, and suggest that those who know what those sources of my inspiration are might tell those who do not. Several of my colleagues have done me the great service of reading portions of this work in advance of its publication. I would like to take this opportunity to thank them all for their wise counsel and gentle correction, while absolving them of all responsibility for the result: Peter Heath, Salma Khadra Jayyusi,

Hilary Kilpatrick, Everett Rowson, Yasir Saqr, Michael Sells, and William Smyth.

I would like to conclude by expressing my heartfelt thanks to the staff of Cambridge University Press. It was Dr Katharina Brett who, by initially asking me the seemingly innocent question as to whether I thought this project was possible, provided me with the instigation to plan and then to write this book. She saw the process through its initial stages, and Josie Dixon and Linda Bree have since offered much needed encouragement and advice. I owe a particular debt of thanks to Patricia Salazar who has edited the manuscript. Her eagle eye has spotted a number of infelicities and obscurities, and the resulting manuscript has much benefited from her careful ministrations. In view of the broad scope of the volume, it is particularly important that I finish with a traditional but crucial act of absolution, by stressing that I remain solely responsible for the errors of fact or judgement that no doubt remain.

Note on translation, transliteration, and further reading

A few words need to be said about various aspects of the text and the conventions that it uses. Firstly, translation: except where indicated in the text itself, the translations in the book are my own.

Secondly, on transliteration: the literary works that are the focus of this volume have been composed in Arabic. Thus, in discussing them in English, a system of transliteration is needed whereby the written symbols of Arabic are represented from the repertoire of the English alphabet. Scholars working in Arabic studies have devised a number of different systems for doing this, in part reflecting the conventions of writing and pronunciation within their own language systems. In English scholarly discourse on this field, the system of transliteration that is most widespread is the one devised by the Library of Congress in the United States, also used with minor adjustments by the British Library. The basic outlines of this system are used in this book.

The Library of Congress system uses a written symbol from the English alphabet to replicate an equivalent written symbol in Arabic. It makes no attempt to reproduce exactly the way in which the Arabic words are pronounced. Thus, while the Arabic names and titles transliterated in this book will give some idea of how the written symbols will sound, the equivalence is not (and cannot be) anything approaching complete. Beyond the usual English alphabet set, two other symbols are used: the left-facing single quotation-mark (ʾ) represents the Arabic glottal stop (called *hamzah*), such as is represented by the hyphen in the word re-enter; and the superscript c (ʿ) represents a sound for which English has no equivalent, but which linguists term a pharyngeal plosive (the name of the Arabic phoneme is *ʿayn*). Furthermore, the Arabic language makes use of several written symbols and pronounced sounds that are not found in the English language system. To represent these sounds and symbols in transliteration, the Library of Congress system makes use of a series of supplementary markings (usually called diacritics) in order to indicate the presence of these intrinsically Semitic phenomena: dots under certain consonants to indicate that they are emphatic and elongation signs (macrons) over vowels to show that their pronunciation time is longer than that of the short vowels.

Lastly, regarding the Guide to Further Reading, bearing in mind the nature and breadth of the subject-matter of this work, it is obviously impossible to provide anything approaching a complete bibliography on any topic or even sub-topic; I might note that the reasons lie not only in the bulk of what would result, but the extreme inaccessibility of some of the sources involved. The Guide to Further Reading, which is divided into sections relating to the various chapters, is thus intended to give samples of work on the particular genre and subject involved; it is my hope that readers who find their interests aroused by this book may use such studies and translations as a trigger to yet further investigations.

Chronology

WORLD

Year	Historical events/people*	Literary events/people†
400		
500		
533	Justinian rules in Constantinople	
600		
624	T'ang dynasty in China	

Note: The date assigned to individual authors is, to the extent known, the date of death.
* Names are listed to coincide as closely as possible with dates of death.
† Names listed to the left are those who may be considered as 'creative writers'. Those listed to the right are critics, historians, and other commentators on the literary and cultural tradition.

MIDDLE EASTERN

Year	Historical events/people[*]	Literary events/people[†]
400		
500		
		al-Muhalhil
533		Imru al-Qays
c. 570	birth of Muḥammad	al-Shanfarā (?)
		Taʾabbaṭa Sharran (?)
		al-Muraqqish
		Ṭarafah
600		
		ʿAmr ibn Kulthūm
		al-Ḥarith ibn Ḥillizah
		ʿAmr ibn Qamīʾah
		ʿAdī ibn Zayd
		Zuhayr ibn Abī Sulmā
		ʿAntarah
622	*hijrah* from Mecca to Medina	Durayd ibn al-Ṣimmah
632	death of Muḥammad	Al-Aʿshā
635	capture of Damascus by Muslims	
636	Battle of Qadisiyyah; defeat of Sāsānī (Persian) army	al-Khansāʾ
637–44	conquests of Syria, Iraq, Egypt	
640	establishment of al-Kūfah and al-Baṣrah as garrison cities in Iraq	Qays ibn Mulawwaḥ (?)
650	standardisation of Qurʾānic text	
656	murder of Caliph ʿUthmān	

WORLD

Year	Historical events/people*	Literary events/people†
700		
725	Bede introduces Christian calendar	
732	Battle of Tours	Beowulf
800		
	Charlemagne crowned Emperor	
820	Norman raids on Gaul	

MIDDLE EASTERN

Year	Historical events/people*	Literary events/people†
657	Battle of Ṣiffīn	
661	assassination of Caliph ʿAlī;	Labīd
	beginning of Umawī dynasty	al-Ḥutayʾah
670	establishment of Qayrawān in Tunisia	Ḥassān ibn Thābit
680	Battle of Karbalāʾ	
685–91	Dome of the Rock built in Jerusalem	
		Jamīl
		Laylā al-Akhyaliyyah
700		
705	building of Great Mosque in Damascus	al-ʿAjjāj
710	Ṭāriq crosses into Spain	al-Akhṭal
705–15	Capture of Bukhārā and Samarkand	
732	Battle of Tours; Charles Martel defeats Muslims	ʿUmar ibn Abī Rabīʿah
		Kuthayyir
		Jarīr
		al-Farazdaq
		al-Ṭirimmāḥ
		ʿDhū al-Rummahʾ
		al-ʿArjī
747	Beginning of ʿAbbāsī revolt in Khūrāsān	al-Walīd ibn Yazīd
750	Fall of Umawī Caliphate; ʿAbbāsī Caliphs come to power	ʿAbd al-ḥamīd al-kātib
755–1031	Umawī dynasty in Cordoba	ibn al-Muqaffaʿ
762	Foundation of Baghdād	Abū Ḥanīfah
		Abū ʿAmr ibn al-ʿAlāʾ
		Ḥammād al-Rāwiyah
		ibn Isḥāq
		Bashshār ibn Burd
		al-Mufaḍḍal al-Ḍabbī
785	Work begins on Great Mosque in Cordoba	al-Khalīl ibn Aḥmad
786–809	Caliphate of Hārūn al-Rashīd	Malik ibn Anas
		Khalaf al-Aḥmar
		Sībawayh
800		
		Rābiʿah al-ʿAdawiyyah
803	Execution of Barmakī family in Baghdād	Abū Nuwās
		ʿAbbās ibn al-Aḥnaf
		Ibrāhīm al-Mawṣilī

WORLD

Year	Historical events/people*	Literary events/people†
853	Book printed in China	
900		

MIDDLE EASTERN

Year	Historical events/people*	Literary events/people†
827	Caliph al-Ma'mūn declares Muʿtazilī doctrine to be orthdoxy; conquest of Sicily	al-Shāfiʿī
		Muslim ibn al-Walīd
832	Foundation of Bayt al-Ḥikmah library in Baghdād	Abū al-Atāhiyah
		al-Aṣmaʿī
		ibn Hishām
		Ibrāhīm ibn al-Mahdī
		al-Kindī
836	Foundation of Samarrā' as ʿAbbāsī capital	Aḥmad ibn Ḥanbal
		Abū Tammām
		ibn Sallām al-Jumaḥī
		al-Khwārizmī
		Aḥmad ibn Ḥanbal
		Isḥāq al-Mawṣilī
		Ziryāb
		Dhū al-nūn al-Miṣrī
869–83	Zanj rebellion	al-Jāḥiẓ
		ibn Qutaybah
		al-Mubarrad
871	Sack of al-Baṣrah by Zanj forces	al-Bukhārī
		al-Kindī
		al-Balādhurī
		ibn al-Rūmī
		al-Buḥturī
		ibn Abī al-Dunyā
		ibn Abī Ṭāhir Ṭayfūr
900		
		Thaʿlab
		al-Yaʿqūbī
901	Establishment of Zaydī state in Yemen	ibn al-Muʿtazz
908	ibn al-Muʿtazz is caliph for one day	
909	Fāṭimī caliphate in Tunisia	
922	execution of mystic, al-Ḥallāj	al-Ṭabarī
		al-Rāzī
		Qudāmah ibn Jaʿfar
		ibn ʿAbd Rabbihi
945	Būyids assume control in Baghdād	al-Ashʿarī
		al-Mutanabbī
		al-Fārābī
		al-Masʿūdī
		al-Iṣṭakhrī

WORLD

Year	Historical events/people*	Literary events/people†
960	Sung dynasty in China	
1000		
1054	Byzantine Church breaks with Rome	
1066	Battle of Hastings	
1091	Normans conquer Sicily	

MIDDLE EASTERN

Year	Historical events/people*	Literary events/people†
		Abū Bakr al-Ṣūlī Muḥammad al-Niffarī al-Qālī Abū Firās Abū al-faraj al-Iṣfahānī
969	conquest of Cairo by Fāṭimī general, Jawhar	
973	foundation of al-Azhar mosque-university in Cairo	ibn Hāni' al-Āmidī al-Ṣāḥib ibn ʿAbbād ibn Ḥawqal
998–1030	Maḥmūd of Ghaznah rules in Eastern Iran	al-Marzubani al-Tanūkhī ibn al-Nadīm
1000		al-Qāḍī al-Jurjānī Abū Bakr al-Khwārizmī Abū Hilāl al-ʿAskarī Badīʿ al-zamān al-Hamadhānī al-Bāqillānī al-Sharīf al-Raḍī ibn Darrāj ibn Shuhayd Abū Ḥayyān al-Tawḥīdī
1031	collapse of Umawī Caliphate in Cordoba	Miskawayh al-Thaʿālibī ibn Khafājah ibn Sīnā al-Bīrūnī
1052	migration of Banī Hilāl across North Africa	Abū al-ʿAlā' al-Maʿarrī
1055	Saljūq Turks capture Baghdād	
1071	Battle of Manzikert: Saljūqs occupy Anatolia	ibn Ḥazm ibn Rashīq al-Qushayrī Wallādah
1085	Christians in Spain capture Toledo	ibn Zaydūn
1091	loss of Sicily to Normans	

WORLD

Year	Historical events/people*	Literary events/people†
1095	Pope Urban announces Crusade	
1100		St Anselm Abelard Archbishop Raymund Peter the Venerable Dominicus Gundisalvi Hildegard of Bingen Gerard of Cremona
1190	Third Crusade	
1200		St Francis Wolfram von Eschenbach
1233	Inquisition in Spain	
1290	Marco Polo returns to Persia from East Asia	St Thomas Aquinas
1291	End of Crusades	Roger Bacon

MIDDLE EASTERN

Year	Historical events/people*	Literary events/people†
1092	Niẓām al-Mulk murdered by Assassins	
1095	Pope Urban calls for Crusade	
1099	Crusaders capture Jerusalem	
1100		
		al-Ghazālī
		ʿUmar al-Khayyām
		al-Aʿmā al-Tuṭīlī
		ibn Ḥamdīs
1147	Second Crusade	al-Ḥarīrī
		ʿAbd al-qādir al-Jīlānī
		al-Idrīsī
		al-Zamakhsharī
1171	end of Fāṭimī Caliphate	ibn Quzmān
1174–93	reign of Ṣalāḥ al-dīn (Saladin)	
		Aḥmad al-Rifāʿī
		al-Wahrānī
		ibn Ṭufayl
1187	Crusaders defeated by Ṣalāḥ al-dīn	
		ibn Rushd
		Usāmah ibn Munqidh
		Shihāb al-dīn Yaḥyā al-Suhrawardī
1200		
		ibn al-Jawzī
		al-Qāḍī al-Fāḍil
		ʿImād al-dīn al-Iṣfahānī
		Maimonides
		ibn Jubayr
		ibn Sanāʾ al-Mulk
1219	Mongols under Jingiz Khān invade Islamic lands	
		ʿAṭṭār
		Jūdah al-Ḥarīzī
1229	Jerusalem handed over to Christians	Yāqūt
		Shihāb al-dīn ʿUmar al-Suhrawardī
1236	Christians in Spain capture Cordoba	ibn al-Fāriḍ
1248	Christians in Spain capture Seville	ibn al-ʿArabī
1250	Mamlūks come to power in Cairo	
1254	King Alfonso estabishes school in Seville	Bahāʾ al-din Zuhayr
		al-Tīfāshī
1256–60	Hūlāgū Khān leads Mongol army to Baghdād	

WORLD

Year	Historical events/people[*]	Literary events/people[†]
1300		
1305	Papacy moves to Avignon	Dante
1337	Hundred Years War between England and France	
1345	Ottomans campaign into Europe	
1348	Black Death in Europe	
1353		Boccaccio
		Petrarch
1362	Ming dynasty in China	
1387		
1400		Chaucer
		Julian of Norwich
1415	Battle of Agincourt	
1429	Joan of Arc	
1445	Gutenburg Bible	
1453	Fall of Constantinople	

MIDDLE EASTERN

Year	Historical events/people*	Literary events/people†
1258	end of ʿAbbāsī Caliphate	
1260	Battle of ʿAyn Jālūt; Mongols defeated by Mamlūks under Baybars	
1261–1520	Mamlūk dynasty rules Egypt	Jalāl al-dīn Rūmī
		al-Shushtarī
		Aḥmad al-Badawī
		ibn Mālik
		ibn Ṣayqal al-Jazarī
		al-Shābb al-Ẓarīf
		al-Bayḍāwī
1291	expulsion of Crusaders from Palestine	ibn Khallikān
		al-Būṣīrī
1300		
1303	Mongols defeated by Mamlūks in Egypt	ibn Manẓūr
		ibn Dāniyāl
1324	Mansā Mūsū, King of Mālī; University of Timbuktū	ibn Taymiyyah
		al-Nuwayrī
1348	Black Death reaches Egypt	Ṣafi al-dīn al-Ḥillī
1349	Muslim missionaries in Nigeria (Kano)	
		Ṣalāḥ al-dīn al-Ṣafadī
		ibn Qayyim al-Jawziyyah
1369	Tīmūr Lang occupies Khūrāsān	ibn Nubātah
1370–80	Tīmūr Lang conquers much of Central Asia	Lisān al-dīn ibn al-Khaṭīb
		ibn Baṭṭūtah
1380–87	Tīmūr conquers Iran	
		Ḥāfiẓ
1400		
		al-Fayrūzābādī
1400	Islam reaches Java	ibn Khaldūn
1402	death of Tīmūr Lang	al-Maqrīzī
		al-Ghuzūlī
		al-Qalqashandī
		al-Ibshīhī
		ibn Arabshāh
1453	capture of Constantinople by Ottomans	

WORLD

Year	Historical events/people*	Literary events/people†
1488	Diaz opens sea-route to Indian Ocean	
1492	fall of Granada to *reconquista*; Columbus sails to the New World	
1498	Vasco da Gama reaches India	
1500		
1509	Portuguese settle in Brazil	
1516		Leonardo da Vinci
		Albrecht Dürer
1521	Protestant Reformation	
1531	Henry VIII of England breaks with Roman Church	
1533	Ivan the Terrible, Czar of Russia	Ariosto
		Copernicus
		Martin Luther
1588	Spanish Armada defeated	Sir Philip Sidney
1600		
	English East India Company founded	
1607	English settlement in Jamestown (America)	Shakespeare
		Cervantes
1618–48	Thirty Years War	
1642	Commonwealth in England	Galileo Galilei
		Descartes
		William Harvey
1661	Louis XIV King of France	
1664	Manchu dynasty in China	Rembrandt
		Milton
		Spinoza
		Molière

MIDDLE EASTERN

Year	Historical events/people*	Literary events/people†
1499	Ismāʿīl establishes Ṣafavī dynasty in Īrān	
1500		
1508	Ṣafavīs capture Baghdād	
		al-Suyūṭī
		Ibn Mālik al-Ḥamawī
1516	Selīm the Grim captures Cairo	
1520–66	Reign of Ottoman Sultan Sulaymān the Magnificent	
1521	Ottoman capture of Belgrade	
1522	Ottoman conquest of Rhodes	Ibn Iyās
1529	Ottoman siege of Vienna	
1549	Ottoman forces reach Yemen	
1550	Sinan builds Suleymaniye Mosque in Istanbul	
1556–1605	Akbar assumes power in Mughal India	al-Shaʿrānī
1600		
1622	English capture Hormuz	al-Maqqarī
1653	Tāj Mahal completed by Shāh Jihān	Ḥajjī Khalīfah (Evliya Çelebi)
		Shihāb al-dīn al-Khafājī

WORLD

Year	Historical events/people*	Literary events/people†
1682	Newton discovers laws of gravity	
1689	Bill of Rights in England	Corneille
		Racine
1700		
		Locke
1704	England captures Gibraltar	Newton
		Defoe
		Galland
		Leibnitz
		J. S. Bach
1768	Cook explores Pacific Ocean	
1776	American Revolution; Declaration of Independence (USA)	David Hume
		Voltaire
		Rousseau
1783	Russia captures Crimea	
1789	French Revolution begins	Sir William Jones
		Gibbon
1800		
1804	Bonaparte Emperor of France	Kant
1813		
1814	First steam locomotive	
1815	Battle of Waterloo	Volney
		Hegel
		Goethe

MIDDLE EASTERN

Year	Historical events/people*	Literary events/people†
1668	Ottoman conquest of Crete	
1683	Ottomans besiege Vienna	
1699	Treaty of Karlowitz	
1700		
		ʿAbd al-Ghanī al-Nābulusī
		Bishop Germanus Farḥāt
1745	Wahhābīs established at Darʿiyyah, Arabia	
1765	English East India Company takes over administration of Bengal	al-Amīr al-Ṣanʿānī
1770–89	Yūsuf Shihāb, Amir of Lebanon	al-Idkāwī
1773	Saʿūdī dynasty in al-Riyāḍ	al-Zabīdī
1774	Treaty of Kuchuk Kaynarji between Russia and Ottomans	
1783	Russia seizes Crimea	
1789–1807	Reign of Selīm III, Ottoman Sultan	
1796	Qajar dynasty in Iran	
1798	Napoleon's invasion of Egypt	
1800		
1803–4	Wahhābīs capture Mecca and Medina	
1805–48	Muḥammad ʿAlī viceroy of Egypt	
1806	Wahhābīs capture Mecca	
1811	Mamlūks massacred on orders of Muḥammad ʿAlī	Aḥmad al-Tijānī
1820–23	Egyptians conquer Sudan	al-Jabartī
1823	Arabic press in Cairo	

WORLD

Year	Historical events/people*	Literary events/people†
1839	British seize Aden	Pushkin
1842	Britain annexes Hong Kong	
1846	War between USA and Mexico	
1848	Communist Manifesto by Marx and Engels	
1854–5	Crimean War	Hegel
		Kierkegaard
		Schopenhauer
1861	American Civil War	Dickens
1871	Unification of Germany	John Stuart Mill
1876	Bell invents telephone	Dostoevsky
		Edward FitzGerald
		Darwin
		Hippolyte Taine
		Marx
1897	First World Zionist Congress	Ernest Renan
1899–1902	Boer War (South Africa)	
1900		
		Nietzsche
1904	*Entente cordiale* between France and Britain	Chekhov
1905	Russo-Japanese War	Tolstoy

MIDDLE EASTERN

Year	Historical events/people*	Literary events/people†
1830	French invade Algeria	
1834	Arabic press in Beirut	Shaykh Ḥasan al-ʿAṭṭār
		Mārūn al-Naqqāsh
1860–61	Civil War in Syria	
1866	foundation of Syrian Protestant College in Beirut (AUB)	Nāṣīf al-Yāzijī
1869	Suez Canal opened	Rifāʿah al-Ṭahṭāwī
1877	Anglo-French control of Egyptian finances	
1881	French occupy Tunisia; ʿUrabī Revolt in Egypt	
1882	British occupy Egypt	
1885	Mahdī's revolt in Sudan; General Gordon killed in al-Kharṭūm	Aḥmad Fāris al-Shidyāq
		Ḥusayn al-Marṣafi
1893	French arrive in Timbuktū	Muḥammad ʿUthmān Jalāl
1898	defeat of Sudanese forces by General Kitchener	Jamāl al-dīn ʾal-Afghaniʾ
1900		
		ʿAbd al-raḥmān al-Kawākibī
		Abū Khalīl al-Qabbānī
		Muḥammad ʿAbduh
		Maḥmūd Sāmī al-Barūdī
1908	Ottoman Sultan ʿAbd al-ḥamīd deposed by Young Turks	

WORLD

Year	Historical events/people*	Literary events/people†
1914–18	First World War	
1917	Bolshevik Revolution in Russia	
1919	League of Nations created	
1929	Financial crash in USA	
1933	Franklin Roosevelt American President; Hitler gains power in Germany	Gustave Lanson
1936	Civil War in Spain	Pirandello
1939–45	Second World War	Freud
1945	Atom bombs dropped on Japan	
1948	Mahatma Gandhi assassinated	

MIDDLE EASTERN

Year	Historical events/people*	Literary events/people†
1909	Anglo-Persian Oil Company founded	
1912	Franco-Spanish protectorate of Morocco	Yaʿqūb Ṣannûʿ
1915	Arab Revolt against Ottoman government	
1916	Sykes-Picot Agreement regarding disposition of Middle East following First World War	
1917	Balfour Declaration	Shiblī Shumayyil Shaykh Salāmah al-Ḥijāzī Muḥammad Taymūr
1919	Popular uprising in Egypt; first proclamation of Muṣṭafā Kemāl (Atatürk) in Turkey	
1920	Turkish War of Independence; revolt in Iraq; French capture Damascus	
1921	Reza Shāh Pahlevī assumes power in Iran	
1922	discovery of Tutankhamun's tomb in Egypt	Farah Anṭūn
1923	Declaration of Turkish Republic	
1924	abolition of the Caliphate; first Egyptian parliament	Muṣṭafā Luṭfī al-Manfalūṭī Shaykh Aḥmad Bamba
1927	beginnings of Muslim Brethren in Egypt	Saʿd Zaghlūl
1929	growing unrest in Palestine	Muḥammad al-Muwayliḥī
1932	foundation of Arab Academy in Cairo	Khalīl Jubrān Ḥāfiẓ Ibrāhīm Aḥmad Shawqī
1933	ʿAbd al-ʿazīz becomes King of Saudi Arabia	Abū al-qāsim al-Shabbī
1935	Italy invades Ethiopia	Rashīd Riḍā Jamīl Ṣidqī al-Zahāwī
1938	death of Atatürk	Mayy Ziyādah Muḥammad Iqbāl
1945	League of Arab States created in Cairo	Maʿrūf al-Ruṣāfī
1947	independence of India; creation of Pakistan	Salāmah Mūsā
1948	war in Palestine; State of Israel established	Anṭūn Saʿādah Ḥasan al-Bannā Khalīl Muṭrān

WORLD

Year	Historical events/people[*]	Literary events/people[†]
1950	Korean War begins	
1954	French leave Indo-China	
1955	Bandung Conference of unaligned nations	Einstein Brecht
1959	Fidel Castro leader of Cuba	
1961	Construction of Berlin Wall	
1963	Assassination of President Kennedy	
1973	Ceasefire in Vietnam	Sartre

MIDDLE EASTERN

Year	Historical events/people*	Literary events/people†
		Khalīl Baydas ʿAlī al-Duʿajī
1951	Muḥammad Mosaddeg Prime Minister of Iran; Ḥusayn becomes King of Jordan	
1952	Revolution in Egypt	
1954	Jamāl ʿAbd al-nāṣir (Nasser) comes to power; beginning of Algerian War of Independence; Czech arms agreement with Egypt	Maḥmūd Ṭāhir Lāshīn
1955	Afro-Asian Conference in Bandung, Indonesia	
1956	Egypt nationalises Suez Canal; Tripartite (British, French, Israeli) invasion of Suez; Sudan, Tunisia, and Morocco gain independence	Badr Shākir al-Sayyāb Muḥammad Ḥusayn Haykal Iliyyā Abū Māḍī
1958	revolution in Iraq; United Arab Republic (Egypt & Syria) created; Lebanese political unrest	Jūrj Abyaḍ
1961	Kuwait independence; Socialist Laws in Egypt; revolution in Yemen	Bayram al-Tūnisī
1962	end of Algerian War; independence	Aḥmad Luṭfī al-Sayyid Mārūn ʿAbbūd
1964	PLO established; King Saʿūd of Saudi Arabia replaced by King Fayṣal	ʿAbbās Maḥmūd al-ʿAqqād Sayyid Quṭb
1967	June War between Israel and Arab states	Muḥammad Mandūr Ḥusayn Muruwwah
1968	Ḥāfiẓ al-Asad becomes President of Syria; Yāsir ʿArafāt leader of Palestine Liberation Organisation	Bishārah al-Khūrī
1969	General Numayrī seizes power in the Sudan; Libyan revolution led by Muʿammar al-Qadhdhāfī	
1970	Aswan High Dam completed; fighting in Jordan (Black September); death of ʿAbd al-nāṣir; Anwar al-Sādāt President of Egypt	
1971	establishment of United Arab Emirates in Gulf	Tawfīq Ṣāyigh
1973	October crossing (Ramaḍān/Yom Kippur War)	Ṭāhā Ḥusayn Maḥmūd Taymūr
1975–88	Lebanese civil war	
1976	Fall of Tall al-Zaʿtar Palestinian refugee camp	

WORLD

Year	Historical events/people*	Literary events/people†
1986	Nuclear accident at Chernobyl	Picasso
1989	Berlin Wall dismantled	
1990	German reunification	
1991	Gulf War	

MIDDLE EASTERN

Year	Historical events/people[*]	Literary events/people[†]
1977	Camp David Accords between Egypt and Israel	
1979	Revolution in Īrān brings Imām Khomeinī to power	
1975–88	Lebanese Civil War	
1981	Assassination of President Anwar al-Sādāt	Ṣalāḥ ʿAbd al-Ṣabūr
1982	Israel invades Lebanon; Sabra and Shatilah Camp massacres	Khalīl Ḥāwī
1987	Palestinian intifāḍah	Michel ʿAflaq
		Tawfiq al-Ḥakīm
		Yūsuf al-Khāl
1988	Nobel Prize for literature awarded to Najīb Maḥfūẓ	
		Mīkhāʾīl Nuʿaymah
		Dhū al-nūn Ayyūb
		Tawfiq Yūsuf ʿAwwād
1990–91	Gulf War: Western forces attack Iraq after its occupation of Kuwait	
		Yūsuf Idrīs
		Lewis ʿAwaḍ
		Yaḥyā Ḥaqqī
1994		Jabrā Ibrāhīm Jabrā
1996		Emil Ḥabībī

CHAPTER I

An essay on precedents and principles

The titles of books are very particular types of beginnings. Practical considerations of space (and of library cataloguing) demand that they consist of relatively few words, and yet they are meant both to attract the reader and to summarise the work's contents and focus. When a book such as this one takes as its topic the vast riches of a literary tradition such as that of the Arabs and when it hopes to take its place in a succession of earlier works on the same subject, the title takes on a very heavy semantic burden indeed. These factors have all impinged upon the process of choosing a title for this work that will be appropriate to both its subject and principles. I would therefore like to use the terms of the title as a conduit to a discussion of the aims and methods of this book.

'Arabic' announces clearly the language in which the literary materials that constitute my primary topic have been composed, but the dual significance of the Arabic equivalent of that adjective, "*arabī*" – referring to both a language and its people – also introduces the notion that this work will be one of 'translation' in the most literal sense: I will be attempting to 'carry' one literary tradition 'across' cultural boundaries into the milieu of English-speaking readers at the end of the twentieth century and, more particularly, the comparative framework of world literature studies. It has to be acknowledged from the outset that, for most of the period under consideration (the sixth century CE till the present), the relationship between the Arabo-Islamic world and the West has been one of almost continuous confrontation, with a concomitant and anticipatable obfuscation of some unpleasant truths on both sides. The Crusades and the reconquest of Spain leading to the fall of Granada in 1492, for instance, both of them traditionally recounted as glorious episodes in the history of Western Europe, take on a quite different significance if viewed from outside such a context. All too often the spatial and attitudinal boundaries between the two cultural systems alluded to above have in fact created barriers to an understanding of the realities of 'the other'. With this background in mind, it is the purpose of the second chapter of this book to provide a linguistic, environmental, and historical context as a basis upon which to build a series of discussions of the literary genres in Arabic. I will examine the features of the Arabic language from both a synchronic and diachronic perspective, as well as its crucial place in the cultural history of the region and peoples that the West has called by a variety of names during the lengthy time-span that is our topic: Moors, Saracens, Turks, the Near East, the Middle East, the Arab world.

'Literary', pertaining as it does to the field of 'literature', invokes a topic of equal breadth. Dictionary definitions refer initially to anything that is written about a particular topic, so that we have, for example, 'scientific literature', and so on. Such indeed is the definition adopted by a major recent project in Arabic literary history, *The Cambridge History of Arabic Literature*. In the Introduction to the first volume in the series, the editors note that, by 'literature' they imply 'virtually everything that has been recorded in writing, apart from inscriptions and purely archival material'. However, alongside this broad definition a more limited and rigorous one has been developed that has found favour with those specialising in the study of literature, most especially within the context of academe, a view reflected by the entry in the *Oxford English Dictionary*, 'writings whose value lies in beauty of form or emotional effect'. It is this latter definition that has provided me with the basic organising principle for the present work; my intention in so doing is not only to establish a clear framework for the discussions that are to follow but also to differentiate the aims and methods of this work from those of most of its predecessors. In this context, two points should immediately be made. Firstly, as Terry Eagleton notes, 'you cannot engage in an historical analysis of literature without recognizing that literature itself is a recent historical invention' (*Literary Theory*, Minneapolis, 1983, p. 219); in a famous essay, entitled 'The Attack on Literature', Rene Wellek examines the history of the term's usage and links the narrower definition to the rise in aesthetics. Secondly, while the Arabic word *adab* is essentially coterminous with the concept of belles-lettres in contemporary critical writings, it has arrived at that meaning via an interesting route, one that begins with something very akin to education and manners before being adopted as the means of defining the varied activities of those important contributors to the cultural values of Arab society who have for many centuries been dignified by the designation *udabā'* (sing. *adīb*) – practitioners, preservers, and teachers of *adab*. The development of this concept, *adab*, is itself a primary topic of the fifth chapter.

Having linked the discussion of 'literature' and '*adab*' in this way, I might perhaps place them both into a single context by drawing attention to the way in which recent intellectual trends in Western literary theory and criticism would seem to present the writer of a work such as this with an interesting dilemma that can be directly associated with issues of definition. During recent decades literary debate within Western academe has been nothing if not lively. A 'post-modern' school of critics has emerged to challenge in a number of ways some of the notions connected with the bellettristic approach to the topic, particularly insofar as the privileged position of the literary text, the question of evaluation, and the concept of canon are concerned. Many contemporary critics now prefer to talk in terms of discourse analysis. The methodology associated with these trends in literary study has allowed a number of widely variant textual types to be the subject of critical approaches. In the trans-cultural context of this book on Arabic literary genres and its organising principles, the dilemma I mentioned above can best be illustrated through the irony that the variety of texts and topics which today are potentially subject to critical analysis within the realm of Western literature studies has been expanded by some theoretical schools to such an extent that the resulting scenario tends to reflect, albeit by way of different criteria, the very same generic and topical breadth that interested the *adīb* during the classical period of Arabic literature. However, I would like to suggest that these contemporary approaches to literature-study in the West, themselves the subject of intense debate and by no means espoused by all participants in the field, need to be placed first within their own context, specifically the history of Western literary criticism during the course of this century. Above all, they need to be regarded – like all such movements – as a reaction to and thus an extension of what precedes them. The application of Western critical methodology to a broader selection of text types is feasible, it seems to me, only within a cultural context in which the close reading of individual texts, stimulated and refined within the realm of literature studies by the almost puritanical rigour of the 'new critics', has provided the study of texts, literary and otherwise, with a solid basis upon which to base broader assessments. While not wishing at this point to indulge in a history of Arabic literature studies in the West, I would venture to suggest that the field has now moved from what I might term a philological phase into a more bellettristic one, but the shift is relatively recent. It is the contributions of a sparse but gradually growing population of scholars and critics in the Middle East and the West to this particular phase in the development of Arabic literary research that inevitably form the primary basis of this volume and thus the decision to use a bellettristic definition of literature.

'Development', a word used in my subtitle, clearly involves a concern with time and chronology, while 'heritage' is concerned with the way in which the readers of the present utilise and evaluate their past, as noted in T. S. Eliot's famous essay, 'Tradition and the individual talent'. It will probably be obvious that the word whose use I am avoiding here is 'history'. In an iconoclastic piece, F. W. Bateson terms literary history a 'non-subject par excellence', suggesting that, while history is concerned with differences, literature involves the study of similarities (*New Literary History*, 2:1, 1970). While such a view may serve perhaps as a useful antidote to literary historical writing that relies excessively on what one might term dynastic logic, it seems to ignore the more synchronic focus of much contemporary historical writing on the one hand, and on the other, an ever-increasing awareness among literature scholars that the almost puritanical demands of the 'new critics' regarding the need to isolate the individual literary text may have served a limited, yet useful purpose in honing our critical skills but has in the longer term deprived us of a rich store of potentially useful information. Inter-textuality and Reception Theory, just to cite two recent theoretical contributions to literature studies, have insisted upon a rediscovery of the relationship with tradition and the societal function of the reader.

Between these different approaches the present work seeks to strike a balance, one that will privilege the literary dimension over the historical. It will make use of categories that are those of literature studies, although there will be frequent reference to political and societal contexts. The chronological dimension will always be implicit. The difference that I hope to establish can perhaps be illustrated by considering the organising principles that have been applied in many other works on this topic in Arabic and other languages, and in particular the method of periodisation that *mutatis mutandis* has been applied in most cases.

The first great temporal divide is one that constitutes an important aspect of Islamic history: that between the Islamic and pre-Islamic periods, the latter being also referred to as the 'period of ignorance' (Arabic, '*Jāhiliyyah*'). Here a period of indeterminate duration is defined by its status as antecedent. The denomination 'Islamic' can be applied in theory to the entire period from 622 till the present day, but is usually used to describe the literary activity of the lifetime of the Prophet Muḥammad and the first four Caliphs. Following this, a new principle takes over, that of the period during which a particular dynasty held actual or nominal sway: firstly, the Umawī, for which Western scholarship has retained the term 'Umayyad' (complete with its Westernised Greek suffix); and then the ʿAbbasī, similarly termed 'Abbasid'. Such a procedure has led almost inevitably to the use of designations such as 'Abbasid poet' to identify such disparate and temporally distant artists as Abū Nuwās (d. *c.* 813), renowned for his wine poetry, and Abū al-ʿAlāʾ al-Maʿarrī (d. 1058), one of Arabic poetry's greatest exponents of philosophical and ascetic verse. Using a different perspective, one might perhaps suggest that there are at least two poets who might merit such a designation: al-Walīd ibn Yazīd (d. 750) as an Umawī poet and Ibn al-Muʿtazz (d. 908) as an ʿAbbāsī, in both cases because they were members of the caliphal family itself. Even before the end of the era termed 'Abbasid', the areas reckoned to be within the Dār al-Islam (region of Islamic dominion) had fragmented into a large number of smaller hegemonies, each controlled by a succession of dynasties that provided sources of patronage for littérateurs. In the context of an examination of various approaches to the organisation of literary historical writing, the case of al-Andalus (as the Iberian Peninsula was called during the period of Islamic [Moorish] rule) and the fact that its literary riches have mostly failed to be integrated into a collective vision of the Arabic literary tradition, may be considered emblematic of the problems raised by methods that place more emphasis on non-literary criteria (such as geography and dynastic history). The issues become even more difficult when it comes to addressing the period which roughly spans the thirteenth to eighteenth centuries, an era designated by yet another kind of title, 'the period of decadence'. Here a combination of factors, among them the rule of large parts of the region by non-Arabic speakers and a perceived preference among the implied audience for Arabic literary works for aesthetic norms considerably at variance with our own, has led – at least until relatively recently – to a widespread ignorance of five centuries of creativity in Arabic aptly reflected in the title generally applied to the period. Beyond the clear problem of our lack of knowledge about such a substantial time-period, there is also the fact that any assessment of the nature of the changes that occurred during the nineteenth century, generally gathered together under the heading of 'modernisation' – involving an encounter with the West and a revival of the heritage of the past, is rendered difficult, or even impossible, by the fact that the real circumstances of the 'pre-modern' remain unclear (a dilemma whose dimensions bring us full circle to the antecedence principle of the pre-Islamic/Islamic divide discussed above). Thus, while renewed contacts with the Western world have clearly played a major role in the developments that have taken place in the Arabic literary tradition during the 'modern period' and the 'revival' that brought it about, there is still room for a good deal of discussion about the relative importance of different factors during its earliest phases.

The principal point to be made following this discussion of traditional modes of periodisation of Arabic literature is that they have no internal consistency, something that seems to me to account in no small part for the many problems that they raise. However, it is not my intention here to suggest that the works that make use of these principles have not made major contributions to the field of Arabic literature studies; I freely acknowledge here that they have constituted the framework within which I began my own study of the field. The works of such scholars as Goldziher, Nicholson, Gibb, Blachère, Huart, Brockelmann, Nallino, to mention just a few of the more famous names, have in many cases brought important Arabic literary texts to the attention of Western readers for the first time, and the surveys they wrote continue to provide a wealth of information about writers and trends. Their works illustrate clearly the crucial role that literature played and continues to play in Arab society. Through their emphasis on the writers themselves, they are able to underline the high social standing that littérateurs enjoyed at court. However, in reflecting for the most part the principles applied in reference works of the source culture, they have emphasized certain aspects at the expense of others. But, before we consider the issues involved in different approaches, there is one crucial and enormous gap in our knowledge of Arabic and Islamic studies in general that needs to be identified from the outset, one for which no group or generation can be held responsible. A sizeable and by definition unquantifiable percentage of Arabic manuscripts on all topics from the early periods of Islamic history remains unpublished and, in some cases, uncatalogued. It is here that the shelf-lists of a Baghdādī book-seller, Ibn al-Nadīm (d. 990), collected into his famous book, *al-Fihrist*, offer us, through listings of titles that we do not possess, a clue as to the extent of what we are missing.

Beyond such regrettable realities as these that stem from a variety of causes (not the least of which is that the field has so few practitioners), we can point out that these earlier accounts of Arabic literature are predominantly concerned with the writings of a literate élite that was almost exclusively male. Recent research into women's writings during the last two centuries suggests that a lively tradition of literature existed behind the closed curtains of the women's quarters, but that, at least till now, the products of such exchanges have not entered the public domain. It does not seem unreasonable to extrapolate the basic outlines of this situation back into earlier periods, noting at the same time that the oral nature of many literary performances (reflected in Edward Lane's surprise and regret at his inability to locate manuscripts or printed versions of the *Thousand and One Nights*, which he was translating while living in nineteenth century Cairo) may be another factor in this context. In cases where women were perceived to have a public societal role (of which the recitation of elegies on dead heroes appears to be one), we do possess examples of their creativity.

A concentration on the writings of this same élite has led to another interesting circumstance involving attitudes, namely the entire question of the significance of popular literature. For, while the Western world became completely fascinated by the narratives of the *Thousand and One Nights* and the fantastic worlds that they invoked following the publication of Galland's translation into French at the beginning of the eighteenth century, most Arab critics have ignored not only them but also the many other collections of popular narrative since they are not considered to be part of the literary canon; the great historian, Ibn Khaldūn (d. 1406), provides one of the very rare exceptions to this trend in his famous work, *al-Muqaddimah*. The situation has been changing more recently, however, with the advent to the educational and cultural institutions in the region of social scientific studies and especially folklore. As we will have occasion to note with reference to all the genres to be discussed in the chapters that follow, it is surely of major significance that the period when élite literature in Arabic was said to be in a 'period of decadence' coincides directly with the efflorescence of popular literature of all kinds.

The Arabic Literary Heritage should thus be viewed as an attempt to present an alternative approach to the production of a survey of Arabic literature. My goals in writing this work very much mirror those of Monique Trède-Boulmer and Suzanne Said, the joint authors of *La littérature grecque d'Homère à Aristote*, Que sais-je? series, (Paris, 1990):

Pour mettre à jour nos connaissances, car les descouvertes papyorologiques revèlent chaque année de nouveaux fragments de poésie ou de prose; pour risquer sur tel ou tel problème particulier une interprétation personelle; mais aussi pour réclasser, avec plus d'equité peut-être, l'héritage antique.

An examination of the materials in Arabic begins with the text that holds an especially privileged position within Islam and Arabic, namely the Qur'ān. It was the urgent need of the Islamic community to record this oral 'recitation' of God's word that may be seen as marking the beginnings of a gradual shift from a predominantly oral culture to a written one. As the Prophet Muḥammad's utterances, preserved in the memories of his companions, were written down and analysed, the recension process required that a number of fields and disciplines be invoked and, in some cases, initiated: a refinement of the writing system (including the establishment of a system of vowelling), a codification of the grammar of Arabic, and a wide variety of philological and critical activities that resulted in making the earliest phases in Arabic literature available to us. In giving prominence to the Qur'ān, as divinely inspired text, as linguistic yardstick, and as motivation for the need to record the pre-Islamic poetic tradition in written form, we acknowledge its central place in almost every aspect of the development of Arabic language and literature. In analysing, albeit briefly, the beauty of the language and imagery of the Qur'ān, we may link the sacred book of Islâm to recent literary-critical studies of religious texts.

The three chapters that follow are surveys of the development of the genres of poetry, bellettristic prose and narrative, and drama. As noted above, the linkages between the genres of Arabic literature, the concept of *adab*, and the terms used to describe their analogues in Western literary traditions, are rarely exact. To cite just a single example: within the realm of narrative, the concept of *adab* admits of categories (travel narratives and biographies, for example) that have not generally attracted the attention of literary critics in the Western world. That said, I will immediately go on to suggest that the often 'fictional' sections of Ibn Baṭṭūṭah's (d. 1377) travel narratives, the clear current predilection among Western writers and readers for biography (as almost any issue of the *London Review of Books* will confirm), and the critical links now being explored between autobiography and fiction, all suggest that the inclusiveness of the Arabic category provides a useful comparative framework for the analysis of narratives.

The final chapter moves away from the literary texts themselves to consider the tradition of criticism that has existed alongside them from the outset. The distinction between the two may seem relatively clear in a modern context, although even there some would wish to obfuscate the distinction, but in earlier times the linkages between them, and indeed between the analysis of the Qur'ānic text and the development of criticism, are particularly close. Many poets have themselves also been critics and anthologisers of poetry, itself of course a major critical exercise; in this combination Abū Tammām (d. 846) and Ibn ʿAbd Rabbihi (d. 940) serve as the forebears of the contemporary Lebanese poet, Adūnīs (b. 1928). It is Adūnīs who avers that, by definition, poetry uses language in different and new ways and that it is thus the role of criticism to follow, rather than to dictate. As a critic, however, he himself has traced the often varied balance between creativity and the trammels of classicism that have marked the relationship between Arabic literature and its criticism.

In recent years several nations have attempted to reflect the political and economic ramifications of what is often termed a 'global vision' in new or revised national educational curricula. As travel opportunities and communications media continue to shrink previously unthinkable distances in space and attitude, such initiatives tend to find a receptive audience among students who are more than ever concerned about the relationship of their studies to a professional career. A frequent component of such plans and their reception is the inclusion of more materials that deal with non-Western cultures, a process that almost immediately reveals a shortage of anthologies and other reference works that, until recently, was little short of scandalous. In the particular case of the region that is represented by the literary tradition of Arabic, the recent award of the Nobel Prize to the Egyptian novelist, Najīb Maḥfūẓ (b. 1911), has provided an interesting opportunity for Western readers to encounter an important world literary tradition to which they have previously had minimal access.

It is with a conscious awareness of this particular situation and the need for an introductory work for a general, non-specialist readership that I have written this book. I wish to emphasise from the start that it is not intended for my fellow-scholars in the first instance. *The Cambridge History of Arabic Literature*, a multi-volume work involving many scholars in the field (including myself), clearly is intended to serve that purpose. This work differs from it in a number of ways. I have already identified a basic difference between the two in the very definition of literature. Beyond that, I have tried to stress the continuity of the Arabic literary tradition and thus have sought as many occasions as possible to provide illustrations of the linkages that connect present and past; this is particularly the case in the introductory section to the chapters on specific genres where features of the great tradition of the past are mirrored in a present-day instance or debate. I might add that, in several of the chapters, I have deliberately made use of the introductory section to recount some of my own experiences with Arabic literature and littérateurs in the region itself; my hope is that those accounts may exemplify the considerable increase in contact with Arab littérateurs and critics which, in my view, is a major and desirable feature of recent Western scholarship. In the interests of readability, I have restricted academic conventions to the very minimum, listing references – where necessary – in parentheses within the text itself. The Guide to Further Reading lists only the most significant works in the field and concentrates on studies in English; sources in other European languages are included only when none is available in English (a not infrequent occurrence in many subfields). Beyond these considerations I should point out that, to cite once again the quotation of Erich Auerbach used at the beginning of the Preface, our knowledge of Arabic literature as a field of specialisation and our studies of it have indeed expanded in recent decades so as to 'become so widely various that their mastery has become the task of a lifetime'. While the need to teach a university-level course on the development of literary genres in Arabic means that I have endeavoured to 'keep pace' with as many aspects of the field as possible, I should make it clear that, in writing about certain genres and periods, I have had to rely extensively on secondary sources in both Arabic and European languages.

But clearly the greatest difference lies in the fact that *The Arabic Literary Heritage* is intended as an introductory survey and has been written with a constant concern for brevity – rarely, if ever, a favoured quality in academic circles. In trying to capture the riches of so vast a literary tradition in so restricted a space, I have been aware that the risks are considerable since what is left out will always exceed what is included by a large margin. However, if readers of this work find themselves tempted to explore the literary heritage of Arabic in more detail and, dare one hope, in the original language, then this work's task of 'translation' will have been achieved.

CHAPTER 2

The contexts of the literary tradition

INTRODUCTION

The Arab League, Arab nationalism; Arabic numerals, Arabic literature; the Arabian peninsula, the *Arabian Nights*. The English language makes use of several epithets to describe the people, language, and region whose literary creativity is the topic of this book. The Arabic language itself, by contrast, has a single word, *ʿarabī*, an attributive adjective derived from what must be one of the earliest words in the history of the language, *ʿarab*, a collective noun that was originally used to describe the nomadic peoples of the central regions of what is now termed the Arabian Peninsula. Quite how far back the existence of the *ʿarab* can be traced is difficult to say, but a group called the *ʿar-ba-a-a*' are cited as components of an army in cuneiform inscriptions dating from as early as 853 BC. At the end of the 1950s the same word, *ʿarab*, was used by Jamāl ʿAbd al-Nāṣir [Nasser], the President of Egypt, when he proclaimed in a speech that 'from the Atlantic Ocean to the Arabian Gulf we are Arabs'. At the time such an expression of unity, a reflection of several decades of Arab nationalist thought and writing, was an aspiration; for many speakers of Arabic it remains so. However, in the wake of more recent realities – not the least of which is the watershed event of the June War of 1967, Nasser's words seem to have a hollow ring to them. For many contemporary littérateurs the phrase 'from the Ocean to the Gulf' becomes a convenient locational phrase through which to criticise their current realities, as when the poet Adūnīs intones in his lengthy poem, '*Qabr min ajl New York*' *A Grave for New York*, 1971:

> The word? You wish to discover its fire? Write then, I say, write! Don't gesticulate, don't copy! Write! From the Ocean to the Gulf I cannot hear a single tongue, nor read a word. All I hear is noise.

In this chapter I will provide a series of contexts that are intended to serve as background for the investigations of the genres of Arabic literature that follow. Firstly I will discuss two particular contexts within which the literary tradition has been created, developed, and recorded: the physical and the linguistic. A more diachronic approach will then be used for an overview of the historical background against which the literary texts were produced; it will be subdivided into two parts, a first that looks at rulers and the changing patterns of authority, and a second that examines some of the intellectual debates against the background of which Arabic literature has been composed.

THE PHYSICAL CONTEXT

The pre-Islamic poet, Labīd, includes the following lines in the opening section of his famous *Muʿallaqah* poem:

> Sites dung-stained and long abandoned after times of frequentation, with their changing seasons of peace and war,
> Fed with spring rains of the stars, hit by the thunder of a heavy rainstorm or fine drizzle,
> Falling from every passing cloud, looming dark in the daytime and with thunder resounding at eventide.

The effect of rain on a desert environment is truly remarkable; the transformations that it brings about are immediate. As Labīd's poem and those of many other poets make clear, the sheer anticipation of its arrival was one of the most positive images in the pre-Islamic poetic repertoire. While water – its presence or absence – was a very practical aspect of life within the desert existence of the earliest poets, it has been a potent image for the modern poet as well, one of fertility, of potential, of revolution. Labīd's twentieth-century successor, the Iraqi poet, Badr Shākir al-Sayyāb (1926–64), devotes a poem to rain ('*Unshūdat al-maṭar*') which evokes the imagery of the earliest poetry in the cause of his country's liberation:

> On the night of departure how many tears have we shed,
> and then, for fear of reproach, pretended it was rain. . .
> Rain . . .
> Rain . . .
> Since our childhood, the skies
> were always cloudy in wintertime,
> and rain poured down,
> but every year, as the earth blossomed, we stayed hungry,
> Never a year went by but there was hunger in Iraq.
> Rain . . .
> Rain . . .
> Rain . . .

And, as desert-dwellers know only too well, water, this same essential, life-giving resource, can also have a potent destructive force. The flash-floods of the *wādī* (stream-valley) can bring sudden death, a fate that is depicted with telling effect both at the conclusion of another *Muʿallaqah* poem from the earliest period of poetry, that of Imru al-Qays, and in the fate of the hero's mother in the novel, *Nazīf al-ḥajar* (The Rocks Bleed, 1990) by the Libyan writer, Ibrāhīm al-Kawnī (b. 1948), who acknowledges spending part of each year deep in the Sahara, an experience that lends his fictional works an atmosphere that provides a direct link between the most contemporary and ancient Arabic literary texts.

Experiments in applying modern technology to the process of desert reclamation are to be found in various parts of the Middle East region, the aim being to make use of arid areas contiguous to agriculturally productive soil for the purpose of increasing the region's food production. However, in recent times increasing concern has been expressed about the long-term environmental costs of this type of experiment, especially in the context of the need to conserve water resources. As the major strategic river-basins of the Middle East region – the Nile, the Jordan, the Litani, the Euphrates, the Tigris, have become the locations for huge water-control projects and as the legal issue of littoral rights and the sheer availability of water impinges upon the already fraught relationship between Israel and its Arab neighbours, between Egypt and the countries to the South, and between Iraq, Turkey and Syria, so has the need to reconcile man's needs with the demands of the environment become yet more urgent. The peoples of Southern Sudan and Somalia are quite as aware of the realities of desert life and the suddenness of its destructive force as were their forebears whose struggle for survival is the primary theme of the poetry which marks the earliest phase of Arabic literature.

The tension between these dualities of aridity and moisture, of death and birth, has been a constant in the Arab world for the entire period represented within these pages. The text of the Qur'ān itself shows an obvious concern with the rigours of daily life in the way it depicts paradise as a well-watered garden. Echoing the 'Garden of Eden' images in Western cultures, the Arabic word for garden and paradise is the same (*jannah*); many analyses of the Islamic garden (and particularly those of the more conducive climes of al-Andalus) show the linkage between the design of gardens and depictions of paradise. This struggle to survive in such a delicate ecological balance continues to affect the lives of people who live in large areas of the Middle East and has a substantial effect on patterns of homogeneity within particular areas and nations. Thus, a nation such as Egypt whose people cling to the fertile Nile Valley region will tend to possess a greater sense of identity than one like the Sudan or Algeria where geographical factors and sheer distances will serve to create real and psychological barriers.

While the coastal regions of the Mediterranean, the Red Sea, the Indian Ocean, and the Gulf, have always served as a base for wide-scale regional commerce, reflected in the famous Sindbad cycle from the *Thousand and One Nights*, the seas of the Middle East do not appear to have roused the interest of Arab littérateurs to any great extent. Perhaps as is the case with English literature, it needed the concern of an islander, the Sicilian Ibn Ḥamdīs (*c.* 1055–1132) who later travelled to Spain, to produce Arabic poetry depicting the sea. In the main however, it is the land that has served as a major means of identity for the Arab people; the fate of the Palestinians, with their annual 'Day of the Land', is a potent contemporary symbol of that sentiment of long vintage. The sea, by contrast, has been viewed as a place of adventure and danger, an alien medium, a symbol of separation and exile, often implicit in accounts of lengthy journeys but rarely described in detail.

The other primary geographical feature of the region is mountains. Northern Iraq, Yemen, Lebanon, and the Maghrib, for example, possess mountain ranges that have played a major role in the cultural life of their people. Mountains are often akin to cultural breakwaters, in that they can afford refuge to minority groups. The Atlas Mountains of the Maghrib have served to create a large divide between those living on the coastal plain and the mountain dwellers; in this case differences of language – Berber, French, and Arabic – only compound attitudinal differences created by different means of subsistence (animal herding and agriculture) and widely variant types of education and culture. In Yemen and Lebanon, they have provided lines of separation between different religious and political groupings, as twentieth-century conflicts in both regions have convincingly demonstrated.

This wide expanse of territory that constitutes the Arab world, with its variety of geographical and climatic features, is peopled by citizens of many nations who speak Arabic and thus trace their linguistic and cultural origins back to the Arabian peninsula. The earliest period in the development of the Arabic language and the poetic expressions through which the nomadic life of the tribe was represented have been idealised throughout the history of Arabic literature. Many of the predominant themes depicted in the literature of the pre-Islamic period–the power of community, encampments, travels, horses, camels, palm-trees–continue to resonate in the minds of Arab littérateurs. The texts of the Qur'ān and prophetic tradition (*ḥadīth*) are filled with references to the image of the palm-tree; the latter source enjoins mankind to 'honour the palm tree which was created from Adam's own clay'. Relics of this aspect of the pre-Islamic way of life endure in colourful ways: the system of metrics (*ʿarūḍ*) devised by the great scholar of al-Baṣrah, al-Khalīl ibn Aḥmad (d. 791), uses the term *bayt* (tent) for the line of poetry, and *sabab* (tent-rope) and *watad* (tent-peg) for the segments of an individual foot. The ancient virtue of *ṣabr* (tolerance of adversity, endurance) was often invoked by the vagabond (*ṣuʿlūk*) poets of the pre-Islamic period in their taunts levelled at the 'soft' life of the tribe, and has since been cited often to explain a willingness to 'bide one's time': in the case of the Crusaders, for example, who were eventually ejected after centuries of occupation. Once again, the Qur'ān provides an appropriate and much cited phrase to reflect this value through the words of Jacob in the Sura of Joseph (*Sūrat Yūsuf*): '*ṣabrun jamīlun*', '[my best plan is] a beautiful patience'. Yet another such traditional virtue is that of hospitality, a quality that, as any visitor to the Arab world knows, remains as prevalent and forceful as ever. This, after all, is a culture in which the poet will describe a man as having 'much ash beneath his cauldron' as a means of denoting his generosity; the amount of cooking that he has done in order to fulfil the requirements of hospitality has caused the wood-ash to form a pile.

When the great social historian, Ibn Khaldūn (1332–1406), wrote the Introduction (*Muqaddimah*) to his book of history, he proceeded to develop a cyclical theory of civilisation that was based on the traditional tribal virtues of the Bedouin, some of which we have just mentioned: courage, endurance, and, above all, group solidarity (*ʿaṣabiyyah*). His model at the time envisaged two elements – desert culture and civilization, with the former continually replacing and invigorating the latter. More recent research in the social sciences (of which Ibn Khaldūn is often cited as the founder) has demonstrated that this twofold model – the settled life of the city as opposed to the nomadic life of the desert – needs to be expanded to include more variegated categories: different kinds of pastoral nomads, migrants, and, with the establishment of more and more urban regions, the institution of the village and its peasant farmers. The growth of cities in the Arab world, and especially the emergence of the great Islamic centres – al-Baṣrah, Baghdad, Cairo, Qayrawān, Fez, and Cordoba, for example – as sources of religious debate and intellectual dynamism, was to have a major impact on both urban and provincial life, frequently to the detriment of both. Cairo, the capital city of Egypt, is perhaps the most extreme example of this, in that fully one quarter of the inhabitants of the entire country live within the city's boundaries. Numerous littérateurs have addressed themselves to the tense relationship between city and countryside. ʿAbd al-wahhāb al-Bayātī (b. 1926), for example:

> The weary harvesters say:
> 'They planted, but we never ate,
> We underlings do the sowing, they eat.
> People coming back from the city – what a blind beast it is! –
> Its victims are our own dead, the bodies of women, decent folk who dream.'
>
> 'Sūq al-qaryah' from *Abārīq muhashshamah*

But people still leave the countryside and pour into the cities; and this is just one type of migration. The discovery of oil and the vast wealth that it has brought to the countries of the Gulf region has led to the migration of huge numbers of workers in search of a living wage.

Industrialisation, the exploitation of oil, improvements in transport and communications, developments in education, all these factors have served to change the nature of the relationship of the nations of the Arab world with other nations and with each other. As we will see in the chapters that follow, all of these phenomena have an impact upon the Arab intellectual's self-view and the way in which that finds a reflection in literature. In spite of all this however, the connection to place and the emotional attachment to the values enshrined in the earliest period of the literary tradition remain strong.

There are two particular 'lenses' through which the Western world examines the Middle East that need to be identified; not so much to avoid their use as to admit the limitations that they impose. Both have been represented, to a certain extent, in the comments that have already been made in this chapter. The first involves treating 'the Arabs' and 'Islam' as monoliths, and indeed often to fuse the two into one. To be sure, the majority of Arabs are Muslims, but there are significant communities of Arabs who are not – the Maronites of Lebanon and the Copts of Egypt, for example. On the other hand, many Muslims are not Arabs; Iranians, for example, (whose Persian language is a member of the Indo-European family), Pakistanis, and large communities in Malaysia, Indonesia, and China. But, beyond these points of information, there lies the assumption that the peoples of a region as diverse in history and culture as the one that we have just described can be described as a single, unified whole on the basis of their being linked by a common language (in itself a problematic notion, as we shall see below). Differences in dialect, in geography, external cultural influences (and especially European imperialism), all these contribute to a diversity that Arab unity, represented by ʿAbd al-Nāṣir's ringing phrase 'from the Atlantic Ocean to the Arabian Gulf we are Arabs', has endeavoured to address. The same principle can be applied to Islam, an entity which the Western world has always found it convenient to treat as a monolith in order to compensate for a failure to investigate its variety. Perhaps we might suggest, adopting de Saussure's well-known categories, that Islam, like other faith systems, clearly stipulates what constitutes its *langue* – the canonical texts that lay down the basis for its principles, but that the *parole*, the actual application in such areas as the difference between the tenets of the Sunnī and Shīʿī communities and the practices of Sufism and popular Islam, presents us with a staggering variety of beliefs and rituals which reflect the world-wide scope of the faith.

The second lens that I have been using is the term 'Middle East', an American term that, along with the European 'Near East', reflects the geographical location of those who coined it. Numerous scholars have addressed themselves to the precise designation of this region, pointing out as they do so that very few of the borders in the region were drawn by its inhabitants. For some the Middle East is coterminous with 'the Fertile Crescent', the 'central lands' of the region – Lebanon, Syria, Jordan, Israel, Egypt. However, in academic terms departments that carry the name Middle East will teach not only Arabic, but also Persian and Turkish (and often others as well), thus including within their purview the broader definition of the Arab world represented by not only ʿAbd al-Nāṣir's Ocean-to-Gulf phrase, but also the Arab nations represented at the United Nations and the Arab League. It is this broader definition of the world of Arabic literature that will be intended when the phrase 'Middle East' is used in this book; indeed, the need to examine the literature of al-Andalus in the West and, on occasion, the lands 'beyond the river' in the East require an even broader definition.

THE LINGUISTIC CONTEXT

Arabic is the official language of a large number of nations in Africa and Asia: Morocco, Algeria, Tunisia, Libya, Egypt, the Sudan, Jordan, Lebanon, Syria, Palestine, Iraq, Saudi Arabia, Kuwait, Bahrain, Qatar, Oman, the United Arab Emirates, and Yemen. These nations make up what is known as the 'Arab world', and, as we point out in the discussion of the bases of Arab nationalism later in this chapter, the Arabic language and its cultural heritage, transcending issues of race, religion, and class, has been one of the most powerful forces in twentieth-century aspirations towards Arab unity. The Arabic language also has official status in Israel, and, because of continuing contacts across the desert regions of North Africa, is used for communication in such states as Senegal, Mauretania, and Chad. If we include within our purview the use of Arabic as the canonical language of Islam, then the spread of nations and peoples becomes enormous, incorporating Iran, Pakistan, Bangladesh, Malaysia, Afghanistan, and Indonesia as Muslim countries, and sizeable communities in many other countries, of which Tajikistan, India, the Philippines, China, France, Britain, and the United States are merely a representative sample. Arabic is also the official language of the League of Arab States founded in Cairo in 1945, and is one of the official languages of the United Nations. Arabic is a Semitic language, and it is generally credited by historical linguists as being the member of that family of languages that has preserved the largest number of features of postulated proto-Semitic. While the languages of both the northern segment of the group – Akkadian in the east, and Hebrew, Ugaritic, and Aramaic in the west, and the southern – Ethiopic and South Arabian, were subject to significant change (and in some cases to extinction) as a result of the different cultures and languages with which they regularly came into contact, the development of Arabic among the nomadic tribes of the Arabian Peninsula seems to have resulted in the preservation of a large number of morphological and syntactic features that not only provides evidence concerning the characteristics of the language from which they all stem but also furnishes comparative data for the analysis of older texts in a language such as Hebrew where the original grammatical structures have been reduced.

Linguists term Arabic one of those languages that are 'diglossic', by which they imply that its native-speakers will use different registers of language according to the requirements of the social situation involved. The first language of every native-speaker of Arabic will be one of a number of colloquial dialects. That language will be used in the home and in day-to-day communication between inhabitants of the dialect area in question. As is the case with any language, there are of course many sub-dialects within each country and region, but one may begin by making a distinction on the broadest scale between the dialects of the Maghrib (Libya and westward) and those of the Eastern countries.

Within the latter group the dialect of Cairo has, by dint of population size and the widespread popularity of contemporary Egyptian media, come to be regarded in the region (and among Western Arabists) as the colloquial that is at least understood (if not spoken) by the largest number of people. Other clusters of dialects include the 'Levantine' (Israel, Jordan, Lebanon, Palestine, Syria) and the Gulf (Saudi Arabia, Iraq, and the Arab Emirates).

The emergence of these dialects seems to have begun with the early conquests of Islam. As the Muslim soldiers from different tribes of the Arabian Peninsula congregated in the garrison cities (*amṣār*) of the border regions (such as al-Kūfah, Fusṭāṭ, and Qayrawān), the practicalities of day-to-day – not to mention, military – living demanded that their different language systems be fused into a *koine* language of communication. In each of these venues this particular type of language began to adopt its own characteristics as speakers of other languages joined the Muslim community and set about learning and then using its language. To these changes implicit in the geographical diversity of the Muslim community in the classical period has been added in the past century and a half a further differentiating factor in the form of neologisms and technical terms culled from the lexica of Western languages, initially Italian as a result of trade with Genoa and Venice, but later French and English. Thus, the Lebanese word for a lorry or truck is *kamiyon* while in Jordan the word is *lūrī*.

For the many inhabitants of the Arab world who receive little or no education the colloquial dialect will be the only language they use to communicate. While a number of television programmes will be broadcast in the colloquial dialect of the region, newspapers and televised news bulletins use the 'standard' language which we will discuss below. This leads to fascinating situations that I myself have witnessed whereby a more literate member of the community gathered around the café's television set will be called upon to explain the details of a news item to the others present. Because of the predominantly oral nature of the colloquial dialects we possess little historical record either of their use in daily communication or of the various types of entertainment that may have been performed in them, but the development of more synchronic attitudes to language as well as other social phenomena that marks what one might term the post-Saussurean era in the twentieth century has led to a significant increase of interest among Arab scholars and Western linguists. In the sphere of literature, the demands of drama for realism on stage have led not only to the performance of plays in the colloquial language but also to the publication of some of the texts of those plays in printed form.

The colloquial dialect is then the first language of all native-speakers of Arabic. Those who attend school and even proceed on to university acquire as a second kind of Arabic language what is known in Arabic as *al-lughah al-fuṣḥā* or simply *al-fuṣḥā*. This is the written form of Arabic that is standard throughout the Arab world and thus a major expression of the Arab individual's sense of identity and unity with his fellow Arabs. While very early examples of the language are to be found in Assyrian, Nabatean (first century BC to fourth century AD), and Palmyrene (first to third centuries AD) sources, the primary yardstick for this standard Arabic language is the Qur'ān, regarded as the supreme and inimitable masterpiece of Arabic. The Qur'ān's clear statement that it is 'an Arabic Qur'ān' and that every sacred revelation comes to its people in their own language initiated a movement of standardisation that, to a remarkable degree, has preserved the classical patterns of standard Arabic morphology and syntax. In the eighth and ninth centuries the grammarians of al-Kūfah and al-Basṛah set about sifting and recording the principles of the language, and local variants that fell outside the framework of such a system of 'regularity' were scrupulously noted, presumably so as to be avoided at all costs; the phrase of a luckless Yemeni, '*akalūnī al-barāghīthu*' (*sic*) (the fleas have eaten me) – with an 'irregular' plural verb-form preceding a plural noun depicting a non-rational being, has become proverbial in this context.

However, in spite of the availability and application of such powerful conservative forces, the written Arabic language did undergo the natural process of linguistic change. From the outset, some countries adopted the language as their own mode of written communication: Egypt, Syria, and Iraq, for example. Others adopted Arabic as part of the process of conversion to Islam, but the indigenous language of the region remained a powerful source of social cohesion – as with Berber in the Maghrib, for example. Persian and Turkish later reassumed their positions as the primary mode of cultural expression for their native speakers while Arabic maintained its canonical status within those spheres (such as the law) where the role of Islam retained its significance. Those inhabitants of the conquered territories who converted to Islam brought to Arabic several features of their own native languages, and this gradual process of adaptation and change was accelerated by the translation movement of the eighth and ninth centuries (discussed in more detail below) whereby works from the Indo-Persian and Greek traditions were rendered into Arabic. As the intellectual centres of the expanding Islamic community now became the bases for scholarship in a huge variety of disciplines – for example, grammar, law, mathematics, astronomy, music, philosophy, medicine, and literature, so did the Arabic language become a clear, subtle and adaptive medium for recording a truly remarkable tradition of learning.

While the great canonical Islamic works of the classical period of Arabic learning show a remarkable degree of unanimity regarding the appropriate level of discourse to be used, the different cultures gathered together within the framework of Islam, the wide variety of subjects that were the object of scholarly research, and the sheer passage of time made it inevitable that elements of difference were also evident in the written language. However, the very regularising instincts of the grammatical tradition and our less than complete knowledge of some six centuries (twelfth to eighteenth) of Arabic linguistic history combine to make it difficult to comment in detail on the effects on written Arabic discourse of a period in which the dominance of other languages (particularly Ottoman Turkish) and the political fragmentation of the Arabic-speaking regions seem to have served in several spheres to narrow the gap separating the structures of the written language–*al-fuṣḥā* – from those of the colloquial dialects. Whatever the case may be, the movement of cultural revival that followed contacts with the Western world in the eighteenth and nineteenth centuries found itself able to revive the classical tradition of language and to reassert the primacy of its principles in the face of yet another process of cultural and linguistic interchange, this time with the forces of European colonialism. Such is the continuing immense prestige of the standard language – the language of the Qur'ān and the classical heritage of Arab-Islamic culture, that the morphology and syntax of modern written Arabic show remarkably little change from those of the classical written language. Organisations such as the Language Academies (*majāmiʿ ʿilmiyyah*) of Damascus (founded in 1919) and Cairo (founded in 1932) have met with the somewhat equivocal success that characterises such institutions everywhere in monitoring language change, most particularly in the lexical realm. Even so, the hallowed place accorded *al-fuṣḥā* within the cultural mindset of the vast majority of Arabic speakers today, whatever their nation, race, or religion, makes it a principal symbol of stability in a context of continual change.

Combining our discussion of these two types of language, the colloquial and the standard, we may suggest that a native-speaker of Arabic operates along a spectrum that starts from a pole represented by the colloquial language. That colloquial language itself will have a number of different levels that will be appropriate for different social occasions: from reprimanding a recalcitrant child, to talking on the telephone to a tradesman, to engaging in persuasive discourse with a policeman who has just stopped the driver for a traffic offence, and lastly perhaps to watching a play on stage or a soap-opera on television performed in the local dialect. Those people who enter the educational system will move along the same spectrum towards the achievement of the status of an educated person. Here the linguistic yardstick is the classical Arabic language and its current manifestation, often termed modern standard Arabic. Quite apart from the chronological distinction implied by the 'classical' language of the cultural heritage and the 'current' (or 'modern'), there are other distinct levels of language at this end of the spectrum also: from discussions among educated people on the media, to news bulletins, to official speeches and sermons, and to some types of drama. Thus, in between the two poles of dialect and standard there are an infinite number of intermediate positions of language-use that will be governed by the education of the speaker in question and the nature of the situation involved. It is part of the social-cultural skill of every educated native-speaker of Arabic to be able to code-switch appropriately between these different registers of language, and it is incidentally in this particular area of socially appropriate language-use that the most interesting regional differences are noticeable. Thus, for example, while in the countries of the Gulf region the language of most public meetings and certainly of speeches and sermons will be standard Arabic, in Egypt the colloquial dialect is considered a culturally appropriate means of communication on virtually all occasions.

Thus far, I have endeavoured to discuss the Arabic language and its development within a context as culturally value-free as possible, a task that, I fully admit, is well-nigh impossible. For, while linguists specialising in the study of Arabic may endeavour to describe the language as it is used by its native-speakers, religion and cultural heritage combine to assign widely variant degrees of prestige to the different types. We can begin by considering the terms themselves. *Al-fuṣḥā* (or *al-lughah al-fuṣḥā*) is in the form of a comparative adjective: it implies 'the language that is more correct'. The dialects by contrast are called *ʿāmmiyyāt* (languages of the populace) or the less pejorative *lughāt dārijah* (current languages). The attitudes implicit in these terms and in a general failure to analyse the large space that inevitably lies between them colour the discussion of the cultural value of many modern literary genres, most especially drama and fiction. They have also served to consign surviving texts of earlier popular literature to the realm of non-literature; this includes the *Thousand and One Nights* itself, a work that was recorded in a form of the written language that reflects the discourse practices of story-telling rather than those of élite literature. Najīb Maḥfūẓ, the 1988 Nobel Prize-winner in Literature, calls colloquial Arabic 'a disease' from which he hopes the people will recover. This attitude may be seen as a reflection of the widely held belief that the dialects are not to be regarded as a distinct and different level of Arabic, each with its own history, but rather a corruption of the classical language that needs to be rectified within the idealised context of an Arab nation unified in its use of a single language.

One of the features of Arabic which links it to the other Semitic languages is the basis of its lexicon on a series of consonantal patterns usually called roots. Thus, the triconsonantal structure K-T-B denotes the semantic field of writing. *KaTaBa* means 'he wrote', *KāTiBun* (the active participle) means 'a writer, scribe, secretary', *maKTūBun* (the passive participle) means 'written, fated', *maKTaBun* (the noun of place) means 'desk, office', *Kitābun* means 'book', *KuTTāBun* means 'Qur'ān school', and so on. The great lexicons of Arabic are arranged on the assumption that the predominant root structure is, as K-T-B suggests, triconsonantal. However, a number of features of the root system combine to call into question the triconsonantal arrangement as an accurate reflection of the language's development. Not only are many of the most basic words in the language biconsonantal ('son', 'father', 'year', 'name', 'language', 'blood', 'lip', and so on), but others consist of a uniconsonantal root (such as F for mouth, also providing *fī* for 'in'). There also exists a quadriliteral root category, a large number of whose members consist of reduplicated biconsonantal patterns (such as *RaFRaFa*, 'to flutter'). It thus seems at least possible that the currently predominant triconsonantal mode of lexical organisation reflects an earlier biconsonantal pattern (or less) to which other consonantal markers were appended.

This algebraic approach to language analysis also makes its way into morphology; incidentally one might suggest that an intellectual community that used such methods to analyse its language was a natural fostering-ground for the mathematical discipline of algebra (*al-jabr*) itself. The consonantal structure of the verb *F-ʿ-L* (to do) becomes the framework which can be used to illustrate the forms of verbs and nouns; they being two of the three categories in Arabic grammar, while the third is particles – whatever is not a noun or verb. Using once again the root K-T-B I can say that *KaTaBa* (he wrote, also the basic morphological pattern for the verb) is of the pattern *Faʿ aLa* while *KāTiBun* is of the pattern *Fāʿ iLun*. When we turn to the verb, we find that each example will have two basic time frames – complete and incomplete, active and passive participles, and a gerund (for example, *QaTaLa*, he killed: *yaQTuLu*, he kills; *QāTiLun*, killer; *maQTūLun*, killed; *QaTLun*, murder), but that each root will also have a number of derived forms that, in most cases, will have a predictable semantic effect on the sense of the root pattern. Using the root *ʿaLiMa* (to know), the *Faʿʿ aLa* form (marked by an elongation in the pronunciation of the central consonant) has a causative force: thus, *ʿaLLaMa* means to cause someone to know, to teach; its passive equivalent is the form *taFaʿʿ aLa*, and thus *taʿ aLLaMa* means to be taught, to learn. My primary purpose in providing these illustrations of Arabic morphology is to demonstrate that the possibilities of rhyme, paranomasia and other plays on the sounds and shapes of words in Arabic are almost infinite. The very fact that Arabic grammatical analysis chooses to emphasize such features of the language may help to explain the great delight that littérateurs have taken from the earliest times in the morphological potential of the language.

Arabic has two types of sentence structure: the nominal sentence which begins with a noun, and the verbal sentence which begins with a verb. Using the two stars of Arabic grammar sentences, ʿAmr and Zayd, and their preferred verb, 'to strike', I can say: *ʿAmrun ḌaRaBa Zaydan* and *ḌaRaBa ʿAmrun Zaydan*, where the English translation of both is 'ʿAmr struck Zayd'. The former is a nominal sentence; the assumption behind the choice of this kind of sentence structure over a verbal sentence is that ʿAmr is to be the topic about whom a particular piece of information is to be imparted. In the verbal sentence emphasis is given to the description of the action that occurred; indeed the first word in the sentence will not only convey the nature of the action, but also the time frame and person and gender of the subject.

The features of the Arabic language, its huge lexicon with a concomitant potential for enrichment and obfuscation, its repertoire of morphological transformations, its exultation in the sheer beauty of the sound of words, these elements have served as the inspiration for generations of littérateurs who have made virtuoso use of the potential it offers.

THE HISTORICAL CONTEXT

Introduction

The breadth of the geographical space into which the Islamic dominions expanded is matched by the length of their recorded history. If we adopt the year AD 622 – the beginning of the *hijrah* era marked by the Prophet Muḥammad's 'emigration' from Mecca to Medina – as a point of reference, then we are talking of some thirteen centuries. However, this time frame also has to be extended backwards. In ch. 1 I noted the primary historical division that is created by the revelation of the Qur'ān to Muḥammad: between an Islamic period and a pre-Islamic one, termed *al-jāhiliyyah* (the period of ignorance). However, as the Muslim community began to realise the need to codify the Arabic language and to assess the accuracy of the carriers (*ḥamalah*, sing. *ḥāmil*) of the Qur'ānic text, the pre-Islamic period came to be regarded as a repository of information that was of extreme value to the emerging scholarly communities in the fields of the Islamic sciences. One of the most illustrious of the early historians, al-Ṭabarī (d. 923), who was one of the first to record the early history of Islam within the broader context of world history and who devoted the lion's share of his account to a detailed investigation of the Islamic period, nevertheless begins his account with the story of the Creation and the Fall and then uses a combination of biblical, pre-Islamic Arabian and Iranian myths as a means of linking together received wisdom concerning the earliest periods in the region that was brought together under the aegis of Islam.

The title of al-Ṭabarī's work of history, *Taʾrīkh al-rusul wa-al-mulūk* (History of Prophets and Kings), clearly announces not only its subject-matter but also its approach to history, one that is primarily concerned with particular types of contributors to history viewed within a diachronic perspective. The tradition of historical writing, of which al-Ṭabarī's work is such an outstanding example, provided the groundwork for a periodisation scheme that has tended to serve the purposes of literary studies as well as historical. Within such an organising matrix, the fall of Baghdad to the Mongol invaders in 1258 comes to be seen not only as a cataclysmic event, but also as the dividing point between a classical era in Islamic culture that precedes it and a period of considerable cultural diversity and aesthetic ambiguity that follows it, only to be broken by the advent of the modern period through a process of cultural revival in the eighteenth and nineteenth centuries. This subdivision of the Islamic (as opposed to pre-Islamic) period into a classical era, a period of decadence, and a modern era finds itself in severe difficulty not only in dealing with the second of the three periods but also in determining what precisely are the cultural factors that link or divide the different eras.

While this study of the Arabic literary tradition has chosen, in the light of these problems (also alluded to in Ch. 1), to analyse the development of genres under organising principles different from the purely dynastic approach, I will now provide a historical context for the literary production that is my primary focus, including reference to those features that are of particular relevance to literature and the status of the littérateur.

Pre-Islamic Arabia

The Arabian city of Mecca (Makkah) is set in the mountains to the east of the Red Sea coast at approximately the halfway point between South Arabia and the lands of the Fertile Crescent to the north. In the period before the sixth century AD it was a major staging-post on the trade-route that brought the products of Yemen, the land of Sabā (Sheba), the proverbial *Arabia felix* of the Roman Empire, to the Mediterranean. Mecca was thus a thriving mercantile community, but it was also renowned for other reasons. Close by were Mount ʿArafāt, a traditional place of pilgrimage, and the town of ʿUkāẓ which was the venue of a celebrated annual poetry festival at which tribal poets would compete. Within the city of Mecca itself was the Kaʿbah, a remarkable sanctuary enclosure that served as the focus for the worship of a number of pagan deities. The guardians of this shrine in the sixth century were the tribe of Quraysh. Apart from cities such as Mecca, another kind of venue at which the more sedentary tribes would cluster was the oasis, which, needless to say, provided other opportunities for commercial activity. One such was the town of Yathrib, some two hundred miles due north of Mecca. It was to this town that Muḥammad travelled in secret in 622. As it became the centre of the new Muslim community, so did its name change to *Madīnat al-nabī* (the city of the Prophet), abbreviated to al-Madīnah or Medina.

The harsh terrain and climate of the central regions of the peninsula seem to have served for the most part as effective barriers to incursions from the outside. To the north and east two tribal confederations served as buffers between the peoples of the peninsula and the two major empires of the region. The Banū Ghassān fulfilled this function *vis-à-vis* the Byzantine authorities based in Constantinople (now Istanbul), while the Banū Lakhm operated from a capital at al-Ḥīrah in Southern Iraq in their dealings with the Sasanian rulers of Persia. The fact that these two mighty empires had been almost continually at war with each other for more than a century is often cited as a partial explanation for the ease with which the entire region was conquered by the Muslim armies.

The Prophet Muḥammad and the first caliphs

It was in the city of Mecca that Muḥammad received his first revelation in about AD 610. He had been taken under the protection of his uncle, Abū Ṭālib, following the death of his father, and had successfully engaged in trade on behalf of a wealthy widow, Khadījah, whose offer of marriage he accepted. Following his custom of contemplating as he wandered the hills near the city, he heard a voice that told him: 'Recite in the name of your Lord who created, created mankind from a blood-clot' Sūra 96. This was to be the first of the revelations that he received for the rest of his life and that were gathered together after his death as the Qur'ān. At first Muḥammad only revealed the messages to his close companions, including his wife and Abū Bakr who later became the first caliph. Abū Ṭālib did not become a convert, but his son, ʿAlī, was another early convert who married Fāṭimah, Muḥammad's daughter. When Muḥammad began to preach his message – of a transcendent God who passes judgement on sinners and of his own role as a prophet, the reaction of the Meccans was one of antipathy to both the content of the message and its implications for their way of life. Following the death of both Abū Ṭālib and Khadījah in 619, the situation of Muḥammad and his followers became progressively more difficult, and in 622 he accepted the invitation of a group of tribal leaders in the oasis of Yathrib to serve as arbiter in their dispute with each other. This *hijrah* (emigration) is a major event in Islamic history in that Muḥammad's arrival in Medina marks the beginning of the formation of the Muslim community that was soon to burst out of the Arabian Peninsula and establish itself as a major world religion.

The ten years that Muḥammad spent in Medina laid the groundwork for the emergence of Islam as a community and system of belief. The revelations of that period were to form the basis for many of the institutions, laws, and societal norms that were to govern the behaviour of Muslims. As the new religious community began to establish its guidelines in this way, some of the groups who had initially welcomed

Muḥammad's arrival began to dissociate themselves. The Jewish tribes of Yathrib that had initially shown appreciation for his role as arbiter and preacher refused to accept the tenets of the new religion that was being expounded to them, in spite of the acknowledgement that it gave to both the 'people of the book' (*ahl al-kitāb*), as Jews and Christians were described in the Qur'ānic revelations, and the Biblical prophets. At this time Muḥammad was inspired to change the direction of prayer for the new community from Jerusalem to Mecca. Meanwhile, relations with the Meccan community remained antagonistic, particularly when the Muslims launched attacks on the Meccan caravan trade. However, after a series of battles that displayed the strength of the new community, an agreement was reached between the two sides in 628 that permitted Muḥammad to lead a large group on a pilgrimage to Mecca in the following year. Many people now converted to the new faith, including figures like Khālid ibn al-Walīd and ʿAmr ibn al-ʿĀṣ who were to play a major role in the spread of Islam in subsequent decades. In 632 Muḥammad again travelled from Medina to Mecca to perform the pilgrimage (*ḥajj*), but died suddenly in June of that year.

At the time of Muḥammad's death no arrangements had been made concerning the authority structure of the community of believers that he had brought together. However, he did bequeath to his successors two sets of sources that were of enormous importance to the development of Islam. The first was, of course, the revelations of the Qur'ān that are regarded by Muslims as God's word to His community conveyed to them in Arabic by one of His messengers or prophets; and Muḥammad is in fact designated as the 'Seal of the Prophets' (*khātam al-anbiyāʾ*). Those revelations were memorised and written down by Muḥammad's followers and later gathered together into textual form through what is known as the Uthmanic recension, since the process of compiling the revelations from various sources, the canonisation of the resulting text, and the eradication of the other versions (by burning), were all realised during the time of the third Caliph, ʿUthmān. The second important source that Muḥammad created was his personal practice during his lifetime (*sunnah*) which was regarded as providing a model of behaviour for the community in those many particular situations for which the corpus of Qur'ānic revelations provided no guidance. The process of collecting, organising, and assessing the 'traditions' (*ḥadīth*) concerning the Prophet's activities became, along with the analysis of the text of the Qur'ān itself, one of the most urgent tasks of scholars within the Muslim community.

After the unexpected death of Muḥammad, the elders of the Muslim community convened a meeting at which Abū Bakr, one of the very first converts to the faith, was chosen as the first holder of the position of 'successor of the Prophet of God' (*khalīfat rasūli l-lāh*) or Caliph. Abū Bakr found himself placed at the head of a religious community (*ummah*) that was to be based on principles that had yet to be codified. Furthermore, the ties that had bound together the various groups attracted to the community during Muḥammad's lifetime were now shown to be not a little ambiguous. Some tribes came to the conclusion that their affiliation with the Muslim community had been annulled by the Prophet's death, and much of Abū Bakr's brief period as Caliph (r. 632–4) was spent in the so-called *Riddah* (apostasy) wars, the process of bringing the Arabian tribes back into the fold by force. It was the decision of Abū Bakr's shrewd successor, ʿUmar ibn al-Khaṭṭāb (r. 634–44), to channel much of this tribal recalcitrance to the benefit of the community by initiating a process of expansion which is one of the most remarkable in world history. In 634 Khālid ibn al-Walīd defeated a Byzantine force in Syria; Damascus fell in 636 and Jerusalem in 638. By 643 ʿAmr ibn al-ʿĀṣ had captured the whole of Egypt. The armies of the Sasanian empire were defeated in the major battle of Qādisiyyah in 637, resulting in the occupation of the entire region of Iraq.

This first wave of conquests was accomplished within little more than a decade of Muḥammad's death. In a second era of expansion, Muslim armies moved across North Africa. The governor of the region, Mūsā ibn Nuṣayr, dispatched a party headed by his Berber commander, Ṭāriq, that reached the Straits separating Africa from the Iberian Peninsula in 710. Crossing the water (during which he passed by Jabal Ṭāriq (Ṭāriq's mountain, Gibraltar), he initiated the conquest of the Iberian Peninsula. By 743 Muslim armies had crossed the Pyrenees and reached the city of Tours in France where, in a memorable battle against the forces of Charles Martel that has been much fêted in Western historical sources, they were defeated and gradually forced back across the Pyrenees. The Muslim forces also moved against the Byzantine borders in Anatolia, and the repertoire of Arabic panegyric records the many occasions in the eighth, ninth and tenth centuries when the two armies were ranged against each other in this region. Further to the east the lands of Transoxania became part of the Muslim dominions by 713.

While the first phase of these campaigns succeeded in uniting the tribes of the Arabian peninsula in a common purpose, questions regarding legitimacy and authority and specifically the mode of succession to the caliphate continued to beset the community in Medina. Traditional tribal feuds found new outlets as squabbles began to develop over the relative importance within the community of the original emigrants from Mecca (*muhājirun*) as opposed to the 'helpers' (*anṣār*) in Medina. When ʿUmar was assassinated in 644, the caliphate was passed to another early convert to Islam, ʿUthmān ibn ʿAffān (r. 644-56), a member of the Banī Umayyah clan. Lacking ʿUmar's frugality and canny instincts, ʿUthmān managed during his caliphate to stir up considerable resentment by appointing members of his own côterie to important positions. These developments succeeded in further alienating the followers of ʿAlī, Muḥammad's cousin and son-in-law, who believed that this method of selection was depriving him of the position that was rightfully his. When ʿUthmān was assassinated in 656, ʿAlī assumed the caliphate, but objections were immediately raised to the legitimacy of his succession. ʿAlī left Medina in order to bolster his claims with the forces living in the two famous Iraqi garrison cities of al-Kūfah and al-Baṣrah, but near al-Baṣrah he was challenged by two of Muḥammad's former companions and the Prophet's wife, ʿĀʾishah. The Battle of the Camel, so-called because fighting raged around ʿĀʾishah's riding beast, was the first one to bring the Muslim community into conflict with itself. ʿUthmān's cousin, Muʿāwiyah ibn Abī Sufyān (whom he had appointed governor of Syria), now entered the continuing struggle for power, and the inevitable confrontation between the rival claims and interests took place at Ṣiffīn on the River Euphrates in 657. After some skirmishes between the two sides, ʿAmr ibn al-ʿĀṣ, the renowned army commander, suggested an arbitration process. Some of ʿAlī's supporters were disgusted by his acceptance of the proposed resolution and abandoned him, becoming known as *al-khawārij* (sing. *khārijī*, 'those who left'). As we will see in ch. 4, it is the odes of their poets – with their rousing calls to battle for the cause – that most replicate the spirit of the tribal poetry of the pre-Islamic era. The angry opposition of these former colleagues, coupled with the arbitrators' decision to request that ʿAlī renounce the caliphate, weakened his support. In 660 Muʿāwiyah proclaimed himself Caliph, and in 661 a Khārijite assassinated ʿAlī in al-Kūfah.

While Muʿāwiyah was able to consolidate his power as leader of the Muslim community from Damascus, opposition to the way in which the Banū Umayyah had been elected to the caliphate continued to fester. The *Khawārij* maintained their steadfast opposition to the tribal basis of much of the discourse within the community and insisted that the election of the caliph, the community's leader, had to be based on personal qualities of devotion. Al-Ḥasan and al-Ḥusayn, the two sons of ʿAlī, became a rallying-point for forces who believed in the right of Muḥammad's own descendants to the position of caliph. When Muʿāwiyah died in 680 and his son, Yazīd, was designated his successor by heredity, al-Ḥusayn refused to acknowledge the new caliph. In a battle at Karbalāʾ in Iraq al-Ḥusayn's small force of followers was defeated by a much larger group of Yazīd's army, and al-Ḥusayn himself, the grandson of Muḥammad, was killed. *Shīʿat ʿAlī* (ʿAlī's party, usually abbreviated to Shīʿah and its adherents to Shīʿīs), now become a vigorous, yet separate, part of Islam, with its own beliefs, codes of law, and rituals.

The decades following the death of Muḥammad thus witnessed not only a period of territorial expansion but also of internal schism. The demands of the *Khawārij* aside, the Muslim community was now split between, on the one hand, the Banū Umayyah and their followers who had gained possession of the title of caliph and who, believing themselves to be adhering to the *sunnah* of Muḥammad (the Prophet's code of behaviour during his lifetime), came to be known by the term Sunnīs, and, on the other hand, those who continued to support the claims of ʿAlī and his descendants, the Shīʿah.

The caliphate

The Banū Umayyah

Most of the sources that record the events of the period of the Umawī (the adjectival form of Banū Umayyah) caliphate (660–750) are the work of historians writing during the period of the next dynasty of caliphs, the Banū ʿAbbās (750–1258). The Banū Umayyah were ousted from the caliphate as the result of a successful revolution in 750. Not only were attempts made systematically to exterminate the members of the family, but also it was clearly in the interests of subsequent writers to portray the era of their caliphate in less than glowing colours. The Umawī caliphs did transfer the focus of authority away from the Arabian peninsula to the city of Damascus in Syria; they did adopt the principle of heredity as the means of determining succession to the caliphate; and the exquisite artwork in their desert palaces does suggest an appreciation for the more secular aspects of life. However, it is worth noting in this context that the more puritanical ideals that these reactions to the Umawī Caliphs seem to reflect and that are also to be seen in the image of the second Caliph, ʿUmar, seem oddly at variance with the picture of Muḥammad himself that can be gleaned from accounts of his life, and especially those to be found in the famous compilation of early Arabic poetry, the *Kitāb al-aghānī* (Book of Songs) by Abū al-faraj al-Iṣfahānī (d. 967).

If the question of the presentation of the Banū Umayyah in Islamic history is a matter for continuing research, there can be no doubt that, once in power, they faced a formidable set of problems resulting from a number of factors. The task of establishing the procedures that would produce order within the Islamic community (*ummah*) was begun by the Caliph ʿAbd al-Malik (685–705), who, among many other things, ordered the construction of the Dome of the Rock in Jerusalem, a site as revered in Islam as in the faith of Jews and Christians, described in the Qurʾān as 'the people of the book' (*ahl al-kitāb*). The domains of Islamic authority had expanded as more sections of the *dār al-ḥarb* (the haven of conflict) were added to *dār al-Islam* (the haven of Islam). The pace of these conquests severely taxed the military and administrative resources of the young community. To control the outlying regions, garrison cities (*amṣār*) were set up: Fusṭāṭ to the south of present-day Cairo, Qayrawān in Tunisia, and both al-Kūfah and al-Baṣrah in Iraq. Lines of communication between these cities, filled with the soldiers of the victorious Muslim armies, and the central administration in Damascus were long, and it is therefore hardly surprising that the *amṣār* became the focal points of much debate and unrest. The two Iraqi cities were particularly famous for this, and as early as the caliphate of Muʿāwiyah, the discreetly named Ziyād ibn Abīhi (Ziyād, son of his father) was dispatched to restore order. As the Islamic communal structure began to take shape, the dissidence of these two cities was converted to more intellectual pursuits, and they became primary centres of research and learning. A stimulating rivalry gradually developed between the two as scholars in both centres made major contributions to Arabic and Islamic learning.

The area now under Muslim control incorporated within its boundaries a variety of ethnic types, languages, and religious beliefs. The society, and especially that in the garrison towns of the outlying areas, found themselves overwhelmed with converts to Islam (*mawālī*). These people did not command the communal respect accorded to the Arab Muslims who had brought Islam from the peninsula to this larger area, but they were Muslims and had to be accommodated within the community. As the *mawālī* flocked to the garrison towns, the countryside became severely depopulated (especially in the fertile regions of Mesopotamia) and at the same time the treasury was depleted; for, without going into the complexities of taxation at the time, the 'people of the book' were required to pay a head-tax (*jizyah*) in addition to the general land-tax (*kharāj*). It was the function of another administrator-caliph, ʿUmar ibn ʿAbd al-ʿazīz (717–20), to begin the process of establishing a community in which the status of Muslim was of primary importance and other modes of identity were secondary. Meanwhile, those who did not wish to convert to Islam were given a contract of protection (*dhimmah*) and were thus known as *dhimmīs*.

The problems that needed to be addressed by the caliph as head of the *ummah* were enormous, and the measures taken by the Umawī holders of the office were not sufficient to quell the increasing resentment within the community. The Banū Umayyah were viewed by the new converts to Islam as tribal chieftains, as secular monarchs, who continued to indulge in their tribal rivalries and to assert a superiority based on their desert origins in the Arabian peninsula. In 747 these feelings among the *mawālī* burst into a full-scale revolt. From a centre in al-Kūfah, the Banū ʿAbbā – descendants of al-ʿAbbās, Muḥammad's uncle – sent Abū Muslim to the distant province of Khurāsān, where he raised the black flags of rebellion against the Banū Umayyah. Gathering support as they proceeded towards Iraq, the leaders of this revolt against the Banū Umayyah claimed the caliphate for Abū al-ʿAbbās (nicknamed 'al-Saffāḥ' (bloodletter)) in al-Kūfah in 749. The forces of the Banū Umayyah were defeated at the Battle of the River Zāb in 750, and all the members of the Banū Umayyah were systematically killed, apart from a certain ʿAbd al-raḥmān (nicknamed 'Ṣaqr Quraysh' (the falcon of the Quraysh)) who managed to escape detection and made his way to Spain. In 755 he was acknowledged as *Amīr* in Cordoba. When his successor, ʿAbd al-raḥmān III, was acknowledged as caliph in 925, the era of a single caliphate – albeit a focus of both support and opposition – was at an end.

The Banū al-ʿAbbās

In the aftermath of the ʿAbbāsī revolution, many of the groups that had participated in the overthrow of the Umawī dynasty found themselves marginalised. The Banū al-ʿAbbās had peninsular tribal links just as strong as those of the Banū Umayyah, but their revolution had drawn its initial strength from the regions far to the north-east of the peninsula and to the east of Damascus. A number of disparate groups had joined their cause in the hope of seeing an end to Umawī rule. The Shīʿah, for example, who had seen the revolt as an opportunity for their group and its beliefs to assume a more central role in the Islamic community, found their claims thwarted once again as the ʿAbbāsī family claimed the caliphate for themselves and chose to adhere to the tenets of Sunnī doctrine. Abū Muslim himself, who had served as primary instigator of the revolt in Khurāsān, was killed, and his death led to further rebellions as his supporters joined the Khawārij and the Shīʿah in opposing the new ʿAbbāsī authority, one that, in their view, had knowingly manipulated them.

The caliphs of the Banū al-ʿAbbās served as heads of the Islamic *ummah* for a period of five centuries, from 750 till the sack of Baghdad by the Mongols in 1258, an era during which the geographic spread of the *dār al-Islam* continued – extending eastward to the borders of India and establishing contacts far beyond that. This lengthy era is usually subdivided into an initial stage when the caliph, as spiritual leader of a community based on the faith of Islam, managed to maintain some form of control over the region, and a second stage – a period of some three centuries – when the caliph was essentially a symbolic figure at the head of the Muslim community, while secular authority was vested in other offices and the separate regions of the Islamic dominions enjoyed substantial amounts of autonomy.

One of the first gestures of al-Saffāḥ's brother and successor, al-Manṣūr (754–75), was to order the construction of a new city at a point where the Tigris and Euphrates rivers come closest to each other. The establishment of the capital in Baghdad – with its Persian name – in 762 marks an acknowledgement of the expansion of the Islamic dominions and the need to move beyond the region and trappings of a purely Arab power centre. The city now became not only a focal point of caliphal authority and power but also a glittering cultural centre that was the cynosure of all eyes in the Islamic regions and far beyond. The move from Damascus and continuing efforts further to internationalise the inner workings of the Muslim community gave increasing importance to the Persian element that had played such a significant role in the military aspects of the revolution itself. As the bureaucracy began to expand and to organise itself into separate divisions of records, taxes, and military matters, so did an increasing number of Persian administrators come forward to fill the new positions. The Caliphs al-Mahdī (775–85) and Hārūn al-Rashīd (786–809) formalised the recognition of this administrative apparatus by appointing members of the Barmak family (of Persian origin) to the post of *wazīr* (the current term in the Middle East for minister), a decision that set in motion a gradual but continuing process whereby the functions of caliphal authority were subdivided and alternative power centres came into existence. The relationship between Hārūn al-Rashīd and Jaʿfar, his Barmakī *wazīr* – vividly portrayed for us in several tales of the *Thousand and One Nights* – is symptomatic of the problems that were to afflict the caliphate from now on. As Jaʿfar's administrative role became more and more significant, the Caliph seems to have become uneasy with this rival focus of popular appeal. In 803 Jaʿfar and many members of his family paid the ultimate price for this miscalculation when Hārūn al-Rashīd gave orders that he be killed and his relatives disgraced.

Following the death of Hārūn al-Rashīd the tensions aroused by this new Persian influence led to conflict. His Arab wife had produced a son, al-Amīn, while a Persian concubine had given birth to another son, al-Ma'mūn. The struggle for succession between the two sons involved the Muslim community in yet another period of civil war that concluded with al-Ma'mūn's victory over his half-brother in 813. This war, needless to say, wreaked havoc not only on the civilian population of the region but also on the loyalties of the army. The practice was now developed of importing Turkish youths into service in order to create a trained and loyal military force. By the time of the Caliph al-Muʾtaṣim (r. 833–42), this new category of soldiers had become such a disruptive element in the life of Baghdad that the Caliph decided in 836 to move them to the purpose-built city of Samarrāʾ further up the River Tigris, and to establish his centre of authority there. During the half-century of rule from Samarrāʾ, the structure of caliphal authority begins to show signs of coming apart. This is illustrated best perhaps by the prolonged Zanj Rebellion (868–83) during which slaves managed to maintain control of large segments of southern Iraq and to sack the city of al-Baṣrah, an event memorialized in a famous ode by the poet, ibn al-Rūmī (d. 896):

I weep for thee, O Baṣrah! It burns like a lighted fire.
I weep for thee, O haven of all this is good. I chew my fingers in grief.
I weep for thee, O dome of Islam! The sorrow prolongs my suffering.
I weep for thee, O pivot of far-off lands! My grief will linger for years to come.

In 892 the Caliph al-Muʿtaḍid decided to return to Baghdad, but the new patterns of authority had now been firmly established. Continuing struggles between the caliph and the administrative apparatus headed by the *wazīr* and the increasing power of the army produced an unstable political situation that provides the theme for a remarkable play, *Mughāmarat raʾs al-mamlūk Jābir* (The Adventure of Mamlūk Jābir's Head, 1972) – analysed in detail in ch. 6 below – by the modern Syrian playwright, Saʿdallāh Wannūs (b. 1941). The ʿAbbāsī Caliph al-Muqtadir (r. 908–32) is involved in a power struggle with his *wazīr*; the latter invites the ruler of a separate dynasty in Iran to send troops to attack Baghdad. The events presented in this modern play served in fact as a prelude for those of 945 when a military group headed by the Persian family of Buwayh assumed effective authority in Baghdad, reducing the role of the caliph to that of a figurehead.

By this time, several regions within the larger area of Islamic dominion were already politically independent. Al-Andalus had been governed by a separate dynasty of the Banū Umayyah since their fall from power in the east. As the ʿAbbāsī authorities in Baghdad dispatched governors to the different areas of the region, several of them established themselves as local potentates and passed on their position through hereditary succession. The Aghlabī dynasty in Tunis dates from as early as 800 and managed to cause considerable consternation in Europe through its conquest of the island of Sicily that was finally completed in 878. In Egypt Aḥmad ibn Ṭūlūn, the builder of one of Cairo's most glorious mosques, was to establish his own dynasty in 868. Other family dynasties also controlled large segments of the Iranian region. The year 945 sees the completion of a process that put an end to effective caliphal power. In the blunt but accurate phrase of Shawqī Ḍayf, the caliph was now like a parrot in a cage. However, while these changes in the role of the caliph may be viewed in a negative light within the context of a unified vision of Islamic dominion, it needs to be observed that they served the purposes of literature well, in that the numerous petty dynasties that emerged from this break-up of authority provided widespread and variegated opportunities for the patronage of the arts, which were fully exploited by littérateurs. Maḥmūd of Ghaznah (r. 998–1030) and Sayf al-Dawlah al-Ḥamdānī of Aleppo (r. 945–67) are two of the more illustrious rulers whose prestige was further enhanced by littérateurs who earned a living under their patronage.

The steady diminution of caliphal authority during the three centuries that precede the sack of Baghdad by the Mongols in 1258 served to amplify still further the already immense variety of the political and cultural landscape. The Shīʿah community had split into a number of groupings according to their beliefs regarding the legitimacy of the Imams who were ʿAlī's successors. One group, called the Ismāʿīlīs after the eldest son of the sixth Imam, were particularly vigorous in their missionary activity. In 910, one of their number, ʿUbaydallāh, arrived in Tunis and succeeded in wresting power from the Aghlabī ruler. Proclaiming himself Shīʿī Caliph, he named the dynasty that he established Fāṭimī after Fāṭimah, the Prophet's daughter and ʿAlī's wife. In 969 Fāṭimī forces captured the capital city of Egypt and established their rule there. Once again, poetry provides us with a commentary on the event which vividly illustrates the dynastic rivalries of the period. The ode by Ibn Hāniʾ (937–73) which celebrates the capture of Egypt by the Fāṭimī general, Jawhar, begins:

> The ʿAbbāsī rulers ask whether Egypt has been conquered; relay the news to them that the deed is done!
>
> Jawhar has overwhelmed Alexandria, escorted by good news and preceded by victory.

Work started immediately on the building of a new city, named 'the victorious' (Al-Qāhirah, later rendered by Italian travellers who visited the region as 'Cairo'), and in 972 a seat of Shīʿī learning, the al-Azhar Mosque, was established at its centre. Cairo now comes to rival Baghdad as a centre of Islamic culture and learning. Further to the west, the cities of Qayrawān in Tunisia and Fās (Fez) in Morocco continue their process of development as intellectual centres around their great mosques. In al-Andalus, the Umawī dynasty reaches its zenith of power when ʿAbd al-raḥmān III (r. 912–61) proclaims himself as Caliph. At this period, the capital city of Cordoba is one of the major intellectual centres of Europe, and Andalusian society is an admixture of races, religions, and languages, living alongside each other in a fertile atmosphere of intercultural exchange that is of incalculable importance in the intellectual history of Europe. The pattern of decentralisation that we have already seen in the east is replicated in the Iberian Peninsula. The Umawī dominions break up into a number of petty states that almost immediately begin to lose territory to the Christian kingdoms to the north. By 1085 Toledo was in Christian hands, part of the process of *reconquista* that was not completed until 1492 when the forces of the redoubtable Isabella of Castile and her husband, Ferdinand of Aragon, captured Granada and expelled the Arab and Jewish communities to North Africa.

Spain was not the only venue where Christian forces were advancing southward. The Normans overran Sicily, completing its conquest by 1091. The region of Syria had witnessed a succession of conflicts and was divided into areas controlled by the Fāṭimī dynasty of Egypt, the Orthodox Christian Emperor of Byzantium, and the Turkish dynasty of the Saljūqs which had taken over the secular administrative authority in Baghdad (with the connivance of the ʿAbbāsī Caliph, al-Qāʾim) in 1055. By the end of the eleventh century the Saljūqs had seized control of much of the region, including the Holy Places in Jerusalem, a situation that led the Byzantine Emperor to appeal to the Pope in Rome for aid. It was clearly in the interest of the Pontiff of the Western Church to be seen to be offering support to his Eastern counterpart. In 1096 Urban II gave a speech in France that called for a crusade that would lead to the recovery of the Holy Places from the hands of the 'infidels'. The First Crusade set out at once, and Jerusalem was captured in 1099 amid gruesome scenes of pillage, slaughter, and bounty hunting. Several decades later (in 1144) Muslim forces, led by Zanjī, the governor of the Iraqi city of Mawṣil, launched a counter-attack. Zanjī's son, Nūr al-dīn, took over the task of ousting the Crusaders and was soon in control of much of Syria. Nūr al-dīn's nephew, the renowned Ṣalāḥ al-dīn (Saladin), managed to seize power in Egypt following the death of the last Fāṭimī Caliph, al-ʿĀḍid in 1171, and, following the death of his uncle, he undertook the conquest of Syria, first overcoming the almost legendary branch of the Ismāʿīlī Shīʿah known as the Assassins (*hashīshiyyūn*) and then capturing Jerusalem in 1191. Another Crusade now provided a golden opportunity for two more European leaders, France's King Philip and England's King Richard (the Lionheart), to lead their forces to the Holy Land in order to feather their own nests in spirit and in kind. In this case as with the Crusades in general, the motivations and character of the Crusader leaders and the significance of the events themselves need to be viewed in a more balanced light than that provided by much historical writing and, in particular, by popular tales such as that of Robin Hood.

Syria and Egypt were now united under the rule of Ṣalāḥ al-dīn, who had already proclaimed himself Sultan in Egypt in 1171. Upon his death in 1193, his successors – the Ayyūbī dynasty – countered numerous attempts by Christian forces to capture both Jerusalem and Egypt. In 1229 a treaty was signed whereby the Holy City was handed over to the Christians, with the stipulation that the Dome of the Rock should be accessible to Muslims and no fortifications were to be constructed. The last Ayyūbī ruler of Egypt, Tūrān Shāh, was overthrown and killed in

1250 by a most unusual and interesting social group, one of the slave regiments of the army called Mamlūks. These slaves, mostly Turks or Circassians, were purchased as boys, and it was a requirement that no native Egyptian or Syrian could join the group. They proceeded to establish a dynasty based in Cairo in which the Sultan had to be a manumitted slave, a regime that lasted until the Ottoman conquest of Egypt in 1516–17. Even then, the Mamlūks retained authority within Egypt under the overall suzerainty of the Ottoman Sultan in Istanbul, and it was not until 1811 that Mamlūk power was finally eliminated when an Albanian Turkish soldier in the Ottoman army named Muḥammad ʿAlī engineered a spectacular massacre following a banquet in the citadel of Cairo that Ṣalāḥ al-dīn had built on the Muqaṭṭam Hills overlooking the city.

From 1218 the easternmost regions of the Islamic dominions – Transoxania and Khurāsān – began to encounter a new and mighty military force, the armies of the Mongol ruler, Jinkiz (Genghis) Khān. The actual advance of the Mongol forces to the south and west was preceded by terrifying accounts of the barbaric treatment meted out to those who resisted the onslaught: wholesale massacres of populations, piles of skulls, lands laid waste by pillage and flood. In 1256, Hūlāgū Khān, Jinkiz's grandson, moved into Iraq, and the ʿAbbāsī capital fell in February 1258. The city and its inhabitants were subjected to a brutal assault: libraries and mosques were destroyed and the entire ʿAbbāsī family was killed by being trampled to death by horses. The Mongols did not pause to celebrate their triumph, but continued to Syria where they captured Aleppo. However, the advance of the Mongol army, its lines of communication and supply stretched perilously thin, was finally halted at the battle of ʿAyn Jālūt in 1260. The great victory of the Mamlūk army and the military feats of their general, Baybars, are the topic of one of the Arab world's favourite popular epics. Retreating to the east, the Mongols established a dynasty – named Ilkhān after the title of their leaders, converted to Islam, and ruled parts of Persia, Iraq and Anatolia into the fourteenth century.

The sack of Baghdad did not in fact lead to the complete disappearance of the ʿAbbāsī line. When Baybars became Sultan of Egypt in 1260, he invited one of the few surviving members of the caliphal family to come to Cairo, where the much reduced caliphal functions were intended to lend some Islamic legitimacy to the ruling dynasty. This caliphal presence continued in Egypt till 1517 when the Mamlūks were overthrown by the armies of the Ottoman Selīm 'the Grim' (1512–20), and the last ʿAbbāsī holder of the title, al-Mutawakkil, was transferred to Istanbul. Thereafter the Ottoman sultans in Istanbul may have made occasional use of the title of 'caliph', but it was not until the nineteenth century that the title and functions of the caliphate were again invoked as a means of making the Ottoman sultan a rallying-point within the context of a pan-Islamic movement for resistance to the colonial encroachments of the Western powers in the Middle Eastern region. The title and office of caliph were finally abolished by the secularist government of Turkey in March 1924.

The Mamlūk and Ottoman periods

The fall of Baghdad is clearly a major watershed in Islamic history. It marks the end of the lengthy period during which the ʿAbbāsī caliphate was based in Baghdad, thus providing a symbolic focus not only for Sunnī Islamic authority but also for the variety of institutions – including the cultural ones – that supported it. However, we have already noted that the process of fragmentation within the Islamic dominions was well under way long before 1258, and the tenth century had witnessed no less than three caliphates – in Iraq, Egypt, and Spain. Thus, even as we acknowledge the cataclysmic effect of the Mongol invasion in the regions of Persia, Iraq, and Syria, we must wonder whether the more distant regions within the Islamic dominions – the Maghrib and Spain, for example – were affected in any significant way. The inhabitants of al-Andalus, for example, had seen their 'petty kingdoms' (*mulūk al-ṭawāʾif*) replaced by two waves of Muslim zealots from Morocco, the Murābiṭūn (Almoravids) in the eleventh century and the Muwaḥḥidūn (Almohads) in the twelfth. In 1232 Muḥammad ibn al-Aḥmar announced his independence and declared himself Sultan. Six years later he entered the city of Granada and established the dynasty that survived until 1492. While the Mongols were moving through Persia and Iraq towards Baghdad, Ibn al-Aḥmar's successors were in the process of building one of al-Andalus's most spectacular monuments, the Alhambra Palace in Granada (named after the dynasty's founder). One cannot avoid observing that, as the great historian, Ibn Khaldūn (d. 1406), surveyed the recent history of the Maghrib into which he was born and the bewildering speed with which dynasties of local potentates came and went, he had no lack of data with which to illustrate the principles of his cyclic theory of civilisation in the famous *al-Muqaddimah* (Introduction) to his work of history.

During the fourteenth century, the suzerainty of the dynasties that held sway in Persia and Iraq was challenged by a new figure whose reputation for brutality rivalled that of the Mongols: Tīmūr Lang (Tīmūr 'the Lame', usually known in English – as in Marlowe's play – as Tamburlaine). From his capital of Samarqand he first subdued the lands of Khurāsān and the Caucasus, destroying cities and farmlands as he went. After a foray into India (where one of his descendants, Bābūr (1483–1530), was to found the Mughal dynasty) he moved against the Mamlūk territories of Syria, capturing Damascus in 1403. However, Tīmūr died suddenly in 1405 while planning yet another campaign to China. His descendants did not replicate his rapacious instincts and were content to remain as rulers of Transoxania and parts of Persia till the beginning of the sixteenth century.

One of the groups that Tīmūr confronted and overcame during his march to the west was the army of the incipient Ottoman dynasty which traced its origins back to ʿUthmān (Turkish 'Osman'), the son of a tribal leader who in the thirteenth century had assisted the Saljūqs in their ongoing conflict against the forces of Byzantium. Having established a base at Būrsa in Anatolia, the Ottomans took their attack to the Balkans, beginning a process of transformation in the region, the results of which continue to make themselves evident in the break-up of the former Yugoslavia in the 1990s. Bāyezīd I (r. 1389–1402) brought most of the Balkans under Ottoman control, and in 1453 his great-grandson, Mehmet Fātiḥ ('the conqueror'), managed to achieve a long-standing goal of the Ottomans when the city of Constantinople, the seat of Eastern Christendom, was captured. The city was renamed Istanbul and for four and a half centuries was to be the centre of a huge empire and bureaucracy. Like Baghdad in earlier centuries, it was also a glittering cultural jewel, providing patronage in the realms of architecture, painting, music, and literature.

The campaigns undertaken during the reign of Sultan Selīm were of a pace and sweep to rival those of the early Muslim conquests. In 1514 he set out to subdue a rival force that had come to prominence in the regions of Iran, the Ṣafavī dynasty which assumed power after the downfall of Tīmūr's successors and, most significantly, had become a vigorous centre of Shīʿite belief. However, while Selīm succeeded in driving the Ṣafavī forces from Anatolia, the Ṣafavī ruler, Ismāʿīl, who had proclaimed himself Shāh in 1501, consolidated his authority in the region which now constitutes Iran (where Shīʿah Islam remains the national religion). Under Ismāʿīl's successor, Shāh

ʿAbbās I (r. 1588–1629), the city of Iṣfahān became a major centre of learning and culture. His contemporary, Queen Elizabeth of England, sent the Shirley brothers as emissaries to his court, and their writings record amazement at the splendours of the court life that they witnessed. Sultan Selīm now turned his attention southward, and by 1517 he had also defeated the Mamlūk armies and entered the city of Cairo. When Selīm died in 1520, the Ottoman Empire included Anatolia, Syria, Egypt, and the western part of the Arabian Peninsula; the Sultan was 'the custodian of the two holy mosques (Mecca and Medina)', a title that has in more recent times been adopted by the Saudi monarchs. Under his successor, Sulaymān (r. 1520–66) – known as 'the lawgiver' and 'the magnificent', North Africa was brought under Ottoman control. In Europe the armies of the Sultan moved beyond their possessions in the Balkans and besieged the Austrian capital of Vienna.

When we bear in mind the sheer scope of the empire that was administered from Istanbul and the length of time that it held sway over the Middle East region, it should not surprise us that the process of decline, which – as ibn Khaldūn had noted – would involve both inside and outside forces, was a gradual one. Among the outside factors mention should be made of the discovery of the Cape route to the Far East; the East India Companies of Holland and England were established in 1600 and 1601 respectively. Furthermore, the tremendous wealth that Spain was bringing to Europe as a result of its conquests in the Americas also served as a major agent of destabilisation in commerce. Within the Ottoman system itself the huge size of the ruling family frequently led to destructive feuds at the time of succession. Equally damaging to stability and authority was the fact that the tight organisation of the armed forces, most especially the much feared janissary infantrymen and the navy, was allowed to slacken. The military units involved became forces of conservatism, not only in politics but in the strategic realm as well. As such, they ceased to be the formidable force that they had previously presented in their conflicts with the European powers. In the seventeenth and eighteenth centuries Ottoman forays into Europe became less and less successful, and the peace agreements that brought them to an end were increasingly detrimental to Ottoman interests. With the Treaty of Karlowitz in 1699 the Ottomans were forced to hand over Hungary to Austria, while in 1774 the Treaty of Kutchuk Kainardji assigned to the ruler of Russia the right to protect Christians living within Ottoman dominions.

The Middle East and the West

In 1826 the Ottoman Sultan, Maḥmūd II (r. 1808–39), seized the opportunity afforded by the unpopularity of the janissary corps to carry out long-needed reforms to the Ottoman armed forces, recasting them along European lines. European trainers were brought in, a new administration was established, and steps were taken to introduce Western-style education (and the translation schools necessary to provide them with materials). Under Maḥmūd's successor, ʿAbd al-Majīd (r. 1839–61), these initial gestures were expanded into a wide-scale process of reform, known under the general title of *tanẓīmāt* (reorganisations): included were such concepts as subjects' rights, freedom of religion, fair assessment of taxes, and the right of all nations to indulge in free commerce. Such measures were not implemented without considerable conservative opposition, but once set in motion, they were to engender changes in all branches of society and to carry the notion of reform to other areas in the region.

Elsewhere in the Middle East, contacts with Europe took a different form. In Lebanon, for example, the Maronite community had maintained ties with the Vatican in Rome since at least the sixteenth century; a Maronite College had been established by the Pope in 1584. In the eighteenth century, a figure such as Bishop Germanus Farḥāt (d. 1732) wrote a wide variety of works, including books of poetry and grammar, that laid the groundwork for the intensified activity that was to follow the advent of Protestant missionaries in the nineteenth century, most prominently from the United States. The involvement of members of several prominent Lebanese Christian families in the preparation of a Protestant translation of the Bible was to provide both opportunity and impetus for their participation in the early stages of the movement of cultural revival known in Arabic as *al-nahḍah*. By contrast, the level of control exercised by the Ottoman authorities elsewhere – in Syria, Iraq, and the Maghrib, for example – over the intellectual community and its modes of communication with the outside world is often cited as a major factor in the comparatively later emergence of such developments in those regions.

It was in Egypt that the meeting of cultures was most abrupt. As the continuing naval war between Britain and Napoleon's France reached beyond the Western Mediterranean, the French Emperor launched an invasion of Egypt in 1798, bringing with him not only an army and navy but also a substantial group of scientists. The Egyptian army, even though bolstered by Ottoman reinforcements, was roundly defeated at the Battle of the Pyramids. However, even though the French force withdrew following a heavy defeat of its navy by Admiral Nelson, the French occupation was to have a major impact. An Albanian Turkish commander of the Ottoman contingent sent to resist the French, Muḥammad ʿAlī, regarded the invasion and occupation as an obvious demonstration of the extent to which the force that he had commanded could be no match for a well-trained army equipped with modern weaponry. It was Muḥammad ʿAlī who stepped into the power vacuum that was left following the withdrawal of French forces, establishing his family as a dynasty that ruled the country until the revolution of 1952.

In 1809 Muḥammad ʿAlī began sending missions of young men to Europe – to Italy initially and later to France – to study European languages and to learn about military technology. A translation school was established, headed by the imam of one of these missions, Rifāʿah al-Ṭahṭāwī (d. 1873). Manuals on warfare and weaponry were translated. Confirmation of the soundness of Muḥammad ʿAlī's plans was not long in coming. In 1832 he turned against his nominal Ottoman overlords, placing his son, Ibrāhīm, at the head of an Egyptian army that established control over Palestine and Syria and even managed to invade parts of Anatolia itself. The resulting crisis brought Britain and France into the picture on the side of the Ottoman Sultan. Under threat of a British naval blockade, the Egyptian army returned to its homeland. The same agreement however gave Muḥammad ʿAlī and his successors the right to rule Egypt with the title of 'Khedive', as well as authorising his continuing control over the Sudan.

These initiatives in creating a cadre of officers and administrators had obvious benefits beyond the purely military sphere, not least through the educational opportunities that were made available to young Egyptians and the expansion in contacts with European commercial concerns that was the result of the country's need for technology and financial assistance. This applied most notably in the agricultural sector where, after wresting control of much productive land from its traditional owners, Muḥammad ʿAlī considerably expanded the production and export of cotton through the construction of a variety of irrigation projects. The process that began in Muḥammad ʿAlī's reign was continued by his successors, most notably the Khedive Ismāʿīl whose declared intention it was to make Egypt part of Europe. He ordered the construction of new quarters of both Cairo and Alexandria based on the street-plans of

Haussmann's Paris. In 1869 his most grandiose project, the Suez Canal, was opened amid the greatest possible splendour. The Egyptian capital was rapidly becoming a bustling cosmopolitan city, and Western business interests, drawn by the attractive commercial climate that Muḥammad ʿAlī's 'concessions' had created, became heavily involved in the financial affairs of the country. The liveliness of the Egyptian commercial and cultural scene was further enhanced in the 1850s and 1860s when, as a consequence of inter-communal conflict in Syria, large numbers of Christians – including many of the most prominent contributors to the earliest phases in the cultural revival – left their homeland and emigrated to Egypt. Others travelled to England and the Americas where they established the *mahjar* (*émigré*) communities that still exist in such cities as New York, Detroit, and São Paulo.

The French occupation of Egypt in 1798 was the first, albeit short-lived, example of a pattern of Western incursions into the Middle East region that was to be a principal feature of the next century and a half. The strategic value of the region, in its own right and as a stage on the way to the Far East, was not lost on the European powers, most especially France and England. The French invaded Algeria in 1830 and gained control over a small coastal area from which their authority was gradually expanded during following decades. A pattern was established whereby the administration and educational system of the countries of the Maghrib were thoroughly gallicised. Furthermore, a large French community settled in Algeria, and the country came to be considered, indeed administered, as part of France itself; Albert Camus (d. 1960), the 1957 Nobel Laureate in literature, played goalkeeper in the Algerian national soccer team. The War of Independence by which Algeria gained its independence from France (1954–62) was by far the longest and most bitterly fought in the entire region. The British meanwhile were also protecting their interests in India by seizing the port of Aden in Yemen for use as a way station in 1839 and using their navy to establish contacts with the various confederacies on the South Coast of the Arabian Gulf. As these strategic interests came to be joined by others that were of a more commercial nature, governments found themselves drawn still further into the complex web of relationships and motivations in the Middle East region. In 1881 France occupied Tunisia in order to protect its interests there, and in the following year, Britain – initially supported by France but later on its own – used the state of Egypt's finances following the conspicuous spending of the Khedive Ismāʿīl as a pretext for occupying the country. In 1904, an agreement was reached between France, Britain, and Spain acknowledging Morocco as a sphere of French influence in exchange for a similar understanding of the British role in Egypt.

Ibrāhīm al-Muwayliḥī, an Egyptian journalist who resided for many years in Istanbul, described the Ottoman dynasty in 1896 as 'lolling around like a lion ruminating peacefully in the reeds on the banks of the Bosphorus'. Sultan ʿAbd al-ḥamīd had suspended the Ottoman parliament following his succession in 1876, and in subsequent decades he ruled as a dictator, surrounded by sycophants and a vast network of spies. In 1908 a group called the Committee for Union and Progress (CUP), generally known as the 'Young Turks', succeeded in forcing the Sultan to reinstate the constitution. Equally significant, a secularist government was installed, and nationalist movements that were developing throughout the vast expanse of the Ottoman Empire were made yet more aware of the increasing weakness of the Ottoman authority structure and of the possibilities of a quest for independence. In 1914 the Turkish government committed its forces to the First World War on the side of Germany.

Many of the seeds of the conflicts that have continued to affect the Middle East to the present day were sown during and immediately after the First World War; in this connection it needs to be borne in mind that the majority of the borders on any current map of the Middle East are the result of agreements among Western powers and not of indigenous factors. When the tribes of the Arabian Peninsula were persuaded to attack Ottoman positions – the 'Arab Revolt' beginning in 1916 in which T. E. Lawrence was a prominent participant – they were given undertakings (in the so-called Ḥusayn–McMahon correspondence) about independence following the conclusion of the conflict in the region. Meanwhile, 1917 saw the publication of the famous Balfour Declaration in which the British government announced its support for the idea of a homeland for the Jewish people in Palestine, with the additional proviso that the interests of the current population not be affected by the implementation of such a plan. With the end of the First World War, the Ottoman Empire was no more. To all extents and purposes, Egypt and Tunisia had been separate entities for some time, but, as the secular state of Turkey now turned inwards under the rule of Muṣṭafā Kamāl (Atatürk), the remaining areas of the Middle East came to be viewed by the Western powers as 'spheres of influence'. Britain and France avoided the need to resolve the many ambiguities contained in the various understandings that they had reached by agreeing to implement the terms of a secret pact that they had drawn up with Russia in 1916, the Sykes–Picot agreement, all the while acknowledging the intentions of a new participant in the international scene, the League of Nations fostered by the American President Woodrow Wilson, by declaring themselves 'mandate powers' who would be responsible to the new international body. In 1920, France was assigned control of Syria (including Lebanon), while Britain assumed control of Palestine (including Transjordan) and Iraq. The French control of the Maghrib and the British of Egypt remained as they had been. In other words, Ottoman control of large segments of the Arab world was replaced by that of European mandate powers, and the hopes of many Arab nationalist groups were crushed.

The years 1919 and 1920 saw popular nationalist uprisings against the policies of British occupying forces in Egypt and Iraq. The years between the two World Wars were to be a period of constant confrontation between the increasingly strident demands of pan-Arab and local nationalisms and the maintenance of the status quo by the mandate powers. In Palestine the British found themselves bogged down in a political quagmire largely of their own making; the few attempts that were made to deal with an essentially impossible situation only managed to antagonise both the indigenous Palestinians and the increasing number of Zionist immigrants. In 1943 an agreement between Sunnīs and Maronites in Lebanon led to the foundation of a Lebanese state, one that was based on a tragically fragile balance between the different communities – as the events of the 1970s and 1980s showed all too clearly. The Saudi family consolidated its control in the Arabian Peninsula, while Western oil interests were permitted to explore the extent of the reserves lying beneath its soil. However, any moves in the direction of independence that may have been granted by the mandate powers during the inter-war period were abruptly swept aside when, in the early 1940s, the armies of the Axis Powers and the Allies fought their way across North Africa.

The aftermath of the Second World War produced changes in hegemonic patterns on both the international and local scale. The emergence of two superpowers, the United States and the Soviet Union, led to a radical shift in the balance of global influence and its effects on the Middle East region. On a more local plane, high levels of cynicism regarding the motives of the mandate powers and resentment towards the sheer corruption of the *anciens régimes* produced a volatile political mixture that was to lead to a series of revolutions in the 1950s, beginning with the overthrow of Muḥammad ʿAlī's dynasty in Egypt – represented by the corpulent figure of King Fārūq (Farouk) – in 1952. The continuing aspirations of Arab nationalists were reflected in the decision to establish a League of Arab States in Cairo in 1945. Within a year, however, this body found itself presented with a major crisis, as the United Nations – the new international body that had emerged from the ashes of the Second World War – announced a partition plan for Palestine and Britain announced a date for its withdrawal. The War of 1948 was the first of many conflicts between the new state of Israel and its Arab neighbours, as they too have failed to resolve the many incompatibilities of the situation into which the decisions of the international community have placed them.

During the 1950s Iraq, Morocco, the Sudan, and Tunisia became independent. Following a prolonged and vicious struggle – called the 'war of a million martyrs', Algeria gained its independence in 1962. The idea of Arab unity, fostered by many writers since the beginnings of the nineteenth century revival and enshrined in the founding of the League of Arab States, took actual form in the United Arab Republic (1958–61) between Egypt and Syria. For the Arab world the 1950s were a period of release and of growing optimism. On the international scene, the successes of Egypt's charismatic president, Jamāl ʿAbd al-Nāṣir (Nasser) – the Czech Arms Deal of 1955, the nationalisation of the Suez Canal, and the subsequent débâcle of the Tripartite invasion of 1956 when the posture of the United States provided France and Britain with a brusque lesson in the new realities of international power – gave both him and the region as a whole a new sense of purpose and influence. Within each country there was a need to reconcile the interests of the many different political configurations that had participated in the revolutionary process: a wide variety of nationalists, communists, and religious groups. While such projects as the reapportionment of land and property through Agricultural Reform Laws was a frequent and popular choice for early implementation, other changes that would create the bases for the new independent and secular society were more difficult to bring about. With regrettable frequency the debate over these issues was quashed by the elaborate systems of security that had been developed. Some writers were prepared to say in retrospect that, after a long period of colonial occupation, the Arab world had woken up to find itself enclosed in a prison.

This difficult process of adaptation and change continued into the 1960s. As the United Arab Republic broke up in some bitterness, the plight of the Palestinian people continued to weigh on the conscience of the Arab world and served as a primary unifying factor. It was this cause that led the Egyptian President and the Arab world as a whole into its biggest disaster, the June War of 1967. Quite apart from the loss of Jerusalem, the West Bank, the Golan Heights, and Sinai, there was the fact that, throughout the initial days of the conflict, the leaders of the Arab world lied to their peoples. All the pretensions of previous decades were swept away, and what ensued was a moral crisis on the broadest scale, one that, in the words of the Moroccan historian and novelist, ʿAbdallāh al-ʿArwī (Laroui), led to 'a searching reappraisal of post-war Arab culture and political practice' (*The Crisis of the Arab Intellectual*, Berkeley, 1976, p. viii).

The three decades since the 'setback' (*al-naksah*) of 1967 witnessed little change in the situation of the Palestinians. When many members of the younger generation decided to resort to a more systematic use of force against Israel by joining the fedayeen (*fidāʾiyyīn*, those who sacrifice themselves), they were expelled from Jordan in a bloody conflict known as 'Black September'. Moving to Lebanon, they became one of the many catalysts in the protracted civil war that erupted in 1975. Even though the Palestinians withdrew from the country following the Israeli invasion of 1982, the Lebanese civil war between the various religious and political factions continued with barbaric ferocity until 1988. Alongside these much reported conflicts, others in different regions of the Arab world have continued off and on for decades: in the south of the Sudan, for example, in the Kurdish regions of Syria, Turkey, and Iraq, in Chad, and in the former Spanish Sahara. When coupled with the Iranian Revolution (1979), the assassination of Anwar al-Sādāt (1981), the Iran–Iraq War of the 1980s, and the Gulf War of 1991, these events do indeed reveal what Albert Hourani terms 'a disturbance of spirits'.

Alongside these significant global events other issues have also had a major effect on Arab society. As many of the most highly populated Arab nations with secular and mostly socialist regimes have endeavoured to promote a sense of national welfare and progress in the course of feeding, clothing, housing, and educating their peoples, they have been forced to establish economic and political alignments, both local and international, within a global context that seems to condemn all but the very richest Arab states to an apparently endless client status as importer of Western goods and trends. The situation has led to some truly enormous disparities. The world's continuing reliance on oil as a primary source of energy supply and the existence of huge oil reserves beneath the deserts of the Gulf region have made some of the least populous and most traditionalist areas in the Arab world into nations of immense wealth. The aggressive programmes of modernisation that such resources have enabled those oil-producing states of the Gulf to implement have not only radically transformed the societies themselves, but have also had major effects on other nations in the Arab world and beyond, most especially through the hiring of large numbers of workers from more populous nations such as Egypt, Bangladesh, Malaysia, and the Philippines. Thus, in the 1990s we see a region deeply divided, as the customary balance in each of the Arab nations – between the Arab and Islamic, the traditional heritage and modern development – continues to be disturbed by factors beyond the control of the majority of the region's inhabitants.

As this lengthy, yet much abbreviated, survey approaches the present day, it becomes more difficult to identify significant patterns of power from among the many continuing alternatives. However, the Gulf War of 1991, during which Western forces came to the aid of Kuwait and Saudi Arabia in the face of an assault launched by Ṣaddām Ḥusayn, the President of Iraq, provides – apart from its more obvious strategic aspects – an interesting example of the way in which a complex of factors involving religion, oil, and politics coalesced in such a way as to provide an excellent illustration of the differing patterns of interest in the region. The regime of Āyatallāh Khomeini and his successors in post-revolutionary Iran was assiduous in exporting its revolutionary Islamic message to other parts of the region, and most especially to the large Shīʿite communities in the Arab world: in southern Lebanon, in Iraq, in Saudi Arabia, and in the other states on the southern shore of the Gulf. To Ṣaddām Ḥusayn and other rulers of the region, these developments were alarming. Ṣaddām Ḥusayn's answer to the challenge was the Iran–Iraq War of the 1980s, during which the Sunnī rulers of the Gulf States gave him significant funding in his attempt to neutralise the power of Shīʿite Iran. The end of the conflict in 1988 brought no real change in the basic situation, even though both sides had lost colossal numbers of young men. However, when the Gulf States demanded repayment of the loans that they had made to Iraq and when market forces conspired to drive down the basic price of oil on which the Iraqi economy depended to a large degree, the Iraqi President sensed a conspiracy against him and decided to make use of the opportunity to resolve a territorial dispute that had existed ever since Britain had carved the lands of Kuwait out of the Ottoman province of al-Baṣrah in the 1920s and acknowledged the Āl Ṣabāḥ as its rulers. With the crushing defeat of Ṣaddām Ḥusayn and the enforcement of sanctions against Iraq, a potent military threat in the Gulf was thwarted. Meanwhile, in an interesting return to the very origins of Islam with which we began this survey, the oil-rich countries of Sunnī Saudi Arabia and Shīʿite Iran – whose relationship ranges from bitter enmity to reluctant coexistence – spend large amounts of money on the propagation and fostering of popular Islamic groups throughout the Arab world, aimed at resisting the incursions of secularist and modernist trends from the West that are regarded as antithetical to the tenets of Islam and the interests of the peoples of the Middle East region.

THE INTELLECTUAL CONTEXT

The Qurʾān and the foundation of the Islamic sciences

The text that resulted from the transcription and collation of God's revelations to Muḥammad – the Qurʾān – presented the incipient Islamic community with an enormous challenge. Perhaps the most profound of the changes brought about by these circumstances was that a society which had relied for centuries on oral communication and memory as its favoured medium of record soon found it necessary to disambiguate the different versions of Muḥammad's utterances by establishing a single written version of them as the canonical source and declaring other versions non-canonical. This decision automatically led to a need to record in written form and to authenticate a wide variety of other sources and to develop modes for prioritising them. The demands of the rapidly expanding Islamic community accelerated the move to a more literate culture in specific areas of concern, but the incorporation into it of converts from the conquered areas guaranteed that the transformation process, once set in motion, would gather momentum. A tradition concerning the recording of the Qurʾān itself – that fragments of it had been preserved on animals' shoulder blades and palm leaves – may perhaps be seen, among other possibilities, as a reflection of a shortage of appropriate surfaces on which to make records in written form. However, if recording materials remained scarce during the initial century or so of Islam, then the introduction of paper from Asia towards the end of the eighth century clearly expanded the availability of resources and contributed further to the use of writing as a medium for both creativity and the preservation of learning. All this said however, it would appear that, alongside the emerging written tradition of literature and its criticism, the oral modes of expression and transmission have retained their hold on the public ear throughout the period covered by this volume.

The status of the Qur'ān as a canonical text served as the basis for the initiation of a series of fields of study that were to develop into the Islamic sciences and therefrom into Arabic literary scholarship. The Egyptian polymath, Jalāl al-dīn al-Suyūṭī (d. 1505), devotes a chapter of his *Al-Itqān fī ʿulūm al-Qurʾān* (Perfection on the sciences of the Qur'ān) to 'fields of study derived from the Qur'ān'. The very act of recording the sound of the utterances in written form required that the alphabetic system be refined in order not only to clarify the distinctions between sets of similar graphemes but also to incorporate symbols for vowels, elisions, and stops. The text itself contained numerous individual words and phrases that reflected the linguistic and religious environment of the Arabian Peninsula in the pre-Islamic era. Such words had to be codified, and their meanings and origins had to be investigated. Thus did Arabic lexicography begin, and with it the search for precedents to the language of the Qur'ān; among principal sources were the sayings of the pre-Islamic soothsayers couched in an ornate variety of the language known as *sajʿ* (rhyming prose) and the highly elaborate poems of an oral tradition that was the most recent manifestation of a process of creativity and transmission that could be traced back for many generations. In all three of these areas – alphabet systematisation, lexicography, and poetry – al-Khalīl ibn Aḥmad of al-Baṣrah (d. 791) was an important pioneer: he devised the system of symbols that identify and govern the sounds of the text of the Qur'ān and that has been used ever since in the teaching of the Arabic alphabet and morphology; he composed a dictionary, *Kitāb al-ʿayn* (Book of ʿAyn), which is arranged on phonetic principles; and he codified the metrical patterns of the pre-Islamic tradition of poetry into a prosodic system (*ʿarūḍ*) that was declared canonical by later generations of critics and has remained as a pillar of Arabic poetics till well into the twentieth century. Alongside these concerns with the recording and analysis of texts there arose a desire to ensure that the principles of the language be systematised, most particularly when mistakes began to creep into the recitation of the sacred text. A tradition has it that the Caliph ʿAlī himself was sufficiently dismayed by such errors that he instructed Abū al-aswad al-Du'alī (d. 668) to prepare a work that would summarise

Arabic grammar, thus commencing a process of codification and debate that was greatly expanded during the eighth and ninth centuries among the intellectual communities in the rival Iraqi cities of al-Baṣrah and al-Kūfah.

Once the revelations of the Qurʾān had been committed to writing, the process of studying and interpreting the text intensified in that it was acknowledged as the Islamic community's primary source in establishing a system of laws that would govern the behaviour of its individual members. Regarding a number of issues – family law, debt, and inheritance, for example – the text was explicit. The Qurʾān's injunctions concerning God's will also led to the identification of the five 'pillars' of Islam: the statement of belief (*shahādah*); the five daily prayers (*ṣalāt*); almsgiving (*zakāt*): fasting during the holy month of Ramadan (*ṣawm*); and pilgrimage to Mecca (*ḥajj*). To these were added a further obligation, that of '*jihād*', a much misunderstood concept that implies 'effort' on an individual and communal level, including the process of spreading the word of Islam to other peoples and defending the religion against its opponents. However, beyond these rituals and obligations there were many areas on which the Qurʾān remains silent; in such cases the community resorted to another source: records of the Prophet's own conduct during his lifetime, the *sunnah*. This in turn initiated another process of gathering information, as accounts of Muḥammad's acts (the Arabic term is *ḥadīth*) were collected and organised by category. In such reports the primary means of authentication was the 'chain' of authorities (*isnād*) that had passed it on; this chain was placed at the very beginning of the report and worked backwards from the most recent transmitter to the contemporary of Muḥammad himself. This process of beginning reports with details regarding its sources becomes a characteristic feature of numerous types of narrative in the Arab-Islamic tradition including some literary ones. As the role that these *ḥadīth* played in providing information to corroborate or establish tenets and modes of conduct came to be more fully appreciated, there developed a tradition of *ḥadīth* criticism that was designed to check on the authenticity of the reports; for not only could the accounts themselves be distorted or fabricated, but those that seemed of dubious origin could be given an aura of probity by being affixed to a chain of distinguished transmitters. At a later date, the reports that were deemed the most reliable were collected into volumes called *Ṣaḥīḥ* (genuine); the two most famous collections were those of al-Bukhārī (d. 870) and Muslim (d. 875). Beyond such potential evidenciary functions the process of collecting and sifting these *ḥadīth* also marks the initial stages in the tradition of Qur'ānic exegesis (*tafsīr*), since the accounts often included discussions of problematic passages that had been recorded from earliest times. It was the great historian, al-Ṭabarī, who was the first to compile a commentary on the Qur'ān that incorporated within it the labours of his predecessors.

The processes of sifting accounts and authenticating sources that we have just described also revealed a need for detailed information on the reliability of individuals, and therefrom on the history of family groups and tribes. Genealogy was thus added to the list of fields with which the Islamic community concerned itself, as scholars investigated the histories of prominent families and their tribal affiliations. All this retrospective searching for details of tribal histories, for linguistic precedents to the lexicon and style of the Qur'ān, and for details regarding customs and beliefs in pre-Islamic times, inevitably led scholars to the greatest repository of such information: the huge corpus of poetry stored in the memories of generations of tribal and professional bards. Indeed the significance attached to the earliest stages of the classical Arabic poetic heritage has long been recognised by such a title: *dīwān al-ʿarab* (the register of the Arabs). The pre-Islamic poems that are available for us to study today and that are regarded as the glory of the Arabic literary heritage were consigned to written form as part of this process of information gathering. Collections of the poems were made according to a variety of criteria: the most well known was that of length, leading to the compilation of *al-Muʿallaqāt* – elaborate, polythematic celebrations of tribal values, and *al-Mufaḍḍaliyyāt*, a collection of shorter poems gathered by the famous bard and transmitter, al-Mufaḍḍal al-Ḍabbī (d. 876), for the education of al-Mahdī, the son of the ʿAbbāsī Caliph, al-Manṣūr. Still other collections were based on tribal affiliation, such as the collection of poems by the Banū Hudhayl.

This brief summary has only sketched the outlines of the immense task that was undertaken by scholars within the Islamic community. From the outset Islam vigorously eschewed anything resembling a priesthood, and the community assigned great value to the scholarly contributions of individuals who devoted themselves to knowledge of the religion; the Arabic word for such people is *ʿālim* (a learned person), and the plural of that word – *ʿulamāʾ* (religious scholars) – came to represent a cogent force within the community, in that the people so named represented the collectivity of its learning on matters of significance for the maintenance and propagation of Islam.

The Changing Intellectual Environment

While religious scholars devoted themselves to the urgent tasks connected with the demands of the incipient religious community, their researches stimulated other scholars to expand their interests in different directions. Much of this initial activity occurred during the period of the Umawī caliphs, when, as was noted above, the rapid expansion of the Arabian peninsular forces over a wide area brought Islam and its tenets into contact with a wide variety of cultures. The new converts assimilated many of the values advocated by the carriers of their adopted faith, but they also retained many aspects of their own indigenous cultures. It was only in 697, for example, during the reign of the Caliph ʿAbd al-malik that Arabic was designated the official language of administration (substituting for the Greek and Persian of numerous functionaries who continued to work in many areas of the Caliph's chancery). That change was clearly a significant beginning to the process whereby a class of bureaucrats, speaking and writing in Arabic, would begin to administer the affairs of the caliphal court and serve as a primary focus for the development of a repertoire of 'polite letters'.

As the functions of this class of administrators (known as *kuttāb*, sing. *kātib* – secretary, scribe) grew in complexity, there came the need to develop codes of conduct and appropriate models of style by which the chanceries at the various levels of authority within the Islamic dominions would facilitate the transfer and exchange of goods, information, and ideas. Pioneers like ʿAbd al-ḥamīd al-Kātib (d. 750) and ibn al-Muqaffaʿ (d. 757) – whose works will be examined in detail in the chapter on narratives below – established through their writings and the style in which they were couched an environment and tradition that came to be known by the designation *adab*, the literal translation of which is 'manners'. The concept of 'polite letters' (one that George Makdisi has linked in a full-length study to the notion of 'humanism') forms the basis for the creation of a cultural milieu and the cultivation of a set of aesthetic norms within which much of the literature that is to be studied in the chapters that follow was conceived and performed. While the term *adab* today is rendered into English as 'literature', its meaning in the earlier periods of Arabic literary creativity went far beyond the bounds currently associated with that word (although it has to be acknowledged that the English term has also narrowed its definitional focus over time). The person who practised, studied, and taught within this cultural realm was known as an *adīb* (pl. *udabāʾ*), and, as the term *adab* itself came to change meaning and incorporate additional areas of interest, its best definition became 'what *udabāʾ* consider part of their area of interest'.

Ibn al-Muqaffaʿ was just one among many scholars and writers of Persian origin who began to make major contributions to Arabic literature and its study. In the crucial ancillary field of grammar, for example, Sībawayh (d. *c.* 794), a pupil of al-Khalīl ibn Aḥmad, wrote a comprehensive study of the written Arabic language that is still revered as a major source on the subject. In addition to the contributions that scholars of Persian provenance were to make, there was also another major influence on the development of Islamic thought, namely that of Hellenistic Greek culture. The fruits of the schools of Athens and Alexandria had been carried to centres in Western Asia; the Nestorian Church played a particularly important role in the process of preserving and transmitting Greek learning through their schools in Nasibin in Syria and at Jundishapur in Persia. The large-scale translation movement that was sparked by the curiosity of the dynamic intellectual community that we have just described spanned a period of at least two centuries; the effort was supported by every segment of the intellectual class that surrounded the institution of the Caliphate. The translations that were undertaken reveal the concerns of a community interested in acquainting itself with a huge variety of topics and in the modes of organising and discussing them: from philosophy to astronomy, from music to pharmacology. The pace of translation activity was greatly accelerated by the personal interest of some of the ʿAbbāsī caliphs. In particular, al-Maʾmūn is remembered in this connection for establishing an institution in Baghdad, *Bayt al-ḥikmah* (The House of Wisdom), that provided a wonderful library and research facility to receive the fruits of such translation activity. The availability of such texts to scholars was to have a major impact on every sector of the Islamic community, and it needs to be added that the preservation of Greek thought through this process remains one of Western culture's continuing debts to the cultural values that were fostered by the intelligentsia of the community.

Given the variety of cultures that were represented within this intellectual milieu, certain biases were bound to make themselves evident. One that has attracted the particular attention of intellectual historians is the movement known in Arabic as the *Shuʿūbiyyah.* The nationalist environment within which so much discussion of the history of the modern Middle East has taken place has tended to encourage a view of this cultural manifestation as an argument between Persian and Arab secretaries and littérateurs over the relative merits of their respective cultural heritages. During the period of the early ʿAbbāsī caliphs, that view can find some corroboration in lines of poetry such as these by Bashshār ibn Burd (d. 783):

> Where is there an emissary to chant to all Arabs?...
> I am a person of high class, raised above others;
> Chosroes is the grandfather through whom I claim precedence,
> and Sāsān was my father...
> Never did he sing camel songs behind a scabby beast,
> nor pierce the bitter colocynth out of sheer hunger...
> nor dig a lizard out of the ground and eat it...

However, the discussion of the heritage of the various groupings within the larger community both preceded and followed this particular period. The Arab tribes, it will be recalled, had squabbled among themselves from the earliest periods of the Islamic era, and the Khawārij – the almost permanent opposition to the central authority – had also castigated the Umawī caliphs in their poetry. The same tendencies are to be found in the eleventh century among the variegated ethnic groupings in al-Andalus. Thus, the *Shuʿūbiyyah* movement needs to be viewed as not so much an expression of nationalist pride in an era in which primary modes of self-identification within the community tended to focus more on adherence to Islam and the use of Arabic as its language, but rather more an attempt to forge the bases for a multicultural intelligentsia. Such a view finds some corroboration in a report recorded by the great prose stylist, Abū Ḥayyān al-Tawḥīdī (d. 1023) in his famous compilation, *Kitāb al-imtāʿ wa-al-muʾānasah* (Book of Enjoyment and Good Company): Ibn al-Muqaffaʿ himself is asked whether he prefers Arabs or non-Arabs and delivers an answer that attempts to capture the qualities of the wide variety of cultures that were incorporated within the *dār al-Islam*.

Within the côteries of the *ʿulamāʾ* (religious scholars) and *kuttāb* (secretaries), a pattern of research and creativity was established that was to serve as a model for other intellectual centres that sprang up as the central authority of the caliphate began to wane. A crucial element of this research activity involved an elaborate system of education whereby scholarship in the various fields of learning was passed on to the next generation. The systematisation of jurisprudence (*fiqh*), for example, led to the foundation by prominent figures of colleges (*madāris*, sing. *madrasah*) at which the various fields of study connected with the *Sharīʿah* would be taught. The college itself was established by attaching a hostel to a mosque so that students who came to study in the 'circle' (*ḥalqah*) of the master could remain with him until they had 'read' with him all the major texts germane to the field, whereupon they would be granted a 'licence' (*ijāzah*) in those subjects in which they had gained mastery.

The major debates

As scholars developed a corpus of authoritative source-works and continued to cast their nets far and wide in search of new fields and sources of information, the values and endeavours that they fostered served as the stimulus for a number of notable controversies regarding matters of belief and practice and the principles that lay behind them.

The development of discrete 'schools' of law (*madhāhib*) and the formalisation of a system of education in jurisprudence indicate the central role that the *Sharīʿah* occupied in a community as a law code that was not limited to certain specific requirements of faith but governed every aspect of the life of the individual. As we have already noted, the Islamic community had soon identified the 'pillars' through which believers could express their individual and communal devotion. During the period of the Umawī caliphate, legal authorities scattered throughout the expanding Islamic domains were constrained to administer justice by adopting and adapting local jurisprudential practice to their own needs in the process of formulating opinions that conformed with the current consensus concerning appropriate Muslim conduct. Meanwhile, the *ʿulamāʾ*, equally scattered among the cities of the Arabian Peninsula and Iraq, studied the text of the Qurʾān and produced commentaries (*tafsīr*) that explicated the text of God's revelation to His people. They advocated the primacy of the Qurʾān as a source of legislation, pointing to clear statements in the text regarding such matters as divorce and inheritance, and went on to note that the *sunnah* of the Prophet collected in *ḥadīth* was a valid basis for the codification of Islamic practice. With the transfer of the centre of caliphal authority to Baghdad in the eighth century came the desire to exert some kind of central control over the variety of scholarly investigations under way. It was in such a context that efforts were made to reconcile the two tendencies within the legislative community. The distinctions and tensions that existed between them are visible in the early codes of Abū Ḥanīfah (*c.* 699–767) and Mālik ibn Anas (*c.* 715–95). It was the important role of al-Shāfiʿī (767–820) to codify and prioritise the relationships between the various sources of law. Both the Qurʾān and the *sunnah* were declared primary in the process of formulating legislation, but to them was added the process of reason that would need to be applied in those situations where interpretation was needed. The *ʿulamāʾ*, those schooled in the doctrine of Islam, were enjoined to make use of analogy (*qiyās*) in order to assess the validity of incorporating new and unfamiliar circumstances into the corpus of law regarding issues that had already been determined. This process of reasoning was termed *ijtihād* (the exercise of independent judgement), and, once the results of such determinations had been found valid by the community of religious scholars, the decision was said to have achieved a state of consensus (*ijmāʿ*) and was considered binding.

The codification and study of the 'principles of jurisprudence' (*uṣūl al-fiqh*) and their elaboration into a huge library of works concerning *Sharīʿah* now gathered momentum. As this corpus of scholarship was collected, examined, and elaborated within the legal colleges (*madāris*), orthodox scholars came to declare that, since all possible circumstances had been elaborated in the legal codes that were available, the 'gate of independent judgement' (*bāb al-ijtihād*) should be considered closed. The principle to be followed was that of adherence to past practice (*taqlīd*). Two points need to be noted here. Firstly, here is a case in which the practice of three of the Sunnī schools of law which we have been discussing – those of Mālik, Abū Ḥanīfah, and al-Shāfiʿī – differs from that of the school of Aḥmad ibn Ḥanbal and the Shīʿah. While Shīʿī law, for example, also acknowledged the primacy of the Qurʾān and *ḥadīth* (in the latter case, demanding that the chain of authorities [*isnād*] include one of the Shīʿite imams), it differed from the view of Sunnī scholars in giving the legal scholar – significantly termed *mujtahid* (someone who exercises independent judgement) – the right to interpret the *Sharīʿah* through reference to the Qurʾān and *ḥadīth* without being bound by the principle of consensus. Secondly, while it may have been the intention of some Sunnī legal scholars to discourage further potentially divisive debate on the complexities of law, actual practice suggests that independent judgement continued to be exercised, primarily through the institution of the legal opinion (*fatwā*) that could be requested from the *Muftī* (jurisconsult). Such an instance occurred, for example, in the final years of the nineteenth century when Muḥammad ʿAbduh (1849–1905), the Muftī of Egypt, delivered the so-called Transvaal *fatwā* concerning the legitimacy of Muslims eating meat slaughtered under Christian supervision.

The development of codes of law that has just been outlined served as a major impetus for the study and explication of the text of the Qur'ān and the elaboration of a system of *ḥadīth* criticism, both of which rapidly accorded the study of the Arabic language itself and the codification of its grammatical system a major status. Beyond such issues lay deeper questions of a theological nature. How was Allāh represented in the Qur'ān, and what was His relationship with human beings? Muslims believe that the 'speaker' in the Qur'ān who enjoins the Prophet to 'recite' is God, and that may help to explain the use of the Arabic word *kalām* (meaning 'speech, discourse') to render the study of theology. The investigation of the nature of God's word to His people as transmitted by His Prophet, Muḥammad, began from a vigorously unitarian position that categorically denied the possibility of God having any associate (*sharīk*), so that the very term 'association' (*shirk*) was synonymous with heresy. The primary focus of theology (and the title given to one of the disciplines within the Islamic sciences) was the study of God's oneness and His 'attributes' (*al-tawḥīd wa-al-ṣifāt*). God is transcendent and all-powerful, and His revelation to His people takes the form of a 'recitation', the Qur'ān. The text of the Qur'ān underscores God's oneness, His power, and His control over human beings, but it also enjoins them to turn away from sin and live a virtuous life. As theologians (*mutakallimūn*, those who studied *kalām*) considered the question of responsibility for sin within such a context, a number of schools of thought emerged. The Khawārij, it will be recalled, separated themselves from the community because they refused to acknowledge the legitimacy of the caliphate, in that they believed ʿAlī and his successors as caliph to have committed mortal sin, thereby automatically becoming unbelievers. This strict interpretation of the linkage between evil and unbelief was countered by another group, the Murjiʿah, who believed that the commission of sin does not lead to severance from the community of faithful.

In the eighth century, these issues were taken up by a movement termed *al-Muʿtazilah* (literally 'those who retire', but coming to imply 'those who take a neutral position'). Beginning with the teachings of Wāṣil ibn ʿAṭāʾ (d. 749) and ʿAmr ibn ʿUbayd (d. 762), both of whom had been disciples in the circle of the renowned scholar and ascetic, al-Ḥasan al-Baṣrī (d. 728), they took an intermediate position ('*manzilah bayn al-manzilatayn*') on the question of sin between that of the Khawārij and the Murjiʿah. Since God is One, they reasoned, He can have no attributes, including that of speech; from this they deduced that the

Qur'ān cannot be uncreated. A central belief of Islam, that God is just, implies that He cannot ordain evil; sin results from the freedom of will that is an attribute of humanity. During the reign of the Caliph al-Ma'mūn (d. 833), who took a personal interest in matters of intellectual debate within Islam–including the restoration of the Caliph ʿAlī to a position of prestige within the Islamic community, the beliefs of the Muʿtazilah, became part of official doctrine. Officials were subjected to a 'test' (*miḥnah*) during which they were asked if God was the Creator of all things; a positive answer–thus including the Qur'ān–implied that such persons believed in the doctrine of the Muʿtazilah. A negative response could lead to unpleasant results. One of the primary opponents of the Muʿtazilah was Aḥmad ibn Ḥanbal, founder of one of the four major schools of law, who rejected the Muʿtazilah's reliance on speculative dogmatics, something that had been much fuelled by the stimulus given to the propagation of Greek learning through the resources of the *Bayt al-ḥikmah* that al-Ma'mūn had founded in Baghdad. Ibn Ḥanbal insisted on a return to the primary sources of Islam. His patience and endurance were rewarded when the Caliph al-Mutawakkil (d. 861) abandoned the doctrine of the createdness of the Qur'ān. Following al-Mutawakkil's decision the Muʿtazilah gradually lost influence within Sunnī Islam, but it retained a strong position among the Shīʿah community till the twelfth century and beyond.

The task of finding a compromise between the two poles of the speculative reason of the Muʿtazilah and the literalism of the traditionalist followers of Aḥmad ibn Ḥanbal was taken up by al-Ashʿarī (d. 935). Initially a follower of the doctrine of the Muʿtazilah he came to believe in the primacy of divine revelation and the need for the literal interpretation of the Qur'ān. Regarding God's attributes, he was prepared to acknowledge the value of the application of reason up to a point, but suggested that true faith required that such issues should be accepted 'without asking how' (*bi-lā kayf*). In addressing the question of free will and predestination he suggested that God foreordained everything but that one of the attributes of humanity was the ability to acquire (*kasb*) freedom of choice regarding action. By reconciling the basic tenets of Islamic tradition with the application of reason in this way, al-Ashʿarī laid the foundations for the further development of an orthodox theology. Through his many pupils and their successors, among the more famous of whom are al-Bāqillānī (d. 1013), al-Qushayrī (d. 1074), and al-Juwaynī (d. 1085), his views were widely disseminated so that the *kalām* of al-Ashʿārī became the most accepted within Sunnī Islam. One of the students of al-Juwaynī was al-Ghazālī (d. 1111), widely acknowledged as 'the proof of Islam' (*ḥujjat al-islām*) and as one of the most significant figures in the whole of Islamic thought. Through his writings, and especially his monumental work, *Iḥyā' 'ulūm al-dīn* (The Revival of the Religious Sciences), al-Ghazālī succeeded in exemplifying the methods and limits of al-Ash'ārī's doctrines, showing how the application of reason could be used to defend the status of the Qur'ān and *ḥadīth* while at the same time quashing the worst speculative excesses of the philosophers. Against this latter group he wrote a notable treatise, *Tahāfut al-falāsifah* (The Incoherence of Philosophers), in which he explored the incompatibilities between the concerns of philosophy and the belief in a divinely revealed system of faith.

The response to al-Ghazālī's attack was written by the great Andalusian philosopher (and Mālikī judge), ibn Rushd (d. 1198). In his direct retort, *Tahāfut al-tahāfut* (The Incoherence of 'the Incoherence') and in other works of which the most significant is *Faṣl al-maqāl* (The Decisive Treatise), he was at some pains to show that any incompatibility that was seen to exist between philosophical investigations and the lessons of the Qur'ān could only result from literalist readings of the divinely revealed text. The demands of philosophy and the need to interpret the Qur'ān in different ways might restrict the audience for such investigations to an intellectual élite, but they did not render the entire activity incompatible with a belief in divine revelation. It is a sign of the significant role that Arab philosophers were to play in the elaboration of transmission of ideas inherited from the Greek tradition that the names of ibn Rushd and his predecessor, ibn Sīnā (d. 1037), Europeanised as Averroes and Avicenna, hold honoured places in the history of European philosophy. The tradition on which they elaborated had, like so many other movements we are discussing here, come into its own within the context of the dynamic intellectual community fostered by the translation activities of the eighth and nineth centuries. Ibn Sīnā's most prominent predecessors were al-Kindī (d. 865) and al-Fārābī (d. 950). Working at the caliph's court during the heyday of the Mu'tazilah, the former maintained the primacy of revelation but insisted that the application of reason was also appropriate. Al-Fārābī, known as 'the second teacher' (*al-mu'allim al-thānī* – Aristotle himself being the first), took a more critical posture towards the arguments of the theologians, endeavouring to find a role for the philosopher within the Islamic community by challenging the former's modes of argumentation. These early contributors to the corpus of philosophical writings in Arabic discussed the metaphysical aspects of the topic within a wide-ranging vision that also incorporated the natural sciences and logic. Al-Kindī, al-Fārābī, and Ibn Sīnā, for example, all wrote treatises on music, and al-Rāzī (d. *c.* 923), known in Europe as Rhazes, composed two 'therapeutic' treatises, one on the treatment of the body, the other on that of the soul.

Ibn Sīnā's own masterwork on medicine, *al-Qānūn fī al-ṭibb* (The Canon on Medicine), renowned for its accurate observation and clarity of expression, was to remain a prominent source in Europe till the seventeenth century. In the realm of philosophy itself Ibn Sīnā begins by acknowledging the way in which al-Fārābī, who had analysed the contributions of Plato and Aristotle, had played a key role in clarifying his understanding of metaphysics. Ibn Sīnā proceeded to compose a series of works that endeavour to reconcile the tenets of Islam with the principles of Aristotelian logic and Neo-Platonist explorations on the nature of the soul; the most famous is *al-Shifā*ʾ (The Cure (of the Soul)), but his works also include a number of fascinating allegories.

Much of our discussion thus far has dealt with intellectual debates on the broadest scale–at the level of the community at large. To be sure, the message of the Qurʾān, which acted as an instigator for much of the research and creativity that we have been and will be studying, was explicit about the need to create a community of the faithful; to the notion of *ijmā*ʿ (consensus) that we have already seen in the context of the discussion of legal studies, we can add from the same verbal source the 'day of community' (*yawm al-jum*ʿ*ah*, Friday) and the communal mosque (*jāmi*ʿ, the gathering place). But, alongside these more public and communal aspects of the Islamic faith and the community that it fostered, the text of the Qurʾān also enjoins believers to read and reflect. Studying the text of the Qurʾān and engaging in acts of private devotion and piety were encouraged alongside the more corporate rituals of public worship. While the 'pillar' of fasting (*ṣawm*) was an obligatory part of the month of Ramaḍān, acts of self-denial and asceticism at other times were also considered meritorious. These particular aspects of the message of the Qurʾān were among the factors that led to the emergence of another major trend in the life of the Islamic community, one that has continued to play a significant role in the propagation of Islam: mysticism (*taṣawwuf*, whence the English word, Sufism), the development of mystical sects, and the search for a 'way' (*ṭarīqah*, path) to achieve 'a closer walk with God'.

As with so many other intellectual currents in early Islamic history, the earliest beginnings of Ṣūfī ideas are traced to the twin Iraqi cities of al-Kūfah and al-Baṣrah. Al-Ḥasan al-Baṣrī, revered by Ṣūfīs and the Muʿtazilah alike as a founding figure, practised a personal life of asceticism and private devotion, emphasising in particular individual responsibility for pious behaviour. As *taṣawwuf* began to assume an identity of its own, it developed particular rituals and, most significant from the literary point of view, an awareness of the allegorical potential of language. The litany of the *dhikr* (repetition of the word 'God') became an important means of obliterating the concerns of the world.

When Ṣūfī sects proliferated in later centuries, some of the elaborations of these rituals came to be seen, perhaps unfortunately, more as acts linked to this temporal existence rather than their original purpose as denials of it; thus the 'whirling dervishes' associated with the Mevlevis, followers of Mawlānā Jalāl al-dīn Rūmī (d. 1273), and other acts of extreme self-denial such as walking on hot coals. On the level of language, mystics began to move from a literal interpretation of the text of the Qurʾān to one which suggested a number of levels of meaning, from the most direct to hidden symbolic signficances only attainable through spiritual experience. The combination of extreme self-denial and a desire for communion with the transcendent produced some of the remarkable utterances of mystics such as Rābiʿah al-ʿAdawiyyah (d. 801), Abū Yazīd al-Bīstāmī (d. 874), and Manṣūr al-Ḥallāj (d. 922), who in an ecstatic moment declared 'I am the Truth' (*anā l-ḥaqq*) and was later executed for heresy. The dangers inherent in the use of language in this extremely allegorical fashion to reflect and comment on the experience of an individual knowledge of God can be seen also in the execution of another prominent mystic, al-Suhrawardī, in 1191 and in the accusations of heresy levelled against the great Andalusian mystical writer, ibn al-ʿArabī (d. 1240), by a number of traditionalist authorities, including ibn Taymiyyah (d. 1328) in the fourteenth century and the Egyptian censor in the twentieth.

The extreme emphasis of mystics on the role of the individual conscience in assessing personal conduct towards God and other people led to opposition from traditionalist theologians who were anxious to codify proper behaviour on a more communal level. The process of reconciling these different views, undertaken by al-Ḥārith al-Muḥāsibī (d. 857), al-Junayd (d. 910), and al-Qushayrī (d. 1072), reached its crowning point in the writings of al-Ghazālī. Beginning a career as a scholar in theology and jurisprudence, al-Ghazālī moved from Nīshāpūr in 1091 and was appointed to a teaching post at the illustrious Niẓāmiyyah College in

Baghdad. His autobiographical work, *al-Munqidh min al-ḍalāl* (Deliverance from Error), records the way in which his increasing scepticism concerning the tenets he was supposed to impart to others led to a serious intellectual crisis. Abandoning his prestigious post he went into retreat for some nine years and adopted the life of an ascetic. This crisis and its resolution permitted him to compose his monumental *Iḥyāʾ ʿulūm al-dīn* (The Revival of the Religious Sciences), a work that succeeded in integrating the various aspects of revelation, canon law, and personal devotion into a single statement of faith.

Al-Ghazālī's achievement in incorporating Sufism into the mainstream of Islamic belief led to a palpable increase in popular interest in the more personal approach to God that the mystical path appeared to offer. An immediate consequence was a growth in Ṣūfī orders (the term for which is *ṭuruq*, the plural of *ṭarīqah*). These orders were, more often than not, named after their founders: thus, the Qādiriyyah order named after ʿAbd al-qādir al-Jīlānī (d. 1166) and the Rifāʿiyyah order after Aḥmad al-Rifāʿī (d. 1183). The rapid expansion of these orders was to lead to a considerable diversification of religious ritual, as local customs that were even remotely adaptable to an Islamic framework were incorporated into the litanies of particular groups and regions. The founders of these orders and other 'holy men' whose piety and beneficial deeds gathered around them a group of followers were often designated by the term 'saint' (*walī*). The abundance of place names (especially in North Africa) that begin with the word 'Sidi' (my lord) marks a practice whereby towns would be named after a local shrine to the *walī* of that name, thereby making it a place of pilgrimage for those with special favours to request of the saint. The mosque-shrine of Aḥmad al-Badawī (*c.* 1199–1276) in the Egyptian city of Ṭanṭā, for example, continues to attract huge numbers to the celebration of his birthday celebration (*mawlid*), itself the topic of ʿAbd al-ḥakīm Qāsim's famous novel, *Ayyām al-insān al-sabʿah* 1969; *The Seven Days of Man*, Evanston, Northwestern University Press, 1996.

This expansion and elaboration of popular Islamic belief aroused considerable opposition among conservative theologians. Ibn Taymiyyah, for example, focused his objections in particular on the speculative explorations of ibn al-ʿArabī, and firmly rejected the practice of saint worship, as he followed the path of Aḥmad ibn Ḥanbal in reasserting the traditionally central function of the Qur'ān and *ḥadīth*. The negative aspects of these Ṣūfī practices to which ibn Taymiyyah and others objected and the extent to which they have continued to exert a major influence on the life of the populace are illustrated by the great twentieth century intellectual, Ṭāhā Ḥusayn (d. 1973), in his famous autobiography, *al-Ayyām* (The Days, 1925). With undisguised contempt, he describes the impact of a visit by a famous mystical 'shaykh' on a poor family that has to provide the best possible entertainment for him, and then goes on to note the shaykh's virtually total ignorance of the basic doctrines of Islam. In a poem from the 1950s entitled '*Khubz wa-ḥashīsh wa-qamar*' (Bread, Hashish, and Moon)–a comprehensive indictment of the cultural values of the Middle East region, the Syrian poet, Nizār Qabbānī (b. 1923), is clearly referring to such rituals when he talks of a people who 'rattle the tombs of saints'.

That the names of ibn Sīnā, al-Ghazālī, and ibn Rushd (and many others in addition) should be well known in medieval Europe–albeit transliterated as Avicenna, Algazel, and Averroes, is one of the more obvious measures of the high esteem in which the intellectual tradition just outlined was held there. In the twelfth century the translation school at Toledo, fostered by its Archbishop Raymund (d. 1152), attracted some of the greatest intellects of Europe to participate in the process of transferring the wealth of learning in Arabic to Hebrew and Latin and thence to the intellectual centres of Europe: John of Seville (d. 1157), for example, Dominicus Gundisalvi (d. 1181), Adelard of Bath (d. 1142), Gerard of Cremona (1114–87), and Michael Scot (d. *c.* 1246). The majority of histories of Islamic thought and Arabic literature have suggested that, at precisely the time when this process of transfer was taking place, the very culture that had been the cynosure of European eyes for so long was entering a period of considerable change, a process that some commentators have dubbed decline, decadence, and even darkness.

It may be reasonable perhaps to expect that, following several centuries of theoretical and empirical research in so many areas (of which we have only touched on a few above), certain scholars felt a need to draw breath, as it were; to collate and elaborate on what was already available. The principle of adherence to already established norms (*taqlīd*), while not considered binding by all schools of law and theology, certainly encouraged efforts at explication, commentary, and elaboration. We have also suggested above that, given the breadth of the area in which Islam was the dominant religious system, the impact of the fall of Baghdad in 1258 – traditionally regarded as a turning-point in the chronology of Arab-Islamic history, needs to be seen in a broader context. The destruction of the ʿAbbāsī capital, with its libraries and colleges, was clearly an enormous loss to the world of Arabic scholarship, but it was an accumulation of 'falls', those of Baghdad, of Constantinople in 1453, of Granada in 1492, and of Cairo in 1516, that transformed the map of the Middle East and its cultural life. For example, the advent of Ottoman rule to large parts of the region introduced the Turkish language as the primary medium of administration. The cultured élite that had been the principal locus and sponsor of literary activity was now constrained to conduct official transactions in a language other than Arabic. If the poetry and belles-lettres of the time (to the rather limited extent that they have been studied) appear to be replete with the rhetorical flourishes that were being so carefully recorded and illustrated by the critical tradition and if much of the society's store of originality seemed to be invested in the more popular literary genres (which are still in need of much more research), then we should perhaps not be unduly surprised.

This apologia for a period that, having normally been denigrated by title, is then skipped over in a rush to encounter the modern, should also make reference to several important figures who during the course of its several centuries (from approximately the thirteenth till the eighteenth) made major contributions to the intellectual tradition of the Arabs. While the series of events (the 'falls') mentioned above clearly represent major shifts in the nature of political power in the region, the processes of change within the cultural environment of literary texts are less obviously identified. In fact much of that environment changed rather little. In the period following the fall of Baghdad, local dynasties–retaining their court protocols and system of patronage for scholars and littérateurs–not merely survived but proliferated. It is thus not surprising that we are able to identify many continuities with the earlier period. In the realm of travel literature, for example, ibn Baṭṭūṭah (d. 1377) continues the tradition established earlier by al-Idrīsī (d. 1165) and ibn Jubayr (d. 1217) of Granada. Ibn Baṭṭūṭah's work, entitled *Tuḥfat al-nuẓẓār fī gharāʾib al-amṣār wa-ʿajāʾib al-asfār* (The observers' delight regarding curious cities and remarkable journeys)–and the reader will no doubt have noticed by now the proclivity of writers at this period for embellishing their titles with rhyming prose (*sajʿ*)–describes the journeys that he took from his native Tangier in Morocco to India and China and later south into Africa. The writing of economic and urban history, and especially descriptions of the prominent citizens and quarters of the Islamic world's great cities, is further developed by al-Maqrīzī (d. 1441), who served as the superviser of weights and measures (*muḥtasib*) in Mamlūk Cairo. His monumental study of the city, *al-Mawāʿiẓ wa-al-iʿtibār fī dhikr al-khiṭāṭ wa-al-āthār* (Admonitions and lessons regarding the mention of districts and monuments), established a model for the analysis of the topography of cities. Ibn Khaldūn (d. 1406), one of the world's most illustrious historians, surveyed the disarming frequency with which ruling dynasties changed in the North-West Africa region in which he himself lived and penned a theoretical Introduction (*al-Muqaddimah*) to his work of history that is universally acknowledged as marking a fresh approach to the study of human societies and their processes of change.

The desire to collate and organise materials into useful forms remained a constant. The earliest known version of the *Thousand and One Nights* as a collection of popular tales dates from about the fourteenth century. Encyclopedias and compilations of fact and anecdote continue to appear in ever more elaborate and varied form (as we will see in ch. 5 below). This predilection for the gathering and analysis of information found a particularly conducive field in lexicography; work on the compilation of the two great dictionaries of the Arabic language, *Lisān al-ʿarab* (Language of the Arabs) and *Tāj al-ʿarūs min jawāhir al-qāmūs* (The Bride's Crown Taken from the Jewels of the Qāmūs), into their present form was begun during the first half of this long period. The *Lisān al-ʿarab* was an elaboration of an earlier work by al-Jawharī; it was completed by ibn Manẓūr (d. 1311). The history of *Tāj al-ʿarūs* is somewhat lengthier: another lexicographer, al-Fayrūzābādī (d. 1414), devoted his life's work to compiling a dictionary, *al-Qāmūs al-muḥīṭ* (The Comprehensive Dictionary), but parts of it were lost; the project was not completed till the eighteenth century at the hands of al-Zabīdī (d. 1790).

Coinciding with the halfway point in this much neglected period is the career of the renowned Egyptian polygraph, Jalāl al-dīn al-Suyūṭī (d. 1505); no single figure, we might suggest, illustrates so well the concerns and priorities of an era whose engagement with the forces of continuity and change has yet to be properly understood. He wrote on an enormous variety of subjects (some scholars put the total of his works at well over five hundred). To the study of religion, for example, he contributed works on the exegesis of the Qurʾān, on *ḥadīth*, and on Sufism; he wrote biographies and works of general history; to philology and grammar he contributed *al-Muzhir fī ʿulūm al-lughah* (The brilliant [work] regarding the sciences of language); and he also composed poetry and a set of *maqāmāt*. The sheer variety of this output reflects the interests of a society that valued versatility and elaboration; one that, above all, gave the highest esteem to those who had such mastery of the Arabic language that they were able to use it not only to inform, but also to divert, to amuse, and to baffle.

Of the comparatively little attention that has been devoted to a study of the literary output of this period the bulk has reflected a confrontation of differing aesthetic principles. Scholars, who have tended to view the texts through a critical prism influenced by European romanticism's quest for unity and originality, have found themselves frustrated by Arabic texts that clearly do not conform with such expectations. Their verdict has been to declare the era lacking in originality and even decadent. The creativity reflected in the variegated nature of the compilation process, the linguistic brilliance of a scholar such as al-Suyūṭī, and indeed the apparent fictionality of a good deal of ibn Baṭṭūṭah's narrative, all these features (that have now begun to attract the attention of a few specialists) have previously been overlooked. The literary output of this entire period, much of which remains unknown, clearly needs to be examined (or re-examined) using the methodologies of less exclusive critical approaches.

The Egyptian historian, ibn Iyās (d. *c*. 1523), has left us an account of the panic that gripped Cairo in 1516 after the defeat of the army of the Mamlūk Sultan al-Ghawrī and of the subsequent arrival in Cairo of the victorious Ottoman troops. The impact that this and other Ottoman conquests had on the political, economic, and social life of the Arabic-speaking world was, of course, enormous, but, as we have noted above, the cultural ramifications–among them the change in administrative language and, in many regions, the tight control over the dissemination of information–were no less significant. Literary production in Arabic continued during the seventeenth and eighteenth centuries, but such is the exiguous state of our knowledge of literary production throughout the Arabic-speaking region that references in the chapters that follow to authors and works from what might be termed the 'pre-modern' period will be few and far between. A mere inkling of the extent to which we may need to revise our highly impressionistic estimates of the literary output of the period comes from the existence of a number of literary salons in Egypt, including that of the above-mentioned al-Zabīdī, at the end of the eighteenth century. Al-Zabīdī dies a few years before another great transition point in the history of the region–Napoleon's invasion of Egypt in 1798, but it is from within the same intellectual milieu that another Egyptian historian, ʿAbd al-raḥmān al-Jabartī (d. 1821), emerges to record in *ʿAjāʾib al-āthār fī al-tarājim wa-al-akhbār* (Wondrous Relics Concerning Events and Biographies) the impact on Cairo's intelligentsia of the discussions between Egyptian intellectuals and the French scientists who accompanied the military expedition. While the invasion itself may have fallen short of its goals, these inter-cultural conversations were an important early example of the series of contacts through which the Arabic-speaking world began to enlarge its acquaintance with the developments in science, technology, and education that had so transformed the societies of the Western world.

The challenge of modernity: the relationship to present and past

The incompleteness of our understanding of the cultural forces that were at work in the Arabic-speaking world in what I will term the pre-modern period clearly makes any discussion of the factors involved in the cultural revival of the nineteenth century (*al-nahḍah*) more difficult. For, while increased contact with the West was clearly a very important part of the process, contacts both within and without the broad compass of the Middle East region were ongoing. In particular, the long-standing tradition of travel (that will be discussed in ch. 5) continued to flourish: the writings of Evliya Çelebi [d. *c.* 1658]), author of the renowned and compendious *vade mecum*, *Siyāhat-nāme*, are renowned in this regard, but there were also numerous Christian Lebanese who travelled widely (such as Ilyās al-Mawṣilī who went to South America in the seventeenth century). Beyond issues of cultural contact, the further question as to whether the indigenous cultural tradition was quite as moribund as previous scholarship has tended to suggest is a topic that requires further research. Certain eighteenth century trends would seem to indicate that an awareness of the intellectual heritage of previous centuries was not entirely lacking. Muḥammad ibn ʿAbd al-Wahhāb (d. 1787), for example, founder of the Wahhābī movement in the Arabian Peninsula, went back to the teachings of Aḥmad ibn Ḥanbal and ibn Taymiyyah and determined to eradicate all the accretions that saint worship and other popular practices had introduced into Islamic ritual. In Egypt, the French scientists who came to Egypt with Napoleon's army at the end of the eighteenth century and compiled the *Description de l'Egypte* found themselves debating issues with intellectuals who were thoroughly acquainted with the riches of the Arabic literary heritage. Al-Zabīdī, for example, whom we cited above as the compiler of the dictionary *Tāj al-ʿarūs*, trained his students to memorise the famous *maqāmāt* of al-Ḥarīrī (d. 1122) and composed poetry in the style of the famous love-poet, Majnūn Laylā. Al-Zabīdī was well acquainted with the historian al-Jabartī, and through the literary salons of the time both men made the acquaintance of Shaykh Ḥasan al-ʿAṭṭār (d. 1835) who was to play a major role in Egyptian intellectual life during the reign of Muḥammad ʿAlī, not least as Shaykh of al-Azhar. Al-ʿAṭṭār himself contributed to the *maqāmah* genre, a tradition that had remained a favoured genre throughout the intervening period at the hands of writers such as al-Zamakhsharī (d. 1143), ibn Nubātah (d. 1365), and al-Suyūṭī and that, with the writings of Nāṣīf al-Yāzijī (d. 1871), Aḥmad Fāris al-Shidyāq (d. 1887), and Muḥammad al-Muwayliḥī (d. 1930)–among many others–was continued well into the twentieth century before being overwhelmed by the introduction of Western fictional genres that proved more adaptive to the political and social circumstances in which the Arab nations found themselves.

At the beginning of the period of cultural revival (*al-nahḍah*) this increasing interest on the part of the Western powers in the Middle East helped initiate a movement in reverse. When Muḥammad ʿAlī, the ruler of Egypt, sent al-Ṭahṭāwī (d. 1873), a pupil of Shaykh al-ʿAṭṭār, to France in 1826 as imam of a mission of Egyptian students, a process was set in motion whereby the Arab World rapidly became aware of major cultural differences between itself and the West. Al-Ṭahṭāwī's famous account of his time in Paris, *Takhlīṣ al-ibrīz fī talkhīs Bārīz* (The Purification of Gold Regarding Paris in Brief, 1834)–note yet again the rhyming Arabic title–is full of observations regarding issues that are exotic in their peculiarity: for example, the institution of parliament and the appearance of women in public.

In the transfer of these and other ideas–the Western concept of 'nation', for example–to the intellectual community of the Arab World two institutions were to play a crucial role. The first was the Translation School that Muḥammad ʿAlī established in 1835 with al-Ṭahṭāwī himself as its director. Priorities focused at first on practical manuals on engineering and military strategy, but gradually the proclivities of the translators themselves led to the appearance of Arabic versions of a number of classic products of European culture. The second institution was the press. In 1828 Muḥammad ʿAlī founded an official gazette, *al-Waqāʾiʿ al-Miṣriyyah* (Egyptian Events), and al-Ṭahṭāwī became its editor in 1841. During the reign of the Khedive Ismāʿīl, who was bent on westernising his country to the maximum extent possible, these two institutions provided a ready vehicle for an increasingly rapid introduction of Western ideas into Egyptian intellectual life. The very atmosphere that Ismāʿīl's policies engendered was also a major factor in the decision of many Syro-Lebanese Christian families to come to Egypt following the civil disturbances of the 1850s, bringing with them the fruit of contacts with European institutions (and especially the Church of Rome) that went back at least two centuries. To the expanding milieu of Egyptian cultural life they were able to contribute a broad experience in the key areas of translation (most notably, of the Bible) and the press, as well as a number of important early experiments in literary genres such as the novel and drama. Thus, the special political arrangements that Muḥammad ʿAlī secured regarding Ottoman control over his country had a major impact on the early period of the modern Arabic cultural revival, chiefly in Egypt itself, but by example in other parts of the Arab World as well. For, while many countries remained under the control of the Ottoman government and its censorship practices (Tunisia, Syria, and Iraq, for example), Muḥammad ʿAlī and his successors were unimpeded in their determination to open up Egyptian society to the new and different ideas of the West. Egypt, with its large population, central geographical position, and lively cultural environment now quickened by the new arrivals from Syria, became the fullest and most often cited example of intellectual developments in the early decades of the twentieth century. Our concentration in what follows on trends in Egypt reflects this tendency.

The imported and the indigenous, the modern and the traditional, the Western and Middle Eastern, the non-Islamic and the Islamic, these pairs and many others became the focus of lively debate in the last decades of the nineteenth century and into the twentieth. We have seen, for example, that the *maqāmāt* of al-Ḥarīrī had remained a yardstick of literary education well into the eighteenth century, and so it is hardly surprising that this very set of classical masterpieces of Arabic literature served as the inspiration for the Lebanese scholar, Nāṣīf al-Yāzijī (d. 1871), who contributed to the emerging neo-classical trend by producing his own set of *maqāmāt* under the title, *Majmaʿ al-baḥrayn* (The Meeting-place of the Two Seas, 1856). During the 1870s and 1880s in Egypt we find, on the one hand, an ever-expanding number of newspapers and specialist journals publishing serialised novels, both translations of European works and initial efforts in Arabic such as *Dhāt al-khidr* (Lady of the Boudoir, 1884) by Saʿīd al-Bustānī, and, on the other, a scholar such as

Ḥusayn al-Marṣafī (d. 1890) writing a two-volume work, *al-Wasīlah al-adabiyyah* (The Literary Method, 1872, 1875), in which he expresses his clear admiration for the models provided by the 'classical' poetic tradition. In such a context Muḥammad al-Muwayliḥī's acerbicly witty analysis of an Egyptian society in cultural turmoil at the turn of the century, *Ḥadīth ʿĪsā ibn Hishām* (ʿĪsā ibn Hishām's Tale, 1898 in newspaper form; 1907 as a book)–invoking the style and narrator of al-Hamadhānī's *maqāmāt* of many centuries earlier, attempts a kind of synthesis of old genre and modern topic. The work is full of accounts of debates between wearers of the turban (the traditional headwear of religious shaykhs) and of the tarbush (the 'fez' that became part of the uniform of the Western-educated bureaucrat), but nothing symbolises the essence of the clash between indigenous and imported values more than the superbly drawn picture of a rustic *ʿumdah* (village-head), a figure of major importance in his own small world, who comes to Cairo, is completely overwhelmed and outwitted by the urbanity of his westernised companions, and comments incredulously in a restaurant on the fashion of eating mushrooms–a food that in his village is only fed to pigs.

Al-Muwayliḥī was a student of Muḥammad ʿAbduh (1849–1905), one of the most significant figures in the debate concerning the role of Islam within a society trying to find a balance between the traditional and the modern. As was the case with many other intellectuals of the time, ʿAbduh was much influenced by the ideas of Jamāl al-dīn al-Asadābādī (d. 1897), an Iranian Shīʿī scholar who is generally known by the name 'al-Afghānī'. A charismatic lecturer and inveterate participant in political intrigue, al-Afghānī was determined to modernise Islam and to make full use of reason to reformulate the faith as a cogent basis for resisting the threat posed by European domination of the Middle East. Muḥammad ʿAbduh was as anxious as his mentor to protect Islamic principles, but in his capacities as judge and later as Chief Muftī of Egypt (from 1889) devoted more of his attention to questions of application. For him, the Qurʾān and *ḥadīth* remained the principal sources of guidance, but, as his pronouncements on matters of legal interpretation make clear, he did not base his judgements on the principle of *taqlīd* (adherence to past practice). If Islam was to survive and remain strong, he argued, it needed to be adaptive.

These calls for modernisation and reform within the context of Islamic thought attempted to provide a means for countering the uncritical importation of Western ideas or at least for the achievement of some form of reconciliation between two different value-systems. The teachings of ʿAbduh in particular had an enormous impact on his numerous pupils and acquaintances in Egypt and elsewhere in the Arab World. This is most obvious perhaps in the career of his most famous pupil, Rashīd Riḍā (d. 1935), a Syrian scholar who came to Cairo in 1897 and one year later began to publish *al-Manār* (The Lighthouse), a journal which publicised the reformist ideas of ʿAbduh. Like many other thinkers whom we have discussed above, ʿAbduh and Riḍā supported the notion of an Islamic faith based on the Qurʾān and the views of the great authorities of the past (the *salaf*). Riḍā, having initially been attracted to Ṣūfī practices, became a diehard opponent of the way in which the accretions attributed to popular Ṣūfī rituals had diluted the basic truths of Islam. What is most significant within the temporal context is that Riḍā rejected any basis for the formation of a state or nation that was not based on Islam, the faith that in its classic form had created a successful model for community. The ideas of ʿAbduh and Riḍā, termed the *salafiyyah* movement, were particularly influential in North Africa (most especially at the hands of ʿAbd al-ḥamīd ibn Bādīs in Algeria) and in the East reached as far as Indonesia.

Riḍā's firm position made him a staunch defender of traditional principles at a time when they were the subject of much debate. In 1925, for example, Riḍā was heavily involved in a famous dispute. ʿAlī ʿAbd al-rāziq, who had studied at both al-Azhar and Oxford University, wrote a famous work, *Al-Islam wa-uṣūl al-ḥukm* (Islam and the Bases of Authority). In the context of the times, it could hardly have been more controversial. During the reign of the Ottoman Sultan, ʿAbd al-ḥamīd (d. 1907), discussions regarding the possible bases of nationhood within traditionalist Islamic circles had focused on a 'pan-Islamic' vision whereby all Muslims would be united under the Ottoman ruler as caliph. While many Muslim intellectuals of Arab origin were opposed to such an idea, they continued to espouse the revival of an Arab caliphate. In 1924, however, the secular Turkish government declared the caliphate abolished. It was in this context that ʿAlī ʿAbd al-rāziq's study on the caliphate appeared. Suggesting that the Prophet's mission had been a spiritual one and not concerned with establishing principles of government, he challenged the legitimacy of the caliphate as an organising principle for Islamic government. ʿAbd al-rāziq was subjected to furious verbal assaults from the religious establishment, and a council of ʿ*ulamā*ʾ at al-Azhar declared him incompetent to hold public office. Riḍā was one of those who took part in this ritual of public rebuttal.

ʿAbduh made a point not only of travelling widely within the Arab world and beyond but also of frequenting many of the intellectual salons of his day. One of the most famous in *fin de siècle* Cairo was that of Princess Nāzlī. Among the members of this group, besides ʿAbduh himself, were several politicians, prominent journalists such as ʿAlī Yūsuf and the al-Muwaylihīs–father and son, the poet Ḥāfiẓ Ibrāhīm, and Qāsim Amīn. In 1899 Amīn aroused a storm of controversy by publishing two studies in which he advocated 'the emancipation of women' (the actual title of his first book, *Taḥrīr al-marʾah*); in this book and a second, *Al-Marʾah al-jadīdah* (Modern Woman, 1900), he follows the method of ʿAbduh by resorting to the basic tenets of Islam as a means of justifying the need to provide education for women, for not only their benefit but also that of society as a whole. Qāsim Amīn was a pioneer in his advocacy of women's rights, and his works, while initially arousing a storm of protest and rebuttal, had an immense influence on the intellectual community in the Arab World. The reaction to his published books shows clearly enough that his views reached a broad public, but the existence of the literary salons of Princess Nāzlī and of Mayy Ziyādah (d. 1941), the famous Palestinian writer resident for many years in Cairo, and the writings of Zaynab Fawwāz (d. 1914), Malak Ḥifnī Nāṣif (d. 1918), and Labībah Hāshim (d. 1947)–much of which has yet to be published in book form, provide equally clear evidence that, while women's voices may not have commanded as much attention in the public domain, they were no less insistent in raising these same issues.

These often intense debates regarding the role of Islam within a process of cultural revival and change occurred within a political and social context in which other forces were tending to marginalise the role of religion. When large segments of the administration of government were being supervised by foreigners, and banks, stock exchanges, the press, and international commerce were stimulating the appearance of a new class of Western-educated bureaucrats and professionals, the diminution of the traditional power of the *ʿulamāʾ* and the emergence of more secular voices and priorities that reflected an increasing awareness of Western political theories was almost inevitable. As the intellectual community expanded its investigations of the history of the Arabic language and the glories of the classical heritage and as opposition to Ottoman suzerainty over large segments of the Arabic-speaking world continued to grow, the concept of an Arab nation, one based on an awareness of a shared language and culture, began to gather momentum. Fostered by such pioneers as ʿAbd al-raḥmān al-Kawākibī (d. 1903) and Najīb ʿAzūrī (d. 1916), who in 1904 founded in Paris a group known as 'Ligue de la Patrie arabe', the movement was given considerable impetus by the Western powers during the First World War. The failure of the Western powers to honour the series of 'understandings' they had reached with their erstwhile Arab allies and the division of the Middle East region into a series of 'mandates' insured that the interwar period would be one of confrontation.

The half-century from 1919 till the June War of 1967 sees the debate on nationalism elaborated in both pan-Arab and local contexts. Arab nationalism in its widest and most ambitious dimensions is developed primarily among the intelligentsia of Iraq and Syria. Two among many prominent contributors to the literature on the subject are Qusṭanṭīn Zurayq (b. 1909) and Ṣātiʿ al-Huṣrī (d. 1964); both stress that, if the larger Arab cause is to thrive, more local concerns need to be sacrificed. These goals took a more ideological form in the writings of Michel ʿAflaq (d. 1989), a Syrian Christian who invoked the notion of *baʿth* (revival) as a rallying cry for Arab national unity and social justice. In 1952 his theories were adopted as the basis for the foundation of a political party, the Arab Socialist Baʿth Party, which for several decades has served as the political ideology for the governments of both Syria and Iraq, although the personality cults of leaders and the very local political concerns that the ideology aims to counter have often caused a wide rift between the two. These more local nationalist movements and parties have existed alongside the broader agenda of a pan-Arab movement, catering to particular classes and groups within each society. In Syria, for example, Anṭūn Saʿādah (d. 1949) established a National Syrian Party in 1932 that was organised along militia lines and became a vigorous advocate of Syrian nationalism. In Egypt, the dashed expectations of the Arabs at the end of the First World War and the popular uprising in Egypt that followed in 1919 brought to the fore the country's great nationalist leader, Saʿd Zaghlūl (d. 1927)–yet another member of ʿAbduh's circle who had been particularly influenced by the writings of one of the primary expounders of Egyptian nationalist principles, Aḥmad Luṭfī al-Sayyid (d. 1963). In 1922 Egypt was granted a degree of independence by the British government, and Zaghlūl's Wafd Party played a significant role within the tortuous politics of the country's parliamentary democracy during the interwar period. However, while Britain may have made concessions regarding Egypt, it continued to maintain direct control over Iraq and Palestine, in the latter of which the increasingly fractious situation was an accurate reflection of two sets of agenda that many recognised from the outset as being completely incompatible.

Najīb Maḥfūẓ's famous set of novels, *al-Thulāthiyyah* (The Trilogy, 1956–57), is one of those great works of fiction that manage to capture the spirit of an entire era in a country's development, and the specific era in question is the interwar period we are discussing. The complications of politics, both national and international, are there of course; not least the 1919 Revolution itself, but also discussions of socialism that reflect the influence on Maḥfūẓ of the great Egyptian Fabian socialist writer, Salāmah Mūsā (d. 1958). But the reader also follows the emergence of women into society, the workplace, and the educational system, and, through the anguished musings of Kamāl–whom Maḥfūẓ admits to be a representation of his own persona–the debates between the traditions of a society based on Islamic values and the often conflicting ideas of modern science. Maḥfūẓ himself was fourteen years old when the conflicts inherent to the course of Egyptian intellectual life burst into the open in two major controversies. The first, that of ʿAlī ʿAbd al-rāziq, we have already mentioned. The second was that of the doyen of Egyptian littérateurs in the first half of the twentieth century, Ṭāhā Ḥusayn (1889–1973), who in 1926 published *Fī al-shiʿr al-jāhilī* (On Pre-Islamic Poetry) in which, laying great stress on the scientific nature of his research, he not only claimed that much of the poetic tradition in question was post-Islamic but also went on to suggest that certain segments of the text of the Qur'ān were fables. Maḥfūẓ is surely reflecting the feelings of an entire generation of younger writers in noting that the publication of this work and the fierce reactions to it had a profound influence on his own intellectual development.

Any progress that may have been made in the 1920s and 1930s towards the goal of independence was immediately lost in 1939. The whole of North Africa became a primary theatre of war, and the strategic imperatives of Britain and France tended to shove aside the negotiated agreements of peacetime. The aggravation of Egyptian politicians at this state of affairs seems to have persuaded them to add the considerable weight of Egypt, with its large population and central position, to the continuing efforts of the pan-Arab movement. The foundation in the Egyptian capital of *Jāmiʿat al-duwal al-ʿArab* (The Arab League) in 1945 was intended to represent and implement the long-awaited aspirations of the Arab nation but since its foundation it has come to symbolise all the complexities of international politics in the Middle East. Indeed, it was immediately faced with the problem that, since the conclusion of the Second World War, has become, in the words of the Moroccan historian, Abdallah Laroui, 'the Arab issue': the fate of the Palestinian people. The series of conflicts, 1948 (*al-nakbah*, the disaster), 1956, 1967 (*al-naksah*, the setback), 1973 (*al-ʿubūr*, the crossing– in Jacques Berque's phrase, 'a semi-success'), and 1982, these are not simply tragedies in the lives of Palestinians but widely regarded by Arab intellectuals as emblematic of a broader societal crisis.

During the 1950s a number of Arab nations gained their independence and set themselves to establish social agenda in a post-colonial era. In the aftermath of revolution many groups who had participated in the removal of the *anciens régimes* discovered that the changes they had hoped and fought for were not to be realised. Here again, Maḥfūẓ's *Trilogy* provides an illustration. At the conclusion of the third volume, *al-Sukkariyyah* (the name of a Cairo street), the two grandsons of the family, Aḥmad and ʿAbd al-munʿim, are both arrested (the year is approximately 1944). The former is a Communist who is questioned by the police about his 'extremist writings', while the latter belongs to the Muslim Brethren. Members of both these groups participated in the concerted campaign against the British occupation and governmental corruption in the late 1940s, but in the uneasy atmosphere of the early years of the Egyptian revolution both were ruthlessly suppressed. Many Communist intellectuals were to spend much of their life in jail, and among them are a number of prominent littérateurs who have provided accounts of their experiences. The Muslim Brethren, a group that had been founded by Ḥasan al-Banna (d. 1949), a student of Rashīd Riḍā, in 1928, also lent its support (and highly organised underground network) to the anti-colonial cause, but it was precisely the breadth and efficiency of its organisation that almost immediately brought it into conflict with the new revolutionary government. In 1954, an attempt was made on (then Colonel) ʿAbd al-nāṣir's life, and many Muslim Brethren were imprisoned, among them Sayyid Quṭb (d. 1966), who had officially joined the Brethren just one year earlier. Quṭb, whose writings continue to play a key role in contemporary religious discourse, was in and out of prison during the 1950s and 1960s and, in spite of an international outcry, was executed in 1966.

The intellectual life in most countries of the Arab world during the 1950s and 1960s was a patchwork of complexities and contradictions. On the international level there were the triumphs of the Bandung Conference (1955) at which the concept of a new Third World non-alignment was formulated, the nationalisation of the Suez Canal in

1956, the creation of the United Arab Republic between Syria and Egypt (1958–61), the conclusion of the Algerian Revolution (1962), all of which led to significant changes in local and international alignments. Within the societies themselves however the debates and controversies of the intellectual community were closely monitored by an elaborate security apparatus, and expression was subject to the tightest control. Those many intellectuals who espoused the goals of the revolution, whether on a broader or more local scale, and who felt themselves able to function within prescribed guidelines eagerly adopted *iltizām* (commitment) as the organising principle of their writing; it was part of the motto of what remains the most widely circulated Arabic literary journal, *Al-Ādāb*, founded in 1953 by Suhayl Idrīs (b. 1923) in Beirut. Palestinian writers, and especially their poets, found a direct incentive for this literary credo within their own particular circumstances, but elsewhere too fiction, drama, and poetry were drawn into an approach to the portrayal of the new societies that was predominantly committed and social realist. Those writers who chose to explore the darker side of the image so carefully constructed by the government-controlled media found themselves imprisoned or worse; for them the most frequent resorts were to silence or exile. Writing in 1989 in the journal, *al-Nāqid* (published in London), the Iraqi novelist Fāḍil al-ʿAzāwī notes that

> when a regime nationalizes mankind in the name of adherence to a national, religious, or class credo, it simply condemns itself to death. The selfsame credo will die when its only goal turns out to be a closed room haunted by specters. The real crisis for Arab man today is above all else that of freedom of conscience.

The bitter aftermath of the June 1967 War led many contemporary Arab intellectuals to undertake a profound re-examination of the foundations upon which their societies are assumed to be based. Many stopped writing altogether, while others sought solace and reaffirmation through an investigation of the classical heritage (*turāth*) of the Arabs and of the bases of cultural authenticity (*aṣālah*). In 1973 Abdallah Laroui published his famous study, *Al-ʿArab wa-al-fikr al-tārīkhī* (*The Crisis of the Arab Intellectual*), in which he condemns the bases of Arab historical writing, while on a more philosophical plane, his fellow Moroccan, Muḥammad ʿĀbid al-Jābirī, investigates the epistemology of Arab thought; in his two-volume study, *Naqd al-ʿaql al-ʿArabī* (Critique of the Arab Mentality, 1984), he resorts to the great debates of the classical period of Islam in order to illustrate the primarily explicative goals and methods of traditional scholarship and therefrom the need for new modes of thought untrammelled by the principles of the past.

During the 1980s and 1990s one of the principal arenas of both action and debate in the Arab world (and elsewhere) has focused on Islamic revival and especially a major increase in popular Islamic movements which, in several countries, have become a prominent political force. The investigations into the heritage of the past that we have just described inevitably highlighted the linkages between the Arabic and Islamic heritage that had tended to be somewhat marginalised during the heyday of nationalism, the push towards independence, and the establishment of a new social order in the post-revolutionary period. In such a context, the Iranian Revolution of 1979 assumes a major importance, in that Iran's active bolstering of self-identity among Shīʿī communities in the Arab world (most notably in Iraq, the Gulf States and Southern Lebanon) has not only galvanised those communities into action–as subsequent events in Iraq, Lebanon, and the Gulf have shown, but has also led Sunnī governments in the Gulf region (and particularly that of Saudi Arabia) to counter the threat posed by their assertive Shīʿī neighbour by encouraging and fostering popular Islamic movements elsewhere in the region. The political and social problems of such countries as Algeria, Palestine, Egypt, and the Sudan have provided fertile ground for the growth of increasingly activist popular Islamic movements. For, if current Arab political and social realities can be attributed to decades of secularist government and a reliance on the West, popular preachers suggest, then Islam–as an indigenous faith system with its own set of values–presents a ready and viable alternative. The extent to which that set of values should be applied or reapplied is now a topic of intense political debate throughout the Arab world, but in 1988, Imam Khomeini, the President of Iran, provided an instance of their strictest application to the world of literature when he issued his infamous death sentence against the British novelist, Salman Rushdie, for allegedly blaspheming the Prophet in his novel, *Satanic Verses*.

Another area of discussion that has enriched debate among the intelligentsia of the Arab world in the post-1967 period and thus been reflected in literary production is that of the status of women in Arab and Islamic society. One of the pioneers in this movement is Zaynab al-Ghazālī, an Egyptian writer who worked with Ḥasan al-Banna and later with Sayyid Quṭb on an organisation of Sisters alongside the Muslim Brethren, a role for which she was imprisoned for five years (1966–71). In her writings she advocates the need for an Islamic state, basing her position on an understanding that, since Islam has provided women with all the rights they need, there is no need to talk in terms of liberation. Al-Ghazālī's fellow countrywoman, Nawāl al-Saʿdāwī (b. 1931), clearly does not share her views. Al-Saʿdāwī has made use of her prominence as both a medical doctor and a writer of fiction to challenge societal norms regarding gender roles and the tendency to keep the open discussion of sexual mores under wraps. Her increasingly strident criticism of the linkage between patriarchal structures and the economic subjugation of women brought her into direct conflict with the repressive cultural policies of Anwar al-Sādāt's presidency, and she was imprisoned for nine months in 1981. Following the assassination of al-Sādāt, she was released, and since that time she has become renowned in the West as the Arab world's most forthright feminist advocate. Another Arab feminist whose works are known in the West is the Moroccan sociologist, Fatimah Mernissi, (Fāṭimah al-Marnīsī, (b. 1940), who discusses the issue of gender in its contemporary Islamic framework from a rather more scholarly and historical viewpoint. For her, it is not so much the status of women themselves that needs to be reconsidered, but rather the relationship between the sexes in marriage and the provisions of Islam that perpetuate male domination.

CONCLUSION

When an English television company made a film series about the Arabs in the 1980s and devoted a programme to the role of literature in society, it was entitled *The Power of the Word.* The choice is entirely appropriate. From the beginnings of the Arabic tradition, literature has been an immensely influential force in society. We might illustrate what appears to be one point of contrast by invoking the old English proverb of uncertain provenance which runs: 'Sticks and stones may break my bones, but names can never hurt me'. No sentiment could be further from the realities of the situation in the world of Arabic literature. Names and words could not merely hurt; they could be the verbal triggers that would start wars. In the hands of a skilled poet, the genre of *hijāʾ* (lampoon) was a weapon much feared by the tribes of the Arabian Peninsula. Words then do indeed have the power to lift up and to crush; '*Hādhā huwa-smī*', (This is My Name), is the modern poet, Adūnīs's, defiant proclamation of the writer's sense of his own identity and significance. Littérateurs in Arab society continue to have at their disposal a formidable mode of expression in order to uplift, persuade, criticise, and entertain. Most significantly, the tremendous emphasis that Islamic scholarship was to place on the creation of a written record of reports, opinions, and ideas did nothing to lessen the prevalence of the oral and public dimension that have been part of the literary heritage from the very outset.

In this chapter I have endeavoured to provide some context for the literary production that is the topic of the chapters that now follow. In spite of its relative length, it is still a riskily concise summary of the cultural background to a large topic spread over a geographical area and span of time that are both extensive. It also needs to be stated explicitly that, by separating these particular contexts from the other chapters, my aim is only to afford myself the opportunity for a greater concentration on the more intrinsically literary qualities of the texts and authors themselves. The contexts we have discussed here–physical, linguistic, historical, and intellectual–are all intrinsic components of the literary production that is the subject of this book.

CHAPTER 3

The Qurʾān: sacred text and cultural yardstick

INTRODUCTION

In the previous chapter I discussed the revelation of the Qurʾān to the incipient Islamic community and then explored the multifarious ways in which that event had an impact on the course of Middle Eastern history and the development of the Islamic sciences. For the Muslim believer the Qurʾān is the primary source on matters theological and legal, but in addition to that it is a daily presence in the life of the community and its individual members. Beyond these aspects of its message however, the recorded text of the Qurʾān is a work of sacred 'scripture', and the miraculous qualities attributed to its style (termed *iʿjāz*) have long been the object of scrutiny by the critical community. More recently, literature scholars have showed renewed interest in works of sacred scripture as literary texts (Alter and Kermode, *The Literary Guide to the Bible*, Cambridge, Mass., 1987, for example), and specialists on the Qurʾān have also contributed to this research. It is these more literary aspects of the Qurʾān that I would like to explore in this chapter, focusing on features that have played a major role in the development of the Arabic literary tradition.

The opening verses of *Sūrat al-ʿalaq* (Sura 96, The Blood-clot) are believed to represent the first of God's revelations to His messenger, the Prophet Muhammad. Their structure and style serve as an excellent illustration of many of the features of Qurʾānic discourse.

> Recite: in the name of your Lord who created (1)
> created mankind from a clot of blood (2)
>
> Recite: and your Lord is most generous, (3)
> He who instructed with the pen, (4)
> instructed mankind what he knew not. (5)

This passage illustrates the primary mode of communication found in the Qurʾān: God, the speaker, addresses His messenger in the second person and instructs him to recite to his listeners, the initially small but ever-expanding community of Muslims. The messages that Muḥammad's early audience heard in Mecca were couched in short rhyming phrases; in the example above the final word in each verse of the two sections (1–2 and 3–5) ends with a rhyming syllable; in 1 and 2, for example, it is *khalaq* and *ʿalaq*. The repetition of the word 'recite' (in Arabic, *iqraʾ*) is a further structuring device. The word *iqraʾ* is the imperative form of the verbal root Q-R-ʾ, a noun derivative of which is the word '*Qurʾān*' itself. The original meaning of this verbal root was 'to recite'; thus the Qurʾān is a 'recitation', a series of utterances, the word of God, transmitted orally by Muḥammad to his listeners. I use the adjective 'original' because the root has since added a further meaning to that of 'to recite', namely 'to read'. That very shift in predominant meaning may be seen as a reflection of firstly the text's own acknowledgement of the function and power of writing (that God 'instructed with the pen') and secondly the juxtaposition within the developing Islamic tradition of the written and the oral. Just as the root Q-R-ʾ has never lost its implicit sense of 'to recite (out loud)', so have Islamic societies throughout the world continued to pay the greatest respect to the oral traditions of their heritage even as they compiled an enormous and varied corpus of textual scholarship.

The impact of the contents of the Qurʾān and their interpretation by generations of scholars is clearly enormous, but equally powerful is the impact of its modes of structure and discourse, whether the medium is that of reading or listening, in the latter case involving the highly skilled art of intonation of the text (*tajwīd*, literally 'making it good').

STRUCTURES

The Qurʾān is subdivided into 114 chapters called suras (*sūrahs*). Each sura has a title; for example, the 96th, the opening of which we cited above, is called *Sūrat al-ʿalaq*. The title is a word that is mentioned within the text of the sura itself. While in many cases the word in question will occur near the beginning of the sura, that is not always the case; in *Sūrat al-shuʿarāʾ* (26, The Poets), for example, the word 'poets' occurs in the 224th verse of a sura with 226 in total. The first sura, called '*al-Fātiḥah*' (The Opening), is in the form of a prayer; its privileged position within the ordering of the text is a recognition of its special status: within Islamic societies the process of 'reading the *al-Fātiḥah*' is a requirement in completing contracts, most especially that of marriage. Apart from the *Fātiḥah*, the suras are arranged by length, starting with the longest,

Sūrat al-baqarah (2, The Cow) which has 286 verses and finishing with a number of extremely short suras; *Sūrat al-kawthar* (108, Abundance), for example, and *Sūrat al-naṣr* (110, Help) each have three verses, and *Sūrat al-nās* (114, The People) has six.

The public recitation of the Qur'ān is considered a meritorious act, most especially during the month of Ramaḍān which is devoted to fasting and meditation. For this and similar purposes, the text is divided up into thirty equal parts (*ajzā'*), one for each day of the month, and each 'part' is also subdivided into halves called *aḥzāb*, (sing. *ḥizb*). These segments, which are purely quantitative and not related to the sura structure noted above, are detailed in the margins in the text so that those who commit themselves, either in private or public, to a reading of the complete text may have a convenient point of reference.

Each sura is prefaced by a section that states its number and title, the place–Mecca or Medina–where the majority of revelations cited in the sura were first recited, the number of verses it contains, and its place in the sequence of revelations; *Sūrat al-zalzalah* (99, The Earthquake), for example, 'was revealed after [*Sūrat*] *al-Ṭalāq*' (65, The Divorce). In addition, twenty-nine of the suras begin with a sequence of letters, the function of which remains a mystery. Some of these sequences, *ALIF-LĀM-RĀ'*, for example, and *ALIF-LĀM-MĪM*, are to be found at the beginning of several suras, while others occur only once. Two of them, *ṬĀ-HĀ* (verse 1 of *Sūrat Ṭaha*, Surah 20) and *YĀ-SĪN* (verse 1 of *Sūrat Yāsīn*, Sura 36) are regularly used as names for male children. Through an interesting exercise in textual analysis, the American scholar, James Bellamy, has suggested that all the combinations of letters can be read, with some judicious emendations, as abbreviations of the '*Bismillah*', the phrase 'In the name of God, the Merciful, the Compassionate'–itself the first verse of *Sūrat al-Fatiḥah*–which was adopted during Muḥammad's lifetime as an invocation at the beginning of each sura (*Sūrat al-tawbah* [9, Repentance] being an exception).

We have already noted that the suras are arranged in order of length; in other words, the later suras are compilations of fewer revelations than the earlier ones. Each of the 'phases' into which Muḥammad's prophetic call is commonly divided–an initial attempt at reconciling his recitations of God's message with the beliefs and expectations of his fellow-townsfolk in Mecca, then a realisation that his words were not being accepted by them, and lastly, the move to Medinah and the foundation of a new religious community–find a reflection in the revelations and thus in the suras into which they are placed.

In the earliest period, when Muḥammad wished to draw the attention of the people of Mecca to the implications of his message, his revelations show very particular structural features. Here, for example, is the beginning of *Sūrat al-Mursalāt* (77, Those Sent Forth):

wa-al-murasalāti ʿurf-an	(1) By the ones sent forth in droves
f-al-ʿāṣifāti ʿaṣf-an	(2) storming in tempest,
wa-al-nāshirāti nashr-an	(3) by the scatterers scattering
f-al-fāriqāti farq-an	(4) cleaving a cleavage
f-al-mulqiyāti dhikr-an	(5) tossing a reminder,
ʿudhr-an aw nudhr-an	(6) excuse or warning,
inna-mā tūʿadūna la-wāqiʿun	(7) what you are promised will happen!
fa-idhā n-nujūmu ṭumisat	(8) When the stars are snuffed out,
wa-idhā s-samāʾu furijat	(9) when the heavens are cleft,
wa-idhā al-jibālu nusifat	(10) when the mountains are pulverised,
wa-idhā r-rusulu uqqitat	(11) when the messengers are assigned a time,
li-ayyi yawmin ujjilat	(12) to what day will they be delayed?
li-yawm il-faṣli	(13) to the Day of Decision.
ma adrāka ma yawm ul-faṣli	(14) What will inform you about the Day of Decision?
waylun yawmaʾidhin li-l-mukadhdhibīna	(15) On that day woe to the liars!

These sections–with their references to natural phenomena, their remarkable parallelisms, and their final and internal rhyme schemes –are a typical feature of many of the suras from the Meccan period. This particular sura is remarkable, in that it begins with a sequence of invocations–an oath-preposition (*wa-* or *fa-*) followed by a participial form in the feminine plural and a noun in the indefinite singular (repeated with exactly the same sound structure at the beginning of suras 37, 51, 79, and 100, and with different sound patterns in a number of others, 52 and 53, for example). It then continues with a second segment (vv. 8-11) that replicates the series of 'when' clauses which serve as the opening for several other Meccan suras (56, 82, and 84, for example); the opening of *Sūrat al-takwīr* (81, The Enshrouding) contains fully fourteen of these phrases. Sequences such as these were apparently similar in structure to the pronouncements of other types of preacher and 'warner' to be encountered in sixth century Mecca, particularly soothsayers (*kuhhān*, sing. *kāhin*). However, the crescendo of images and sounds that marked the beginning of several of these early revelations recited by Muḥammad to the people of his native city were followed by a new and disturbing message, often preceded by a question ('What will inform you about...?'), which contained clear warnings concerning the inevitability of God's judgement that awaited sinners.

In the imagery and sounds of these invocations of nature and the elements we can see the message of the Qur'ān being revealed to the people of Mecca in not only their own language ('an Arabic Qur'ān', as *Sūrat Yūsuf* [12, Joseph] declares in verse 2) but also a formal structure that they would recognise. That this process of 'recognition' became problematic for Muḥammad in his prophetic mission is clear from the text of the Qur'ān itself: it was necessary to distinguish the revelations of God to his Prophet from these other types of homiletic utterance, and verses 41 and 42 of *Sūrat al-ḥaqqah* (69, The Indubitable) are unequivocal on the subject:

> It is the saying of a noble Messenger,
> not that of a poet; how little you believe!
> nor of a soothsayer; how little you remember!
> a revelation from the Lord of the worlds.

Part of the problem in the association that the people of Mecca made between Muḥammad's recitations and those of poets and soothsayers lies in the fact that they all sought to exploit the sound qualities of Arabic by resorting to the cadential rhythms of *saj*ʿ (lit. 'the cooing of a dove', but thereafter 'rhymed and cadenced discourse'), a style and structure that makes full use of the morphological potential of Arabic (described in the previous chapter and amply illustrated by the transliteration of the Arabic text just provided). The traditional English 'translation' of the Arabic word has been 'rhymed prose', a reflection of the later use of *saj*ʿ in prose writing and especially the narrative genre known as the *maqāmah* (discussed in ch. 5). However, even though the early development of the style is not known to us, several features suggest the possibility of a link to the very earliest stages of Arabic poetry. While the presence in the above quotation from sura 77 of rhyme, parallelism, and imagery–and the 'different' discourse that characterises many modern definitions of poetry–are more than sufficient for a modern reader to declare segments from many suras 'poetic', the quotation from the text of 'The Indubitable' reminds us that, in Mecca before the *hijrah*, any such generic similarities had to be disavowed. The Qur'ān was unique: it was neither prose nor poetry, but the revelation of God to His people.

This desire to preserve the concept of the uniqueness of Qur'ānic style led conservative scholars to disavow the connection with *saj'* and indeed to deride it; the 'poetics' of *saj'* have, in fact, been the subject of remarkably little interest among critics, a notable exception being Ḍiyā' al-dīn ibn al-Athīr (d. 1239) who asserted unambiguously that the large part of the Qur'ān is in *saj'*. Indeed, while the comparative brevity of the later suras lends a particular emphasis to the role of *saj'* units within the structure of the sura, the elements of the *saj'* style are also much in evidence throughout the Qur'ān. Turning to the longer suras, we find that *Sūrat al-baqarah* (2, The Cow), for example, contains 286 verses, of which 264 form part of a rhyming sequence, those based on the rhyme *ūn/īn* being the most prevalent. The beginning of the sura notes that it is a 'Medinan' sura, only a single verse (v. 281) being attributed to the time of Muḥammad's final pilgrimage to Mecca in 632.

This lengthy sura contains a number of different types of discourse. One of the most remarkable is in the form of a direct address from God to His Messenger (v. 186):

> If My servants ask you about Me, indeed I am near;
> I answer the call of the caller when he calls Me.
> So may they respond to Me and believe in Me.
> Perhaps they will be rightly guided.

The sura also contains injunctions and homiletic narratives couched in verses that are considerably longer than those of the early Meccan period. Specific obligations incumbent upon the community of believers are presented in the form of a series of imperatives that begin with the phrase: 'O you who believe...' These segments provide instructions on such matters as food, retaliation, wills, fasting, divorce and its consequences, and – at the very end of the sura – debt. A single verse (196), detailing some of the obligations connected with the pilgrimage and visitation (*'umrah*) to the holy cities of Mecca and Medina, serves as an excellent illustration of both the length and tone of the verses from the Medinan phase of Muḥammad's mission:

Complete the pilgrimage and visitation to God; if you are prevented, then such offerings as are feasible. Do not shave your heads until the offerings reach their place. If any of you is sick or has a pain in his head, then redemption comes through fasting, alms, or sacrifice. When you are safe, whoever enjoys the visitation up to the pilgrimage, then such offerings as are feasible. Anyone who can find none, then for you a three-day fast during the pilgrimage and a seven-day fast following your return, making ten in all. That is for those whose family is not present in the Holy Mosque. Fear God and know that God is dire in retribution.

The dynamic nature of the process of revelation and its reception by the community can be gauged by the implied questioners who are reflected in a further set of segments beginning with the phrase 'They will ask you about…', and which provide clarification on such matters as drinking and gambling, the treatment of orphans, the direction of prayer, and fighting during the holy month; the response to the inquiry is prefaced with the word 'say' (*qul*):

They will ask you about orphans. Say: The best is to do well by them. If you mingle with them, they are your brethren. God knows the corrupter from the doer of good. Had God so willed, He would have harried you. He is mighty and wise. (v. 220)

The narratives invoke the careers of Moses, Abraham, Saul, and David, and references to Jesus and Mary, as a means of addressing the message of the revelations to the 'People of the Book' (Jews and Christians) and of showing the way in which the new calling to which Muḥammad's audience was being summoned incorporated the Judeo-Christian prophetic tradition within it, and at the same time placing the mission of Muḥammad to his people within the same prophetic framework.

The sections created by these different types of address are set off by verses that draw attention to God's power and generosity; verse 164 may serve as an example of the language of such statements and of the increased length of the rhyming unit:

Indeed in the creation of the heavens and the earth, the difference of night and day, the ship that plies the seas to people's profit, and the water that God releases from the heavens, thus reviving the soil after it has died and placing all kinds of beast in it, in the turning of the wind, and the clouds employed between heaven and earth, in these things are signs for the intelligent.

Sūrat al-baqarah, an elaborate and lengthy collection of prophetic narratives, commands, warnings, and statements concerning God's transcendent authority, ends with a prayer:

O Lord, do not fault us if we forget or err;
O Lord, do not give us a charge like that of those who went before us;
O Lord, do not burden us beyond our abilities;
Pardon and forgive us, and show us mercy;
You are our protector; grant us victory over the unbelievers.

Sūrat al-nisāʾ (4, Women) is another lengthy sura from the period in Medinah, and shows many of the same structuring features that we have just described: detailed instructions to the community in imperative form concerning points of doctrine and law (and particularly, as the title implies, concerning the status of women); and responses to points that have been raised regarding the revelations, now introduced by the specific verb 'They will ask you for an opinion (*istaftaw*)'. The structure noted above, 'They will ask you about. . ', is used to introduce another segment (v. 153ff.) addressed to the People of the Book; it includes a lengthy passage on the death of Jesus and invokes the names of many Judeo-Christian prophets.

We gave you revelation just as We did to Nūḥ and the prophets who came after him; We gave revelation to Ibrāhīm, Ismāʿīl, Isḥāq, Yaʿqūb, the Tribes, ʿĪsā, Ayyūb, Yūnus, Hārūn, Sulaymān; and we gave Dāʾūd the psalms.
(v. 163)

Believers are enjoined to obey God and His messenger (v. 59), and particular wrath is reserved for those people who, having joined the faithful, began to have doubts when conflicts arose between the small community of Muslims in Medinah and the people of Mecca; these doubters were termed 'hypocrites' (*munāfiqūn*), and verse 138 shows a certain grim humour in proclaiming their fate:

Give the hypocrites the good news: they will have a gruesome punishment.

This survey of a few of the shortest and longest suras in the Qurʾān attempts to identify some of the discourse features that are involved in the structuring of the Qurʾān as a whole and of its individual suras. The entire text clearly exhibits features of the style known as *sajʿ*, although, as Muḥammad's prophetic mission develops and expands, the need to differentiate the revelations of the Qurʾān from other kinds of public recitation may have served as an impetus for the significant change that occurs in the length and inner patterns of the rhyming structures. Within each sura the different revelations are grouped together in the order established by the process of recording the Qurʾān in written form and especially by the recension of the third Caliph, ʿUthmān. The text that emerged from that process, with injunctions and narratives often spread over several suras, became the object of intensive study and commentary. Its variations in structure and discourse came to be seen as accurate and reasonable reflections of the more than twenty-year period during which the utterances were recited and of the mode by which they were put into textual form. Within such a framework the placement of various segments of a series of prophetic revelations in different suras, for example, and the juxtaposition within a single sura of passages from different periods and on divergent topics came to be regarded as characteristics of Quranic discourse and revered as such. In the straightforward phrase of commentaries: 'some parts of the Qur'ān provide explanations of others'.

These very same features that, within the tradition of Islamic scholarship, have been considered as contributors to the Qur'ān's unique textual qualities have served to bemuse and frustrate many Western readers of the Qur'ān. In this context, a famous remark of Thomas Carlyle establishes some kind of yardstick for transcultural misapprehension. The Qur'ān, he declares, is 'a wearisome, confused jumble, crude, incondite... Nothing but a sense of duty could carry any European through the Koran'. While we note in passing Carlyle's invocation of the 'sense of duty' that appears to have characterised the motivations of many nineteenth-century students of the Middle East, we should also draw attention to the missed expectations that seem to colour his comment: for the sequential logic and structural unities of Biblical discourse that had had such a powerful effect on the development of English literature, and for narrative techniques such as those that Erich Auerbach discusses in the first chapter of his famous work, *Mimesis*. It is expectations such as these that appear to have led the authors of the relatively few studies of the literary aspects of the Qur'ān in Western languages to concentrate on those suras and segments that conform with such criteria. There is, for example, *Sūrat al-raḥmān* (55, the Merciful), in which the rhyming syllable of the title (*ān*) becomes the rhyme for the entire sura, and the repetition after each verse of a 'refrain'–'O which of your Lord's benefits will you both disbelieve' (*tukadhdhibān*)–creates the effect of a responsorial psalm. However, a sura that has attracted the attention of commentators in both Arabic and other languages for its unusual structural unity and narrative qualities is *Sūrat Yūsuf* (12, Joseph). The elements of the narrative–Joseph's dream and its interpretation, the duplicity of his brothers, the attempted seduction of Joseph by Potiphar's wife, the imprisonment and recognition scenes–these are all well known from the account in Genesis (Chs. 37–50); the craftsmen who made the splendid thirteenth-century stained glass in Chartres Cathedral's north aisle provided worshippers with a beautifully structured visual analysis of the episodes in the story.

The Qur'ānic version of the narrative opens with a passage that provides a framework for the text as a whole: after a set of the 'opening letters'–*ALIF-LĀM-RĀ'* (discussed above)–the text declares that the recitation is 'an Arabic Qur'ān', a statement the implications of which have had a vast impact upon ritual practice throughout the Islamic world. The third verse of the sura then provides confirmation of the very qualities to which we have just alluded: it announces that 'We will tell you the best of stories'. The perfect chiastic symmetry of the Joseph narrative gives the central portion–his imprisonment and the homily that he delivers (vv. 37–42) – a tremendous importance. And, just as aspects of the narrative, especially the betrayal of Joseph by his brothers, possessed a powerful symbolic resonance within the Christian tradition, so are the words of Joseph to his fellow-prisoners clearly intended to convey a powerful and important message to the hearers of Muḥammad's recitation in Mecca:

> It is not for us to make any association with God; that is part of His bounty to us and all people, but most of them show no gratitude. (38)
>
> O my prison-companions, which is better: to have a number of different gods or God the One and All-powerful? (39)
>
> The entities you worship other than Him are mere names that you and your ancestors have named, and God has not revealed to them any authority. Judgement belongs to God alone; you should worship no other god than Him; that is the proper religion, but most people do not know. (40)

The elaborate way in which the narrative establishes a web of situations–the telling of the dream, the plotting of the brothers, the resigned patience of Jacob (the quality of *ṣabr* [v. 18] that has been highly regarded as an Arab trait since pre-Islamic times), the betrayal, the attempted seduction, and the imprisonment, and then proceeds to resolve them in reverse order–the discovery of the 'trickery' (*kayd*) of Potiphar's wife and companions (which in turn becomes a common motif in Arabic writing), the encounter with the brothers, their confession of guilt, the reuniting of Jacob with his long-lost son, and the fulfillment of the dream–all this serves as a wonderfully appropriate framework for the message that Muḥammad conveyed to the people of Mecca concerning the power of the One God and the authority that He gives to His chosen prophets.

Sūrat Yūsuf certainly contains the longest connected narrative in the Qur'ān, a fact that, in the context of its original reception, raises interesting questions concerning the precise context in which it was revealed. Its undoubted narrative qualities have made it a particular favourite for analysis within the as yet small library of works analysing the literary qualities of the Qur'ān. As we noted above, the Qur'ān includes a number of other homiletic narratives and parables, some of them scattered in different suras. A particularly rich source of somewhat shorter narratives is *Sūrat al-Kahf* (18, The Cave). In it we find firstly the story of the seven sleepers of Ephesus (vv. 9–26) which tells the legend of a group of Christians persecuted during the reign of the emperor Decius (249–51) who resort to a cave (whence the sura's title) and fall into a profound and lengthy sleep; verse 25 says that the period involved is 309 years. When they wake up, they find themselves in a new era in which Christians are no longer persecuted. At the hands of the modern Egyptian playwright, Tawfīq al-Ḥakīm (d. 1987), this legend is turned into a five-act play, *Ahl al-kahf* (The People of the Cave). Returning to *Sūrat al-Kahf* itself, we next encounter a remarkable parable concerning two men to each of whom a vineyard is assigned: the passage is characteristically framed, being introduced by God's instruction to Muḥammad that he should 'Make for them a simile' and brought to a conclusion by a typical Qur'ānic device of closure, the expression of God's power: 'God is surely the best in recompense and best in outcome' (vv. 32–44). At verse 60 begins one of the Qur'ān's most fascinating tales, that of Moses and his encounter with a figure called al-Khaḍir. With a young companion Moses embarks on a quest to find the 'meeting place of the two seas', during the course of which the two encounter 'one of Our servants' (v. 65). Moses is set a challenge: not to ask any questions concerning this person's deeds, however odd they may seem. The series of seemingly violent and illogical actions that this person perpetrates are eventually explained to the all too humanly impatient Moses. The story leads directly into a further tale which may provide a clue to its origins of the Moses narrative, that of 'the man with two horns' (*dhū al-qarnayn*), generally associated with the romance of Alexander. This portion of the tale, introduced by the phrase that we noted above: 'They will ask you about...', describes God's injunction to Alexander to deal with the corrupt peoples of Gog and Magog. It too closes with an expression of the truth of God's promises (vv. 83–98).

These are just a few of the many stories that are invoked in the Qur'ān in order to provide illustrations and warnings to Muḥammad's audience. As the contemporary study of narratives acknowledges the move beyond the conventions of what Bakhtin terms a 'monologic' narrative perspective to an appreciation of more fragmentary modes of verbalising the complexities of the human consciousness and as the literary analysis of the sacred texts of many faiths and cultures addresses itself to the many types of narrative that they contain, the tales, legends and parables that we have just discussed (and other examples that we have not) clearly demand further study.

LANGUAGE AND IMAGERY

In the previous chapter we alluded to the language situation in the Arabian Peninsula at the time of the revelation of the Qur'ān. Analysis of that situation is complicated by the fact that the Muslim community continued to rely primarily on memory and oral communication as modes of preserving and transmitting the sacred text until it was realised that many of Muḥammad's contemporaries (the so-called 'carriers' of the revealed message) who served as the Muslim community's corporate memory were dying. Thus, while we can note that the tradition of pre-Islamic poetry serves as a clear historical precedent for the language of the Qur'ān and that the language of the Bedouin of the Peninsula became an authoritative source for 'correctness' during the period when Muslim scholars began the process of codifying Arabic grammar, we possess little information about the status of the language of the Qur'ān in the context of the general linguistic situation in the Arabian Peninsula at the time of its revelation. The entire topic is still the subject of considerable debate.

In several verses the text of the Qur'ān notes that it is couched in 'a clear Arabic language' (*lisān ʿarabī mubīn*; see *Sūrat al-Naḥl* (16, The Bee), v. 103, for example, and *Sūrat al-Shuʿarāʾ* (26, The Poets), v. 195). Furthermore, the root of the word *mubīn* is found in another significant passage regarding language: *Sūrat Ibrāhīm* (14, Abraham) v. 4 declares that 'We have never sent down a prophet with anything but his own people's language so that he may make things clear (*yubayyin*) to them'. The statements, reports, and implied questions ('They will ask you about...') that are included in the suras of the Qur'ān make it clear that

God's message was indeed recited by Muḥammad in a language that was comprehensible to his listeners. In view of the enormously important role that the language of the Qur'ān was to play in every aspect of the life of Muslim society, it is hardly surprising that there has been a good deal of scholarly debate over the linguistic features and social context of the language of the Arabian Peninsula at the time of the revelations to Muḥammad. However, it is generally agreed that the languages of the Qur'ān and of the corpus of pre-Islamic poetry are essentially the same and share particular and distinctive characteristics. An example of one such feature occurs in verse 4 of *Sūrat al-Qadr* (97, Power): 'In it the angels and the spirit come down', where the verb for 'come down' (*tanazzalu*) is lacking the prefixed 't' for the incomplete timeframe that characterises the morphological expectations of Arabic grammar as it was later codified.

Concordances of the Qur'ān list a number of words that appear to be of non-Arabian provenance; Arthur Jeffrey in his *The Foreign Vocabulary of the Qur'ān* (Baroda: Oriental Institute, 1938), lists some 275 such items. It needs to be said from the outset that the very notion of 'foreignness', when dealing with the necessarily adaptive language situation in a commercial centre such as that of Mecca, is somewhat problematic. While the Arabic language of the desert nomads may have been less subject to linguistic change than its northern Semitic cousins, the various towns, oases, and tribal confederations were far from being isolated from social and commercial contacts with regions to the north and south. Later scholars such as Jalāl al-dīn al-Suyūṭī (d. 1505) abandoned their forebears' reluctance to acknowledge the presence of such lexical items within the Qur'ānic text and suggested that in fact many of the words were already part of Arabic vocabulary before the time of the revelations to Muḥammad.

As many of the examples we have already cited show clearly, the language of the Qur'ān is often used with excellent figurative effect, providing further illustration of the close linkage between metaphor and the homiletic. In his Epistle to the church at Ephesus, for example, St Paul compares the adherence to a faith to donning armour ('putting on the whole armour of God') before providing a veritable check-list of weaponry linked to aspects of belief (Ephesians 6. 11–17). The Qur'ān uses the metaphors of blindness and deafness to convey unbelief: 'God has removed their light and left them in darkness, not seeing; deaf, dumb, blind; they shall not return' (*Sūrat al-Baqarah* (2, The Cow) vv. 17–18). Those who follow other gods have 'gone astray', and just as those who do not believe have had the light removed, so do those whom God has guided to belief have the light, an image which provides one of the Qur'ān's most extended and beautiful images:

> God is the light of the heavens and the earth; the likeness of His light is as a niche with a lamp in it; the lamp is in a glass, and the glass is like a pearly star kindled from a blessed tree, an olive from neither East nor West, its oil almost giving light even though no fire has touched it; light upon light. God guides to His light whomever he wishes. (*Sūrat al-Nūr* (24, The Light) v. 35).

And, along with the more direct comparisons implicit in the similes of this passage, we find others that are more intricate in their linkages: those who spend their money in vain and do not believe in the Day of Judgement are likened to 'a smooth rock with soil on it; a rainstorm strikes it and leaves it barren' (*Sūrat al-Baqarah* (2, The Cow) v. 264); that very Day is depicted as one 'when we roll up the heavens just like the scroll for texts, (*Sūrat al-Anbiyā'* (21, The Prophets) v. 104); and, in the depiction of God's wrath against the people of 'Ād, a wind was sent down that 'snatched up people like the stumps of uprooted palm-trees' (*Sūrat al-Qamar* (54, The Moon) v. 20).

All these features of the discourse of the Qur'ān are encapsulated into the religious and critical doctrine of *i'jāz*, the 'inimitability' of God's revelation to Muḥammad. It is enshrined in the *tahaddī* ('challenge') verses, such as 'If you have doubts concerning what we have sent down to our servant, then produce a sura like it' (*Sūrat al-Baqarah* (2, The Cow) v. 24), and 'If mankind and the jinn got together to produce the like of this Qur'ān, they would not produce its like' (*Sūrat al-Isrā'* (17, The Night-Journey) v. 88). The existence of this doctrine has deterred most writers from attempting to take up the implicit challenge; one who did was Arabic's most famous poet, who thereby earned himself the name by which he is generally known, 'al-Mutanabbī', (he who claimed to be a prophet). Such exceptions aside however, the language and style of the Qur'ān endure as yardsticks of Arabic eloquence, to be admired, cited, and, in particular, recited.

THE ROLE OF SOUND

At the beginning of this chapter I drew attention to the oral dimension in not only the process of the original revelation of the Qur'ān but also in the continuing practice of the Islamic community. Once the Qur'ān was established and canonised in textual form, the overwhelming bulk of learning devoted to its study has been concerned with the written dimension–with the Qur'ān as text, and that has been reflected in the contents of this chapter. However, the oral dimension continues to exert its enduring influence on society. The ability of a devout Muslim to memorise the entire text and to recite it at will remains today what it has always been, a sign of a complete Islamic education, starting at the *kuttāb* (Qur'ān school) where the text is taught by rote. The great Egyptian littérateur, Ṭāhā Ḥusayn (d. 1973), provides us in his autobiography (translated into English as *An Egyptian Childhood*) with a memorable account of the entire process and of the pride his family felt when he became a *ḥāfiẓ* (one who has committed the Qur'ān to memory). The 'recitation' of the Qur'ān (its original meaning, it will be recalled) remains a daily phenomenon, enjoined upon the faithful: 'chant the Qur'ān [a chanting]' (*Sūrat al-Muzammil* (73, The Enwrapped) v. 4). Indeed, the advent of powerful modern means of communication has served to amplify this effect: not only is *tajwīd*, the traditional craft of chanting the text of the Qur'ān, readily available on radio and television as a celebration of the sounds of the sacred text that may be heard and watched several times a day, but also at the mosques of Middle Eastern cities the often heavily amplified voice of the '*mu'adhdhin*' fills the air with his elaborate intonations as he summons the faithful to prayer five times daily.

In discussing the structure of some of the shorter suras in the Qur'ān, I drew attention to the shortness and parallelism of phrases, and to repetition and rhyme, most especially those connected with the style known as *saj'*. If such features are transferred from the purely textual to the acoustic realm, their impact is, needless to say, even greater: words and chant, message and sound, combine to carry the significance of the revelation to even higher levels of understanding and emotional response. The practitioner of *tajwīd* is required to possess a beautiful voice; emphasis can be given to specific consonants and vowels through elongation, and 'n' and 'm' are singled out for 'nasalisation' (*ghunnah*). When the chanter uses these techniques to accentuate the assonantal features of passages such as verse 17 of *Sūrat al-Baqarah* (2, The Cow) noted above: '*ṣummun bukmun 'umyun*', or the opening verse of *Sūrat al-Qadr* (97, Power): '*innā anzalnāhu fī laylati l-qadri*' and then blends this technical repertory into the rise and fall of traditional chant, the effect on the listener transcends that of words alone. In a memorable passage from *Mountolive*, the British novelist, Lawrence Durrell, manages to capture the atmosphere engendered and the emotions of the participants:

They waited now with emotion for that old voice, melodious and worn with age, to utter the opening strophes of the Holy Book, and there was nothing feigned in the adoring attention of the circle of venal faces. Some licked their lips and leaned forward eagerly, as if to take the phrases upon their lips; others lowered their heads and closed their eyes as if against a new experience in music. The old preacher. . .uttered the first *sura*, full of the soft warm colouring of a familiar understanding, his voice a little shaky at first but gathering power and assurance from the silence as he proceeded. . .His listeners followed the notation of the verses as they fell from his lips with care and rapture, gradually seeking their way together out into the main stream of the poetry, like a school of fish following a leader by instinct into the deep sea.
(1961 ed., pp. 240–41)

William Graham, the author of a study on the oral aspects of scripture and particularly of the Qur'ān, describes in his Preface his meanderings through the quarters of Cairo during the fasting month of Ramaḍān and mentions how 'the drawn-out, nuanced cadences of the sacred recitations gave the festive nights a magical air as the reciters' penetrating voices sounded over radios in small, open shops, or wafted into the street from the doorways of mosques and from under the canvas marquees set up specially for this month of months in the Muslim calendar' (*Beyond the Written Word*, Cambridge, 1987, p. x).

As with any linkage between sacred text and musical setting, the ritual chanting of the Qur'ān clearly has a powerful effect on listeners. As numerous accounts show, that effect will often assume an enhanced form in the rituals of the Ṣūfī community; the gathering of a brotherhood (termed *ḥaḍrah*) will include not only recitations from the Qur'ān but also texts in praise of God (*dhikr*) and mystical poems such as the *Burdah* of al-Būṣīrī (d. 1296). It is the heightened intensity brought about by this particular kind of experience and in particular the prevalence in many regions of Ṣūfī orders whose rituals make full use of it that have led to an uneasy tension between popular practice in many Muslim communities and the orthodoxy espoused by conservative scholars who have always viewed the impact of music on believers with a healthy suspicion. This has prompted a continuing debate concerning the acceptability of *tajwīd* and its linkages to music. However, there would appear to be a general consensus that, as is the case with other liturgical traditions, the intent of the musical aspect is to enhance the effect of the sacred message rather than to supersede it; as long as such a balance is maintained, this art that links recitation and chant so as to enhance the believer's devotional experience is condoned.

QURʾĀN AND ARABIC LITERATURE

The doctrine of *iʿjāz*, confirming the Qurʾān's miraculous nature, demanded its severance from the statements of humans couched in such forms as poetry and *sajʿ*; its relevation may be associated with a period and a language, but it is by definition unique. This very inimitability, while discouraging all but a few from any attempt at emulation, has only served to enhance its influence on the course of Arabic literature and its study. In spite of the clearly oral nature of its original revelation, its form as canonical text and the role that it plays within the Islamic community turns it into '*al-kitāb*' (*the* book). It becomes the paradigmatic text, and its language, structures, and images pervade the whole of Arabic discourse. Citations from its text occur in all periods and genres, and, through the traditional processes of memorisation and the kudos attached to them, communal awareness of its every word is such that quotations and allusions are rarely felt to need any further reference.

In the realm of poetry the language of the Qurʾān and particularly its imagery became a rich source for allusion and citation. When the Caliph-poet, ibn al-Muʿtazz (d. 908), wrote his *Kitāb al-badīʿ* (Book of Tropes) with the purpose of codifying poetic devices, the Qurʾān was a principal source in providing him with examples of the use of imagery. The poets' resort to the Qurʾān as a source of imagery and allusion is not limited to the more obvious genres such as poems of asceticism (*zuhdiyyah*) and the inspirational odes of Ṣūfīs, but can also be seen in the more overtly 'political' poetry, for example odes in praise of the Caliph – as leader of the community of faithful – and his entourage. The quest for forgiveness and the depiction of paradise provide thematic links between the message of the Qurʾān and the tradition of love poetry (*ghazal*) that emerged as an independent genre in the early decades of Islam; many of the stock images of this genre and of the *khamriyyah* [wine poem] were adopted by Ṣūfī poets as means of providing a symbolic representation of the believer's aspiration for closer contact with the Almighty. With the famous Ṣūfī poet, ʿUmar ibn al-Fāriḍ (d. 1235), the use of this repertoire of images leads to frequent confrontations with the forces of orthodoxy concerning the interpretation of the balance between the literal and symbolic levels of their poetry. With the most famous exponent of wine poetry in Arabic, Abū Nuwās (d. *c*. 813), the antinomian stance is unambiguous: his defiance of the postulates of orthodox belief goes so far as to make use of the Qurʾānic theme of 'right guidance' to direct his listeners not in the direction of a righteous way of life but rather towards the sources of the finest wine. If we are to believe the speaker in his later poems, then the same Qurʾānic source becomes the avenue for a genuine quest for repentance.

In modern times the Qurʾānic themes of divine retribution against sinful peoples and the ephemerality of human existence have provided fertile images through which poets can express their political opinions: in his famous poem, '*Unshūdat al-maṭar*' [Hymn to the rain], Badr Shākir al-Sayyāb (1926–64) invokes the fate of the ancient Arabian people of Thamūd as a warning to modern oppressors; the Egyptian poet, Ṣalāḥ ʿAbd al-Ṣabūr (1931–81) invokes Qurʾānic phrases used to express the unchallengable power of God as creator – able to say 'be' at birth and 'he was' as a prelude to death – as the text for a homily delivered by a member of the older generation in the middle of a poem that salutes his people's endurance in the face of continuing adversity, '*Al-Nās fī bilādī*' (The people in my country).

While poetry in Arabic antedates the revelation of the Qurʾān, the emergence of a bellettristic prose tradition (the topic of ch. 4) can be considered a consequence of the revelations to Muḥammad, in that it reflects both the needs of the bureaucratic class within the growing Islamic community and the expanding fields of interest of the scholarly community. ʿAbd al-ḥamīd al-kātib (d. 750) whose writings are generally recognized as being among the earliest monuments of this tradition shows a complete familiarity with the Qurʾān and makes copious citations from it in his epistles which were to serve as models of polite discourse. The predilection of this bureaucracy for compendia of information about an amazing variety of topics sees its most sophisticated realisation in the works of ʿAmr ibn Baḥr, nicknamed al-Jāḥiẓ (*c.* 776–869); in an anecdote from his *Kitāb al-bukhalāʾ* (Book of Misers) we follow the increasing despair of the narrator as he listens with ever increasing incredulity and exasperation to the lengths a miser from Marw in Khurāsān will go to in order to preserve oil in a lamp, but, even in such a context, the conclusion takes the form of the famous 'light' verse from the Qurʾān that we cited earlier (*Sūrat al-Nūr* (24, The Light) v. 35).

The genre of the *maqāmah* which retained its popularity well into the twentieth century is linked to the Qurʾān in both direct and indirect ways: directly through the use of *sajʿ* structures that inevitably provoke echoes of the cadences of the sacred text; indirectly through the homiletic message that can be inferred from the often nefarious antics of the picaresque characters who people the vignettes. Another source of narratives that provides a direct link to the Qurʾān is the *Thousand and One Nights*. Many writers–particularly in the context of feminist criticism–have pointed out that the major theme of the collection's renowned frame story, that of Shahrazād and King Shahrayār, is the 'wiles of women'; it is Shahrazād's function to tell stories as a means of diverting the King from his custom of killing a succession of concubines after discovering his own wife *in flagrante* with a slave. This theme finds its *locus classicus* in *Sūrat Yūsuf*, the betrayal of Joseph by the Pharaoh's wife. It is verse 28 of that sura that provides the 'technical term' for this enduring theme: *kayd* (guile, trickery). Within this same enormous collection of narratives the gloomy tale of the 'City of Brass' can be seen as an elaborate homily on a predominant theme in God's message in the Qurʾān, the ephemerality of the life in this world: its narrative and especially its many *zuhdiyyah* poems are intended to provide 'warnings' and 'lessons' to the prudent. The very phrase invoked at the conclusion of many tales–that they provide '*ʿibrah li-man yaʿtabir*' (a warning to those prepared to learn)–is itself a strong echo of Qurʾānic discourse.

In more recent times Najīb Maḥfūẓ's controversial novel, *Awlād ḥāratinā* (1959/1967; *Children of Gebelawi*, 1981; *Children of the Alley*, 1996) provides us with an example of not only a modern narrative genre being used to invoke themes, images, and language found in the Qurʾān but also the continuing confrontation between creative writers and religious orthodoxy regarding the interpretation of such works. Maḥfūẓ uses allegory as a vehicle for narratives of the careers of four Qurʾānic prophets, Adam, Moses, Jesus, and Muḥammad, and their attempts to bring God's message to a human community ever prone to violence. In a fifth section of the work a new 'leader', ʿArafah ('scientia'), brings strange new powers to his communal functions and manages to kill the remote figure of Jabalāwī who has exerted control over the 'quarter' from his house outside the walls. It goes without saying that this Egyptian intellectual's linkage of prophetic missions with human needs and passions, and the suggestion that religion is the loser in a confrontation with modern science has endeared neither him nor this novel to Islamic authorities, a point that was given additional emphasis in 1988–the year in which Maḥfūẓ won the Nobel Prize in literature–when *Awlād ḥāratinā* was directly linked with another fictional work that invokes the Qurʾān, Salman Rushdie's *Satanic Verses*.

CONCLUSION

The above examples are intended as a small sample of the myriad ways in which the text of the Qurʾān has been a continuing influence on every aspect of the Arabic literary tradition. Quotations from and allusions to the Qurʾān–prayers, phrases, individual words–are as much a given in the Arabic literary tradition as themes and citations from the Biblical text are in English literature and the societies of its publics. When Ingmar Bergman entitled one of his films 'Through a glass darkly', we must assume that his premise at that time was that his audiences would be, at least to some degree, aware of the reference to St Paul's Epistle to the church at Corinth; I use the words 'at that time' because the movement to render the Biblical text into modern English has since turned the title of Bergman's film into 'in a mirror dimly'. The walls of Jericho, the Gadarene swine, the eye of the needle, these are a tiny sample of phrases and images that have become part of the allusive repertoire of English literature. Bearing in mind the continuing status of the Qurʾān within the societies of the Middle East, it is hardly surprising that it has provided just as many analogues to the creators of the Arabic literary tradition.

Having now examined its status as the founding monument of the Muslim community and explored some of the more literary aspects of the text itself, we will now turn to consider the genres that emerged and developed within the framework of that community. Our survey begins with poetry, considered from the outset as the great repository of Arab creativity and values.

CHAPTER 4

Poetry

INTRODUCTION

In November 1988 I attended the Mirbad Festival of Poetry in Iraq. On one of the evenings the attendees were all gathered in the town hall of al-Baṣrah in Southern Iraq, a city renowned in earlier times for the Mirbad Square where, as we will see below, poets (such as the redoubtable lampoonists, al-Farazdaq (d. *c.* 729) and Jarīr (d. 732) would gather and more recently for the statue of one of Southern Iraq's most illustrious modern poetic sons, Badr Shākir al-Sayyāb (d. 1956). Sitting next to me on this occasion was another invited guest, the French novelist, Alain Robbe-Grillet. After listening patiently for a while to the ringing tones of several poets, he asked me if any of them had changed the theme from the predominant topic of the last several days. I responded in the negative and went on to point out that these poets were all faithfully replicating the role of their predecessors, eulogising the ruler and celebrating his glorious victories. After all, this was 1988. Even though from a broader perspective the Iran-Iraq War had just come to an inconclusive end, the southern Iraqi peninsula of Faw which had earlier fallen to Iranian forces had been recaptured. Poets lined up to glorify the event. The opening ceremonies in Baghdad had produced new odes from Nizār Qabbānī from Syria, Muḥammad Fayṭūrī from the Sudan, and Suʿād Al-Ṣabāḥ from Kuwait, and on this particular evening in al-Baṣrah the theme was being re-echoed in a welter of imagery and bombast.

Just two years later, the army of Iraq invaded Suʿād Al-Ṣabāḥ's homeland of Kuwait, and Arabic poetry was again called upon to fulfil one of its traditional roles. On this occasion, Arab nations were pitted against each other and could use the common medium of their shared literary language. In a wonderful revival of ancient traditions, each side in this most conservative part of the Arab world unleashed not merely its contemporary military might but also the literary heritage's ultimate poetic weapon, the lampoon (*hijā'*). The media carried stinging attacks against the rulers of the other side in the conflict. It is reported that, in order to raise (or rather, lower) the tone of this verbal conflict, poets were hired from the Yemen. That country contains the region's greatest repository of trained poets currently involved in the practice of some of Arabic poetry's most ancient functions, a society where certain day-to-day issues can still be resolved through poetry competitions (the topic of Steven Caton's wonderful study, *Peaks of Yemen I Summon*).

Arabic poetry has always been regarded as the *dīwān al-ʿarab* (the register of the Arabs), a resort in times of sorrow and happiness, of defeat and victory, an expression of the Arab people's cultural ideals and greatest aspirations. In the Western world today, poetry's impact on society appears to be restricted to a small côterie among the highly literate (unless, of course, we include that poetic expression that is accompanied by popular music). The Poet Laureate in Britain will publish occasional poems to acknowledge particular events. At Oxford University the Professor of Poetry will be selected through an ancient process and then proceed to 'lecture' on the topic. In the United States, the more literate presidential candidates will even invite a poet to deliver a celebratory ode at their inauguration: Robert Frost did so at John F. Kennedy's, and Maya Angelou at Bill Clinton's. However, these occasional public glimpses of poetry seem to reflect a relatively infrequent and unenduring role for poetry that stands in marked contrast to its continuing presence in the daily life and consciousness of most Arab societies. For, while the Arabic poetic tradition has witnessed many changes during the course of its centuries-old development and indeed a modernist trend of considerable vigour and variety (that will be examined later in this chapter) is now exploring numerous new avenues of creativity, in its more traditional guises poetry continues to be called upon to fulfil the visible public function it has upheld through the centuries. As we suggested in ch. 2, words in the Arabic-speaking world are powerful and effective weapons; contrary to the English adage, names can indeed hurt. As a result, poetry – society's most highly effective projector of words and names – matters. Its practitioners are considered as figures important enough to be invited to support the policies and personae of their rulers and conversely to be hounded, exiled, or imprisoned if they do not. The Iraqi-born poet, Muẓaffar al-Nawwāb, surfaces somewhere in the Middle East and recites a poem that condemns virtually every ruler in the Arab world in the most withering terms. The poem is recorded and circulated on cassette throughout the region. He meanwhile vanishes again before he can be caught by one of the several secret police organisations who would like to 'disappear' him.

In the Arab world, as elsewhere, poetry finds itself faced with formidable rivals in the form of contemporary media that may not be replacing the role of the more traditional literary genres – élite and popular – in any direct way but clearly are providing attractive and easy alternatives to the occasions for which so much of the wonderful tradition of Arabic poetry was intended. Evening recitations of popular poetic romances, for example, find it hard to compete with televised soap-operas, most especially when a younger generation does not wish to undertake the rigorous training in order to learn the repertoire and improvisatory craft from its elders. And yet, poetry continues as an enduring presence in the lives of contemporary Arabs, most especially among intellectuals; as the novelist, Jamāl al-Ghīṭānī, puts it: 'For me poetry is the opening of each day, the initial point of my energy; it is one of the sources of my vision, not merely regarding literature but existence as a whole'.

POETRY

As just noted, poetry is indeed 'the register of the Arabs'. A good deal of what has been preserved of the heritage of the past consists of what can be termed occasional poetry. We learn, for example, through the famous *Muʿallaqah* of Zuhayr ibn Abī Sulmā (d. *c.* 607) of the means by which tribal conflicts in pre-Islamic Arabia could be resolved, while the poetry of al-Ṭirimmāḥ (d. *c.* 730) reflects the religious fervour of the Khawārij, the group that 'went away' from the other divisions within the Muslim community after the arbitration at the Battle of Ṣiffīn in 657. The odes of Abū Nuwās (d. *c.* 803) and Bashshār ibn Burd (d. 784) give us insight into the tensions that arose when new converts to Islam brought with them many of the values of their own cultural traditions and sought to challenge the hallowed norms of the earlier poetry. Abū Tammām (d. 846) and al-Mutanabbī (d. 965) are two of many poets bequeathing to later generations ringing odes in praise of a caliph whose forces have just won a great battle for the cause of Islam. Within a very different political and strategic balance modern Arab poets such as Ḥāfiẓ Ibrāhīm (d. 1932) and Abū al-qāsim al-Shābbī (d. 1934) compose poems in support of nationalist causes, while at a point of the most extreme adversity – the June War of 1967 – Nizār Qabbānī (b. 1923) reflects savagely 'On the margins of defeat'.

For the critic, Qudāmah ibn Jaʿfar (d. 922), poetry is 'discourse that is metred, rhymed, and conveys meaning'. This formalistic approach to the definition of poetry marked the emergence of a new trend in critical thought which is examined in detail in ch. 7. What is significant here is that this set of what would appear to be definitional minima came to be adopted as a prescriptive device; the formula was used to exclude types of writing that did not match those criteria. Separate manuals on rhyme and metrics were already in existence; in the latter case, the system of al-Khalīl ibn Aḥmad which had identified fifteen metrical patterns and organised them into 'circles' became the canonical norm. The community of critics moved beyond these basics to consider other facets of poetry: ʿAbd al-qāhir al-Jurjānī (d. 1078) considers the function of the image, analysing those that appeal to reason (*ʿaqlī*) and to the imagination (*takhyīlī*). By the time of the Andalusian poet-critic, Ḥāzim al-Qarṭajannī (d. 1285), Qudāmah's definition remains intact but is considerably elaborated to include an appeal to the imagination and a consideration of mimetic efficacy.

In 1898 Qudāmah's definition is still being cited by an Egyptian critic like Muḥammad al-Muwayliḥī (d. 1930), but again with elaboration and of an interesting kind: poetry, he says, is 'one of the conditions of the soul'. Here a new voice is entering the picture, one that is picked up as part of the same newspaper discussion by al-Muwayliḥī's friend, the poet Ḥāfiẓ Ibrāhīm. Poetry, says Ibrāhīm, is 'a science to be found along with the sun'. It is hidden deep in the souls of men, rather like electricity; what the soul is to the body, poetry is to discourse. Rather than sticking with Qudāmah's pedantic definition, he suggests, critics should regard poetry as being anything that has an effect on the soul. In what may be seen as a prescient statement he suggests that, while metrical discourse provides many wonderful examples of the poetic, it is not out of the question to consider some prose writers as showing similar qualities. Ḥāfiẓ Ibrāhīm's opinions brought forth howls of protest at the time, many of them suggesting that his judgement had clearly been 'polluted' by readings in the poetry of other cultures, but the course of twentieth century developments in Arabic poetry provides eloquent vindication of his judgements.

The Syro-Lebanese poet, Adūnīs (a pseudonym of ʿAlī Aḥmad Saʿīd, b. 1928?), has discussed the nature of poetry in a number of his works. For him, poetry has a distinct purpose, that of renewing language, of changing the meaning of words by using them in striking new combinations. Through his own poetic creativity and critical writings, Adūnīs has continued to assert the centrality of poetry to the political life of the Arab world and to affirm and underline the completeness of the shift from a time when poems that did not conform with a set of prescriptive formal norms were thereby excluded from the very category of poetry to one in which it is the poet who chooses the subject-matter and language of the poem and thereby determines anew in each case what the nature of the poem will be.

As this brief and highly selective montage illustrates, the composition and reception of Arabic poetry have gone through processes of enormous transformation during the approximately fourteen centuries of which we possess records. The mention of the recording process here draws attention to the fact that the poetic heritage to which we have access consists of what transmitters, philologists, and critics who lived and worked at the various political and cultural centres of the Islamic dominions decided to be worthy of preservation, a process that involved the transfer of what was delivered orally to written form. One part of the poetic heritage of the Arabs that is missing from such a picture is all but an occasional glimpse of the more popular poetic forms; for that reason we must be grateful that the renowned historian, ibn Khaldūn (d. 1406), provides a small but invaluable sampling of such compositions as part of his *al-Muqaddimah*, and indeed recent research on contemporary manifestations of popular poetic genres offers suggestive links to what was clearly a lively tradition.

In what follows we will try to trace some of the major features of this lengthy and varied process of development, beginning with the role and status of the poet as the practitioner of the art, and then considering the structures and themes of the poems themselves.

THE POET

Person and persona

The author in English is someone who increases (Latin *auctor*), and the poet someone who does (Greek *poietes*); thus the interesting dimensions of etymology. The poet in Arabic is one who senses, *shāʿir*; in the more elaborate version of the eleventh century poet-critic, ibn Rashīq (to be discussed in ch. 7), the poet is someone who perceives things that other people cannot. Such a view of the poet encouraged the notion that such people were born, not made; that the poetic gift was the consequence of innate rather than acquired qualities; not that certain skills did not have to be learned, but that the spark of intangible genius had to be already present for a poet to become really great. These assumptions concerning the nature of poetic talent led early Arab critics to assign greater credit to 'natural' poetry (*maṭbūʿ*) than to 'artificial, contrived' (*maṣnūʿ*); the breaking down of such categories, which, almost by definition, accorded greater credit to earlier poetry rather than contemporary, was to occasion much critical debate (discussed in ch. 7). The Egyptian poet, Aḥmad Shawqī (d. 1932), writes in the Introduction to his collected poetry published in 1898 that the poet should fulfil three conditions: he must be convinced that poetry is part of his own nature; he must possess both learning and experience; and he must treat poetry as a lasting occupation and not merely a frill.

This designation of poets as those who have unique qualities of perception assigns them a function that transcends that of composing in a particular way, a role in society that is akin to that of a shaman. Poets within pre-Islamic Arabian society were believed to be gifted with insight, and their utterances possessed special power. With this in mind, the clash between poets and Muḥammad that is reflected in the revelations of the Qurʾān (and particularly in the Surah on Poets (26), where poets are said to be followed by the deluded and to say things they do not do) can be placed into a different context. Superficial readings of these passages have led some commentators to suggest that Muḥammad disliked poetry and, by extension, music, something that is hard to justify in view of the fact that Ḥassān ibn Thābit (d. 673) is known as the Prophet's poet and that one of the most famous collections of early Arabic poetry, the significantly named *Kitāb al-aghānī* (Book of Songs) of Abū al-faraj al-Iṣfahānī (d. 967) is full of accounts of Muḥammad listening to poetry and music. It would appear that what is being addressed in the revelations of the Qur'ān is the power that poets continued to exert at a time when Muḥammad was endeavouring to introduce the new message of the Qur'ān into a society which detected similarities between the two types of expression; hence the force of the passage already noted in the previous chapter *Sūrat al-ḥaqqah* (69, The Indubitable):

> It is the saying of a noble Messenger,
> not that of a poet; how little you believe!
> nor of a soothsayer; how little you remember!
> a revelation from the Lord of the worlds.

The Arab poet then possesses 'the power of the word'; as Caton notes with reference to the poetic tradition in Yemen today, 'the poet has power over men, and poetry is a deeply political act' (*Peaks of Yemen I Summon*, Berkeley, 1990, p. 40). In the earliest stages of the literary tradition the emergence within a tribe of the Arabian peninsula of a truly gifted poet was a cause for great rejoicing, as ibn Rashīq notes; the presence of such a figure was a matter of supreme importance, in that words were the most effective of weapons. The poet would rouse the tribe with eulogies (*madīḥ*) extolling the chivalry and generosity of its leaders and men; would remind them of the qualities of fallen heroes in elegies (*marthiyyah*), a category in which women poets seem to have played a prominent role; and, deadliest of verbal weapons, would cast aspersions on the qualities of enemy tribes, their leaders and womenfolk, in vicious lampoons (*hijā'*). In such a societal context, the poet was, to cite Kilito, 'as indispensible as the chief or soothsayer'. In an interesting reversal that only serves to underline the significance of these functions, poetic personae were created to reflect the anti-tribal scenario, the so-called vagabond (*ṣuʿluk*) poets such as Ta'abbaṭa Sharran (a nick-name meaning 'he who has put evil in his armpit'), ʿUrwah ibn al-Ward, and al-Shanfarā. While these ostracised figures often stood in solidarity with each other, the vision that their poetry presents is one that relishes antisocial behaviour and the hardships of life alone in the desert environment. Hunger, thirst, and discomfort are habitual states that need to be overcome; since human beings are so fickle in their loyalties, the vagabond poet's truest friends are the less attractive of the region's animal creatures, the wolf and the hyena – a renowned scavenger and devourer of corpses. Their scoffing at the need for tribal solidarity and their glorification of deprivation, solitude, and the company of wild animals only serve to emphasise for poetry's audience the benefits that affiliation was able to provide. That there was also a class of itinerant 'professional' poets who would earn their living by proceeding from one court and occasion to another seems confirmed by the accounts of the life of a poet such as al-Aʿshā (literally, 'night-blind', d. *c.* 630), renowned for his wine and hunt descriptions, whose search for a livelihood seems to have taken him across the length and breadth of Arabia. Such was the repute of his poetry that he was invited to mediate in intertribal disputes; the loser would not only suffer the effects of an adverse ruling but would be lampooned for his pains.

With the advent of Islam some aspects of the poetic function changed. Clearly, the establishment of new cultural centres outside the Arabian peninsula – Damascus, Baghdad, Cairo, Qayrawān, Marrakesh, Fez, and Cordoba, to name just a few – and the vibrant cultural admixture that populated them created new and expanded opportunities for the patronage of littérateurs and, given the predominant position of poetry, of poets in particular. Inevitably much cultural activity gravitated towards these glittering courts and the rulers and urbane bureaucracies that peopled them. For several centuries scholars and poets in search of norms of language and poetic excellence would continue to resort to the Bedouin of the desert for confirmatory data. Indeed in the third century of Islam the great poet, al-Mutanabbī, is said in his youth to have honed his poetic skills in this way, known in the pedagogical literature as going into the *bādiyah* (Arabian desert). But his career is probably the most emblematic of the role that the truly gifted poet came to play within the fabric of Islam, especially following the break-up of central authority that, as we observed in ch. 2, can be seen as beginning with the establishment of an alternative Umawī amirate in al-Andalus in the eighth century. The poet is now an important court functionary, and poetic careers are made or broken according to the extent that talent is recognised. The negative side is shown in the career of ibn al-Rūmī (d. 896) who complains bitterly in some of his poems about a lack of recognition. Some lines of Abū Saʿd al-Makhzūmī, a poet at the court of the Caliph al-Ma'mūn, express what may be an extreme of frustration:

> Dog and poet are in one and the same situation; would I
> were not a poet!
> Just look at the way he has to stretch out his palm asking
> for food from all comers!

On the other hand, poets like al-Buḥturī (d. 897) and al-Mutanabbī feel sufficiently confident of their status to drop unsubtle hints about the lack of appreciation they feel from their patrons. 'When I am dealt with badly', says the former in his famous ode contemplating the Persian ruins at Ctesiphon, 'I'm liable to spend the morning in a different place from the night before'. Al-Mutanabbī, the greatest exemplar in Arabic of 'have poem, will travel', whose clashes with rulers and fellow poets seem to reflect actual personality as much as poetic persona, goes even further in his poetry addressed to the great ruler of Aleppo, Sayf al-dawlah al-Ḥamdānī. The poet fulfils his ancient function by delivering a heroic ode in celebration of a glorious victory against the Byzantines at the battle of al-Ḥadath (954), but he cannot finish without reminding his patron that he, Sayf al-dawlah, may have won the victory, but it is the poet who is responsible for preserving the event for future generations. Frequent requests for remuneration expressed in these terms apparently went unheeded, and a marked cooling in the ruler's attitude made it advisable for al-Mutanabbī to move on, and so he did; to Egypt, where he lauded the regent, a former slave named Kāfūr, in glowing tones before discovering that here too his worth was not properly estimated. 'I am rich', he declaimed in one of the series of withering lampoons that he left behind as he moved on yet again, 'but my wealth is all in promises'.

We still encounter vestiges of this tradition of the patronised poet, habitué of court and literary salon, during the earlier phases of the modern period of Arabic literature. Criticisms of the Egyptian court poet, Aḥmad Shawqī, tend to harp on his close ties to the royal household, contrasting his way of life and access to privilege with those of Ḥāfiẓ Ibrāhīm, who was viewed as the people's poet and one whose voice best reflected Egyptian nationalist aspirations in the wake of British occupation of the country. Gradually however, the emergence of new modes of publication, expanded educational opportunities, and changing local and international configurations provided the basis for a different readership and focus for literary texts. Nationalisms, pan-Arab and local, served as a major standard under which the Arab poet sought to express sentiments both corporate and individual, and no more so than in the odes of the Tunisian, Abū al-qāsim al-Shābbī, composed in the 1920s and 1930s. The period following the Second World War, involving not only political and social upheavals but also the fate of the Palestinian people in the wake of the 1948 conflict, saw this poetic role intensified. The rallying cry was now 'commitment', and many poets addressed themselves to the urgent issues of the time: for Palestinians like Maḥmūd Darwīsh and Samīḥ al-Qāsim, the topics were both obvious and immediate – loss of land and of human rights. For other poets as varied as Nizār Qabbānī, ʿAbd al-wahhāb al-Bayātī (b. 1926), and Ṣalāḥ ʿAbd al-Ṣabūr (d. 1981), the topics to which their poems were addressed were the concerns and aspirations of an educated and mostly middle-class readership that found itself confronting the injustices and complexities of life in the newly independent societies of the Middle East.

We have concentrated thus far on the poet's public face, and indeed the way that contemporary poets choose to comment on significant issues in society (and often provoke a firestorm of criticism in so doing) marks the continuation of an ancient role. The shift away from the patronage of an influential individual or office towards that of the broader societal community has led the poet to a new sense of individual responsibility. Darwīsh expresses the new priorities clearly in a poem entitled 'About Poetry' ('*An al-shiʿr*'):

> Our poems are without colour, taste, or voice.
> If they carry no light from house to house,
> if the simple cannot grasp their meanings,
> it is better to discard them;
> then we can go on for ever ... with silence! ...
> A poet will say:
> If my poems delight my friends
> and annoy my enemies,
> then I am a poet
> and I ... will speak.

This assertion of individuality has not been without its risks for the modern Arab poet in the latter half of the twentieth century. As long as the poet's sense of commitment has coincided with the political and social priorities of the government concerned, all has remained relatively well and the poetry has reached its intended audience. But, when the poet has chosen to 'speak' in a manner not pleasing to the authorities, the process of suppressing the poetry – and, all too often, the poet – has not been difficult. Adūnīs considers this changing role of the poet within a more historical context. A poem entitled 'I Told You' ('*Qultu la-kum*') begins:

> I told you: I have listened to the seas
> reciting their poetry to me; I have listened
> to the bell aslumber in the sea-shell;
> I told you: I have sung my songs
> at the devil's wedding, at the fairytale banquet ...

Here the modern poet adopts a vigorous first-person voice to assert – at least in one reading – that the sources of poetic inspiration are many and that poets, throughout the Arabic literary heritage perhaps, have applied their poetic talents to reflect the various sources of inspiration, both internal and external – even 'the devil's wedding' – to which they have addressed their verses. It is now the responsibility of the individual modern poet alone to select those inspirational moments and occasions, both public and private, for celebration in poetic form; the consequences of doing so – whether they be recognition, imprisonment, exile, or death – are the poet's also. Adūnīs's poem draws our attention not only to the modern poet's insistence on seeking an individual voice, but also to the tension between the public and personal which has marked the poetic function from the outset. We have already suggested that a poet such as al-Mutanabbī and the noisy critical controversy that surrounded his poetic career give us some insight into the motivations of the individual voice found within his poetry; the poetic persona is certainly a major one, but we also seem to catch a glimpse of the person behind it. With many other poets, the linkage between the individual voice and the public persona remains pleasingly, indeed poetically, ambiguous. When ʿUmar ibn Abī Rabīʿah (d. 711) composes poems that describe his Don Juanesque encounters with the ladies of Meccan society, we are given an intimate glimpse into the society of his time that many commentators have chosen to link closely to the poet's own lifestyle; at all events, it creates a poetic vision that is considerably different from the traditional love poetry associated with the tribal life of the desert (both to be discussed below). At a later stage, the verses of Abū Nuwās (d. *c.* 815), Arabic's ribald poet *par excellence* and, at least in the *Thousand and One Nights*, a regular member of Hārūn al-Rashīd's night-time côterie, seem to reflect a richly complex persona's quest for meaning, at one moment indulging to the utmost in all the sins of the flesh and boasting of his 'heroic' exploits, and then recognising the essential frivolity and ephemerality of life and the inevitablity of judgement:

> Lo! Grey-haired old age has surprised me by its
> appearance; how evil and ill-starred it is!
> I have repented of my mistakes and of missing the
> designated times [of prayer].
> So I pray You, God – all praise to You! – to forgive, just
> as You did, Almighty One, with Jonah!

When the Andalusian poet, ibn Zaydūn (d. 1071), who has been jilted in love by the Umawī princess, Wallādah, composes a poem in which the palace of al-Zahrāʾ near Cordoba is invoked to recall happier times, the sentiments expressed in his concluding line seem on a quite personal level:

> Now I give praise for the time we shared;
> You have found solace, but we have remained devoted.

The social contexts within which much Arabic poetry was composed were indeed of a kind that many songs had to be sung at 'the devil's wedding'; furthermore, such patronised surroundings were the very ones that could provide the facilities for recording and archiving the best examples of the poet's craft. However, as the few instances we have used above suggest, such circumstances do not seem to have in any way deterred resourceful poets from expressing more individual concerns – the degree of subtlety involved varying in accordance with personality, occasion, and patron.

Viewing the status of the Arab poet from a contemporary perspective, one thing that may seem somewhat striking is the extent to which the balance of poets during the earlier centuries of the Arabic heritage – at least those whose works have come down to us – is overwhelmingly male. That is not to say, of course, that there is a complete lack of female poets: among the more famous names in that category are al-Khansāʾ (d. *c.* 640), renowned for her elegies on her brother; Rābiʿah al-ʿAdawiyyah (d. 801), the famous Sufi poetess; and Wallādah (d. *c.* 1077), Umawī princess of al-Andalus. While research is insufficient to make any firm judgements, it seems plausible to posit the notion that the process of recording women's poetry was directly linked to levels of education and literacy; thus the contents of their poetic heritage which were stored in the memory and passed on through successive generations were for the most part not committed to written form. This situation has, needless to say, changed considerably in the modern period due to enhanced educational opportunities and different attitudes to publication. Female poets have now joined their male counterparts as vigorous contributors to the social and political life of the contemporary Arab world.

Training

The curricula for the Islamic sciences that were refined by scholars and later bequeathed to the West included within their purview the training of poets. By the tenth century poetry had been subsumed within the syllabus that was part of the formation of an *adīb* (littérateur, a term to be discussed in detail in ch. 5). The aspiring poet, ibn Rashīq tells us, needs to memorise the poetry of the ancients, study grammar, tropes, rhyme, and metre, and then familiarise himself with genealogy. The entire system was based on a process whereby the apprentice came under the tutelage of a mentor who was a respected poet.

The trainee phase was that of the 'bard' (*rāwī*); it involved learning the rudiments of the craft by memorising the poetry of a senior poet, performing the odes of the master and others, and perfecting the various aspects of the creative process. Once these tasks had been successfully completed, the aspiring poet would gradually be invited to imitate the best examples of other poets, and finally achieve a level of competence which would permit him to create his own compositions. The efficacy of the system is well illustrated by a chain of illustrious names from the earliest period provided for us by Ṭāhā Ḥusayn: Ṭufayl had ʿAws ibn Ḥajar as his bard; ʿAws had Zuhayr ibn Abī Sulmā; Zuhayr had his son, Kaʿb ibn Zuhayr; Kaʿb had al-Ḥuṭay'ah; al-Ḥuṭay'ah had Jamīl Buthaynah; and Jamīl had Kuthayyir ʿAzzah – thus over successive generations did bard-trainee become illustrious contributor to the poetic tradition. If such chains of transmission from the earliest period provide some evidence of the development of a poetic career, then recent studies of contemporary traditions within the Arabian peninsula suggest that aspects of the system remain in place. In both Saudi Arabia and Yemen, for example, the description of the skills that trainee poets are expected to master very much echoes that of ibn Rashīq described above: control of rhymes and metres, and knowledge of a repertoire of themes and motifs. Yemeni society is one that regards poetry as a central contributor to its political and social life, and children are introduced to poetic discourse through attendance at all kinds of gatherings where they listen to songs, pick up aphorisms, and participate in word games. Their first steps in poetry may involve participation in the chorus at a communal session at which a poem is to be performed; each member of the society has been introduced to the repertoire in this way and is expected to be both an expert listener to and participator in the poetic event. As was presumably the case in the earliest period, those youngsters who display a particular affinity for poetry become the apprentices of major poets.

The transfer from a culture that preserved and transmitted its cultural treasures by oral means to one that recorded them in written form obviously led to changes in this training process, but the basic requirements remained the same: the spark of poetic genius was, of course, a given, but to it was still appended the need for prolonged and intensive exposure to the treasures of the poetic heritage through memorisation. The modern poet who is encouraged to cultivate such gifts is now able to find inspiration from a number of sources and especially through readings of the treasures of his own and other traditions: first and foremost, the collections (*dawāwīn*, sing. *dīwān*) of the renowned poets of earlier centuries collected and preserved within the highly elaborate system of Islamic education, but also through engagement with the works of the great poets of world literature. Some of the greatest among the modern Arab poets – one thinks of Badr Shākir al-Sayyāb and Adūnīs – are notable for the extent to which their poems, for all their modernity, show a familiarity with the language and imagery of the poetic heritage. Meanwhile, it is in those areas where the cultural norms of the past remain strongest – among the Bedouin of the desert and in the Arabian Peninsula – that we continue to find clear echoes of the training processes that have been responsible for turning the truly gifted from apprentice poets into masters.

Performance

'No poem can be completely apprehended', says Robert Phillips, a poet and public reciter of poetry, in the book review of the *New York Times* (12 February 1995), 'until its music is *heard*'. He cites Stanley Kunitz's colourful phrase that 'the page is a cold bed'. The performance of Arabic poetry has been a constant from the outset. One of the earliest accounts that we possess finds the illustrious poet, al-Nābighah (d. *c.* 604), adjudicating a poetry competition as part of the annual fair held at the Arabian market-town of 'Ukāẓ. Within the context of tribal rivalries and the kind of training process that we have just described such occasions were clearly of major significance in that reputations could be won and lost as new generations of poets endeavoured to rival the artistry of their seniors and outperform their contemporaries. This tradition of poetic competitions, jousts, and duels continues today. While many competitions based on written submissions are organised on national and international levels (some of them, such as the King Faisal and Sultan 'Uways prizes, of considerable value), jousts of improvised oral poetry are still to be found. One such type is the Lebanese *zajal* tradition. Two poets, one often an itinerant professional and the other a local poet (termed a *zajjāl*), will determine a topic for the night's competition; it will usually be in the form of an oppositional pair such as black and white. Each poet will bring a small chorus which will have rehearsed a verse appropriate to whichever of the pair of opposites they are supporting and which will be repeated after every strophe that the *zajjāl* improvises on his chosen topic. The other *zajjāl* has the interval during which the other poet's chorus is singing its verse to come up with his own improvised response. And so the evening proceeds, often lasting for several hours.

Alongside these somewhat spontaneous and local types of occasion which lie at the more popular end of the performance spectrum, there have always been, of course, more official events at which the poet has been expected to fulfil a more corporate function, whether the venue was a tribal gathering, court ceremony, or day of national remembrance. Such occasions would include celebrations of victory in battle (like that of al-Mutanabbī mentioned above), prominent events in the lives of the ruling dynasty – births, weddings, funerals, and religious festivals. For the most formal gatherings (for which the Arabic term is *majlis*) the subject matter of these poems would be a matter of court protocol. According to a poem of Bashshsār ibn Burd (d. 783), his love poetry was so popular in court circles that his patron, the Caliph al-Mahdī, told him to avoid the topic; as the poet notes, 'the Caliph has forbidden me, and, whenever he does so, I do so as well', although one has to add that the poem in itself is a distinct boost to his own poetic ego and indeed the contents of his *Dīwān* suggest that the interdiction referred to did not seem to have lasted for too long. Later in the evening when the ruler gathered with his boon-companions (*nudamā'*) and slave-girls (*jawārī*), the *majlis* would have a more intimate atmosphere and the topics for poetic performance were considerably less constrained, at least if we are to credit some of the accounts concerning the poet, Abū Nuwās, and al-Mahdī's son, the Caliph Hārūn al-Rashīd. Here again, al-Iṣfahānī's *Kitāb al-aghānī* is replete with accounts of both formal and less formal occasions for musical and poetic performances by such illustrious singers as Ibrāhīm al-Mawṣilī (d. 804), Ibrāhīm ibn al-Mahdī (d. 839 – as his name implies, the son of the Caliph, al-Mahdī), and, most virtuoso of all, Isḥāq al-Mawṣilī (d. 849, son of Ibrāhīm).

In earliest times the occasion for poetic performance would have been a tribal gathering, whether it involved the members of a single grouping around a campfire in the evening or a larger annual gathering of tribal confederacies. Current practice in countries like Yemen may not be an entirely accurate guide to earlier times, but, in the almost total absence of recorded information on the topic, it may provide some clues. Coffee is being served, and there is much noise as the group converses. When the poet is ready to begin, he will clear his throat to request silence and then start declaiming. The two halves of the first verse of the poem will both end with the rhyming syllable, and the poet will repeat the first line so that the audience has a clear sense of both rhyme and metre. The audience listening to the performance is thoroughly familiar with the occasions, motifs, and facets that make up the poetic craft and will be quick to express its approval of excellent lines (often requesting their repetition) and criticism of less satisfactory efforts through silence or bodily gestures of disapproval. When the group as a whole expresses a general feeling of restlessness through fidgeting and other bodily gestures, the poet-reciter is rapidly made aware of the need for a break in his performance; a particular section of a lengthier ode may be terminated with an appropriately gnomic sentiment.

Certain genres that have been mentioned above were discussed in terms of performances involving both poet and chorus, which leads to a discussion of the tantalising topic of the role of music in poetic performance; tantalising because, as Owen Wright shows in a unique chapter, information on the topic is virtually non-existent (ch. 21, '*Arabic Literature to the End of the Umayyad Period*', Cambridge History of Arabic Literature, I, 1983). The *Kitāb al- aghānī* (Book of Songs), Abū al-faraj al-Iṣfahānī's (d. 967) collection of early Arabic poetry, suggests a linkage between poetry and song; indeed the collection itself includes accounts of the careers of some of the most famous singers from the early period of Islamic history, including al-Dalāl, ibn Surayj (d. *c.* 716) and al-Gharīḍ (d. early eighth century). Furthermore, while almost every aspect of the debate surrounding the two famous Andalusian poetic genres, the *muwashshaḥ* and *zajal* (to be discussed below) is a topic of intense debate, there seems little doubt that both were compositions for singing. In this, as in other aspects of the presumably crucial contribution of music to the performance of Arabic poetry, surmise marks the limits of our current ability to assess the nature of its role.

THE POEM

Collections

A collection of Arabic poems is usually called a '*dīwān*', a word that originally meant a military list but was then applied to various modes of collection and organisation; it thus incorporated at different periods the notion of 'chancery', 'collected poems'. The early philologists who gathered poems into collections used a variety of organisational criteria. Some were named after the tribe under whose protective umbrella the works had been conceived and performed: thus the poems of the Banū Hudhayl. Others were named after their compilers: the *Mufaḍḍaliyyāt* of al-Mufaḍḍal al-Ḍabbī, for example, and the *Aṣmaʿiyyāt* of al-Aṣmaʿī. Still others were clustered around particular motifs; one of the most cherished was heroism, *ḥamāsah*, providing the title for a number of collections of which the most renowned is that of the poet, Abū Tammām. However, the most favoured organising principle for collections of Arabic poetry has been and remains the gathering of the works of a single poet (the *Dīwān* of al-Mutanabbī, for example).

Until relatively recently it was not the practice to give Arabic poems descriptive titles. The majority of collections by early poets frame the poems themselves within a series of short statements that recount the occasion for which the poem was composed and/or performed: upon the death of a prominent person, for example, or in celebration of a significant event in the life of the community (occasions and categories that will be explored in more detail below). A preferred mode of sequence for the collected poems was an alphabetical one based on their end-rhymes. The most famous poems were often referred to in this way: thus, the vagabond poet, al-Shanfarā's, most famous ode is known as 'the L-poem of the Arabs' (*lāmiyyat al-ʿArab*); ibn Zaydūn's love poem to the Princess Wallādah is known as his 'N-poem' (*nūniyyah*), and one of ibn al-Fāriḍ's best known mystical love poems as his 'M-poem' (*mīmiyyah*). Another method of identification is through the opening of the poem: thus, Imru al-Qays's *muʿallaqah* poem is instantly recognisable through its renowned, if formulaic, beginning: 'Halt, you two companions, and let us weep ...' (*qifā nabki*). As the Arabic poetic tradition developed and particular genres came to be recognised as separate entities, the *dīwān* of the poet was often subdivided into categories. Abū Nuwās's collected poetry, for example, contains large separate sections of love poems addressed to males and females (*ghazal*) and wine poems (*khamriyyah*); in addition to anticipated sections on eulogy, lampoon and elegy, there are also others gathered around the themes of hunting, asceticism, and reprimand. With Abū Tammām's *Dīwān* we find separate sections on eulogy, lampoon, elegy, love, chiding, description, boasting, and asceticism.

During the ensuing centuries these organisational principles of the poetic *dīwān* – based in the first instance on an alphabetisation of end-rhyme consonants and, if quantity, variety, and repute demanded it, on a subdivision into separate categories – changed remarkably little. The *dīwān* of Aḥmad Shawqī, the twentieth-century Egyptian neo-classical poet, contains most of the categories listed for that of Abū Tammām, to which are appended others on history, politics, society, humour, and 'varia'. However, as we have already noted, political and social developments in the Arab world during the twentieth century have led to significant changes in the status and role of the poet. Thus, in addition to the new creative environment within which poets sense a need to speak with a more individual voice, there is also a marked transformation in modes of communication with their public in that the advent of modern print technology provides a broader, swifter, and readier means of contact. Journals, magazines, and newspapers regularly publish poems, and, given the right political circumstances (admittedly a large proviso in certain regions), such works can be gathered into publishable collections. Thus, with a poet like Badr Shākir al-Sayyāb, for example, whose early death allows us to assess the collected poems of a contemporary writer, each *dīwān* published separately comes to be regarded as representative of the poet's art at a particular phase in his career. The Arab world's most popular poet in the latter half of the twentieth century, Nizār Qabbānī, has garnered a sufficient following to be able to found his own publishing house, and he thus profits directly from the publication of his enormous *dīwān* and its continuing supplements.

Rhyme and metre

Arab poets today reflect a variety of attitudes towards the heritage of which they are the heirs. Thus, while the majority now regard poetry as being marked by the difference and even difficulty of its discourse and believe that decisions regarding form and structure are part of the creative process itself and cannot be predetermined, other poets – fewer in number, to be sure – continue to find their preferred means of poetic expression through adherence to the forms of earlier poetry and the expectations that accompany them. Thus, while the different categories of poem that will be discussed below are all characterised by their resort to language that draws attention to itself, the means by which such difference is displayed show considerable variation.

The form of the pre-modern Arabic poem on a printed page suggests symmetry. The lines are laid out so as to emphasize the end-rhyme of each line (*bayt*). The gap that separates the two halves of the line indicates the point at which the metrical pattern (according to the prosodic system of al-Khalīl ibn Aḥmad) is repeated; while this space will often also mark the division between two distinct segments of syntax, the sense of the line may be carried over from the first half to the second. In the case of the *qaṣīdah* the resulting columns of neatly margined print are a primary characteristic of printed editions, and the lack of such patterning is a distinct feature of modern poetry. In the case of the other types of poem that will be discussed below, the layout on the page might be more varied, but the visual symmetry of the verbal patterns is intended to underline the principles of rhyme and metre that lie behind the poetic composition.

Rhyme in Arabic is based on sound; there is no concept of visual rhyme. In the majority of poems the rhyming element (termed *al-rāwī*) is the final consonant in the line, although a poet such as al-Maʿarrī (d. 1057) set himself in his collection *Luzūm mā lā yalzam* a greater challenge of incorporating the vowel sound of the previous syllable as well. While some of the categories of poem that will be discussed below exhibit different rhyming patterns, the scheme of the predominant form – the *qaṣīdah* – is that of the monorhyme at the end of each line of the poem, that rhyme normally being found in both halves or hemistiches (*miṣrāʿ*) of the first line as a means of acquainting the audience with the nature of the rhyming sound. While this monorhyme scheme is the most predominant within the poetic tradition, there are a number of other patterns: one such is the 'doublet' (*muzdawijah*), which may well have entered the Arabic tradition in imitation of the Persian *mathnawī*; the pattern involved is that the two halves of each line rhyme: aa, bb, cc, and so on. This alternative rhyme scheme appears to have stimulated a number of Arab poets to extend the process into a more strophic type of patterning, via 'triple-rhyme' (*muthallathah*) to 'quintuple-rhyme' (*mukhammasah*) – aaaaa, bbbba, cccca, and so on. Poems that followed this kind of pattern – beginning with a rhyme 'a', then a series of strophes with a specific number of lines rhyming on 'b' and so on, and each ending with the repeat of the rhyme 'a' – were termed *musammaṭ*, based on the Arabic word *simṭ* meaning 'a string, thread'. We will explore some of the poetic categories involved below.

Following the Second World War, Arabic poetry moved beyond earlier experiments with different types of rhyming scheme and even with blank verse (a short-lived experiment which had little success) and abandoned rhyme as a defining element. After initial experiments with *shiʿr ḥurr* (an Arabic translation of *vers libre* (free verse) that subsumed a number of different experiments), many poets moved on to experiment with the prose poem (*qaṣīdat al-nathr*). In contemporary poetry the sound elements traditionally associated with rhyme have been replaced by such features as assonance and repetition.

By the time of Qudāmah ibn Jaʿfar (d. 922) the mention of metrics (*ʿilm al-ʿarūḍ*) had come to imply an adherence to the system developed by al-Khalīl ibn Aḥmad of al-Baṣrah. He had recorded, it will be recalled, the rhythmic pulses that he heard in listening to early Arabic poetry. The system was one that quantified sound patterns into two categories: one that was fixed, termed *watad* (the Arabic word for 'tent peg'); and one that was variable, *sabab* (meaning 'tent rope'). The different sequences of pulses that he recorded were formed into five continuous chains in the form of circles; by starting the chain at different points on the circle, he came up with fifteen independent metres. Relying on different combinations of *watad* and *sabab* al-Khalīl identified eight different types of metrical foot (*tafʿilah*) which were designated through the use of the blank morphological pattern F-ʿ-L. Thus, a pattern that consisted of one 'short' followed by two 'longs' (u - -) is said to be of the *faʿūlun* pattern. Predictable combinations of these feet would make up the major unit of metrics, the line (*bayt*, in early Arabic the word for 'tent'). By way of illustration, the first half of the first line of Imru al-Qays's *muʿallaqah* (that adopts one of the most favoured metres named *ṭawīl*) is analysed thus:

```
----> 
qifā  nab--ki min  dhikrā  habībin    wa-manzili
 u -   - | u -    -    - | u -    - | u   -   u u
faʿūlun      mafāʿīlun    faʿūlun      mafāʿīlun
```

The half-line (which would be repeated in the same pattern in the second half) consists of two feet, each of which is repeated in the pattern 1 2 1 2 : the foot *faʿūlun* consists of one fixed *watad* (u -) and one variable *sabab* (-). The other foot of the *ṭawīl* metre, *mafāʿīlun*, consists of the same fixed *watad* (u -) and two examples of the variable *sabab* (-) which, as the final foot demonstrates, the poet may choose to replace with an unstressed syllable (u).

The metrics of a sizeable percentage of Arabic poetry can be analysed using al-Khalīl's system; it is just one of the remarkable achievements of a scholar who contributed much to the study of Arabic language, literature, and music. However, within this context we need to keep al-Khalīl's account of his procedure in mind: that he had recorded what he heard. The process of converting his description into a prescriptive metrical system for the identification of what constituted poetry (and what did not) was not without its problems. Quite apart from the fact that certain lines and categories of poem do not seem to conform with this system, it is in connection with the subject of music and accompaniment that a strict adherence to al-Khalīl's system as sole criterion in this area becomes problematic. Several scholars, both Arab and Western, have argued that beyond the concerns with the demands of a quantitative-syllabic system, there must also be an underlying stress pattern. From the point of view of a performance that might have involved instrumentalists, percussion, or both, such a view seems more than reasonable. However, apart from discussions of the much vexed question of the Hispano-Arabic strophic genres (to be discussed below), the texts are unforthcoming on this subject and, in the absence of further evidence concerning performance practice, we are left to speculate.

We noted above that in the aftermath of the Second World War Arabic poetry went through a period of profound change. In addition to the abandonment of rhyme as a *sine qua non* of poetry, the metrics of al-Khalīl were initially adapted as part of a movement known under the general heading of free verse (*shiʿr ḥurr*). At first, the notion of the line of poetry (*bayt*) as the basic unit was discarded in favour of the single foot (*tafʿilah*), thus permitting poets to vary the length of the line while preserving the basic metrical pulse and, if they wished, the rhyme also. However the abandonment of the dictates of the classical tradition had served to open the proverbial floodgates. In the revolutionary atmosphere of the late 1940s and 1950s, Arab poets were not inclined to replace one set of rules with another. The heading *al-shiʿr al-ḥurr* becomes a banner under which traditional norms were set aside and a whole series of poetic experiments were conducted. With the advent of the prose poem (*qaṣīdat al-nathr*) all ties to the requirements regarding rhyme and metre as defining elements of poetry were severed. It needs to be emphasised once again that many Arab poets continue to compose poetry in *qaṣīdah* form, most particularly for those formal occasions on which the glories of the past need to be invoked, but for the majority of contemporary poets it is the moment of poetic inspiration – the words, phrases, and images that it invokes – that alone provides the organising principles for the sound and structure of the poem that emerges.

Categories

Qiṭʿah and *Qaṣīdah*

The filter that affords us the opportunity to assess the earliest forms of Arabic poetry takes the form of the process initiated by the community of Muslims when it found itself faced with the urgent need to interpret the text of the Qurʾān that had been revealed to them. Since the corpus of pre-Islamic poetry emerged as its most ready and obvious linguistic precedent, philologists set out to collect as much of the poetic heritage as possible, using as their primary source the bards and poets of the Arabian tribes and urban centres who had learned the poetry of the desert. As a consequence of this procedure, a poetic tradition that presumably extended back over several centuries was collected and sifted in a highly intense effort aimed at retrieving the linguistic heritage of a society that had preserved and transmitted its poetic expression through the memory rather than the written word. Many of the texts that were recorded through this process clearly represented the most prized products of the poetic tradition, poems varying in both length and structural complexity that constitute the most recent versions of a performance practice going back through many generations of bards. Alongside these types of poem were other shorter examples, some of which seem complete in their own right while others appear to represent fragments of lengthier structures, perhaps favourite parts of longer poems selected from the memory of a particular bard in order to illustrate a theme, image, or section of the poem.

If the Qur'ān provided a strong motivating force for the collection of the earliest examples of Arabic poetry, it may also have provided a disincentive for a similarly intensive effort devoted to the collection of examples of at least one other kind of composition that shows strong links to the poetic, namely the kind of discourse known as *saj*ʿ. We have already explored the difficulties connected with this particular style and its linkage to the Qur'ān in ch. 3, but it needs to be stated that, while *saj*ʿ has not been subjected to anything like the critical examination that has been devoted to poetry in all its guises, it was nonetheless a prevalent mode of discourse in pre-Islamic Arabian society and, as we will see in ch. 5, was later to become a major feature of bellettristic writing. Whatever the posture of the critical tradition towards this form of expression may have been at different periods, the fact that it consists of identifiable structures that show not only rhyming patterns but also carefully cadenced phrases suggests at least an affinity with that form of discourse that we refer to as poetic.

Returning to those poems that are regarded as providing models of the earliest forms of Arabic poetry, it is possible that the shorter of the two primary types, called the *qiṭʿah*, is antecedent to the lengthier, the *qaṣīdah*, but the process referred to above, whereby several centuries of poetic creativity were recorded in an intensely concentrated manner, served to obscure the stages in the development of the poetic genres themselves. Indeed, such was the prevalence of the *qaṣīdah* in the centuries that followed that most critical investigations of poetic origins were focused on its features at the expense of the *qiṭʿah*. The shorter form often served as a monothematic poem for a particular occasion, a brief elegy on a fallen hero or an account of a raid or encounter. A comparison of examples of the *qiṭʿah* with those of the *qaṣīdah* seems to justify the surmise that the latter may have developed as a concatenation of several themes culled from the former into a more elaborate, polythematic structure. Indeed, the most famous examples of the pre-Islamic *qaṣīdah*, the seven – according to some compilers, ten – poems collected under the title '*al-muʿallaqāt*' which were performed (and preserved) as carefully orchestrated celebrations of the mores and environs of Arabian society, are not only liturgical events that rehearse for their audience the virtues of social cohesion but also highly effective propaganda devices for bolstering the chivalrous spirit of the tribe's fighting heroes and blunting the resolve of the enemy.

With the term *qiṭʿah* (meaning 'piece, segment') we can say that etymology and poetic function seem to coincide, but the word *qaṣīdah* presents more of a problem. The verbal root Q-Ṣ-D implies both intention and moderation; a *qaṣd*, for example, is an aim or purpose. Whichever of these semantic fields was intended to be the most prevalent, the early *qaṣīdah* was certainly a poem that was intended to convey a message. Examples of the genre from different periods display a degree of variation on the apparent structural principles of the initial segments of the poem, but the arrival at the crux is, more often than not, clearly marked within the poem's textual form and was presumably even more so in public performance. Indeed, in many poems the point is made through resort to a direct imperative. Here, for example, are some lines from a *qaṣīdah* by the elder of two poets called al-Muraqqish (sixth century) taken from Sir Charles Lyall's still affecting version of the collection of al-Mufaḍḍal al-Ḍabbī (d. *c.* 786), *al-Mufaḍḍaliyyāt*:

> O camel-rider, whoever thou mayst be, bear this message,
> if thou lightest on them, to Anas son of Saʿd, and
> Harmalah:
> 'Great will be the virtue of you twain and your father, if
> the man of Ghufailah escapes being slain!'

or these lines by the famous itinerant poet, al-Aʿshā (in Michael Sells's more contemporary version):

> To Yazīd of the Banī Shaybān
> bear this word:
> Abu Thubayt,
> stop gnawing at your heart!
>
> Stop carving at the grain
> of our ancient name
> that nothing can harm
> as long as burdened camels groan.

The 'message' section of the *qaṣīdah* may not always be marked by such a clear transitional device as these examples provide, but the section in which the poet publicly extols the qualities of his fellows – valour, endurance, patience, liberality, and so on – is intended to provide the putative addressee of the poem with clear signals as to the appropriate response.

One of the problems associated with the analysis of the *qaṣīdah*'s structure has been the extent to which the description that ibn Qutaybah (d. 889) provided in the introduction to his *Kitāb al-shiʿr wa-al-shurʿarāʾ* [Book of Poetry and Poets] was used as a norm. In attempting to encapsulate the form of the Arabic *qaṣīdah* for the purposes of a work of reference, ibn Qutaybah was, of course, extrapolating backwards from a cultural environment that had undergone significant changes; and, to be fair, it also needs to be observed that he prefaces his much-cited description with the phrase 'Some literary folk say . . .' What those particular people did say is that the *qaṣīdah* is a tripartite structure, consisting of a nostalgic opening (*nasīb*), leading through a 'release' (*takhalluṣ*) to a travel section (*raḥīl*), and finishing with the message of the poem in the form of praise of tribal attributes (*fakhr*), lampooning the enemy (*hijāʾ*), and moral aphorisms (*ḥikam*). Like all such attempts to encapsulate a literary genre – let alone one that was already of several centuries' duration, this one serves as a convenient summary of the primary features of a number of Arabic *qaṣāʾid* (convenience being a primary principle of ibn Qutaybah's writing). However, the creativity of the poet ensured from the outset that this generalised pattern was not the rule. Thus, for example, the opening of the *qaṣīdah* does indeed often take the form of an invocation of the beloved's name; ʿAmr ibn Qamīʾah begins a poem:

> Umāmah is gone far from thee, and there is left for thee only to ask after her the place where she dwelt, and the vision of her that comes when thou dreamest –
>
> Its appointed time is when night closes in, and as soon as dawn breaks it refuses to stay any longer,

while the *muʿallaqah* of the great poet-cavalier, ʿAntarah (d. *c.* 615), creates the same mood, although accompanied by an interesting comment about poetic convention:

> Have the poets left anywhere
> in need of patching? Or did you,
> after imaginings,
> recognize her abode?

O abode of ʿAbla in al-Jiwāʾi,
speak! Morning greetings,
abode of ʿAblah,
peace!

ʿAmr ibn Qamīʾah's ode provides a succinct illustration of ibn Qutaybah's model; the fourth and fifth lines provide a wonderful example of the transfer to the travel section:

Sooth, fear seized my heart when they proclaimed their purposes, and
men said, 'Our comrades are preparing for an early departure';
And the two captains of the caravan hurried her swiftly away at earliest
dawn, after stirring up the male camels to rise from the place where
they couched–

and, after the animal description that is ushered in by these lines, the eighteenth line brings a complete shift; after the initial sections of the poem we have reached the goal:

How then dost thou sever the tie that binds thee in sincerity to a man
of glorious fame, who desires not to withdraw from it?

The famous *Burdah* ode of Kaʿb ibn Zuhayr, 'Suʿād is far gone from here' – so called because, once the poet had announced his repentance of his anti-Islamic position and his intention of joining the community of faithful, the Prophet Muḥammad is alleged to have wrapped the poet in his own mantle (*burdah*) – provides another example of the nature of the transition from the earlier portions of the poem to its core. The poem begins with a description of the beloved's absence and then proceeds to an elaborate depiction of a camel and its lithe movements, but line 34 informs us:

On both sides of my camel rumour-mongers say: Descendant of
Abū Sulmā, you are as good as dead,

and Kaʿb's intention is made clear a few lines later when he announces:

God's Messenger has threatened me with death, I was told;
but I hope for pardon from him.

The goal of ibn Qutaybah's description then seems to be the provision of some basic parameters for an analysis of structure that would match that of a substantial number of early Arabic poems in *qaṣīdah* form. Indeed his decision to include such an account may have been aimed at identifying a 'classical' model for the post-Islamic *qaṣīdah* at a time when the genre had already gone through a process of change and poets were challenging the normative values of the ancient poetic tradition. In fact, a sizeable percentage of the earliest corpus of poetry shows considerable variation on his basic model. To provide just one of the more famous examples of poems that vary or elaborate on the pattern, the *muʿallaqah* of ʿAmr ibn Kulthūm, a piece of tribal boasting *par excellence*, makes mention of the beloved, but not until the poet has opened his performance (according to accounts, at the court of King ʿAmr of al-Ḥīrah) in a rather different fashion:

> Ho there, maid, bring a morning draught in a goblet,
> and do not stint on the best vintages of ʿAndarīn!

More recent analyses of this cherished repertoire of early Arabic poetry have examined the structure of the *qaṣīdah* in more mythopoetic terms, seeing the total poem as a dynamic process that shifts from moments of absence, deprivation, and nostalgia to those of presence, plenty, and celebration of life. The older mode of analysis that saw each line as a discrete and carefully crafted jewel of language and the poem itself as 'a string of pearls' has been rejected in favour of analyses that view the *qaṣīdah* as a kind of suite. Viewed within such a matrix (which appears to have much in common with the analysis of quest narratives and of rites of passage), the beginning of the poem finds the poet halting at an abandoned campsite, evoking images of both the absence of the present and companionship of the past; the atmosphere is one of loss, yearning, and nostalgia. These memories lead on to a process of separation, whereby the poet begins a journey into the dangerous world of the desert, a sphere of loneliness and 'liminality'. His companion is the she-camel (*nāqah*), the preferred mode of transport in such inhospitable climes but also a protector and lifeline. The constant danger associated with this journey and the complete reliance on animal traits leads to some elaborate depictions of the camel, one of the most famous of which is that of Ṭarafah in his *muʿallaqah*. These segments of the poem not only describe the beast in its own right but also incorporate often lengthy images whereby its sterling qualities are compared to those of other desert animals – the onager, ostrich, and oryx, for example – each one identified by its own characteristic epithet (such as 'flat-nose' for the oryx). The amazing variety of ways in which this central confrontation with the unknown is elaborated within the early poetic tradition makes it abundantly clear quite how much such descriptions were prized by their audience. With this ritualistic sequence complete, the poet is then able to reintegrate himself into his society in a kind of homecoming ritual. The audience that has shared with the poet (and his bard) a full awareness of the perils that have been transcended now waits to hear the qualities of the group extolled in a boastful celebration of aggregation and solidarity. Here the closing section of the *Muʿallaqah* of Labīd, perhaps the greatest poetic expression of tribal mores, provides a splendid illustration. To the accompaniment of feasting, drinking, and gambling, the poem closes with a paean to the tribe that serves as man's primary source of security in his struggle against fate and the rigours of desert life.

The *qaṣīdah*, like other literary genres, was not to remain frozen in one static structural pattern based on the models provided by its earliest examplars. With the advent of Islam came the recording of the Qurʾān and the beginnings of its textual tradition, the move away from the Arabian Peninsula, and the development of an increasingly cosmopolitan Muslim community. In fact, the earliest stages in the history of that community provided occasions for elements of continuity within the poetic tradition. We have already noted the famous *burdah* poem of Kaʿb ibn Zuhayr, and to it can be added the poetry of Ḥassān ibn Thābit (d. *c.* 673), called 'the Prophet's poet', which celebrates the exploits of Muḥammad and pours scorn on his foes. One of Muḥammad's principal aims in his lifetime had been to replace the unit of the tribe with another type of community (*ummah*) based on the tenets of Islam, but, whatever initial cohesion may have been achieved during Muḥammad's lifetime, the aftermath of his death showed many tribes reverting to their former affiliations and enmities. Furthermore, the early history of the Muslim community itself was rife with doctrinal schisms and personal rivalries, all of which provided a continuingly fertile environment for the traditional mode of lampooning (*hijāʾ*). Most famous here were the famous 'flytings' (*naqāʾiḍ*), primarily between Jarīr (d. *c.* 732) and al-Farazdaq (d. *c.* 732) but also involving al-Akhṭal (d. *c.* 710) and al-Ṭirimmāḥ (d. *c.* 723); they will be discussed in detail below. Al-Ṭirimmāḥ devotes some of his poetry to a celebration of the cause of the Khawārij, those who had left the community in disgust after the arbitration at the Battle of Ṣiffīn; the rallying-cries to opposition and battle, the exultation of a glorious martyrdom, these recall both the confrontation with danger that characterises the earlier poetry and the new attitude to martyrdom and the imminence of death subsumed within the Islamic belief system, the tenets of which the Khawārij viewed themselves alone as being the true upholders.

However, while the poems composed during the initial stages of the post-Islamic era continued to display facets of the earlier tradition, the gradual process whereby allegiances shifted from those based on a system of tribal confederacies to that of the growing community of Muslims and their leaders inevitably had an effect on the generic purpose of the Arabic *qaṣīdah*. This type of poem, which had been an important element in the communal assertion of the tribe's self-identity and sense of chivalry (*ḥamāsah*), came to assume a more specifically panegyric function. The poem was now addressed to a specific figure, more often than not a patron who was to be recognised as protector of the Muslim community (or a subset of it); its primary function was to extol this leader's virtues as a representative of Islam and its community of believers. Furthermore, the emergence of an elaborate court system, with its accompanying panoply of bureaucrats and courtiers, also demanded of the poet that he be prepared to serve as an entertainer as well as morale-booster and propagandist. As a result of these changing expectations, the *qaṣīdah* – which, we suggested above, appears to have originated as a polythematic amalgamation of various types of shorter poem (*qiṭʿah*) – now takes on a different structural logic for its new context and function. While the latter part of the poem focuses on eulogising the patron or other members of the court, earlier sections come to reflect the changed realities of performance context by moving away from the motifs of journeying through the desert and halting over encampments – concepts far removed from the courts of Baghdad or Cordoba and their mixture of Arab and non-Arab côteries. Thus, while Ghaylān ibn ʿUqbah (d. 735), a poet of the Umawī period best known by his nickname 'Dhū al-Rummah', is affectionately remembered as 'the last of the Bedouin poets' because of his continuing adherence to the conventions of the earlier poetry, Abū Nuwās (d. *c.* 803) reflects changing attitudes by using some of his openings to take pot-shots at the conventions of the traditional *qaṣīdah*:

> Some poor wretch turned aside to question a camp-ground;
> my purpose in turning aside was to ask for the local pub.

Within this new social context and purpose for the *qaṣīdah*, the evocation of the structural elements and imagery of early Arabic poetry now becomes the subject-matter of allusion. Such are expectations among the court audience with regard to erudition and urbane values that these archaistic elements continue to maintain a vigorous, albeit transformed, presence within the poetic tradition. Poets were, needless to say, eager to exploit the predilections of their audience to the full by using the intertextual possibilities that these motifs offered in order to exhibit the extent of their awareness of the tradition. As an example, we can point to the frequency with which references to ancient sites and buildings are incorporated into later examples of the *qaṣīdah*; many are the poems, for example, that include mention of the twin Iraqi palaces of al-Khawarnak and al-Sadīr as a means of recalling memories of a glorious past. These and other evocative devices become one part of the stock in trade of occasional poets at the widely scattered courts of the Islamic dominions. Their ringing *qaṣāʾid* in praise of rulers remain a central element in the Arabic poetic tradition, seen most famously in the odes that al-Mutanabbī (d. 965) addressed to a sequence of rulers, but also in the works of many other poets among his contemporaries and successors, including, to cite just two examples, ibn Hāniʾ (d. 975), court poet of the Fāṭimī Caliph al-Muʿizz in Tunis and ibn Darrāj (d. 1030) of al-Andalus. Eulogies (*madīḥ*) in *qaṣīdah* form, whether of rulers or religious figures, are the primary focus of the élite poetic tradition that has come down to us from the pre-modern period; among the more notable poets are al-Shābb al-Ẓarīf (d. 1289), ibn Nubātah al-Miṣrī (d. 1366), and Ibn Mālik al-Ḥamawī (d. 1511). The form continues well into the twentieth century where it is represented by the occasional poems of Aḥmad Shawqī (d. 1932), Khalīl Muṭrān (d. 1949), and other exponents of neo-classical poetry.

As the *qaṣīdah* was gradually transformed into a panegyrical vehicle for court occasions, its practitioners made use of the potential of its new structural logic to illustrate the extent of their 'anxiety of influence' towards the earlier poetic heritage. Meanwhile, the less complex *qiṭʿah* form maintained its independent and less formal status, adopting and adapting some of the other themes that had been part of the earlier poets' repertoire. This led to the emergence of such genres as the *ghazal* (love poem) and *khamriyyah* (wine poem) as separate entities in their own right (to be discussed below).

Rajaz

Commentaries on the Arabic poetic tradition link the *qiṭaʿah* and *qaṣīdah* into a single category known as *qarīḍ*. In that way the two structures that we have just analysed can be distinguished from another type of poem known as *rajaz* (also the name assigned to its metrical pattern). In this distinction we once again seem to be faced with the results of the process whereby the earliest phases in the development of the Arabic language and its cultural expressions were recorded. If we give credence to the idea that *sajʿ* does indeed represent an early manifestation of the poetic in Arabic, then *rajaz* emerges as a further step in the development of a mode of discourse characterised by its rhymes and rhythmic pulses. One of the primary types of early *rajaz* poem is the camel-driver's song (*ḥidāʾ*), and the commentators note that the form was especially conducive to spontaneous compositions of such a kind. It would appear however that the philologists who set out to discover the precedents of the Qurʾān in the pre-Islamic poetic tradition regarded the poetry in this form as a less authentic source for those models of lofty vocabulary and correct grammar that were their goal. The clear distinction that appears to have been drawn in the earliest period between *qarīḍ* and *rajaz* thus seems to reflect a view of the latter as a less exalted genre of poetic composition.

With this early history of the *rajaz* in mind, it is somewhat ironic that the studies undertaken at the schools of language study at al-Baṣrah and al-Kūfah (described in ch. 2 above) led certain poets in the period of the Umawī Caliphs to make use of the *rajaz* in order to compose virtuoso poems that have as a major purpose to explore the limits of Arabic lexicography. Al-ʿAjjāj (d. *c.* 717) and his son, Ruʾbah (d. 735), are particularly famous for their efforts in this domain. It needs to be added that the poem in *rajaz*, the *urjūzah* – with its more variable metrical and rhyming patterns than those of other metres subsumed within al-Khalīl's 'canonical' system – comes to be used by a number of Arab poets and for a variety of purposes: a hunt poem with ibn al-Muʿtazz (d. 908), for example, and a 445-line chronological account of the exploits of the Andalusian Umawī Caliph, ʿAbd al-raḥmān III (d. 961), composed by the famous poet-anthologist, ibn ʿAbd Rabbihi (d. 940). It is perhaps a sign of the reintegration of *rajaz* that the *urjūzah* poem was often described as *qaṣīdah muzdawijah* (a doublet ode), referring to the rhyming pattern (aa, bb, cc, etc.) involved. That is the rhyme adopted in ibn ʿAbd Rabbihi's poem mentioned above, and it was especially popular for a number of types of didactic poem on matters historical, astronomical, and grammatical; the last category is famously represented by the *Alfiyyah* of ibn Mālik (d. 1274), a thousand-line poem about Arabic grammar that, as Ṭāhā Ḥusayn's (d. 1973) autobiography of his childhood, *al-Ayyām* (*An Egyptian Childhood*) clearly shows, was the bane of several centuries of Arab schoolchildren who had to memorise it.

The prescriptive tendencies of the critical tradition may account for the fact that such variations on and adaptations of the hallowed *qaṣīdah* form are not plentifully represented in the collected works of the famous poets. However, it seems clear that, at least from the tenth century onwards, structures with different rhyming patterns – gathered together under the general heading *muṣammat* ('*simṭ*' meaning 'a string of thread') – became increasingly popular, adopting a variety of rhyming patterns in threes, fours, and fives (*muthallath*, *murabbaʿ*, and *mukhammas*).

The seven types

In quantitative terms the categories of poem that we have mentioned thus far would appear to constitute those that the recorders of the Arabic literary tradition thought most worthy of preservation for posterity. The *qaṣīdah* had become the preferred mode of expression for the more public and ceremonial occasions, while other categories were reserved for less official gatherings and for more personalised avenues of creativity. In addition to these categories there were others, most of which emerged at later stages in the history of the Muslim community and as a consequence of the interplay between the various cultural heritages involved. Commentators have often been inclined to dub these categories as 'popular' (*shaʿbī*), a designation that is not a little problematic in that it fuses and confuses aspects of language and performance occasion. The audience attending ceremonial occasions at which *qaṣā'id* were recited would indeed be listening to a level of language that was not their normal mode of daily communication but had long been universally recognised as the only appropriate discourse for such events in the life of the Muslim community. However, there would also be many other types of less official occasion at which the recitation of poetry would be expected and welcomed, and for such events the type of language to be used would be adjustable in accordance with the nature of the audience and its linguistic predilections. Thus, any exclusive association of the literary language with the élite classes of society and the colloquial with the populace would be a false dichotomy; poetry which made use of levels of language other than the high literary was not 'popular', if by that is intended the notion that it was restricted to a plebeian audience. In the realm of language, it is true, of course, that the upholders of the grammatical and philological tradition – based in turn on the kind of language of which the Qur'ān itself was the inimitable model – have always fiercely condemned any writers whose works showed a 'lapse' into a level of language that appeared to replicate the lexicon or syntax of the colloquial dialect; indeed a technical term was coined for such usages, *laḥn*, implying incorrectness. Such strictures regarding the canonical status of the literary level of language (called *al-lughat al-fuṣḥā*, the more correct language) have tended to create a bipolar attitude to Arabic diglossia that has, in large measure, overlooked the obvious reality that the language possesses the infinite number of levels of 'interlanguage' between the two poles of 'literary-élite' (*fuṣḥā*) and 'popular-colloquial' (*ʿāmmiyyah*), levels that are inevitably reflected in a variety of literary genres in both prose and poetry. Indeed this issue of language, audience, and cultural attitude will confront us again when we consider the subject of *adab* and popular narratives in ch. 5.

With such linguistic postures in mind, we must consider ourselves fortunate in that a few poet-critics make a point of recording, alongside the categories of poem already mentioned, a seemingly lively tradition of what we will term 'less official' categories of poem. Later critics talk in terms of 'the seven types' of poem (*al-funūn al-sabʿah*): *qarīḍ* (i.e. *qiṭʿah* and *qaṣīdah*), *kān wa-kān*, *dubayt*, *muwashshaḥ*, *qūmā*, *mawwāl*, and *zajal*. The Iraqi-born poet, Ṣafī al-dīn al-Ḥillī (d. *c.* 1339), for example, composed an invaluable study of these genres entitled *al-ʿĀṭil al-ḥālī wa-al-murakhkhaṣ al-ghālī* (one of the more delightfully oxymoronic and therefore untranslatable of Arabic titles, roughly 'The unadorned now bedecked, the cheapened made costly') following the earlier example of the Egyptian poet, ibn Sanāʾ al-Mulk (d. 1211), who had written a study of the *muwashshaḥ* with the equally colourful title, *Dār al-ṭirāz* (The House of Brocade). Al-Ḥillī divides the categories of poem in two different ways: according to variations in metre and rhyme, and according to language. Three are said to be '*muʿrabah*', meaning that they require the use of fully inflected literary Arabic (within which, as he colourfully notes, any lapse is unforgivable): *qarīḍ*, *muwashahah*, and *dubayt* (also known as *rubāʿī* (quatrain), the type of poem more famous within the Persian tradition and exemplified by the quatrains of the famous algebraist, 'Umar al-Khayyām, later rendered into English versions as 'The Rubaiyat' by Edward FitzGerald). Three other types are termed '*malḥūnah*', implying that a kind of language unacceptable to the grammarians is the norm: the *qūmā*, the *zajal*, and the *kān wa-kān* ('once upon a time'), the last of which began, as its name implies, as a story-telling type among Baghdādī poets but became an occasion for didactic and wisdom tales. For one type of poem, the *mawāliyā*, al-Ḥillī suggests that either kind of language is permitted, although the colloquial level is said to be more prevalent.

The lion's share of al-Ḥillī's study is devoted to the *mawāliyā* and the *zajal*. The former type of poem is alleged to have originated in Iraq, and al-Ḥillī's attention to it is based in large measure on the fact that it conforms for the most part with the expectations of the *basīṭ* metre of al-Khalīl's system, consisting in its written forms of four rhyming lines. Under the alternative name of *mawwāl*, the *mawāliya* is also a popular category of folk poetry known in several countries within the Arab world; in this case the rhyming scheme described above is altered in an interesting fashion, in that series of lines of varying lengths are introduced between the third and fourth lines of the original rhyming structure (i.e. from 'aaaa' to 'aaa bc ---> a'). Regarding the *zajal* al-Ḥillī notes with disarming candour that 'the majority of people cannot distinguish between the *muwashshaḥ* and the *zajal*'. He is here alluding to just one of the many debates and controversies that continue to swirl around these two categories of poem; when we add to their uncertain origins the sweeping cross-cultural generalisations that have been made by previous generations of scholars and the sensitivities associated with national myths, we soon realise that we are broaching one of the most contentious realms of contemporary Arabic literature scholarship. The following is thus an attempt to tiptoe across a room floored with eggshells.

As just noted, the very origins of both genres are not clear, nor indeed is the issue of which is anterior to the other (in spite of the common assumption that the *muwashshaḥ* is the earlier). It does seem clear that the *muwashshaḥ* was committed to written form before the *zajal*, but, since the latter allowed non-literary language into the body of the poem whereas the former did not, such an eventuality is hardly surprising. Perhaps what is most significant in any attempt at analysing the two is that they were intended for singing. The well-known effects that song will have on the seeming immaculacies of written texts and the scant nature of our knowledge concerning the musical tradition involved combine to make discussions of the two categories of poem that much more problematic.

The *zajal* (a word meaning literally 'shout') is a strophic poem composed in a language that permits the introduction of non-literary Arabic within the poem itself; such language might take the form of Arabic or Romance dialectal forms. It seems reasonable to suggest that, within the framework of a cultural environment such as that of al-Andalus, such distinctions came to be not a little blurred. The structure consisted of alternating segments: those which had independent rhymes were called *aghṣān* (sing. *ghuṣn*), and those that had dependent rhymes *asmāṭ* (sing. *simṭ*, a linkage to the *musammaṭ* categories mentioned above). The *zajal* was said to be 'complete' (*tāmm*) if it began with a prelude (*maṭlaʿ*), a section that shared its rhyme with the *asmāṭ*; if the poem had no prelude, it was given the somewhat pejorative designation 'bald' (*aqraʿ*). A simple pattern might thus be: 'aa bbb a ccc a' and so on; a more complex one: 'aba ccc aba ddd' and so on (where 'aba' represents the repeated pattern of the *simṭ* and 'ccc, ddd' the varying patterns of the *ghuṣn*). As al-Ḥillī notes at a later stage in the *zajal*'s development, there was a good deal of variation in both rhyming and metrical patterns. This has led in turn to the suggestion that as a song the *zajal* was intended primarily for a solo performer and one of considerable virtuosity.

The *muwashshaḥ* category (the word meaning 'girdled') shares some of the same structural characteristics: the majority of examples begin with a prelude (*maṭlaʿ*) and consist of a number of *asmāṭ* that share a rhyme with it and of *aghṣān* that do not. However, the content of the *muwashshaḥ* replicates many of the themes and images of the *qaṣīdah* tradition, and especially the conventions of courtly love poetry. What is most significant about the *muwashshaḥ* however is that its final *simṭ* (rhyming segment) is termed the *kharjah* (envoi) and is in the form of a quotation, or, some scholars would maintain, a deliberate attempt to imitate and surpass another poem or song. What initially attracted the attention of scholars to this category of poem is that in some examples the *kharjah* draws attention to itself, firstly by giving the appearance of being a popular song in either Romance dialect or colloquial Arabic and secondly by having content of an extremely earthy quality. For example, a *muwashshaḥah* by al-Saraqusṭī al-Jazzār (a poet of Saragossa, *fl.* eleventh century) begins with an anticipated expression of love-agony: 'Woe to the lovelorn wretch, my frame is in the grip of disease'. It finishes however with the female voice of the *kharjah* expressing sentiments in a rather different tone: 'Mamma, that boy's all mine, "legit" or otherwise.' Thus, in the *muwashshaḥ* pattern, the *maṭlaʿ* (if there is one), the *asmāṭ*, and the *kharjah* all share the same rhyme and metre, leading to the conjecture that they represent those segments of a performance text different from that of the *zajal* in that they are intended for a chorus of some kind while the variable *aghṣān* are for a soloist.

In considering the metrical analysis of the *zajal* and *muwashshaḥ* we confront two seemingly irreconcilable schools of thought: the one suggests that, since the poems are composed in Arabic, their metrics must be analysed according to the quantitative-syllabic system of al-Khalīl described above – with some slight adjustments; the other insists to the contrary that the poems were composed in al-Andalus and thus reflect the stress-based system of Hispanic poetry and song. Leaving aside an issue noted earlier – namely that the relationship of al-Khalīl's system of analysis to patterns of stress and musical performance is not clear, we can take note of the fact that a social milieu as diverse as that of al-Andalus might be expected to engender poetic forms that were a blend of influences from the various communities who participated in its cultural life. That such poems should not conform with the expectations of either culture's norms, indeed that they should illustrate their trans-cultural goals through difference, is not an unexpected consequence. And so, the debate continues . . .

Neither the *zajal* nor the *muwashshaḥ* remained frozen in time, but underwent the normal processes of generic change. It is from the later compilations and analyses of the likes of ibn Sanā' al-Mulk and Ṣafī al-dīn al-Ḥillī that one attempts to extrapolate backwards to their beginnings. With regard to the *zajal*, its most famous exponent is clearly ibn Quzmān (d. 1160) who manages to obfuscate the issues of definition and structure still further by composing songs that blur the distinctions between the two categories, producing examples of what Samuel Stern called 'the *muwashshaḥ*-like *zajal*'. In fact, ibn Quzmān, who in addition to being a poet was also a Cordoban nobleman and minister, provides an excellent example of the *zajal*'s use as a 'popular' medium in very genteel company: he is abundantly aware of the 'classical' tradition against which he is tilting (expressing in his poetry his desire to be distinguished from earlier poets like Jamīl Buthaynah [d. 701] and Abū Nuwās) and can write a *zajal* poem in which the final section, replete with the usual repertoire of eulogy (*madīḥ*) addressed to a patron, is preceded by a depiction of an encounter with a Bedouin prostitute that is astoundingly racy. The general acceptability of the *zajal*, with its variable characteristics, is seen through its different manifestations encountered in other regions of the Arab world: in the hymns of the Maronite liturgy, for example, and in a vigorous tradition of contemporary poetic jousting in Lebanon that boasts of its own celebrity poets. In a retrospective on the development of the *muwashshaḥ* we find that the *kharjah* appears in a number of linguistic guises: a small percentage in Romance, a larger number in colloquial Hispano-Arabic, and a majority in literary Arabic, illustrating perhaps a kind of formalisation process whereby a poetic category of Andalusian origin was adopted into the broader repertoire of the Arab poet. As the *muwashshaḥ* made its way eastwards, it continued to serve as a medium for the poetic expression of a variety of themes: indeed ibn al-ʿArabī

(d. 1240) and al-Shushtarī (d. 1269), both prominent Andalusian theologians who travelled to Syria, composed their own examples. Among many other famous exponents were the renowned secretary, al-Qāḍī al-Fāḍil (d. 1200) and the critic, Ṣalāḥ al-dīn al-Ṣafadī (d. 1362). As Moreh shows in his study of the early phases in the development of modern Arabic poetry, the *muwashshaḥ* was still a particular favourite among poets in the nineteenth and early twentieth centuries, and most notably for those Lebanese Christians who make up the *émigré* (*mahjar*) school in the Americas. (*Modern Arabic Poetry 1800–1970*, Leiden, Brill, 1976)

To conclude this brief review of these two fascinating categories of Arabic poem we might note that it remains an as yet unanswered question as to whether the existence of this Andalusian tradition of courtly love poetry as song (one word for which in Arabic is *ṭarab*, from the verbal root Ṭ-R-B) is to be linked to the subsequent emergence in Provence of another group of singers of poetry known as 'troubadours'.

THEMES

The above discussion of 'categories' of poem has focused in the main on more formal aspects of the poem, but inevitably reference has also been made to subject matter. We described the early *qaṣīdah*, for example, as polythematic, and suggested that it brought together within a single liturgical performance medium several topics of communal concern that were also the focus of shorter individual poems. We also observed that during the early centuries of Islam many of the themes brought together within the context of the tribal *qaṣīdah* were to become separate categories in their own right. In such cases, the categorical name of the poem often described the theme: thus, the *ghazal* as 'love poem', the *khamriyyah* as 'wine poem', and the *ṭardiyyah* as 'hunt poem'.

From the earliest stages of the critical tradition Arabic made use of the concept of the goal or purpose of the poem (*gharaḍ*, pl. *aghrāḍ*) as a means of discussing thematic content. Each purpose within what may be regarded as the most basic triad involved the element of praise. First and most significant was eulogy (*madīḥ*) involving praise of the living. Here the primary role of the poet was to praise. The poem would wax hyperbolic in extolling the virtues of the community and its leader(s); with the advent of the caliph's court and other seats of power, the language of these encomia of wealthy patrons would become flamboyant. Secondly, and stemming directly from the first, was the antithesis of praise: invective and lampoon (*hijā'*), whereby the virtues of the speaker's community would be enhanced by often scurrilous depictions of the faults of those inimical to it. Insult was the weapon in this case, and the target would be subject to withering ridicule. If the basic syntax of eulogy involves 'he is/they are', then that of lampoon may initially appear as 'he is/they are' (fools, cowards, impotent, cuckolds, etc.) but is clearly intended to invoke in the audience a sense of *schadenfreude* and thus to serve as an inverse reflection of its own virtues – 'he is/they are not'. The third element of praise is that of the dead, namely elegy (*rithā'*); here the syntax is 's/he was', combining a sense of grief and consolation for loss with a rehearsal of the dead person's virtues that serve as an appropriate celebration of communal ideals.

As the above comments suggest, each of these primary poetic modes tended to bring with it a particular mood. Overriding the different occasions at which the poems would be performed and the atmospheres that they engendered were the universal values to which the society adhered: that of '*muruwwah*', akin to a code of chivalry in its broadest sense, and of the above-mentioned '*ḥamāsah*', a combination of heroism and *élan*. Early critics analysing the ways in which eulogy, lampoon, and elegy serve as celebrations of these communal values identify a series of further elements that contribute in different combinations to the poem's larger 'purpose': the love theme (*nasīb*), description (*wasf*), boasting (*fakhr*), and aphorism (*hikmah*). In the work of the renowned critic, Qudāmah ibn Jaʿfar (d. 922), we find that the list of the *aghrāḍ* of poetry has been expanded by the addition of the comparison of the similar (*tashbīh*). Thus to the basic notion of '*gharaḍ*' as 'purpose' expressed through different modes and performance contexts were later added other aspects more associated with modes of poetic analysis.

It is these different modes of thematic organisation that will now be utilised as the basis for a survey of the Arabic poetic corpus. It is as well to emphasise from the outset what is reasonably obvious: that any such selection cannot be anything but a minute sample of a heritage of enormous variety and richness, one that retains its long-standing position as the great repository of the Arab world's most cherished values and traditions. In order to accommodate within our own purview the different categorisations that we have just discussed, we will begin by elaborating on the three major modes that reflect the preferred organising principles of the poetic collections themselves – eulogy, lampoon, and elegy, and append to them a discussions of 'description' (*wasf*). We will then discuss particular themes, many of which came to constitute separate categories within the collected works of poets – the wine poem, the love poem, and so on. In the modern period, the changing role of poetry and poets has meant that the topics and imagery of some of these earlier types of poem have become more matters of allusion than primary focus, but themes such as love and heroism have – one might say, inevitably – endured, transcending all processes of change.

Madīḥ: eulogy, panegyric

> You are a very sun and other monarchs are stars; when your
> light gleams bright, other stars disappear.

Thus the poet, al-Nābighah (d. *c.* 602), addressing al-Nuʿmān ibn al-Mundhir, the ruler of al-Ḥīrah. At a later date al-Mutanabbī appears to follow suit in a *qaṣīdah* addressed to Sayf al-Dawlah, ruler of Aleppo, that celebrates the latter's recovery from illness:

> Light is now restored to the sun; it had gone out, as
> though the lack of it in its body were a disease.

Al-Mutanabbī's disease image finds a still later echo in a eulogy composed by a poet who was a Circassian grandee of Damascus, Manjak Pāshā al-Yūsufī (d. 1669), when he lauds his patron with the following line:

> Intellects are cured of disease by his prudence; in his
> shadow the steadfast religion stands secure.

Conservative literalist critics in quest of a protocol for reading canonical texts were quick to point out that these poets (and others like them) are lying; poetry, they suggested, does not tell the truth. As we will observe in ch. 7 on criticism, the poet-critic ibn Rashīq (d. 1064) is among those who point out that, while such verdicts may be correct on one, rather narrow, level, they are essentially missing the point. It is not the province of poetry to be concerned about what Churchill once called 'terminological inexactitude'; indeed hyperbole has always been part of the stock-in-trade of the panegyrist. As we noted above, the *qaṣīdah* of the pre-Islamic poet was a celebration of the life and values of the tribe, and the generic expectations within which it functioned were clearly understood, indeed established, by its audience. During the Islamic period, the addressee of the *madīḥ* poem – be he caliph, *wazīr*, or sultan – now served as an authority-figure to a large and diverse community. Poetry composed in such a person's honour transcended the individual level to become an intrinsic part of the the society's political and social fabric. The repertoire of communally accepted codes under which such poems were composed and performed were thus part of a system of publicity and propaganda that helped in the establishment of the society's sense of identity, the maintenance of its core values, and its relationship to the heritage of the past.

In the earlier discussion of the structure of the earliest examples of the tribal *qaṣīdah* it was noted that the third and last section was intended as a celebration of the virtues of aggregation and solidarity. The sheer delight in belonging to a community could be reflected in a variety of ways, for example Labīd's depiction of bibulous assemblies and of gambling in his renowned *Muʿallaqah.* But, while such descriptions would be regularly invoked to display some of the advantages of tribal membership, the more direct form of poetic propaganda took the form of panegyrics addressed to tribal rulers, of boasts (*fakhr*) concerning the manly qualities (*muruwwah*) of the tribesmen, and of aphorisms (*ḥikmah*) that would reflect the philosophy of life as envisaged by the tribal society. A superb illustration of this poetic environment is the *Muʿallaqah* of Zuhayr ibn Abī Sulmā (d. *c.* 607). Its historical context is the War of Dāhis and Ghabrā', a lengthy conflict between the tribes of ʿAbs and Dhubyān that had originally been triggered by some skulduggery during a horse race and then degenerated into a sequence of revenge killings. Two chieftains, Harim ibn Sinān and al-Ḥarith ibn ʿAwf, made an enormously generous offer to bring the cycle of violence to an end, offering three thousand camels over a three-year period to settle the dispute and cancel the blood-wits involved. Within pre-Islamic Arabian society the gift of so huge a number of camels was a significant gesture, and the structuring of Zuhayr's poem shows considerable dispatch in reaching its point. At line 15 the intervention of the two chiefs is described, and their generosity (*karāmah*) is accorded fulsome praise:

> You have brought ʿAbs and Dhubyān together again after lethal conflict
> and the stench of death;
> We will achieve peace, you both said; should property and charitable
> words be needed, so it shall be.
> Thereby you placed yourselves in the best position, far removed from
> obstinacy or crime,
> Two great men of high rank in Maʿadd; may you be guided aright!
> Whoever condones a treasure-trove of glory will himself be glorified!

As is well known, generosity and hospitality have always been an intrinsic part of the value-system of Arabian culture; that a man should have a pile of ash under his cooking-pot is a clearly understood metaphor for generosity. Indeed the name of another poet, Ḥātim al-Ṭāʾī (d. *c.* 605) became proverbial for such qualities. But the gesture of these two chieftains is clearly of an unusual kind. What makes it even more so is that a hotheaded tribesman named Ḥuṣayn ibn Ḍamḍam (significantly named in Zuhayr's poem, line 38) behaves in a reckless manner that threatens the fragile fabric of the peace settlement. The two chiefs – showing, it must be said, a good deal of patience in adversity (*ṣabr*) – remain steadfast in keeping their side of the bargain and give more of their property. As Zuhayr notes at the conclusion of one version of his poem:

> We asked, and you gave; we asked again, and you gave again.
> He who asks too much, will find himself deprived.

While Labīd's *muʿallaqah* celebrates the tribe through reference to the courage, generosity, and loyalty of its members, Zuhayr's poem concludes with a montage of moralistic utterances. His panegyric completed, he pronounces himself weary of the cares of an impermanent existence:

> I have grown weary of the cares of life; whoever lives eighty years will
> inevitably grow weary.

These panegyrical sections in celebration of the tribal values of bravery, fidelity, and generosity, coupled to an appreciation of the routines, comforts, and securities of communal living (they still being, incidentally, a central part of the twentieth-century Arabian poetic tradition described by Sowayan and Caton) find an exact obverse in the poems of the vagabond poets (*ṣaʿālīk*). The *locus classicus* for this anti-tribal posture is the already mentioned 'L-poem' (*Lāmiyyah*) of al-Shanfarā. The mood is established from the very first line:

> Sons of my mother, stir up the breasts of your riding
> animals; for I am inclined to a tribe other than you . . .

and the poet proceeds to illustrate his scorn at the supposed securities of tribal life by piling up a series of lines beginning with a negative that state exactly what he is not: a thirsty shepherd, a stay-at-home asking for his wife's opinions, a skirt-chaser, one scared of the dark, and so on. The persona of the *ṣuʿlūk* poet is of one ostracised from society, relishing loneliness, danger, and the inevitable imminence of death. For such a person the advantages of integration into the tribe, as celebrated in the boasts and panegyrics of the tribal *qaṣīdah*, are not available, and indeed not desired; his is a life of liminality, and the attitudes and hardships depicted in his poetry serve to confirm for the bard's audience the wisdom of communal living.

This earliest tradition of Arabic panegyric poetry, with its established ideals and repertoire of images, was to see its context transformed in the seventh century with the advent of Islam. The career of the Prophet Muḥammad, the institution of the caliphate and resulting schisms, the transfer of the seat of caliphal authority to the city of Damascus, and the gradual emergence of an elaborate and cosmopolitan court bureaucracy, all these factors contributed to a change in generic purpose and performance context. The many tensions that marked the initial phases in the development of the religious community are wonderfully captured in the famous *burdah* poem of Kaʿb son of Zuhayr that was discussed above. The authentically pre-Islamic vision of the first half of the poem ends abruptly with the introduction of the poem's purpose: an account of the poet's dangerous position and the recitation of the poem itself as an act of contrition and conversion. At the close of the *qaṣīdah* the mood switches back to the past as Kaʿb makes use of his praise of the Prophet and his company as a point of transfer back to the mounted warriors of the pre-Islamic vision.

As was noted in the previous chapter, the revelations of the Qurʾān had cast a negative light on the social function of poets, most especially in the context of a messenger endeavouring to reveal God's word to a community. That said, it is evident that Muḥammad was quick to realise and utilise poetry in the cause of Islam. Indeed Ḥassān ibn Thābit (d. *c.* 670) was dubbed 'the Prophet's poet', and the biography (*sīrah*) of the Prophet (discussed in the next chapter) contains reference to a number of poems composed by Ḥassān that serve as records of particular events, such as the Battle of Badr in 624, a crucial victory for the forces of the incipient Muslim community against their Meccan opponents, and Muḥammad's early death in 632. Ḥassān's panegyric poems also mark the beginning of a particular strand of *madīḥ* poetry devoted to praise of the Prophet; during the centuries when the influence of popular mystical movements was at its height – extending from the thirteenth century well into the twentieth, this subgenre was to find particular favour as a mode of invoking the Prophet's intercession, a ritual that is seen most notably in the widespread popularity of another poem termed '*burdah*', that of al-Būṣīrī (d. 1295); it hardly needs to be added that the practice is roundly condemned by conservative theologians such as ibn Taymiyyah.

The unexpected death of Muḥammad was followed by the withdrawal of many tribal groupings from the Muslim community, and the early years of Abū Bakr's Caliphate were spent in the so-called *Riddah* Wars whereby seceding groups were returned to the fold. The question of caliphal legitimacy and succession soon became a cause for murder and schism. With these facts in mind, it is hardly surprising that the mood of defiance and the pride in hardship that had characterised the boasting segments of much pre-Islamic poetry were readily transferred to the several opposition groups engendered by such internal dissension – the Shīʿah and especially the Khawārij (both to be discussed in more detail below). Meanwhile the panegyrical aspect of the poem was co-opted by the Umawī caliphs. Their claim to legitimacy had come as a direct result of a much disputed process of arbitration that had followed a resort to armed force, namely the initially indecisive Battle of Ṣiffīn (657) against supporters of the Caliph ʿAlī. The tradition of panegyric poetry now became a means of bolstering their position as leaders of the Muslim community and as rulers and commanders-in-chief of ever expanding dominions; it was called on to legitimate their authority in a period fraught with religious schism and political tension. The poet who was known as 'the poet of the Umawī Caliphs' was the Christian, al-Akhṭal (d. 710), whose verses invoke the qualities eulogised in the earlier tradition of panegyric but for the new purpose of glorifying the grandeur of a figure and indeed a dynasty that combined spiritual and temporal rule:

> Their ancestry is complete, and God Himself has selected them; the ancestry of any other clan is obscure and worthless.
> On the Day of Ṣiffīn, with eyes lowered, reinforcement came to them when they sought a favour from their Lord.
> You are from a house that has no peer when nobility and number are reckoned.

Al-Akhṭal was a member of the tribe of Taghlib, and his two famous contemporaries, Jarīr (d. 732) and al-Farazdaq (d. 729) both belonged to the Tamīm confederacy. Much of their poetry, and most especially the 'flytings' (*naqāʾiḍ*) that they aimed at each other (to be discussed in the section on lampoon below), provides an excellent reflection of the political tensions of the era through their continuing concern with and use of tribal affiliation for purposes of both boasting and ridicule, all this in conjunction with the centralising aspirations of the Caliphate that they eulogised so fulsomely in their verses.

When the ʿAbbasī caliphs shifted the seat of power from Umawī Damascus to their new, purpose-built, capital of Baghdad in 756, they were not only 'distancing' themselves geographically and psychologically from the domains of their predecessors, but also acknowledging the major role that their more northern and eastern affiliates, particularly the Persians, had played in bringing them to power. The role of the caliph as spiritual head of the Muslim community and supreme ruler of a vast empire was clearly symbolised in the design of the new capital through the placement of the palace firmly at the centre. While the early ʿAbbasī caliphs may have been at some pains to contrast their conduct and priorities with the more secular proclivities attributed to the Umawī caliphs (mostly, it needs to be said, by historians who wrote during the ʿAbbasī period), the demand for panegyric that would celebrate the achievements of Islam through the personage of its caliph remained constant. Indeed, opportunities for the panegyrist were to become more plentiful. In addition to the ʿAbbasī caliph in Baghdad, other focuses of power made their influence felt: the Umawīs, now removed to their new centre in Cordoba (initially as *amīr* but, after 931, as caliph) and Fāṭimī dynasty in Tunisia and thereafter in Egypt. The earliest poetic expression of tribal rivalries could now be matched by caliphal ones, as when the Andalusian poet, ibn Hāniʾ (d. 972), a supporter of the Fāṭimī Caliph, al-Muʿizz, throws the capture of Cairo in 969 in the face of the ʿAbbasī caliph in Baghdad with the opening phrase:

> 'Has Egypt been conquered?' the sons of al-ʿAbbās will ask. Tell them
> that the matter has been concluded!

As the ʿAbbasī caliph's hold on central authority began to weaken and its more temporal functions came to be exercised at a local level by numerous petty dynasties, the accomplished Arab poet found himself with no shortage of opportunities for patronage.

As the performance venue for Arabic panegyric poetry shifted from a tribal gathering in the evening air of the desert or a gathering in the courts of pre-Islamic rulers to the pomp of the caliphal court in Damascus and later Baghdad, involving both the official ceremonial of the ruling élite and somewhat less panoplied occasions for eulogising ministers, grandees, courtiers, and bureaucrats drawn from an increasingly wide variety of cultural backgrounds, so did the generic purpose and organising logic of Arabic *madīḥ* undergo a transformation. In a widely quoted study Stefan Sperl examines some of the structural implications of the change (*Mannerism in Arabic Poetry*, Cambridge University Press,

1989). With the gradual evolution of the wine, love, and hunt themes found in examples of the early *qaṣīdah* as separate genres, the panegyric poem, he suggests, develops a new sequential logic, adopting a pattern of strophe-antistrophe: the first part presents a vision of the ruled segment of society, impermanent and temporal, while the second portrays the authority of the ruler himself, a symbol of continuity and prestige who upholds the spiritual and secular values of the community. A famous example of this movement is one of Arabic's greatest ceremonial panegyrics, the poem composed by Abū Tammām to celebrate the victory of Muslim forces over the Byzantines at the Battle of Amoreum (838). Accounts tell us that astrological predictions concerning the outcome of the battle had been negative, but that the Caliph, al-Muʿtaṣim, had ignored their counsel. A stirring account of the battle, the demeanour of the victorious and defeated, and the stalwart attitude of the caliph, are all part of the central core of the poem:

> God's Caliph, may God reward your efforts on behalf of the roots of
> religion, Islam, and honour!

but Abū Tammām opens his panegyric with a memorably gnomic line, packed solid with poetic devices, which posits the superiority of the sword over the pen and thus links the poem's introduction to its core through a linkage of the battle's prelude to its outcome:

> The sword conveys truer tidings than books; its cutting edge separates
> the serious from the flippant.

The blind poet, Bashshār ibn Burd (d. 784) was cited in ch. 2 for his stalwart advocacy of the Persian cultural heritage during the *shuʿūbiyyah* debates. His poetic career, mostly spent in al-Basrah, was sufficiently long to permit him to compose panegyrics for members of both the Umawī and ʿAbbāsī caliphal families and their respective retinues. A panegyric addressed to Khālid al-Barmakī, minister of the Caliph al-Mahdī (d. 785), provides a good illustration of the role that the theme of generosity now comes to play in the relationship between eulogiser and eulogised:

> While not every wealthy personage shows munificence, by my life
> Ibn Barmak has shown generosity towards me.
> I have used my poems to milk his palms, and they have flowed
> copiously like rain-clouds in a thunderstorm.

Bashshār's panegyrics serve as excellent examples of the changing relationship between the opening of the *qaṣīdah* and the central section devoted to its principal purpose. The nostalgic references to the deserted encampment and the absent beloved will still occur as reminders of the inherited values of the past, but the quest for a more expeditious linkage of exordium to the recipient of the eulogy (more often than not mentioned by name) introduces a variety of other themes as possible preludes; in the case of the more ceremonial poems the goal, illustrated by Abū Tammām's example above, is the maximally gnomic phrase. One mode of variation is well illustrated by a famous panegyric *qaṣīdah* addressed by al-Buhturī (d. 897) to the ʿAbbāsī Caliph, al-Mutawakkil (d. 861), who had moved the caliphal abode of Samarrā'. The mood created by the opening is a familiar one:

> Turn aside to the dwelling of Laylā, so we may greet it,
> yea, and ask it about some of its people.

The place in question, it emerges, is the luxurious palace at Samarrā' with its ornamental lake, all of which pales into insignificance when the magnificence and virtue of the caliph are taken into account.

Bashshār is credited by the Arabic critical tradition as one of the pioneers in a movement that sought to exploit the new interest in the intrinsic lexical and syntactic riches of Arabic by rendering the language and imagery of poetry more complex, a trend which became known as *badīʿ*, an adjective implying newness and creativity. While this trend is visible in all the genres of poetry that we are considering in this chapter, the ceremonial aspect of the panegyric and, one might say, the generic proclivity of the genre towards hyperbole made the Arabic *madīh* poem a primary vehicle for *badīʿ* expression. Abū Tammam is the poet whose name is primarily associated with the critical controversies that raged around the function of *badīʿ* and the contribution to the poetic tradition of the modernist poets (*muḥdathūn*), a debate that will be explored in detail in ch. 7. The opening line cited above, with its contrasts, parallelisms, and wordplay, is just one famous example of the work of a poet who, it would appear, courted controversy through the challenges that he posed to his audiences. As the later critic, ʿAbd al-qāhir al-Jurjānī (d. 1078) pointed out, it was the impact of the unfamiliar juxtapositions in his imagery in particular that made him such an important catalyst for change within the Arabic poetic tradition:

> No veil can distance my expectations from you; for, when the heavens
> are veiled by cloud, much is hoped from them.

The Arab poet whose career and disposition personify the role of court poet, most especially as panegyrist, was Abū al-Ḥusayn, generally known by his nickname, al-Mutanabbī (d. 965); he is the Arab occasional poet *par excellence.* Yet another victory against the Byzantines at al-Ḥadath (954) afforded him the opportunity to declaim an ode that replicates the occasion and moment of the Amorium ode of his predecessor, Abū Tammām. The audience at the court of Sayf al-dawlah, Ḥamdānī ruler of Aleppo, heard an opening that is equally gnomic and, if anything, yet more complex in its devices:

> Resolutions come in accordance with the worth of the resolute; noble
> deeds come in accordance with the worth of the noble.
> In the eyes of the puny, puny deeds seem important; in the eyes of the
> important, important deeds seem puny.

Even in English translation (deliberately literal) the wordplay of these much quoted verses and the values – resolution, nobility, and a becoming modesty – that they invoke conjure up an image of a fabulous occasion upon which al-Mutanabbī proclaimed this glorification of an Islamic ruler and his heroic deeds, making every possible use of the pun created by the ruler's name, 'Sword of the State'. Steeped in the tradition of Arabic poetry from its earliest times, al-Mutanabbī's panegyrics fuse the imagery of his pre-Islamic and Islamic predecessors with the elements of the 'new' *badīʿ* trend to create some of Arabic's most memorable poems, individual verses of which have remained since their first delivery part of the proverbial repertoire of the Arabic literary heritage:

> The worst of places is one where there is no friend; the worst thing
> a man can acquire is something that soils his reputation.

This line comes from a poem addressed by al-Mutanabbī to Sayf al-dawlah after the latter chose to favour another poet, his own relative, Abū Firās al-Ḥamdānī (d. 968), over al-Mutanabbī and served as a warning and harbinger of his departure to other, more promising, climes. Those turned out to be the Egypt of the Ikhshīdī regent, a manumitted slave named Kāfūr. Perhaps nothing illustrates al-Mutanabbī's mercurial personality and the close linkage between panegyric and its obverse, lampoon, better than the succession of poems that he addressed to that ruler. Upon his arrival, the poet greets his new patron:

> O father of musk, the face for which I have yearned, the time for
> which I have hoped . . . ,
> You have not gained kingship merely by wishing, but through
> hair-whitening times,

but, when the anticipated munificence does not match the poet's expectations, he secretly departs, leaving behind some of the most scabrous invective in the entire literary tradition:

> Nothing can be more vile than a stallion with a penis, being led by
> a serving-girl with no womb;
> The nobility of every people come from among themselves; among
> Muslims however they are paltry slaves.

In Harold Bloom's terms (*The Anxiety of Influence*, London, 1973), al-Mutanabbī is certainly the strongest of the strong Arab poets, the anxiety of whose influence was felt by all his successors, and this in spite of the often rancorous opposition against him and his poetry that began during his own lifetime and became something of a growth industry after his death. His panegyrics in particular became models for that kind of literary flattery known in the tradition as *muʿāraḍah* (imitation with the goal of surpassing the qualities of the original). One such example is the work of Ṣafī al-dīn al-Ḥillī (whose work on poetic genres was cited above). Challenged by the Mamlūk ruler of Egypt to produce an imitative panegyric, al-Ḥillī comes up with a rather overblown piece:

> A monarch who views the exhaustion of noble deeds as relaxation,
> while the comforts of palaces he reckons annoyance.
> Through noble deeds and resolutions desert wastes become seas and
> seas desert wastes.

The rulers of the Arabic-speaking world continued to employ poets to observe and celebrate the various occasions associated with their position: coronations, weddings, victories, birthdays, returns from the pilgrimage to Mecca, and so on. In the nineteenth century, the Lebanese writer, Aḥmad Fāris al-Shidyāq (d. 1887) composes a panegyric in honour of Queen Victoria; in the twentieth, Aḥmad Shawqī (d. 1932) celebrates the coronation of King Edward VII. Shawqī's relief that the Ottoman Sultan (as Caliph) has escaped an assassination attempt clearly replicates the lexicon of his forebears:

> Good health to you, O Commander of the Faithful! Your safety is safety
> for the true faith.
> Good health too to Ṭā-Hā, the Book, and a community for whom your
> continued existence means survival and life.

In another panegyric the Egyptian poet is full of praise for the victories of Muṣṭafā Kamāl Pāshā, the Turkish army commander, urging him to replicate the exploits of one of the generals of early Islam:

> God is greatest! How joyous is victory! O Khālid of the Turks, repeat
> the exploits of the Arab Khālid . . .

but, when the government of that same commander, now known as Kamāl Atatürk, announces the abolition of the Caliphate in 1924, Shawqī's joy at victory turns into sorrow and anger:

> Wedding songs now resound as wailing; in the midst of celebrations
> death is announced.

Occasions such as these and poems to mark them may have been a feature of the early decades of this century, but political and social developments in the Arab world – the rise of nationalism as a response to European colonial incursions, the struggle for independence, and the quest for individual rights – have during the first half of the twentieth century led to the emergence of an entirely different set of imperatives and priorities for the poet. In more literary terms, romanticism, the emergence of the individual voice, and, at the hands of poets such as ʿAlī Mahmūd Ṭāhā (d. 1949) and Abū al-qāsim al-Shābbī (d. 1934), a linkage between the two, have all but eradicated the notion of the poet as patronised artist. The rallying-cry of the Arab literary world in the 1950s was 'commitment' (*iltizām*), whereby the individual writer was supposed to devote his art to the cause of his nation – whether pan-Arab or local – and its people. Following the Suez débâcle in 1956, the Egyptian poet, Aḥmad ʿAbd al-muʿṭī Ḥijāzī (b. 1935), addresses a poem to the President of his country, Jamāl ʿAbd al-nāṣir (Nasser), that is certainly a panegyric but, equally certainly, a heartfelt expression of pride and support:

> Poets, I would have you write
> that here I behold the leader uniting the Arabs
> crying out: 'Freedom, justice, and peace'.

The contemporary Arab poet composes as an individual; poetry is rarely for purchase. To which many poets would add that the history of the region in the latter half of the twentieth century has provided little cause for panegyric of either rulers or occasions.

Hijāʾ: lampoon, satire, invective

The well-aimed barb, the personal smear, these now common and even accepted features of media-dominated political campaigns in our current era of Western politics have a very ancient history in the Arabic poetic tradition. Invective against one's foes (*hijāʾ*) – negative advertising, if you will – is found in poetry from the very earliest stages. As we have already noted, the poet, possessor of the verbal capacity to elevate and demolish, is a much cherished and feared member of the society. A line attributed to ʿAmr ibn Qamīʾah makes the point unequivocally:

> Many's the tribal poet loaded with rancour I have tamed, so his folk
> have felt puny and ashamed.

Hijāʾ is the opposite of panegyric. Abū Tammām uses a line of poetry to acknowledge that not only are panegyrics addressed to tribe or patron and lampooning of the adversary often part and parcel of the same process, but also that, if the former is not properly controlled, it becomes the latter.

> If a poet wishes to eulogise someone and keeps it up for too long,
> he is actually lampooning him.

Arabic poetry provides us with many examples of this combination. Accounts of the occasion on which two of the *Muʿallaqāt* were alleged to have been first performed provide an excellent illustration. After a prolonged war, the tribes of Bakr and Taghlib sought mediation through the king of al-Ḥīrah. The poet, ʿAmr ibn Kulthum, begins by expatiating upon the Taghlib tribe and its prowess. This inappropriate use of the occasion goads al-Ḥārith ibn Hillizah, the poet of Bakr, into a retort that puts his braggart rival and the pretensions of his tribe firmly in their place:

> We turned our attention to the Banū Tamīm. As we observed the month
> of truce, their daughters were our servant-girls.
> On the open plain even their great men could not hold their ground; nor
> did it help the dishonoured to run away
> The men of Taghlib who fell were unavenged, covered in death by the
> dust of oblivion.

This same combination of boasting (*fakhr*) and invective is found in the two ceremonial panegyrics that were discussed above. In Abū Tammām's *qaṣīdah* to the Caliph al-Muʿtaṣim, he relates how the Byzantine Emperor, Theophilus,

> Turned and fled after the spears had turned his speech into silence;
> his bowels all the while were in uproar,

while al-Mutanabbī's *qaṣīdah* addressed to Sayf al-dawlah questions the judgement of the Byzantine Domestikos before showing him in the same plight:

> Does the Domestikos advance each day, while his very neck scolds his
> face for advancing? . . .
> He fled, thanking his friends for escaping the sword-blades which were
> already too busy cleaving heads and wrists.

And, as we have already noted with regard to the L-poem of the vagabond (*ṣuʿlūk*) poet, al-Shanfarā, the process whereby an ostracised persona cocks a snook at the comforts of tribal life while boasting about the hardships of a lonely existence is an integral part of the reception of such poems.

As the above examples have shown, the most readily available targets of lampooning and invective were the chivalry of men (*muruwwah*, literally 'manliness') and the honour of women. Throughout the centuries both have provided ample scope for scurrilous attacks on adversaries. In particular, the good repute of the womenfolk of the family and tribe (the *ḥarīm*), a word with semantic connections to the notions of sanctuary and the need for protection, has always been and continues to be a primary means by which (masculine-based) honour is maintained and assessed. *Hijāʾ*, the obverse of approbation, thus becomes, almost automatically, a major means for calling such honour into question. Al-Ḥārith's taunt to ʿAmr about the latter's womenfolk being used as serving-girls is taken several stages further by the Khārijī poet, al-Ṭirimmāh, in his invective against the poet, al-Farazdaq:

> The smith [meaning al-Farazdaq] has, I am told, fornicated with an
> old hag named Qufayrah, because he could not achieve what I have;
> If you had any nobility in you, you would not have slept through the
> night of al-Naqā while Jiʿthin [al-Farazdaq's sister] was raped.

As an indication of the nature of the honour code involved in this particular case, the 'rape' referred to here seems to have involved a man deliberately brushing against Jiʿthin's shoulder. Nevertheless, this incident is sufficient to make of al-Farazdaq's sister a prominent figure of satirical reproach in the *hijāʾ* poems of his poetic opponents. In a continuing *hijāʾ* contest (a tradition that dates back to the pre-Islamic period and known as *naqāʾiḍ* ('flytings')), al-Farazdaq becomes a primary figure in Arabic poetry's most famous episode of poetic jousting, with Jarīr as his most prominent opponent, but also involving other poets such as al-Akhṭal and al-Ṭirimmāḥ. In fact, Jarīr and al-Farazdaq belonged to different clans within the same tribal confederacy (Tamīm), but that did not stop them from lambasting each other with a display of ever increasing vulgarity that seems to have become a major spectator sport. Their rivalry was in every sense 'the talk of the town', accurately reflecting the political tensions and intra-tribal rivalries that so characterised communal life during the Umawī period. Indeed this prolonged poetic exchange gives every appearance of having been continued primarily for the sake of the audience who would gather at the Mirbad Square on the edge of the city. Each poet was well aware of the poetic talents of the other; when al-Farazdaq died, Jarīr composed what appears to be a heartfelt elegy for his longtime poetic 'adversary'.

In spite of the direct and often lewd purpose of the poetic barbs they aimed at each other, both poets seem anxious to acknowledge their debt to the heritage of earlier times. They often begin their poems with thoroughly traditional exordia in the form of nostalgic *nasīb*s and pitch their scurrilous jibes in the language and imagery of the tribal *qaṣīdah.* Within such terms of reference they take up their roles with a relish and go at it hammer and tongs. In a sequence of poems, Jarīr, much feared for his pointed invective, chooses to turn the insult to al-Farazdaq's sister into a sexual orgy of major proportions. One of them begins in traditional fashion before broaching the main topic:

Hail to the dwellings at Suʿd; for love of Fāṭimah I have these dwellings ...
Is al-Farazdaq an ape? Stricken by lightning he was turned around ...
Do you recall how Jiʿthin screamed, while your goal was women's amulets and veils?
When the disgrace of Jiʿthin's evil was known, weren't you afraid of it being brought to light?

Of al-Farazdaq himself, he says:

Al-Farazdaq's mother gave birth to a fornicator; what she produced was a pygmy with stubby legs;
Poor al-Farazdaq had no Muslim neighbour, someone to look after an ape who can't sleep at night.

Springing to the defence of his sister's and therefrom his tribe's honour, al-Farazdaq responds in kind with a series of retorts. In some of his poems the verbal savaging of Jarīr's tribe, unfortunately called Banū Kulayb ('sons of the puppy', thus affording al-Farazdaq an opportunity for all sorts of variations on the 'sons of bitches' theme) is preceded by a *nasīb* that mentions his cousin-wife, Nawār, whom he had tricked into marriage and was then forced – to his undying regret – to divorce:

I address my companion in consolation, after the ladies turned aside from the dunes of al-ʿAqar,
Exhausted by the sighs of a heart that groans in longing for Nawār ...
To the folks in trouble from Kulayb, dogs squatting under tiny tents,
Women in a fix whose veils cannot hide their disgrace ...

a theme that is elaborated in increasingly obscene detail in later poems:

> The women of the Banū Kulayb spend the evening sitting on their backsides by the alley corners,
> Peddling their vaginas for coins like a market: Hey ho, they shout, come and get it!

Among those who witnessed this extended joust was Bashshār ibn Burd, and in several *hijāʾ* poems addressed to poetic opponents his tone and vocabulary suggest that he has been a careful listener. However, as we noted in ch. 2 (where a poem was cited that lampoons traditional Arab values while glorifying Persian ones), the predominant motif of Bashshār's *hijāʾ* poetry was not the kind of tribal rivalries exemplified by the contest between Jarīr and al-Farazdaq but rather the new and more promising arena represented by the tensions and sensitivities that were aroused by the diverse cultural backgrounds of the expanding Muslim community. While the examples of *hijāʾ* by Jarīr and al-Farazdaq that were cited above were from poems that open in a traditional way, Bashshār follows the trend found in many of their other poems by getting straight to the point. Talking sarcastically about a tribe of al-Baṣrah who have been boosting their numbers with new, non-Arab converts, he says:

> I have checked on the Banū Zayd: among their seniors there is no prudence; among their juniors none of unsullied repute . . .
> To their numbers they append sin-children, so that their throng surpasses everyone else's.

Abū Nuwās, secure perhaps in his status as renowned poet at the court of the Caliph Hārūn al-Rashīd, manages to talk sarcastically about the latter's renowned minister, Jaʿfar al-Barmakī (Hārūn's faithful and long-suffering companion on many escapades in the *Thousand and One Nights*):

> This is the ape era. So just bow down and say: To hear is to obey.

In another poem he comments on the minister's tight-fistedness:

> Every day that God increases Jaʿfar's worldly wealth, I see him getting progressively meaner.

The poet is even prepared to comment sarcastically on Jaʿfar's ill-starred marriage to Hārūn's sister, ʿAbbāsah, a union that is said to have led Hārūn to order his minister killed and his dismembered body displayed on the bridges of Baghdad.

> If you find pleasure in removing some rascal's head,
> Don't kill him with a sword; just marry him to ʿAbbāsah!

Arabic poetry's *locus classicus* for this type of sarcastic attack-poem lies – once again – with al-Mutanabbī, notably his series of *hijāʾ* poems (one of which was excerpted above) that he left behind when he departed Kāfūr's Egypt in a clearly disappointed rage. In another poem from the same series he insults the eunuch regent before once again alluding to the thematic linkages between panegyric and lampoon that we alluded to above:

Till I met this eunuch, I always assumed that the head was the seat
  of wisdom,
but, when I looked into his intelligence, I discovered that all his wisdom
  resided in his testicles . . .
Many's the panegyric I've recited to that rhinoceros, using verse and
  charms,
but it was not a panegyric for him but rather a lampoon of mankind as
  a whole.

Such invective and satire remains a continuing feature of the politics of court life within the Islamic dominions. Ibn ʿUnayn describes the court of Ṣalāḥ al-dīn al-Ayyūbī (Saladin) in this fashion:

Covetousness and lies, that's all people see now as the reason for God's gifts.
The Sultan is lame, his secretary is half-blind, and the minister is humpbacked.

Beyond these verbal assaults on persons in authority, other figures and traits become targets for satirical humour. Here is Bahāʾ al-dīn Zuhayr (d. 1258) on the subject of elaborate beards:

An idiot with a huge, billowing beard.
I searched hard within it for signs of a face, but I failed.
It's someone I know, but that beard has made him anonymous.
Just one tenth of a tenth of it would suffice ten men.
It looks like a rain-cloud hovering over the land.

The changing political circumstances in the Arab world during the course of the twentieth century have radically transformed the social context of Arabic poetry and thus of *hijāʾ*. Burning issues, and especially cultural debates and rivalries, have continued to serve as stimuli for exchanges of insult and jousts. In some societies such as those of the Arabian Peninsula, the traditional modes and contexts have been maintained; indeed, as we noted at the very beginning of this chapter, the Gulf War of 1991 provided such an occasion, and reports suggest that Yemeni poets resorted to the very same below-the-belt themes that so characterise the exchange between Jarīr and al-Farazdaq. However, the post-revolutionary period in most Arab societies (roughly coinciding with the second half of the twentieth century) has been one in which the freedom of writers has been heavily circumscribed – to put it mildly, and, as a consequence, *hijāʾ* directed against authority figures of the kind we have just described has diminished considerably. One poet stands out as an exception to this general rule: Muẓaffar al-Nawwāb (b. 1934). His disgust with the entire authority structure of the Arab world spills out into poetry of a withering, venomous sarcasm:

> The son of Kaʿbah is having sex . . .
> The world's prices must wait!

Rithāʾ: elegy

In her autobiography, *Riḥlah jabaliyyah, riḥlah ṣaʿbah* (1985; *A Mountainous Journey*, London, 1990), the Palestinian poetess, Fadwā Ṭūqān (b. 1917), describes how her elder brother, the poet Ibrāhīm Ṭūqān, introduced her to the treasures of Arabic poetry. Opening Abū Tammām's famous anthology of early poetry, *al-Ḥamāsah*, he recited to her an ancient elegy (*rithāʾ*) by an unknown poetess (usually attributed to either Umm al-Sulayk or the mother of the infamous vagabond poet, Taʾabbaṭa Sharran):

> He wandered the desert in quest of an escape from death, but he perished.
> If only I knew what it was – a terrible error – that killed you . . .
> Whatever track a young man follows, the Fates lie in wait.

Ibrāhīm Ṭūqān explains to his younger sister that he selected this particular poem to show what beautiful Arabic poetry was composed by women.

The *rithāʾ* poem in Arabic (*marthiyyah*, pl. *marāthī*) was intended to memorialise and eulogise someone who had recently died; in earliest times, that often implied death in tribal conflict or as a result of one of the many ways by which desert life could be an agent of imminent death. The large number of elegies composed by women that have been recorded suggests that this communal function was a particular province of women poets, the poems themselves being part of the funeral ritual. The two most celebrated names in the early history of this type of poem are Tumāḍir bint ʿAmr, renowned under the name of al-Khansāʾ (d. before 670), and Laylā al-Akhyāliyyah (d. 704).

Al-Khansāʾ mourns the deaths in tribal conflict of a brother, Muʿāwiyah, and a half-brother, Ṣakhr. In fact, her grief at their loss is the overarching theme of her entire poetic output. The type of lament that is so associated with her name begins directly with a proclamation of the tragedy and the name of the dead hero:

When nights bring disaster, I will never find among folk the likes of
Muʿāwiyah . . .
nor will I see another cavalier like the white knight whenever valour and
prowess raise him to the heights.

or this *marthiyyah*, one among many written in tribute to her half-brother:

When night draws on, remembering keeps me wakeful
And hinders my rest with grief upon grief returning
For Ṣakhr . . .

The initial salute to the dead hero will often be followed by an account of the dire event itself and a recounting of his virtues, particularly as a warrior in battle. Continuing with the same Ṣakhr poem:

. . . What a man was he on the day of battle,
When, snatching their chance, they swiftly exchange the spear-thrusts.

The *rithāʾ* will often end with words of advice for the tribe, and, if the incident is part of a continuing feud, with calls for retribution against those who carried out the foul deed. While other examples can be used to illustrate these features, al-Khansāʾ's elegies are renowned (and have thus been preserved and cherished) for the way in which she personalises her grief:

O Ṣakhr! I will ne'er forget thee until in dying
I part from my soul, and earth for my tomb is cloven.
The rise of the sun recalls to me Sakhr my brother,
And him I remember also at every sunset.

(Nicholson, *Eastern Poetry & Prose*, Cambridge, 1922, p. 19)

In the case of Laylā al-Akhyāliyyah, the focus of her grief is a beloved named Tawbah; among the few recorded poems that make up her *dīwān* is this *marthiyyah*:

Splendid knight you were, O Tawbah, when high points came together
and lowlands were raised.
Splendid knight you were, O Tawbah, not to be surpassed on the day
of your endeavour.
Splendid knight you were, O Tawbah, when the timorous would seek
your protection; splendid too were your fine deeds.

While the performance of short elegies memorialising the slain heroes of the community seems to have been a particular function of women poets, there are also many examples of elegies, both short and long, composed by men. It has been suggested that longer and more complex forms are more characteristic of male elegaic poetry and that the shorter poems by male poets are recorded extracts of longer compositions, but, given the modes whereby the poetic tradition was transmitted and consigned to written form, such notions are difficult to confirm. Certainly, a point of difference can be shown in the way that an early poet-warrior such as Durayd ibn al-Ṣimmah (d. 630) manages to inject into one of his elegies for his slain brother, ʿAbdallāh, a vivid and particularised depiction of tribal conflict:

> My brother yelled out when we were separated by horsemen; when
> he called, he did not find me one to hold back.
> I reached him to find spears piercing his body like the fall of shuttles
> on an outstretched weave . . .
> I kept the horsemen away from him till they gave up, while a flow of
> black blood overwhelmed me . . .
> The horsemen have slain a warrior, they shouted; is it ʿAbdallāh they
> have killed, I asked.
> If indeed it is ʿAbdallāh who has left his space empty, he was not one
> to shirk a fight, nor was his aim untrue . . .
> As a youth he did youthful things, but then, when the grey hairs
> appeared, he bade farewell to frivolity.

Durayd's poem is a typical poetic product of the continuing pattern of raids and battles among the tribal confederacies of the Arabian peninsula – of which the Wars of Basūs and of Dāḥis and Ghabrāʾ have already been mentioned as examples – affording ample occasion for poems of praise for heroic warriors coupled with boasts of prowess and calls for vengeance. One of the most famous examples of this subgenre is a *rithāʾ* poem attributed to the famous vagabond poet, Ta'abbaṭa Sharran. The poem describes how the death of a relative at the hands of the rival tribe of Hudhayl has been savagely avenged:

> In the glen there a murdered man is lying –
> Not in vain for vengeance his blood is crying.
> He has left me the load to bear and departed:
> I take up the load and bear it true-hearted . . .
> First, of foeman's blood my spear deeply drinketh,
> Then a second time, deep in, it sinketh . . .
> O'er the fallen of Hudhail stands screaming
> The hyena; see the wolf's teeth gleaming!
> Dawn will hear the flap of wings, will discover
> Vultures treading corpses, too gorged to hover.

Nicholson, *Eastern Poetry & Prose*, 15–17

This heroic spirit – reflected in the themes of fighting for a worthy cause, confronting the inevitability of death, mourning lost comrades, and calling out for revenge – is carried over into the Islamic period most noticeably in the poetry of groups opposed to the policies of the central authorities; the anthologies record poems and extracts by poets of the Shīʿah and Khawārij. Shīʿī poets such as Kuthayyir ʿAzzah (d. 724–also renowned as a love-poet) and al-Kumayt (d. 743), who was killed for satirising the Umawī governor of Iraq, certainly used their poems to express opposition to the interests of the Umawī dynasty, but the spirit of fierce defiance and struggle that is so much a part of the early desert poetry is best reflected in the work of Khārijī poets. ʿImrān ibn Ḥaṭṭān (d. 703) mourns the loss of one of the group's warriors thus:

> Shed tears for Mirdās and his death, my eye; O Lord of Mirdās, let me join him!
> He has left me in despair, to mourn in a desolate dwelling that was once abustle . . .
> For a while I mourned for you, then my heart despaired; but that could not dispel my tears.

while, in elegising another Khārijī hero, the poet says:

> I am wary of dying in my bed; I hope to die beneath a rain of spear-heads . . .
> Some may have this world as their concern; as for me, by God the Lord of the Kaʿbah, I abhor it!

Another Khārijī poet, ibn Abī Mayyās, expresses exultation at the vengeance wreaked on the fourth Caliph, ʿAlī, who was assassinated by a Khārijī named ibn Muljam:

> However costly, no dowry can rival in value the death of ʿAlī; no deadly attack can equal that of ibn Muljam.

These poems provide ample evidence of the way in which many of the genres and themes of the pre-Islamic poetic tradition were readily adapted to the religious and political tensions that so characterised the era of the Umawī caliphs. On the official and even ceremonial level, a poet such as al-Farazdaq, whom we have encountered above as a notable lampoonist and who was a recognised supporter of the Shīʿah cause, could find himself called upon to elegise al-Ḥajjāj, the notorious governor of Iraq, who had been utterly ruthless in suppressing the varying manifestations of opposition to the Umawī caliphs in Damascus. He does so in a poem that replicates a traditional *marthiyyah* pattern: the announcement of the dead hero at the beginning of the poem and the dreadful impact of the event itself, a recounting of the funeral rites, a reference – in this instance probably recited through gritted teeth – to the 'pastoral' qualities of the elegy's subject, and finally a reference to the consolation that is to be found in the sterling qualities of the Umawī caliph.

The patronage afforded to poets within the elaborate structures of the caliphal court and other centres of authority provided a plethora of occasions for elegies of this official kind. In the context of such exalted halls, the poet was expected to transform the death of a member of the ruling élite from a context of purely personal grief into a matter of major communal significance. Upon the death of the mother of Sayf al-dawlah, the Ḥamdānī ruler of Aleppo, for example, al-Mutanabbī composed an elaborate ceremonial elegy for the occasion. Beginning in that gnomic fashion for which his poems are so renowned, the poet notes that he is no stranger to adversity; this tragedy however is more than he can bear. The deceased lady is then extolled in fulsome fashion; the poet draws attention to her generosity and, more controversially, her beauty – a gesture that was roundly criticised in a work on al-Mutanabbī's faults by al-Ṣāḥib ibn ʿAbbād (d. 995), a prominent arbiter of taste whose contributions will be considered in the following chapter. The imagery evokes the by now familar play on nostalgia and absence:

> Under compulsion you now reside in a place far removed from the winds of south and north;
> Veiled from you is lavender scent, kept away is the dew of rains
> In a house where every dweller is a stranger, long absent, all ties severed.

As with al-Farazdaq's elegy, the poet concludes with a stirring address to his patron:

> Sayf al-dawlah, seek help in forbearance; for what are mountains when compared with yours?
> You offer people counsel in consolation and in defying death in the fickle chances of war.

Through the agency of the *marthiyyah* composed by the patronised poet a family loss becomes a communal tragedy, and yet the presence of the enlightened Muslim ruler is a continuing source of consolation. The sense of disaster becomes more intense, needless to say, when the very fabric of Islamic society is attacked. In 871 for example, al-Baṣrah, the garrison city and port in southern Iraq that had become a major intellectual centre, was devastated by the Zanj, an army of slave labourers. Ibn al-Rūmī (d. 896) composed a *marthiyyah* (cited above in ch. 1) bewailing the fall of the city and the massacre of its inhabitants; the repetitions which mark the beginnings of so many lines give the elegy a plangent quality:

> What sleep is there after the enormous catastrophes that have beset al-Baṣrah?
> What sleep is there now that the Zanj have flagrantly violated the sanctuaries of Islam itself? . . .
> My heart is seared with grief for you, poor al-Baṣrah, with flames of burning fire . . .
> My heart is seared with a grief for you, dome of Islam, a grief that prolongs my affliction;
> My heart is seared with a grief for you, port from lands afar, that will linger for many years . . .

The poet describes the massacre of the city's people, old and young, male and female, and the destruction of its buildings, before invoking the most ancient of images:

> My two companions, turn off the road to al-Baṣrah the resplendent, but as one who is sick and unwell,
> and question the city – yet there will be no answer, for who is left to speak?

The elegy ends with a call for swift retribution, and the poet makes a clear linkage between the ancient call for blood-vengeance and the present imperatives of the community of faithful:

> Pursue vengeance for the people's blood; such a deed will
> be like endowing their bodies once again with spirits . . .
> You people, the city's shame clings to you, for religions
> are like blood-ties.

In the ensuing centuries the *marthiyyah* continues to fulfil this role as public record of the community's direst moments. Ibn al-Mujāwir (d. 1204) recounts the fall of the al-Aqṣā Mosque in Jerusalem to the Crusaders:

> The entire domain should weep over Jerusalem and proclaim its sorrow and grief;
> Mecca should do likewise, for it is Jerusalem's sister; and it should protest to ʿArafāt itself the treatment meted out.

Following the Mongol destruction of Baghdad in 1258 a poet from al-Kūfah, Shams al-dīn al-Kūfī, pays a return visit to the shattered city:

> What of the homes whose people are no longer my people, whose neighbours are not mine?
> By my life, what befell Baghdad after you was death, destruction, and torch . . .
> After you left, I went to the house, and stood helpless before it.
> I questioned it, but without speech; I spoke but with no tongue . . .
> It replied: When all was overthrown, they left, exchanging scorn for glory.
> The vicissitudes of fate have obliterated them as they did of old to the monarchs of Persia.

The Egyptian historian, ibn Iyās, rues the fall of Cairo in 1516 to the Ottoman army under Sultan Selīm the Grim:

> Mourn for Egypt, struck by a calamity so grave that it affects mankind as a whole.

In the twentieth century it is the Palestinian people that has often faced disaster; the corpus of its poetry contains, not surprisingly, many echoes of the elegaic tradition. In an elegy entitled 'My Sad City' ('*Madinatī al-ḥazīnah*') Fadwā Ṭūqān, whose introduction to the genre by her brother opened this section, echoes the words of ibn al-Rūmī many centuries earlier:

> Children and songs vanished
> No shadow, no echo.
> In my city sorrow crawled naked
> With smattered tread.
> In my city all is silence . . .
> O my silent, sad city
> At harvest time
> Are grains and fruits on fire
> Has everything thus come full-circle?

Another modern Palestinian poetess, Salmā Khaḍrā' al-Jayyūsī, mourns her homeland's martyrs:

> I know that they died 'so the homeland might live on' . . .
> I know that, yet the grief in the depths of my heart does not know
> I weep for every eye that has lost the light of life,
> Every soul that flowed out through opened lips.

Along with these examples of the more public type of elegy, the poets' *dīwān*s contain many expressions of grief in a more personal context. Al-Mutanabbī mourns his grandmother in a famous poem, and the Shīʿī poet, al-Sharīf al-Raḍī (d. 1016) writes a touching ode on the death of his sister. The lengthy elegy that Abū al-ʿAlāʾ al-Maʿarrī (d. 1958) composed on the death of a close relative was a heartfelt expression of the deepest sense of loss, providing a *locus classicus* for the 'ubi sunt' (where are they now?) theme that is so prevalent in the tradition of Arabic ascetic poetry (*zuhdiyyah*) – to be examined below – of which he was such a prominent exponent:

> Lighten your tread; I think the surface of the earth is nothing but the bodies of the dead,
> so proceed slowly in the air and do not trample the remains of God's servants underfoot.

However, few elegies can match the poignancy of those that recount the agonies of that most awful of family tragedies, the death of a child. Ibn al-Rūmī is one such father who mourns his middle son, Muḥammad:

> Short indeed was his time between cradle and grave; he had not even forgotten the cradle when he was enclosed in the grave …
> My eyes! Be generous with your tears; for I have given the earth the most precious gift I possess …
> Though you [my son] may be alone in a desolate house, I am just as desolate among the living …
> God's peace be with you – a greeting from me and every rain-cloud endowed with thunder and lightning.

Bashshār ibn Burd laments the loss of a son of the same name:

> After Muḥammad's death I feel a stranger, yet with his passing death is no longer a stranger to us …
> I have endured the loss of the best of boys; he is taken from me and, but for faith in God, I would have prolonged my grief.

A similar, albeit less intense, kind of personalised sentiment often emerges in the elegies that poets compose for their departed colleagues. We have already noted Jarīr's poem on the death of his longtime adversary, al-Farazdaq. In the early decades of the twentieth century, Aḥmad Shawqī (d. 1932) who took full advantage of the new opportunities that the press offered to publish elegies on a number of literary figures, Arab and Western, found himself delivering an elegy on this long-time neo-classical companion in poetry, Ḥāfiẓ Ibrāhīm (d. 1932) a few months before his own death. Beginning with the wish that the roles of the two had been reversed, Shawqī acknowledges Ḥāfiẓ's role as a neo-classical poet, punning on his friend's own name as he invokes the great poets of the past:

Preserver [Ḥāfiẓ] of literary Arabic, guardian of its glories, leader of the eloquent,
You continued to proclaim the virtues of the past and protected the authenticity of the ancient poets.
You renewed the style of al-Walīd [al-Buhturī] and brought the world the magic of al-Ṭā'ī [Abū Tammām].

In closing he salutes his fellow poet and, by implication, all others from the heritage of the past whose verses have been recorded:

You have left to the world everlasting eloquence, bequeathed to generations of children;
On the morrow time will remember you; for fate is still a fair dispenser of reward.

Wasf: description.

The three modes that we have just discussed – eulogy, lampoon, and elegy – subsume within their purview a large percentage of ancient Arabic poetry. From the earliest stages they were identified by collectors and anthologisers of the poetic tradition as rubrics under which themes and the values that they reflected could be most effectively categorised. In addition to these three primary purposes (*aghrāḍ*), those who set about analysing the poetic corpus also identified a fourth feature, that of description (*wasf*). As we have already noted, many poems were polythematic structures that would regularly incorporate more than one purpose: a section boasting about the prowess of the tribe's warriors might also pour scorn on the effeminate qualities of their foes; indeed an elegy intended to honour a dead hero might conclude with a eulogy to a living ruler. Descriptions of a wide variety of phenomena were an intrinsic feature of these various segments of the poem; indeed the poet-critic ibn Rashīq, who, as we have already seen, is always a highly quotable summariser of the features of the poetic tradition that he inherited, notes that actually the bulk of Arabic poetry could be subsumed under the heading of description.

In ch. 2 it was observed that Arabian tribes eked out a living as animal herders and that this livelihood naturally led them to prize horses and camels in particular for their hardy qualities. They travelled and lived within an environment that was both inhospitable and fragile. This centrality of desert animals to the life and symbolic code of the community is graphically illustrated by the vast wealth of vocabulary used to depict them within the poetic corpus; some of the most colourful lexemes take the form of reserved epithets (snub-nose, thick-hump, red-colour). The lonely wolf of the poems of al-Shanfarā and Imru al-Qays howling at dead of night to his mates, the extended similes in Labīd's *muʿallaqah* that lead him to include elaborate depictions of a pair of onagers speeding across the desert at the different seasons and of the female oryx protecting its calf against the attacks of hunting dogs, these passages certainly provide the Western reader with vivid images of an unfamiliar landscape. Here, for example, is part of the wonderful scene that ʿAbīd ibn al-Abraṣ (d. *c.* 554) narrates in comparing his horse with an eagle swooping down to pounce on a fox:

She spent the night, stock-still, on a hillock, like an old crone whose children have died,
She was still there at dawn on a frigid morning, the frost dripping off her feathers.
Then in a trice she spotted a fox, the barren desert between them . . .
Swiftly she rose in the air towards him and then swooped downwards.
Terrified at the sound of her wings, he raised his tail, the reaction of one in a panic.
She grabbed him and dropped him from on high; beneath her the prey is in torment.
She smashed him to the ground and crushed him, and the sharp stones ripped his face apart.
He was screaming all the while, but her talons were embedded in his side and his chest was ripped apart.

While admiring the startling vivid imagery of such a passage, one should not overlook the way in which the themes it represents, the fight for survival and adaptability to a fickle environment, interact so powerfully with the lives of the human communities sharing the same terrain. Those groups made up the audience that would listen with relish as their poet used the *qaṣīdah* to celebrate their most prized memories and aspirations, including in his performance lengthy and elaborate descriptions of their beloved animals. These passages thus acquire a tremendous symbolic resonance and inevitably become a primary locus of the Arabic poetic tradition's classical ideals. The very size of the repertoires of poetry and anecdote dealing with desert flora and fauna that were gathered into anthologies beginning in the eighth century–al-Jāḥiẓ's *Kitāb al-ḥayawān* (Book of Animals) being merely the most renowned among many – serve to illustrate the enduring value that was attached to them. Indeed, reactions to the poetry of Dhū al-Rummah suggest that his repute may have suffered because of his emphasis on these 'classical' elements. For, while to some critics his continued resort to desert imagery makes him 'the last of the (desert) poets', to others the increasingly vigorous and closely focused modes of eulogy and satire – as practised by Jarīr, al-Farazdaq, and others – was more in tune with what were admittedly contentious times.

The most elaborate and famous depictions of animal life are to be found in the central section of the early *qaṣīdah*, where the poet narrates a dangerous journey by camel into the desert wastes. The qualities of the trusted riding-beast are catalogued in great detail and compared with those of a variety of other denizens of the desert. When the poem turns to the process of reintegration and tribal solidarity, there is opportunity for a wide variety of other description. Labīd, it will be recalled, talks about gaming and feasts. Ṭarafah's *muʿallaqah* includes one of the most famous descriptions of a camel (*nāqah*) in the entire poetic corpus before re-entering the tribal fold with a notable picture of his preferences in entertainment:

> Seek me out at the tribe's assembly and you will find me; if you track me to the taverns, you will find your target too.
> My companions gleam like stars, and in comes a singing-girl wearing a striped blouse and scented gown;
> Her neckline is wide-open, and her exposed skin is soft to the touch of my companions.
> When we ask her to sing for us, she starts, improvising in leisurely fashion with a languid glance;
> As she repeats her song, her voice sounds to me like the cries of an oryx-mother looking in vain for her spring fawn.

The latter part of Imru al-Qays's *muʿallaqah* includes a much cited picture of a horse, both as idealised riding animal and as proficient hunter, but the poem closes with a vivid picture of the desert after a thunderstorm, linking in a single scene the violence of sudden death and the promise of new growth:

> The storm pours its rain on Kutayfah, uprooting the lofty *kanahbul* trees,
> Then passes over Mount al-Qanān in a deluge, so that the goats have to leave their favoured spots,
> And on Mount Taymāʾ not a single palm-trunk or dwelling is left standing, unless bulwarked with stones . . .
> It unleashes its load on the desert of Ghabīṭ, like a Yemeni with loaded bales.
> At daybreak, the valley-birds sound as though they have drunk a draught of mulled wine,
> while at twilight the beasts who have drowned in its remote parts look like roots of wild-onion.

The changes that have already been noted above in connection with the performance context and generic purposes of the *qaṣīdah* and therefrom with its structural logic inevitably led to a transformation in the role of description. In the panegyric poem (*madīḥ*) in particular, the journey section (*raḥīl*) becomes less of an exploration of the risks of solitude and more of a process of directing oneself towards the *mamdūḥ*, the person to be eulogised. While a poet like Dhū al-Rummah endeavoured to maintain the validity and authenticity of the pre-Islamic vision, the imagery that had been contained within the lengthy depictions of desert scenes and animal qualities becomes a classical repertoire of nostalgia for the glories of a lost past – in Jaroslav Stetkevych's terms (*The Zephyrs of Najd*, Chicago, 1993), Arabia's Najd as a kind of Arcadia. Here, for example, is ibn Khafājah (d. *c.* 1039), the great Andalusian poet, so remote in both time and place:

> Is Najd aware that in my eyes tears are welling which pour down, while grief extends between them?
> O tents of Najd, Tihāmah and Najd stand between us, a broad pace for night-travel, and the camel's gentle tread.
> O oryx of Najd, hardships are many through the dictates of destiny, and few indeed are the loyal.

While many poets continued to make use of the ancient sites and place names of Arabia as focuses of nostalgic resonance in their poems, other poets chose to reflect changes in poetic venue and audience by addressing the heritage of the past through a resort to different locations and structures. A short panegyric addressed to the caliph al-Mahdī by the poet Abū al-Atāhiyah (d. *c.* 825) opens with,

> My grief for the brief while spent between Khawarnaq and Sadīr.

Here the twin sites are not located in the Arabian desert (as, say, al-Dakhūl and Ḥawmal in the opening line of Imru al-Qays's *muʿallaqah*) but instead are the names of two palaces at al-Ḥīrah in Iraq, the hunting lodges of pre-Islamic Lakhmī kings and their Sāsānī Persian overlords. They set the scene for a depiction of an earthly paradise:

> When we were in the chambers of paradise, afloat in a sea of pleasure . . .
> They pass around the choicest of the crimson wine . . .
> And slender maids visit us after the tranquility of their boudoirs,
> Plump-buttocked, wearing bangles at their waists . . .

And then, in the midst of this luxuriance, the poet tells how he urges on his riding-beast to the palace of 'God's trustee' before bringing the poem to a somewhat abrupt conclusion six lines later.

For al-Buḥturī, generally acknowledged as one of the finest exponents of descriptive poetry in Arabic, the resort in times of adversity is to another Sāsānī monument, the ruins of the palace at Madā'in (Ctesiphon), the so-called *īwān* of Chosroes (Kisrā). The poem opens with an assertion of the poet's rectitude and of regret that his worth has not been recognised. He turns his camel towards Madā'in,

> seeking consolation from adversity and grieving for an abode of the House of Sāsān that had decayed.

He notices a striking wall-painting that depicts a battle at Antioch in 540 between Persian and Byzantine forces and visualises the fighting. Given a draught of wine by his companion, the poet imagines that the monarch Anūshirwān himself is offering him the drink; the building has been restored to its former glory and is filled with embassies and entertainers:

> As though, when I have achieved the limit of my perception, I can see ranks and people,
> Delegations standing in the sun, ruing the delay as they wait in line . . .

By reviving glorious memories of the past in this way, al-Buhturī seeks to reassure himself and his patrons that true mettle of this kind is the soundest foundation for a polyethnic community:

> After this I see myself more attached to people of nobility as a whole, drawn from every origin and base.

It is at the site of another palace that the Andalusian poet, ibn Zaydūn (d. 1070), recalls blissful times of old spent with his beloved, Wallādah:

> Longingly I recalled you in al-Zahrā', when the horizon was cloudless and the face of the earth gleamed,
> When at eventide the breeze grew languid, as though it pitied my plight and showed compassion;
> The garden smiled to reveal its silvery fountains, as though you had loosed necklaces from around the throats of maidens.

It has to be said that the lingering affection seems to have been entirely one-sided in that Wallādah's own poetry about ibn Zaydūn is excessively uncomplimentary:

> For all his virtue ibn Zaydūn loves rods inside trousers.
> If he spotted a penis up a palm-tree, he'd turn into a whole flock of birds,

the final phrase being an evocation of the fourth verse of *Sūrat al-fīl* (105, The Elephant). Whatever the wishful thinking involved, the poet is here invoking a place that has tremendous nostalgic significance for him personally, but the regret so poignantly expressed in this and other poems needs to be placed in a wider context. His beloved, Wallādah, was a princess in the Umawī house of Andalusian caliphs centred in Cordoba. The caliphate had been abolished in 1031 and replaced by the so-called party-kings (*mulūk al-ṭawāʾif*). The great caliphal capital had lost much of its prestige, and the glittering palace of Madīnat al-Zahrāʾ had been burned. Another poet, ibn Shuhayd (d. 1035), had already lamented Cordoba's fate and reminisced about the glorious times of the past when,

> The palace, the court of the Banū Umayyah, was the provider of all
> things, while the Caliphate was yet more munificent.

Ibn Zaydūn's choice of the burned out ruins of an Umawī palace as the site for a nostalgic and wistful contemplation on his ill-starred love for Wallādah thus assumes a much broader significance.

Ibn Zaydūn's image of the garden introduces another favourite topic of the Arabic poem. Bearing in mind the visual splendour of the gardens in Andalusian palaces such al-Ḥamrāʾ (Alhambra) in Granada, we should not be surprised to discover that they are a much favoured topic of poets. Ibn Khafājah was cited above for his resort to imagery of the desert, but he can also set his scene,

> In a garden where the shade was dark as ruby lips and blossoms sprung
> up as white as pearly teeth;
> In it danced the tree-branch after sipping the soil; the collar-doves sang,
> and the brook clapped with joy.

The basic Arabic word for garden (*jannah*) also carries connotations of Paradise, and the Qurʾān itself is not alone among sacred texts in linking the two. In a phrase that is repeated on many occasions throughout the text, the faithful who perform good works are promised a paradise where they will find 'gardens with rivers flowing underneath them' (for example, *Sūrat al-baqarah* (Surah 2, The Cow) v. 25). Given the Arabian environment into which the Qurʾān was originally revealed, the difference between this promised haven of bliss and the realities of daily life was great indeed. As the Muslim community expanded beyond the Arabian environment and became acquainted with a wide diversity of cultures and climes, the development of the concept of garden as an earthly replication of paradise seems a natural consequence. The delights of the hereafter and the path towards them were a subject of contemplation for some poets, but for the most part it was to the garden as terrestrial paradise that poets devoted the most attention. Al-Buḥturī describes one such in Iraq:

> Many are the gardens in the Jazīrah, the Tigris frolicking with their rivulets;
> They reveal emeralds to your gaze, all scattered; the light enhances their gleam,
> Strange delights that catch the eye when the sun reveals their hue . . .
> When a breeze rustles the branches, it is as though maidens were walking there . . .

while ibn al-Rūmī describes,

> Many are the gardens where the earth flaunts its beauty like a girl in fine clothes,
> Decked in brocade, but the weavers here are night and morning clouds skilled with the stitch.

The garden is above all the place of encounter with the beloved, and, as the above examples show, its most prized attributes are hers. The tradition is carried on by ibn al-Muʿtazz:

> Pomegranate trees, their fruits looking like carnelian boxes filled with pearls;
> Amid the branches they seem like virgin cheeks laid on green coverlets.

And, with al-Ṣanawbarī (d. 945), the garden extravaganza reaches its acme:

> Many a narcissus, with its white and yellow, is doubled in beauty;
> Pearl and gold are blended in it, as are musk and ambergris.

He describes the city of Damascus thus:

> For its inhabitants the world of Damascus is serene; you will not see the like of it elsewhere . . .
> In it crystal streams flow through gardens that grow brocade.
> Thus, there are apples to rival cheeks, and lemons that would not discredit breasts.

In a final twist of the garden theme we can point to an interesting flight of the imagination by Ṣafī al-dīn al-Ḥillī. He composes a poem in which the garden serves as the venue for an argument, not between humans but among a group of flowers; the iris claims authority over the rose and lily, and the other flowers protest.

Groups of *wasf* poems, particularly those that continue this predilection for the portrayal of aspects of nature, remain a feature of *dīwāns* of Arab poets until the modern period. An eighteenth century poet such as ʿAbd al-ghanī al-Nābulusī (d. 1731) composes a line devoted to the depiction of a flower:

a carnation in the garden, resembling drops of blood on the water-surface,

while twentieth-century poets such as Aḥmad Shawqī and Khalīl Muṭrān (d. 1949) devote several of their *wasf* poems to portrayals of nature; in Shawqī's case one such poem devoted to the Bois de Boulogne in Paris becomes an occasion for a nostalgic remembrance of his time in France. However, in Muṭrān's famous poem, 'Evening' ('*al-Masāʾ*'), we catch a glimpse of that process of change whereby the emphasis shifts (to cite Charles Rosen, referring to Schiller) from 'the evocation of the beauties and the delights of a pastoral existence [or] the virtuosity of the artist's imitation of the objects of Nature' to 'the correspondence between the sensuous experience of Nature and the spiritual and intellectual workings of the mind' [*The Romantic Generation*, 129]. This change is seen in its fullest bloom in the poetry of Khalīl Jubrān (d. 1931), notably in his 'Processions' ('*al-Mawākib*'), a lengthy contemplation of the human condition that advocates a return to the primitive realm of the forest (*al-ghāb*):

In the forest is life to be lived, and, did I have gathered within my grasp the passing of days, it is there that I would scatter them.

The romantic poet situating himself in the midst of nature is personified by ʿAlī Maḥmūd Ṭāhā (d. 1949) in 'Rustic Song' ('*Ughniyah rīfiyyah*'):

When the water strokes the shade of the tree and the clouds flirt with the moonlight . . .
I have taken my place in its shade with distracted heart and downcast eyes.

The most vivid contrast to these idyllic pictures of nature, the countryside, and gardens is provided by the city, that haven of political and administrative complications and of all that is cruel and corrupt. The Egyptian poet, Aḥmad ʿAbd al-muʿṭī Ḥijāzī (b. 1935), uses a 'Basket of Lemons' ('*Sallat līmūn*') to symbolise the ways in which the metropolis exploits the surrounding countryside:

A basket of lemons left the village at dawn.
Green it was till that cursed moment and laden with dewdrops,
Floating on waves of shade;
In its verdant slumber it was the birds' own bride.
Ah me!
Who alarmed it so?
Which hungry hand plucked it at today's dawn
And under cover of earliest twilight brought it
To congested, crowded streets,
Rushing feet, cars burning petrol
As they move by!
Poor thing! ...

In ch. 2 we cited part of a poem by al-Bayātī on the destructive nature of urban society, but perhaps the most richly complex and savage poetic attack on a city is that of Adūnīs in 'A Grave for New York' ('*Qabr min ajl New York*') – composed in the 1970s at the time of the Vietnam War:

New York:
A woman, statue of a woman
In one hand she holds up a scrap of paper we call freedom,
so called by another piece of paper we term history,
While with another hand she throttles a baby called the earth ...
New York plus New York equals the grave or whatever emerges from it;
New York minus New York equals the sun.

To return to our starting-point in this section devoted to the somewhat anomalous category of *wasf*, a large percentage of Arabic poetry in all its variety can be reckoned as fitting its terms of reference. The topics that have been selected for illustration here are intended purely as examples, culled from a wealth of poetry and image which the contemporary poet has to confront, exploit, or reject.

Ghazal: love poetry.

Honoré de Balzac's story, 'Sarassine', analysed by Roland Barthes in *S/Z* (1970), talks at one point about 'a girl of sixteen whose beauty embodied the fabled imaginings of Eastern poets. Like the Sultan's daughter, in the story of the Magic Lamp, she should have been kept veiled ... ' If we leave aside Balzac's perhaps anticipatable evocations of the fantasy worlds of the *Thousand and One Nights*, the 'imaginings' of Eastern poets are part of a tradition of Arabic love poetry (*ghazal*), the origins of which coincide with the earliest period in Islamic history. (We should point out here that the important tradition of *ghazal* in both

Persian and Turkish literature which developed at a later date is essentially a separate genre.) The verbal root GH-Z-L has as a basic meaning the spinning of thread, but, from the earliest stages of Arabic lexicography and the recording of its poetic evidence, the idea of the lover spinning a charming thread of conversation with the beloved has made the root the primary semantic base for the expression of love, the use of the eyes in flirting, and, through a charming extension to the world of fauna, the delicate attributes of the gazelle.

The precedents to the emergence of *ghazal* as a separate genre in Arabic can be seen most clearly in the opening section of the pre-Islamic *qaṣīdah*, known as the *nasīb*, a structural feature that recent studies of the modern Arabian tradition (such as those of Sowayan and Kurpershoek) show to be still predominant. The mood in a large number of *nasīb* sections is one of nostalgia for times that are for ever gone; of longing, absence, and wistful memories. ʿAlqamah's Salmā, Labīd's Nawār, Ṭarafah's Khawlah, Zuhayr's Umm ʿAwfā, al-Aʿshā's Suʿād, Laylā, and others, and, in the Umawī period, Dhū al-Rummah's Mayy, these are all female names used by the poets to invoke memories of the image of a now far-distant beloved, leaving the speaker of the poem, often in the company of companions, to question, to remember, to regret. Ṭarafah begins his *muʿallaqah*:

> Khawlah has left traces by the outcrops of Tahmad, that show like tattoo traces on the hand.

Labīd's *qaṣīdah* echoes the statement but without naming the beloved, and then goes on to note:

> Since the time when I knew the company of these ruins so well, many years have gone by, months sacred and otherwise . . .

When he comes to mention Nawār by name, it is in the context of absence:

> Nay, what do you recall of Nawār? She is far away, and all links, both strong and weak, are severed.

These themes may perhaps be viewed as the natural expression of poetic sentiment in a society where gender roles were closely monitored, and occasions of aggregation (such as the annual 'gathering of the clans' during a month when all conflicts were suspended) might be followed by prolonged months of desert travel. Al-ʿArjī (d. 738) echoes the complaint of Labīd when he says:

> We spend a complete year without meeting, unless it is on the pilgrimage,
> if she undertakes it;
> And what of Minā and its folk, if she does not?

The most renowned of the *muʿallaqāt*, that of Imru al-Qays, begins in a way that fits the pattern; indeed it is the *locus classicus* for the image:

> Tarry, my two companions, and let us weep for the memory of a beloved
> and a place, at the sand-dune's edge between al-Dakhūl and Ḥawmal.

However, Imru al-Qays's poem then proceeds to break the above pattern. Indeed it is fondly remembered – and, as we will see in ch. 7, roundly condemned by the conservative critic, al-Bāqillānī – for the series of episodes following this beginning in which the beloved, indeed a series of beloveds, is very much present:

> The day I entered ʿUnayzah's howdah; 'Curses on you!' she protested,
> 'you'll make me dismount'.
> All the while the howdah kept swaying. 'You've hobbled my camel, Imru
> al-Qays', she said, 'so get down'.

This scene is followed by a description of another woman (referred to as 'the jewel (lit. 'the egg') of the boudoir') which, in its sheer extravagance, was to become another *locus classicus* as the portrayal of a male-narrated ideal of feminine beauty and deportment. However, the poet's inclusion of his own name in the above line also suggests that the focus of these episodes is not so much the mutual aspects of relationships with women, but rather a narcissistic account of his own success as a lover; the depiction of his prowess as a hunter of women, one might suggest, precedes that of an animal hunt which is so prominent a feature of the latter part of the poem.

It is against this background that the *ghazal*, essentially a new development in Arabic poetry, emerged in the early days of the community of Muslims; the location was the Ḥijāz region of the Arabian peninsula with its twin holy cities of Mecca and Medina. This conjunction may at first seem an odd one, but we should recall that, while Islam engendered tremendous changes in many aspects of life, other activities continued as they had always done. One of the latter was commerce. Thus, while the armies of the new Muslim community were carrying the new faith to much of the region at the eastern end of the Mediterranean, the Ḥijāz region itself, protected as always by its forbidding geographical surroundings, continued as a thriving commercial centre, while at the same time adjusting to its new role as a centre of Muslim pilgrimage (which, in the case of the Kaʿbah in Mecca, was a continuation of pre-Islamic practice). The Prophet Muḥammad himself, it will be recalled, had earned a wide reputation while managing the commercial interests of his first wife, Khadījah, in Mecca, and his renown as a mediator was a primary factor in the decision of the tribes at Medina to invite him to serve in that capacity. It was from this mercantile aristocracy of Mecca that one of Arabic's greatest love poets, ʿUmar ibn Abī Rabīʿah (d. 712), emerged; indeed, so great is his repute that the adjective ʿUmarī is regularly employed to refer to the unrestrained Ḥijāzī type of *ghazal*.

While ʿUmar was on occasion capable of writing poems which replicated the themes and moods of the pre-Islamic tradition, the genuine innovation that he brought to love poetry was to relinquish the mood of nostalgia – love in the past tense – in favour of a view of love as a Don Juanesque sport very much in the present. In so doing he was very aware of using the scenes from Imru al-Qays's *muʿallaqah* as precedent. Indeed the similarity can be shown to be even closer: during Imru al-Qays's detailed description of the 'lady of the boudoir' ('*bayḍat al-khidr*'), he leads her away from the encampment:

> I took her with me; as we walked, she was pulling the hem of an
> embroidered garment over our footsteps.

This image is exactly replicated by ʿUmar:

> Behind me they dragged the hems of their garments, of soft material, so
> that the footsteps should not be discovered.

However there is a major difference: once Imru al-Qays has described the lady's beauty, he closes the scene with a gnomic verse about 'the follies of men' before moving on to other topics; on the other hand, ʿUmar's companions are his lover's maids sneaking him out of the encampment disguised as a woman. For ʿUmar, amorous conquests are a continuing goal; love is a game, a process of overcoming obstacles. The love poem is peopled by those expressing love and their inamoratae, but important roles in the narrative are also given to confidants with whom to share secrets and informers whose task it is to thwart the passionate intentions of the lovers. In a spirit of prankish irreverence, ʿUmar chooses some of his most exotic targets from among pilgrims to Mecca. He – or, perhaps more accurately, his poetic persona – is found 'standing on the corner, watching all the [pilgrim] girls go by':

I spotted her at night walking with her women between the shrine and the [Kaʿbah] stone.
'Well then', she said to a companion, 'for ʿUmar's sake let us spoil this circumambulation.
Go after him so that he may spot us, then, sweet sister, give him a coy wink'.
'But I already did', she said, 'and he turned away'.
Whereupon she came rushing after me.

Besides providing an illustration of decidedly unholy behaviour in the sacred mosque in Mecca, these lines also illustrate some of the features that made ʿUmar's poetry so popular. Once again emulating Imru al-Qays but expanding considerably on the model, ʿUmar introduces realistic segments of flirtatious conversation in his poems, expressed in a level of language less complex than that of the ceremonial tribal *qaṣīdah*s of old. The essential narcissism of the persona is reflected in a particular delight in assuming the role of the female beloved and using the occasion to illustrate quite how devastating are his attractions to the opposite sex. The comments of Hind are a renowned example of this:

One day, they claim, as she stripped to bathe herself, she asked our neighbour:
'Tell me, by God! The way he depicts me, is that how you see me, or does he show no restraint?'
'Ah', they replied with a chuckle, 'To every eye the one who is adored is beautiful!'

The popularity of these poems was considerably enhanced by the availability of a group of renowned singers who set the lilting, gentler rhythms of ʿUmar's poetic escapades to music. The famous collection, *Kitāb al-aghānī* (Book of Songs) by Abū al-faraj al-Iṣfahānī (d. 967) is an invaluable source on the musical entertainments of the earliest period in Islamic history. Particularly famous among the musical interpreters of ʿUmar's poetry were ibn Surayj (d. 726) and al-Gharīḍ.

Many poets followed the playful lead established by ʿUmar's poetry, including al-ʿArjī quoted above. However, if the accounts of trysts and escapades are to be believed, some of them carried their play in dangerous directions. Both ibn Qays al-Ruqayyāt (d. 704) and Waḍḍāḥ al-Yaman (d. 708) wrote poems depicting the attractions of Umm al-Banīn, the redoubtable wife of the Umawī Caliph al-Walīd ibn ʿAbd al-Malik; while the charm of the former's tribute seems to have delighted the lady, the latter poet was allegedly put to death for taking his playfulness beyond the realm of poetry.

Another development in Arabic love poetry took the *ghazal* in a very different direction; since some of the poets who typify the trend, and especially the poet Jamīl (d. 701), came from the Banū ʿUdhrah tribe, this trend is usually termed ʿUdhrī. The absence, longing, and distance characteristic of the *nasīb* of the earlier poetry are no longer matters of nostalgia, capable of being transcended by reference to other concerns and generic tribal benefits, but now become a lifelong situation, in fact an obsession. Differentiating the lives of many of these poets from the elaborate repertoire of narrative that was appended to their collected poetry (found, for example, in Abū al-faraj al-Iṣfahānī's *Kitāb al-aghānī*) is virtually impossible and probably beside the point. The story of Jamīl involves a breaking of the tribal code regarding contact between the sexes. In this connection, it is interesting to note Lila Abū Lughod's observation concerning life among the Bedouin of the Western Desert of Egypt today:

> [L]ove relationships pose such a threat to the system that they are the object of stringent control through symbolic manipulation ... Modesty, including the denial of attachment to unrelated members of the opposite sex, is construed as a moral virtue–for women, the ultimate one. *(Veiled Sentiments*, Berkeley, 1986, p. 208)

Jamīl publicly revealed his feelings towards his beloved, Buthaynah. This attack on the honour of the tribe and especially of Buthaynah's family (maintained and enforced by her male relatives and particularly her father) led to a complete ban on any further contact between Jamīl and his beloved. Thus was established the classic situation of the ʿUdhrī love poem.

> Did you but realise how crazed I am with love, you would forgive me; if you did not, you would do wrong ...
> As long as I live, my heart will adore you; should I die, my echo will trail yours among the graves.
> O to meet my fate suddenly, if the day of my reunion with you is not destined to happen!
> You and the promise you give are nothing but the lightning of a cloud that brings no rain.

and in another poem:

> I see all other lovers except you and me happily enjoying the delights of this world.
> You and I walk as if we were two prisoners pledged to our enemies.

Here love is a never-ending, unachievable aspiration, its beginnings and lack of consummation willed by fate. In a replication of certain aspects of a religious devotion, the poet-lover places his beloved on a pedestal and worships her from afar. He is obsessed and tormented; he becomes debilitated, ill, and is doomed to a love-death. The beloved in turn becomes the personification of the ideal woman, a transcendent image of all that is beautiful and chaste. She is a gazelle pasturing in gardens and woods; her radiance gleams like the sun or moon. The cheek, the neck, the bosom, and, above all, the eyes – a mere glance – these are the cause of passion, longing, devastation, and exhaustion; the arrows and spears that they direct towards the beloved pierce the heart.

The tradition's greatest example of this compulsive and somewhat masochistic adulation is the poet, Qays ibn Mulawwaḥ (d. 688), the beloved of Laylā, whose obsessions did indeed make him crazed (*majnūn*); he is thus known as Majnūn Laylā. The collection of poetry attached to his name is surrounded by an elaborate repertoire of fable. Like Jamīl, he too will be faithful to the grave and beyond:

> Should our spirits meet after death, with high ground separating our graves,
> the echo of my voice will thrill to the echo of Layla's, though I be dust in the ground.

and in a touching conceit:

> An oryx passed by me looking lost. 'Are you Laylā's brother?' I asked.
> 'So they say', it replied.

The illustrations that we have provided of these two strands of love poetry, emerging from the Arabian peninsula in the seventh century, show clear differences. However, while many of the ghazals composed by poets such as ʿUmar ibn Abī Rabīʿah and al-ʿArjī do represent a significant new development in Arabic poetry, their collected works also contain a number of poems that continue to acknowledge the patterns of the past. During the processes of expansion and cultural fusion that characterise the early centuries of Islam, these different types of love poetry exist alongside each other. In addition, some scholars identify a more ribald variety connected with the 'frontier' atmosphere of garrison cities in Iraq such as al-Kūfah. The plentiful supply of entertainers of various kinds, offering a wide spectrum of comforts, provided a ready supply of topics for a distinctly baudy repertoire (categorised as *mujūn* poetry).

We have already encountered Dhū al-Rummah contemplating the traces of his beloved, Mayy's, encampment and indeed of al-Farazdaq bemoaning the loss of his ex-wife, Nawār. The centrality of the *ghazal* during the period of the Umawī caliphs can perhaps be shown most strikingly by the fact that one of the most prominent of its poets was none other than al-Walīd ibn Yazīd (d. 744), one of the Umawī Caliphs:

She came to me, smothering me with kisses, svelte, as though musk were in her mouth.
'May I be your ransom!' she said, 'Come in; no one knows we are here. My soul will ransom yours against illness'.
Thus we spent the night in bed, without sleep, clasping each other from the heat of our passion.

As the *ghazal* genre develops, elements of the idealised love theme that are particularly associated with the ʿUdhrī tradition become integrated into the broader repertoire of love poetry. Indeed, as we will note in the section on religious poetry below, ʿUdhrī tropes and images are readily adopted by Sufi poets at a later stage in order to provide a mode for the expression of another kind of devotional state, that of the mystic in quest of the transcendental experience.

Within the gradual process of generic change Bashshār ibn Burd is once again an important participant. His love poems addressed to his beloved, ʿAbdah, reflect the familiar sounds and images of the past:

ʿAbdah has an abode; it speaks not to us, but looms like lines of writing.
I question stones and a collapsed tent-trench, but how can such things give an answer?

So popular were these ʿAbdah poems (which contain much reference to the lover's suffering, to sleepless nights, and to the reproachful beloved) that, if we are to credit the contents of the poet's own verse, the Caliph al-Mahdī forbade him to write any more. Bashshār however can also replicate the conversational tone of ʿUmar ibn Abī Rabīʿah:

Many's the buxom maid who has told her companions: 'You people, this blind man is amazing!
Can someone who cannot see be in love?' With tears streaming, I replied: 'Though my eyes may not see her face, in my heart it exists as an image'.

and in still another poem he can wax quite racy:

Her arm shows traces of a bite, and mine does too;
Anklets gleam on her leg, and there is the sound of heavy breathing.
The gazelle's palm slackens, and with streaming tears she says: 'Leave me alone!
Go away! You're not the way they described. By God, you're a disgusting lecher!'

A poet who found particular favour with the Caliph, Hārūn al-Rashīd, was ʿAbbās ibn al-Aḥnaf (d. after 808). His *ghazal* poetry is primarily concerned with the hopelessness of love, and the persona in his compositions seems resigned to a relationship of deprivation. The beloved's pedestal is now elevated to the sky:

> The very sun she is, residing in the heavens; so console the heart as best you may!
> Never will you ascend to her, nor will she descend to you . . .

and their love is both pre-ordained and destined to be retold:

> Your heart and mine are a novelty, created to be mutually attracted in a sincere love,
> exchanging a desire that will make of us a tale to be told in East and West.

However, it is al-Ḥasan ibn Hāni', renowned under his nickname Abū Nuwās (the man with the curl), whose name is most closely linked with the côterie of Hārūn al-Rashīd (particularly in the cycle of Hārūn tales in the *Thousand and One Nights*) and of his successor, al-Amīn (d. 813). Many of his contributions to both love and wine poetry can be seen as the creations of an iconoclast eager to confront and contest the behavioural and cultural norms of his time. His love poems, divided between those addressed to women (*mu'annathāt*) and those to men (*mudhakkarāt*), cover a broad spectrum that ranges all the way from the deprivations associated with the ʿUdhrī love poem to depictions of sexual encounters that reflect his own bisexual predilections. Here he speaks in a more traditional vein:

> The passionate lover suffers exhaustion; emotion affects his every mood;
> If he weeps, he has every right to do so, for it is no joke.
> You laugh distractedly while the lover is wailing.
> You wonder at my illness; t'were a miracle for me to be well!
> No sooner is one tie to you broken than another returns.

Running through his collection of love (and especially wine) poetry there is an ongoing confrontation between his playful, ribald persona and a penitent alter ego:

> 'Hello!' said the Devil as he swooped down. 'Greetings to a penitent whose penitence is sheer illusion!
> What about a sensuous virgin-girl with a splendid bosom
> And a cascade of black hair down her back, its colour replicating the darkest grapes?'
> 'No', I replied. 'Then what about a beardless youth whose plump buttocks are all aquiver,

One who resembles a virgin in her boudoir, yet on his throat there is no necklace?'
'No', I said again. 'Then what about a notorious youth renowned for his singing and dancing?'
'No', I replied. 'Everything resembling what I've told you', the Devil continued, 'is sheer common sense.
You'll change your tune, you fool! Of that I've no doubt!'

Within the broad domain that these poets established for the *ghazal* genre their successors were able to develop and elaborate on its repertoire of image and conceit. Muslim ibn al-Walīd (d. 823), for example, who is regarded as one of the pioneers of *badīʿ*, earned the nickname 'victim of the lovelies' (*ṣarīʿ al-ghawānī*) for his love-poems that emphasise the desperate state of his infatuation. The *ghazal* now has a fixed place in the collected works of many poets; among the more famous who have already been mentioned are ibn al-Rūmī and ibn al-Muʿtazz, yet another caliph-poet:

I passed by a flower-covered grave in the midst of a garden, covered in bay-leaves like anemones.
'Whose grave is this', I wondered. 'Be gentle with it', the soil responded, 'it's a lover's grave'.

Far removed from the desert wastes of Arabia, al-Sharīf al-Raḍī (d. 1015) deliberately invokes the shade of Imru al-Qays in order to express his own sense of desolation:

You two riders, stop for me and fulfill my purpose; give me news of the Najd:
Has the vegetable garden bloomed, or has the acacia grove with its willow and laurel received its share of rain?

The cultural environment of al-Andalus, initially at the caliphal court and later at the number of smaller centres of political patronage provided by the 'party kingdoms' (*mulūk al-ṭawāʾif*), provided a rich environment for the elaboration of the *ghazal* tradition. Ibn ʿAbd Rabbihi (d. 940), the compiler of the famous literary anthology, *al-ʿIqd al-farīd* (The Unique Necklace), includes a section on love poetry that refers to most of the poets mentioned above and expresses a preference for the more courtly variety, something that also emerges from his own contributions to the genre. In addition to the renowned ibn Zaydūn whose storm-tossed affair with the princess, Wallādah, was described above, ibn Ḥazm (d. 1064) and ibn Khafājah (d. 1138) are renowned for their love poetry; the former is also the author of a manual on love, *Ṭawq al-ḥamāmah* (The Dove's Neck-ring), which is examined in more detail in the following chapter. Further insight into the inner dynamics of the tradition of Andalusian love poetry is provided by the recorded verses of the famous poetess, Ḥafṣah bint al-Ḥājj al-Rakūniyyah (d. 1190). Her beauty, it appears, aroused the passion of Abū Saʿīd, son of the ruler of Granada, but she responds caustically to his poetic advances:

> You who would lay claim to the head position in love and passion,
> Your poetry has arrived, but its composition failed to please me.

Some of the poetry that she composed for other occasions (and admirers) has been preserved:

> I visit you or you me; my heart is always inclined to what you desire.
> My mouth is a pure, sweet spring, and the branches of my locks afford plenteous shade.

However, it is with Andalusian strophic poetry, the *muwashshah* and *zajal* (the forms of which were discussed earlier in the chapter), that *ghazal* makes some of its most innovative contributions. Early examples of the *muwashshah* poem are seen by some scholars as reflecting the cultural complexities of Andalusian society by juxtaposing a series of strophes and verses that bear an ʿUdhrī stamp with a final strophe – often a popular song – that is decidedly different. One of the fiercest of such contrasts occurs in an anonymous poem in ibn Sanāʾ al-Mulk's collection, *Dār al-ṭirāz* (House of Embroidery). It opens with the traditional repertoire of infatuation and suffering:

> He who has endowed eyelids with the qualities of Indian swords,
> And caused sweet basil to sprout on the side of his cheek,
> Has sentenced the infatuated lover to tears and sleeplessness;
> How can one keep silent?

With the final strophe (*kharjah*) of the poem we encounter an entirely different voice:

> Come on, my sweet, show some resolve! On your feet and give me a kiss! Embrace my breast and lift my anklets all the way up to my earrings. My husband's been called away.

The contrast is less stark in another *muwashshahah* by al-Aʿmā al-Tuṭīlī (the blind poet of Tudela, d. 1126) where the *kharjah* is in the colloquial dialect:

> You look sick! So what's with you? As time goes by, you'll forget about me,

and, by the time of ibn al-Khaṭīb (d. 1374), a prince who for the diversity and polish of his writings was accorded the title '*Lisān al-dīn*' (Tongue of the faith), a lengthy *muwashshaḥah* addressed to the ruler of Granada can conclude with a *kharjah* that has essentially been 'classicised':

> Does a gazelle realise how it has kindled the heart of a lover who released it from its covert?
> It burns and palpitates like a firebrand fanned by the east wind.

Ibn Quzmān (d. 1160), the acknowledged master of the *zajal*, uses his poetry to boast about his prowess as lover and poet; he is quite explicit about his allegiance to poetic forebears:

> I am a man in love, by God!
> My state shows I'm speaking the truth.
> And in *zajal* I'm the tops.
> Like a drawn sword poetry pierces my mind, and chainmail itself will not stop my tongue.
> Spare me, please, the religion of Jamīl and 'Urwah!
> Al-Ḥasan [Abū Nuwās] is a model for people!

Such is the enduring nature of the *ghazal* repertoire of landscape and image that we have just explored that in the eighteenth century we can still listen to the poet known as 'the prince of Ṣanʿāʾ' (*al-amīr al-ṣanʿānī*, d. 1768) proudly proclaiming:

> ʿUdhrī love is my art. Should I pine, do not blame me!
> In love I am unique; neither mention nor extol any other . . .
> Should you drink of the wine of love, then take it from my vat;
> Should you be ignorant of some aspect, then ask your questions of me.

The Majnūn Laylā legend becomes the source of Aḥmad Shawqī's (d. 1932) most famous poetic operetta, its songs remembered (like those of ʿUmar ibn Abī Rabīʿah many centuries earlier) through the popularity of song:

> Laylā! Someone calls out that name – Laylā; and in my heart a rapture takes wing, uncontrollable!
> Laylā! the name is for ever implanted in my ear, in my very soul, like the sound of birds in the forest.

The generation of romantic poets that came after Shawqī laid great stress on the centrality of the individual and the role of the soul in the imaginative process. As in the European literary traditions to which they had turned for critical insight, much of the poetry that emerged from such inspiration was devoted to the topic of love. As noted above, it was among the poets of the emigre communities in the Americas (*mahjar*) that the most accomplished examples of early romantic poetry are to be found. Iliyyā Abū Māḍī (d. 1957) finds his idealised beloved, Salmā, contemplating at sunset:

> The clouds scurry across the spacious heavens as though scared,
> while behind them the sun is yellow-hued with brow wrapped.
> The sea a silent teak, humble as ascetics,
> but your gaze is pallid as you stare at the distant horizon.
> Salma, what preoccupies your thoughts?
> Salma, of what are you dreaming?

while, writing in Brazil, Ilyās Farḥāt (d. 1977) questions nature about his beloved:

> I ask the morning breeze about her, the flowers in the garden, the breezes in the lavender;
> How often I have said that, when we meet, my passion will suffice to quench thirst!

Instigated by a number of groups and movements – the Mahjar poets in the Americas, the Dīwān group and later the Apollo group in Egypt, romantic poetry saw its heyday in the 1930s and 1940s. The range of expression is wide: from the pleasures of ʿAlī Mahmūd Ṭāhā's (d. 1949) universe of love, to the wistful mood of Ibrāhīm Najī (d. 1953), and the mellifluous language of Saʿīd ʿAql's (d. 1991) symbolist visions:

> Olive-skinned beauty, dream of childhood,
> Reluctance of skittish lips!
> Do not draw near. Remain, for my morrow,
> a lovely idea . . .

For ʿUmar Abū Rīshah (b. 1910) the love poem was a vehicle for a newly liberated expression of the relationship between man and woman, whereas, for Ilyās Abū Shabakah (d. 1947), the passions of love become a source of nightmarish visions of personal agony and intolerant humanity. Sin, guilt, and lust are central themes of his collection, *Afāʿī firdaws* (Serpents of Paradise, 1938), and his preoccupation with them finds partial redemption through the prolonged process of composing '*Ghalwāʾ*', a poem addressed to Olga, the woman who was eventually to become his wife. A similarly tortured vision of love is later seen in the work of Tawfīq Ṣāyigh (d. 1971) whose collection, *Qaṣīdat K* (K's Poem,

1960), shows the emotional impact of his obsessive relationship with an English woman named Kay.

The gradual emergence of Arab women as a participating force in the public life of many Arab countries during the latter half of the twentieth century and the increased educational opportunities that have become available have served as the societal context within which the female voice has been able to offer fresh visions of love and gender relationships to the repertoire of Arabic poetry. Nāzik al-Malā'ikah (b. 1923), a pioneer in the process of change in the formal aspects of the poem, plays an important role here, as does the Palestinian poetess, Fadwā Ṭūqān, some of whose poems, not unnaturally, link the theme of love to the fate of her homeland. As Fadwā Ṭūqān expresses it:

> In my homeland, O poet,
> in my precious homeland,
> there waits a lover,
> a fellow countryman;
> I shall not waste his heart . . .
> I am a female, so, whenever your whisper
> strokes my heart, please
> forgive its vanity.

The poetic voice of the modern Arab woman can be illustrated through numerous exemplars. From among them we choose an extract from a poem in the collection *Fī al-bad' kānat al-unthā* (In the Beginning was the Female, 1988) by the Kuwaitī poetess, Su'ād al-Ṣabāḥ (b. 1942); the feelings expressed by the speaker provide yet another linkage to the earlier tradition, one that echoes the sentiments expressed in ibn Quzmān's *zajal* cited above:

> I am tired of traditional words
> about love,
> I'm fed up with the *ghazal* of the dead,
> flowers of the dead;
> sitting down to dinner every night
> with Qays ibn Mulawwaḥ
> and Jamīl Buthaynah,
> and all the other permanent members
> of the 'Udhrī Love Club.
> Please try to deviate a bit from the text,
> try to invent me.

The name of one modern Arab poet is most closely linked to the theme of love: Nizār Qabbānī (b. 1923). Throughout his lengthy career he has garnered for himself enormous and widespread popularity by using his poems to express the younger generation's quest for liberation from the trammels of traditional morality. In his poems discretion is thrown to the winds:

> Wake up from a night of burning passion
> and put on your folded gown.
> Wake up; the dewy morn will
> expose your scandalous desires.
> You with the roving breast, cover up
> your bosom and voracious nipple.
> Where are the clothes you scattered
> in a moment of unrivalled pleasure?

He can adopt the female voice in order to declare a passionate love (an echo perhaps of the narcissistic mood of his distant forebear, ʿUmar ibn Abī Rabīʿah):

> When will you realise how much I adore you, you man for
> whom I would sell the entire world and its contents?
> For love of you I have challenged entire cities and will
> continue to do so . . .

but the same female voice can also express utter revulsion:

> You sent a servant to throw me out
> into the street,
> You who planted sin in my loins
> and broke my heart.
> 'My master's not at home', he told me.
> Oh yes, he's at home, a thousand times at home,
> But he's a coward now he knows
> that I am pregnant.

The forthrightness with which Qabbānī has addressed love in its various aspects has also led him to compose a number of searing indictments of Arab society and its values, including '*Khubz wa-ḥashīsh wa-qamar*' (Bread, Hashish, and Moon) from the 1950s and '*Hawāmish ʿala daftar al-naksah*' (Commentary on the Notebook of the Disaster) in 1967 following the June War. In the following extract the vocabulary of love becomes immersed in a modern poem of political protest:

> Ah, my darling!
> What is this nation that treats love like a policeman?
> A rose is considered a conspiracy against order;
> A poem is a secret opposition pamphlet.

What is this nation, drawn like a yellow locust
crawling on its belly 'from the Ocean to the Gulf' . . .
talking like a saint by day,
and reeling around at night over a woman's navel.

Khamriyyah: wine poetry.

In *Risālat al-ghufrān* (The Epistle of Forgiveness), a narrative by the poet-philosopher, Abū al-ʿAlāʾ al-Maʿarrī (d. 1057) – to be discussed in the following chapter, a shaykh is taken on a tour of the next world in order to find answers to a burning question: How have some famous forebears, particularly those who lived during the pre-Islamic era, managed to obtain forgiveness for their conduct during their time on earth? Among those whom the shaykh meets are a number of poets whose fate is clearly in question because they have composed verses in celebration of wine (*khamr*). Many composers of *qaṣāʾid* wrote elaborate bacchic segments as part of the larger, polythematic structure; they range from the celebrated opening of the *muʿallaqah* of ʿAmr ibn Kulthūm to often elaborate descriptions of the qualities of wine and of bibulous occasions; those of ʿAlqamah ibn ʿAbadah, Labīd, and ʿAdī ibn Zayd are among the most famous. All these poets are questioned by al-Maʿarrī's shaykh, but among the first figures to be approached is the most famous of the pre-Islamic winepoets, Maymūn ibn Qays, the much travelled professional bard known as al-Aʿshā ('night-blind', d. *c.* 630?). In one of his most famous odes, he boasts:

I have gone to the tavern in the morning, with a bold, brazen, bawdy
  butcher in my tracks . . .
Reclining I have outdone my rivals for a sprig of sweet-basil and a dry
  wine from a moist jug.
As long as it is available, they only wake up to yell 'Give me more' after
  the first and second draft.

With al-Aʿshā's renown established by such verses and many others like them, the shaykh is curious to know how he is faring. The poet narrates how, just as he was being hauled away to the nether regions, ʿAlī (the fourth Caliph) appeared. Al-Aʿshā reminded him of his poem in praise of Muḥammad, and that proved sufficient to persuade ʿAlī to ask the Prophet to intercede on the poet's behalf, the condition being that he drink no wine in Paradise. The shaykh later questions Ḥassān ibn Thābit, the 'poet of the Prophet', asking how the poet could introduce the theme of wine into a eulogy of the Prophet himself. The poet replies (and here we can appreciate the ironic tone of al-Maʿarrī's voice in this narrative) that he was only decribing the phenomenon, not participating himself; and, in any case, the poet continues, the Prophet was not the puritanical figure that some subsequent scholars have made him out to be.

The driving force behind the shaykh's questions is, of course, the series of injunctions in the Qur'ān concerning the consumption of wine. In one of the 'they will ask you about . . . ' segments that were discussed in ch. 3 – *Sūrat al-baqarah* (2, The Cow, v. 219), the Prophet is questioned about wine and gambling (the game known as *maysir*, involving the shuffling of arrow-shafts). The reply is somewhat equivocal: 'Say: both involve major sin and benefits for people; but the sin is greater than the benefit'. In other passages, however, the import of the message is unambiguous: 'O you who believe, wine, gambling, idols, and divining arrows, these are an abomination, the work of the devil. Avoid such things, then you may prosper'. (*Sūrat al-māʾidah* [5, The Table, v. 90]). These and other proscriptions regarding wine-drinking are incorporated into official Islamic doctrine (although, as one might anticipate, there is considerable debate as to the precise definition of *khamr*). However, the application of any such rigid behavioural norms in a developing Muslim societal environment that remained culturally pluralistic and fractious provided – almost automatically – a ready device through which poets could exhibit a sense of defiance against received orthodoxy and publicise their non-adherence to such doctrines, whether in earnest or as a creative posture. It is within such a context that the *khamr* theme of the earliest period is developed into a separate genre in its own right, the *khamriyyah*.

That the court of the Umawī caliphs was hardly oblivious to the delights of wine (or, at the very least, to listening to poetry on that topic) can be illustrated not only in the celebrated poems of the Christian poet al-Akhṭal, who, as we noted above, numbered among the most prominent court poets of his period, but even more by the compositions of one of Arabic's most celebrated masters of the wine-poem, the Umawī Caliph, al-Walīd ibn Yazīd (d. 744):

Cast off hidden cares with frivolity; thwart fate by enjoying the daughter of the grape . . .
How I long to drink from a maid of noble descent on her wedding-day,
Resplendent in her jewels, wondrous to behold,
As though her glass contained a firebrand gleaming into the watcher's eye.

Here the poet-caliph illustrates the developing imagery of the wine-poem and its emerging cast of 'characters': the drinkers are challenging the fates (not to mention the tenets of the dominant faith), and the shape of the bottle and the promise that it offers is likened to that of a beautiful woman. These and other images are brought to their full flowering by the acknowledged master of the Arabic wine poem, Abū Nuwās.

Abū Nuwās's name has already occurred several times in this chapter on poetry, as is only fitting for a poet who was fully cognisant of the early heritage of Arabic poetry and of the primary Islamic canonical sources but whose creative persona was clearly unwilling to be trammelled by the perceived dictates of either. We have already seen him kicking against the traces by poking fun at the desert imagery found in the exordium (*nasīb*) of the early *qasidah* and introducing ribald elements into the *ghazal* poem. However, it is in the wine-poem (*khamriyyah*) which, at the hands of al-Walīd ibn Yazīd and several other lesser-known poets, had by now become recognised as a separate genre, that his iconoclastic instincts are best combined with his poetic genius. In al-Maʿarrī's *Risālat al-ghufrān* those poets who lived before Islam or who did not indulge in wine-drinking during their lifetime are fully supplied with the promised wine of paradise, but it is the aim of Abū Nuwās's poetic world to create a replication of the heavenly realm on earth. It is a fools' paradise, of course, and, since it directly confronts and challenges the behavioural norms of the society, it is also fraught with risk. The sheer defiance of the poetic persona and his drinking companions (*nudamāʾ*) turns them into something akin to war heroes:

> This conflict is not one that grieves people with oppression;
> In this case, we kill them, then resurrect the dead.

For this defiance, this heroism, to be effective, there is no use for secrecy: rather it must be flaunted:

> Ho, give me wine to drink, and tell me it's wine! Don't do it secretly when it can be done in the open!
> To see me sober would be a swindle; when I am roaring drunk, that's the real boon!

Abū Nuwās's *khamriyyah* has a repertoire of characters and images; in some cases, it is akin to a narrative. The primary resort with his rowdy group is the tavern which may have to be opened at a very late hour by the owner:

> Many's the lady publican I've roused from sleep, long after the Gemini has set and the Vulture Star is in the sky.
> 'Who's knocking?' she asks. 'A whole gang', we reply, 'short of goblet and in need of wine'.

The world into which the publican admits them is one where glasses gleam like stars ('like the sun, their gleam like the very Pleiades in exquisite glass') and bottles – slender-necked and unsealed, full of fine, old wine – are at the same time old crones and lithe virgin maids. Above all, in Abū Nuwās's poetry, the wine is served by the *sāqī*, a youth whose beauty is depicted in extravagant and sensual terms; as are the sexual encounters to which he entices the group:

> 'We must have sex', we say. 'How about a youth', she suggests, 'gleaming like a gold dinar, with a certain langour in his eye' . . .
> She brings him in. He's like the very moon at full; you would imagine there was magic in him, though there is none.
> One after another we went to him; he provided the breaking of a fast of absence.
> Thus we spent the night, observed by God in our evil doings, plumbing without pride the lewdest depths of sex.

Into this scenario the figure of the 'blamer' (*ʿādhil*) familiar from the tradition of love poetry, is also introduced, but it is usually a cue for further boasts:

> Put away your blame; it is merely an incitement. Instead, cure me with that which is itself the disease.

The persona in Abū Nuwās's poetry seems bent on advertising quite how naughty it can be. He is not alone, of course, in choosing to explore (and exploit to the full) the many and various modes of challenge to orthopraxis, but his mischievous citation of phrases culled from the text of the Qur'ān itself clearly illustrates a conscious process of confrontational allusion. In the words of the modern poet-critic, Adūnīs, 'the insolence of the clown purifies and liberates. It is a celebration which holds in it the promise of something capable of going beyond this culture of orders and prohibitions to a culture of freedom . . . Values are transformed through this symbol, and sin becomes the only virtue'. Abū Nuwās's achievement, especially in the *khamriyyah* genre, in crafting a different kind of poetic expression, in Adūnīs's view, 'result[ed] in an almost complete transformation of the language of poetry' (*Introduction to Arab Poetics*, London, 1990, pp. 61, 50).

The *khamriyyāt* of Abū Nuwās cast a giant shadow over the subsequent tradition of wine poetry in Arabic. The motifs and images that become an intrinsic feature of the false worldly paradise opened up by his poetry make their way into the works of Arab poets composing in a variety of forms and genres. In al-Andalus, they are to be found in *muwashshaḥ* and *zajal* poems, and also in the traditional *qaṣīdah* poetry. Ibn Ḥamdīs (of Sicilian origin, d. 1132) writes:

> When a glass reaches one of our drinking-companions, he takes it gently with his ten fingers
> and imbibes a vine-intoxication which sends his wakeful eye to sleep without his even being aware.

Ibn Khafājah's (d. 1138) inspiration is also obvious:

> I greeted the lady publican's tavern by night and in reply she bade me welcome...
> and brought me a flaming red wine gleaming starlike in its cup.

Replicating not only Abū Nuwās but also one of his immediate successors, ibn al-Muʿtazz (d. 908), Ṣafī al-dīn al-Ḥillī (d. 1349) draws attention to the attractions that wine-making Christian monasteries (and their monks) provided:

> I roused a monk from sleep whose mellifluous voice accompanied us when he prayed or spoke.
> Opening the door he let us in ... and brought us a superb vintage with a bouquet, well aged in its vat.
> He filled the cup till it overflowed on his hand, and gave me to drink after he had drunk himself...

The hope with which ibn Mālik al-Ḥamawī (d. 1511) finishes one of his *khamriyyāt* reflects the penitential voice that is also present in some of Abū Nuwās's poems:

> Should I be daunted by sin, God is possessed of beneficence.
> Mighty, Forgiver, erasing the gravest of sins and burdens.

In contrast with the public and declamatory nature of the panegyrical *qaṣīdah*, the *ghazal* and *khamriyyah* emerge as genres intended to express more private, personal types of sentiment, reserved perhaps for intimate, rather than ceremonial, occasions. This may at least help to account for the readiness with which the poetic repertoire of both genres came to be adopted by those poets who wished to find modes of expression suited to those more private, personal, and indeed ecstatic, forms of devotion associated with Sufism. When the most famous of the Sufi poets who wrote in Arabic, the Egyptian ʿUmar ibn al-Fāriḍ (d. 1235), begins his Ṣūfī *khamriyyah*,

> In remembrance of the beloved we drank a wine through which we became drunk before ever the vine was created.
> For a cup it has a full moon; it is a sun circled by a new moon; when it is mixed, how many a star appears!

we are being introduced to a world where the imagery of love and wine constitutes a surface beneath which an elaborate code is at work. The 'beloved' here refers to God, while 'wine' serves as the medium through which a state of oblivion can be achieved; the gleaming of the stars represents sparks of inspiration that the mystic can receive once that state has been reached.

The *dīwān* of ibn al-Fāriḍ is generally regarded as marking the high point in Arabic mystical poetry, a genre in which, among the various literary cultures within the Islamic dominions, pride of place is generally accorded to Persian poets, notably ʿAṭṭār (d. *c.* 1230), Jalāl al-dīn Rūmī (d. 1273), and Ḥāfiẓ (d. 1390). The tradition upon which ibn al-Fāriḍ builds sees some of its earliest manifestation in the poetry of the renowned female mystic, Rābiʿah al-ʿAdawiyyah of al-Baṣrah (d. 801), whose lifespan thus partially overlaps that of al-Hasan al-Baṣrī, an important figure in the early development of Sufi thought and practice. In an often quoted poem of hers the linkage of the themes of devotion and love is direct, somewhat redolent of the poetry of famous European ecstatics of a later era such as Hildegard of Bingen (d. 1179) and Julian of Norwich (d. early fifteenth century):

> For You I have two loves: one of longing, the other
> because You are worthy of it.
> As for the one of longing, the mention of Your name
> diverts me from that of all others.
> As for the love of which you are worthy, that resides in
> Your lifting the veil for me so that I may behold You.
> There is no praise for me in one or the other, but in both
> the praise is Yours.

The love theme, and especially the notion of suffering in love that, as we have already noted, was an intrinsic feature of the ʿUdhrī tradition, was further developed in the poetry of the Egyptian mystic, Dhū al-nūn al-Miṣrī (d. 861). The idea of such longings leading to martrydom in the cause of divine love is most famously represented by the renowned figure of Manṣūr al-Ḥallāj (d. 922), whose execution turned him literally into a martyr and a central symbol of the uneasy tensions between Sufism and Islamic orthodoxy. With him the vocabulary of love signifies at another level of meaning:

> The hearts of lovers have eyes which see what other
> beholders do not see,
> Tongues confiding secrets that remain hidden from
> distinguished clerks,
> And wings that fly featherless towards the realm of the
> Lord of the Worlds.

and, in a more controversial vein:

> With the eye of my heart I saw my Lord. 'Who are you?' I asked. 'You', He replied,

and, as the ecstatic vision takes over, the unification of aspirant with the transcendent becomes complete:

> I am You, without doubt. So Your praise is mine,
> Your Unity is mine; Your defiance is mine.

It was the literal interpretation of such poetic transports that served as a contributing factor in al-Ḥallāj's trial and execution for heresy, a process captured with notable success by the modern Egyptian poet-playwright, Ṣalāḥ ʿAbd al-Ṣabūr (d. 1981) in *Maʾsāt al-Ḥallāj* (1965; *Murder in Baghdad*, Leiden, 1972).

Those mystics who composed poetry during the four centuries that separate al-Ḥallāj and ibn al-Fāriḍ expressed their devotion and quest for the ascetic life in relatively stark and unadorned verse. Looking back from the poetic output of the two Ṣūfī masters of the thirteenth century, ibn al-Fāriḍ and ibn al-ʿArabī (d. 1240), Martin Lings, one of the most sensitive interpreters of this tradition (see, for example, *ʿAbbasid Belles-Lettres*, Cambridge History of Arabic Literature, II, 1990, ch. 14), suggests that the changes evident in their poetry seem to result more from an awareness of developments in the more secular court tradition than to any line of continuity stretching back to al-Ḥallāj and his predecessors. In the case of ibn al-Fāriḍ we have already quoted the opening lines of his *khamriyyah*, where the images of bacchic verse are intended to direct the initiate towards deeper levels of contemplation, but that poem's combination of the bacchic and erotic – the devotee is instructed to take his wine pure and not to shun the 'beloved's white teeth', i.e. the Prophet's word – is expanded into a much broader expression in the poet's '*al-Tāʾiyyah al-kubrā*' (Great Poem rhyming on T, also known as '*Naẓm al-sulūk*' (Poem of the Path)), in which, following an opening verse,

> The palm of my eye gave me love's wine to drink, and my cup is the visage of the one who is beyond beauty,

the devotee explores over 760 lines the soul's journey in quest of God, filtered through the imagery of his relationship with his 'beloved': his suffering and self-denial, his instructions to his fellow devotees, and his desire for union. Such was the impact of this and other poems of ibn al-Fāriḍ that he was revered as a 'saint' (*walī*) within his own lifetime and later castigated by orthodox scholars as a heretic; even so, as a recent work by Homerin records, his tomb in Cairo remains a Ṣūfī shrine to this day. Ibn al-Fāriḍ's contemporary, ibn al-ʿArabī, was also revered during his own lifetime and earned his own share of opprobrium from orthodox scholarship; as noted earlier, he was even accorded the curious distinction of having his books banned for a period by the Egyptian Ministry of the Interior during the 1980s. During a stay in Mecca, ibn al-ʿArabī was apparently inspired by an affection for his host's young daughter to write a collection of poetry, *Tarjumān al-ashwāq* (Interpreter of Desires), a work whose poems are replete with the desert imagery of the early Arabic tradition, not least a variety of names for the beloved. So convincingly authentic was this imagery and so complex its layering of symbolism that he found himself thereafter constrained to add a commentary on it in order to counteract more secular interpretations of its content, noting, for example, that these 'beloveds' serve as symbols of divine beauty. The following lines, often quoted, illustrate not only the links to the tradition of Arabic love poetry but also the resonances of ibn al-ʿArabī's language:

> O Marvel! A bower amidst the flames,
> My heart is now capable of every form,
> A meadow it is for gazelles, for monks a monastery;
> A shrine for idols, for pilgrims the very Kaʿbah;
> The tables of the Torah, the book of the Qur'ān.
> Love is my faith. Wherever its camels may roam,
> There is found my religion, my faith.

Later generations of scholars continued the process begun by ibn al-ʿArabī himself, drawing attention to the many potential imports contained within the symbolically layered poetry of these two great Sufi poets. Among the most prominent was ʿAbd al-ghanī al-Nābulusī (d. 1731) whose *al-Ṣūfiyyah fī shiʿr ibn al-Fāriḍ* (The Sufi Text on ibn al-Fāriḍ's Poetry), for example, contains a line-by-line analysis of many of his great forebear's poems.

It is symptomatic of the tremendous devotional following attracted to popular Sufi movements over large areas of the Islamic dominions that a single poem composed by an Egyptian poet named al-Būṣīrī (d. 1296), also known under the title of '*al-Burdah*' (the mantle), was to become one of the most commented-upon poems in the whole of Arabic. A 161-line record of the life of Muḥammad, its division into subsections detailing aspects of his prophetic mission made it an ideal poetic vehicle for use in the *ḥaḍrah*, the gathering at which members of Sufi brotherhoods would conduct their rituals of worship and listen to devotional texts. This poem also begins with a gesture to the early tradition:

> Is it from a memory of neighbours at Dhū Salam that you have mixed
> with blood tears that flowed from an eye?
> Has the wind blown from Kāẓimah's quarter, or a lightning flash
> gleamed in the dark by Idam?

After a lengthy exordium the poet moves on to praise Muḥammad and recount the details of his life and mission. The process of incorporating the poem into the ritual of an evening *ḥaḍrah* is recounted in ʿAbd al-ḥakīm Qāsim's (d. 1990) novel, *Ayyām al-insān al-sabʿah* (1969; *The Seven Days of Man*, 1997):

> 'Begin reciting the *Burdah* poem of al-Būṣīrī, Shaykh Aḥmad Badawī', Ḥājj Karīm intoned, clapping his hands in pleasure.
>
> Aḥmad Badawī … was the appropriate person to lead the group in the recitation of al-Būṣīrī's poem. The *Burdah* was full of music, and his voice had its own timbre. He was the one to bring the reading to a peak of emotion.
>
> 'Aid us, Master Būṣīrī!'

The presence of such references to al-Būṣīrī's poem (and indeed to ibn al-Fāriḍ's poetry in some of Najīb Maḥfūẓ's works) points to an interesting linkage between present and past through the invocation of literary texts that illustrate the continuing quest for the transcendent. However, while the mellifluous complexities of ibn al-Fāriḍ and ibn al-ʿArabī may continue to delight adherents and disturb orthodoxy, it is the figure of the martyred al-Ḥallāj that provides many modern writers with a potent symbol. In addition to the already mentioned play by ʿAbd al-Ṣabūr, we may mention in closing Adūnīs's poem, '*Marthiyyat al-Ḥallāj*' (Elegy for al-Ḥallāj), in which the political defiance of the martyred Sufi is transported into a modern Arab world much in need of such qualities:

> O star, arising from Baghdad
> laden with poems and birth,
> O poisoned green pen
>
> Nothing remains for those who come from afar
> bringing thirst, death, and ice.
> In this "resurrectionist" land
> Nothing remains, save you and presence.

Ṭardiyyah: hunt poetry.
That the *muʿallaqah* of Imru al-Qays, that yardstick of the Arabic poetic tradition to which we have frequently had recourse, is just one among many earlier poems that contain a vivid description of a hunt is evidence enough of the antiquity of the Arabs' delight in this quest for food and sport. The tradition continues unabated today. In the Arabian peninsula the oryx has been hunted almost to extinction, although more recently cars have been the preferred mode of transport rather than riding-animals; the Saudi government has now introduced measures to try to preserve the relatively small stock of the species that remains. Besides weapons like the bow and spear (and, more recently, guns), specific types of animals and birds have traditionally been used to assist in the hunting of prey. Among the former, the category of hound known as *saluqi* (saluki) were particularly preferred; among birds, the falcon (*ṣaqr*), a sport that first came into vogue during the period of the Umawī caliphs. The continuing popularity of the latter among the nations of the Arabian Gulf was brought home to me personally in a very vivid fashion when in 1988 I spent a somewhat uneasy flight from Abu Dhabi to Bahrain seated alongside an extremely large falcon (hooded, I am glad to say) that was serenely perched on the leather-padded arm of its proud owner.

The shaykh who does the rounds of paradise in al-Maʿarrī's *Risālat al-ghufrān* encounters one of the earliest of Arabic's hunt poets, the Christian ʿAdī ibn Zayd of al-Ḥīrah (d. 604), who proceeds to regale him with some of his hunt poetry before inviting him to join him in a round of heavenly sport. In dealing with the hunt theme, we once again witness a process whereby such episodes within the larger framework of the pre-Islamic *qaṣīdah* become the topic of separate *qiṭʿah* structures during the Islamic period. As with the other genres we have discussed above, it appears to be in the *dīwān* of Abū Nuwās that the *ṭardiyyah* is first categorised as a separate entity.

The majority of the poems of this type have a stock opening: the hunter ventures forth in the early morning, and his faithful hound is with him. The opportunity thus presents itself to evoke not only the atmosphere of the early Arabic *qaṣīdah* but also its delight in depicting the qualities of animals in loving detail:

> I go out in the early morning, with me my dog seeking game in my company.
> We mount the outcrops with him and send him after the gazelles . . .

The dog possesses heroic qualities:

When a fox appears at the mountain foot, 'Ho!' I yell to my dog, and
he is roused like a hero,
A brave-hearted dog, a splendid worker, well trained, perfect in every
quality . . .

and is a relentless pursuer:

I have trained a dog for the chase, straight as an arrow,
with collar and rope on his neck . . .
He tears away from the squawk of the sand-grouse as he
weighs in the balance the spotted hares.
They discover he is a tyrannical apportioner: for bones
crushing, for skin rending . . .
Praise be to God for his gifts!

Abū Nuwās even provides an elegy for one of his prized hounds:

O my sorrow for the death of my dog, a sire among hounds!
With him I had no need of falcons!
He removed the need for a butcher or for purchasing
fetcher servants.

Ibn al-Muʿtazz also contributes to the repertoire of poems on this theme:

The dog-trainer brought out a slender saluki hound that he
had often used,
well trained, a wind-daughter – when you ask that she run,
he sends her even faster;
tongue sticking out of mouth the way daggers split
through their sheathes.
She grabs her prey without pause, just as suckling mothers
hug their children.

The identification of the *ṭardiyyah* as a separate category of topic-based poem during the Islamic period seems to reflect the particular tastes and predilections that characterised the court life and sporting activities of the Umawī and early ʿAbbāsī caliphs (including ibn al-Muʿtazz himself). While the hunt and chase, and indeed the animals involved as chaser and chased, continue to appear as images in court panegyric and indeed in poems that depict the continuing chase of love, the *ṭardiyyah* poem itself appears to have fallen out of favour, at least with those who were entrusted with the task of committing the poetic record to written form.

Zuhdiyyah: homiletic poetry.

Among the many tales in the expanded version of the *Thousand and One Nights* (a process examined in detail in ch. 5), is '*Madīnat al-nuḥās*' (The City of Brass). During the reign of the Umawī Caliph, ʿAbd al-Malik ibn

Marwān, the Amīr Mūsā ibn Nuṣayr is sent on a journey to locate the bottles in which King Solomon has imprisoned the demon spirits known as *jinn*. Numerous sinister beacons point the travellers towards a mysterious 'city of brass'. The journey to the city is frequently interrupted by pauses in front of weird statues and pillars, on each of which are written poems that warn about the ephemerality of life on earth and the failure of humanity to reckon with what is to come. The journey, in fact the entire tale, is a lengthy homily on mortality and sage conduct. It serves as a splendid vehicle for the story-teller to include *ad libitum* copious examples of sermons in verse addressed directly to mortals:

> O man, consider what you see and take heed before you go
> on your final journey.
> Offer provision of charity for your benefit, for every
> house-dweller will depart.
> Consider too those who embellished their houses; under the
> earth they have become a pledge for their deeds.
> They built, but to no avail; they stored up goods, but
> their wealth was useless when their lifespan came to an
> end.

Upon hearing many examples of this type of poetry, the Amīr Mūsā spends much of the journey in tears; indeed such is the cumulative effect on him that at the conclusion of the tale he asks the caliph for permission to retire to a life of contemplation in Jerusalem.

The word *zuhd* means literally asceticism, and the type of poetry that was to become the *zuhdiyyah* stresses the inevitability of death and thus an avoidance of life's excesses in favour of a path of self-denial and contemplation. The world created by such poetry is one of stark contrasts. Humans in their mortality are weak, at the beck and call of death whenever God so decrees; 'dust thou art, and to dust thou shalt return'. The coming of the Day of Judgement is inevitable; evil-doers will be punished, and the pious will earn their reward. Those who accrue wealth and power in this lifetime will discover its worth when the great leveller places their mortal remains in the grave. This aspect of the general theme, often referred to as the *ubi sunt* motif and repeated many times in the poetry of the 'City of Brass' tale, finds a very early expression in the poetry of the great Khārijī poet, al-Ṭirimmāḥ (d. *c.* 723), and is closely echoed in a famous modern poem, '*al-Nās fī bilādī*' ("The People in My Country", 1954), by the Egyptian poet, Ṣalāḥ 'Abd al-Ṣabūr. One of the ways in which he uses the poem to illustrate the social tensions between traditional religious beliefs and the spirit of modern Egypt is to have the speaker's uncle deliver a homily to a group of men in his village:

So-and-so built himself palaces and raised them high,
forty rooms filled with shining gold.
One weak-echoed evening came the Angel of Death
with a small notebook in his fingers.
So-and-so was the first name on his list.
The Angel stretched out his stick
with the secret of the two letters 'Be'
and of the words 'He was',
and down into Hell rolled the spirit of So-and-So.

Examples can be found in the pre-Islamic poetic corpus that acknowledge an awareness of the impermanence of life and imminence of death; the works of ʿAdī ibn Zayd (cited above for his hunt poetry) are often mentioned in this connection:

I have never seen the likes of young men, deluded by
passing time, who manage to overlook its consequences . . .
Their souls imagine that death's destruction will never
reach them, while random fates aim a straight arrow.

While such sentiments clearly form one kind of precedent to the later emergence of the *zuhdiyyah* poem, the Qurʾān's specific and frequent references to God's judgement and to rewards and punishments based on deeds and attitudes in life clearly provided a rich source of inspiration. The message is unambiguous:

Those who prefer this world and its embellishments, we
will pay them full measure for their deeds there, and
their rights will be observed.
They are the people who in the next world will have only
Hellfire; whatever they have created will be as nought;
their previous deeds will be futile.

(*Sūrat al-Hūd* (11, Hud), vv. 15 and 16)

while *Sūrat al-Humazah* (104, The Backbiter) adopts the rhyming style of the early Meccan surahs to make the same point:

Woe to every backbiter, prevaricator
amassing wealth and counting it,
supposing his wealth will make him eternal.
No, no! Verily he will be cast into the Crusher.
What will inform you about the Crusher?
The fire of God set alight
towering over hearts
enveloped over them
in extended columns.

Warnings and injunctions such as these, coupled with *ḥadīth* that gave accounts of the Prophet's own behaviour during his lifetime, provided a ready repertoire of homiletic materials for those who would disseminate the more contemplative and ascetic aspects of the message of Islam; one of the most illustrious of such figures during the first century of Islam was al-Ḥasan al-Baṣrī (d. 728). Homilies and moral pronouncements were among the types of record that were committed to written form in collections, and the ideas and values that they contained were often couched in poetic form. The following lines, for example, are attributed to the famous grammarian, al-Khalīl ibn Aḥmad (d. 791):

> Live as seems right to you. Death is your mansion, and
> there is no escape from it.
> A house may be wealthy and glorious; the wealth will
> vanish, and the house will collapse.

During the period of the Umawī caliphs, a judge named Sābiq al-Barbarī (d. early eighth century) earned a wide reputation for his sermon-poems, but the genre is regarded as reaching its acme with the work of two poets, both of whom were suspected of adhering to heterodox beliefs. The earlier of the two, Ṣāliḥ ibn ʿAbd al-Quddūs, sounds familiar themes:

> Humans collect, and time divides; while fate tears things
> apart, they keep on patching.

but he also included in his poetry references to certain dualistic beliefs which, in the politically sensitive early decades of the ʿAbbāsī caliphate, were regarded as suspect; on the orders of the Caliph al-Mahdī he was executed as a *zindīq* (heretic) in 784. The second and more famous poet, Abū al-Atāhiyah (d. 826), managed to circumvent such accusations. Like most poets, accounts of his career come supplied with anecdote. One suggests that he devoted himself to *zuhdiyyāt* after failing in love, while another records that he demanded of his contemporary, Abū Nuwās, that he relinquish the field of *zuhd* poetry and concentrate instead on his obvious forte, namely the poetic genres that focus on the celebration of life's pleasures. The relative balance of sections in each poet's *dīwān* lends some credence to the story, and yet Abū Nuwās's does include a section devoted to *zuhdiyyāt* and their cautionary message:

> Death is ever near us, never far removed.
> Every day brings death's call and the wailing of keening
> women . . .
> How long will you frolic and jest in delusion
> When every day death glows to the flint of your life?

Whether or not this story concerning a proposed subdivision of speciality (an interesting notion in itself) has any veracity, Abū al-Atāhiyah's concentration on this genre was sufficient to make him Arabic's *zuhdiyyah* poet *par excellence*. His poetry insists on the reality of humanity's mortality: death is inevitable and life a purely transitory phase that it is pointless to prolong:

> How lofty the hopes to which you have clung!
> How insistently you have relished the ephemeral world!
> Good man, make ready to leave – family and wealth,
> For death is a certainty in every circumstance.

It is God alone who possesses the power:

> Take heed! We are all dust. Who among humans is immortal?
> From their Lord do they come and to Him do they all return.

Wisdom therefore demands that humans in their impotence adhere to God's injunctions through piety and good works. They should be satisfied with what is enough (*kafāf*) and not embark on a useless quest for riches; those who do so and abuse others in the process know their reward:

> Daily sustenance should meet your needs. How great is the sustenance of those who die!
> God is my sufficiency in every matter; in Him is my wealth and to Him do I express my need.
> If what suffices does not meet your needs, then the entire earth cannot do so.

The poetry of Abū al-ʿAlāʾ al-Maʿarrī (d. 1058) participates in the same *zuhdiyyah* tradition. Yet the poetic voice of this blind philosopher-poet, one of the most famous in the whole of Arabic literature, is less concerned with homiletics than with philosophical reflection tinged with pessimism. Such was his fame as a scholar that in 1008 he travelled from his native Syria to Baghdad in order to participate in the intellectual life of the great caliphal capital. However, he only stayed for some eighteen months, leaving in disillusion to return to his home-town where he spent the rest of his life. Some of the themes of the *zuhdiyyah* are certainly present in his poetry,

> The finest of time's gifts is to forsake what is given;
> God extends a predatory hand to what He has provided.
> Better than a life of wealth is one of poverty; a monk's
> garb is better than a king's fine clothes.

and,

> Charity doesn't involve a fast that causes fasters to fade
> away, nor is it prayer and woolen garments on the body.
> No! It involves casting evil aside and clearing your heart
> of rancour and envy.
> As long as beasts and cattle are still afraid, the lion's
> talk of abstinence remains invalid.

but al-Maʿarrī is constantly wondering about the meaning of a life that to him brings only misery. One of his most famous expressions of this gloomy vision is:

> If only a child died at its hour of birth and never
> suckled from its mother in confinement.
> Even before it can utter a word, it tells her: Grief and
> trouble is all you will get from me.

Such a life-view is a constant theme of al-Maʿarrī's great collection *Luzūm mā lā yalzam* (Adherence to What is Not Required [usually abbreviated to *al-Luzūmiyyāt*]), the title of which refers to his self-imposition of a more elaborate rhyming pattern than required by the poetic canon. For al-Maʿarrī every heartbeat is a further step towards the grave, and death itself is a relief from hardship:

> My clothing is my shroud, my grave is my home; my life is
> my fate, and for me death is resurrection.

However, as Sperl points out in his book on mannerism, along with the gloom and doom of al-Maʿarrī's pessimism comes a sardonic tilt against the orthodoxies of his era and those who advocated them. These lines are among the more obvious in expressing what is a constant in his poetry:

> In your time the ʿ*ulamā*ʾ have been lost, and over them
> hovers the blackest darkness;
> Error smothers our people since the black mare has lost
> her clear colouring.

One interpretation of the second line is that the 'black mare' (*dahmā*ʾ) is a reference to the ʿAbbāsī caliphate, which, in a nice touch of *badī*ʿ (the device known as *tajnīs* [paronomasia]), al-Maʿarrī introduces into the line a second time to match the same word ('*dahmā*ʾ') in the sense of 'people, crowd'.

Like the hunt-poem described above, the *zuhdiyyah* does not appear to have retained its currency to any significant extent among al-Maʿarri's successors. Those poets who did turn their attention to the genre hark back to the message and style of Abū al-Atāhiyah. Sharaf al-dīn al-Anṣārī (d. 1264), for example, exhorts his listeners:

Where are the quavering hearts, the copious tears
For the sins committed, too countless to describe? . . .
Weep many tears then till you imagine your eyelids to
bleed,
And seek God in order to gain the blessings of His
goodness.

MODERN ARABIC POETRY

In the opening chapter of this book I suggested that one of the primary goals behind its mode of organisation was to emphasise continuities. In the preceding sections of this chapter on Arabic poetry I have attempted to illustrate the different ways in which themes and genres (*aghrāḍ*, to give them their Arabic term once again) developed during the pre-modern period and for modern poets became material for evocation or allusion (and, in the case of radical change, for rejection). However, the terms 'modern', 'modernity', and 'modernisation' – topics of many conferences and volumes in both Middle East and West – imply a posture that acknowledges the continuing processes of change and in particular a way of looking at or confronting the heritage of the past. Thus, while the previous sections have sought to illustrate linkages between past and present, I will close this chapter with a section that investigates the differences that mark its modern manifestations.

In discussing the Middle East's encounter with modernity, Marshall Hodgson notes that 'the individual lifespan came to embrace enormous, even shattering, historical changes, which a person had somehow to confront'. [*Rethinking World History*, 228] We suggested earlier that in this context Egypt's experience is not typical of the more gradual process of change which characterised most other regions of the Arabic-speaking world, but the very abruptness of its confrontation with the need for change – in the form of Napoleon's invasion in 1798 – provides a convenient model. On the broader regional scale Egypt found itself facing a vastly superior military and technological power, a sample of the kind of might that would buttress the European colonialising ventures of the later nineteenth century. However, as Egypt's ʿ*ulamāʾ* also discovered during Napoleon's invasion, this confrontation with the might of post-industrial Europe also involved an exposure to new types of learning and new modes that were to become available to disseminate it, most notably printing and the press. The resulting awareness on the part of Arab intellectuals of principles of Western parliamentary representation and the gradual implementation of secular systems of education and law, all these contributed to a radical break with the traditions of the past; and, as many commentators have observed, the process of introducing such changes into society was taking place at a pace considerably faster than had been the case in the Western context.

Faced with such forces, poets found themselves constrained to confront both the Western other, simultaneously the symbol of their nation's occupation by foreign forces and the impetus for many of the social changes in which they found themselves involved; and the self, as they sought to come to terms with the 'anxiety of influence' implicit in their relationship or confrontation with the poetic past. Changes within society itself – expanded educational opportunities, the emergence of a middle class, and, albeit at a more measured pace, the changing role of women in society, these contributed to the emergence of new audiences for poetry and a very different system of patronage. This change in poetic role was, of course, founded on and bolstered by the very notion of the individual, a person with rights and citizen of a nation, and by the consequent quest for a personal voice through which to reflect on these rapidly changing realities. All these features help to explain why in the early decades of the twentieth century a generation of Arab poets turned away from the directions that Arabic poetry had initially taken during the early stages of the revival (*al-nahḍah*) movement and found their inspiration in the poetry of European Romanticism. The neo-classical trend against which they were reacting had sought its models in the poetic heritage of the past. In the poetry of Maḥmūd Sāmī al-Bārūdī (d. 1904), Aḥmad Shawqī (d. 1932) and Ḥāfiẓ Ibrāhīm (d. 1932) in Egypt, form and occasion tended to echo the repertoire of the earlier tradition. That is a judgement on their collected poetry, but it should in fairness be added that each of them also composed some poems which made gestures to modernity, particularly in choice of themes. This trend is particularly noticeable in the poetry of Jamīl Ṣidqī al-Zahāwī (d. 1936) and Maʿrūf al-Ruṣāfī (d. 1945) in Iraq, both of whom seemed anxious to rid the classical *qaṣīdah* form of its lofty and detached associations. It should be added that, as modern Arabic poetry has witnessed the enormous processes of change that we are about to discuss, a number of poets, including Badawī al-Jabal (b. 1907), Bishārah al-Khūrī (renowned under the pen-name of 'Al-Akhṭal al-Ṣaghīr', d. 1968), and Muḥammad Mahdī al-Jawāhirī (b. 1900), continued to compose much admired poetry that maintains the neo-classical tradition while addressing itself with vigour and commitment to the concerns of the present. As Salma Khadra Jayyusi notes in her study of movements in modern Arabic poetry, for example, al-Akhṭal al-Ṣaghīr's poetry combines classical and romantic sensibilities in a way that makes him an important foundation for the emergence of a later generation of romantic poets in his native Lebanon.

Between these two approaches to poetry and modernity a key bridge role is often assigned to Khalīl Muṭrān (d. 1949), a Lebanese poet who spent most of his career in Egypt and is known as 'poet of the two regions'. While the bulk of his poetry is of the more occasional variety (panegyrics and elegies, for example) and thus places him in the company of Aḥmad Shawqī and Ḥāfiẓ Ibrāhīm, the language and mood of a few poems, '*al-Masā*'' ('Evening'), for example, which was cited earlier, affords an illustration of the kind of sensibility that seems to reflect Muṭrān's hopes for the future. Those aspirations find their clearest expression in a 'Brief Statement' prefaced to his 1908 collected poems in which he lays considerable emphasis on the unity of the poem and the creative role of the individual poet.

Romanticism, as a reaction against the definitional strictures of classicism, found its earliest creative impulse among Arab writers living within a set of communities that were themselves the consequence of a major change, the *émigré* (*mahjar*) communities of the Americas, North and South. Far removed from the watchful eye of conservative critics, these predominantly Christian poets found themselves exercising their poetic creativity in a cultural environment in which they were almost automatically exposed to the literary and philosophical heritage of their newly adopted abodes. These influences were to have a profound effect on the way that a whole generation of Arab poets looked at the role and especially the language of poetry; in this latter regard, many of them were also much influenced by the language and cadences of the new Protestant translation of the Bible into Arabic that had been completed in the latter half of the nineteenth century. In order to provide each other with support in both writing and publication, these writers established their own cultural societies: *al-Rābiṭah al-qalamiyyah* (The Bond of the Pen) founded in New York in 1920, and *al-'Uṣbah al-Andalusiyyah* (The Andalusian Group) founded in São Paulo, Brazil in 1932. Of the northern group the undisputed leader is Jubrān; indeed he led from the front in his use of different forms – revivals of earlier strophic structures such as the *muwashshaḥ* and early experiments with prose poetry – and above all in his sensitivity to the creative potential of language. As has often happened within the Arabic poetic tradition, a refrain from his most famous poem, '*al-Mawākib*' ('Processions', already quoted above), is now known throughout the Middle East in the hauntingly beautiful musical version sung by Fayrūz:

> Give me the lyre and sing, for singing is the secret of
> existence,
> And, though it all vanish, the melody lingers on.

Jubrān's colleague in New York and the northern group's most significant critical writer was Mīkhā'īl Nuʿaymah (d. 1988). His most searing poetic statement reflects his experience as an American soldier of Arab descent who has fought in the First World War. The speaker in '*Akhī*' ('My Brother') localises the issue from the outset by noting the possibility that 'someone from the West' may brag about his accomplishments. However, as he notes in the final stanza, the Arab world has nothing to brag about:

> My brother! Who are we, with neither homeland, people,
> nor neighbour?
> Whether asleep or awake, our garb is shame and disgrace.

In other poems and especially in his collection of critical articles, *al-Ghurbāl* (The Sieve, 1923), Nuʿaymah displays his advocacy of change in a less pessimistic vein. But of the poets in the northern group it is Īliyyā Abū Māḍī (d. 1957) whose works best illustrate the tensions involved in this process of change in poetic sensibility. For, while his earlier poetry shows the influence of earlier and contemporary models, his most famous collection, *al-Jadāwil* (Brooks, 1927, with an introduction by Nuʿaymah) is generally regarded as a major contribution to the development of Arabic romantic poetry. Song has once again made one of its poems, '*Ṭalāsim*' ('Charms'), widely known in the Arab world, and, in spite of its wayward length, the opening stanzas do establish a characteristically quizzical tone:

> I came, I know not where from, but I came.
> I had seen a way before me, so I took it
> And I will continue, whether I wish or not.
> How did I come? How did I see my way?
> I do not know.

In another poem, '*al-ʿAnqāʾ*' ('The Phoenix'), the poetic voice expresses a yearning for contentment:

> I am not the first to be infatuated with this beauty, for
> she is the world's aspiration as much as mine ...

The quest is in vain, but at the poem's conclusion there is a discovery:

> Grief crushed my spirit, and it flowed with tears. Just
> then I spotted her and in my very tears touched her.
> It was only when such knowledge was of no avail that I
> discovered the one I had lost to be with me.

Among the southern group of poets the most prominent names are Rashīd al-Khūrī (d. 1984) and Ilyās Farḥāt (d. 1980), both of whom are recalled for their advocacy, albeit from a substantial distance, of the cause of Arab nationalism, and the Maʿlūf brothers, Fawzī (d. 1930) – author of the famous long poem '*ʿAlā bisāṭ al-rīḥ*' ('On the Wind's Carpet', 1929) – and Shafīq (b. 1905).

The work of these poets was transmitted to the Middle East, not only through publication in the region itself (such as that of Fawzī Maʿlūf's poem in the Lebanese journal, *al-Muqtaṭaf*), but also through journals published in America (such as Abū Māḍī's *al-Sāmir*) that were sent back to the Arab world and personal correspondence. The introduction of Nuʿaymah's critical collection, *al-Ghurbāl*, was written by ʿAbbās Maḥmūd al-ʿAqqād, one of the most prominent early advocates of romantic ideals in Egypt. Al-ʿAqqād and his two colleagues, ʿAbd al-raḥmān Shukrī (d. 1958) and Ibrāhīm al-Māzinī (d. 1949), became avid devotees of the school of English romanticism as students, and, even though the group later split apart in acrimony, the causes that they espoused were still gathered around the title of the journal that they published in two parts in 1921, *al-Dīwān*. Part of the process involved debunking the pretensions of neo-classicism, and al-ʿAqqād undertook the mission with gusto in his attack on what he regarded as the outmoded artificiality of Shawqī's public poetry. As al-ʿAqqād's introduction to Nuʿaymah's collection also shows, the Egyptian poet-critic regarded it as part of his function to stand guardian at the gate of change and to monitor some of the more radical changes being advocated by the *mahjar* poets and others. It has to be admitted that he was considerably more successful in this role than as a poet, and for that reason it is no small tragedy that the best poet of this trio, Shukrī, was the object of a savage attack in *al-Dīwān* penned by his erstwhile colleague, al-Māzinī.

The creativity, whether in poetry, criticism, or both, of these pioneers laid the framework for the heyday of Arabic romantic poetry – the inter-war period stretching into the 1940s, a good deal of which has been cited above in the sections on description and love poetry. For the Arab nations these were years of social turmoil and of confrontation with the Western powers. Following the lead of earlier romantic poets like Nuʿaymah and members of the South American *mahjar*, the renowned Tunisian poet, Abū al-qāsim al-Shābbī (d. 1934), was fired by the fervour of nationalist sentiment and sought to rouse his people in stirring tones:

> If a people ever wills to live, then fate must respond.
> Night must be revealed, and chains be severed.
> Whoever is not embraced by a desire for life dissolves in
> the air and vanishes
> So woe to the one who can find no solace in life from
> the blows of an all-powerful nothingness.
> Thus did the universe of beings speak to me, in the voice
> of its veiled spirit.

Al-Shābbī, whose published lecture, 'Poetic Imagination Among the Arabs' is a stirring statement of the ideals of romanticism, died at a tragically early age. Many of his poems are suffused with an awareness of death's imminence, and yet, in '*Al-Ṣabāḥ al-jadīd*' ('The New Morning'), he insists on transcending the gloomy foreboding:

> Be silent, you wounds and griefs!
> The age of lamentation, the era of madness are over.
> Morning has dawned from beyond the centuries . . .

The final stanza is a parting of great poignancy:

> Farewell, farewell, mountains of cares,
> Mist of grief, path of hell!
> My raft has set off on the vast ocean
> And I have spread the sail. So, farewell, farewell!

Much of al-Shābbī's poetry was published for the first time in Cairo, where another group of poets, *Jamāʿat Apollo* (The Apollo Society) was fostered by the supportive environment provided by a guiding figure, Aḥmad Zakī Abū Shādī (d. 1955). Unlike the other groups we have just mentioned, the Apollo Society was less polemical in its attitudes, endeavouring to stress continuity rather than confrontation; its first two presidents were Aḥmad Shawqī and Khalīl Muṭrān. For a period of just two years (1932–34), its journal, *Apollo*, was an important meeting-place for discussions about poetry, and it is not a little ironic that its closure came about as a result of a dispute involving al-ʿAqqād, an advocate of the modern, as we have seen, but only on his own terms. Abū Shādī himself was a prolific poet, the author of nineteen collections; *al-Shafaq al-bākī* (Weeping Twilight, 1926–27) alone contains some 1,380 pages. He was also an inspiration for the creativity of others: in addition to al-Shābbī, the most significant names are Ibrāhīm Nājī (d. 1953) and ʿAlī Maḥmūd Ṭāhā (d. 1949). These poets and their *mahjar* predecessors were an acknowledged influence on another writer who died tragically young, the Sudanese poet Yūsuf Bashīr al-Tījānī (d. 1937), whose poetry succeeds in fusing these modern sensibilities and a thorough acquaintance with classical poetry culled from a traditional Islamic education into verses that are marked by a unique mystical quality:

> True being, how vast its extent in the soul!
> Purest silence, how firm its links to the spirit!
> Everything in existence walks in the folds of God;
> This ant in miniature is the sound of His echo.

During these same decades, the Palestinian poet, Ibrāhīm Ṭūqān (d. 1941) cast an increasingly angry eye on the ever worsening situation in his homeland and sought to rally people to the national cause:

> You people, your foes are not such as to be gentle and
> merciful.
> You people, before you is nothing but exile, so get ready.

Ṭūqān also composed love poetry, some of it acknowledging the attractions of the opposite sex in a playful vein, other poems venturing into the realms of pornography. For Ṭūqān, as for Ibrāhīm Nājī and ʿAlī Maḥmūd Ṭāhā, the game of love was one to be embarked on without guilt, but for their Lebanese contemporary, Ilyās Abū Shabakah (d. 1947), the animal desires provoked by love involve the horrors of sin and shame. While a later collection like *Ilā al-abad* (For Ever, 1945) may give expression to a more innocent and blissful love, the process of achieving that state sees the poet's persona laying bare his personal agonies; and no more so than in his appropriately named collection, *Afāʿī firdaws* (The Serpents of Paradise, 1938), to which we alluded above. The following lines are from his much quoted poem, '*al-Qādhūrah*' ('Squalour'):

Close the gates of paradise in the face of a poet who
plucks the strings of Hell as he chants.
If in his eye there blazes the fire of hate, in his
luminous heart resides a generous space for love.
With his spirit he senses the paradise of life, yet all he
sees is a Hell ever looming!

Alongside these developments in the 1930s and 1940s there emerged a group of symbolist poets. In view of the strong ties that have continued to link Lebanon with France and its culture, it is not surprising that most of the practitioners of this trend were of Lebanese origin or that they sought their models among the French symbolist poets. Indeed, the most influential of the Arab symbolists, Saʿīd ʿAql (b. 1912) was throughout his career a fervent advocate of Lebanese nationalism ('Phoenicianism') and also of following the Turkish lead by adopting the European alphabet; indeed his poetry collection, *Yārah* (1961, of which he himself recorded some extracts) was composed in the Lebanese dialect and published in Latin characters. However, ʿAql's true significance lies in the groundwork that his poetry laid for future developments in Arabic poetry. ʿAql's etherial creations, couched in a symbolic language of great beauty, may have been criticised by his successors for their supreme detachment from 'reality', but the more perceptive of poetic critics have come to realise the debt that those same successors owe to ʿAql in paving the way for the effective use of symbols during the decades following the Second World War.

With the post-war period came inevitable changes on the political and social fronts. Such was the impact of political corruption, continuing foreign occupation and interference, and the loss of Palestine in 1948, that the impetus for radical change – independence, self-determination, and social justice – became overwhelming. The 1950s were a decade of revolution in the Arab world, and literary genres were inevitably a part of the process. As we have already noted, 1947 saw the appearance of two attempts to achieve a final break with the demands of *qaṣīdah* structure; Nāzik al-Malāʾikah, the author of one of them, proceeded to develop a new prosodic system that relied on the unit of the poetic foot rather than the line as a whole. However, the movements that we have just described were determined to sweep away *anciens régimes*, and that of poetry was no exception.

In retrospect it is possible to see the changes in Arabic poetry since the 1950s as the major step in the direction of modernism. The achievements of the romantic movement were certainly considerable. The strong hold of the classical tradition (and its neo-classical manifestations) had been lessened; there had been a move from a patronised public voice to a more individual one, and poetic language had extended beyond the familiar repertoire of imagery to explore new associations of meaning. However, romantic poetry had veered in the direction of sentimentality, and symbolists like Saʿīd ʿAql were defining the aesthetics of their creations in terms of the sheer beauty of sound. These tendencies, not to mention the continuing prevalence of the *qaṣīdah* form, were to be challenged by a younger generation of poets. The political corruption and social injustice that for them symbolised the desolation of the Arab world were to be stimuli for poetic creativity that focussed on oppression, poverty, injustice, and exploitation and supported revolutionary change. If the title of T. S. Eliot's famous poem, 'The Wasteland', provided an emblematic text for so many Arab poets who read it in either the original or translation, then the rallying-cry of 'commitment' (*iltizām*) which came to prevail during the revolutionary decade of the 1950s afforded poetry (and other genres) a yardstick for social relevance.

Iraq, suffering under the joint burdens of British occupation and the corrupt regime of Nūrī al-Saʿīd, was a particularly fertile ground for the new, defiant voice of committed poetry, and also for the pattern of exile that has all too often been the automatic corollary of such expressions. ʿAbd al-wahhāb al-Bayātī (b. 1926), still exiled from his homeland and recently deprived of its citizenship, and Badr Shākir al-Sayyāb (d. 1964) graphically depict the conditions in which their fellow Iraqis live and work. Al-Bayātī's poem, '*Sifr al-faqar wa-al-thawrah*' ('The Book of Poverty and Revolution') begins:

From the abyss I call to you.
My tongue is parched . . .

before proclaiming:

Departing ships,
Migrating swan . . .
Word,
Artist's brush . . .
All these have I hailed
with the words:
'Let us burn,
So sparks will shoot from us
To light the revolutionaries' cries
And rouse the cock dead on the wall.'

The speaker of al-Sayyāb's poem, '*Unshūdat al-maṭar*' ('Song of the Rain'), generally acknowledged as one of the greatest poems in modern Arabic, is in exile and contemplates a future of untapped potential:

In every raindrop
A red or yellow flower-bud.
Each tear of hungry and naked people,
Each drop spilled from the blood of slaves,
Each is a smile awaiting new lips,
A teat rosy on a babe's mouth
In tomorrow's youthful world, giver of life.
Rain, rain, rain,
Iraq will blossom with rain.

The speaker hears distant thunder gathering on mountains and plains, preparing for a storm that will sweep away, like the vengeful God in many Qur'ānic stories, those 'thousand vipers who are sipping the nectar from a flower dew-fed by the Euphrates'. While, for these poets, the city is the seat of tyrannical and corrupt political authority, it also represents the crushing power of the modern, technological metropolis to destroy the oppressed peasantry who flock to it in search of a livelihood. The Sudanese poet, Muḥammad al-Faytūrī (b. 1930), takes up this favourite theme of poets who responded to the call of commitment in '*Aḥzān al-madīnah al-sawdā'*' ('Sorrows of the Black City'):

When darkness erects
Over city streets
Barriers of black stone,
People extend their hands
To the morrow's balconies . . .
Their days are ancient memories
Of an ancient land,
Their faces, like their hands, gloomy . . .
You might think they are submissive,
But actually they are on fire!

For the poets of Palestine this general sense of oppression and alienation acquired a more particular and intense focus as their homeland became the arena of conflict in 1948 following the declaration of the State of Israel. Questions of land, home, and identity, confrontations with violence, injustice, and exile, these cogent factors prompted a number of poets to adopt the defiant voice of resistance. Most famous among them is Maḥmūd Darwīsh (b. 1942), whose poems range from the directly confrontational, as in '*Biṭāqat huwiyyah*' ('Identity Card'):

Write it down!
I'm Arab,
And my card number is fifty thousand;
I have eight children
And a ninth ... is due late summer.
Does that annoy you?

to the more lyrical, although even in such poems (the renowned '*'Āshiq min Filasṭīn*' ('Lover from Palestine'), for example) the central message of exile, return, and confrontation is still present:

Wherever, however you are,
Take me and bring colour back
To my face and body
And light to my heart and eye ...
Take me as a verse from the book of my tragedy,
As a toy, a stone from my house,
Then our next generation
Will remember the way back home!

For Palestinian poets like Darwīsh, Samīḥ al-Qāsim (b. 1939), and Rāshid Ḥusayn (d. 1977), confrontation with the realities of the Israeli state was an almost daily event. For others, the dimensions of exile – within the Arab world and beyond – contributed to a somewhat different voice, still challenging, yet more nostalgic. One such was Tawfīq Ṣāyigh (d. 1971), whose personal life became emblematic of the fate of the exiled Palestinian but who managed to transcend these difficulties in poetry that was to be a major contribution to the development of prose poetry in Arabic. We have alluded above to the poems that expound his agonised love for an English woman named Kay, but his collected works provide numerous examples of the sorrow, frustration, and anger that accompanied the continuing loss of identity. There is also a quest for a resolution of the internal conflicts resulting from his profound Christian faith. The conclusion of a poem of very direct reference, '*Al-maw'iẓah 'alā al-jabal*' ('The Sermon on the Mount'), would seem to be linking these latter two concerns:

I know he will return,
And I await his return.
(Our cemetery is now on yonder hill.)
He will return to it, abandoning the crowds,
Seeking a headrest ...
Maybe he will open his mouth
And I may hear: 'Blessed are ... '

Exile is also a prominent theme in the poetry of Ṣāyigh's Palestinian colleague, Jabrā Ibrāhīm Jabrā (d. 1994). However, while Jabrā's works – in poetry, fiction, and criticism – reveal a similar experience of living 'In the Deserts of Exile' ('*Fī bawādī al-nafy*', the title of one of his poems), he also served an invaluable function by using his superb knowledge of English and its literature to make available through translation to the littérateurs of the Arab world some of the most significant works of English writing – including the tragedies of Shakespeare, and sections from Sir James Frazer's *The Golden Bough*. While the power of myth in fostering the national sense of identity had already become clear to a number of Arab writers who had studied in the West – including Jubrān, (Kahlil Gibran), Nuʿaymah, Lewis ʿAwaḍ, and Muḥammad Mandūr, Jabrā's translation of Frazer (1957) aroused enormous interest. As poets in the 1950s and 1960s sought fresh sources of inspiration through which to express their reactions to new political and social realities within the larger Arab world and their particular nations – a process that inevitably required an exploration of the complex relationship with the Middle East of the past, the ancient figures of Tammūz, Ishtār, and Adonis, and symbols of regeneration such as the Phoenix (*al-ʿAnqāʾ*) and Christ, became newly powerful symbols of both indigenous cultural values and modernity in poetic expression.

As has been noted earlier in this chapter, a primary role in the process of 'modernising' Arabic poetry involved changes in form: the move to free verse forms (*shiʿr ḥurr*) and to the prose poem (*qaṣīdat al-nathr*). Building on earlier experiments, the true pioneers here are Nāzik al-Malā'ikah and Badr Shākir al-Sayyāb. With his tragically early death in 1964, al-Sayyāb in particular had established himself as the first undisputedly great modern Arab poet, moving beyond concerns with form to a wonderful fusion of theme and technique through the invocation of ancient myth and the power of imagery. The example provided by his poetry was to be carried on by a generation of poets who, for all too brief a period, were his contemporaries. Many of them were members of a circle of poets and critics that gathered around the Beirut journal, *Shiʿr* (Poetry), founded by Yūsuf al-Khāl (d. 1987) in 1957. Al-Khāl's weekly Thursday gatherings provided a venue for discussions of poetry and modernity. He himself translated many prominent English-language poets into Arabic (including Whitman, Eliot and Pound), and his famous poem '*al-Biʾr al-mahjūrah*' ('The Deserted Well') provides a good illustration of the way in which myth was invoked in new poetic form and language to form a powerful contemporary message of rebirth:

If I could spread my forehead
On the sail of light,
If it were granted to me to remain,
Would Ulysses return, I wonder,
The Prodigal Son, the Lamb,
The Sinner stricken with blindness,
So that he might see the Way?

Al-Khāl's Lebanese contemporary, Khalīl Ḥāwī (d. 1982), shares many of his poetic qualities, but his vision is a much darker one. Ḥawī, who had also studied in the West and completed a Cambridge doctorate on Jubrān, uses '*al-Baḥḥār wa-al-Darwīsh*' ('The Sailor and the Dervish') to explore the clashing myths of East and West: the former with its vision of the great achievements of Western culture which to Ḥāwī's dervish had left behind nothing but 'ash from time's refuse', while to the latter the magical Orient remains a haven of story-tellers, 'lazy tavern, myths, prayer, and the languid shade of palm trees'. And, if his poem '*al-Jisr*' ('The Bridge') holds out some hope for a future generation that 'will deftly cross the bridge in the morning . . . to a new East, my own ribs laid out for them as a firm crossing', by the 1960s the always-questioning mood of Ḥāwī's poetic voice has assumed a yet grimmer tone. '*Al-Aʿzar 1962*' ('Lazarus 1962'), a work often seen as an uncanny prediction of the events of 1967, begins:

Deepen the hole, grave-digger,
Deepen it to a depth with no limits
Ranging beyond the orbit of the sun . . .

Ḥāwī's suicide during the Israeli invasion of Lebanon in 1982 was his own final and devastating statement of a defiance and despair that he had already expressed so graphically in his poetry.

Al-Khāl's closest colleague among the *Shiʿr* group was ʿAlī Aḥmad Saʿīd (b. 1928), universally known by his pen-name, Adūnīs. After the fruitful experimentation represented by *Shiʿr* and its côterie had succumbed to the machinations of politics typical of the 1960s, Adūnīs proceeded to establish his own journal, *Mawāqif*, which since that time has served as the primary platform of modernism in Arabic poetry. Indeed through both his own poetry and his extended writings on modernity and its relationship to the cultural heritage Adūnīs has come to personify the vanguard of change in the cultural life of the Arab world; in an environment where the role of literature has always been so closely linked to political processes, such a posture has brought him both renown and contumely. Quite how far the process of change in poetic creativity has gone can be gauged by comparing the form-based definition of poetry (still the prevalent norm in the 1940s) as 'discourse in metre and rhyme' with Adūnīs's notion that it is 'a vision (*ru'yā*)' and thus 'a leap outside of established notions'. The very function of poetry, he suggests, is to use language in innovative ways; if the transformation of meaning leads to difficulty and indeed obscurity, that should not inhibit the enjoyment of the poem's reception. Viewed in these terms, poetry comes close to T. S. Eliot's notion of a 'superior amusement', although it should immediately be added that such an association is not meant to imply any direct influence since Adūnīs readily acknowledges in his critical writings the influence of not only modernists among Arab poets of the classical period such as Abū Nuwās and Abū Tammām but also French poets from Mallarmé and Rimbaud to St John Perse. This approach to poetic language has tended to polarise debate within the community of modern Arab poetry. A poet and critic with very different views, for example, is the Egyptian, Ṣalāḥ ʿAbd al-ṣabūr – in this case a close reader of Eliot, whose modernity did not require such transformations of language. The portrait he paints of his fellow-countrymen in '*Al-nās fī bilādī*' ('People in My Country') is affectionate, yet disarmingly equivocal:

> People in my country are rapacious as hawks . . .
> Their laughter hisses like flame on firewood.
> They kill, steal, drink, and belch,
> But they're human,
> Good-hearted as long as they have a handful of coins,
> And they believe in fate.

With regard to Adūnīs, even critics of his approach to language acknowledge that he is the true modern successor of the great classical creators of the poetic image, such as al-Buḥturī. One often cited example from the short poem, '*Waṭan*' ('Homeland'), will illustrate:

> To a father who died green like a cloud
> On his face a sail,
> I bow . . .

The sail image, an aspiration to movement, provides a linkage to al-Khāl's poem cited above, but the striking conjunction of verdure – youth and fertility – and cloud – with its promise of rain and rebirth, a potent symbol for both the pre-Islamic poet and al-Sayyāb, creates a powerful sense of unfulfilled potential. Adūnīs's poetic oeuvre is replete with similar examples of his continuing quest for new and unusual combinations of words into arresting images. For him, *tajdīd* (innovation) is the means whereby Arabic and its speakers must learn to confront their past and find meaning for their present; he remains the Arab world's modernist poet *par excellence*.

The influence of Adūnīs's poetry and theoretical writing on younger generations of poets has been considerable, but the emulations of those less gifted than he and less aware of the poetic heritage have not met with critical or popular success. Meanwhile, many poets of Adūnīs's own generation – for example, ʿAbd al-wahhāb al-Bayātī, Aḥmad ʿAbd al-muʿṭī Ḥijāzī, and Nizār Qabbānī – have continued to forge their own paths through the tumultuous decades that have witnessed war and destruction in Palestine, Lebanon, Iraq, and the Gulf, and the concomitant vogues and conflicts within the cultural sector. If these figures continue to constitute the major figures in modern Arabic poetry, then a somewhat younger generation has come to the fore at a more recent stage; among a host of possible names we would cite Saʿdī Yūsuf (b. 1943) in Iraq, Maḥmūd Darwīsh (b. 1942) in Palestine (and in exile), Muḥammad ʿAfīfī Maṭar (b. 1935) and Amal Dunqul (d. 1982) in Egypt, Muḥammad al-Māghūṭ (b. 1934) in Syria, and Muḥammad Bannīs (b. 1948) in Morocco.

Arabic poetry today finds itself in a confrontation with another aspect of modernity, one that is having a considerable impact on all literary genres: the media. The case of Egypt, clearly the centre of the Arabic media, shows that there are positive and negative aspects to the situation. For, while television and cinema (not to mention videotapes and the Internet) have enormous potential for the dissemination of culture of all kinds, it is poetry of all literary genres that seems to be taking a back-seat in this confrontation between one medium that is highly visual and another that provokes and relies on the power of the imagination. Even so, it remains the case that, when tragedy strikes – as it continues to do in the war-torn region that is the Middle East, the resort of the Arabic-speaking people is to poetry, the public literary mode that best reflects their sense of self-identity, history, and cultural values.

CHAPTER 5

Belletristic prose and narrative

INTRODUCTION

A regular perusal of book review periodicals such as those published in London and New York provides confirmation of the fact that biography has become a popular, perhaps the most popular, genre among what is often termed the general reading public. The craft of the biographer has always seemed at its most obvious in those works devoted to prominent public figures, and not least politicians. The arts of inclusion and omission have ensured that the existence of several biographies of the same prominent personage and the widely divergent pictures that they manage to create provide ready corroboration of our increasing awareness of the linkages between biography and fictional genres and, in more general terms, of the fuzziness of the lines that separate genres which have been reckoned as factual from those that have not. Most particularly, recent research on the fascinating genre of autobiography, that ultimate act of self-arrogation, has served to identify unequivocally the intimate connections between that literary activity and fiction. With the subversion of the more legislative tendencies of genres that were so abhorred by Benedetto Croce, varieties of writing in such topics as history, biography, travel, as well as fiction, all come to be viewed as types of narrative, thereby sharing a number of structural and aesthetic features but differentiated by the contract that they establish with the reader, that contract itself being subject to varieties of manipulation by the author.

Modern Arabic fiction provides us with some interesting illustrations of this move beyond the more traditional generic borders and the various ways in which its possibilities are being exploited by creative writers. Emile Ḥabībī leads his reader on an inter-textual romp as he explores the illogicalities of the life of Palestinians in Israel in *al-Waqāʾiʿ al-gharībah*... (1972–74; translated into English as *The Secret Life of Saeed the ill-fated pessoptimist*, 1982), the very title of which – considerably abbreviated here – invokes the stylistic extravagance of earlier centuries. The narrators of several of ʿAbd al-raḥmān Munīf's (b. 1933) novels relate their narratives with a concern for the variety of possible versions that characterises the traditional story-teller (*ḥakawātī*), and the same concern with replicating older narrative modes within the framework of a modern novel characterises Ilyās Khūrī's *Riḥlat Ghandī al-ṣaghīr* (1989; *The Journey of Little Gandhi*, 1994). Jamāl al-Ghīṭānī (b. 1945) shows what is perhaps the greatest proclivity in this direction, using citations and virtuoso pastiches of historical, topographical and mystical writings as vehicles for his fiction.

This immensely creative variety of modes whereby generic categories have been and are being blurred serves as an excellent preliminary to this chapter in which we will explore literary works in Arabic which fit within the terms of reference identified by Leder and Kilpatrick in a most useful article: 'Works principally in prose, in which there is a pervasive concern with artistic expression as well as the communication of information'. (*Journal of Arabic Literature* 23:1 (March, 1992), 2). The goal, indeed the necessity, of transcending distinctions between fact and fiction and between the different types of writing that have traditionally been assigned to one or the other category provides an excellent basis on which to examine the various genres of belles-lettres in Arabic that are expressed in other than poetic form and to consider the tensions that exist between the norms of the classical tradition and the preferred discourses of modern writers.

In the contemporary Arab world, fiction, and especially the short story, is clearly the most popular mode of literary expression, having supplanted poetry in that role at some point in the mid-twentieth century. The factors involved in such a shift are too numerous and complex to explore in any detail here, but would seem to involve, among other things, changes in educational priorities, the influence of Western culture, and, most particularly, the impact on public tastes of modern media such as cinema and television. By contrast, in earlier centuries the prose genres existed in the shadow of a poetic tradition which, as we saw in the previous chapter, was the most prevalent force in the cultural life of society. At certain stages in the Arabic literary tradition poetry was regarded as the only mode of literary expression; as we will note in the chapter on criticism, discussion of 'the two crafts' (poetry and prose) is a later development. Thus, any retrospective study of the development of bellettristic genres and of the precedents to the emergence of modern narrative in Arabic finds itself confronted with an earlier tradition of writing in which not only was the balance between poetic and non-poetic expression tilted firmly in favour of the former but also the criteria and societal function of the latter were substantially different from their contemporary manifestations. One of the more surprising consequences of that difference can be illustrated by the contrasting attitudes of Western and Middle Eastern cultures to the Arab world's greatest collection of narratives, the *Thousand and One [Arabian] Nights* (originally translated into French by Antoine Galland and published in 1704). A Western world which has for two centuries avidly devoured, adapted, and bowdlerised the contents of this great store of tales discovers that, to quote Pellat, 'Arab scholars have never been able to consider [the *Thousand and One Nights*] worthy of the slightest esteem, seeing in it merely a trivial diversion incompatible with the tastes which a true believer should profess'. (*Encyclopedia of Islam*, 2nd edn. (1954 *et seq.*), 'Hikaya'). It is only relatively recently that these huge collections of narrative have become the object of interest among the critical community in the Arab world. The 'different criteria' to which I have just drawn attention will thus be studied in detail below, not least because I intend to include in this chapter a discussion of not only those works that have been incorporated into the traditional canon but also the varieties of narrative (such as the *Thousand and One Nights*) that have not.

QUESTIONS OF DEFINITION: *ADAB* AND BELLES-LETTRES

The origins and development of a corpus of belles-lettres in Arabic are directly linked to the concept of *adab*, a term that has undergone a number of transformations in meaning over the centuries. In modern times *adab* serves as the equivalent of the English word literature (in its narrower sense); in the Arab world I am described as *ustādh adab* (a professor of literature (studies)). Consulting a modern bibliographical source such as the bibliographical periodical, *al-Fihrist*, we find under the heading '*adab*' subheadings on such familiar literary topics as: style, structuralism, pessimism, aesthetics, prizes, love, war, religion, symbolism, poetry, emotion, women, drama, criticism, modernism, romanticism, death, and realism. There are also references to articles and books on '*al-adab al-muqāran*' (comparative literature). In earlier centuries, however, the term *adab* was used to describe a field that was considerably broader in scope. The original meaning of the verbal root from which the noun *adab* is derived implied inviting someone to a meal, and from that developed the notion of enriching the mind, particularly by training in the social norms of politeness. The ideas of intellectual nourishment, manners, and education, were thus present from the outset and remained important features of the concept as it developed and expanded within the general framework of the Islamic sciences. Within these terms of reference, *adab* was something that could be studied, taught, and learned. The person involved in those activities was the *adīb* (pl. *udabāʾ*), a term which in modern times is usually translated by the French term littérateur but which in earlier centuries identified a scholar and mentor whose areas of interest included such fields as grammar, poetry, eloquence, oratory, epistolary art, history, and moral philosophy (the fields noted by George Makdisi in *The Rise of Humanism* (Edinburgh, 1990)) and whose social status was a reflection of the love of learning and urbanity that were characteristics of the intellectual community within which the *adīb* fulfilled his function.

As the *udabāʾ* continued to practise their role as pedagogues and arbiters of literary taste, the concept itself underwent a process of change. However, as we search for parameters whereby works were included and excluded from this category, it seems possible to identify certain criteria as constants throughout the process of change. Firstly, audience: *adab* grew out of the environment of a cultured, 'literate' élite and was addressed to and reflective of the moral and cultural values of such an audience. Secondly (and derivative of the first), there is the matter of language: *adab* works were composed in the written Arabic language (*al-ʿarabiyyah al-fuṣḥā*) of which the Qurʾān was the (inimitable) model. Thirdly, textual medium: following the transfer, exemplified by the Qurʾān itself, from a culture that relied to a large extent on oral transmission of information and opinion to one that adhered to a system of laws and norms developed by generations of scholars working with textual sources, *adab* came to focus on texts, the written word – a process much enhanced by the introduction of paper to the region in the late eighth century, and chose not to concern itself with those forms of creativity that were not composed in or consigned to written form. Many *adab* works were, of course, a faithful record of the kinds of verbal debate and erudite exchanges that would characterise the variety of occasions – soirées (*musāmarāt*), sessions (*majālis*), and conferences (*muḥādarāt* – at which intellectuals and wits were gathered together. However, with the development of the status of the *adīb* as practitioner and teacher, *adab*, elevated language, and text came to be closely associated with each other to the exclusion of other types of creativity that did not match those criteria.

As the tradition of *adab* expanded and diversified in its functions as both instruction and entertainment, the majority of works preserved for posterity that were subsumed within its definitional borders took the form of compilations of information and anecdote on an astonishing array of subjects. Their themes ranged from the morally uplifting to the socially marginalised, and the organising principles that governed the ordering of their subject-matter ranged from the surface logic of chronology and geography to the apparently random collection of information that had in common only the fact that it was exotic and curious. There were also genres – types of fictional narrative, tales of history and travel, and autobiographies – that clearly bear the stamp of an individual author, but, as Abdelfattah Kilito has shown in a most interesting study (*L'auteur et ses doubles*, Paris, 1985), we need, in the context of *adab* works, to adjust our concept of authorship and originality in order to incorporate within it the contributions which the collectors of these many compilations, the *udabāʾ*, made to the library of Arabic belles-lettres.

Before we turn to the bellettristic works that were produced under the rubric of *adab* from its earliest manifestations in the chanceries of the Umawī court, we should consider the examples of prose writing that have been preserved from the pre- and early-Islamic periods, some of which were to furnish significant stylistic and structural features to the genres that were to develop within the *adab* tradition itself.

THE EARLIEST TEXTS IN PROSE

As we noted in the previous chapter on the Qurʾān, the revelations of God to Muḥammad included a number of narratives of different kinds. Particularly during the Meccan period, these included many rhyming passages replete with colourful imagery which, from the reactions of Muḥammad's listeners recorded as questions and comments in the text of the Qurʾān, were frequently confused with the discourse used by soothsayers and other popular preachers. We also noted that the recording of the revelations in textual form and the canonisation of that text – the Qurʾān – by the Caliph ʿUthmān marks the beginning of a vast exercise of recovery and analysis which involved tracing the precedents to the beginnings of Islam in the cultural and linguistic heritage of pre-Islamic Arabia and organising the modes whereby such a huge amount of information could be preserved, sifted, and studied. This movement was responsible, for example, for the recording of the poems from the oral tradition of pre-Islamic Arabia that had been passed down by bards from one generation to the next, and provided philologists and grammarians studying the language of the Qur'ān with their richest source of linguistic comparison. But the same motivations also led to the preservation of a number of other categories of text which provide samples of early Arabic prose. Yet again, the circumstances surrounding the transmission and recording of these works raise the possibility of later accretions to whatever may have been the original, but, as is the case with the poetic tradition, one must presume that, if the texts were accepted by the scholars of the time as authentic samples of their cultural heritage, then they can be regarded at the very least as accurate reflections of not only the original context but also its modes of transmission.

The oldest and most basic mode by which information was transferred is known in Arabic as the *khabar* (meaning a report, pl. *akhbār*); today *Al-Akhbār* is not only the name of a Cairene newspaper, but also the Arabic term for radio and television news. It is a distinct characteristic of *akhbār* from the earliest times that they announce clearly their status as narratives by recording in detail the series of sources through whose mediation the information has become available, working back from the present into the past and finally to the alleged point of origin. This structure (known in Arabic as the *isnād* (chain of authorities)) takes a form similar to the following: 'X told me that he had heard Y telling a story which he had heard from Z, to the effect that he had been present when the following occurrence happened . . . ' The actual account that follows the *isnād* is termed the *matn* (the report itself). The placing of such information regarding the narrative act and its sources at the beginning of the report is characteristic of a large number of narrative genres in Arabic. In the tales of the *Thousand and One Nights*, for example, the narrator of Shahrazād's narrative opens each night with a clear indication that she is continuing her narration. As we will note below, such an opening device is also a feature of the *maqāmah* genre.

A series of accounts which are, no doubt, as much a mirror of the intertribal rivalries of the early stages in the development of the Muslim community as they are of the spirit of the pre-Islamic era itself are the *akhbār* known collectively as the *ayyām al-ʿarab*, the narratives of the wars and battles in pre-Islamic times through which the fighting men of the clan avenged wrongs and resolved their conflicts with other tribes. The War of Basūs, for example, set in an atmosphere fraught with tribal rivalries and family tensions, began with the slaying of a prized she-camel and degenerated into a prolonged period of intertribal strife; its heroes, including the poet, al-Muhalhil, and battles became celebrated during the Islamic period (as were many tales of pre-Islamic chivalry and tribal solidarity) in a popular romance, that of al-Zīr Sālim, which finds a modern interpretation in the play of that name (1967) by the Egyptian playwright, Alfred Faraj (b. 1929).

Another characteristic mode of expression from the 'period of ignorance' is the rhyming utterances of the soothsayers, with their terse phraseology and prolific use of parallelism and colourful imagery. This very particular style of composition and delivery was echoed not only, as noted above, in the Meccan-period *sūrahs* of the Qur'ān but also in a variety of examples of composition from the early period of Islamic history: testaments (*waṣāyā*), proverbs, sermons, and orations (*khuṭab*). The great compilations that will be considered below – the *Kitāb al-aghānī* (Book of Songs) by Abū al-faraj al-Iṣfahānī (d. 967) and the *Al-ʿIqd al-farīd* (The Unique Necklace) of Ibn ʿAbd Rabbihi (d. 940), for example – illustrate the continuity of the tradition between the pre-Islamic and Islamic periods by providing examples of these genres during the lifetime of Muḥammad and the era of the early caliphs. Along with the extant examples of early legal texts, treaties, and the beginnings of official chancery documents, they form part of the recorded legacy of the early period in the development of the Muslim community in the seventh century.

The circumstances surrounding the early history of the Muslim community were described in ch. 2: the unexpectedly early death of the Prophet Muḥammad; the disagreements over the modes of appointment and affiliations of the early caliphs; and the conflicts and schisms that resulted. When the third caliph, ʿUthmān ibn ʿAffān, declared a single version of the revelations to Muḥammad to be the only authorised Qur'ān, he may have resolved the issue of the canonicity of the central source of divine guidance for the community, but there remained numerous other areas of conduct and belief on which the Qur'ān is silent. Faced with these many situations the community resorted to reports on what the Prophet had said and done, and the source of such information was a host of accounts (*akhbār*) recorded in the memories of the Prophet's companions and followers who had been part of his larger côterie.

Bearing in mind the disagreements and conflicts to which we have just drawn attention, it should not surprise us that not only did discrepancies begin to arise over the particulars of Muḥammad's utterances but also reports of questionable authenticity or expressive of the interests of a particular group began to circulate. By the end of the seventh century it was clear that, in order to disambiguate the sources for the code of belief and behaviour for the Muslim community in a number of areas, it was necessary to make a record of the statements and actions of Muḥammad during his lifetime. The movement thus set in motion provides Arabic literature with two important types of text that were to have a significant influence on the development of a tradition of prose literature: the *ḥadīth* – a report of a statement by Muḥammad on a particular issue or occasion, and the *sīrah* – the record of the Prophet's life.

With the collection of accounts concerning the life and conduct of the Prophet, the *isnād* segment of each account (*khabar*) described above now assumes an increased significance, in that it provides religious scholars with the evidence needed to check the authenticity of a report, the acceptance of which would have potentially major implications for the determination of appropriate conduct within the Muslim community. The *ḥadīth* accounts themselves vary widely in both length and degree of elaboration. Among the lengthier ones are those which elaborate on references found in the Qur'ān. The *ḥadīth al-ifk* (the slander *ḥadīth*), for example, provides considerable detail on the incident in which the Prophet's wife, ʿĀ'ishah, the daughter of Abū Bakr (later to become the first caliph), is slandered. The account dwells on her own emotions as the events unfold and on the tensions that inevitably arise between Muḥammad and his loyal companion until the entire issue is resolved. The account of the *isrā'*, Muḥammad's journey by night, is also elaborated. In the Qur'ān, *Sūrat al-isrā'* (17, v. 1) begins with the statement: 'Glory be to the One who took His servant by night from al-Masjid al-Ḥarām [in Mecca] to al-Masjid al-Aqṣā which We have blessed, to show him some of Our signs. He is the Hearer and Beholder.' Commentaries on the Qur'ān have offered different interpretations of the meaning of 'al-Masjid al-Aqṣā' (the furthest mosque). The more allegorical explanation sees it as a reference to heaven, whereas literalist authorities have taken it to mean the mosque in Jerusalem. To the basic framework of this account the *ḥadīth* sources add a good deal of detail. The angel Gabriel leads Muḥammad to a winged animal named Burāq on which he undertakes his journey. In Jerusalem he encounters Abraham, Moses, and Jesus, all of whom perform the prayers with Muḥammad as their imam. Moses is given a particular role in the story, in that, when God informs Muḥammad that Muslims should pray fifty times daily, it is Moses who urges the Prophet to return and request a lower number. Even when the number is reduced to five, Moses's response is: 'Your community is not capable of five prayers. Return to your Lord and pray to Him for relief for your community'. Muḥammad declares himself ashamed to do so, and God's injunction remains at five. (See J. C. Burgel, in *Critical Pilgrimages*, Texas, 1989, p. 57.)

The process of compiling the vast collection of reports that make up the *ḥadīth* collections – the second major source on matters of doctrine and behaviour after the Qurʾān itself, occurred in several stages, each involving different principles. The first stage (at the end of the seventh century) involving collections of materials preserved by companions and followers of the Prophet (named *ṣuḥuf*, sing. *ṣaḥīfah*) was the reflection of a growing concern over the loss through death of many key figures in the process of evaluating the authenticity of the number of reports concerning the Prophet. By the mid-eighth century, collections were being organised by category (*muṣannaf*); the best known example is *al-Muwaṭṭaʾ* by Mālik ibn Anas (d. 770), the founder of one of the four major 'schools' of Islamic law. However, while this mode of organising such a large corpus of materials assisted greatly in the process of codifying the legal system, it did not address the increasing problem regarding *ḥadīth* of dubious authenticity. By the end of the eighth century, scholars were beginning to pay closer attention to the issues raised by the *isnād*; the kind of compilations that they produced, arranged according to the names of the Prophet's companions who served as the source of the account, was termed *Musnad* (from the same verbal root as *isnād*). One of the most famous examples of this kind of *ḥadīth* collection is that of yet another founder of a school of law, Aḥmad ibn Ḥanbal (d. 855), whose *al-Musnad* consists of some 30,000 *ḥadīth*. By the ninth century, the science of *ḥadīth* scholarship had refined a critical process that permitted the compilation of the two most famous collections, those of al-Bukhārī (d. 870) and Muslim ibn al-Ḥajjāj (d. 875) who are referred to together as '*al-Shaykhān*' (the two chiefs). Their works, called *al-Jāmiʿ al-ṣaḥīḥ*, are collections of *ḥadīth* that conform with the criteria for the most authenticated reports, termed *ṣaḥīḥ* (authentic). That term represented the highest category of authenticity, a *ḥadīth* whose chain of transmitters shows no weakness (*ʿillah*); below this category were other examples of *ḥadīth* that were 'fine' but not flawless (*ḥasan*) and 'weak' (*ḍaʿīf*). Alongside these compilations of the *ḥadīth*, critics also set themselves to categorise the transmitters, using yet another scale from *thiqah* (completely reliable source) to *kadhdhāb* (arch-liar). Al-Bukhārī is the author of such a study, *Kitāb al-rijāl al-kabīr* (Major Work on Men (authorities)).

In addition to the obvious significance that this increasingly elaborate process of authentification and codification had for the establishment of a system of law and conduct in the Muslim community, we need to stress that the processes involved and the critical methods that were developed by scholars transcended the areas of Qurʾān and *ḥadīth* research. As we will note in the chapter on criticism, the methods developed in the recording and sifting of *ḥadīth* were also used to categorise poetry and poets. Such was the nature of the intellectual environment created by the needs and priorities of the Muslim community that many scholars who made major contributions to the Islamic sciences also contributed to the development of the *adab* tradition.

Alongside and linked to trends in *ḥadīth* scholarship, an elaborate tradition developed to provide accounts of Muḥammad's life. Under the title '*al-sīrah al-nabawiyyah*' (the biography of the Prophet) numerous works were compiled throughout the pre-modern period. The earliest compilation appears to be that of Wahb ibn Munabbih (d. 732), but the most famous work to appear under this title is that of Muḥammad ibn Isḥāq (d. 767), as edited by ibn Hishām (d. *c.* 833). As the tradition developed, compilations became extensive and elaborate, incorporating materials from a wide variety of sources: one of the largest later exemplars is *al-Sīrah al-shāmiyyah* (The Syrian biography [of the Prophet]), the work of Muḥammad al-Ṣāliḥī who died in 1535. In addition to these specific works, segments devoted to the Prophet's biography are also to be found in numerous other types of text, such as Qurʾān commentaries (*tafsīr*), *ḥadīth* compilations, and histories. Furthermore, subgenres, such as the *maghāzī* – works specifically devoted to episodes of raids and treaty-signing in which Muḥammad was involved, are often subsumed within the category of *sīrah*.

The primary focus of the *sīrah* compilations was Muḥammad's life, with accounts of his contacts with family, companions, and adversaries, descriptions of battles and negotiations, and citations of correspondence. The collections (and segments of larger works) comprise a mixture of anecdotes, battle narratives, miraculous tales, and poetry; there are elaborations on incidents depicted in the Qurʾān, tales concerning the lives of Prophets mentioned in the Qurʾān (such as Adam and Moses), and discussion of the genealogy of Arabian tribes. While much of this material is of relevance to the life of Muḥammad and to any account of his prophetic mission, scholars have noted that, as is the case with the *ḥadīth*, the inclusion of certain types of material (the segments on genealogy, for example) is clearly also a reflection of the ways in which adherents of the various factions within the Muslim community made carefully selected use of the sources available to provide precedents in order to validate their claims to legitimacy.

From the many types of expression in the early-Islamic period that are mostly in prose, we have focused in particular on the categories of *ḥadīth* and *sīrah* because the textual features that they display and the methods developed to compile and analyse them can serve as models for other types of individual work and compilation that are subsumed within the framework of this chapter. Some of those text-types have already been mentioned in the course of our discussion: commentaries on the Qurʾān (*tafsīr*) and historical writings are two such. To them we can add that of *ṭabaqāt* (classes), works which placed categories of people – jurisconsults, grammarians, and poets, for example – into groups according to particular characteristics or qualities. A further feature of all these variegated genres is that they participate in the long-standing predilection for invoking the great heritage of Arab (and indeed Middle Eastern) fables and legends. As we have already noted, such tales could be invoked not only for the sheer delight in narrative (a tendency that was to find expression in another type of *sīrah* – the *sīrah shaʿbiyyah* – in which the composers of popular romances made use of the ancient tales of tribal glory as the basic material for lengthy sagas that served as one of the great repositories of narrative creativity among the Arabs) but also in order to foster a sense of communal identity and to forward the claims to prominence of one religious or ethnic group against another.

THE DEVELOPMENT OF *ADAB*

Beginnings

By the end of the seventh century, the sheer dimensions of the area contained within the *dār al-Islam*, comprising an increasingly elaborate mixture of races, religions, and languages, demanded that the central administration of the caliphate in Damascus develop and maintain a sizeable and diverse chancery system. While the early caliphs of the Umawī house may have been willing to allow such administrative functions to be carried out in the languages of the personnel involved and indeed to make use of the same procedures as had obtained during the pre-Islamic period, the Caliph ʿAbd al-Malik (d. 705) required that Arabic become the language of chancery documents. As the personnel in those departments, the secretaries (*kuttāb*, sing. *kātib*) – in effect a newly emerging class of bureaucrats – grew in number and as their tastes became more urbane and cosmopolitan, the growing complexity of the administrative apparatus and the shift to Arabic as the mode of communication made it necessary not only to establish terms of reference within which the system of communication would function but also to develop texts and methods through which the desired norms of discourse and matters of taste could be inculcated into trainees. The process of meeting these somewhat practical needs was later to be subsumed within the fascinatingly complex cultural debate known as the *shuʿūbiyyah* (mentioned in ch. 2), the process whereby those converts to Islam whose cultural background was not that of the Arabian peninsula sought to challenge the implied superiority of the values that the members of the Arabian tribes had brought to the increasingly cosmopolitan Muslim community. It was thus within the exciting era when that community found itself forced to confront its new cultural complexities that we can trace the early stages in the development of *adab*, a mode of discourse that would reflect the educational needs and cultural taste of this urbane (and often contentious) class of *kuttāb*.

The administration of the caliph's authority centred on a number of departments (Arabic *dīwān*); the chancery was termed *dīwān al-rasāʾil* (the correspondence department). The process whereby the secretaries of that department (*kuttāb*) would archive documents received from rulers and administrators in various governorates and then compose appropriate letters (*rasāʾil*, sing. *risālah*) in reply provided the initial context for a focus on the study and teaching of prose style. The word *risālah* shares with the English word 'epistle' the notion of a text of enduring significance and even of instructional intent, and it is in the realm of the *risālah*, the process of offering advice, and most especially, advice on good government, that the first monuments of Arabic belles-lettres are to be found. Once again, there is a link to the multi-cultural environment of the early eighth century and, in this case, the desire of ʿAbd al-Malik's son, the Caliph Hishām (d. 743), to see the Muslim community's perspective expanded through the translation of works from other cultural traditions. The head of Hishām's chancery was Sālim Abū al-ʿAlāʾ, who may well have been the translator of an advice manual on secretarial conduct towards the ruler perhaps based on Aristotle's correspondence with Alexander; whether or not he is the translator, his status as a pioneer in the development of *adab* needs to be acknowledged.

The name more usually associated with the earliest manifestations of a school of *kuttāb* writing is one of Sālim Abū al-ʿAlā's pupils, ʿAbd al-ḥamīd 'al-Kātib' (d. 750), who served as secretary to the last of the Umawī caliphs, Marwān II, and who, according to one version, died with his master. ʿAbd al-ḥamīd wrote several Epistles, including what appears to be the earliest example of the 'Mirror for Princes' genre, an Epistle to ʿAbdallāh, Marwān's son, in which ʿAbd al-ḥamīd describes in detail the appropriate deportment and behaviour of the good ruler towards his entourage and subjects before turning somewhat abruptly to the more practical aspects of military strategy, troop organisation, and intelligence. In our current context, however, it is ʿAbd al-ḥamīd's Epistle to the Secretaries that is more germane. After a splendid exordium which provides an interesting glimpse of the status to which holders of the rank of *kātib* aspired, he goes into considerable detail about the training and duties of the office. His advice is proffered in the most direct of styles:

> Then perfect your calligraphy, for it is the ornament of your writings. Recite poetry, and get to know its themes and less familiar aspects; the glorious battle-days of the Arabs and Persians as well, their tales and sagas. Such things are enjoined on you so as to conform with your high-reaching aspirations. Do not overlook computation either, for that is the basic skill of the tax official.

While the subject-matter of ʿAbd al-ḥamīd's Epistle to the Prince seems to reflect the admixture of Arabic and Persian influences that were so characteristic of this period, his writings display a thorough acquaintance with the genres and language of early Arabic prose. The Epistles reflect a complete familiarity with the Qur'ān, its tropes and structures, and his style, with its predilection for balanced phrases and parallelisms, is a product of a keen awareness of the styles of not only the Qur'ān but also the other early Arabic sources that we have just analysed. His important status was widely recognised: the renowned bibliographer, ibn al-Nadīm (d. 991?), for example, notes that: 'epistle-writers are indebted to him in that they followed his path; he is the one who smoothed the way in developing a stylistics of letter-writing'.

In spite of such verdicts however, ʿAbd al-ḥamīd's name is often linked to, and more frequently overshadowed by, that of his contemporary, the Persian *kātib* originally named Rūzbīh who adopted the

Arabic name, ʿAbdallāh Ibn al-Muqaffaʿ (d. 757). About him ibn al-Nadīm says that: 'he was the ultimate in style and eloquence, one of those who translated Persian works into Arabic, equally fluent and eloquent in both'. Alongside his knowledge of and pride in Persian culture that grew out of his upbringing, a period of study in the Iraqi intellectual centre of al-Baṣrah led him to develop a strong attachment to the Arabic language and an awareness of both its heritage and potential as an instrument of expression; from a later context an anecdote in the *Kitāb al-imtāʿ wa-al-muʾānasah* of Abū Ḥayyān al-Tawḥīdī (d. 1023) – a major prose writer whose works we will examine below, recounts ibn al-Muqaffaʿ being asked by a group in al-Baṣrah to compare the relative merits of different peoples. Showing an awareness of the controversial nature of such an exercise in intercultural comparison, ibn al-Muqaffaʿ responds with an appreciation of the Arabs for 'the soundness of natural endowment, correctness of thought, and acuteness of understanding' (see Ilse Lichtenstadter, *Introduction to Classical Arabic Literature*, New York, 1974, pp. 353–5). Like ʿAbd al-ḥamīd, ibn al-Muqaffaʿ contributed a manual on the politesses of court officialdom, the *Kitāb al-adab al-kabīr* (Major Work on Courtly Etiquette); a variety of other works are also attributed to him, including an imitation of the style of the Qurʾān itself. However, such were the cultural and political controversies in which he seems to have involved himself (he was executed in 757 by the Governor of Iraq) that it is difficult to disambiguate the details of his life and beliefs, not to mention the attributions that have been made to such a personification of the intercultural rivalries of the time. One feature of his career that is not in doubt is his major role in the realm of translation, in this context, as elsewhere (as Walter Benjamin has shown in a famous essay in the topic), a major conduit of cultural cross-fertilisation and change. Ibn al-Muqaffaʿ applied his bilingual skills and stylistic sensitivity to the process of translating a number of works from the Persian tradition, the most famous of which is a collection of animal fables of Indian provenance concerning wise government, the *Panjatantra*, which he rendered into Arabic as *Kalīlah wa-Dimnah* (from the Pahlavi title of the work). Named for two jackals who appear at the beginning of the collection, the work consists of a series of tales that are evoked by Bidpai, a wise philosopher, in response to questions posed by a king named Dabshalim. The way in which each section begins and the transition mechanism to the tale itself is illustrated by this example:

King Dabshalim ordered Bidpai to tell the tale of someone who, having been successful in the achievement of his goals, finds himself immediately losing what he has acquired. The Philosopher responded that the process of achieving a laudable goal is frequently less difficult than that of retaining it. The person who is unable to retain what he has acquired is like the tortoise in the following tale . . .

In spite of wide variations in the textual sources of this translation by Ibn al-Muqaffaʿ, what may be termed a 'tradition of the text' has become firmly established within Arab-Islamic culture, and its format and style have come to be seen as major contributors to the development of a tradition of Arabic belles-lettres.

Ibn al-Muqaffaʿ's career coincides with the tense period of conflict that marked the transition from the Umawī to the ʿAbbāsī caliphate; indeed his life was cut short by order of the Governor of Iraq appointed by the second caliph of the Banū ʿAbbās, al-Manṣūr (d. 775), to whom ibn al-Muqaffaʿ had allegedly addressed one of his original works, *Risālah fī al-ṣahābah* (Epistle on the (Caliph's) Entourage). It was al-Manṣūr who determined to reflect the new political and social balance of the Muslim community by ordering the construction of a new capital and moving the caliph's court away from Damascus and further to the east. While the capital city was beginning to fulfil its function as a focus of the caliph's authority, thus initiating the process that would eventually turn it into a cultural centre of unrivalled influence, the two traditional centres of learning in Iraq – al-Kūfah and al-Baṣrah – witnessed the heyday of their prestige. Al-Khalīl ibn Aḥmad (d. 786) pioneered the study of prosody, music, and lexicography, and his eminent pupil, Sībawayh (d. 792), compiled a work of grammar which is regarded as the *locus classicus* of the Arabic language system and is still known and revered as simply *al-Kitāb* (The Book). The work of compilation and analysis was continued by philologists who conducted what we would now term fieldwork by travelling to the desert (*bādiyah*) and recording from bards and story-tellers the memorised tribal lore of generations. As a result of these continuing efforts by scholars such as Abū ʿAmr ibn al-ʿAlāʾ (d. 770), and his successors, including Abū ʿUbaydah (d. 824) and al-Aṣmaʿī (d. 831), a large corpus of textual materials on language and poetry became available that was to serve as the basis for investigations by future generations. This transfer process serves to illustrate a gradual but important shift in focus away from the language and values of the desert towards those of the more cosmopolitan intellectual centres; while the desert and its tribes remain a continuing resort for those in search of classical ideals (such as the poet, al-Mutanabbī, mentioned in ch. 4), the primary locus of Arabic literary energy is now the city and its institutions. Since most of the names that we have just mentioned were connected with the 'Baṣran school' which maintained a healthy rivalry with al-Kūfah (somewhat analogous with that between Oxford and Cambridge or Harvard and Yale), we should also mention among members of the 'Kūfan school' the eminent grammarian, al-Kisāʾī (d. 804), who in the view of the scholarly community of Baghdad succeeded in besting Sībawayh himself, and the philologists, ibn al-Sikkīt (d. 857) and Thaʿlab (d. 903).

If the court life of the later Umawī caliphs had seen a growth in administrative personnel and a burgeoning debate over the cultural parameters of the community, the move to the city of Baghdad, the foundation of institutions of learning and translation, and the increasing emphasis on the outward trappings of official life at the court provided a fruitful environment for research and debate that fostered further and intensified development in the realm of *adab*. One of the most individual writers to emerge within this period was the long-lived 'al-Jāḥiẓ' (the goggled-eyed one), the nickname by which ʿAmr ibn Baḥr (*c.* 776–869), one of the greatest polymaths in the whole of Arab-Islamic culture, is generally known. The style of writing that he developed and the huge variety of topics to which he addressed himself were uniquely his own and were soon recognised as the products of a prodigious, unrivalable intellect. Thus, even though the course of *adab* was to move in other directions, we must now pause to acknowledge the achievements of one of Arabic's greatest littérateurs.

Al-Jāḥiẓ

Essayist, anthologiser, stylist, wit, polemicist, al-Jāḥiẓ is acknowledged as the master of classical Arabic prose. Of African origin and trained in the intellectual centre of al-Baṣrah, he quickly became renowned for his polymathic interests; stories concerning him abound, for instance concerning his habit of renting bookstores for his own personal use so that he could devour the contents of their various offerings. A bewildering variety also characterises the works of al-Jāḥiẓ that have been preserved, a variety that, al-Jāḥiẓ's innate intellectual gifts apart, is a reflection of the atmosphere of his time – one of religious and cultural controversies, of translation from the Greek and Persian cultural traditions, and of assimilation of new ideas. Charles Pellat, the French scholar who devoted much of his career to a study of his works, reckons the total number at approximately two hundred.

In his writings al-Jāḥiẓ involved himself directly in the religious and political controversies of his times. In a number of essays he explores the relative merits of the prominent families of pre-Islamic Arabia in order to provide evidence for the legitimacy of the ʿAbbāsī caliphs against the rival claims of those who, disapproving of the policies of Caliph al-Maʾmūn, expressed their opposition in terms of continuing adherence to the claims of the Umawī house. It was al-Maʾmūn who also instituted the dogma of the Muʿtazilah school as official doctrine, and al-Jāḥiẓ, trained in that school by the famous al-Naẓẓām (d. *c.* 840) in al-Baṣrah, explores one of the school's central points of debate, the createdness of the Qurʾān, in his *Kitāb khalq al-Qurʾān* (Book on the Createdness of the Qurʾān), which includes a fascinating account of the procedures of the inquisition (*miḥnah*) involving the illustrious *ḥadīth* scholar, Aḥmad ibn Ḥanbal.

However, while these works provide a sample of the extent to which al-Jāḥiẓ involved himself in the intellectual debates of his day, he is better remembered (and recorded) for his thoroughly innovative contributions to the compilation genre. In these works al-Jāḥiẓ took on the formidable task of exploiting the stimulating intellectual environment provided by this cosmopolitan community as a starting-point for a project aimed at integrating an appreciation of the literary heritage of the Arabs – in all its formal variety – into the new cultural milieu. In so doing, he made a vigorous and effective contribution to the continuing *shuʿūbiyyah* controversy. His *Kitāb al-ḥayawān* (Book of Animals), for example, is, on the surface, a vast collection of poems and stories about animals, but such is al-Jāḥiẓ's encyclopedic knowledge that he is unable to resist indulging in asides on all manner of topics; thus alongside stories about snakes, foxes, camels, birds, rats, and a notable tale about a dog suckling a baby during a plague that is quoted by the contemporary novelist, ʿAbd al-raḥmān Munīf, in his novel, *Al-Nihāyāt* (Endings), we find other information on philosophy and society and even a description of his teacher, al-Naẓẓām. The *Kitāb al-bayān wa-al-tabyīn* (Book of Clarity and Clear Expression) is another huge reference work that provides a similarly discursive compilation of anecdotes and information on ideals of expression. Al-Jāḥiẓ's broader and more specific goals may be seen, I believe, in the following extract:

> Like people themselves, discourse falls into categories: it can be either serious or trivial, beautiful and fine or vile and nasty, entertaining or the reverse. It's all Arabic . . . For me, there is no speech on earth as enjoyable and useful, as elegant and sweet to the ear, as closely linked to sound intellect, liberating for

the tongue, and beneficial for improving diction as a course of prolonged listening to the way the eloquent, intelligent and learned Bedouin talk. In general people have been correct in their verdicts, but I would claim that trivial expressions and ideas go hand in hand. Sometimes there may be a need for triviality: it may be much more entertaining than a display of elaborate pomposity and a whole series of lofty ideas, but then a wry anecdote can be even more fun than a steamy one. (al-Maqdisī, *Taṭawwur al-asālīb al-nathriyyah fī al-adab al-ʿArabī*, Beirut, 1968, pp. 171–2.)

In addition to these collections which represent al-Jāḥiẓ's very individual contribution to the process of educating and even acculturating the class of bureaucrats, he also compiled anthologies that address themselves to questions of proper behaviour and morals. Here too, his range is astonishingly broad, including discussions of character traits such as envy and pride and explorations of emotion, including essays on the qualities of singing slave-girls (*qiyān*) and homosexuality. By far the most famous in this category is *Kitāb al-bukhalāʾ* (The Book of Misers), misers being a category which, in a culture that regards hospitality and generosity as behavioural norms, clearly offers a heaven-sent opportunity for an exploration of very peculiar people and situations. Such proves to be the case, and the work is the greatest outlet for al-Jāḥiẓ's wit and exploitation of irony. The work includes a whole series of anecdotes about the people of Khurāsān, who are alleged to specialise in miserliness; and, within the broader category of Khurasanians, the people of Marw are said to be the acknowledged masters of the trait. One anecdote tells of a man from that town who, upon entering a room, discovers that the owner of an oil lamp is using, as an 'economy' measure, a small and completely saturated stick of wood to keep the lamp's wick upright; using all manner of curses about waste and hellfire, the man from Marw instructs the poor lamp-owner to use a metal needle instead. As the narrator then notes, he learned on that day the unchallenged 'superiority' of the people of Marw in this particular category. And, in what can only be regarded as an entirely appropriate gesture to the early tradition that we have just described, the entire sequence of anecdotes about what we may term 'lamp economy' ends with a citation of the complete verse about lamps from the Qur'ān that we cited in the chapter on the Qur'ān (*Sūrat al-Nūr* [24, The Light], v. 35). In yet another lengthy tale, the narrator makes the mistake of challenging a landlord's account of his expenses and is treated to a tirade against tenants that might be recognised by many a modern estate agent.

Among the most characteristic aspects of al-Jāḥiẓ's works are their style and structure. His training in al-Baṣrah ensured that he could take advantage of the corpus of scholarship on the various aspects of language that had been developed by scholars in that city, and he set himself not only to make use of that learning in his own writing but to make significant additions to the corpus itself. His style exploits to the full the morphological potential of the Arabic language. The richness of his vocabulary and the complex periods that he weaved within the boundaries of Arabic syntax combine with his pedagogical bent, predilection for debate, and ready wit, to create a style that his successors acknowledged as both masterly and inimitable. It was presumably a combination of these same traits that led to the predominant aspect of the structure of his works, namely their tendency to digress. The *Kitāb al-bayān wa-al-tabyīn*, for example, which came to be regarded as a major source for critical principles, is, as we noted above, a collection of anecdotes and observations that are a perfect reflection of the thought processes of a polymath who, in the midst of discussing a particular point, is suddenly reminded of an ancillary issue and feels no compunction about following it. The cut and thrust of debate, the sheer delight in anecdote, and the desire to learn and to pass on that learning, these are all primary features of the career and personality of this genius of Arabic literature, and they are all mirrored in the style and structure of his works.

While posterity was virtually unanimous in its estimation of al-Jāḥiẓ's greatness, the religious politics of his time – in which he himself had been a participant – were to cause him difficulties towards the end of his long life. In 847 Caliph al-Mutawakkil abandoned official adherence to the dogma of the Muʿtazilah which al-Jāḥiẓ had espoused, and reasserted the uncreated nature of the Qurʾān. This change is often cited as the reason for al-Jāḥiẓ's decision to return to al-Baṣrah where he died in 869. In Baghdad meanwhile there developed what some came to regard as a school separate from the traditional centres of al-Kūfah and al-Baṣrah and dedicated to the propagation of more traditional Sunnī beliefs. In the field of *adab* its primary exponent was ʿAbdallāh ibn Qutaybah (d. 889), who incidentally came from the Marw region (although no record of his prowess as a miser has come down to us).

VARIETIES OF *ADAB*

Manuals and compilations

While some later writers aspired to imitate aspects of al-Jāḥiẓ's genius, it was ibn Qutaybah whose works provided the principal model for emulation by the bureaucrat class. While he was of Persian descent himself, he seems to have been particularly conscious of the negative influences of the ongoing *shuʿūbiyyah* debate that may initially have served as a stimulus to an innovative cultural environment but had tended over time to degenerate into a less productive process of name-calling. Ibn Qutaybah was the author of a number of works including important studies on *ḥadīth* and problematic passages in the Qur'ān, but he made use of his status as virtual tutor to the Baghdad administrative class to produce a variety of works that aimed at bringing about the reconciliation of a number of different groups and schools. By contrast with the somewhat wayward genius of al-Jāḥiẓ, ibn Qutaybah's view of the role of *adab* was more practical, prosaic perhaps. Following the lead of ʿAbd al-ḥamīd and ibn al-Muqaffaʿ he wrote a manual for bureaucrats, the very title of which, *Adab al-kātib* (The Bureaucrat's Manual of Etiquette), confirms the now firmly established linkage between the administrative class and *adab*. The work itself covers all manner of topics: from the naming of people and animals, to sections on food, weapons, and clothing, and practical instructions on handwriting, syntax and morphology. His *Kitāb al-shiʿr wa-al-shuʿarāʾ* is a massive anthology of Arabic poetry arranged chronologically from Imru al-Qays and Zuhayr ibn Abī Sulmā to Abū Nuwās and ʿAbbās ibn al-Aḥnaf. As we will note below in the chapter on criticism, much attention has been focused on ibn Qutaybah's introductory remarks to the collection, and not least his opinion that modern poets should not consider themselves bound to copy their predecessors. With his *Kitāb al-maʿārif* he made an important and early contribution to the writing of history, gathering into a single work stories from the Bible, pre-Islamic narratives from Arabia and Iran, and accounts of the first two centuries of the Muslim community. However, in the context of the development of a compilation tradition, ibn Qutaybah's most significant contribution is *ʿUyūn al-akhbār* (Springs of Information), a work divided into ten separate sections, the general organising principles of which serve as a precedent for a huge number of similar contributions to *adab* that were to appear in ensuing centuries. Each section is devoted to an entirely different topic: war, nobility, eloquence, asceticism, and friendship, for example, and a final section on women. For each subject ibn Qutaybah collects a number of anecdotes and extracts of poetry, the purpose being, as he instructs his readers in a tone of pedagogic fervour in the Introduction, 'that you should insert it into your conversation in meetings and make it part of your style whenever you put pen to paper'.

With the different approaches and styles of al-Jāḥiẓ and ibn Qutaybah as two key points in an expanding field, the tradition of *adab* proceeded to diversify, adopting a variety of forms and subjects that, as we noted earlier, cannot be conveniently related to any system of genres and topics that we recognise today but that were nevertheless united in their continuing goal to instruct, enlighten, and entertain. *Adab* and the role of the *adīb* came to represent both process and product: the process of contributing to the corpus of materials that would maintain and enhance the status of *adab* and the aesthetic norms of its practitioners, and the products of the education, diversion, and somewhat precious self-fulfilment that the corpus provided. Such products found a ready market among the côterie that would attend formal and informal soirées at the caliph's court or at the residences of wealthier notables and courtiers. Among the primary participants in the repartee on such occasions was the boon-companion (*nadīm*) whose task it was to maintain the good humour of the ruler; compilations of anecdotes and fables provided him with an appropriate and ready repertoire with which to divert and amuse his distinguished audience. Musical entertainment would be provided by distinguished male and female vocalists; the musical talents and alluring qualities of singing girls (*qiyān*) are the particular focus of an epistle of al-Jāḥiẓ that was noted above. Within the environment of such salons the maintenance of proper modes of etiquette was the province of arbiters of taste who were termed 'refined' (*ẓurafāʾ*, sing. *ẓarīf*). The above-mentioned *Kitāb al-aghānī* of al-Iṣfahānī is a primary source for accounts of the behaviour of rulers and their confidants on such occasions, while the *Kitāb al-muwashshā* (The Book of Brocade) of al-Washshāʾ (d. 936) provides a virtual manual of *ẓarīf* etiquette.

The contexts for the sharing and propagation of the principles and products of *adab* were *majālis* – literally sessions but essentially salons of the cultured élite, and *amālī* (the plural of *imlāʾ*, dictation), a term that gives us an important insight into the way in which students of this field (and others) would be required to read texts dictated to them by their masters. Both these words make their way into the titles of a number of compilations; one of the most famous of the former category is *al-Majālis* of Thaʿlab (d. 904), the famous grammarian of al-Kūfah, and of the latter, *al-Amālī* of al-Qālī (d. 967), a philologist who settled in Spain after receiving his education in Baghdad.

The model that had been established by ibn Qutaybah with *ʿUyūn al-akhbār* – a collection of information and anecdote organised by topic, was adapted by the great Cordoban poet and littérateur, ibn ʿAbd Rabbihi (d. 934), in his *al-ʿIqd al-farīd* (The Peerless Necklace). Divided into twenty-five sections entitled 'precious stones', it provides examples of various types of literary expression, poetry (including that of the compiler, for which this collection is a major source) and proverbs, as well as discussions of prosody and other literary topics. It still retains its status as one of Arabic's most favoured literary thesauri.

As literary salons (*majālis*) began to fashion their own modes of disputation and aesthetic vogues, so did the collections of texts that interested and diverted them become more elaborate and fanciful. Over the centuries this literary genre – for that is what these compilations really are – went through the normal processes of generic transformation that reflected the tastes and ideologies of the era in question; it has to be admitted that scholars are only just coming to terms with the need to assess (in some cases, reassess) the changing parameters of selection within this important mode of cultural expression. Compilations differ, for example, in the critical posture of the compiler towards the arrangement of his materials and in the categories of choice: among the latter are textual mode (prose and/or poetry), length of segment, and the question of the inclusion of the contemporary along with the old. Thus, al-Tanūkhī's (d. 995) *Kitāb nishwār al-muḥāḍarah wa-akhbār al-mudhākarah bi-alfāẓ al-mukhālafah* (Book of Shared Conversation and Memorable Information by means of Contrasted Expressions) consists primarily of narratives, while *Muḥāḍarāt al-udabāʾ wa-muḥāwarāt al-shuʿarāʾ wa-al-bulaghāʾ* (Talks by Littérateurs and Conversations Among Poets and Rhetoricians) by al-Rāghib al-Iṣfahānī (d. 1108) includes (as its title implies) a variety of genres; both incorporate contemporary materials. A selection of other famous examples of *adab* encyclopedias include: *Kitāb al-imtāʿ wa-al-muʾānasah* (Book of Enjoyment and *Bonhomie*) by Abū Ḥayyān al-Tawḥīdī (d. 1008), a collection of erudite and often witty conversations, *Tamthīl al-muḥāḍarah* (Exemplary Discussion) and *Laṭāʾif al-maʿārif* (Book of Wonderful Information) by al-Thaʿālibī (d. 1038), and *Rabīʿ al-abrār* (Springtime of the Innocent) of al-Zamakhsharī (d. 1143), a large and thematically organised collection of short quotations in both prose and poetry. Al-Thaʿālibī's *Laṭāʾif al-maʿārif* provides an illustration of the contents of a 'varia' compilation: the opening chapter is concerned with recording a totally undifferentiated series of 'first people' (to plant date-palms, to clip his moustache, to speak Arabic, and so on); it is followed by a pair of chapters on nicknames, and leads to a ninth chapter concerning 'interesting and entertaining pieces of information about various happenings and strange coincidences' [*Laṭāʾif al-maʿārif of Thaʿālibī*, p. xii]. As the tastes of the court audience for such modes of instruction and entertainment developed, this predilection for the curious and diverting extended in a number of directions. One such was still further into the realm of interesting and exotic stories. Collections were made of fables about every conceivable topic and drawn from many cultures. Al-Jahshiyārī (d. 942) is reported by ibn al-Nadīm (the compiler of the catalogue of works known as *al-Fihrist*) to have gathered a huge and carefully organised collection of tales from Arabic, Persian, Indian, and Greek sources, but regrettably the work has not come down to us. The titles of later collections that were preserved continue to reflect many of the same organising principles and intended audience as those we have already discussed: al-Ibshīhī's (d. *c.* 1446) manual for rulers, for example, *Al-Mustaṭraf fī kull fann mustaẓraf* (The Ultimate on Every Refined Art), is a diffuse collection of short, improving narratives, while his contemporary, ibn ʿArabshāh (d. 1450) – biographer of Tīmūr Lang (Tamerlaine) – produces a collection of fables, *Fākihat al-khulafāʾ wa-mufākahat al-ẓurafāʾ* (Fruit of Caliphs and Humour of the Refined), that incorporates a good deal of material drawn from Persian sources. A particularly favoured topic is that of amazing information (*ʿajāʾib*), 'tall tales' of the exotic and unbelievable that were presumably intended to amaze and even terrify, and, in so doing, to underscore for the audience the pleasing security of its own existence. Echoes of this vogue for tales of the unique, dangerous, and bizarre – and particularly those culled from the accounts of the lengthy journeys of merchants, administrators, and other travellers – are clearly seen in the Sindbad voyages that were later to be included by Antoine Galland in the *Thousand and One Nights* (which will be discussed in more detail below).

The changes in generic purposes and audience implicit in these titles and the works that they represent are also reflected in language and style. By the tenth century writers had access not only to a number of grammatical works that codified the elaborate system of morphology and syntax of Arabic but also to the lists of lexicographers who had begun the enormous process of recording its wonderfully diverse vocabulary. The application of this expanding branch of knowledge to the craft of *kātib*, illustrated by the manual genre of which ibn Qutaybah's *Adab al-kātib* is a fine example, was elaborated in a number of works, of which we would cite *Adab al-kuttāb* by Abū Bakr al-Ṣūlī (d. 948?) and *Kitāb ṣināʿat al-kitābah* (Book on the Craft of Writing) by Qudāmah ibn Jaʿfar (d. 938). Students of the workings of contemporary bureaucracy will appreciate the coupling of the latter of these works with a truly appropriate topic, *Kitāb al-kharāj* (The Book on Land-tax). A further contribution to the enhancement of artistic prose and epistolary style is *Kitāb al-tāj* (Book of the Crown) by Abū Isḥāq al-Ṣābī (d. 994) who practised the craft himself as head of chancery to the Buwayhī Sultan, ʿIzz al-dawlah. However, as the ties that had linked many early pioneers of artistic prose writing (ʿAbd al-ḥamīd and ibn Qutaybah, for example) to the principles and practices of the religious sciences, and particularly *ḥadīth* scholarship, were gradually loosened, the epistolary school of writing was increasingly influenced by the tastes espoused by the *habitués* of literary salons. Stylistic priorities shifted away from a primary concern with the details of linguistic correctness and stylistic clarity towards a quest for the decorative and refined. This gradual process of transformation can be gauged in part by contrasting the titles we have just cited: the practical and specific language of those cited in this paragraph with the often more elaborate and fanciful words and images exemplified by the titles of compilations discussed in the one preceding it. The most famous literary salon of the era, that of ibn ʿAbbād (d. 995), a minister of the Buwayhī rulers who is renowned as 'al-Ṣāḥib' (the master), provides an excellent illustration of not only the process of change but also of the turbulent cultural background that lay behind it.

Ibn ʿAbbād's teacher and predecessor as minister in Rayy (near Tehran) was Abū al-faḍl ibn al-ʿAmīd. In his great literary thesaurus, *Yatīmat al-dahr fī maḥāsin ahl al-ʿaṣr* (Solitaire of the Ages concerning the Qualities of the People of the Era), al-Thaʿālibī characterises ibn al-ʿAmid as 'the primary epistolographer of his age', while the historian, Miskawayh (d. 1030), who also served as librarian to the court at Rayy, comments that 'in *adab* and epistolography he had no rivals in his own time'. These writers and others are agreed on his pioneer role in leading the stylistic tastes of the school of bureaucratic prose-writing (dubbed '*inshāʾ dīwānī*' or 'chancery-composition') towards a greater emphasis on embellishment and elaboration, availing itself of the artifices of *sajʿ*, the tropes of *badīʿ*, and citations of poetry and proverbs.

Such features are difficult, if not impossible, to illustrate in translation, but, while the extract that follows (from a letter sent by ibn al-ʿAmīd to a colleague who had set himself in opposition to the Buwayhī ruler) cannot capture all the aspects of the style and especially the end-rhymes of each phrase, it does at least illustrate the parallelisms, repetitions, and contrasts:

As I write to you, I waver between hope for you and despair of you, between reaching out to you and avoiding you. Your previous esteem is self-evident, your former service is clearly established. The least of the two would demand careful attention and require both protection and concern, but to them you now append a matter of malice and betrayal and attach dissension and revolt. The least part of it subverts your deeds and wipes out everything attributed to you.

When Abū al-faḍl ibn al-ʿAmīd's son, Abū al-fatḥ, who succeeded his father in the ministerial position, was disgraced and executed, al-Ṣāḥib ibn ʿAbbād took over the post. He proceeded to enhance still further the reputation of Rayy as a major intellectual centre, attracting to his côterie many illustrious figures: the grammarian ibn Fāris (d. 1005), the critic al-Qāḍī al-Jurjānī (d. 1001), and, among significant contributors to the development of artistic prose, Abū Bakr al-Khwārizmī (d. 993), Badīʿ al-zamān al-Hamadhānī (d. 1008) whose pioneering role in the development of the *maqāmah* genre we will explore below, and Abū Ḥayyān al-Tawḥīdī (d. 1023). Clearly what attracted many of these figures to the city was not only the prestige attached to a political figure such as al-Ṣāḥib but also the peerless library that he had assembled; to all of which the opportunity to exchange information and debate with such a remarkable aggregation of scholars provided additional incentive.

Al-Ṣāḥib ibn ʿAbbād himself was a major scholar and writer in his own right; in addition to works on theology, history, and philology, he published works of criticism (a review of the alleged plagiarisms of the poet al-Mutanabbī, for example) and a collection of poetry. Like his teacher, however, his repute rested mainly on his collected letters, large portions of which are to be found in another famous literary anthology of the era, *Zahr al-ādāb* of al-Ḥuṣrī (d. 1022). His letters reveal the breadth of his learning, the unruffled ease with which he was able to exert his political authority, and, from a stylistic point of view, the ways in which he began the process of altering the balance between old and new styles that had characterised the epistles of his teacher and explored the boundaries of a more elaborate aesthetic. The controversy which al-

Ṣāḥib's adoption of this style provoked was intense, but an assessment of its aspects is made particularly difficult by the fact that not only were many littérateurs who praised its qualities to the skies beholden to him for their livelihood but also he himself seems to have been possessed of a particularly vituperative personality. We possess samples of nasty exchanges between him and both Miskawayh and Abū Bakr al-Khwārizmī, but the most vivid (if not the most accurate) picture of his personality comes to us from the pen of one of Arabic's most illustrious prose-writers, Abū Ḥayyān al-Tawḥīdī.

Al-Tawḥīdī is regarded by many critics as the *adīb* whose works most closely approximate the virtuosity of al-Jāḥiẓ himself. His life story and especially his travels from court to court in search of employment reflect the hardships and frustrations (and occasionally the rewards) of anyone who aspired to a professional writing career during the fractious times that resulted from the demise of the beliefs of the Muʿtazilah as the official doctrine of the caliph and the search for a compromise position. It was within this environment that al-Tawḥīdī, a Sunnī, spent much of his life working in the courts of rulers under Buwayhī (Shīʿī) suzerainty. He was thus constrained by circumstances to conduct himself with considerable diplomacy and tact, a demeanour for which, to judge by his works, his personality was singularly ill-equipped. Part of that personality, its complexes and frustrations, seems to have been involved in his decision late in life to burn all his writings.

Among his works is an essay in praise of al-Jāḥiẓ, and it seems clear that al-Tawḥīdī was anxious to emulate the achievement of his great predecessor. To the tradition of *adab* compendia he contributed not only *Kitāb al-imtāʿ wa-al-muʾānasah*, but also *al-Baṣāʾir wa-al-dhakhāʾir* (Insights and Treasures), a collection of anecdotes and proverbs, and *al-Muqābasāt* (Book of Comments), which consists of 106 short discussions of a philosophical, grammatical, and literary nature of which the following is a selection: 'Concerning the author's experience with certain doctors', 'Useful anecdotes concerning higher philosophy', 'Statements on asceticism and shunning the world', and 'On friends, true friendship, the philosophy of love and passion, and definitions of sound philosophy'. This last theme seems to have preoccupied al-Tawḥīdī throughout his life, in that he began a separate work on the subject during the earlier part of his career and returned to it later in life. At the time of his death in 1023 it remained unfinished.

In 974 al-Tawḥīdī attended the *majlis* in Baghdad conducted by Abū al-fatḥ ibn al-ʿAmīd, the son of Abū al-faḍl discussed above. Such were al-Tawḥīdī's accomplishments that not only did he become a prominent member of Abū al-fatḥ's *majlis*, but also, upon the early demise of the latter, found himself invited to Rayy by al-Ṣāḥib. However, al-Tawḥīdī's high hopes that he would be welcomed at the salon and library as an *adīb* were disappointed; instead he found himself assigned the lowly task of copyist. By about 980, al-Tawḥīdī's pride had been battered enough, and he returned to Baghdad. The result of his rancour at the treatment he had received is *Kitāb mathālib al-wazīrayn*, also known as *Akhlāq al-wazīrayn* (Book on the Foibles of the Two Ministers), the two in question being Abū al-fatḥ ibn al-ʿAmīd and al-Ṣāḥib ibn ʿAbbād. One of the more scurrilous contributions to the literature of the period, it nevertheless gives us much insight into the workings and rivalries of political and cultural life. Invoking the example of an earlier essay of al-Jāḥiẓ comparing the qualities of two men and assuring his readers of his 'impartiality', he proceeds to reveal the seemier side of his patrons' conduct:

[My informant told me that] al-Ṣāḥib ibn ʿAbbād used to say: Even with all this recklessness and debauchery, Abū al-fatḥ ibn al-ʿAmīd is better than his father. Abū al-faḍl was a roaring bull, a braying ass; he would even impugn his own son's reputation . . .

But didn't ibn al-ʿAmīd hear what al-Ṣāḥib had to say about him?

Oh yes, indeed! Abū al-fatḥ would retort that al-Ṣāḥib's rhyming prose showed signs of dissipation and loose living, while his script suggested someone who was paralysed or had the pox. Whenever he shouted, it sounded as though he was gambling in a pub. I've never laid eyes on him without thinking that some idiot's just given him some 'medicine'. He's stupid by nature, but there's some good in him too. Then there are days when his stupidity gets out of control. At that point all his goodness disappears, and decent, respectable and cultured people find themselves subjected to fits of jealousy, arrogance, and boorish behaviour.

As these extracts show with abundant clarity, al-Tawḥīdī's service at the salon of al-Ṣāḥib ibn ʿAbbād brought into contact two men who were not only among the most significant *adīb*s of the period but also personalities with a highly developed sense of their own importance. Al-Tawḥīdī may perhaps claim a measure of 'impartiality' when he acknowledges in his own remarks both the political skill and wide learning of al-Ṣāḥib, but the depth of his resentment at the treatment he received from such an illustrious patron finds full vent in the montage of scabrous anecdotes that he compiles.

The intellectual centre at Rayy, with its collection of scholars drawn together by the attractions of patronage and a great library, is one example of a trend that inevitably accompanied the decentralisation of authority within the vast region that now constituted the Muslim community. With the rise of local dynasties, each requiring its own bureaucracy, those practised in the practicalities of the epistolographer's art and the various fields of *adab* were presented with a wealth of opportunities for patronage. Abū Bakr al-Khwārizmī, for example, who is credited with the further enhancement of the ornate style of prose, found service at the illustrious court of Sayf al-dawlah al-Ḥamdānī in Aleppo where his colleagues included the poets al-Mutanabbī and Abū Firās and the philosopher, al-Fārābī. A century or so later, the court of Ṣalāḥ al-dīn provided another conducive environment for a number of eminent writers whose epistles are regarded as marking the acme of the *inshāʾ dīwānī* style. The most illustrious of these writers was al-Qāḍī al-Fāḍil (d. 1200), who served as minister and spokesman for Ṣalāḥ al-dīn. His report to the caliph in Baghdad concerning the recapture of Jerusalem in 1144 provides a good example of the extent to which mannerisms were the vogue in Arabic epistolary prose; sun and moon, heavens and darkness, and the entire panoply of battle imagery is brought to bear on the triumph of Islam and, of course, Ṣalāḥ al-dīn himself. One of al-Qāḍī al-Fāḍil's subordinates was an equally famous writer, ʿImād al-dīn al-Iṣfahānī (d. 1201) whose account of Ṣalāḥ al-dīn's career, entitled *Barq al-Shām* (The Lightning of Syria), is regarded as the authoritative source and at the same time a model of *inshāʾ*. The career of a third figure, al-Wahrānī (d. 1179) who travelled to Egypt from Algeria in quest of employment, shares some of the features of al-Tawḥīdī's experience noted above. Apparently confined by the pre-eminence of al-Qāḍī al-Fāḍil and ʿImād al-dīn to a position as copyist, al-Wahrānī turned his attention to the writing of a series of epistles that imitate or parody other genres: rental contracts, oaths, letters of judicial appointment, and so on. These interesting contributions to the under-studied topic of humorous writing in Arabic have been gathered together under the title of *Manāmāt al-Wahrānī wa-maqāmātuhu wa-rasāʾiluhu* (Al-Wahrānī's Dreams, *Maqāmāt*, and Epistles).

An accurate reflection of the stylistic sophistication achieved by the *udabāʾ* and *kuttāb* of these various courts is provided by the work of Ḍiyāʾ al-dīn ibn al-Athīr (d. 1279), *Al-Mathal al-sāʾir fī adab al-kātib wa-al-shāʿir* (The Current Ideal for the Literary Discipline of the Secretary and Poet). A training manual for all those with a broad interest in the cultivation of learning and its transmittal in stylish form, it sets out to demonstrate that, in spite of a traditional prejudice in favour of poetic expression, bellettristic prose has developed to a stage where it displays aesthetic qualities of equal merit. That ibn al-Athīr's message was heeded by his successors is indicated by the fact that the ensuing centuries witnessed the continued production of literary compilation that included instructions to writers along with varieties of other information and anecdote. Of these the most frequently cited are two compendia with quite different focuses: *Nihāyat al-arab fī funūn al-adab* (The Goal of Desire concerning the Categories of *Adab*) by al-Nuwayrī (d. 1332) which resembles many of the earlier models cited above by including information on the heavens, mankind, animals, and plants, as well as a history of the Arabs up to his own time; and *Ṣubḥ al-aʿshā fī ṣināʿat al-inshāʾ* (Morning for the Night-blind regarding the Craft of Secretarial Style) by al-Qalqashandī (d. 1418), a detailed survey of every aspect of the bureaucratic function, from filing techniques and types of ink, to matters of political acumen, grammar, geography, and history.

The compilation of manuals, thesauri, and compendia of which we have just provided a sample reflects the processes of change within the administrative sector of the Islamic community and its modes of education. While the *adab* tradition, reflecting its origins in *politesses*, retained a concern for the maintenance of norms of behaviour and the conservation of the legacy of the past, it is not surprising – bearing in mind the increasingly diverse cultural environment in which it was studied and taught – that many of its practitioners set out to explore new modes of expression and to broaden the aesthetic expectations of the community of *adab* readers. The wide variety of anthologies that were produced reflect the tastes and needs of a class whose interests were broad and open; communication was to be not merely informative but also enlightening and entertaining. And, while admiring the stupendous labour and erudition involved in the collecting of the many large compilations of information and anecdote, we should not overlook the originality that informed the critical tasks of selecting and ordering the materials and of crafting the style in which they are couched. One of the most colourful illustrations of such originality is provided by *Maṭāliʿ al-budūr fī manāzil al-surūr* (Rising of Full Moons in/regarding the Abodes of Delights) by al-Ghuzūlī (d. 1412), a manumitted Turkish slave who lived in Damascus but also travelled to Egypt. This anthology describing all kinds of worldly delight is arranged in the form of a house; sections on site, neighbours, doors, gardens, food, and hygiene all evoke pertinent selections of poetry and anecdote. One section is devoted to 'soirées of the leisured classes', and it is followed by others on poets, singers, secretaries, and physicians. The entire assemblage concludes with a glimpse of the world to come and the male and female servants who will cater to the believers' needs.

Monographic works

The compilations of information and anecdote that we have just discussed were organised around topics and themes that were also the subject of monographic works; the earliest compilations were, one must assume, collected from already existing written or oral repertoires on individual topics. As we have already noted, al-Jāḥiẓ compiled a large collection of poetry and anecdote about animals in his *Kitāb al-ḥayawān*, they being the topic of subsections of works such as ibn Qutaybah's *Adab al-kātib* and, at a much later date, al-Nuwayri's *Nihāyat al-arab*. In citing opinions concerning changes in taste within the community of *kuttāb* and *udabāʾ*, we have also made use of other sources that focus on a single area, for example the large anthologies of poetry and anecdote such as al-Thaʿālibī's *Yatīmat al-dahr* and al-Ḥuṣrī's *Zahr al-adab*. To these must be added the most famous literary anthology of them all, the *Kitāb al-aghānī* (Book of Songs) of Abū al-faraj al-Iṣfahānī (d. 967). This work in twenty-four volumes is a major source of information on Arabic poetry, poets, culture, and history from the pre-Islamic period till the compiler's own times. It is notable not only for the skilful way in which poetry and anecdote are interwoven to create a narrative portrait of the career of each poet, but also for the fact that, as the title of the collection implies, we also receive invaluable information concerning the musical tradition that was a significant aspect of the performance of poetry.

Al-Jāḥiẓ, it will be recalled, also wrote individual works on a variety of topics, from misers and singing slave-girls to envy and rhetoric. His successors in *adab*-writing endeavoured to match the versatility of his themes and the different lessons they were intended to impart. Like his informative works on schoolmasters, scribes, and singers, that, for all their stylistic elegance, were presumably intended to provide a catalogue of the behaviour of particular social groups, later writers prepared works on such categories as the blind and women. On the other hand, we must assume that his work on misers, a topic to which a separate section is devoted in a number of compilations (those of ibn

Qutaybah, for example, ibn ʿAbd Rabbihi, al-Ḥuṣrī, and al-Nuwayrī), was not intended to function in the same manner, but rather to provide a repertoire of witty and often scabrous anecdotes that might well instruct by negative example but were also clearly intended for amusement. To the *Kitāb al-bukhalāʾ* (Book of Misers) by al-Jāḥiẓ we can add another collection by al-Khaṭīb al-Baghdādī (d. 1071), an illustrious *adīb* to whom we owe a further addition to this list of fascinating social types, gatecrashers. *Al-Taṭfīl wa-ḥikāyāt al-ṭufayliyyīn wa-akhbāruhum wa-nawādir kalāmihim wa-ashʿārihim* (Gatecrashing and tales about gatecrashers, their way-of-life, and choice titbits of their conversation and poetry), seems mostly concerned with expressions of disapproval regarding the practices involved, and yet the work finishes with the equivalent of a how-to-do-it manual. This aspect links it to a further sub-genre that focuses on varieties of confidence tricks (*ḥiyal*). There is a substantial corpus of works on the organisations and activities of beggars – 'the mendicant's code' (*adab al-kudyah*). One such work is *al-Mukhtār fī kashf al-asrār wa-hatk al-astār* (Choicest Items regarding the uncovering of Secrets and rending of Veils) composed by the widely travelled Damascene scholar, al-Jawbarī (thirteenth century), at the request of his Turkman patron; it takes the lid off, as it were, the repertoire of ruses practised on the public by rogues. Other kinds of group such as the *futuwwah* (originally meaning 'chivalry') began as fraternities devoted to laudable goals, but were gradually taken over by the criminal class and turned into gangs of thugs; this is certainly the way that they emerge into the modern era as seen in some of the novels of Najīb Maḥfūẓ, most notably *Awlād ḥāratinā* (1959/1967; *Children of Gebelawi*, 1981) and *Malḥamat al-ḥarāfish* (1977; *The Harafish*, 1994). The ambivalent attitude – of interest and disapproval – towards these denizens of the lower echelons of society that emerges from these and other similar works is creatively exploited in the *maqāmah* genre which will be discussed in more detail below.

A theme that lent itself very well to the predilections of anecdote-compilers for tales that would contain the maximum amount of incident and surprise was '*al-faraj baʿd al-shiddah*' (Escape from hardship). Among early works under this title are those of al-Madāʾinī (d. 849) and ibn Abī al-Dunyā (d. 894), but the most famous collection is that of the judge, Abū al-ḥusayn al-Tanūkhī (d. 994). Divided into fourteen sub-categories of deliverance – some dealing with context (prison, love, encounters with animals), others with means (use of prayers, dreams) – al-Tanūkhī assembled a collection which makes use of materials from his *Nishwār al-muḥāḍarah* noted earlier. The originality of the presentation of the anecdotes (and, some scholars maintain, of their contents as well) makes of this work a frequent point of reference in the development of imaginative narratives in Arabic. Here is a brief anecdote as an example:

The judge Abū al-Ḥusayn mentioned in his book and said: ʿUmar ibn Hubayrah fell on really bad times. One day his condition made him feel so indolent, downcast, and aggravated that his family and retinue suggested that he ride over and see the caliph. If the caliph sees the way you are, they said, he might do something nice for you; or, if he asks you how you are, you can tell him. So ʿUmar rode over and went in to see [the Umawī Caliph] Yazīd ibn ʿAbd al-Malik. After standing there for an hour, he addressed the caliph. Yazīd looked at him and noticed that ʿUmar seemed really different, and it disturbed him.

'Do you need to leave the room?' he asked. 'No', ʿUmar replied.

'Something's the matter', the Caliph said.

'Something's hurting me between my shoulders', he said, 'but I don't know what it is'.

'Look and see!' the Caliph ordered. They looked and found a scorpion between his shoulders that had stung him several times. Before he left, he had been appointed governor of Iraq. Thereafter Yazīd would talk about his fortitude and high-mindedness. (*Al-Faraj baʿd al-shiddah*, Baghdad, 1955, pg. 229).

There is, of course, no shortage of other themes that can be utilised to illustrate what is essentially an organisational spectrum: from compilations of anecdote and poetry arranged with the deliberate intent of providing variety, to others that are focused on a particular topic, and to monographic works that are the topic of this section. From among them we will focus on the theme of love, one that introduces a variety of its own in that we may subsume under the general heading works that range from explorations of divine love – most especially within the context of Sufi writings, to a variety of compilations and studies on the delights and/or perils of profane love, to the most explicit of sex manuals. In his '*Risālah fī al-ʿishq*' (Epistle on Passion), ibn Sīnā (d. 1037) discusses the intellect (*ʿaql*) and passion (*ʿishq*) as two qualities that are intrinsic to 'the necessary existent' (*wājib al-wujūd*), the balance between them being an important aspect of moral judgement and the relationship of humanity to the divine being. For Sufis, the concept of love, the agonies and delights that it engenders, and, above all, martyrdom in its worthy cause – all of them prominent themes in earlier love poetry – become symbols of a continuing struggle whereby the believer endeavours to mortify the demands of the flesh in a quest for transcendent experience. In this they viewed themselves as adhering to the dictates of a *ḥadīth* ascribed to the Prophet: 'Whoever loves, remains chaste, and then dies, dies as a martyr.' The Sufi figure whose entire career personifies this martyrdom for mystical love is al-Ḥallāj whose ecstatic utterances led to his execution in 922. The title of one of the most prominent anthologies on the subject, in its mystical and more earthly manifestations, illustrates the same theme: *Maṣāriʿ al-ʿushshāq* (Demises of Lovers) by Jaʿfar al-Sarrāj (d. 1106), later expanded by al-Biqāʿī (d. 1480) as *Aswāq al-ashwāq fī maṣāriʿ al-ushshāq* (Markets of Desires concerning Demises of Lovers).

Turning to the treatment of love in its more secular aspects, we still encounter in many works a concern with adherence to dictates elicited from the texts of the Qurʾān and *ḥadīth*; the concept of desire (*hawā*) is regularly linked with the lower self (as opposed to the intellect (*ʿaql*)) which, in the phrase from Sūrat Yūsuf (12:53) in the Qurʾān, 'encourages evil'. Such an attitude emerges clearly in the famous work, *Dhamm al-hawā* (Condemnation of Desire), an anthology compiled by ibn al-Jawzī (d. 1200), a Baghdādī preacher who resorts to *ḥadīth* and other sources in warning believers against the perils of passionate love. What might be termed the 'Summa' among such works is *Rawḍat al-muḥibbīn wa-nuzhat al-mushtāqīn* (Meadow of Lovers and Diversion of the Infatuated) by ibn Qayyim al-Jawziyyah (d. 1350), a companion of ibn Taymiyyah (d. 1328), the renowned conservative theologian and opponent of Sufism. A major and original contribution to *adab* writing, this work explores the essence of desire (*hawā*) and passion (*ʿishq*) in the context of giving advice to a young man faced with the conflict between the joys of love and the ever-present perils of sin. In so doing, he addresses himself to many of the issues that had been raised by his predecessors within the corpus of love literature; he condemns the notion of martyrdom in love (hardly surprising in view of ibn Taymiyyah's attitude to Sufi practices), and regards as scandalous the approach adopted in what is the most individual and popular work on profane love in Arabic literature, *Ṭawq al-ḥamāmah* (The Dove's Neck-ring) by the renowned Andalusian jurisprudent and poet, ibn Ḥazm (d. 1064). Ibn Qayyim is clearly disturbed by the way in which ibn Ḥazm's work appears to condone and indeed elucidate the techniques associated with surreptitious glances and secret trysts, and we might add that, in addition to these features of the work that ibn Qayyim finds so disturbing, the somewhat surprising candour with which ibn Ḥazm discusses the escapades of Andalusians who appear to be his contemporaries adds considerably to both its value and delights. The following extracts replicate to a degree the unusually intimate, indeed confidential, narrative tone that ibn Ḥazm adopts in this charming work:

Love has characteristics which are easily recognised by intelligent people ... Lovers will always rush to the spot where their beloved is to be found and make a point of sitting as close as possible; they will drop all other work that might take them away and scoff at any weighty matter that might cause them to leave. When they have to go, their walk is always very slow. I express the notion in poetry as follows:

> When I leave you, it is as though I am being led away
> like a captive;
> when I come to you, I am propelled like the full moon
> traversing the heavens;
> and, if you arise, then so do I, my slowness rivalling
> that of the stars fixed high in the firmament ...

Weeping is another manifestation of love, although in this aspect people are quite different. Some, for example, weep copious tears, whereas others remain dry-eyed. I am among the latter, because I chew frankincense for my heart condition ...

On a personal note, when I was young, I fell in love with a blonde, and ever since I haven't liked brunettes even though they may have been paragons of beauty. I find that since those earlier days it's simply become part of my make-up, and nothing else pleases me. The very same thing was true of my father (God be pleased with him), and that's the way he went to his grave.

It was qualities like these that made *Ṭawq al-ḥamāmah* so appealing to European tastes and ensured that it would be translated into a number of languages. Other sorts of appeal were, no doubt, at work when it came to the task of translating *al-Rawḍ al-ʿāṭir fī nuzhat al-khāṭir* (The Perfumed Garden for the Delight of the Heart), a sex manual written by Shaykh al-Nafzāwī (fifteenth century) at the behest of Muḥammad al-Zawāwī, the *wazīr* of Tunis (who is addressed at the beginning of many chapters). In the English-speaking world, the work became renowned through the abiding interest that Sir Richard Burton had in such materials; his translation is actually an unacknowledged transfer into English of a French version published in Algiers in 1850. Burton seems to have overlooked an earlier survey of sexual practices by another Tunisian, al-Tifāshī (d. 1253), with the provocative title, *Nuzhat al-albāb fī-mā lā yūjad fī kitāb* (Delight of Hearts concerning what will never be found in a Book), perhaps because it had not been translated at that time, but more likely because Victorian sensibilities would have fought shy – at least in the public domain – of a work that devotes so much attention to homosexual practices. Even al-Nafzāwī's manual concerning the most private and sensual of intercourse between humans is placed by its author in the context of gratitude to God for His gifts to humankind; indeed the section describing the most gymnastic sexual acts is prefaced with a verse from the Qur'ān: 'Your womenfolk are a field for you, so go to your field as you wish' (*Sūrat al-baqarah* (Sura 2, The Cow), v. 223).

Adab and the writing of history and geography

In *On Autobiography* (Minneapolis: University of Minnesota Press, 1989), Philippe Lejeune notes that literary genres 'constitute, *in each era*, a sort of implicit code through which, and thanks to which, works of the past and recent works can be received and classified by readers' [my emphasis]. As our discussion thus far has endeavoured to show, the term *adab* was used over a period of many centuries not only to identify the aesthetic norms of an intellectual élite – the gradually shifting terms of reference under which research, writing, and teaching on a wide variety of topics was conducted, but also to designate the corpus of works that were the result of such activities. In turning to a consideration of some of those topics – history and geography in particular – within the context of *adab*, we confront an interestingly varied cluster of text-types. During the first century of Islamic history, it will be recalled, the development within the community of scholars of new fields of learning and modes of expression had taken place within the context of a society constrained to adapt itself to the new realities that had been created by its assimilation of conquered territories and converted peoples. It is thus to be expected that the process of recording events and creating the biographies of those who participated in them was accompanied by and often fused with a description of the new and often distant places where the events had occurred. As the intellectual community's appetite for information and enlightenment increased, the fields of history and geography (and their sub-genres) are often blended together, and their areas of focus can be seen as operating along a single, broad-scaled continuum. The broadening of the concept of 'history' represented by these tendencies within the *adab* tradition provides an interesting parallel to recent challenges to disciplinary boundaries in Western scholarship which have led to a shift from the use of genres as means of establishing differences towards an approach that examines affinities between types of writing long reckoned discrete; a situation in which Hayden White, for instance, can describe historical texts as: 'verbal fictions, the contents of which are as much *invented* as *found* and the forms of which have more in common with literature than they have with those in the sciences.' (*Tropics of Discourse*, Baltimore, 1979, p. 82)

Some of the types of early writing in prose that we examined above – the battle accounts of pre-Islamic times (the *ayyām al-ʿarab*) and of Muḥammad's lifetime (the *maghāzī*) and the biography of Muḥammad himself (the *sīrah*), are, needless to say, historical data organised according to particular principles; they constitute some of the earliest examples of the generic requirements that characterise a good deal of historical writing in Arabic. As we also noted, the task of collecting and sifting such massive amounts of information as were needed by the Muslim community included processes of authentification. That in turn led to the gathering of data on a variety of individuals, tribes, and categories. Such data were organised into 'classes' (*ṭabaqāt*) for easy reference, and the *ṭabaqāt* collections that resulted – on physicians, jurisconsults, poets, theologians, grammarians, and Sufis, to name just a few of the categories – provided a wealth of biographical information. As these examples suggest, one approach to the recording of historical data consisted in the collection of accounts (*akhbār*) clustered around particular topics; those scholars whose concern was with the varieties of text gathered together under this principle were known under the title of *akhbārī*. Alongside this category of historical research there developed another that was concerned with the linkage of events to chronology. The current Arabic word for history, *tārīkh*, is a slight adaption of the gerund form *taʾrīkh* which literally means 'the assignment of a date, the process of dating'. The task of *taʾrīkh* in its initial stages was the preparation of chronologies and annalistic records; its practitioner was the *muʾarrikh* (historian, assigner of dates).

These earlier contributions to the historical archive served as the bases for the development of historical studies on a broader scale that strove to present a unified vision of the increasingly large and diverse community of Muslims. In our brief assessment above of ibn Qutaybah's role as a compiler of manuals for bureaucrats, we have already drawn attention to his *Kitāb al-maʿārif* (Book of Knowledge), an early essay in historical writing that, with its readership clearly in mind, draws on a variety of sources. Among his contemporaries three names stand out for their contributions to the development of historical writing. The first is al-Balādhurī (d. 892), whose *Kitāb ansāb al-ashrāf* (Book on the Genealogies of the Noble) expands on previous biographical collections by organising information around the tribes and families of important figures within the Muslim community, with a particular concentration on the caliphs of the Umawī family. In his *Kitāb futūḥ al-buldān* (Book on the Conquests of Countries) he documents the processes of conquest and settlement within each province, thus answering an urgent need of the administrators of the widespread Muslim community. A second writer is al-Yaʿqūbī (d. *c.* 900) whose travels over a wide area permitted him to record a good deal of local and often original information. His *Tārīkh* (History) deals first with pre-Islamic cultures, such as those of Israel, India, Greece, and Africa, before turning to an account of the early centuries of Islam up to his own time; the version that he presents of events during the troubled first century AH is just one obvious reflection of his own Shīʿite sympathies. Most prominent of these three figures, however, is al-Ṭabarī (d. 923), whose *Kitāb taʾrīkh al-rusul wa-al-mulūk* (Book of History of Prophets and Kings) is the great monument of Arabic historical writing and, because of its very comprehensiveness, a transition point to new developments in historical writing. Al-Ṭabarī set himself to record the historical traditions of the Arabs, and the great value of his work lies in the fact that, as the compiler of a major commentary (*tafsīr*) on the Qurʾān, he adopted the same standards of authentification of sources in his work of history. Reports of all kinds were collected, many of them contradictory, but the *isnād* (chain of transmission) for each one was provided. The information is laid out in annalistic form, the primary organising principle being the chronology created by the reigns of the caliphs. As several writers have pointed out, his work of history fails to represent the full breadth of the Islamic dominions either in his survey of the pre-Islamic period or in his coverage of his own times; concentration is on the Eastern part with which he is most familiar, while al-Andalus gets particularly short shrift. However, in that al-Ṭabarī's monumental work – now available complete in English translation – provided the Muslim community with a comprehensive and chronologically organised account of its history, compiled in accordance with the strictest standards of authentification demanded by Qurʾān and *ḥadīth* scholarship, its exalted status within the tradition of Arabic historical writing is clearly deserved.

A significant change in Arabic historical writing is brought about by al-Masʿūdī (d. 956) who combines historical and geographical information into a unified narrative framework (a feature which, as has been noted by several scholars, may reflect an awareness of the writings of Greek historians such as Herodotus). Even more widely travelled than his predecessor and fellow-Shīʿite, al-Yaʿqūbī, al-Masʿūdī's peregrinations took him from Persia to the borders of China, the Red Sea, Ceylon, and Palestine. The enormous work that he compiled under the title *Akhbār al-zamān* (Accounts of Time) has not come down to us, but a digest published under the colourful title, *Murūj al-dhahab wa-maʿādin al-jawāhir* (Golden Meadows and Jewelry Mines) immediately became a major and popular source; the great historian of the fourteenth century, ibn Khaldūn, terms al-Masʿūdī *imām li-al-muʾarrikhīn* (a model for historians). Al-Masʿūdī begins his work with a survey of geographical phenomena – the creation of the world and a description of the earth, before surveying the ancient history of the peoples subsumed within the *dār al-Islam* and the history of Islam up to the year 947. What contributes to the originality of this work is not only the way in which it incorporates a personal knowledge of many regions and peoples into a continuous narrative but also the attractive and lively style in which the author couches his account, itself a reflection of the developing norms of *adab* writing and of his unusual open-mindedness to other peoples, cultures, and religions.

In subsequent centuries the writing of universal histories tended to reflect the variety of organising principles adopted by these pioneers, although the majority of writers followed the model of al-Yaʿqūbī and, in particular, al-Masʿūdī, by incorporating geographical information in their works. Prominent among such works were *Tajārib al-umam* (The Experiences of Peoples) by Miskawayh (d. 1030), *Al- Muntaẓam* (The Well-arranged) by ibn al-Jawzī (d. 1200), *al-Kāmil fī al-taʾrīkh* (The Complete Work on History) by ʿIzz al-dīn ibn al-Athīr (d. 1232 – the brother of the above-mentioned Ḍiyāʾ al-dīn), *Taʾrīkh al-Islam wa-ṭabaqāt al-mashāhīr wa-al-aʿlām* (History of Islam and Classes of Renowned and Eminent People) by al-Dhahabī (d. 1347), and *Al-Bidāyah wa-al-nihāyah* (The Beginning and End) by ibn Kathīr (d. 1373), the organising principles of which, not to mention their aspirations to universal coverage, are evidenced by their very titles. The *Kitāb al-ʿibar wa-dīwān al-mubtadaʾ wa-al-khabar fī ayyām al-ʿArab wa-al-ʿAjam wa-al-Barbar* (Book of Lessons, the Record of Subject and Predicate on the Times of Arabs, Non-Arabs, and Berbers) by ibn Khaldūn (d. 1406) is similarly universal in its approach, but a number of features differentiate it from the other works that we have just listed. In the first place, ibn Khaldūn was born in Tunis and spent much of his life at courts in North Africa and al-Andalus; the knowledge that he acquired from those experiences is reflected in the comprehensive coverage of Western Islam that he provides. Secondly, his work makes use of a wide variety of sources, and, most significant from a literary point of view, includes discussion of popular literary forms within his survey of Arabic literature. However, what has made him the most famous historian to have written in Arabic is that, based in no small part on his own knowledge and experience of the rapidity of political transformation in North Africa and al-Andalus, he wrote an introduction (*Muqaddimah*) to his larger work in which he elaborated a theory of cyclic civilisational change involving the relationship between the peoples of the desert and the settled regions. He suggests that, through a process of softening that is the natural product of a sedentary and urban existence, the desert tribes lose their fierce, warrior-like qualities and are then prey to incursions from other tribes who still possess the qualities that they themselves have lost. The civilising process itself instigates dynastic decline, and so the cycle continues. This pioneering exercise in synchronic analysis has led many to see ibn Khaldūn as the founding father of the social sciences.

As the focus of political power moved from a model based on a single centre of caliphal authority in Baghdad to one with a number of widely scattered centres of authority – Cordoba, Cairo, Aleppo, Qayrawān, to name just a few – in each of which a local dynasty held sway, so did the writing of histories with a regional focus, early examples of which already provided much information for the compilers of the broad-scaled studies, increase and diversify. The significance of Mecca and Medina – the two holiest sites in Islam – had ensured that they would be early topics of city-histories; one such is *Taʾrīkh Makkah* (History of Mecca) by ibn al-Azraq (d. 834). The prominence of Baghdad is reflected in the *Kitāb Baghdād* (Book on Baghdad) by ibn Abī Ṭāhir Ṭayfūr (d. 893), a strangely anonymous figure given the frequency with which his writings are cited (he is, for example, a major source for al-Ṭabarī). As its title implies, it is a city-based history that focuses not only on the topography of the city itself but also on its prominent citizens, prime amongst whom are the caliphs of the ʿAbbāsī family.

Histories devoted to regions east and west abound: of Yemen by al-Ḥamdānī (d. 945) and al-Ḥakamī (d. 1175); of the Maghrib by ibn ʿAbd al-ḥakam (d. 870), ibn Raqīq al-Qayrawānī (*fl.* early eleventh century), and ibn Saʿīd (d. 1286). The case of al-Andalus is an interesting one, in that, while its intelligentsia showed an abiding interest in events and trends in 'al-Mashriq' (the East), writings literary and otherwise make clear that there was also a tremendous sense of local pride in the achievements of Andalusian culture. Many prominent scholars contributed to recording the history of the region: ibn Ḥabīb (d. 853), the theologian-poet ibn Ḥazm (d. 1063), and Lisān al-dīn ibn al-Khaṭīb (d. 1374). At a considerably later date, al-Maqqarī (d. 1631) of Tlemçen, looks back over the illustrious history of al-Andalus in a work written long after the fall of Granada in 1492 which carries the colourful and even nostalgic title, *Nafḥ al-ṭīb min ghuṣn al-Andalus al-raṭīb* (Waft of Fragrance from al-Andalus's Luscious Branch). The strategic importance of Egypt has always ensured that its history would be eventful, and two of its later historians were on hand to record momentous events: ibn Iyās (d. 1523) records in his *Badāʾiʿ al-zuhūr fī waqāʾiʿ al-duhūr* (The choicest Blooms concerning the incidence of Dooms) the events surrounding the fall of Cairo to the Ottoman armies under Sultan Selim 'the Grim', and in 1798 ʿAbd al-raḥmān al-Jabartī (d. 1822) records in *ʿAjāʾib al-āthār fī al-tarājim wa-al-akhbār* (Remarkable Reports on Biography and History) his reactions to the arrival in Egypt of French forces under Napoleon and, equally important, the encounters between the Egyptian intelligentsia and the French scientists who accompanied the expedition. At any earlier date, al-Maqrīzī (d. 1441) who held the post of *muḥtasib* in Mamluk Cairo and was thus responsible on the practical level for the honest use of weights and measures in the markets and on a broader plane for public morality in general, introduces a good deal of economic insight into his works, based no doubt on his own practical experience. Most famous among them is *al-Mawāʿiẓ wa-al-iʿtibār fī dhikr al-khiṭaṭ wa-al-āthār* (Lessons to be drawn from a mention of Districts and Remains), which gives increased emphasis to the topographical aspect of city-history. This '*khiṭaṭ*' genre, which provides a detailed survey of streets, buildings and their histories, was expanded and updated in the nineteenth century by ʿAlī Mubārak (d. 1893) in his *Al-Khiṭaṭ al-Tawfīqiyyah al-jadīdah* (Modern Districts of Cairo [during the reign of the Khedive Tawfīq]).

Many of these different types of historical record included (and, in some cases, largely consist of) biographies of prominent figures in the city or region. The continuing interest in genealogy ensured that the compilation of biographical records would remain a prominent part of historical scholarship. An important work in this category is *Taʾrīkh Baghdād* (The History of Baghdad) by al-Khaṭīb al-Baghdādī (d. 1071), in that, in addition to supplying topographical detail on the city, he provided biographies of prominent citizens arranged in alphabetical order. Al-Khaṭīb's compilation provided a model for other city-based works, such as the enormous *Taʾrīkh madīnat Dimashq* (A History of the City of Damascus) of ibn ʿAsākir (d. 1175) and *al-Iḥāṭah fī akhbār Gharnaṭah* (Comprehensive Book on the History of Granada) by ibn al-Khaṭīb. The principles on which these more locally focused works were based were expanded in major collections of biographical data that were collected by Yāqūt (d. 1229) in his *Irshād al-arīb* (Guidance for the Intelligent) and, most notably, by ibn Khallikān (d. 1282) whose biographical dictionary, *Kitāb wafayāt al-aʿyān* (Book on the Deaths of Prominent People), was expanded by al-Ṣafadī (d. 1362) in a work entitled *al-Wāfī bi-al-Wafayāt* (The Complement to the 'Deaths'). While the bulk of the information provided in these works is biographical, the compilers occasionally include autobiographical accounts which tend to record incidents that reflect well on the subject involved rather than provide insights into aspects of personality; one among many examples that provides interesting insight into the career of a prominent figure is the autobiography of ibn Sīnā, contained within the biography of the philosopher by his pupil, Abū ʿUbaydah al-Juzjānī (*fl.* eleventh century). However, some individual works do stand out because of the glimpses they afford of the personae of their authors. In *Al-Munqidh min al-ḍalāl* (Deliverance from Error) al-Ghazālī looks back in his latter years and surveys the circumstances of his life, one that led him to a spiritual crisis in 1095 and to a 'deliverance' whereby he withdrew from public life and began a course of contemplation – a process that was to engender the hugely important works which he contributed to Islamic scholarship. In a second, more robust and worldly, example, Usāmah ibn Munqidh (d. 1189) uses the hindsight afforded by old age to record a life full of incident in *Kitāb al-iʿtibār* (Book of Example). He recounts the adventures of a fighter against the Crusaders but is equally anxious to share with his readers the pleasures of hunting and literature along with a wealth of anecdote about himself and others.

While the Muslim community was clearly in need of geographical works that would describe the territories brought within the *dār al-Islam* by the Muslim conquests, there was also a need for other works of a more directly practical nature. Messengers and administrators had to travel on business from the centres of authority to the provinces and from one province to another, frequently traversing unknown terrain in the process. Among the first to respond to these needs was ibn Khurradādhbih (d. *c.* 885), apparently an official in the postal service, whose *Kitāb al-masālik wa-al-mamālik* (Book of Routes and Realms) is from one point of view a listing of itineraries, but the expectations of *adab* are also met through the inclusion of other types of information, including poetry. Among other works of what we might term descriptive geography were the *Kitāb al-buldān* of the widely travelled al-Yaʿqūbī (whose contribution to historical writing was mentioned above), the *Kitāb al-masālik wa-al-mamālik* of ibn Ḥawqal (d. *c.* 990) – itself a continuation of an earlier work of al-Iṣṭakhrī (d. 961), and *Aḥsan al-taqāsīm fī maʿrifat al-aqālīm* (The Best Divisions for Knowing the Regions) by al-Muqaddasī (d. *c.* 1000), a work which is generally agreed to point to the future for both the rigour of its method and the elegance of its style. A century later, al-Idrīsī (d. 1165) composed a famous work for King Roger II, the Norman ruler of Sicily, under the title *Nuzhat al-mushtāq fī ikhtirāq al-āfāq* (The Dilectation of the One Who Desires to Traverse the Horizons) but also known as *Kitāb Rūjār* (Roger's Book) which provided not only a comprehensive geographical survey of the known world but also a series of maps to accompany the text. It is one of the first Arabic works to be printed in Rome (1592) and through translations into European languages was regarded as the most famous work of geography in Arabic. It was the invaluable contribution of Yāqūt, whom we mentioned above in connection with biographies, once again to bring together parts of the vast amount of information contained in these and other works in a geographical dictionary, a kind of gazetteer of place names arranged in alphabetical order, the *Muʿjam al-buldān* (Dictionary of Countries).

To the practicalities of communication were added the demands of commerce and diplomacy. 'The Voyages of Sindbad', originally a separate story tradition but later incorporated into the *Thousand and One Nights* collection, provides a clue as to the extent of the trade-routes plied by Arab mariners; the same linkage of navigation, the figure of Sindbad, and narrative, provides a creative impulse for the modern Egyptian writer, Ḥusayn Fawzī (1900–88) and, more recently, for the American novelist, John Barth, in his *The Last Voyage of Somebody the Sailor* (1991). A repertoire of manuals on navigation parallel to the *masālik* genre described above for land travel was developed. On the diplomatic front we have the fascinating account of ibn Faḍlān who was dispatched by the Caliph al-Muqtadir in 921 on an embassy to the Volga region and returned to record in his *al-Risālah* (The Treatise) the details of his encounters with the Slavic and Turkic peoples whom he met during his travels.

Quite apart from these motivations to travel and explore, Islam enjoined believers with the obligation to perform the pilgrimage to the holy city of Mecca. These often lengthy travels from the various peripheries of the Islamic world to its original centre were divided into stages (*marāḥil*, sing. *marḥalah*); as part of al-Jāḥiẓ's sequence of tales about the implausibly miserly traits of the people of Marw in his *Kitāb al-bukhalā'* (Book of Misers), he records in disbelief how, when they alight at one of these staging posts, they all go off on their own and eat their food in isolation. Two of the most renowned works of travel in Arabic begin by announcing that they are to be accounts of the pilgrimage, and both involve a journey from west – the Maghrib – to east, but both are also fulsome reflections of the linkage that was established very early in the tradition of Islamic scholarship, namely that travel provided a wonderful opportunity for learning; in the words of the traditional phrase: 'seek knowledge, though it be in China'. The pilgrimage of Ibn Jubayr (d. 1217) of Granada was, he tells us, an act of expiation for the sin of drinking. The *Riḥlah* (Journey) takes the form of a precisely organised chronological narrative of visits to the cities of Egypt, Syria, and Arabia, culminating in the description of Mecca itself. His descriptions are elaborate and often emphasise the more remarkable and unusual aspects of the places involved, an effect that is underlined by his hyperbolic mode of expression. In this he differs from his successor in this genre, Ibn Baṭṭūtah (d. 1377) of Tangier, whose *Tuḥfat al-nuẓẓar fī gharā'ib al-amṣār wa-ʿajā'ib al-asfār* (Delight of the Beholders Regarding Exotic Cities and Remarkable Journeys) continues the focus on the unusual (as his title clearly illustrates) but is written in a less complicated style. If ibn Jubayr's primary focus was the pilgrimage itself, ibn Baṭṭūtah seems to have been gripped by a genuine wanderlust, in that, between 1325 and 1349, he visited Africa, Constantinople, Russia, India, Ceylon, and China, following that with a shorter visit to Spain and Niger in 1353. As with ibn Jubayr (and Herodotus) ibn Baṭṭūtah gathered together in his work all kinds of information about the places he visited. In addition, he appears to have suffered the misfortune at one point in his travels of losing his notes, so that parts of the dictation of his account to ibn Juzayy had to be reconstructed from memory. That the chronology of his narrative should be less precise, indeed less evident, than that of ibn Jubayr, and that certain recorded events should have proved to be 'misplaced' is thus not surprising. Whether completely accurate or not, ibn Baṭṭūtah's narrative remains a remarkable and enjoyable record of a tradition that combined the adventure of travel with a quest for knowledge.

The contribution of mystical discourse

During the course of our survey in the second chapter of the backgrounds against which the Arabic literary tradition developed, we noted that the energies of the Islamic scholarly community were initially devoted to the analysis of the Qur'ān and the use of both it and other authoritative sources as bases for the development of systems of dogmatics and jurisprudence. Alongside this emphasis on the more legislative and communally based aspects of belief and practice, there emerged a perceived need for more personal modes of approach to the transcendent God through prayer, contemplation, and spiritual reflection. A variety of types of homiletic and contemplative discourse had already been part of the broad-scaled project of compilation that we have already described: sermons (*mawāʿiẓ*, sing. *mawʿiẓah*) for example, and testaments (*waṣāyā*, sing. *waṣiyyah*), two genres that offered the believer spiritual and ethical counsel. One of the acknowledged masters of the sermon genre was al-Ḥasan al-Baṣrī (d. 728), whose repute is based both on the personal example that he set in his scholarship and personal behaviour and on the attractive style in which his admonitions are couched. Gathered together by his disciples, his admonitions were regarded as models of style and were cited in the works of such major figures as al-Jāḥiẓ and ibn ʿAbd Rabbihi. These foundations provided a base for the development of a more specifically mystical discourse, a process in which pioneer status is given to Dhū al-nūn al-Miṣrī (d. 861) whose innovative writings made use of allegory and parable as means of establishing interpretive layers through which to express the mystical path to spiritual ecstasy in terms of love and other more worldly sensations. Another renowned Ṣūfī teacher was al-Junayd (d. 910) who made use of the epistle (*risālah*) genre to impart his wisdom to his Sufi brethren. One of al-Junayd's pupils, al-Daqqāq, served as master to al-Qushayrī (d. 1072) whose Epistle (usually known as *al-Risālah al-Qushayriyyah*; English translation, *Principles of Sufism*) served both to provide a systematic analysis of Ṣūfī tenets and, equally important, to exclude from consideration many of the more peculiar beliefs and practices that continued to attach themselves to the mystical path. Beginning with a chapter on 'repentance' and proceeding through the major principles of mystical belief and practice (asceticism, for example, humility, contentment, sincerity, remembrance of the name of God (*dhikr* – the term for Sufi rituals), freedom, sainthood, and love), al-Qushayrī makes use of the dicta of all his famous mystical forebears in a work that cogently advocates the role of Sufism within Islam. The same linkage was also central to the thought of Shihāb al-dīn ʿUmar al-Suhrawardī (d. 1234), one of several contributors to mystical thought of that name, as expressed in his manual of Sufi practice, *ʿAwārif al-maʿārif* (The Benefits of Knowledge). For that reason, he needs to be clearly distinguished from his fellow-townsman, Shihāb al-dīn Yaḥyā whose contribution will be discussed below.

The popularity of Sufism as a devotional path and the systematisation of its principles by a number of highly respected scholars contributed to the emergence of mystical brotherhoods (*ṭarāqah*, pl. *ṭuruq*) that burgeoned throughout the Islamic world from the twelfth century onward. Among the most notable of these are the Qādiriyyah named after ʿAbd al-qādir al-Jīlānī (d. 1168), the Rifāʿiyyah named after Aḥmad Abū al-ʿAbbās al-Rifāʿī (d. 1182), and the Naqshbandiyyah named after Muḥammad Bahāʾ al-dīn Naqshband of Bukhārā (d. 1389). With the establishment of such linkages of brotherhood and devotion, it is not surprising that an elaborate tradition of hagiographical writing developed. In a number of collections of virtuous deeds (called *manāqib*) a wide variety of miraculous actions are attributed to famous figures like al-Jīlānī and al-Rifāʿī. As we have noted with regard to other fields, the careers of the more prominent Sufis are gathered into large compilations, such as *Ṭabaqāt al-ṣūfiyyah* (Sufi Classes) by al-Sulamī (d. 1021) and the huge collection, *Ḥilyat al-awliyāʾ* (Jewel of the Saints), by Abū Nuʿaym al-Iṣfahānī (d. 1038).

The imagery and discourse of Ṣûfī writing provides the tradition of Arabic prose with some of its most beautiful models. Following the example provided by Dhū al-nūn, Muḥammad al-Niffarī (d. 965) recorded his own experiences of the transcendent in two works, *Kitāb al-mawāqif* (Book of Stations) and *Kitāb al-mukhāṭabāt* (Book of Intimations); the elements of imagery and repetition (here transcending its normal poetic role in the sonic realm to attain the more insistent function of entrancement) combine with an aphoristic and homiletic tone to remarkable effect:

STATION OF A SEA

He stationed me in a sea, but did not name it. He said to me: I do not name it because you belong to Me, not to it; when I let you know of other than Me, you are the most ignorant of the ignorant. The entire universe is other than Me. That which calls to Me and not to it, it is of Me. If you respond to it, I will punish you and will not accept what you bring. I cannot avoid having you; my entire need is in you. So seek bread and shirt from me. I bring delight. Sit with me, and I will make you happy; none other will do so. Look at Me, for I look at no one but you. When you bring me all of this and I tell you it is sound, you are not of Me, nor I of you. (Station 39)

Servant, satisfy your eye, I will satisfy your heart;
Servant, satisfy your legs, I will satisfy your hands;
Servant, satisfy your sleep, I will satisfy your waking;
Servant, satisfy your desire, I will satisfy your need . . . (Intimation 34)

The works of scholars such as al-Qushayrī and al-Ghazālī sought to place Sufi thought and practice within the larger framework of Islam as a whole. However, such gestures of reconciliation did not prevent other Sufi scholars from pursuing their own paths, challenging the norms of established dogma as they explored and expounded on the nature of the transcendental experience. Two of the most notable and controversial figures in this area were Shihāb al-dīn Yaḥyā al-Suhrawardī (d. 1191) and Muḥyī al-dīn ibn al-ʿArabī (d. 1240). The second Shihāb al-dīn from Suhraward, Yaḥyā, made use of his profound knowledge of philosophy to integrate the concepts of the Greek philosophy and particularly Neo-Platonism with concepts from Zoroastrianism, into a system that considered the place of the individual within God's universe. His views were focused around the notion of *ishrāq* (illumination): that human beings exist in a world of darkness and that it is God's divine light that illumines their path. However, his speculative explorations on this topic and, in particular, the nature of revelation and the role of prophethood within it – well developed by the time he moved to Aleppo in his early thirties, ran afoul of the conservative religious establishment at a particularly sensitive moment during the ongoing conflict with the Crusaders. Executed on the order of Ṣalāḥ al-dīn, he thus shared the fate of his mystical forebear, al-Ḥallāj (d. 922) and was thereafter distinguished from other bearers of the name al-Suhrawardī as *al-maqtūl* (the one who was killed).

No less controversial in his speculations was Muḥyī al-dīn ibn al-ʿArabī, known to his admirers as *al-shaykh al-akbar* (the supreme master), whose contributions to the tradition of Ṣūfī poetry were briefly discussed in ch. 4. He was born and educated in al-Andalus, and his travels throughout the Maghrib region had already earned him a wide reputation as a Sufi divine when he decided – inspired by a dream, he tells us – to undertake the pilgrimage to Mecca in about 1202. Visiting Cairo, Baghdad, and Konya, as well as the holy cities of Arabia, he eventually settled in Damascus. His deeply textured writings, an accurate reflection of their author's intense spirituality and powerful imagination, are allusive and complex to the point of obscurantism. For centuries they have taxed the interpretive skills of the most erudite, and traditionalist scholars have regarded them as dangerously speculative and even heretical; for them 'Muḥyī al-dīn' (the reviver of the religion) was rather to be thought of as 'Māḥī al-dīn' or 'Mumīt al-dīn' (the eraser or slayer of the religion).

It was a period spent in Mecca that provided the inspiration for his monumental, thirty-seven-volume *al-Futuḥāt al-Makkiyyah.* Written over a period of several years and interrupted by visits to other cities where his ever spreading reputation had preceded him, the *Futuḥāt* bring together within a single work speculative theology, philosophy, a personal spiritual diary, and information about other Sufi masters, to become a virtual *summa* on esoteric wisdom in Islam. Later in his life, ibn al-ʿArabī was inspired – by a command from the Prophet Muḥammad in another dream, he tells his reader – to compose *Fuṣūṣ al-ḥikam* (The Gem-settings of Wisdom), a commentary on the Qurʾān based not on the numerical order of the Surahs but rather on the prophetic narratives; in a series of meditations each prophet – Adam, Noah, Moses, Solomon, Jesus, and so on – becomes the locus for a discussion of one aspect of God's divine self-manifestation. The first chapter, for example, is on Adam, and takes as its topic the 'wisdom of divinity':

> When the real willed
>   from the perspective of its most beautiful names
>   which are countless
> to see their determination
> or you could say
> when it willed to see its own determination . . .
> to reveal itself through itself
> its mystery
>   for the self-vision of a being through itself
>   is not like its self-vision through something outside
>   which acts like a mirror
>
>   its self appearing to it
>   in a form
>   in a plane of reflection
>
>   a form which could not occur
>   without the existence of such a plane
>   and the self-manifestation in it

and when the real had brought into being
the universe
a vague, molded shape
without a spirit
it was like an unpolished mirror . . .

(Michael Sells, *Studia Islamica* (1986): 125)

For ibn al-ʿArabī the image of the mirror is a central one; the divinity of God is thereby reflected in the apportionment of part of His attributes to Prophets and 'saints' (*aqṭāb*, sing. *quṭb*). They are particular examples of the heights to which humanity can strive in its quest towards the ideal of the 'perfect man' (*al-insān al-kāmil*). These concepts are all part of his overarching principle, 'the oneness of the universe' (*waḥdat al-wujūd*), whereby everything that is or might be is to be understood as a manifestation of the divine attributes of God illustrated by His 'beautiful names' and explored through the mystical path.

If al-Ghazālī's writings fostered the integration of Sufi thought into the framework of Islamic scholarship, then ibn al-ʿArabī carries the exploration of esoteric meaning to its highest point. While continuing along the path of his Sufi forebear, al-Ḥallāj, he avoided the latter's fate through the creative use of allegory, allusion, and an elaborate system of coded imagery. Such discourse features insured that his works would be the inspiration for succeeding generations of mystical poets (among whom are some of the most notable within the tradition of Persian mystical verse, including Jāmī (d. 1492)). The very extent of ibn al-ʿArabī's own travels through west and east of the Islamic lands was to have an immense effect on the further development of mystical thought and the movements that expounded it.

The five centuries following the death of ibn al-ʿArabī saw a vast increase in the influence of Sufi brotherhoods. The teachings of their leaders and the rituals that their initiates performed became a major component of popular Islamic religious devotion, a trend that aroused the opprobrium of conservative theologians such as ibn Taymiyyah. A natural consequence of this increase in the role and influence of Sufism at all levels of society was the composition of an enormous library of works intended for the inspiration of these communities: collections of miraculous tales concerning prominent Sufis and compendia of devotional texts. Alongside this ever expanding store of hagiographic material the work of Ṣūfī scholars continued to enrich the Islamic sciences; two eminent examples are al-Shaʿrānī (d. 1566) and ʿAbd al-ghanī al-Nābulusī (d. 1731), whose writings stand out not only for their variety but also for the distinguished style in which they were couched.

The contribution of Sufi writings to the development of Arabic prose literature is immense and generally underestimated. As much of the material discussed in this chapter has shown, *adab* texts were mostly written within the milieu of court structures where *udabāʾ*, after carrying out their primary functions as civil servants, would have both the time and environment for study and teaching; the peripatetic career of Abū Ḥayyān al-Tawḥīdī in quest of such appreciation provides a good illustration. In a word, such authors and the works they wrote were, more often than not, patronised. To adopt Sufi terminology, this might be termed the *ẓāhir* (external, evident) trend within the *adab* tradition, that which took the visible world as its topic and source of inspiration. Much Sufi writing, on the other hand, uses the *ẓāhir* as a base from which to embark on an inward journey of contemplation, investigating the unknown, the metaphysical, and the transcendent; its focus is that which is *bāṭin* (internal, hidden). This concern with the more individual and personal level led those who wrote under its inspiration to develop new modes of expression and imagery that greatly enriched the literary repertoire. In the eloquent words of Jamāl al-Ghīṭānī, the Egyptian novelist who has himself been much inspired by Sufi writing (his novel *Kitāb al-tajalliyyāt* (Book of Illuminations) is modelled on the work of ibn al-ʿArabī), 'Sufi expression presents a challenge to fixed, established patterns and an adventure into the unknown that aspires to limitless horizons'. It is on the basis of an increasing awareness among modern authors of the features of Sufi discourse that the works of a writer such as al-Niffarī (cited above) have been a source of inspiration; thus has the Arabic literary heritage provided for its modern literary heirs a means through which to explore the dimensions of modernity.

Journeys of the imagination

The debates over the place of philosophy and mysticism within the system of Islamic belief, which had preoccupied the minds of such great scholars as ibn Sīnā and al-Ghazālī, were reflected in several works in which writers used more indirect and allegorical modes to explore the dimensions of esoteric wisdom. One of the more famous allegorical treatments within the tradition is *Ḥayy ibn Yaqẓān, asrār al-ḥikmah al-mashriqiyyah* (Alive the Son of Awake, the Secrets of Eastern Wisdom). This allegory of the cosmic order served as inspiration for a number of writers, including the philosopher ibn Sīnā, but its most famous elaboration is that of the Andalusian philosopher, ibn Ṭufayl (d. 1185), who clearly acknowledges the influence of his great predecessor in philosophy. Ibn Ṭufayl's version clearly fascinated Western scholars from an early date in that by the fourteenth century it had already been translated into Hebrew and was later rendered into Latin by Edward Pococke, son of the first holder of Oxford's Laudian Chair in Arabic, in 1671 and then into English in 1674.

At the beginning of the work, the narrator informs a friend who has asked him to reveal the secrets of philosophy as expounded by ibn Sīnā that he will make use of a story already used by 'the great master' (*al-shaykh al-ra'īs*, as ibn Sīnā is named) to illustrate the nature of the path ahead. The story he tells is that of Ḥayy ibn Yaqẓān, born in a process of spontaneous generation, who lives on an island. Through contemplation and speculation he gradually learns to appreciate the rational nature of the cosmos and to develop a code of ethics. He then moves on from such earthly considerations to achieve a level of ecstatic contemplation, about which, as the narrator tells his friend, he can only provide hints since words are incapable of depicting it. It is at this point that Ḥayy – 'philosophus autodidactus' in the words of Pococke – comes into contact with Asāl, the inhabitant of another island where social behaviour is governed by the teachings of a true religion. Ḥayy returns with Asāl to his island and endeavours to explain his acquired wisdom to them, but his teachings are given a cold reception. Realising the nature of the human condition and his hosts' inability to comprehend the essence of his insights, Ḥayy, accompanied by Asāl, returns to the other island. Recovering the state of ecstasy he had known before, Ḥayy lives the rest of his life along with his companion in tranquil contemplation. In closing the story the narrator notes that his purpose has been to make a hidden branch of learning more explicit, but that he has nevertheless preserved a certain veil of allegory thick enough to exclude those unworthy of looking behind it.

The theme of a visit to the afterlife is adopted as the framework for two other famous works of the imagination. In *Risālat al-tawābiʿ wa-al-zawābiʿ* (Treatise of Familiar Spirits and Demons) the narrator of the Andalusian poet, ibn Shuhayd (d. 1035), meets the spirits of a number of prominent littérateurs – poets such as Imru al-Qays, Abū Nuwās, Abū Tammām and al-Mutanabbī, prose writers such as ʿAbd al-ḥamīd, al-Jāḥiẓ, and Badīʿ al-zamān al-Hamadhānī, and critics. However, it is the final section which may explain the rationale for this erudite and witty work: the narrator meets a number of animals, including a donkey and a goose, who duly provide their critical opinions on works of literature, suggesting that ibn Shuhayd was prompted to invoke the spirits of his forebears in order to counter some negative criticism among his local contemporaries. The other work is the *Risālat al-ghufrān* (Epistle of Forgiveness) by the renowned ascetic philosopher-poet, Abū al-ʿAlāʾ al-Maʿarrī (d. 1057). Having received from one ʿAlī ibn al-Qāriḥ a letter containing questions regarding aspects of heresy and belief, al-Maʿarrī decided to preface his response with an imaginary tour of the afterworld, during the course of which the Shaykh would be permitted to visit Paradise and Hell and interview various literary personages concerning their behaviour during their lifetime and its consequences. During the visit to Paradise he discovers that several pre-Islamic poets have been forgiven. The famous wine-poet, al-Aʿshā, has abandoned his former ways. When Ḥassān ibn Thābit, 'the poet of the Prophet', is challenged to justify a seemingly risky verse in his famous 'Mantle Poem' (*Burdah*), he observes that the Prophet was not as puritanical as some people imagine. Visiting Hell, the Shaykh encounters Imru al-Qays, Bashshār ibn Burd, and several other poets, including the famous vagabonds, Taʾabbaṭa Sharran and al-Shanfarā. In the second part of the work al-Maʿarrī finally broaches the task of responding to his correspondent's comments and questions on aspects of heresy. He notes with a certain resignation that his statements on belief have been misinterpreted and that he is 'slandered just as the Arabs slander the ghoul'. Such protestations notwithstanding, the level of scepticism to be found in this and other works of his was such that it is hardly surprising that, in R. A. Nicholson's colourful phrase, it managed to 'set up a minatory wagging of pious beards' (*Journal of the Royal Asiatic Society* (1900): 639).

Maqāmāt

The genre of fictional narrative that became the most widespread and popular was the *maqāmah*; indeed it managed to retain that status until well into the twentieth century. There is still much scholarly debate concerning the origins of the genre. Al-Hamadhānī (d. 1008) – as noted above, a member of the court circle of Rayy, is considered to be its pioneer, and indeed such was his stylistic virtuosity that he was dubbed 'the wonder of the age' (*Badīʿ al-zamān*). Rather than term him the 'inventor' of the genre however (an improbable concept in any case), it seems more accurate to suggest that he managed to fuse together a number of already existing elements into a form that proved to be an ideal reflection of the aesthetics of his and subsequent ages.

The original meaning of *maqāmah* involves a place of standing. From there it came to mean a tribal assembly, to which was gradually attached the sense of an occasion for the delivery of an uplifting message. Al-Hamadhānī chose to use, indeed to play on, these oratorical and homiletic dimensions by placing them into a societal context and by couching his narratives in a discourse that both exploited the potential of the Arabic language and evoked numerous inter-textual linkages. The societal aspect is represented by the placement of the scenario of many *maqāmāt* among the beggar fraternities of the cities of Islam, thereby reflecting the ever changing nature of the broader Islamic community as it endeavoured to deal with the tensions aroused by such factors as multiethnic contact, religious and cultural controversies, and increasing commercialism. The stylistic element was, no doubt, a product of the move towards elaboration that al-Hamadhānī had witnessed among his colleagues and rivals in Rayy and Baghdad, in that he adopted the increasingly popular *sajʿ* (rhyming prose) as the stylistic vehicle for his *maqāmāt*, thereby invoking reference not only to the many genres that made use of the style – epistles, sermons, and the like, but also to the language of the Qurʾān and the cadences and images of poetry.

The sentences and phrases of the *maqāmah*'s *sajʿ* are preceded by an opening formula in the form of an abbreviated *isnād* (the process of tracing the line of transmission familiar from the *ḥadīth* concerning the Prophet and other types of report). In the case of al-Hamadhānī, each *maqāmah* begins with the phrase: 'ʿĪsā ibn Hishām reported to us and said'. This ʿĪsā, a fictional character who is nevertheless named after one of al-Hamadhānī's contemporaries, is one of two figures whose interaction forms the framework of the series of short narratives contained within the *maqāmāt*. The other character in the duo is named Abū al-fatḥ al-Iskandarī. His attitude to life is summed up in a number of short poems which conclude the *maqāmāt*:

Use every device to obtain your daily bread and do not balk at any ruse,
Undertake any enormity; for – there's no escaping it – man is feeble.
(*Maqāmah* of Baghdad)

May God never put the likes of me at a distance; for where, O where, can you find the likes of me?
God only knows how stupid people are; I have fleeced them with ease.
I have asked of them charity in bulk, but in return I have merely given them a measure of deceit and lies. (*Maqāmah* of Mawṣil)

Abū al-fatḥ is a trickster, a master of disguise; he is never what he at first seems. In the majority of the *maqāmāt* ʿĪsā's role is as his companion and foil, his uncoverer; the recognition of the identity of Abū al-fatḥ reveals the trickery that he has been working on his audience. In other *maqāmāt*, however, ʿĪsā fulfils a different function. In the Baghdad *maqāmah*, for example, it is ʿĪsā alone who dupes a country yokel into providing him with a lavish free meal before watching the wretched individual being pummelled into paying the bill. In the Maḍīriyyah *maqāmah*, ʿĪsā does not appear at all; instead the sight of a wonderful stew-like dish (*maḍīrah*) triggers in Abū al-fatḥ's memory an occasion when he encounters a *nouveau riche* merchant who insists on showing him every feature of his ultimate suburban residence, not least the toilet.

It is traits such as these in al-Hamadhānī's *maqāmāt* that have aroused the interest of Western scholars in quest of fictional narratives that appear to replicate some of the features of their Western counterparts and perhaps serve as possible antecedents for the emergence of the modern tradition of Arabic fiction. The glimpse that they afford of a segment of society other than the court is indeed a lively one, and the picaresque scenario within which their stories unfold provides an antecedent to the later emergence of that genre in Spain that suggests tantalisingly interesting, but as yet unsubstantiated possibilities of transmittal. To the 'narratives' that we have briefly described above can be added others, such as the two-part *maqāmāt*, that of the Lion – with its tale of desert travel, youthful heroism, and deceit – and the almost farcical events of the *maqāmah* of Mawṣil, with ʿĪsā and Abū al-fatḥ first convincing a family that a dead man is actually still alive and then escaping under a hail of blows after their victims realise that they have been cruelly deceived and secondly offering to divert a flood from a village through a thoroughly rigid performance of prayers and then abandoning the worshippers in mid-prostration (a scenario later adopted as a motif by the Egyptian short-story writer, Yūsuf Idrīs). However, while these tales are indeed lively and entertaining, they are not representative of the bulk of al-Hamadhānī's *maqāmāt*. Other examples are far more static in nature and serve rather to provide replications, or perhaps pastiches, of different types of occasion and text: the *maqāmah* of al-Jāḥiẓ, for instance, takes the form of a literary circle (*majlis*) where the works of al-Hamadhānī's great predecessor are discussed in learned (and critical) terms. The *maqāmah* of Ṣaymarah recounts a lengthy and elaborate morality tale whose narrator is Abū al-ʿAnbas al-Ṣaymarī (d. *c.* 888), an actual poet, story-teller, and boon-companion (*nadīm*) of the

Caliph al-Mutawakkil. Al-Ṣaymarī tells the reader how a life of good living and lavish generosity towards the social élite lead him to bankruptcy and societal oblivion; wandering far and wide, he gathers stories and practical experience as well as considerable wealth before returning to Baghdad. Learning of his return, his former côterie of acquaintances beg his forgiveness for their callous behaviour and are delighted to be invited to a lavish meal. When they are all sufficiently drunk, their host invites a barber to shave their beards. Unable to appear in public, his guests' businesses suffer and their relatives invoke curses against al-Ṣaymarī. However, when the caliph's minister is consulted on the issue, he is much amused and declares al-Ṣaymarī's actions justified. Here indeed, to cite the phrase much used in the *Thousand and One Nights* is 'a lesson for those who would learn it' (*ʿibrah li-man yaʿtabir*).

Al-Hamadhānī's *maqāmāt* are indeed significant contributions to Arabic literature: insightful, witty, and stylistically brilliant, they simultaneously invoke and reflect the urbanity of an intellectual milieu in its search for new directions and its critical readings of established genres. If it is the function of comedy to convey to its audience a sense of satisfaction through watching others behaving in variously inappropriate ways, then al-Hamadhānī's *maqāmāt* may be regarded as an interesting set of counter-narratives that invoke the language and modes of various types of Islamic text and thereby provide an ironic framework that challenges their readers (and originally their audience) to adopt a critical posture towards the kinds of morality and behaviour presented in these witty vignettes.

Al-Hamadhānī's pioneer status is acknowledged by his great successor in the genre, Abū Muḥammad al-Qāsim al-Ḥarīrī (d. 1122), in the introduction to his set of *maqāmāt*. We have already noted that al-Hamadhānī's examples have been interpreted in a number of ways by different audiences, but it is clear from the model presented by al-Ḥarīrī and his successors in the genre that it was in the realm of stylistic virtuosity and its use for homiletic purposes that the *maqāmah* became for several centuries a popular mode of bellettristic prose expression; to such an extent in fact that the role of al-Hamadhānī was largely eclipsed by the enormous amount of attention paid to the work of his famous successor.

With al-Ḥarīrī, the basic scenario of the *maqāmah* remains the same, but the names are different: the narrator is now called al-Ḥārith ibn Hammām, and the chameleon-like character whom it is his role to uncover is named Abū Zayd al-Sarūjī. The continuing ambivalence of the narrator towards his partner in narrative is well captured by al-Ḥārith himself when he notes in *al-Maqāmah al-wabariyyah*: 'As I weighed Abū Zayd's benefit and harm in the balance, I was at a loss as to whether to scold or thank him'. A few of al-Ḥarīrī's *maqāmāt* share the narrative qualities of some of al-Hamadhānī's examples that were mentioned above: that of Damascus, for example, depicts a desert journey, while others are concerned with Abū Zayd's feuds with his wife. However, al-Ḥarīrī's introduction specifies that he will be providing examples of other types of text, and this transtextual aspect, already present in al-Hamadhānī's *maqāmāt*, now becomes a more predominant feature. In several *maqāmāt* – those of Tannis and Rayy, for example – Abū Zayd is a hell-fire preacher, advocating asceticism (*zuhd*) and reminding his listeners of the ephemerality of this world and all its goods. In the *maqāmah* of Samarqand he delivers a homily; in that of Thebes he becomes a legal scholar untangling complex situations; in the *maqāmah* of Sāsān, he delivers his last will and testament to his son, handing over to him the position of chief of the beggars' fraternity. Other *maqāmāt* take the form of a *majlis*: Abū Zayd's learning is shown through his discussions of metaphor and plagiarism in poetry (the *maqāmāt* of Ḥulwān and Poetry), of syntax (Qaṭīʿ), and of the comparative virtues of epistolary and financial expertise (Euphrates).

We suggested above that al-Hamadhānī's adoption of *sajʿ* as the stylistic medium for his *maqāmāt* was already an indication of the essentially textual (rather than narrative) focus of this new genre. With al-Ḥarīrī, master grammarian and author of a study of language usage, *Durrat al-ghawāṣṣ fī lughat al-khawāṣṣ* (The Pearl of the Diver concerning the Language of the Elite), this stylistic and textual aspect comes to the fore. Thus, whereas one can conceive of al-Hamadhānī improvising his brilliant vignettes in the public domain, al-Ḥarīrī's *maqāmāt* reflect the deliberate touch of a virtuoso creating his works within the more private world of the written text and crafting each example into a masterpiece of language. His *maqāmāt* are longer, and poetry assumes a much more prominent place within the structure of the text. Beyond that, however, al-Ḥarīrī provides examples of linguistic virtuosity that is unparalleled in Arabic literature: *al-Maqāmah al-marāghiyyah*, for example, contains a letter in which there is an alternation between words whose graphemes carry no dots and others in which every grapheme carries a dot; *al-Maqāmah al-raqṭāʾ* (Black Speckled with White) contains a similar letter where the same principle is applied to alternate graphemes within individual words. Reflected here is the delight of an intellectual côterie in observing a virtuoso probing the limits of human creativity in language, linked at the same time to a celebration of the sheer variety of textual examples that such language can invoke and imitate. As Abū Zayd informs his audience in *al-Maqāmah al-qahqariyyah* (backwards, in that it contains a letter than can be read in either direction), 'Here are a couple of hundred phrases, comprising both *adab* and homiletic wisdom; anyone who follows such a path will encounter neither discord nor argument'.

After the death of al-Ḥarīrī, the *maqāmah* became a favoured mode of bellettristic expression in Arabic, its continuing popularity as a genre serving as one of the more obvious manifestations of the literary élite's predilection for elaborate forms of prose discourse. *Saj*ʿ, with its celebration of rhyme, deftly structured discourse, and lexicographical virtuosity, permeated most areas of expression, from the increasingly elaborate titles of books on all topics to the more formulaic segments of popular narratives like the *Thousand and One Nights*. Authors of works chose the *maqāmah* as the vehicle for their writing projects on a wide variety of topics, but the narrative structure established by al-Hamadhānī and followed to a certain extent by al-Ḥarīrī clearly did not provide a pattern that their successors felt called upon to replicate. The famous philologist, al-Zamakhsharī (d. 1143), who, in addition to the already mentioned *Rabīʿ al-abrār*, composed commentaries on the Qur'ān, a major source work in Arabic grammar, *al-Mufaṣṣal*, and a compilation entitled *Aṭwāq al-dhahab fī al-mawāʿiẓ wa-al-adab* (Golden Necklets on Homilies and *Adab*), informs his readers in the Introduction that he was prompted in a dream to complete fifty *maqāmāt*. Written in the polished *saj*ʿ of a philologist and grammarian, they open with an invocation to Abū al-Qāsim (al-Zamakhsharī) and offer homiletic advice on various topics to the author himself; through question and command they proceed to issue warnings and counsel to the reader. The second *maqāmah*, entitled 'Fear of God', illustrates the tone:

> O Abū al-Qāsim, life is short and to God is the resort, so what means this delinquency? The fripperies of life have led you astray, and the demon of desire has made you stumble. Were you as shrewd and sensible as you claim, you would have done things that were more worthy of you ...

More similar to al-Ḥarīrī's work are *al-Maqāmāt al-luzūmiyyah* by al-Saraqusṭī (from Saragossa in Spain, d. 1143). Even though these *maqāmāt* do not carry particular titles, they reflect and discuss travel throughout the world of Islam, from the Arabian peninsula to China.

Once again the collection recounts the antics and impostures of a pair of 'characters'; one is from ʿUmān, named Abū Ḥabīb, and he is joined by al-Ṣāʾib ibn Tammām whose narratives are themselves often narrated by another narrator named al-Mundhir ibn Humām. While al-Saraqusṭī does not set out to rival the verbal acrobatics of al-Ḥarīrī, the style of his writing and the variety of his themes (including two *maqāmāt* on literary topics) show clearly the inspiration that he drew from his illustrious forebear. (It is worth noting parenthetically at this point that al-Ḥarīrī was also the inspiration for the *maqāmāt* that Judah al-Ḥarīzī (d. 1225), the Andalusian Jewish littérateur, wrote in Hebrew.) In his *al-Maqāmāt al-zayniyyah* ibn al-Ṣayqal al-Jazarī (d. 1273), a teacher at the Mustanṣiriyyah College in Baghdad, debates issues of jurisprudence and grammar, while indulging in some Ḥarīrian linguistic feats: the seventh *maqāmah*, entitled '*al-Sanjariyyah*', extols the work of al-Ḥarīrī and then proceeds to replicate his feat in producing a segment that can be read forwards or backwards, and the *al-Maqāmah al-Ẓifariyyah* is also called '*al-ṣādiyyah*' because it contains a segment in which every word contains the consonant '*ṣād*'. Since the Egyptian writer, al-Suyūṭī (d. 1505) is renowned as one of Arabic culture's major polygraphs, it is hardly surprising that his collection of *maqāmāt* should be primarily a display of immense erudition. In a few *maqāmāt* that appear to have been composed early in his career (those of Asyūṭ and Mecca, for example), we find mention of a narrator and hero, Hāshim ibn al-Qāsim and Abū Bishr al-ʿAlabī respectively. However, others of his thirty *maqāmāt* show little concern with narrative structure and are more in the form of articles or epistles on a variety of topics; in fact, al-Suyūṭī seems to be expatiating on subjects that he treats at length in other works – grammar, for example, plagiarism, the wiles of storytellers, and the false rituals and beliefs associated with Sufi practice. One *maqāmah* is a stalwart defence of the beliefs of the famous Egyptian Sufi poet, ibn al-Fāriḍ (d. 1245), citing all manner of textual authorities on the subject of Islamic orthodoxy, while another, '*al-Maqāmah al-miskiyyah*' (of musk), appears on the surface to be a survey of four perfumes but is almost certainly also a comparison of the political acumen of four Mamlūk rulers who were vying for power at a particular point in al-Suyūṭī's writing career.

The influence of al-Ḥarīrī's *maqāmāt*, already seen in many of the works we have just mentioned, is particularly evident in the records of literary activity in Egypt in the seventeenth and eighteenth centuries. Shihāb al-dīn al-Khafājī (d. 1653) composed a commentary on al-

Ḥarīrī's *maqāmāt* and produced some examples of his own, as did the poet, al-Idkāwī (d. 1770). The intellectual salon of al-Zabīdī (d. 1791), most renowned as the compiler of the dictionary, *Tāj al-ʿarūs* (The Bridal Crown), became a virtual centre for Ḥarīrī scholarship and imitation, including among its members Shaykh Ḥasan al-ʿAṭṭār (d. 1835) who not only wrote several *maqāmāt* (including one concerning his contacts with French scholars in 1799) but also served as mentor to Rifāʿah al-Ṭahṭāwī, who in 1826 was appointed the religious leader of the first Egyptian educational mission to France.

During the nineteenth century writers in Egypt, Iraq, and Syria turned to the *maqāmah* genre as an appropriate vehicle for participating in the changing cultural environment in which they were living. The popularity of the genre reflected not only its continuity in Arabic literary discourse (as just illustrated) but also the new intellectual stimuli provided by contacts with European culture (as reported, for example, in al-Ṭahṭāwī's famous work, *Takhlīṣ al-ibrīz fī talkhīṣ Bārīz* [The purification of gold concerning the summary of Paris, 1834]), the increasing pace of publication made possible by the availability of printing presses, and the rapid spread in popularity of the newspaper medium as a means of bringing the treasures of the literary heritage to the attention of an ever expanding readership. From among the many authors who contributed to this trend two writers stand out: Nāṣīf al-Yāzijī (d. 1871) and Aḥmad Fāris al-Shidyāq (d. 1887). Al-Yāzijī, a scholar of the Arabic language and admirer of al-Mutanabbī's poetry, read the *maqāmāt* of al-Ḥarīrī in the French edition of Sylvestre de Sacy and felt inspired to write his set. *Majmaʿ al-baḥrayn* (The Meeting-point of the two Seas, 1856) – the title itself being a quotation from the Qurʾān (*Sūrat al-Kahf* (18, [The Cave], v. 60) – is a genuine exercise in neo-classicism, in that it seeks to revive the glories of al-Ḥarīrī's classic work; in his Introduction, al-Yāzijī states his intention of using rare words and recherché usage, and the *maqāmah* of Sarūj consciously noted that it is in quest of the spirit of Abū Zayd al-Sarūjī, the renowned 'hero' of al-Ḥarīrī's *maqāmāt*. While al-Yāzijī's work reflects the priorities of an intellectual community anxious to rediscover its classical heritage, al-Shidyāq's work points in new directions. He too was renowned for his knowledge of Arabic; he participated in the translation of the Bible into English and for many years was editor of the influential newspaper, *al-Jawāʾib*. His famous work, *Al-Sāq ʿalā al-sāq fī-mā huwa al-Fār-yāq* (1855), the very untranslatability of the title illustrating an intrinsic part of its generic purpose, often resorts to the *sajʿ* style for rhetorical effect; he himself describes the process of writing in the style as being like walking with a wooden leg. The book contains four *maqāmāt*, one for each section; the one on medical terminology is of sufficient lexical complexity to require a separate glossary. The narrative is concerned with 'Fār-yāq's' travels to Europe – London, Paris, and Cambridge – and his encounters with cultural difference; a particular focus of that difference involves the status of women, something that involves the pointed comments of 'Fāryāqah', his wife. The names 'Fār-yāq' and 'Fār-yāqah' are here cited in quotation marks because both consist of the first part of al-Shidyāq's first name, Fāris, and the last part of his family name; they suggest not only that this work provides al-Shidyāq with the opportunity to explore some of the interesting dimensions of autobiographical writing but also that al-Shidyāq is using the femininisation of his own name, 'Fār-yāq', to explore sexual difference within his own society and in its contacts with others. Al-Shidyāq's treatment of this and other issues makes it clear that the entire book is intended, much in the style of Rabelais, to be a deliberate act of confrontation, and no more so than in his anti-clerical comments (he himself came from the Maronite Christian community) which include a listing of a large repertoire of Arabic terms for the private parts of the body. *Al-Sāq ʿalā al-sāq* is thus thoroughly subversive and ironic, as al-Shidyāq flaunts his linguistic virtuosity as a means of challenging many of the cherished norms of his society. The fictionalisation of the autobiographical, the evocation of the individual voice, and the focus on societal issues, these all look ahead to the emergence of a fictional tradition in the twentieth century.

The narrator of al-Shidyāq's *maqāmāt* is named al-Ḥāris ibn Hithām, a clear parody of the name of many of the narrators in the *maqāmāt* works that we have just surveyed. When Muḥammad al-Muwayliḥī (d. 1930) began to publish his contribution to the genre as a series of newspaper articles under the title, 'Fatrah min al-zaman' (A Period of Time), in 1898, he took the process back to its origins; his narrator is none other than ʿĪsā ibn Hishām, the narrator of al-Hamadhānī's *maqāmāt* of some nine centuries earlier; the linkage is made even clearer with the publication of the episodes in book form in 1907 as *Ḥadīth ʿĪsā ibn Hishām* (ʿĪsā ibn Hishām's Tale). In spite of this obvious salute to the genre's purported originator, al-Muwayliḥī chooses to follow the model of al-Shidyāq rather than the more neo-classical gesture of al-Yāzijī. ʿĪsā ibn Hishām is the narrative persona for the author, and, in the company of a pasha resurrected from the times of Muḥammad ʿAlī some eighty years earlier, he becomes an active participant in a lively and highly critical survey of life in the city of Cairo under British occupation at the turn of the century, and most notably its arcane legal system both secular and religious. In the latter part of the work, ʿĪsā and the Pasha watch in amusement and disgust as a rustic village headman (*ʿumdah*) is introduced by a Westernised fop to the ersatz attractions of 'modern' Cairo and in the process loses much of his wealth and reputation. Al-Muwayliḥī is also a master of style and uses *sajʿ* to introduce each episode in the newspaper; he also cites traditional text-types and lines from a wide selection of classical poets. In a clear reflection of the views of his primary mentor, Muḥammad ʿAbduh (d. 1906), al-Muwayliḥī also incorporates into his narrative some savage criticism of traditional religious attitudes to change, as part of which he composes wonderful parodies of almost incomprehensible sermons and learned disquisitions. *Ḥadīth ʿĪsā ibn Hishām* thus serves in an important bridging capacity, invoking styles, texts, and names from the past as a vehicle for a critical analysis of society that would be the primary generic purpose of modern fiction.

In spite of the increasing popularity of European fictional genres, fostered by a host of new magazines and journals that published translations in serial form, al-Muwayliḥī's model of the *maqāmah* as a modern vehicle was emulated by several other writers: Ḥāfiẓ Ibrāhīm (d. 1932), the famous Egyptian poet, for example, and the Iraqi journalist, Sulaymān Fayḍī al-Mawṣilī (d. 1951). Most interesting of all is the example of Bayram al-Tūnisī (d. 1961) who published *maqāmāt* in a variety of newspapers during his much travelled career. Abandoning al-Muwayliḥī's concentration on the élite of society, Bayram takes the *maqāmah* back to its original focus on the poorer segments of society and their perpetual striving for the means of survival, often involving varieties of trickery. Both titles and the narrators' names continually point to the author's intention of subverting the goals of the genre's stylistic medium in the direction of a more popular focus: among the *maqāmāt* we encounter 'al-Funughrafiyyah', 'al-Tilifuniyyah', 'al-Sīnamabtughrabfiyyah', 'al-Autumubiliyyah', and 'al-Camp Cesariyyah' (named after a resort district of Alexandria). The naming of narrators, that had always served composers of *maqāmāt* as an opportunity for imitation of the examples created by al-Hamadhānī and al-Ḥarīrī, is now taken to parodic lengths: 'al-Shaykh Saʿrān ibn Falsān' (Shaykh Lunatic son of skint), 'al-Qāriḥ ibn Shayṭān' (Festerer son of Satan), and 'al-ʿĀjiz ibn ʿImyān' (Impotent son of the blind).

The works of Bayram al-Tūnisī and other twentieth-century authors (including ʿAbd al-salām al-ʿUjaylī [b. 1919], the illustrious Syrian writer of fiction) who have occasionally resorted to the *maqāmah* as a mode of expression show the continuing attraction to the educated readership of Arabic literature of this flamboyant genre that, while addressing itself to a wide variety of issues, exults in the sheer delight of exhibiting its own virtuosity.

POPULAR NARRATIVES

Introduction

In 1703 Antoine Galland, a French scholar who had made several visits to the Middle East, published the first two parts of *Mille et une nuit*, a translation of a manuscript collection of stories that he had acquired. Between 1704 and 1717 he was to publish other volumes in the series, completing the translation of the manuscript and adding to it some other tales from the oral repertoire of an obscure figure named Hanna from Aleppo, among them those of Aladdin and Ali Baba. The tales were organised into some 280 'nights', and were built around a frame story involving a King named Shahrayār who takes vengeance for the infidelity of his wife by marrying a virgin every night and killing her at dawn. Shahrazād, the daughter of the King's minister, takes it upon herself to put an end to the King's behaviour by means of storytelling, stopping her narration of a series of exciting tales at a crucial point that always coincides with the dawn – thus providing a *locus classicus* for the principles of serialised narratives.

The appearance of Galland's translation is one of the most remarkable success stories in the history of publishing. It was being rendered into English before the initial publication was complete, and within a decade the collection had been translated into the majority of European languages. The immense popularity with which these versions were greeted inevitably led to questions concerning the collection itself. Its title, for example, suggested the presence of many more tales than were included, although it emerged that the use of 'a thousand and one' in the title was merely suggestive of a very large collection; proverbially large numbers have thus progressed via a thousand and one from the Biblical forty to today's trillions. This interest also prompted the preparation of printed Arabic versions: the first began to appear in Calcutta in 1814, and a second was published in 1835 from the Būlāq Press that Muḥammad ʿAlī had founded in Cairo. Galland had in fact already translated another set of tales besides those contained in his manuscript and the others he had translated from Hanna the Aleppan's transcription, namely 'The Voyages of Sindbad', and had added it to his collection. The Arabic editions that were published in the nineteenth century give evidence of the efforts that had been made to supplement the basic collection, bringing the total number of nights up to the anticipated thousand and one.

Scholarly interest had also been aroused by this phenomenon. Philology being the queen of humanistic research at the time, much attention was devoted to a search for other manuscripts and sources. Influences and common bases in other cultural traditions were not hard to trace, but the search for manuscripts proved harder. As Edward Lane commented in the 1830s, 'when a complete copy of "The Thousand and One Nights" is found, the price demanded for it is too great for a reciter to have it in his power to pay'. The key word in this extract is 'reciter', in that it draws our attention to an intrinsic feature of the *Thousand and One Nights* (or *The Arabian Nights* as they were often called in English) in its indigenous setting and the fascinating issues relating to its reception. Although evidence on this topic is scanty in the extreme, one must assume that this huge collection is (or, at the very least, became) one among many examples of the huge repertoire of oral narratives that were performed on public and private occasions in the regions of Asia and North Africa. The principal reason why Lane found it so difficult to purchase any manuscript copies of the tales was that they had not been recorded in that medium; such copies as did exist were for the use of the *ḥakawātī* (story-teller), a figure who was till relatively recently one of the most prominent participants in the communal life of Middle Eastern societies (and who has now been adopted by modern dramatists as a ready-made Brechtian device). In other words, the rare copies of texts that were available were mnemonics. The literary community of the Arab world may have joined in listening to these tales on numerous public occasions, but otherwise seems to have paid them little attention.

In the Western world meanwhile the popularity of the *Thousand and One Nights* increased. There were many translations of the Arabic versions (as opposed to those that used Galland's French translation), and the variety of purposes reflected in the different approaches to translation provides us with interesting insights into the tastes of the European readership at the time. The language of the collection had been that of the *ḥakawātī* (whose gesturing cues form part of the recorded text of the second Calcutta edition of 1839–42), a register that, needless to say, contained a good deal of colloquial usage and was thus quite different from the elaborate style of *adab*. The editor of the Būlāq edition, Shaykh al-Sharqāwī, records with a disarming candour how he endeavoured to polish the language of the collection so as to remove traces of this 'lower' and 'non-literary' language. In rendering the texts into English, translators had to select an appropriate level of the target language; Edward Lane and Sir Richard Burton, for example, chose to exoticise their English versions by couching them in a style redolent of the King James Bible, thus creating a curious disjuncture between the impact of the original (in its authentic context) and the English translation. However, in other ways their versions differ considerably. Lane's complex persona found the sensuality of many of the narratives too much to bear, leading him to produce a heavily bowdlerised version. Burton on the other hand went in entirely the opposite direction (in the process plagiarising large segments of the version of Joseph Payne); his version included 'anthropological footnotes' and to it were later added 'supplemental nights', the entire extravagant package turning his translation into an instant collector's item. The images of the exotic Orient – with its swashbuckling adventurers, dusky maidens, magic lamps, fabulous riches, and wicked viziers – emerged from these and earlier versions, to become the contents of children's books, and to be performed in Christmas pantomimes (which, through an irony, were mostly based on Aladdin and Ali Baba, two of Galland's tales that were not part of the original collection). This exoticisation of the Middle East was, of course, also tailor-made for Hollywood extravaganzas, as a number of films, especially those devoted to the Sindbad voyages, make clear. The negative side of this creation of false stereotypes emerges clearly from the 1993 animated cartoon of *Aladdin*; the effects of such continuing cultural stereotyping and the resulting misunderstandings are the major topic of one of modern Arabic's greatest works of fiction, al-Ṭayyib Ṣāliḥ's *Mawsim al-hijrah ilā al-shamāl* (1967; *Season of Migration to the North*, 1969).

Here then is an interesting case of cultural contrasts. A work that had a major influence on any number of artistic genres in Western culture (one thinks for example of the lush Scheherazade scores of Rimsky-Korsakov and Ravel) and whose enormous popularity in the West has been responsible for the creation of so many stereotypes regarding the Middle East, has until recently been completely neglected as an object of study by the culture that fostered it. One of the first studies of the collection to be published in Arabic was that of Suhayr al-Qalamāwī (b. 1911), which she completed as a doctoral thesis in the 1930s, significantly under the supervision of Ṭāhā Ḥusayn who had been exposed to the reception of the *Thousand and One Nights* in Europe during his studies in France. The advent to academic institutions in the Arab world of several twentieth-century disciplines, especially folklore, linguistics, and anthropology, has almost automatically led Arab scholars to investigate various aspects of this great collection and many others like it, less famous in world terms to be sure, but within the Arabic context of equal significance as contributions to the heritage of popular narrative. Meanwhile, the *Thousand and One Nights* is still not immune to controversy in its host culture: in 1985, a senior official in the Egyptian Ministry of the Interior declared that the collection offended public morals and ordered it banned. After a few months of intense critical debate, the order was rescinded, not least because many writers had pointed out that jurisdiction over the collection, as one of the greatest monuments of world narrative literature, could no longer be restricted to the purview of a single country or cultural tradition.

Types of popular expression

The decision to include a survey of popular narratives within a work like this brings with it problems beyond those of transcending traditional categories. On the broadest scale, the generic divide that appears to separate élite and popular literature is, as John Carey points out in *The Intellectuals and the Masses* (1993), essentially a misleading one. In the Arabic context, the discussion of such narratives involves consideration of the various levels of the Arabic language and the cultural values attached to them. As I have already noted, the literary tradition has had no compunction about evaluating texts on such a basis, not only through its choice of terms (*al-fuṣḥā*, the more élite language, and *al-ʿāmmiyyah*, the language of the *plebs*) but also through the aesthetic criteria of the *adab* tradition. Secondly, the narratives within our purview are not all solely prose narratives; the *Thousand and One Nights* is just one among many collections of tales in which the *ḥakawātī* (story-teller) is at liberty to include within his narration large segments of poetry (as is the case with classical *adab*), a judgement that he will make according to the occasion of the performance and the desires and reactions of his audience. Lastly, research on Arabic prose genres of all types shows that tales with particular plots and themes would make their way into both 'élite' and 'popular' collections; tales concerning miraculous escapes, for example, are as much part of the material of the *Thousand and One Nights* as of the more explicitly titled *al-Faraj baʿd al-shiddah* of al-Tanūkhī (discussed above). Al-Tawḥīdī, whom we also discussed above, remarked somewhat superciliously in his *Kitāb al-imtāʿ wa-al-muʾānasah* that stories such as those in the *Thousand and One Nights* were 'for women and children', but listeners within his own culture and countless readers world-wide have clearly challenged his verdict.

In our discussions above of historical, geographical, and religious works, we have noted that many writers – al-Ṭabarī and al-Masʿūdī for example – made use of the legends and fables that form part of the earliest lore of the Arabs. Those who collected and transmitted reports (*akhbār*) were *ipso facto* also *quṣṣāṣ* (story-tellers). The stories of pre-Islamic lovers (like Laylā and Majnūn), of tribal wars (the *ayyām al-ʿArab*, such as the Basūs War between Bakr and Taghlib), of ancient Near Eastern heroes and prophets, these made their way into not only the works of those who contributed to the world of Islamic scholarship but also the repertoire of story-telling; indeed the Arabic word *sīrah* was used not only to describe biographies of the Prophet Muḥammad (as noted earlier) but also these collections of tales, the usage being specified by the addition of the adjective 'popular' (*al-sīrah al-shaʿbiyyah*). To these sources were added other types of narratives: animal fables and proverbs, such as those of the legendary figure of Luqmān (who gives his name to Surah 30 of the Qur'ān); stories of semi-legendary poets such as Ḥātim al-Ṭāʾī, accounts of whose generosity have made his name proverbial; stories of conquest and *jihād*, tales of the expansion of Islam, of the Crusades, of the defeat of the Mongols; stories of migrations of peoples; and, of course, collections of humour, moralising anecdotes, accounts of pranksters, and tall tales of all kinds – the wily exploits of ʿAlī Zaybaq (the name means quicksilver) and Aḥmad al-Danaf (the 'mange'), and the numerous situations involving the Middle East's primary jokester, Juḥā, a character claimed by almost every nation in the region as its own (known within the Persian and Turkish traditions as Naṣr al-dīn (Nasreddin)):

One of Juḥā's neighbours came to ask him if he could borrow his donkey. Juḥā apologised and said that his donkey wasn't there. Just then the donkey let out a loud bray. The neighbour commented that he seemed to be in luck because the donkey was there after all.

'What's with you?' expostulated Juḥā. 'Do you believe my donkey rather than me?!'

The compilation of different types of narrative was, as we have noted above, part of the larger process of gathering all sorts of information during the initial centuries of Islam. Scholars have traced back references to collections of tales as far as the eighth century; ibn al-Nadīm (d. 990), the Baghdādī bookseller and compiler of *al-Fihrist*, declares that he has encountered several complete copies of *Hazar Afsāneh* (A Thousand Stories), the Persian version of the core collection. As we have noted elsewhere, the eighth to tenth centuries were a period of intense activity in the collection, sifting, organising, and anthologising of all kinds of reports and information. However, in the context of popular narratives, it is not surprising, given the oral nature of the processes of transmission and performance of the tales themselves, that there is a dearth of textual sources and thus the precise chronology for the development of the large collections is not clear. Information concerning the different versions of the *Thousand and One Nights* collection is the most complete. It suggests that a core collection made up of an Indo-Persian frame-story and accretions from the Baghdad of Hārūn al-Rashīd (from the ninth century onwards) made its way to Syria and thence to Egypt; Muhsin Mahdi has published (1984) a reconstruction of the collection as it was in the fourteenth century extrapolated back from manuscripts belonging to the Syrian stemma (including Galland's manuscript now in the Bibliothèque Nationale). The period from the thirteenth to the eighteenth century, when a large number of compilations of all kinds – anthologies, dictionaries, and commentaries – were being produced, also sees the heyday of popular narrative. Even in the 1830s Lane gives vivid descriptions of street performances by story-telling specialists of all kinds: some dealt with the epic tales of ʿAntar, the pre-Islamic poet, others with Abū Zayd, the hero of the migrating tribe of the Banī Hilāl. Here as elsewhere however, such performers who thrived on the popular demand for their tales have not been able to rival the attractions of films, videos, and television. Public narration is a dying craft.

The major narrative collections

The Western reception of the *Thousand and One Nights* and the complex history of its compilation that we have just described have made it the most famous collection of Arabic narratives of popular provenance, but the precise nature of its origins – as oral or written corpus – remains obscure. What is clear however is that the popular tradition did engender many lengthy sagas, romances, and epics that were intended for public performance, each one constituting a narrative event that might extend over several evenings or be intended to celebrate a particular occasion (such as a wedding, for example, or a safe return from the pilgrimage or a long journey) or as entertainment during the nights of Ramaḍān. Furthermore, each one was a mirror of the culture's sense of its own history and cultural values.

The material for some of these narratives has the same provenance as many of the different kinds of *akhbār* collections that were listed above. The repertoire of *ayyām al-ʿArab* (tribal wars of pre-Islamic times), for example, is put into extended narrative form in the saga of *Al-Zīr Sālim* (Prince Sālim) which tells of the lengthy War of Basūs between the tribes of Bakr and Taghlib. Also of Arabian provenance is the huge *sīrah* of *Sayf ibn Dhī Yazan*, a work that seems to have been compiled in about the fourteenth century, in that one of its villains is named Sayf Arʿad, a ruler of Ethiopia at the time. However, while this *sīrah* may represent the anxiety of fourteenth century Egyptians at the threat of attack from the south, the setting of its eponymous hero, Sayf ibn Dhī Yazan, is South Arabia during pre-Islamic times, the temporal disjuncture being vivid enough proof of the lack of concern that these narratives have with the niceties of chronology. While fighting wars to repel the attacks of Ethiopians – accounts that are redolent of the *maghāzī* (raids) and *futūḥ* (conquest) collections discussed above, Sayf undergoes a variety of adventures, not the least of which is a visit to the fabled land of Wāq al-wāq, an island paradise peopled by women where he becomes infatuated by a beautiful bird-woman named Munyat al-nufūs (Soul's desire). As many scholars have pointed out, this land of Wāq al-wāq is a prevalent theme in Arabic literature of all types; in this particular context, Sayf's encounter is replicated as an episode in the tale of Ḥasan from Baṣrah in the *Thousand and One Nights*. If Sayf ibn Dhī Yazan is frequently rescued from dire straits by the intervention of women, another *sīrah* takes the process one stage further: *Sīrah al-amīrah Dhāt al-Himmah* has a female warrior-princess as its heroine. Dhāt al-himmah (she who is possessed of resolve) is originally named Fāṭimah; abandoned by her father who is disappointed that she is not a son, she is a born warrior. She avoids marriage, but is drugged at the instigation of the villain of the piece, ʿUqbah the judge, and raped by her foster-brother. She bears a son, ʿAbd al-wahhāb, who is black, and he joins his mother in any number of battles. This further huge collection consisting of some seventy separate episodes is also known as '*sīrat al-mujāhidīn*' (of the strivers for Islam), suggesting a linkage to the textual tradition on *jihād* (the propagation of Islam). The context presented in the collection is the period during the Umawī and ʿAbbāsī caliphates when Islam was expanding its domains and thus confronting not only other communities of faithful such as the Christians of Byzantium but also questions of belief within the Muslim community itself. As with the other works being discussed here, we are not, of course, dealing with historical data, but these narratives, which show such delight in the sheer pleasure of telling and listening to stories, still manage to provide another avenue of insight into the concerns of the culture within which they were created. Similarly fixed in time by the events that it depicts is the *sīrah* of *al-Ẓāhir Baybars*. It recounts the glorious victory of the Mamlūk Sultan over the invading Mongols in the thirteenth century and has thus become a favourite for those audiences desiring to listen to a narrative that reflects the traditional virtues of strategic resourcefulness and courage in battle. The way in which these very qualities have endeared the *Baybars sīrah* to its listeners is used to telling effect by the modern Syrian playwright, Saʿdallāh Wannūs (b. 1941), in his play, *Mughāmarat raʾs al-Mamlūk Jābir* (The Adventure of Mamlūk Jābir's Head, 1972). Intended as a reflection on the post-1967 period in the Arab world, the play uses an incident of intrigue drawn from the era of the ʿAbbāsī caliphate. Part of the stage dynamics involve the use of a *ḥakawātī* who adamantly refuses the audience's request for a narration of *Sīrat Baybars*, pointing out that such a tale of heroism and victory is entirely inappropriate for the times in question.

During the nineteenth century *Sīrat ʿAntar*, a romance about the famous pre-Islamic poet-cavalier, ʿAntarah son of Shaddād, and his beloved and cousin, ʿAblah daughter of Mālik, was sufficiently well-known in the Western world that it too was translated into several languages (including a partial translation into English) and Rimsky-Korsakov made an episode from the huge collection the subject of one of his earliest orchestral works. Born as a black child (an echo of the theme of Dhāt al-himmah's child) as a result of a union between the tribal chief and a black slave, Zabīdah, ʿAntar is initially ostracised; it is his tremendous courage and strength that come to earn him the grudging respect of the tribes. When he falls in love with the beautiful ʿAblah and her father refuses to contemplate a union, the stage is set for a whole series of impossible tasks that ʿAntar has to carry out in order to earn the right to marry his lady-love; in the process he must overcome seemingly insuperable odds, fighting against a series of implacable enemies – among them the King of Persia and the Crusaders, for chronology matters little in this context – and dealing with the never-ending skulduggery of his uncle and prospective father-in-law. In all this, ʿAntar's bravery, chivalry, and generosity to friend and foe alike are matched by the qualities of his beloved, ʿAblah, who is often subjected to the indignities of capture, confinement, and the lewd advances of rogues; these are occasions upon which, as the narrative informs us, she lashes out at her abusers with the tongue of a scorpion. Time and time again, ʿAntar performs heroic deeds, restores the peace, rescues his beloved, and kills his and the tribe's foes – often composing poems for the occasion, only to find himself confronted by yet another obstacle. Thus does the saga become almost indefinitely extendable.

Among the most widespread of the *sīrahs* and certainly one of the most famous is that of the *Banū Hilāl*; researchers writing in English, for example, have recorded versions in Egypt, Nigeria, and Tunisia. Once again, we are dealing with an enormous collection of narrative; in this case the geographical spread and social variety of the local traditions mean that there is considerable difference in style and contents, each one emphasising those episodes and elements that are of particular significance to that particular region. Thanks to the efforts of modern folklorists, we are fortunate to have recordings of actual performances of this still-living tradition of oral narrative. This is a tale of migration, of the Banū Hilāl who left the Arabian peninsula in the tenth and eleventh centuries and travelled via Sinai to Egypt. Initially sent south to Upper (southern) Egypt, they were dispatched westwards in the eleventh century as part of the struggle between the ʿAbbāsī caliphs in Baghdad and the rival Shīʿī Fāṭimī caliphs in Cairo. The historian, ibn Khaldūn, records the impact of this large-scale migration on the communities that they encountered on the way and on their arrival in Tunisia. Like the other *sīrahs* we have discussed above, the *Sīrat Banī Hilāl* has its hero, Abū Zayd al-Hilālī, another personification of the courageous warrior, and a number of friends and foes who help or impede the progress of the tribes towards their goal.

In this short survey of some of the narrative collections that are a part of the popular heritage of Arab culture, I have emphasised context, themes and characters (and especially heroes, villains, and beloveds). In discussing these works however, it is important to remember that each of the textual versions that we possess constitutes a written recording of one particular performance, and that the collections as a whole – in multiple volumes – represent a repertoire of tales built around a core theme and set of characters that would rarely, if ever, be performed complete. Audiences, while familiar, to be sure, with the episodic structure of the complete narrative, would request to hear a particular segment of the larger whole: the segment in *Sīrat ʿAntar* in which he captures a herd of camels, for example, or Sayf ibn Dhī Yazan's encounter with the beautiful bird. The narration of these segments would be occasions that were spread over a number of evenings, and the *ḥakawātī* would adjust his performance in accordance with the occasion and the duration of the segment in question. It is in this context that Susan Slyomovics's published version of a performance of an episode from *Sīrat Banī Hilāl* (1987) is such a revelation. For not only were certain parts of the performance enhanced by the use of drums and, in some cases, a small troupe of instrumentalists, but also by different types of language: prose narration to establish context, to segue from one incident to another, and to provide – as it were – footnotes to the narrative; rhyming prose (*sajʿ*), the predominant mode of narrative discourse recited in the local dialectal pronunciation, its rhymes and rhythms providing the *ḥakawātī* (and his musicians) with any number of ways of enhancing the mood of the narration; and poetry, fulfilling its traditional role as the loftiest ideal of Arabic literary discourse. All these modes could be used – inserted, substituted, omitted – in accordance with a number of factors: the virtuosity of the performer (*ḥakawātī*), the nature of the occasion and the amount of time it offered, and the whims and reactions of the audience. It is in such a context that we come to realise that the extreme variation in the recorded versions of individual tales – the amount of poetry included in some of the tales in the *Thousand and One Nights*, 'The City of Brass', for example – and in their English translation may represent the different circumstances in which the tale was performed as well as the editorial instincts of the translator.

The Thousand and One Nights

The most famous collection of Arabic popular narrative, the *Thousand and One Nights*, shares many features with those we have just discussed, although the reception of its translated versions in the West and the consequences of its world-wide popularity have served to complicate the investigation of its provenance and authenticity. It too contains tales of adventure, of war, of trickery, and of love; it also includes a number of animal fables like those of Luqmān. Furthermore, some of the tales are set in particular historical periods; notable in this category are those devoted to incidents involving the Caliph Hārūn al-Rashīd, his famous minister, Jaʿfar al-Barmakī, and his boon-companion, the poet Abū Nuwās. However, whereas it is possible with the other *sīrah* collections to assign a general title containing the name of a hero or heroine to the often divergent collection of incidents and stories, the unique set of circumstances surrounding the compilation (and expansion) of the famous *Thousand and One Nights* collection, as outlined above, have furnished it with features that set it somewhat apart from the others. Shahrazād, the daughter of the King's minister, is a prominent participant in the frame-story of the collection, but thereafter she becomes a story-teller *par excellence*, using her frame-narrative–with its continuing threat of a violent conclusion if her narrative strategy should fail–as a context (and pretext) for the telling of other narrators' stories. The entire collection thus becomes a narrative about story-telling, its general goal being to offer, in the phrase repeated throughout the collection, 'a lesson for those who would learn' (*ʿibrah li-man yaʿtabir*).

The frame-story of the collection performs a number of functions. It introduces the situation within which the primary characters will fulfil their roles. The way in which the brother kings, Shāhzamān and Shahrayār, dispense justice in response to their wives' infidelity is echoed in numerous tales involving rulers and their treatment of people; the Caliph Hārūn al-Rashīd numbers prominently among such types. The behaviour of the wives themselves is taken as yet another illustration of the 'wiles of women' (*kayd*) theme, which, as we saw in the chapter on the Qur'ān, finds a *locus classicus* in *Sūrat Yūsuf* (12, Joseph). But, beyond the thematic bases that are established, there is the narrative structure itself. Even within this outer frame, the sequence is interrupted by other tales. Shahrazād's father, the minister, warns his daughter that her fate may be that of the farmer who could understand the talk of animals, leading in turn to the animal fable concerning 'the Ass and the Bull' and the discussion between the dog and the cock that revolves around the best way to keep wives in order – by beating them. Once the perfidy of their wives has been revealed, the two kings go on a journey, during which they encounter a huge column emerging from the sea. It turns out to be a demon, whereupon they both hide up a tree (a position that is in itself to become a kind of topos). The genie carries a box on to the beach and promptly falls asleep. The box opens, and a beautiful woman emerges; she has been snatched away on her wedding night. She demands that the two kings come down and make love to her. When they refuse, she threatens to wake the demon. After the two kings have obliged, she demands their rings and adds them to the 572 others that she already possesses. The kings return home chastened; they too have learned a lesson of a sort (*ʿibrah*), and the result is the killing of their wives, the need for Shahrazād's stratagem, and the start of the story-telling process. The overall purpose is to prevent killing, and the narrative technique involves the suspense of building to a climax and then abruptly cutting off. Shahrazād weaves her narrative thread (so well captured by the solo violin in Rimsky-Korsakov's *Scheherazade*) for a thousand and one nights – at least, after the eighteenth century. At the conclusion of the final tale, that of 'Maʿrūf the Cobbler', Shahrazād asks the king whether he has abandoned his idea of killing her and brings in their sons to bolster her request. The king agrees, and the collection appears to end on a happy note. It is the modern Egyptian dramatist, Tawfiq al-Ḥakīm, who explores the new dilemmas the king will now have to face in his play, *Shahrazād* (1934).

The original collection of tales – as translated by Galland – gives every indication of being arranged in a way that will develop these themes. 'The Porter and the Three Ladies of Baghdad', for instance, is a wonderfully elaborate narrative structure, in which story-telling is a way of avoiding threatened violence and listening without question is a requirement for avoiding chastisement; and this is not the only occasion when the Caliph Hārūn al-Rashīd, during one of his tours of the city in disguise, finds himself constrained to follow the explicit instructions of his subjects. The descriptions of sexual play and the elaborately crafted parallelisms of the tales within tales become vehicles for the creation of suspense and its resolution, at the same time involving a sheer delight in the power of the language of story. 'The Story of the Murdered Girl' (also known as 'the Three Apples') is a thoroughly convincing crime narrative, again involving Hārūn al-Rashīd, whose demeanour towards his minister, Jaʿfar, shows striking parallels to that of King Shahrayār within the frame-story. A box is found in the River Tigris, containing the dissected body of a beautiful woman. Jaʿfar is set the seemingly hopeless task of finding the murderer. Two men confess to the crime; much to Hārūn al-Rashid's surprise, they do so without being tortured. They turn out to be the woman's husband (first cousin and father of their boy children) and her father. An inner narrative now reveals a tale of deceit and violence, involving one of the couple's children and Jaʿfar's black slave. The grotesque violence with which the husband has killed and cut up his totally blameless wife is only justified by his feelings of regret (and those of her father), while the proven guilt of the slave is expiated when Jaʿfar, the guilty slave's master, volunteers to tell an even more unbelievable tale in exchange for the slave's pardon. Story-telling here not only prevents killing, but obtains pardon for it.

To this core collection of tales, containing, as we have just indicated, examples of great variety, were added others of different types. There is, for example, a large cluster of animal fables, the most famous of which is 'The Animals and the Man', a story found in the *Epistles* of the *Ikhwān al-ṣafā'* (Brethren of Purity) in which a series of animals recount their negative experiences in dealing with the human species. The lengthy and complex 'Tale of 'Umar al-Nu'mān' is, to all intents and purposes, a miniature *sīrah*, involving a number of sub-tales of battles and loves, all in the context of contacts between Christian and Muslim rulers and the eventual triumph of Islam. The collection also contains a large number of love-stories, some reflecting the hopeless affliction mirrored in early examples within the poetic tradition, others bringing the lovers into close proximity with each other. One of the most notable is 'Ghānim ibn Ayyūb with Hārūn al-Rashīd and Qūt al-Qulūb'. As the title implies, this is a multi-episodic tale in which the Caliph, Hārūn al-Rashīd, moves beyond his function as facilitator or observer to become a full participant. A merchant named Ghānim, locked out of his city one day, witnesses a procession of eunuchs carrying a coffin. He eavesdrops as the eunuchs tell some particularly spicy tales; when they depart, he investigates the coffin, and to his horror finds a beautiful maiden inside – yet another woman in a box; she is drugged but still alive. He is at once in love, and, when she wakes, his tokens of affection are reciprocated. However, when he takes her to his house, everything remains chaste. Finally however, the maiden has to reveal to Ghānim that she is none other than Qūt al-Qulūb (Nourishment for the heart), the favourite concubine of Hārūn al-Rashīd; the Caliph's wife, Zubaydah, has become jealous of her rival and has taken advantage of her husband's temporary absence to get rid of her. The scene now switches to the Caliph's palace, which is in mourning for the 'death' of Qūt al-Qulūb. Inevitably, Hārūn learns that Qūt al-Qulūb is not dead, and Ghānim and his family are placed in mortal danger. However, when Qūt al-Qulūb explains to the Caliph that Ghānim has been entirely honourable, he relents; he gives Qūt al-Qulūb to Ghānim, and, in one of those neat resolutions for which the Hārūn of the collection is renowned, he is married to Ghānim's sister, Fitnah. This tale of the eventual triumph of true love handles the pacing of its different episodes and the switching between scenarios with considerable finesse, features that help explain why this tale was one of the first to be adapted for stage production in the nineteenth century (by Abū Khalīl al-Qabbānī in Damascus).

The collection contains a number of travel-tales. 'The City of Brass' is a prolonged reflection on the ephemerality of life in this world; the poems of asceticism and denial that occur in profusion in some written versions of the tale ram home the message of the '*ubi sunt*' theme, and it is no wonder that Amīr Mūsā ibn Nuṣayr spends a large part of the journey in tears. Beginning as the story of a quest (at the behest of the Umawī Caliph, ʿAbd al-Malik) for the bottles in which Solomon had imprisoned the demons, it becomes a symbolic journey that reaches the 'City of Brass', a place with no visible entrance, a model of human delusion where nothing is the way it seems to be; those whose faith does not shield them from such delusions die. Recitations of such a tale were intended, one imagines, to have a strongly homiletic function, the length of the narration being directly related to the balance that the story-teller wished to establish between the different structural elements and the narrative and poetry that comprised them. A far different kind of audience was surely anticipated for the most famous travel tale of all, 'Sindbad the Sailor', a separate set of narratives that was added to the core collection. The structural patterns of Sindbad's seven separate voyages makes it clear that this discrete set of tales possesses a unity of its own, besides being a participant in the larger *Thousand and One Nights* collection. In fact, the sixth voyage finishes with a meeting with the caliph, suggesting perhaps that at some point the narrative came to an end with that tale; that the seventh voyage is the one that shows the most variation – completely different tales are included in the various versions – suggests that it may have presented the *ḥakawātī* with an opportunity to include a further tale of Sindbad's adventures that reflected either his own preference or the occasion of the performance. Sindbad's tales of adventure and commerce on the high seas are marked by a high degree of symmetry and, at the joins between the voyages, of formulaic repetition. Shahrazād narrates the story of Sindbad the Sailor narrating his tales to another Sindbad – the Landsman or Porter – who not only listens to the tales but is repaid with food and money for doing so; in this instance, listening to stories is profitable, thus reflecting one of the hero's principal motivations. Each tale begins with a voyage from al-Baṣrah in Iraq; some kind of disaster occurs; Sindbad finds himself washed up on some strange shore where humans, semi-humans, or animals do peculiar things. He has to resort to a variety of stratagems to avoid enslavement, capture, and even death, some of which involve acts of considerable violence: in the fourth tale, for example, he kills a succession of spouses who, like him, have been buried along with their deceased partner. The end of escape – and the continuation of the sequence of tales – apparently justifies the means. Thereafter, he finds himself in several of the tales living among the folk of the land, until a ship appears, whereupon he begins the return voyage, recording all the wondrous phenomena he sees on the way. This particular set of tales clearly reflects the abundant repertoire of travel writing that was discussed earlier in this chapter, while the carefully maintained structural symmetry of the tales may be viewed as an illustration of the relative stability of one of the oldest and most popular narratives in the cultural tradition.

Of the tales in this huge collection, it is the most fantastic – of magic rings and lamps, of 'genies' and the instantaneous, yet varying changes they bring about – that have become the most popular in the West. 'Aladdin' (ʿAlāʾ al-dīn) is the most famous of these, of course, although, as we noted above, it is not part of the core collection but was added to the French translation by Galland. Another such tale is that of 'Maʿrūf the Cobbler', the final tale in the collection. In another lengthy and richly structured narrative, Maʿrūf, a poor and henpecked man of Cairo, is transported to a remote land where he meets a childhood friend named ʿAlī. They decide to try 'the caravan-on-the-way trick': that they have arrived ahead of a caravan loaded with the most precious items imaginable. The commercial sector of the city is duly impressed, and a line of considerable credit is opened. Maʿrūf falls into the part with gusto and liberally distributes money to the poor. The merchants become suspicious and take their concerns to the king and his minister. The former however sees an opportunity for profit also; he puts the treasury at Maʿrūf's disposal and marries him to the princess, his daughter. The minister meanwhile, who was himself an aspirant for the princess's hand, is deeply envious and suspicious. The princess is told by her father to find out the truth about her husband, and he tells her his true situation. However, she has fallen in love with her husband and sends him away for his own safety. At this crucial point, Maʿrūf stumbles on a magic ring, creates his fabulous caravan, and returns to the city in triumph. Maʿrūf's fortunes seem to be secure, but the two inimical forces in the tale are not finished. The minister steals the ring, but the princess retrieves it; he is thereafter executed. And in a return to the beginning of the tale, Maʿrūf's shrewish wife reappears. Maʿrūf kindly takes her in, but, when she too tries to steal the ring, she is cut down by Maʿrūf's son by the Princess, she having died in the meanwhile. As the tale and the collection conclude, the many strands in this multi-textured narrative have been pulled together; all the forces inimical to the just King Maʿrūf have been eliminated and his line of succession is secure. The same, of course, applies to Shahrayār, who, through his sons by Shahrazād the story-teller, can share the feeling.

The *Thousand and One Nights* has been a popular resort for modern writers in all genres; motifs, images, and complete stories from the collection have been adopted in a continuing process that illustrates the central place of this and the other collections in the collective consciousness of the Arab world. Bearing in mind the histrionic talents that a story-teller would bring to bear in the narration of his tales, it is hardly surprising that drama should be one of the genres where the inspiration of this collection is most marked. We have, of course, only mentioned a small fraction of the tales here, but even within such a small sample, we can note, in addition to Tawfīq al-Ḥakīm's *Shahrazād* already mentioned, that Shawqī ʿAbd al-Ḥakīm and Alfred Faraj have both written plays based on 'Maʿrūf the Cobbler', while Saʿdallāh Wannūs has written a play about the production of a play, namely Abū Khalīl al-Qabbānī's work based on 'Ghānim ibn Ayyūb'. For many modern poets, Sindbad, the traveller, has become – rather like the Flying Dutchman – the symbol for a somewhat desperate search for meaning; or, from a slightly more optimistic perspective, for the notion that it is the journey, the process, that is the point, not the goal itself.

PRESENT AND FUTURE

This brief survey of the enormous riches of the popular narrative tradition in Arabic is obviously merely an introduction, and not only to the works themselves but also to the increasing body of literary-critical research on the collections as narratives, much of it during the last fifty years or so. This continuing interest in such a huge and largely unstudied cultural resource, not to mention the tendency of a number of contemporary littérateurs to resort to varieties of narrative from the past as sources of inspiration, suggests that it will be necessary to re-examine the criteria under which different types of expression in Arabic have been judged to be 'élite' or 'popular' literature. That is not, of course, to suggest that differentiations of that kind may not be necessary or useful, but rather that questions of language and audience – to list just two possible criteria – point to the need to examine a variety of types of writing (popular histories, for example, and anecdotes that lend themselves to both 'learned' and 'vulgar' adaptations) in terms that may prefer to categorise literary works at numerous points along a spectrum rather than through a binary division.

MODERN FICTION

Beginnings

When Najīb Maḥfūẓ, the Egyptian novelist and Nobel prize-winner, published a work in 1982 entitled *Layālī Alf Laylah* (Nights of a Thousand Nights), his invocation of the title of Arabic's most famous collection of narratives and the subtle change in its wording clearly invoked a renowned intertext. Indeed the work opens with a section that introduces a ruler named Shahrayār and contains other segments devoted to Maʿrūf, Sindbad, and Qūt al-Qulūb. However, this convenient linkage between a recent work by the Arab world's most illustrious novelist and the tradition of earlier narratives that we have just discussed is more a reflection of relatively recent developments in modern Arabic fiction than the culmination of a lengthy process of influence stemming from the beginnings of the modern literary revival (*al-nahḍah*). In those initial stages, evocations of the narratives of earlier centuries were rapidly superseded by the newly imported Western genres of fiction. During the course of the twentieth century these genres – the novel and short story – have become the most popular modes of literary expression. We will now examine the process whereby they were integrated into the Arabic literary tradition and then explore the various directions they have taken.

The changes that occurred in the creation and reception of Arabic narratives during the nineteenth century were the consequence of a combination of factors. First there is translation activity, itself a natural outcome of renewed or intensified contacts with the West. The efforts of Rifāʿah al-Ṭahṭāwī and his students in Egypt and of numerous Christian families in Lebanon may initially have had other, more focused goals: the translation of military materials in the former case, and of the Bible in the latter. But it was virtually inevitable that the interest of such a cadre of translators should turn to literary works, beginning with the processes of translation, adaptation, and imitation, but then leading to the appearance of the earliest examples of modern Arabic fiction. A second pair of factors can be grouped under the heading of 'press', implying on the one hand the establishment of printing presses and the increasing availability of books and journals (and libraries in which to make them accessible, such as the Egyptian Dār al-Kutub founded in 1870), and on the other the rapid expansion in the number of newspapers in the second half of the century. When the civil disturbances in Syria led to the migration of many Christian Syrian families to Egypt, two of the most active literary traditions in the region were combined, a process that resulted in Egypt being generally recognised, most especially in areas like the Maghrib and Iraq that remained under Ottoman suzerainty, as the primary source of cultural innovation in the region. The foundation of general and specialised newspapers – dailies, weeklies, and monthlies – provided ample space not only for the political debates surrounding the presence of foreign occupying forces and the need for nationalist movements to resist them but also for cultural discussions about the need for a balance between the indigenous and the imported, the traditional and the modern, the teachings of Islam and those of Western culture.

It was in this socio-political environment and for a broader readership founded on entirely new modes of access that initial attempts at fiction were written; research suggests that, as in other cultural contexts, women constituted a sizeable portion of the readership involved. Clearly there was no shortage of current topics to address, and yet the very earliest examples looked elsewhere for subject-matter. An early favourite for translation (in almost every Middle Eastern country) was Dumas's *The Count of Monte Cristo*, and the historical romance novel immediately acquired a wide audience. The popularity of this and many other similar works serialised and published in the 1880s and 1890s gives us some idea of tastes at the time and also points to some of the perceptions as to both what the generic purpose of the novel was thought to be and what direction(s) it might take – at least initially. It was part of the literary (and commercial) genius of the Lebanese *émigré* journalist, Jūrjī Zaydān ((d. 1914), to appreciate that this trend could be adopted for educational and even nationalist purposes. In a whole series of historical novels, he portrayed in fictional form significant events from the history of the Arabs and Islam; each one incorporates a local 'human-interest' story, often including a pair of lovers. Following Zaydān's example, a number of writers made use of such journals as *Al-Riwāyah al-Shahriyyah* (monthly novel) to publish historical fiction, including Nīqūlā Ḥaddād (d. 1954), Yaʿqūb Ṣarrūf (d. 1927), and Faraḥ Anṭūn (d. 1922).

While this library of romantic fiction played an invaluable role in developing both a readership and a sense of national and local identity, it did not focus on the societal issues of the times – the great topic of the Western novel in the nineteenth century. We noted earlier that it was the works of pioneers like al-Shidyāq and al-Muwayliḥī that played an important role in laying the groundwork for the later development of a fictional tradition that would address contemporary issues, but that they did so through highly ornate recreations of earlier genres and styles. Alongside the neo-classical modes of expression that addressed themselves to the problems of the day and the adventure novels that did not, the columns of the press were also the publication venue for the first attempts at creating fictional narratives that would be new in content, form, and style. ʿAbdallāh Nadīm (d. 1896) and Yaʿqūb Ṣannūʿ (d. 1912) wrote witty vignettes that exploited mimicry of specific dialectal speech patterns to portray particular character types, and especially those operating in those social contexts where Western and indigenous cultures came into contact. Muṣṭafā Luṭfī al-Manfalūṭī (d. 1924) published a series of moralistic and sentimental 'essays' in which he made use of fictional contexts as a means of discussing pressing social and moral issues. Jubrān Khalīl Jubrān (d. 1931) addressed himself to conflicts of gender and generations in a series of early stories in Arabic. And in 1913 a young Egyptian named Muḥammad Ḥusayn Haykal (d. 1956), recently returned from France, published a novel, *Zaynab*. Filled with nostalgic depictions of the Egyptian countryside and of discussions of social philosophy, it criticises Egyptian society and its attitudes to marriage through a portrayal of the agonies of love among Egyptian peasants. That the novel was initially published under a pseudonym points to the ambiguous status of fiction in the minds of the upper-class intelligentsia to which Haykal's family belonged, but, as a work that reflected the concerns of a new readership in its topic, form, and style, it is clearly an important landmark.

While what we term the novel may provide the earliest examples of modern Arabic fiction, it was the short story that was the first to achieve maturity within the Arabic tradition. Its generic features were adopted with relish by Arab writers during the early decades of the twentieth century; it has now developed into the most favoured mode of literary expression in the Arab world. That it is wonderfully adaptive to the demands of a variety of world cultures is well known, but in the case of the Arab world its popularity is clearly also linked to the status of the littérateur in society and the fact that, even for the most prominent authors, writing literature cannot constitute a career.

The short story

The short story is the youngest of Western fictional genres. Whether or not we accept the notion that the short story came to fruition in its most vigorous form in those societies that had gone through processes of revolution – thus Russia, France and the United States, as opposed to Germany and Britain, it was certainly the genre of fiction that first achieved maturity in the Arab world of the twentieth century, affording a suitable literary vehicle through which to explore aspects of daily life during a period of considerable social and political upheaval.

Any number of writers on the short story (many of whom are themselves short-story writers) have noted that the genre demands of its writer a good deal of artifice, since our experiences of life do not come in the form of stories that are short. Whether the author creates a character vignette à la de Maupassant or portrays a segment from a larger context or series of events, the encapsulation of scene, character, and mood demands a craft that combines very particular powers of observation and use of language akin to that of a poet. While the narratives that pioneer writers such as Nadīm and al-Manfalūṭī published in Egyptian newspapers in the late nineteenth century may not contain all the features of the short story noted by Western critics – its 'ingenuity of design' (V. S. Pritchett), for instance, or its 'more neat plotting functions' (V. Shklovsky), there can surely be no denying the concision of their expression – the stock in trade of any journalist, while their short narratives certainly reflect 'the nervousness and restlessness of modern life' (Pritchett again) as it impacted upon Egyptian society at the time. In Lebanon, both Jubrān Khalīl Jubrān and Mīkhāʾīl Nuʿaymah (d. 1988) addressed themselves in their earliest stories composed in the first two decades of this century to one of the most hotly debated topics of the period: the position of women in society. The trials of 'Mārtā from Bān', snatched from the rural simplicity of her home and placed into the dens of iniquity in the evil city and of 'Wardah al-Hāniyyah' who deserts a comfortable home with a husband she hates in order to live with her real love, these stories are told by Jubrān with both passion and sentimentality. Mīkhāʾīl Nuʿaymah's early stories show a greater sense of both subtlety and detachment, something that stems in no small part from his extensive readings in the Russian masters of the short story such as Chekhov and Gogol; their influence is clearly visible in the themes and techniques of stories such as *Sanatuhā al-jadīdah* ('Her New Year') and *Maṣraʿ Saṭṭūt* ('Saṭṭūt's Death').

These early writers who addressed themselves to current social issues and participated in the crafting of new forms and styles provided a base on which a new generation could develop the genre. In Egypt the acknowledged pioneer in that process was Muḥammad Taymūr (d. 1921), who, in spite of his early death, made a major contribution to the development of the short story. He was followed by a group of writers known as *al-madrasah al-ḥadīthah* (the new school) – including such major figures as Maḥmūd Taymūr (younger brother of Muḥammad, d. 1973), by far the most prolific writer in the group, Yaḥyā Ḥaqqī (d. 1993?), and Maḥmūd Ṭāhir Lāshīn (d. 1954). Within different time frames other regions had their analogues: in Iraq, for example, Maḥmūd al-Sayyid (1903–37) and Dhū al-nūn Ayyūb (1908–88); in Palestine, Khalīl Baydas (1875–1949); in Tunisia, ʿAlī al-Duʿājī (1909–49); and in Lebanon, Tawfīq Yūsuf ʿAwwād (1911–89). Their generation refined the structure and language of the short story into a concise and evocative medium through which many of the issues confronting their own society could be addressed.

One of the most favoured types of story among this group of writers was the vignette: the first part of the story consists of a character sketch of an individual whose name or description often provides the title; once this unusual person has been portrayed, the narrative proceeds to describe one particular incident. Nuʿaymah's *Abū Baṭṭah*, for example, is the story of an aged porter who can still lift enormous weights; when challenged one day by a huge barrel, he has a heart attack and dies. Maḥmūd Taymūr's *ʿAmm Mitwallī* tells the story of a poor man from the Sudan who has come to Cairo; his behaviour leads people to the conclusion that he is the expected Mahdī (the title of a later revised version of the story) and follow his pronouncements until it becomes clear that he has become absolutely mad. Ibrāhīm al-Māzinī (d. 1949) adds an additional element to this type of story by lacing many of his examples with his particular brand of farcical humour; in *Ḥallāq al-qaryah* ('The Village Barber') for example, a city-dweller vacationing in the countryside decides that he needs a shave; even though his host tries to dissuade him, he insists, and, when the 'barber' arrives, it emerges that he is the local sheepshearer and that his equipment is more appropriate for the latter activity.

The ability of the short story to provide encapsulated portraits of broader social institutions made it a powerful tool in the analysis of a topic that just a few decades earlier had been essentially off-limits: the family and in particular the role of women within its structure. At this early stage in a lengthy process, the calls for reform within the society were reflected in a somewhat didactic tone, as in stories like Maḥmūd Taymūr's *al-Ḥājj Shalabī* and *al-Muhallil*, both of which are concerned about the exploitation of Islamic laws regarding divorce and remarriage, or Ayyūb's *Sāqiṭah* ('Fallen Woman'), one of many tales about the fate of prostitutes. Short stories from across the Arab world address themselves to every aspect of family life: the frustrations of teenagers living in a fishbowl society that watches their every move, the stages of marriage and divorce, the treatment of children, and the functioning of the larger Middle Eastern family with its many generations living in close proximity. As changing societal attitudes and improving educational opportunity bring more women writers out of the confines of the family home and into the public domain, these same topics are addressed from an entirely different perspective. Suhayr al-Qalamāwī (b. 1911) and Ulfat Idlibī (b. 1912) are among the first generation of women writers who use their stories to illustrate the female view on the life of women within the Arab family and society at large.

During the 1930s the romantic spirit that characterised much of this fiction led some writers in the direction of sentimentality, culminating in the immensely popular oeuvre of Iḥsān ʿAbd al-Quddūs (d. 1990). While this trend may have gained the short story a considerable readership, it was left to other writers to develop the more artistic aspects of the craft. Prime amongst them was Yaḥyā Ḥaqqī, a member of the 'new school' mentioned above, who wrote a relatively small output of stories, and yet each one reveals the concern with details of form, language, and mood that characterise the greatest exponents of the genre. Paying the greatest attention to authenticity of setting through imagery and language, Ḥaqqī produces exquisite narratives that explore motivations while providing the reader with a vivid picture of Egypt in all its variety of people and place. *Qiṣṣah min al-sijn* ('A Story from Prison'), for example, is set in the countryside of Upper Egypt and tells the story of a law-abiding peasant whose life falls apart when he is bewitched by a beautiful gypsy girl; the girl's companions even poison his faithful dog. *Kunnā thalāthat aytām* ('We Were Three Orphans') tells the story of a brother left responsible for his two sisters when their parents die; setting up house in an expensive flat in order to improve their prospects, it is he who falls into the snares of love; the story finishes with the proverb, 'he went hunting, but he was the one who got caught'. These qualities in Ḥaqqī's writing are brought to superb heights in his famous novella, *Qindīl Umm Hāshim* (1944; *The Saint's Lamp*, 1973). Among other writers who contributed to the development of the craft of short-story writing, we would mention Tawfiq Yūsuf ʿAwwād, whose stories are notable for their depiction of rural life and the hypocrisies of authority, Maḥmūd al-Badawī (d. 1985), ʿAbd al-salām al-ʿUjaylī (b. 1919), and Samīrah ʿAzzām (d. 1967).

To these aspects of theme, language, and form, Yūsuf Idrīs (d. 1991) adds an instinctive genius for the genre, producing volume after volume of stories that seem to be an apt reflection of both the dysfunctional nature of his rural upbringing and his own wayward amd colourful personality. Beginning with an outburst of productivity in the 1950s, Idrīs captures as never before the life of the Egyptian provinces and the abject poverty of the older quarters of Cairo. Incidents and character types of extraordinary variety are portrayed with an intimacy and vividness that reflect not only a profound familiarity with the environments involved but a remarkable ability to depict the sensory aspects of the scene in a new blend of language that Idrīs made entirely his own (and to which the redoubtable Ṭāhā Ḥusayn, ever the guardian of the language's probity, roundly objected). *Arkhaṣ layālī* ('The Cheapest of Nights') finds a man in a village wading through hordes of children and cursing the hole in the sky from which they fell to earth; unable to find anything else to do, he heads to his house and, climbing over the sleeping bodies of his own children, warms himself with the body of his wife. *Mārsh al-ghurūb* ('Sunset March') depicts the increasing desperation of a street-seller of juice, clicking his cymbals together in vain as people speed past him on their way home.

While the realistic short story, in its more or less didactic forms, clearly matched the era of revolutionary political and social change of the 1950s, it soon found itself confronting the unpleasant realities of a new set of regimes for whom the littérateur's depiction of social conditions was expected to conform with certain implicit or explicit expectations. Yūsuf Idrīs was far from being the only Arab writer whose political opinions sent him to prison, and, along with many other writers, he turned in the 1960s to a more allusive and symbolic mode as a means of reflecting a period of enormous uncertainties. Short stories now become allegories of complete alienation and the quest for meaning, for consolation through sex and drugs. Najīb Maḥfūẓ's masterpiece, *Zaʿbalāwī*, is such a quest through the older quarters of Cairo; the narrator has 'an illness for which there is no cure', and he visits a number of 'stations' on his way to a devoutly desired encounter with a 'saint' named Zaʿbalāwī. He fails to find him, and yet the search is not a complete failure in that, as the narrative returns to its starting-point, the narrator has learned that an entity with the supernatural powers needed to cure him exists. Maḥfūẓ continued this pattern of writing throughout the 1960s, and, in the wake of the June War of 1967, his stories become cryptic examinations of societal roles and values in an age of total disillusion with the present and immediate past. Yūsuf Idrīs also contributes stories in the form of parables: *Al-Āurṭā* ('The Aorta') paints a horrifying picture of the human herd instinct, impervious to any concern for the fate of the individual; *Al-ʿUṣfūr wa-al-silk* ('The Bird on the Wire') is a typical product of Idrīs's imagination, as a small bird, making love to its mate, shows its awareness of the power of international commerce and diplomacy by defecating on the telephone cable that is transmitting so many important messages of contemporary civilisation. During this period, Idrīs continues his exploration of changing sexual roles: *Bayt min laḥm* ('House of Flesh') is a superbly evocative picture of sexual tension within a fatherless family of women, the atmosphere being conveyed in a sensual language that is almost tactile. The subject is often treated with a good deal of humour: in *Akbar al-kabāʾir* ('The Greatest Sin of All') the house of a Sufi shaykh is made to sway by two forces, the motions of his dervish colleagues as they perform their rituals and the activity on the roof where his wife is having sex with her lover. One of Idrīs's last stories, *Abū Rijāl* ('Leader of Men'), confronts the topic of homosexuality: a gang leader whose prowess is challenged loses his credibility when his sexual preferences are revealed.

A peer of Idrīs in short-story writing is the Syrian writer, Zakariyyā Tāmir (b. 1931), who has also worked in television and written stories for children. He too is concerned about the tensions arising from changing sexual roles within society. Both *Wajh al-qamar* ('The Face of the Moon') and *Al-Thalj ākhir al-layl* ('Snow at the End of Night') depict families in which the presence of a marriageable daughter in the household causes tensions to its male members; while the former includes a dream of childhood rape, the latter leads the girl's brother to reject the thought of committing a *crime d'honneur* in defence of his family's prestige. Tāmir is equally well known for his symbolic narratives of alienation and oppression, stories that take the reader into an illogical world, a universe of sheer cruelty and callousness. The very relationship between title and beginning is often intentionally disconcerting: *Jūʿ* ('Hunger') opens with the sentence, 'Aḥmad was not a king', using the lack of any logical connection as a means of drawing the perplexed reader into the core of the narrative. Each story is couched in a style whose terseness and clarity suggests a naive detachment from what is being narrated that is as disturbing as it is misleading; a style that, in its subtlety and imagery, turns many of his stories into virtual prose poems.

Among other figures of primary importance in developing the craft of the short story, we should mention the Iraqi writer, Fu'ād al-Tikirlī (b. 1927), whose small output nevertheless manages to reveal his mastery of the structuring of the genre; *Al-Tannūr* ('The Oven') is a masterpiece of ironic play between the reader and an utterly unreliable narrator. The Moroccan novelist and critic, Muḥammad Barrādah, has also made some notable contributions to the experimental short story; his collection, *Salkh al-jild* (Hide Flaying, 1979) reveals the subtle worlds of an author much concerned with the expression of different levels of consciousness. In Egypt, Yūsuf al-Shārūnī (b. 1924) and Edwār al-Kharrāṭ (b. 1926), both influential writers and critics, present an interesting contrast: al-Shārūnī's stories are immaculately constructed narratives that show an awareness of many of the narrative strategies of the contemporary short story and yet are couched in a style that is stark and unadorned; al-Kharrāṭ, on the other hand, relishes his ability to compose his symbolic and ambiguous stories in a style that is highly elaborate and image-laden.

The writers mentioned thus far have been mostly male. Women writers of the short story, taking their lead from pioneers such as Suhayr al-Qalamāwī, Ulfat Idlibī, and Samīrah ʿAzzām, have been making major contributions to every aspect of the genre. During the 1950s and 1960s, Laylā Baʿalbakkī (b. 1936) and Colette Khūrī (b. 1937) published works of fiction that showed a new frankness in their discussion of relationships between the sexes; Baʿalbakkī's story, *Safīnat ḥanān ilā al-qamar* ('Spaceship of Tenderness to the Moon') was considered sufficiently subversive to have her charged in court with an offence against public decency; she was acquitted. The successors of these courageous pioneers, writers such as Ḥanān al-Shaykh (b. 1945), Salwā Bakr (b. *c.* 1950), and Laylā al-ʿUthmān (b. 1945), have been able to contribute to the Arabic short-story tradition works of considerable artistry and social insight.

The short story has now become the most popular mode of Arabic literary expression. Large numbers of collections are published annually throughout the Arab world; for many decades Egypt and Lebanon were generally regarded as the primary centres of publication, but more recently the output in the countries of the Gulf states, the Arabian peninsula, and the Maghrib has been an addition in both quantity and variety. We might note parenthetically here that, whereas in the West the publication of a collection of stories by a single author is a privilege reserved for only the most famous and distinguished exponents of the art, the reader of contemporary Arabic literature tends to be overwhelmed by story collections of truly bewildering variety in theme and accomplishment. Virtually every newpaper and journal will publish a work of fiction – a short story or a segment of a novel – weekly or monthly; there are magazines devoted entirely to the genre, and annual prizes for composing short stories. That this represents a change in the relative popularity of literary genres earlier this century seems clear, but the current political and economic status of those in the Arab world who feel the inspiration to create works of fiction is such that the short story presents itself as the ideal mode through which to apply that creative urge to a fictional reflection of individual concerns and the complexities of modern life.

The novel

In our survey of the early history of modern Arabic fiction above, we noted that the early popularity of the novel genre was engendered in large part by the serialised publication of historical romance novels. This tendency was one of several factors that made the development of an Arabic genre which would replicate the structures, styles, and generic purposes of the nineteenth-century novel in the West a complex and even disjointed process in comparison with that of the short story. Quite apart from social attitudes to the writing of fiction reflected in the pseudonym adopted by Haykal in *Zaynab*, the prerequisites to the emergence of an indigenous novel tradition were formidable. The ability to project aspects of 'life on a large scale', to place realistically drawn characters into authentic environments, and to do so in a style that was palatable to the newly emerging readership, these were skills that needed a prolonged and concentrated period of application and technical development, something that was and, in many cases, remains, a luxury that many would-be novelists cannot afford.

As was the case in other literary genres, a number of geographical and cultural factors – not the least being the emigration of many Syrian families to Egypt in the 1860s and 1870s – made the Egyptian tradition an early focal point of both creativity and emulation. Elsewhere in the Arab world, the timetable involved was different, often considerably so. In the countries of the Maghrib, for example, the deep penetration of

French culture into the educational system has meant that the balance between French and Arabic expression remains a hotly debated issue, with programs of *taʿrib* (Arabicisation) endeavouring to promote the use of Arabic within the cultural milieu. The first Algerian novel in Arabic, for example, is Aḥmad Riḍā Hūhū's *Ghādat umm al-qurā* ('Maid of the City') published in 1947, and the first by an Algerian woman writer is Aḥlām Mustaghanimī's *Dhākirat al-jasad* ('Body's Memory', 1993). Under Ottoman suzerainty (and censorship) Iraqi literature was kept under tight control and tended to adhere to traditional modes; Sulaymān Fayḍī al-Mawṣilī, for example, following the model of al-Muwayliḥī in Egypt, published his book of memoirs and observations as *Al-Riwāyah al-Īqāẓiyyah* in 1919 ('The Īqāẓ Narrative', '*Īqāẓ*' being the name of the newspaper he published). A few historical romances were also published, but it was not till the 1920s, when the British mandate was in effect, that the Iraqi novel began to address pressing contemporary issues. The cultural milieus of the remaining areas of the Gulf and Arabian peninsula were yet more traditional; it is the profound changes brought about by the discovery of oil, particularly in the realm of education and publication, that have provided the opportunities within which contemporary fiction is fulfilling its role as an effective commentator on the processes of social transformation.

In any historical survey of the development of the novel, Haykal's *Zaynab* clearly occupies an important position; some critics have gone so far as to dub it 'the first real Arabic novel', noting that, unlike its predecessors, it depicts Arab (in this case, Egyptian) characters in a contemporary and indigenous setting. To a certain extent that is true, but it needs to be noted that, even when compared with the descriptive detail of al-Muwayliḥī's work of a decade earlier, *Zaynab* comes up short on authenticity. The countryside is depicted with the overwhelming sentiment of a writer studying abroad and recalling it in its most idealistic and romanticized garb – man at one with his environs.

In Egypt, the 1920s witnessed further advances in the continuing debate on the status of women. An Egyptian feminist union was founded in 1923, and there was a significant increase in publications by and for women. As we noted above, much of the creative energy engendered by this political and social ferment found an outlet in the short story. Male and female characters were portrayed in vignettes culled from real-life situations within the family and in society at large; their tales were told in a language which decades of experiment, not least in the columns of the press, had turned into an expressive and adaptable means of communication with the expanding readership of fiction. In 1926 Ṭāhā Ḥusayn made an enormous contribution towards the development of the multi-faceted aspects of novel-writing when he published in serial form a fictionalised account of his early childhood, entitled *Al-Ayyām* (The Days, 1925; *An Egyptian Childhood*, 1932), the narrative features of which – especially the ironic play between the narrator and the protagonist (his childhood self) – have rightly earned it a significant place in the history of the development of modern Arabic fiction.

In addition to the fact that would-be novelists needed considerable amounts of time in order not only to develop the various aspects of the craft of fiction but also to complete the composition of a lengthy narrative, novel-writing faced another challenge, that of achieving a degree of social respectability. For, while novels of historical and adventure romance continued to provide popular escapist entertainment and, at the hands of a Jūrjī Zaydān, could also be part of a broader educational and nationalist project, attempts at using the novel to reflect and challenge contemporary realities, and especially the life of the family and its patterns of sexual conduct, broached an extremely sensitive area – all the more so in an era when the traditional norms concerning the status of women were the subject of intense debate. It was during the 1930s that a group of writers in different parts of the Arab world accepted the challenge of establishing the novel in Arabic as a ready and powerful literary mode whereby to explore these and many other topics of current concern and to experiment with aspects of technique. The dual role of the West as the seat of colonial hegemony and of cultural influence was a favourite topic: Tawfīq Yūsuf ʿAwwād's novel *al-Raghīf* ('The Loaf', 1939), explores the tensions created by the conflict during the First World War; Shakīb al-Jābirī's *Naham* ('Greed', 1936) and Dhū al-Nūn Ayyūb's *al-Duktūr Ibrāhīm* ('Doctor Ibrāhīm', 1939) both discuss the impact of a period of study in Europe on Arab students – a favourite theme of Arab writers from the outset and one which finds its most distinguished expression in Yaḥyā Ḥaqqī's novella, *Qindīl Umm Hāshim* (1944; *The Saint's Lamp*, 1973), and al-Ṭayyib Ṣāliḥ's *Mawsim al-hijrah ilā al-shamāl* (1966; *Season of Migration to the North*, 1969). In *Ibrāhīm al-kātib* (1931; *Ibrāhīm the Writer*, 1976) Ibrāhīm al-Māzinī brings his well-known humour and insight to the portrayal of a number of characters and situations in a story of the narrator's love for three women. Tawfīq al-Ḥakīm contributes several notable works: *ʿAwdat al-rūḥ* (1933; *Return of the Spirit*, 1990) provides a lively colloquial dialogue as a means of introducing his reader to the tensions of a large Egyptian family living through the tensions of life in Egypt in 1919; *Yawmiyyāt nā'ib fī al-aryāf* (1937; *The Maze of Justice*, 1947) is a beautifully constructed picture of the Egyptian countryside in which a young urbanised Egyptian makes a mostly vain attempt to explain the machinations of Egyptian law to the bemused peasantry. One of the most accomplished Egyptian novels of this period, notable by contrast for its apparent lack of autobiographical content, is also one of the most neglected: Maḥmūd Ṭāhir Lāshīn's *Ḥawwā' bi-lā Ādam* (1934; *Eve Without Adam*, 1986), which explores the tortured feelings of a woman who falls in love with the brother of the girl she is tutoring and whose despair leads her to suicide.

It was also during the 1930s that another Egyptian writer, Najīb Maḥfūẓ (b. 1911), set himself the task of tying together all these various strands of the novelist's craft by undertaking a systematic survey of the themes and techniques of Western fiction. In 1939 he published the first of three novels set in ancient Egypt (as part of a much larger project), but the political and social tribulations of his homeland during the Second World War provided a powerful incentive for him to turn the novelist's eye on the ills of the present day. Over a period of five decades Maḥfūẓ has taken as his major theme the novel's primary topic: the city – in his case, Cairo and, to a lesser extent, Alexandria, and the aspirations and sufferings of its middle class of artisans, traders, and bureaucrats. These are venues and subjects with which he is intimately familiar, and in a vast outpouring of fictional creativity he has portrayed them with a subtlety and humour that has made his oeuvre a base upon which generations of younger writers have been able to build and a point of reference from which modernist experiments of great variety have branched out. The Nobel Laureate in Literature for 1988, he is widely recognised as the founding father of the Arabic novel.

By the time the Egyptian Revolution of 1952 had swept away the *ancien régime*, Maḥfūẓ had penned a series of novels that showed in graphic detail the political corruption and social disparities that had bred such discontent. In each case a particular district of old Cairo, depicted with the loving attention of one who is intimately familiar with the area, became the focus for a story that explored the aspirations of Egyptians and the many ways in which they were crushed by forces over which they had no control. The three-volume Trilogy, *Bayn al-qaṣrayn* (1956; *Palace Walk*, 1990), *Qaṣr al-shawq* (1957; *Palace of Desire*, 1991), and *al-Sukkariyyah* (1957; *Sugar Street*, 1992), uses the ʿAbd al-Jawwād family as the focus for a huge canvas of Egyptian political and cultural life from

1917 till 1944, placing the loves, dreams, ideas, and foibles of successive generations within the inexorable forward march of time and the often painful processes of change. The readership of the Arab world as a whole, searching for new directions in the post-independence era, found in Maḥfūẓ's masterpiece a graphic illustration of the circumstances that had brought about the profound political and social transformations that occurred in Egypt and elsewhere during the 1950s. However, while the need for change had united disparate groups and classes in a common goal (as *al-Sukkariyyah* clearly shows), the direction of the newly independent nations and their political agenda were very unclear. In many Arab countries the post-revolutionary period was one of ambiguity and retribution; along with socialism came the trappings of a police state. For novelists who penned works that showed a commitment to governmental policies, the rewards often came in the form of positions in the new cultural hierarchy. For those, on the other hand, who chose to challenge those policies or to point out the ambiguities of the period, the result was imprisonment, exile or worse; the long list of novelists who have been imprisoned and the repertoire of novels that discuss the prison experience – including notable contributions from Ṣunʿallāh Ibrāhīm (*Tilka al-rāʾiḥah*, 1966; *The Smell of It*, 1961 and ʿAbd al-raḥmān Munīf (*Sharq al-Mutawassiṭ* (East of the Mediterranean, 1975) – is a sobering commentary on the lack of a genuine freedom of expression that has been the lot of most Arab writers in the second half of the twentieth century. Maḥfūẓ's response to this situation was a fictional silence that was broken in 1959 by a very different kind of work, an allegorical novel that treated one of his favourite topics, the role of religion in the history of mankind and the dilemma of its relationship to modern scientific knowledge. *Awlād ḥāratinā* (1959, 1967; *Children of Gebelawi*, 1981; *Children of the Alley* 1996) follows the course of mankind's history of faith through a series of leaders who attempt to provide a moral and spiritual base that will bring the unruly conduct of the gangs in the community under some sort of control. It is this religious aspect, and especially the overarching figure of Jabalāwī who is eventually killed by ʿArafah (*scientia*), that has made this work Maḥfūẓ's most controversial piece of fiction; it was immediately banned in Egypt and during the Nobel year of 1988 led to a sentence of death from a popular preacher which was almost carried out in October 1994.

When Maḥfūẓ did turn his attention to the course of the Egyptian revolution in the 1960s, it was in a series of highly allusive works that move away from the depiction of the community as a whole to explore the alienated world of the individual. Using a newly economical language to provide details of place and time, these novels – beginning with *al-Liṣṣ wa-al-kilāb* (1961; *The Thief and the Dogs*, 1984, and culminating with *Thartharah fawq al-Nīl* (1966; *Adrift on the Nile*, 1993) and *Mīrāmār* (1967; *Miramar*, 1978) – constitute a rising crescendo of disillusion and anger towards the rulers of Egypt and the grim atmosphere that their societal machinations had created. The June War of 1967 came as a brutal confirmation of the scenario that Maḥfūẓ and others had painted, and once again Maḥfūẓ wrote no novels for a time, concentrating instead on a series of lengthy and cryptic short stories. When he did return to the novel, it was in changed circumstances: he himself had retired, and Anwar al-Sādāt had become president on the death of ʿAbd al-nāṣir [Nasser]. This was an unsavoury period of political retribution, of 'looking back in anger'. To Maḥfūẓ's personal disillusion over the way that the revolution's promise had been thwarted, obvious enough in works like *al-Marāyā* (1972; *Mirrors*, 1977) and *al-Karnak* (1974; *Al-Karnak*, 1988), was now added a deep antipathy to the president's personality and style and to the open-markets policy (*infitāḥ*) which served to exacerbate the class divisions within Egyptian society. Novels such as *Malḥamat al-ḥarāfīsh* (1977; *The Harafish*, 1994), *Al-Bāqī min al-zaman sāʿah* (Just One Hour Left, 1982), and *Yawm qutila al-zaʿīm* (The Day the Leader was Killed, 1985) show a society of glaring contrasts, one in which basic amenities such as housing remain a dream and there is little mobility. As Maḥfūẓ has aged, his work has also become more retrospective and wistful. In some works he has repeated earlier experiments in structure and language; in others – such as *Riḥlat ibn Faṭṭūmah* (1983; *The Journey of Ibn Fattouma*, 1992) and *Layālī alf laylah* (1982; *Arabian Nights and Days*, 1995) – he has looked for inspiration in the narrative genres of the classical tradition. And with age has come also a certain nostalgic tone; both *Qushtumur* (the name of a cafe, 1989) and *Aṣdāʾ al-sīrah al-dhātiyyah* (1994; *Echoes of an Autobiography*, 1997) – the latter a remarkable evocation of classical Sufi writings – take the reader back to earlier days in the narrator's life, days of hopes and loves, and of struggles both physical and intellectual.

The sheer quality and quantity of Maḥfūẓ's output make him the doyen of Arab novelists, but his remarkable career has also coincided with a period of tremendous growth in the popularity of fiction throughout the Arab world. As the novel has attained a position of prestige that allows, indeed requires, it to fulfil its primary generic purpose as a reflector and advocate of social change, so male and female writers have begun to experiment with a variety of techniques in the process of exploring the significant issues of the time. As noted above, the constraints of work situation often serve to make the composition of novels something of a spare-time activity for many writers, but a few authors have now successfully undertaken the challenge of replicating the mammoth scale of Maḥfūẓ's *Trilogy*. ʿAbd al-raḥmān Munīf's quintet of novels, published under the general title *Mudun al-milḥ* (1984–88; in English thus far, *Cities of Salt*, 1984; *The Trench*, 1991; and *Variations on Night and Day*, 1993) is a carefully crafted and highly critical fictional study of the impact of the discovery of oil on the traditional life of Saudi Arabia and the morals of its rulers; the work is banned in Saudi Arabia and its author has been deprived of his citizenship. The Libyan novelist, Ibrāhīm al-Kūnī (b. 1948), who has written a historical study of the peoples of the Sahara, introduces the readers of his novels to an unfamiliar landscape and environment, the nomadic tribes of the deserts of North Africa, the harshness of their existence, and the complexities of their contacts with the Islamic and non-Islamic peoples to the south. Lengthy works such as *al-Majūs* (The Magi, 1991) and *al-Saḥarah* (The Sorcerers, 1993) take their readers far from the modern cities of the Middle East and place them into a transient society that invokes many of the images and values of the earliest stages in the Arabic literary tradition.

Oil and desert are, of course, closely linked as themes, in reality as in fiction. The discovery of oil in the early twentieth century has guaranteed that the Middle East will remain for the nations of the West a focus of strategic and economic concern. As the Gulf War of 1991 has already proved convincingly, it needs to be added to the large number of points of potential and actual conflict in the region, many of which have, not unnaturally, been the topics of works of fiction. Principal among them is the fate of the Palestinian people; while the focus of some works has been on the conflicts themselves – 1948, 1956, 1967, 1973, and 1982, the most accomplished pieces of fiction have dealt with the life of the fragmented community during the interstices. The works of Ghassān Kanafānī (assassinated in 1972) are emblematic of a period when, for all the empty rhetoric from Arab leaders and with the indifference of the rest of the world, little was done to ameliorate the situation of the exiled Palestinians; *Rijāl fī al-shams* (1963; *Men in the Sun*, 1978), captures the situation with superb artistry, as three Palestinians from different generations suffocate to death as they try to escape to Kuwait inside a water-tanker. Completely different but equally powerful is Emil Ḥabībī's (d. 1996),

Al-Waqāʾiʿ al-gharībah fī ikhtifāʾ Saʿīd Abī al-naḥs al-mutashāʾil (1972, 1974, 1977; *The Secret Life of Saeed, the Ill-Fated Pessoptimist*, 1982). One of the finest exercises in irony in all of Arabic fiction, it depicts the wise fool, Saʿīd, coping in his unique way with the crushing realities of the life of a Palestinian living in the State of Israel. Different again are the novels of Jabrā Ibrāhīm Jabrā (d. 1994) which portray the alienation and nostalgia of the Palestinian intellectual community condemned to a life of exile so well depicted in a poem of Tawfīq Ṣāyigh (d. 1971):

> 'Your passport?'
> without it no entry
> and you don't carry one
> so no entry. (*Qasidat K*, Poem 24)

Novels like *al-Safīnah* (1970; *The Ship*, 1985) and *al-Bahth ʿan Walīd Masʿūd* (The Search for Walīd Masʿūd, 1978), make excellent use of the multi-narrator technique to portray the agonies of the exiled Arab intellectual and specifically the plight of the Palestinians as emblematic of the region as a whole. Saḥar Khalīfah (b. 1941) has taken as a major theme in her novels the often tortuous relationship between the peoples of Israel and the West Bank; in *al-Ṣubbār* (1976; *Wild Thorns*, 1985) we see the reverse of Kanafānī's *Men in the Sun*, in that a Palestinian man returns from the Gulf in order to disrupt the daily transfer of workers from the West Bank to jobs in Israel. When he blows up a bus transporting workers, not only is he himself killed but his own townsfolk on the bus die too, and, as an automatic consequence, his family's house is blown up.

Other conflicts have also provided inspiration for novels. If settings during the First and Second World Wars now fulfil a purely historical function, the prolonged War of Liberation in Algeria (1954–62) is still a potent memory, and no more so than in the vivid narratives of the Algerian novelist, al-Ṭāhir Waṭṭār (b. 1936); in two works, he creates the character of *al-Lāz* (1974, 1982), a fighter for the nationalist cause who spies on the French. The novels explore not only the events of the war itself but also the complexities of the social fabric, between city and provinces, between religious and secular, a situation that has been highlighted by recent events in the country. Social complexity of an even greater kind has been a feature of Lebanese communal life, and the civil war during the 1970s and 1980s, with its linkages to the Palestine question and other regional issues of hegemony and control, was a fertile breeding ground for societal chaos, reflected in vivid detail in several distinguished contributions to fiction. The early pioneer, Tawfiq Yūsuf ʿAwwād, may actually be seen as foretelling the conflict in his novel, *Ṭawaḥīn Bayrūt* (1972; *Death in Beirut*, 1976), in which a Shīʿite girl from South Lebanon encounters the fault-lines in the social structure during her time in Beirut. However, it is Ḥanān al-Shaykh's (b. 1945) *Ḥikāyat Zahrah* (1980; *The Story of Zahrah*, 1986) that, again using a Shīʿite girl as its focus, reveals in most graphic and accomplished detail the full scale of the insane destruction that the armies of the various political and religious subgroups rained upon each other. The same atmosphere of normalised violence and despair characterises the several novels of Ilyās Khūrī; the narrator of *Riḥlat Ghāndī al-ṣaghīr* (1989; *The Journey of Little Ghandi*, 1994) continually questions the author as he finds himself placed into a nightmare world in which personal relationships and narrative linkages of any kind are tenuous and death is an ever present reality.

The Arabic novel has also addressed itself to a whole series of other confrontations and problems within the society itself, many of them antedating the achievement of independence but affected in different ways by the policies of the newly independent regimes. One such issue was the nature of the relationship between the city and the rural life of the provinces. A number of Egyptian novelists have addressed this topic, including ʿAbd al-raḥmān al-Sharqāwī (d. 1987), Yūsuf Idrīs (d. 1991), Fatḥī Ghānim (b. 1927), and Yaḥyā al-Ṭāhir ʿAbdallāh (d. 1981); the works of Yūsuf al-Qaʿīd (b. 1944) such as *Akhbār ʿizbat al-Minaysī* (1971; *New from the Meneisi Farm*, 1987), ʿAbd al-ḥakīm Qāsim in *Ayyām al-insān al-sabʿah* (1969; *The Seven Days of Man*, 1989), and of Bahāʾ Ṭāhir in *Sharq al-nakhīl* (East of the Palm Trees, 1985) are notable examples of this subgenre. In countries such as Algeria and Syria where the relationship between the urbanised littoral and the countryside has always been tense, works of fiction devoted to the topic have a particularly fervent quality; thus, ʿAbd al-ḥamīd ibn Hadūqah's *Rīḥ al-janūb* (South Wind, 1971) and al-Ṭāhir Waṭṭār's *al-Zilzāl* (The Earthquake, 1974) from the former, and ʿAbd al-nabī Ḥijāzī's *al-Sindyānah* (The Oak-Tree, 1971) from the latter.

Given the nature of the changes that have occurred at every level of Arab society, it should come as no surprise that the institution of the family has been subjected to enormous pressures during the latter half of the twentieth century, nor that those pressures have been the subject of much fiction. A number of authors have created works that explore crisis situations in family life, often brought about by the death of the father: Maḥfūẓ's *Bidāyah wa-nihāyah* (1951; *The Beginning and the End*, 1985) and Fāḍil al-Sibāʿī's (b. 1929) *Thumma azhar al-ḥuzn* (Then Sorrow Bloomed, 1963) are two examples of this theme. The presence of the father-figure is often a cause of tension, particularly when the changing expectations of the female members of the family are concerned: Suhayl Idrīs's *al-Khandaq al-ghamīq* (The Deep Trench, 1958) may be named after a district of Beirut, but the title also tells of a deep generational rift between the father and the children of the family who object to his imposition of conservative norms of behaviour. A number of Maghribī novelists paint a gruesome picture of family life and, in particular, of the tyrannical role of the father within it: Muḥammad Barrādah, for example, in *Luʿbat al-nisyān* (1987; *Game of Forgetting*, 1996) and Muḥammad Shukrī in his 'fictional autobiography', *Al-Khubz al-ḥāfī* (1982; *For Bread Alone*, 1973), but the most shocking picture is painted by the Algerian novelist, Rashīd Abū Jadrah (Boujedra) (b. 1941), most notably in *La Répudiation* (1969; *al-Taṭlīq* (Repudiation), 1982), and *al-Marth* (The Soaking, 1984). A number of women novelists have expressed themselves on this topic in increasingly forthright terms. Particularly noteworthy are Laylā Baʿalbakkī with *Anā aḥyā* (I Am Alive, 1958), a pioneer in the forthright fictional expression of women's liberation, Laṭīfah al-Zayyāt (b. 1925) with *al-Bāb al-maftūḥ* (The Open Door, 1960), and Ghādah al-Sammān (b. 1942) with *Bayrūt '75* (Beirut '75, 1975) and *Kawābīs Bayrūt* (Beirut Nightmares, 1976). Loudest of all in expressing her opposition to traditional, male-dominated family values is the Egyptian writer, Nawāl al-Saʿdāwī (b. 1930) who, in addition to serving as a courageous publicist of women's issues in Egypt, has also written several works of fiction, the most famous of which is *Imraʾah ʿinda nuqṭat al-ṣifr* (1975; *Woman at Point Zero*, 1983), the story of a prostitute who is killed for the murder of her pimp. The courageous way in which Baʿalbakkī, al-Sammān, al-Shaykh, and al-Saʿdāwī have expressed their feminine vision of current Arab social realities in such a frank fashion – often at the risk of personal attacks from the more conservative segments of society – has served to open up fictional creativity to a richer and variegated exploration of gender relationships with the family and society as a whole.

As this brief survey of themes makes clear, the complexities of life within contemporary Arab society, as elsewhere in what has become known as the Third World, has provided plenty of incentives for alienation and despair: the loneliness of the individual confronting faceless bureaucracies, the frequent transfer of 'home' from place to place – often from rural countryside to an inimical city, and the apparently endless hegemony of external organisations and governments over the political and economic affairs of the region. Maḥfūẓ's turn from the communal of his pre-revolution novels to the individual in those of the 1960s is replicated in the work of a number of other writers who have found in the exploration of the psychological traumas of the individual a conducive vehicle for their fictional experiments. We have already drawn attention to the repertoire of novels about prisons and the loneliness and alienation that they of necessity engender, but the theme of exile, be it physical and external or psychological and internal, has also been a feature of much writing, as in Ḥannā Mīnah's (b. 1924) *al-Thalj ya'tī min al-nāfidhah*, 1969, ʿAbd al-ḥakīm Qāsim's (d. 1990) *Qadar al-ghuraf al-muqbiḍah* (Fate of the Oppressive Rooms, 1982), Jūrj Sālim's (d. 1976) *Fī al-manfā* (In Exile, 1962), and Ḥabībī's *Ikhṭiyyeh* ('Oh dear', 1985), set in a transformed city of Haifa that is now divorced from its Arab past and site of a static internal exile.

The intangible essence of the novel genre lies in its role as an agent of change and thus the necessity of its susceptibility to the very phenomenon that it depicts. In the rapidly changing societies of the Arab world there has been no lack of material with which to fulfil its generic purpose, and Arab writers have made use of its changing nature to the fullest extent. Like many of their Western colleagues they have chosen to represent the complex and fragmented conditions that confront them through what Frank Kermode has described as 'a recognisable estrangement from what used to be known as reality'. Narrative coherence is no longer a given; it is often eschewed. Chronological time is fractured through flashbacks (as, for example, in Jabrā's works) or through the cinematic sweep of Ḥalīm Barakāt's novel of the June 1967 War, *ʿAwdat al-ṭā'ir ilā al-baḥr* (1969; *Days of Dust*, 1974); the reliability of a single, omniscient narrator is replaced by the different versions of several narrators and then by a challenge to the entire concept as the narrators of the fiction of Muḥammad Barrādah and Ilyās Khūrī argue with their 'authors' about the course of the narrative in which they are involved. This is, of course, one aspect of the process of 'metafiction', what Frank Kermode describes as 'the use of fiction as an instrument of research into the nature of fiction'. One of the most remarkable examples of this narrative strategy is *ʿĀlam bi-lā kharā'iṭ* (A World Without Maps, 1983), a joint work of ʿAbd al-raḥmān Munīf and Jabrā Ibrāhīm Jabrā, that is interesting not only because of its actual authorship but also because one of the characters is in the process of writing a novel and discusses the process at length. At the hands of many contemporary Arab novelists the process of composition involves an elaborate process of textual play. Ḥabībī evokes all manner of styles and references, Arab and Western, as he covers the bitter realities of daily life in Israel with a layer of improbable erudition. In *Maʿrakat al-zuqāq* (Struggle in the Alley, 1986) Rashīd Abū Jadrah's schoolboy protagonist has to make vocabulary lists for his classroom courses in Latin and Arabic; in the latter case the text involved is an account of the Muslim conquest of Spain, and the exercise prompts in the boy's imagination a comparison between life in eighth-century Spain and in post-revolutionary Algeria. Jamāl al-Ghīṭānī (b. 1945) and ʿAbd al-raḥmān Munīf incorporate into their works of fiction segments from, and pastiches of, the works of the classical littérateurs we have mentioned earlier in this chapter (including al-Jāḥiẓ and ibn ʿArabī), while, as we noted above, two of Maḥfūẓ's novels of the 1980s adopt the discourse features of ibn Baṭṭūṭah's travel narratives and the characters of the *Thousand and One Nights*.

This briefest of surveys of the Arabic novel tradition can only begin to convey the enormous role that the genre continues to play in the cultural life of the region. While the Arabic language remains a barrier for a Western readership, the award of the Nobel prize to Maḥfūẓ in 1988 has led to a certain increase in interest on the part of Western readers; while Maḥfūẓ himself has been the primary beneficiary of such interest, other novelists, such as Munīf and al-Shaykh, have also attracted attention. The current focus on women's writing also insures that the writings of Nawāl al-Saʿdāwī are widely available. As examples of Arabic fiction begin to enter anthologies of world literature and other modes of access, a broader readership will become aware of the spirit of defiance and experimentation that makes the Arabic novel such a lively artistic medium.

CONCLUSION

The cumbersome title of this chapter is an appropriate indication of the definitional difficulties associated with the material included in it and, it needs to be added, with any attempt to find a context within which to analyse the literary production of a cultural system (particularly a non-Western one) different from our own. The changing nature of the phenomenon of *adab* during the earlier period and the way that it now represents the – equally problematic – concept of 'literature' provides one cluster of problems, while the exclusion of popular genres, and particularly narratives, from the pale is another. Different parameters are clearly involved here, and we have not tried to hide them. Furthermore, at certain times radical changes have occurred; in the early modern period, for example, the expansion of the press did indeed engender a rapid popularity for the newly imported Western genres of fiction that tended to overwhelm the more traditional genres such as the *maqāmah*.

That said however, much contemporary literary criticism has been at pains to break down the barriers between different types of text. To illustrate the point, Roland Barthes is prepared to analyse a wide variety of texts, while Hayden White points out the invalidity of many of the criteria that have been used to compartmentalise biography, history, and fiction into separate categories. For a work such as this, whose organisational principle implies continuities rather than ruptures, perhaps the most convenient aspect of current narrative writing in Arabic is that the use and imitation of the themes, structures, and language of classical Arabic prose genres – popular as well as élite – is now regarded by many authors as a modernist gesture.

CHAPTER 6

Drama

INTRODUCTION

In 1963 the drama tradition in Egypt was enjoying a wave of popular esteem. The particular complex of societal factors that is needed in order for a theatre tradition to develop and flourish seemed to be in place: a significant group of younger playwrights was composing works that were being accepted for performance by the censorship authorities, transferred to the stage, performed to considerable popular acclaim, and reviewed by a group of accomplished critics who were well acquainted with the traditions of world drama. It was in this year that the prominent Egyptian short-story writer and playwright, Yūsuf Idrīs, ever provocative, chose to publish a series of articles in the Cairene literary monthly, *Al-Kātib*, under the title, 'Towards an Egyptian theatre' (*Naḥwa masraḥ Miṣrī*). Whatever yardstick one may wish to use in deciding what the terms 'theatre' and 'drama' may imply in the Arab world context–a point we will discuss in detail below, there can be little argument about the fact that by 1963 an Egyptian tradition of modern Arabic drama was well over a century old. In the light of such a period of development and the popular acclaim being afforded the medium, the title of Idrīs's articles was something of a challenge to received wisdom on the drama genre in Arabic and the course that its development had taken.

Surveying the development of the drama genre up to that point, Idrīs suggests that, while the processes of translation, 'arabisation', and adaptation may have been able to transfer certain elements of drama into the Egyptian context, and indeed while certain Egyptian playwrights may have produced accomplished works that made use of local themes, the end result of all this creative activity was still culturally derivative. There remained a disjuncture between Arabic drama in Egypt and the indigenous cultural tradition. Were there, Idrīs wondered, no examples of drama to be found within the heritage of the Egyptian people? Could it be seriously claimed that the Egyptians, of all people, were 'undramatic' when one took into account the number of social occasions at which they habitually performed in public fora in one way or another? Idrīs's response to these questions transcended mere affirmation to the point of illustration, taking the form of a remarkable and innovative play, *Farāfir*, that was performed in 1964. However in the context of the series of articles he continued by exploring the nature of the dramatic in the Middle East and the West and the kinds of drama performance that had been popular in the pre-modern period of Middle Eastern history. In particular, he identified one popular genre, the *sāmir* (evening entertainment), as a model for the exploration of the possibilities of an indigenous Egyptian drama tradition and proceeded to apply his notions in the script of *Farāfir*.

Idrīs was writing, of course, at a time when many countries in the Arab world, freed of colonial occupation, were searching within their own heritage for alternatives to the seemingly inevitable hegemony of Western cultural models and values. His quest for a purely Egyptian genre of drama needs to be placed into such a historical and societal context. However, the questions that he raised at that time and the answers he provided constitute a conveniently modern point of reference through which to consider the nature of drama in its Arab world context and the types of dramatic event that were the precedents to the modern tradition.

DRAMA AND ARABIC DRAMA

The theoretical beginnings of the European dramatic tradition which Idrīs is confronting in his comments are generally agreed to be found in the *Poetics* of Aristotle where he tells his readers that drama is based on the principle of *mimesis* or representation, a process that involves impersonation. An expansion, indeed a corollary, of this classic definition is represented by the notion that, in order to fulfil its dramatic function to the full, a play needs to be acted, performed; such a process requires a place where the drama may be presented – a theatre of one kind or another, and an audience who will engage themselves in the performance with both their eyes and ears. As Shakespeare himself expresses it in the Prologue to *King Henry the Fifth*,

> For 'tis your thoughts that now must deck our kings,
> Carry them here and there, jumping o'er times,
> Turning the accomplishment of many years
> Into an hour-glass;

For the most part, the 'action' will involve actors performing on stage by using gestures and dialogue as means of representing the deeds and emotions of characters in order to 'show' the import of the play being presented. The very complexity of the process of dramatic communication, from creation via production to audience reception, clearly represents a potentially substantial extension of the author-text-reader continuum of other 'textual' genres; it is one that has from the outset presented playwrights with a wealth of opportunity for experiment and critical analysts with an equal wealth of theoretical applications. Thus, while in the Greek tradition the relationship between the performance on stage and the audience was viewed as one that involved the stimulus of the audience's empathy followed by a sense of katharsis, more recent trends, particularly those associated with the plays and productions of Piscator and Brecht, have endeavoured to prevent such empathy; in fact, to distance the audience from the action so that the performance can fulfil a more educational purpose. J. L Styan has provided (in *Drama, Stage and Audience*) a threefold schema through which to explore the different aspects of this wonderfully complex semiotic relationship, especially in its more experimental aspects: the categories he employs are venue, time, and people. These three axes provide a means of representing the several dimensions of the dramatic medium: the first invokes the issues associated with the stage and theatre building; the second the relationship between actors and audience; and the third the often problematic continuum from author via producer to society.

Within the context of that broad concept known as society the history of drama shows that the genre has managed to fulfil a number of functions, including those of liturgy, entertainment, and education. The presentation of a single play or a complete theatre festival has always been an 'occasion' in every sense of the word. In origin the genre was connected to religious or communal festivals, as in the case of much Greek and Roman drama. In a more popular vein, the drama was co-opted by medieval Christianity through the often lengthy cycles of plays recorded in the archives of such English cities as Chester, Wakefield, and York, or in the Oberammergau Passion play. Such events as these were originally contributions to other significant occasions, although in a contemporary context their performance will be an occasion in its own right. The development of that particular genre that combines drama and music, namely opera, has come to involve a societal occasion of some elaboration, requiring not only lengthy rehearsals on the part of the performers but also ornate and expensive costumes on the part of the audience, as those attending Covent Garden in London or the newly rebuilt Cairo Opera House can attest. Above all, the very fact that drama is the most public of all literary genres, a performance, an act of impersonation and showing in front of an audience, has also made it in many, if not most, cultures and historical periods the focus of political oversight – in a word, censorship. To cite Millett and Bentley:

Especially in a definitely socialized art like the drama, prejudice, fear, ignorance, and prudishness are likely at any moment to interfere with at least the performance of a drama that affronts some vocal section of the community. (*The Art of the Drama*, London, *c.* 1935, p. 172)

Within the Western tradition of drama the performance element gravitates towards the formalities and conventions of the theatre as structure, something that led Brecht to frame part of his own dramatic theory in terms of the effect of the theatre's 'walls' on audience response to the performance. In the same way the script of the play has assumed the status of a text. The works of Sophocles, Racine, Shakespeare, Goethe, Pirandello, and Chekhov are regarded as major contributions to the literary heritage and have joined the list of canonical works of Western culture, a status confirmed in numerous ways, not least by their presence on the reading lists of national school curricula. As performance and text, as theatre and participant in a cultural canon, drama in the Western world claims a place in society's evaluation of its heritage in literary form, something that affords it an élite status.

It is as part of the nineteenth-century cultural renaissance in the Arab world that the literary community encounters and adopts the generic tradition that we have just outlined. In that any consideration of the development of Arabic drama within the broader context of the Western theatre tradition involves widely variant cultures with differing processes of historical development and literary influences, there seems little purpose in exploring within the Arabic literary heritage the causes for a lack of examples of types of drama that can be conveniently linked to the Western tradition. As many writers have observed, patterns of literary development do not conform with any such niceties. However, while close similarities may not exist, there are, as Yūsuf Idrīs's remarks cited above imply, a number of indigenous genres which exhibit dramatic qualities. Indeed, as we will note below, many modern playwrights have had recourse to themes and techniques from such works in the process of composing plays that utilise and adapt the heritage of the past as a clear assertion of a sense of modernity. In order to illustrate such linkages of past to present, we will briefly discuss a few of these early types of dramatic performance within the Arabic tradition.

Mirroring the combination of religious memorial and public performance that marks the medieval mystery plays mentioned above (to which might be added the liturgy of the Stations of the Cross), a first example can be provided by a performance tradition that survives from great antiquity till the present day. Within the Shīʿite communities of the Middle East (and thus especially in Iran), there is a tradition of the *taʿziyah* (a term implying both mourning and consolation), a passion play which serves as a commemoration of the death of the Prophet Muḥammad's grandson, al-Ḥusayn, at the battle of Karbalāʾ in AD 680. Performances of this particular form of drama take place during the Islamic month of Muḥarram and consist of a highly ritualised public performance: the participants in the presentation process through the streets and perform a series of tableaux in which the events of the martyrdom are re-enacted in a way that often results in scenes of intense emotion among the audience, a phenomenon that has been commented on by local and Western observers for many centuries.

The period preceding the nineteenth century renaissance in the Arab world – an era that, as we noted above in Chapter 1, on principles, spans no less than five centuries – witnessed an efflorescence of a variety of popular genres, many of which can be considered as dramatic. Prime amongst these was the shadow play (*khayāl al-ẓill*) in which coloured figures were manipulated by wires from behind a transparent screen. Through one of those coincidences of which Arabic literature scholarship needs many more in order to fill out details of its history, we are fortunate to possess the manuscript of three 'plays' composed by the Egyptian Shams al-dīn Muḥammad ibn Dāniyāl (1248–1311), for this particular form. It is clear from the introduction to his plays that the genre was not a new one in his day; one of the purposes that Ibn Dāniyāl has in recording these examples is to provide fresh materials for a medium where much of the material has become hackneyed. The plays themselves clearly fall into the realm of comedy, intending to show up the very worst foibles of mankind, most particularly where matters sexual are concerned, and anticipating, as Northrup Frye notes, that an audience will play a vigorous role in extrapolating the mostly explicit social message through its own participation in the interplay between stage and recipients. The contents are bawdy to the point of obscenity. In one play, *Ṭayf al-khayāl*, the chief character is named Prince Wiṣāl, a name that implies sexual congress. Every conceivable kind of phallic image is used within the text of the play. Further farcical and scatological effects are provided by having the characters stumble, babble, and fart on stage. In another play, *ʿAjīb wa-gharīb*, every form of profession, particularly those of the less desirable elements of the populace, are explored. Such a societal context, when coupled with the virtuoso use of language to be found in these plays – in poetry and rhyming prose, has led several scholars to draw attention to the way in which the plays mirror the *maqāmah* genre that we examined in the previous chapter on narrative genres.

A particularly popular and widespread form of this type of presentation was the genre known as *karagöz*, a name that either may be derived from the name of the character in its Turkish tradition, in which case it means 'black face'; or else it may be an adaptation of the name of a Mamlūk ruler of Egypt, Qaraqūsh. This genre bears a very close resemblance to the traditional Punch and Judy show, perhaps not so common at the end of the twentieth century as it was in this writer's childhood. In imitation of what would appear to be a Chinese tradition, a single performer would wrap himself in a tent-like structure and proceed to manipulate hand-held puppets on a stage above his head. A number of sketches involving different characters might be involved, but the basic hero would always be Karagöz – Everyman, the bumbling and boisterous simpleton, who would endeavour to outsmart any pretentious hypocrite who chose to stand in his way, usually resorting to beatings as the preferred mode of resolving disputes. Because of the limitations of the medium itself, the sketches would involve more slapstick than dialogue, but perhaps their greatest virtue was their adaptability to local circumstances so that they could serve as effective means of political and social criticism. In the view of several commentators, it was precisely this feature of the genre that accounted for its demise in the late Ottoman period.

One final aspect of the 'dramatic' during the pre-modern period concerns a particular function that has been much exploited by modern dramatists: the *ḥakawātī* or story-teller. Certain manuscripts of the collections of popular tales (the MacNaughten *Thousand and One Nights*, for example) make it clear that performers of these enormous collections of tales would not restrict their public performances to speech and the dimension of sound. As Edward Lane records in *Manners and Customs of the Modern Egyptians*, his unique account of Cairene life in the 1860s, story-tellers would accompany themselves on musical instruments and would gesticulate at appropriate points in the narrative. It is clear not only from these accounts but also from those of contemporary folklorists who have been providing us with invaluable accounts of performances and audience reactions that the occasions on which tales from such collections were, and in regrettably rare instances still are, 'performed' were dramatic events in every sense of the word. That several contemporary playwrights should invoke the figure of the *ḥakawātī* in order to provide a Brechtian distancing mechanism to their dramas and that a prominent group of Palestinian actors should call themselves the Ḥakawātī Troupe is clearly no accident.

BEGINNINGS IN SYRIA AND EGYPT

European travellers have provided us with accounts of performances of these types of public performance from all parts of the Middle East; in certain areas, the genre of shadow play has lasted well into the twentieth century. Alongside these accounts we encounter – particularly during the period of Western colonial expansion into the region – descriptions of performances by Western troupes for residents from European countries and the local cultural élite who could, at least partially, understand performances in one or other European language. Thus, the Egyptian historian, ʿAbd al-raḥmān al-Jabartī, apparently a somewhat bemused member of the audience, gives us his own account of a performance in 1800 by a French troupe during the French occupation that followed Napoleon's invasion of Egypt in 1798. Nor is it surprising that Egypt's most Mediterranean city, Alexandria, should be the site of an Italian theatre by the 1840s. However, such encounters as these remain essentially unidirectional. It is a member of the Christian community in Lebanon who reverses the direction and thus serves as the founding father of the modern Arabic tradition of drama.

Mārūn al-Naqqāsh (d. 1855) was a member of a prosperous family of Lebanese businessmen who knew both French and Italian. He returned from a visit to Italy in 1847 determined to transfer some of the theatrical performances that he had seen to his own society. In 1848 the play, *Al-Bakhīl* (The Miser), was performed in his own home where a stage had been constructed. As the title suggests, the theme of the play shares much in common with Molière's play of the same name, but the script was no mere slavish copy. In an introductory speech to the performance, al-Naqqāsh draws his audience's attention to the existence of two types of performance that he has seen, one involving music called 'opera' and the other not (termed *prosa*). The dialogue in al-Naqqāsh's play is mostly in verse, but a certain amount of regional characterisation is provided by a resort to dialects for some of the characters. The majority, perhaps all, of the play was sung, in that, to cite al-Naqqāsh, the presence of singing would make the new genre more palatable to its audience. This linkage between dramatic performances and music has remained a predominant feature of much modern Arabic drama, not least in the plays of Aḥmad Shawqī which are mostly recalled through the rendition of poems within them as recorded by famous Egyptian singers.

Spurred on by the success of his initial experiment al-Naqqāsh adapted a tale from the *Thousand and One Nights* for his second and most successful play, *Abū al-Ḥasan al-mughaffal aw Hārūn al-Rashīd* (Abū al-Ḥasan the simpleton or Hārūn al-Rashīd, 1849–50). Here too he serves as a pioneer for the future and a link to the past, in that this greatest of all story collections – a product of the popular heritage that we have examined above – in which he finds his theme becomes a major source of inspiration for contemporary playwrights in the 1950s and after. This tale concerning the ʿAbbāsī Caliph, Hārūn al-Rashīd, and his *wazīr*, Jaʿfar, and the way in which they have some fun at the expense of Abū al-Ḥasan, who in an unguarded moment, wishes that he could have real power, provides much opportunity for comedy and for some none too subtle insights into the realities of authority. Al-Naqqāsh wrote a third play, *Al-Salīṭ al-ḥasūd* (The jealous man with a forked tongue, 1853), but these early manifestations of the potential popularity of drama were cut short when he died of a fever two years later. The legacy was not lost however, in that his nephew, Salīm (d. 1884), continued and expanded on his repertoire; in 1876 he took the al-Naqqāsh troupe to the more conducive atmosphere of Egypt.

Al-Naqqāsh had to obtain a decree from the Ottoman authorities before he could perform plays in his home. *Al-Bakhīl*, whose action is already labouring somewhat under the combined weight of music and ornate poetry, is hampered by the presence of a fulsome speech in praise of the Ottoman Sultan in Istanbul – presumbly a *sine qua non* of performance at the time. Just how sensitive the situation was can be illustrated by the career of another pioneer, the Syrian dramatist, actor, and troupe manager, Abū Khalīl al-Qabbānī (1833–1902). In the early 1870s he was encouraged by the Ottoman governor, Ṣubḥī Pāshā, and later by Midḥat Pāshā (1822–83), the famous reformer, to put on some plays, in particular yet another piece inspired by the tales of Hārūn al-Rashīd to be found in the *Thousand and One Nights*. The conservative religious establishment in Damascus, already deeply suspicious of the permissibility and probity of this new medium, was aroused to a fury by the appearance on stage of Hārūn al-Rashīd the Caliph in disguise and obtained a decree from Istanbul ordering the theatre to close. The circumstances surrounding the performance of al-Qabbānī's plays at this time is the subject of an interesting exercise in contemporary experimental drama by another Syrian playwright, Saʿdallāh Wannūs, entitled *Sahrah maʿa Abī Khalīl al-Qabbānī* (A Soirée with Abū Khalīl al-Qabbānī, 1972). Incidentally, Wannūs, an assiduous student of the history and theory of drama, also adapted the story of 'Abū al-Ḥasan al-mughaffal' which al-Naqqāsh used for a later play, entitled *Al-Malik huwa al-malik* (The King's the king, 1977). In Wannūs's play about al-Qabbānī, we witness the struggles that this pioneer of Syrian and Arabic drama had to wage, not only to enable his plays to be performed in the face of political uncertainties (reflected in Wannūs's play by the presence of the Ottoman governor who sits centre-stage on a chair and is regularly replaced) and religious opposition, but also to persuade his audiences that the dramatic genre was one where the role of the audience was to observe and listen rather than to participate with both words and actions. For, while al-Qabbānī also made copious use of music in his performances, the language of the plays was always literary Arabic; as Wannūs tries to show clearly in his play about al-Qabbānī's tribulations, the dignity of the occasion was regarded as being of crucial importance to the new genre's chances of acceptance and success within Arab society. In 1884 al-Qabbānī emulated the al-Naqqāsh family by moving his troupe to Egypt. There he enjoyed a very fruitful two decades of work, directing numerous plays by himself and others until his theatre was burned down in an act of arson in 1900. By training and maintaining an acting troupe that would perform a variety of plays on stage in literary Arabic and by fusing together the elements of drama and music into a medium that would attract a growing audience to the theatre, al-Qabbānī was a major contributor to the complex process of acculturation that was involved in the early development of the Arabic drama tradition.

The Egypt to which the troupes of al-Naqqāsh and al-Qabbānī travelled provided a much more conducive atmosphere for these and other pioneers in Arabic drama. The Khedive Ismāʿīl, who had ruled the country since 1863, had set himself to replicate within Egyptian society as many aspects of Western culture as possible. The city of Cairo had been extended to the banks of the Nile by building a new quarter (called Ismāʿīliyyah, of course) modelled on the plan of Haussmann's Paris with a network of broad boulevards and squares. Where this new city adjoined the old, a large square had been opened up to accommodate the new Cairo Opera House. Verdi's *Aida* had been commissioned for the opening of the house which was to coincide with the celebration in 1869 of the opening of another of Ismāʿīl's grandiose projects, the Suez Canal; in the event Verdi's newest opera was unfinished, and *Rigoletto* took its place. Just half a mile from the site of the Opera House, foreign acting troupes regularly performed plays on an open-air stage in the newly refurbished Ezbekiyya Gardens. It was among these troupes that another pioneer of modern Arabic drama, Yaʿqūb Ṣannūʿ (d. 1912), obtained his early practical experience in the theatre.

Like al-Naqqāsh, Ṣannūʿ had previously encountered the genre at first hand in Europe. He had been born into an Egyptian Jewish family, but, as a youth his precocity attracted the attention of a member of the ruling family, and he had been sent to further his education in Livorgno, Italy. In the early 1870s he determined to gather together a troupe of actors to perform in Arabic on stage. Details of the particular plays have not come down to us, but they appear to have combined dialogues with episodes of music and singing in much the same way as al-Naqqāsh had done. News of these performances attracted the Khedive's attention, and Ṣannūʿ was invited to perform a set of plays before a large and prestigious audience in the Khedive's private theatre in Qaṣr al-Nīl. The plays presented on this occasion were all relatively brief, and the comic nature of their content can be deduced from the titles: *Al-Bint al-ʿaṣriyyah* (Girl of the times, also called *Al-Ānisah ʿalā mūḍah* (Miss à la mode)), *Ghandūr Miṣr* (Posh Egyptian), and *Al-Ḍurratān* (Rival Wives). The story has it that, during the interval between the first two plays and the last, the Khedive called Ṣannūʿ forward and pronounced him to be the 'Molière of Egypt'. This was before he had seen the last play which concerns the problems associated with polygamy, particularly where a second wife is considerably younger than the first. By the end of the performance, the Khedive was not quite so laudatory, having seen this play as an attack on his own conduct. Ṣannūʿ was admonished to be somewhat more subtle if he wished his theatre to remain open. In fact, Ṣannūʿ's theatre did not remain open for long, being closed down in 1872 for reasons that are not entirely clear. The Khedive, increasingly intolerant of Ṣannūʿ's satirical attacks in the press that continually criticised his behaviour and policies, sent him into exile in 1878. Ṣannūʿ

joined a number of prominent Egyptian intellectuals in France from where he made use of his newspaper, *Abū Nazzārah Zarqā'* (The Man with Blue Glasses (yet another reference to himself)), to intensify his attacks on his erstwhile patron. In an echo of both al-Qabbānī's tribulations in Syria and Wannūs's play that uses them as a vehicle for an exploration of the communicative potential of contemporary Arabic drama, Ṣannū''s *Molière Miṣr wa-mā yuqāsīhi* (The Travails of the Molière of Egypt), published in Beirut some forty years after its original conception, provides an interesting, if not necessarily factual, account of the difficulties faced by a theatre director in dealing with the financial and artistic demands of his own troupe.

Ṣannū' was not shy about recording the extent of his own accomplishments, and it is difficult to assess exactly how many plays he himself composed. We have reports of performances of many of them, but an edition of the extant scripts was not published until 1963. Some of the plays are of purely historical interest, such as *Būrṣat Miṣr* (The Egyptian Stock Exchange) which sets a comic view of a double courtship ritual against the background of the many risks associated with speculation on the newly established Stock Exchange where large sums of money were being won (and, more often, lost) in cotton futures. More accomplished as a contribution to the performance tradition of early Arabic drama was *Abū Riḍā wa-Ka'b al-Khayr*, in which a rich widow agrees to help her servant, Abū Riḍā, in his quest for the love of her maid, Ka'b al-Khayr.

There are many features of Ṣannū''s contribution that are important within the history of modern drama in Arabic. In the first place, they were composed in the colloquial of Cairo. While they did in many instances include episodes of music and singing, this aspect of the performances that had so characterised the performances of al-Naqqāsh and al-Qabbānī was gradually diminished. These adjustments in the type and role of language within the performance clearly represent an important change in the nature of the process of communication between stage and audience and served to provide a medium that was more representative of European models of the genre. Added to these factors was Ṣannū''s decision to include within his troupe actresses, albeit non-Egyptians, to perform the female roles.

Within the Egyptian context, mention must also be made of another important figure, Muḥammad 'Uthmān Jalāl (1829–94). Jalāl was a member of the Translation School that played such a key role in the transfer of prominent works of European culture to the Arab societal medium. In Jalāl's case this took the form of a remarkably accomplished transformation of Molière's *Tartuffe* into an Egyptian version, *Al-Shaykh Maṭlūf*, published in 1873 but not performed on stage till 1912. What is so important about this and other translation efforts by Jalāl (including three other plays by Molière published in 1889) was not merely the authenticity of the resulting texts couched in the Arabic poetic genre of *zajal* and the colloquial level of language into which the original text was transposed, but also the highly successful process whereby the characters and scenario were 'Egyptianised'.

As the brief account above makes clear, Egyptian audiences in the latter half of the nineteenth century found themselves presented with an extremely varied fare within the larger context of the theatre. At the opera one could watch Verdi operas (not unknown for their histrionic potential, particularly when the talents of tenors in touring opera companies are concerned). On the stage there were plays based on traditional tales of romances which were performed in the literary language by a constantly expanding collection of troupes. Such performances, involving a collection of managers and actors which now combined the skills of Syria and Lebanon with those of Egypt, continued to be a fusion of the dramatic and the musical. Elsewhere, there were other performances of a more popular kind in terms of both themes (with emphasis on domestic farce and socio-political satire) and language. The reaction of audiences to this wealth of opportunity ranged from the obvious appreciation of the educated élite to sheer bemusement among large segments of the populace. What, for example, was one supposed to make of women who not only appeared unveiled in public, but also portrayed their emotions on stage with such apparent facility? In this particular context it is as well for us to recall that these reactions were by no means restricted to the Arab world in the nineteenth century: the eighteenth-century founders of the Theatre Royal in my native city of Bristol almost immediately encountered opposition from the city fathers because it was presumed to be a den of wickedness; performances were only allowed to continue when announced as being 'specimens of rhetorick'. In spite of the best intentions of al-Qabbānī and others who concerned themselves with the promotion of the dignified nature of this newly imported literary genre, audience reaction often suggested quite the opposite. Indeed for certain members of the audience the occasion clearly had all the attractions of the burlesque. We possess two notable descriptions from the period: one of a prominent English resident, Sir Ronald Storrs, the other by a significant contributor to modern Arabic narrative, Muḥammad al-Muwayliḥī. Storrs attended a performance at the Opera House where 'the Pashas arrived fairly late and remained in a twilight sleep until the ballet, when, as if at the word of command, they awoke and raked the *ballerine* with powerful prismatic binoculars' (*Orientations* (1945), pg. 27). Al-Muwayliḥī does not name the precise location where the drama that his characters witness took place, but proceeds to describe a performance in which

> The curtain went up to reveal a group of actors and actresses on stage. They started performing something best described as halfway between chanting and singing. Whatever it was, human nature revolted against it...

and, in spite of the best efforts of the narrator to explain the moral and educational role of drama, another character seems clearly to echo the views of the Ottoman censors with al-Qabbānī when he suggests that

> Nothing in the Islamic faith permits women to participate in this art form...It's no part of Islamic literature to have plays dealing with Islamic history, its Caliphs and devout men, acted out in public in a fashion which makes use of love and singing as its basic attractions.
> quoted from Allen, *A Period of Time* (1992), p. 369.

It is worth our while to pause for a moment at this point and observe the extent to which the tensions that still impact upon the drama genre in Arabic today are present at the outset. First of all, we may identify the obvious factor of external control exerted by the government and its agencies over every aspect of the complex process of transfer from the playwright's conception to the audience's reception, the complex sequence that we outlined at the beginning of this chapter. Playwrights can be confronted by censorship authorities and theatres can be closed. But beyond this ever present practicality there is also a number of linguistic and aesthetic considerations that continue to impinge, sometimes creatively, sometimes not, on the process of development in the drama medium. By the turn of the century one can already see an obvious split in the medium of theatre performance between the essentially comic fare that is expressed in the spoken language of the audience and the more serious, literary intentions of those who aspire to a higher form of art performed in the written language of the cultural heritage of Arabic, a theatrical mode that is accompanied by interludes of music and singing. Of these two it is the comic that has always proved the more popular, a fact that continues to arouse the complaints of the theatre establishment in Egypt. However, it has been the exploration of the cultural underpinnings and performance potential of each of these two poles that became the task of the generation of playwrights, managers, and actors who succeeded these pioneers. At a later stage in the developmental process, the most successful phase in modern Arabic drama involved, as we will see below, a process of exploiting the large area of potential creative space in between the two.

As is the case with the other genres we are studying in this work, it was during the early decades of this century that many of the issues connected with this confrontation of different heritages and cultural values were explored by playwrights and the troupes who performed their works. Indeed playwrights found a good deal of inspiration for their works in the cultural confrontation itself. Faraḥ Anṭūn (d. 1922), a Lebanese Christian journalist and writer who was a member of the community living in Egypt, criticises the aping of Western bourgeois values in *Miṣr al-jadīdah wa-Miṣr al-qadīmah* (Modern Egypt, Old Egypt, 1913), a play with a rather complicated plot which was performed by the famous troupe of Jūrj Abyaḍ in the 1920s. Anṭūn also addressed the theme through a historical play about the Crusades, *Al-Sulṭān Ṣalāḥ al-dīn wa-Mamlakat Urūsalīm* (Sultan Ṣalāḥ al-dīn (Saladin) and the Kingdom of Jerusalem, 1914), in which, needless to say, the message is more concerned with the broader issues associated with Western incursions into the Middle East. Anṭūn was one of the earliest playwrights to experiment with the issue of levels of language to be used in dramatic works. His solution, that of scripting the high-class roles in the standard written language and the low-class ones in the colloquial, was one that proved effective within the theatrical milieu of the times; it was imitated by a number of writers. However, while acknowledging its ingenuity – particularly at such an early stage in the development of modern Arabic drama – we have also to admit that it made use of a criterion (class) to create a distinction that did not actually exist in linguistic terms.

The Crusades provide the theme for a significant historical play by another dramatist of the period, Ibrāhīm Ramzī (1884–1949), *Abṭāl al-Manṣūrah* (The Heroes of al-Manṣūrah, 1915), a work in which the famous Queen of Egypt, Shajarat al-durr, plays a prominent part. Ramzī, a translator of numerous Western playwrights into Arabic, reflects the growing sophistication of the theatre medium by the attention that he devotes in his scripts to stage directions, the scenario, and the costumes to be worn. Like Anṭūn, he too wrote an important play that addresses itself to the societal issues associated with Westernisation,

Dukhūl al-ḥammām mish izayy khurūguh (Going in Bathhouses isn't like Leaving Them, 1916). This work written entirely in the colloquial language explores the already popular theme of the clash between the values of the city, usually presented by varieties of venal characters from both sexes, and the more traditional provinces, personified by the figure of the rustic *ʿumdah* (headman of the village), this being a principal theme of the latter part of al-Muwayliḥī's famous piece of narrative, *Ḥadīth ʿĪsā ibn Hishām* (1907). In the skilful hands of the great actor-playwright, Najīb al-Rīḥānī (1892–1949) – with his famous character, Kishkish Bey, this theme was to thrive in Egyptian comedy well into the twentieth century. Ramzī's play is an accomplished early contribution to the development of comic drama in Arabic, one that turns away from the more traditionally popular slapstick varieties of farce in favour of a greater attention to the prejudices and foibles that, through portrayal of attitude and clever use of language, may serve as an equally effective source of entertainment.

The most important figure of the period however is Muḥammad Taymūr (1891–1921), not so much for the dramatic works that he wrote during his brief life, but more for the directions in which his critical writings pointed. Taymūr came from an illustrious and wealthy family of littérateurs: his father, aunt, and brother were all major writers, and he himself contributed to a number of genres, not least the short story. After spending three years in France and coming to understand both the effectiveness of the drama and the perceived faults of its Egyptian manifestation, he set himself to identify criteria for good drama and performance of it, ruing in particular the prevalence of performances of translated works and the lack of what can only be termed local colour in the indigenous tradition, most notably in the matter of language. As if to prove his point, Taymūr appears to have completely recast his play, *Al-ʿUṣfūr fī al-qafaṣ* (Bird in the Cage, 1918) – in which a miserly landlord finds himself outmanoeuvred by his Levantine maid and his own son – from a first version in the written language to an expanded four-act work in the colloquial. With another play, *ʿAbd al-Sattār Efendī*, 1918) – a more farcical piece involving a usual cast of characters, henpecked husband, shrewish wife, marriageable daughter, and manipulative and nubile maid, Taymūr sets himself to provide a counter to the popularity of the roles being played by actors such as Najīb al-Rīḥānī. For the first performance of the play, Taymūr made use of the famous troupe of Munīrah al-Mahdiyyah (d. 1965). The title role was played by none other than al-Rīḥānī's rival, ʿAzīz ʿĪd, the role of the son by another famous actor, Zakī Ṭulaymāt, and the important role of the housemaid being taken by Rūz al-Yūsuf who was to become one of the most famous figures in Egyptian drama.

This period saw the heyday of a number of theatre companies, many of which were offshoots from the Syrian troupes that arrived in the latter decades of the nineteenth century, those of Iskandar Faraḥ (who counted among his protegés Najīb al-Rīḥānī, ʿAzīz ʿĪd, and the famous singer, Shaykh Salāmah al-Ḥijāzī (1852–1917)), and of Jūrj Abyaḍ (1880–1959). Both as director and actor, Abyaḍ set himself to represent the classic aspect of Arabic drama, establishing through his acting contributions to his own productions a yardstick for the more histrionic qualities of the literary level of language as a medium of drama. By contrast, a host of actors and troupes, Yūsuf Wahbī, ʿAlī al-Kassār, and ʿAzīz ʿĪd, for example, concentrated on more popular fare. Another of these troupes was that of the two brothers, ʿAbdallāh and Zakī ʿUkāshah, who built a theatre alongside the Ezbekiyya Gardens in 1920, and used it to offer performances that would endeavour to strike some kind of balance between the various extremes that the combination of language and cultural attitudes had engendered. Among the young writers whose plays were performed by this troupe in the 1920s was one who, fearing the societal opprobrium associated with the theatre milieu, chose to sign the scripts of a series of plays as Ḥusayn Tawfīq. Using his real name, Tawfīq al-Ḥakīm (1898–1987), this young man was to become the acknowledged doyen of Arabic drama this century. However, before we consider the course of his career, we should consider briefly the beginnings of drama in other parts of the Arab world.

BEGINNINGS ELSEWHERE IN THE ARAB WORLD

The above account illustrates the way in which Egyptian society in the latter half of the nineteenth century was able to provide a testing ground for the development of drama that was conducive and stimulating not only to indigenous talent but also to those littérateurs from other Arab countries who found within its borders a refuge from unfavourable political and social conditions elsewhere. It is for this reason that we have devoted our attention thus far to developments in drama and its performance within a single country, one that for a considerable period served in effect as the spawning ground for the developing traditions of two separate regions. In other areas of the Arab world the situation was much less favourable, and thus the time frames involved are quite different.

The case of Abū Khalīl al-Qabbānī that we have noted above provides a ready illustration of the methods through which the strict censorship prevalent within the Ottoman provinces (other than Egypt) was applied. A very public medium such as the theatre was a readily available and thus inevitable target for such attention. As numerous commentators on the development of drama in the area of Ottoman Syria (thus including Lebanon) have pointed out, the dampening effects that censorship was almost bound to have on creativity, when coupled with the departure of large numbers of Christian writers – beginning in the 1860s and continuing well into the twentieth century, were to have deleterious consequences for the theatre. After what one writer has termed a series of 'false starts', it was not until the period following the Second World War that a tradition of drama began to develop in the region.

In other regions of the Arab world, the stimulus needed to persuade members of the literary community to take the initial steps in establishing a local tradition of drama seems to have taken the form of visits from touring theatre companies. An Egyptian troupe visited Tunis, for example, as early as 1908, and by 1932 there were four local companies in existence. One of them visited Morocco in 1923 and aroused sufficient interest for a local company to be created in the following year. Jūrj Abyaḍ's famous Egyptian troupe toured widely and had a similar impact during a visit to Iraq in 1926. However, there remained much to be learned about the drama genre in all of these countries: the preparation of scripts, the training of actors, and performance practice on stage. The complexity of the process was such that many decades were required to bring Arabic theatre in these regions to genuine fruition. In all these aspects Egypt continued to provide the major and central example of a drama tradition at a more advanced stage of development.

THE ACHIEVEMENTS OF TAWFĪQ AL-ḤAKĪM

Tawfiq al-Ḥakīm must be reckoned one of the most significant figures in twentieth-century Arabic literature. His literary career, primarily within the realm of drama but also including (as we have already noted) major contributions to the early development of fiction, is essentially coterminous with the drama's achievement of a literary status within Egypt, a process in which he was the major proponent. The triumphs and failures that are represented by the reception of his enormous output of plays are emblematic of the issues that have confronted the drama genre as it has endeavoured to adapt its complex modes of communication to the societies of the Arab world. The problems that they raise, some of which have already been alluded to in the sections above, remain central to any discussion of the present state and future direction of the genre.

When al-Ḥakīm's parents sent their son to Paris in 1925 to complete a doctorate in law, it was, no doubt, their hope to put an end to the brief career of 'Ḥusayn Tawfiq'. Quite the opposite proved to be the case. Like many other Egyptian students who have been sent to Europe to study, al-Ḥakīm steeped himself in Western culture, reading avidly (although rarely the law texts he was supposed to be studying), attending concerts and performances of plays and opera, and conversing with the wide variety of intellectuals in the French capital. Above all, he imbibed the sense of the role and power of the dramatic medium in its Western form and determined to replicate it in the context of his own society. He returned to Cairo in 1928 without a law degree, but filled with ideas for literary projects, some of them already in draft form. He found the theatre scene dominated by the comic presentations of Najīb al-Rīḥānī and ʿAlī al-Kassār and by the histrionics of Yūsuf Wahbī. At first, al-Ḥakīm attempted to reconcile the vision of drama with which he had returned with the actual situation in which he found the genre upon his return, writing a series of plays of which one, *Raṣāṣah fī al-qalb* (A Bullet Through the Heart, 1931), a work written in a fast-moving colloquial language about the misadventures of a lovesick young man, is a genuine contribution to the development of what might be termed non-slapstick comedy. It is perhaps typical of the situation in which al-Ḥakīm found himself at this time that squabbles over the way to convey its comic content and over the lead role resulted in its not being performed till much later.

The cause of 'serious' drama, at least in its textual form, was in the process of being given a boost by one of the Arab world's greatest littérateurs, Aḥmad Shawqī, 'the prince of the poets', who during his latter years penned a number of verse dramas with themes culled from Egyptian and Islamic history; these included *Maṣraʿ Kliyūbatrā* (The Death of Cleopatra, 1929), *Majnūn Laylā* (the name of a famous *ghazal* poet, 1931), *Amīrat al-Andalus* (The Spanish Princess, 1932), and *ʿAlī Bey al-kabīr* (a ruler of Egypt during the eighteenth century), a play originally written in 1893 and later revised. However, in spite of the superb quality of much of the poetry in these works, they gained popularity mostly through the medium of music as famous singers came to adopt favourite poetic segments from the plays almost as signature tunes. Between the popular traditions of farcical comedy and melodrama and the performance of translated versions of European dramatic masterpieces, there still remained a void within which an indigenous tradition of serious drama could develop. Al-Ḥakīm's desire to replicate the European tradition was thus timely in the extreme, and it is for that reason that the publication and performance of his play, *Ahl al-Kahf* (The People of the Cave, 1933) is such a significant event in Egyptian drama.

The story of 'the people of the cave' is to be found in the eighteenth Sūrah of the Qur'ān as well as in other sources. It concerns the tale of the seven sleepers of Ephesus who, in order to escape the Roman persecution of Christians, take refuge in a cave. They sleep for three hundred years, and wake up in a completely different era – without realising it, of course. In al-Ḥakīm's play their number is reduced to three. While they are greeted as symbols of resurrection by their amazed hosts (including the ruler's daughter, Priskā, who shows an uncanny resemblance to the daughter of the earlier ruler, including her name), they find that they are unable to adapt to the changed circumstances and return, one by one, to the cave from which they emerged. The play ends with a dramatic touch, as Priskā decides to join them. In its use of overarching themes such as that of rebirth into a new world and a predilection for returning to the past, al-Ḥakīm's play obviously touches upon some of the broad cultural topics that were of major concern to intellectuals at the time, and, because of the play's obvious seriousness of purpose, most critics have chosen to emphasise such features. However, the tale itself, with its various venues, discoveries of the changes in time, recognition encounters, and anguished attempts at adaptation, provides ample opportunities for dramatic effect, and al-Ḥakīm makes good use of them. The dialogue is composed in the literary language and at certain points certainly encourages a more declamatory style of delivery, but there are also lively passages of conversation.

As if to show that the establishment of a literary tradition of drama had been a preoccupation of his for some time, al-Ḥakīm produced another major work within a year, *Shahrazād* (Scheherazade, 1934). While the principal character is, of course, the famous narrator of the *Thousand and One Nights* collection, the scenario for this play is set after all the tales have been told. Having been cured of his vicious anger against the female sex by the story-telling virtuosity of the woman who is now his wife, King Shahrayār now abandons his previous ways and embarks on a journey in quest of knowledge, only to discover himself caught in a dilemma whose focus is Shahrazād herself:

SHAHRAZĀD: Do you still want me to reveal my secret?
SHAHRAYĀR: Shahrazad?!
SHAHRAZĀD: Why are you looking at me that way?
SHAHRAYĀR: Don't make fun of me!
SHAHRAZĀD (in a whisper): You don't deserve it!
SHAHRAYĀR: What are you saying?
SHAHRAZĀD: What do you want to know?
SHAHRAYĀR: You know that full well!
SHAHRAZĀD: You want to know who I am.
SHAHRAYĀR: Yes.
SHAHRAZĀD (with a smile): I'm a beautiful body. Isn't my body gorgeous?
SHAHRAYĀR (yelling): To Hell with your gorgeous body!
SHAHRAZĀD: And I've a kind heart. Haven't I got a kind heart?
SHAHRAYĀR: To Hell with that too!
SHAHRAZĀD: Are you going to deny you loved my body and heart?!
SHAHRAYĀR: That is all in the past...past. (as though talking to himself) Today I'm just a wretched man.

Through a linkage to the ancient goddess, Isis, Shahrazād emerges as the ultimate mystery, the source of life and knowledge.

When the National Theatre Troupe was formed in Egypt in 1935, with the poet Khalīl Muṭrān as its director, the first production that it mounted was *The People of the Cave*, staged at the Cairo Opera House. Bearing in mind what we have noted above about the complexities of stage production, it is hardly surprising that performances of al-Ḥakīm's play were a failure. Not only were the theatre personnel, accustomed to performing and producing farces and melodramas, unprepared to put on performances of such a piece, but, equally important, the audience seemed unprepared or unwilling to appreciate a play in which the action on stage was so limited in comparison with the more familiar types of drama. On the other hand, these plays received a warm reception from prominent literary critics of the time. The most famous, Ṭāhā Ḥusayn, a diehard defender of the literary language, termed *The People of the Cave* 'a significant event, not just for modern

Arabic literature, but the whole literary tradition of Arabic'. His review of *Shahrazād* is laudatory, but the more guarded comments that he makes point to issues that were to dog al-Ḥakīm and Arabic drama for some time:

Shahrazād, like *The People of the Cave*, represents a new art form in our modern literature. I cannot claim that it represents the highest ideal in drama or anything close to it, but I will say that it is a carefully wrought work of art...In this play I cannot fault al-Ḥakīm's grammatical usage and his occasional long-windedness as I did earlier with *The People of the Cave*...It would be impossible to have this work acted in Egypt at the moment for two extremely obvious reasons. The story is too highbrow for most audiences who flock to the theatre; only the intelligentsia would enjoy it. Secondly actors who could perform this play and present it authentically in a fashion appropriate to its beauty and precision do not yet exist in Egypt...This is therefore a play to be read rather than acted...

The audience reception for these plays and comments such as this last one led al-Ḥakīm to develop the notion that his plays were indeed contributions to 'théâtre des idées', plays intended for reading rather than performance. However, in spite of such critical controversies, he continued to write plays with philosophical themes culled from a variety of cultural sources: *Pygmalion* (1942), an interesting blend of the legends of Pygmalion and Narcissus; *Sulaymān al-ḥakīm* (Solomon the Wise, 1943), and *Al-Malik Ūdīb* (King Oedipus, 1949). These plays, along with the prefaces in which al-Ḥakīm outlined his own rationale for writing them, have occupied a large share of the critical debate about his status in the development of modern Arabic drama, but it is perhaps a reflection of the issues we have raised above that *Shahrazād* only received its first stage performance in the 1960s; even then, in spite of improvements in both acting techniques and stage production, it was not a success.

Bearing in mind both that al-Ḥakīm was holding posts in the Egyptian civil service, first as a public prosecutor and later in the Ministries of Education and Social Affairs, until 1943, and that he managed to produce a number of works in fictional form, his continued devotion to the cause of serious drama is all the more remarkable. Some of his frustrations with the performance aspect were diverted by an invitation in 1945 to write a series of short plays for publication in newspaper article form. These works were gathered together into two collections, *Masraḥ al-mujtamaʿ* (Theatre of Society, 1950) and *al-Masraḥ al-munawwaʿ* (Theatre Miscellany, 1956). The fact that these plays were to be published in printed form only and in a newspaper at that appears to have given him a sense of release from the trammels that clearly beset his attempts in the more public sphere, and he chose a set of topics that were at once more topical and conducive to livelier dialogue. Several are concerned with the foibles of mankind, none more so than *ʿImārat al-muʿallim Kandūz* (Boss man Kandūz's Block of Flats) in which a rapacious property owner's real estate and his daughters' prospects for marriage become intertwined with hilarious results. But the most memorable of these plays is *Ughniyyat al-mawt* (Death Song), a one-act play that with masterly economy depicts the fraught atmosphere in Upper Egypt as a family awaits the return of the eldest son, a student in Cairo, in order that he may carry out a murder in response to the expectations of a blood feud. As the Egyptian critic, ʿAlī al-Rāʿī, rightly notes, these short plays, while perhaps a distraction from al-Ḥakīm's quest for a public receptivity for serious drama, served to hone his skill in couching topics of more direct relevance to the present day in a more fast-paced framework.

The Egyptian revolution of 1952 found al-Ḥakīm serving once again in a civil service role, this time as Director of the National Library (Dār al-Kutub), a position he had accepted at the request of Ṭāhā Ḥusayn. By now he was the unchallenged doyen of the Egyptian, and to a large extent the Arab, theatre scene. As such, his response to the societal changes brought about by the revolution was a significant one, namely the play *Al-Aydī al-nāʿimah* (Soft Hands, 1954). The 'soft hands' of the title refer to those of a prince of the former royal family who finds himself without a meaningful role in the new society, a position in which he is joined by a young academic who has just finished writing a doctoral thesis on the uses of the Arabic preposition *ḥattā*. The play explores in an amusing, yet rather obviously didactic fashion, the ways in which these two apparently useless individuals set about identifying roles for themselves in the new socialist context. By the time the play comes to an end, jobs have been found for the two men, and, as is often the case, marriage is used as a means of symbolising the new situation, one through which al-Ḥakīm's desire for social reconciliation is clearly expressed.

While this play may be lacking in subtlety, it was certainly a popular reflection of an era of immense political and social change; in the context of al-Ḥakīm's development it clearly illustrates the way in which he had developed his technique in order to broach topics of contemporary interest, not least through a closer linkage between the pacing of dialogue and actions on stage. In 1960 al-Ḥakīm was to provide further illustration of this development in technique with yet another play set in an earlier period of Egyptian history, *al-Sulṭān al-ḥāʾir* (The Sultan Perplexed). The play explores in a most effective manner the issue of the legitimation of power. A Mamlūk Sultan at the height of his power is suddenly faced with the fact that he has never been manumitted and that he is thus ineligible to be ruler. The best legal minds are brought to bear on the subject, and the Sultan is informed that there is no avoiding a sale in which he will be the commodity on offer. The Sultan is purchased by a woman who is generally believed to be a madam and the owner of the local house of pleasure. A dispute now erupts involving the Chief Justice and the Sultan's wily Minister. It becomes clear that, unless the Sultan wishes to follow his Minister's advice and resort to the use of force to solve his dilemma, he will have to accede to his purchaser's wish that he spend the night in her house. The Sultan agrees to do so, only to discover that the woman in question is a respectable and cultured widow. Outside the house meanwhile, the decision is made to shorten the night by ordering the muezzin to sound the call to prayer early. Even though she has been robbed of part of her payment, the woman manumits the Sultan as agreed. The play ends with the Sultan commanding that the woman be afforded every honour.

By 1960 when this play was published, some of the initial euphoria and hope engendered by the Revolution itself, given expression in *al-Aydī al-nāʿimah*, had begun to fade somewhat. To be sure, there had been some spectacular successes: the ignominious withdrawal of British and French forces following the Suez débâcle of 1956, and the building of the Aswan High Dam. But the Egyptian people found itself confronting other political realities: the use of the secret police to squelch the public expression of opinion, for example, the personality cult surrounding the figure of ʿAbd al-Nāṣir (Nasser), and the obvious problems associated with the newly created United Arab Republic with Syria. In such a historical context al-Ḥakīm's play can be seen as a somewhat courageous statement of the need for even the mightiest to adhere to the laws of the land and specifically a plea to the ruling military regime to eschew the use of violence and instead seek legitimacy through application of the law. Beyond these issues of political and social significance however it needs to be noted that, with this play, al-Ḥakīm uses history as the basis of a drama that has action, lively dialogue, and much comic impact. It is both a contribution to Arabic dramatic literature and excellent entertainment. That it should also have enjoyed popular acclaim on the stage is a tribute to al-Ḥakīm's tenacity in pursuing his goals.

Al-Ḥakīm's devoted services to the cause of the literary language, in both fictional and dramatic form, were rewarded in May 1954 when he was elected to the Arabic Language Academy in Cairo; the speech of recommendation was made by Ṭāhā Ḥusayn. With such a credential behind him and the 'winds of change' engendered by the Revolution blowing all around him – not least in the expression by many writers of the need for commitment (*iltizām*) in literature, al-Ḥakīm once again addressed himself to the search for the most appropriate level of language to use in drama. The play, *al-Ṣafqah* (The Deal, 1956), is very much a product of its time, the period of post-revolutionary agricultural reform: the central theme is the same as that of 'Abd al-raḥmān al-Sharqāwī's famous novel, *al-Arḍ* (The Earth, 1954), namely, land, its ownership, and the exploitation of poor peasant farmers. But what is of particular interest within a survey of al-Ḥakīm's oeuvre is that he not only continues his exploration of current political and social topics, but succeeds to a large degree in facing some of the other problems connected with drama performance that we have discussed above: one such is the question of the techniques of the theatre building itself, staging, scenery, and the like. In this play the scenario is outdoors, focusing primarily on a village square – something that at least was a beginning to the process of addressing the question of the broader audience for drama for whom the theatres in the big cities were both physically and metaphorically inaccessible. Al-Ḥakīm's most experimental gesture here was to couch the dialogue in something he termed 'a third language', one that could be read as a text in the standard written language of literature, but that could also be performed on stage in a way which was not exactly the idiom of the colloquial dialect but was certainly comprehensible to a larger population than the literate élite of the city, thus combining with the scenario feature just mentioned in broadening the potential audience for the play. Needless to say, al-Ḥakīm's search for a middle ground in this and other plays (such as *al-Warṭah* (The Bind, 1966)) did not satisfy the proponents of either side in the continuing dispute over the appropriate language for Arabic drama, but its acknowledgement of the existence of a myriad different levels of language between the literary and colloquial poles was at the very least a successful attempt at compromise. There is perhaps an irony in the fact that another of al-Ḥakīm's plays of the 1960s, *Yā ṭāliʿ al-shajarah* (1962; *The*

Tree Climber, 1966), was one of his most accomplished works from this point of view, precisely because its use of the literary language in the dialogue was a major contributor to the non-reality of the atmosphere in this absurdist drama involving extensive passages of non-communication between husband and wife.

Al-Ḥakīm continued to write plays during the 1960s, among the most popular of which were *Maṣīr ṣarṣār* (1966; *The Fate of a Cockroach*, 1973) and *Bank al-qalaq* (Anxiety Bank, 1967). Following the 1967 débâcle and especially during the presidency of Anwar al-Sādāt, al-Ḥakīm tended to play the role of elder statesman of the Egyptian literary establishment and as such was frequently involved in cultural controversies. The most notable of these occurred in 1974 at the height of Sādāt's campaign to expose the foibles of the Nasser era when al-Ḥakīm decided to publish a manuscript that had previously only circulated privately. Entitled *ʿAwdat al-waʿy* (Return of Consciousness), it cast a very critical eye over the Nasser era and aroused a large amount of discussion and contumely.

The links between literary creativity and the press have always been strong during the developmental period of modern Arabic literature. In the 1970s such a relationship had been formalised by the prominent Cairene daily, *al-Ahrām*, in that three of the Arab world's greatest littérateurs, were supplementing their meagre revenues from literary publication by writing regular columns, each of them the acknowledged master of a particular genre: Tawfīq al-Ḥakīm, the dramatist; Najīb Maḥfūẓ, the novelist; and Yūsuf Idrīs, the short-story writer. That al-Ḥakīm should have been assigned the largest office of the three was, one must assume, an acknowledgement by his colleagues of his undoubted status as one of the major pioneer figures in modern Arabic literature and, in the particular realm of theatre, of his overarching role as the sole founder of an entire literary tradition, as Ṭāhā Ḥusayn had earlier made clear. His struggles on behalf of Arabic drama as a literary genre, its techniques, and its language, are coterminous with the achievement of a central role in contemporary Arab political and social life.

EGYPTIAN DRAMA AFTER THE REVOLUTION

Such is the prestige of Tawfīq al-Ḥakīm within the theatre tradition in Arabic that we have used his entire career as a means of illustrating the fortunes of the genre as a whole. Following the Egyptian Revolution of 1952 a complete generation of younger playwrights came to the fore who were able to build and expand upon the basis that had been laid by al-Ḥakīm himself and by other prominent pre-revolution dramatists such as Maḥmūd Taymūr (1894–1973) and ʿAlī Aḥmad Bākathīr (1910–69), the latter of whom had been much inspired by the verse dramas of Aḥmad Shawqī. In the decade preceding the 1967 war it appears to have been a deliberate policy of the Egyptian government to allow the drama to serve as a safety valve for public opinion at a time when censorship was otherwise extremely tight; as one critic puts it, drama served as a kind of 'popular parliament'. In what may be regarded as an uncanny resemblance to the favourable conditions for drama that Egypt provided in the nineteenth century, this policy was to provide a conducive societal context for the development of a lively theatre tradition that was not replicated elsewhere in the Arab world. A number of theatres and companies received financial backing from the Ministry of Culture; several excellent directors returned from study and practice abroad to apply their craft in new and experimental ways; and a cadre of drama critics was provided, through the journal *al-Masraḥ*, with a means of discussing the theoretical issues involved in production and of criticising the performances themselves. For many this particular decade in the recent history of Egyptian drama remains a focus of nostalgia, a time when every aspect of the dramatic endeavour – from its conception in the mind of the writer to its reception by a numerous public – seemed to promise an exciting future.

This younger generation of playwrights had, for the most part, been participants in the demonstrations that marked the fraught period in Egyptian political and social life following the Second World War. It is hardly surprising that these strident calls for social transformation were accompanied by a demand for a change in the societal role for literature; in a word, for commitment (*iltizām*). The 1952 Egyptian Revolution and its ramifications outside of Egypt itself provided a ready political and social context and impetus for such a movement, and playwrights were among the first to appreciate the potential linkages between the goals of committed literature and the genre in which they would couch their creative writing. First among this new generation was Nuʿmān ʿĀshūr (1918–87). His play, *An-Nās illī taḥt* (Downstairs Folk), was produced in 1956 and was an instant sensation. Here was a work of Egyptian drama that, during a period of profound and disruptive societal transition, addressed itself to a serious contemporary subject, namely the modes of interaction between people from a variety of professions and classes, all of whom inhabit a single building owned by

Bahīga Hānem. The play is written in a colloquial dialect that allows for a good deal of verbal repartee while retaining the authenticity of the social functions that each character represents. With the deft use of a comedy that has been liberated from the more physical stage actions associated with popular farce, ʿĀshūr managed to present his audiences with a play in which they could recognise the problems and foibles of their neighbours and themselves. ʿĀshūr repeated this formula in two further plays, *Al-Nās illī fo'* (Upstairs Folk, 1957), dealing with the fate of the upper classes of Egyptian society following the Revolution, and, the best of the triad, *ʿĀʾilat al-dūghrī* (Straight-ahead Family, 1962), a less optimistic piece that reflects the doubts of a period when the Revolution's initial flush of success had to some extent been replaced by serious concern about its future direction. Here the middle-class family implied by the title struggles on the brink of financial ruin as its members desperately try to improve their lot; the tensions involved lead to a breakdown of the family's very structure.

There was, needless to say, no shortage of interesting and relevant topics for the playwright within a society that was going through a period of such rapid and profound transformation. Many writers followed ʿĀshūr's early lead, and the 1960s proved to be a particularly fertile decade, with distinguished contributions from such writers as Saʿd al-dīn Wahbah (b. 1925), Maḥmūd Diyāb (1932–83), and ʿAlī Sālim (b. 1936). Both Wahbah and Diyāb concentrated initially on the life of the village. Most notable among Wahbah's plays of this type is *al-Sibinsā* (The Guard's Van/Caboose, 1963), a heavily symbolic play that revolves around the discovery in a provincial village of a 'bomb' and its subsequent disappearance; the true nature of this bomb and the role of the title in symbolising the processes of social transformation are made clear when at the end of the play one of the village peasants yells out to Darwīsh, the village opportunist:

> Don't try running away, Darwīsh! There's no escape for you and your Pāshās and Beys! Where are you going to hide? The bomb's going to explode, and everything will come crashing down with it. The country's full of bombs, and they're all going to explode. Everything up front will go to the rear. First-class passengers will be in the guard's van, and vice versa.

Diyāb's *Al-Zawbaʿah* (The Storm, 1964) is a brilliant work that succeeds in portraying the tensions that are aroused in a village community by the news that Ḥusayn Abū Shāmah, a villager who has been framed for a crime he did not commit and has spent the last twenty years in jail, is about to be released and has vowed vengeance. The resulting atmosphere leads to a series of dramatic revelations concerning the real perpetrators of the crime that led to Ḥusayn's imprisonment. Even though it eventually emerges that Ḥusayn has actually died several years ago, the dynamics of village authority have been changed for ever. Not least among the reasons for the forceful impact that this play had in performance was that the language chosen by Diyāb was not merely colloquial but the particular dialect of the Sharqiyyah province where the action of the play is set.

Both Wahbah and Diyāb also had considerable success with other plays that focused on different aspects of society. Wahbah's *Sikkat is-salāmah* (Road to Safety, 1965) brings a cross-section of Egyptian professionals face to face with death as their car is marooned in the desert, while *Bīr al-sillim* (The Stairwell, 1966) shows the way in which the incapacitation of Shubrāwī – an unseen father-figure whose illness causes him to lose his traditional moral hold over his wife and children, is exploited by each member of the family, apart that is from his daughter, ʿAzīzah. Diyāb was one of many writers to be completely overwhelmed by the defeat in the 1967 June War. His first work to appear following this major cataclysm was a group of three one-act plays, *Rajul ṭayyib fī thalāth ḥikāyat* (A Good Man in Three Stories, 1970), in which the effective creation of an atmosphere of callous indifference on the part of various symbols of authority reflects the black despair of the period.

ʿAlī Sālim's mode of confronting the unpleasant realities of his intellectual and political surroundings has been through comedy, seen at its most enjoyable in his pointed satire of the all-pervasive triumph of bureaucracy. In his first play, *An-Nās illī fi-s-samāʾ t-tāminah* (People in Eighth Heaven, 1966), we are taken to a 'heaven' where scientists have created an automatic paradise in which non-rational sentiments such as love can have no place. But Sālim's sarcasm finds its readiest target in *Bīr al-qamḥ* (The Wheat-pit, 1968), in which the archaeological discoveries of an amateur Egyptologist, ʿAmm Ḥusayn (who is a waiter in normal life), lead to a take-over of the dig by the official academic and governmental bureaucracy and to a chaos so complete that the importance of Ḥusayn's original discovery is itself buried. While Sālim's talent clearly lies in the medium of satire, he has also written a number of more serious dramas, of which *Kūmīdiyā Ūdīb aw anta illī ʾatalt al-waḥsh* (The Comedy of Oedipus, or You're the One Who Killed the Beast, 1970) is the most accomplished. In this play, Sālim takes the characters from the

Greek myth of Oedipus, but places them in the environment of the ancient Egyptian city of Thebes. They are used as a vehicle for the exploration of the ways in which political authority can be manipulated and the media can be exploited to persuade and mislead the populace. Bearing in mind the relevance of these themes to Egyptian political life at the time of writing and the closeness with which the theatre in Egypt has been monitored, it is hardly surprising that Sālim chose to couch his bitter criticism in the form of a 'comedy' about Oedipus.

Most of the dramatists whom we have considered thus far write on the assumption that the question of language use has been resolved in favour of the colloquial. Indeed the plays that we have discussed did receive a warm reception from Egyptian audiences who saw their experiences and concerns reflected in plays in their normal language of communication. However, for those playwrights who wish to continue al-Ḥakīm's efforts by carrying Arabic drama to a broader Arab world audience, the problem of language remains. One dramatist who has addressed himself to this issue is Alfred Faraj (b. 1929). *Ḥallāq Baghdād* (The Barber of Baghdad, 1963), while not his first contribution to the drama, was the work that secured him a popular audience. The play actually consists of two separate tales, one from the *Thousand and One Nights* and the other from a collection attributed to the great classical littérateur, al-Jāḥiẓ. Disguised caliphs, damsels in distress, tyrannical viziers, and incredible twists of fate are all orchestrated around the meddlesome prattle of a barber who vows to see justice done in spite of the best efforts of authority–a theme, needless to say, with echoes in modern, as well as earlier, times. Among the features that particularly appealed to critics who attended performances of this play was Faraj's gift at developing a dialogue that made use of a simplified version of the written language, thus contributing in no small way to the pacing of the drama and, not insignificantly, to its potential for presentation to audiences elsewhere than Egypt. In this context, Faraj's own opinions on the language of Arabic drama are of considerable interest:

> The question of language use in drama cannot be resolved now; it may also prove difficult in the future...The way in which a new, fully dramatic language will emerge can only come about through serious efforts in the spheres not only of written and colloquial languages but also in the middle languages between the two poles. (*Al-Majallah*, July 1965: 127)

Faraj also enjoyed considerable success with *Sulaymān al-Ḥalabī* (Sulaymān from Aleppo, 1965), a complex and fast-moving drama about a young Syrian student who murders the French General Kléber in Cairo during the brief French occupation of the country at the end of the eighteenth century, and *al-Zīr Sālim* (Prince Sālim, 1967), based on the events of the famous popular narrative set in pre-Islamic times (mentioned in ch. 5). Both these works, with their tendency to rely on a montage of rapidly changing scenes, were a severe test of their director's ingenuity; it is perhaps a measure of the standards of this era that both plays were received with popular acclaim. However, Faraj's most accomplished play from all points of view takes him for his source materials back to the *Thousand and One Nights*: *ʿAlī Janāh al-Tabrīzī wa-tābiʿuhu Quffah* (ʿAlī Janāh from Tabrīz and Quffah, his henchman, 1969). Once again, a theme from the classical heritage – that of a 'wealthy' merchant whose caravan laden with fabulous goods has been delayed and who needs 'temporary credit' – conveys its message very directly to a contemporary audience. Those watching the action of the play–as merchants fall over themselves to grant credit, as the King marries his daughter to ʿAlī the merchant, as the justifiably suspicious vizier is constantly subverted in his attempts to discover the truth, and as ʿAlī himself dispenses all his wealth to the poor of his host city – needed no additional cues to see this picture of an idealist dreamer surrounded by greedy opportunists and yes-men as both a wonderfully entertaining and well structured piece of drama and as an allegory of their own contemporary political realities.

We began this chapter with a retrospective that used as its point of departure some articles on Egyptian drama written by Yūsuf Idrīs. Idrīs was one of a group of writers who began by contributing examples to the kind of drama of social commentary that we have described above, but who went on to explore the more experimental and absurdist aspects of the genre; and no more so than in al-*Farāfīr* (The Farfūrs, 1964), the play that he presented as evidence of the application of the theories he had explored in his articles. This two-act play invokes features of drama from a number of sources: the traditional genres that we have described above; the *théâtre en ronde* with actors placed within the audience itself; and the more farcical aspects of popular comedies. As the persona of the 'author' who opens the performance gradually loses control of proceedings, the audience finds itself involved – seemingly literally – in a wide-ranging discussion of the nature and justification of authority and the use of employment in a futile search for meaning in life. As the twin characters of the Master, born to give orders, and the Farfūr, a stooge doomed to everlasting submission to commands, argue about possible jobs in the face of their wives' demand that they earn money, the possibilities for humorous repartee are endless. The following two extracts from the first act are taken from a succession of such exchanges:

FARFŪR: How about being an intellectual?
MASTER: And what are they supposed to do?
FARFŪR: Absolutely nothing.
MASTER: How can that be?
FARFŪR: If you need to ask that question, you're clearly not going to be an intellectual!

MASTER: How about me driving a cab?
FARFŪR: How good's your vision?
MASTER: Excellent.
FARFŪR: Do you know your way around Cairo?
MASTER: I know every single street.
FARFŪR: D'you think you can sit for a whole hour without raining curses on everyone's religion?
MASTER: Certainly!
FARFŪR: Then there's no way you can be a cabbie.

Carried forward by the comic potential of this type of colloquial dialogue and by a brilliant production of the play by Karam Muṭāwiʿ in Cairo's Pocket Theatre, *al-Farāfīr* was a tremendous popular success, until its broader and essentially nihilist message was emphasised by critics, at which point it was closed down. In later plays, Idrīs was to expand on his explorations of this darker side, most notably in *al-Mukhaṭṭaṭīn* (a *double-entendre* meaning both Men in Stripes, and Programmed Men, 1969), which paints a truly Orwellian picture of a nightmare futuristic society controlled through the media by a figure significantly named Brother. But, in spite of Idrīs's success in using these plays to depict some of the socio-political problems confronting modern man, each of the works shows structural flaws, particularly an unwillingness to exert some editorial control over length. A greater mastery of dramatic economy is shown by Mīkhāʾīl Rūmān (1927–73), whose images of contemporary man as a victim of 'the system', most notably in *al-Wāfid* (The New Arrival, 1965), are brilliant and chilling visions of the callous anonymity beloved of mindless bureaucracy.

This period of efflorescence in Egyptian drama coincided with an increase of scholarly and governmental interest in the revival of the heritage of Egyptian folklore. Among those associated with this movement were at least two dramatists, Shawqī ʿAbd al-Ḥakīm and Najīb Surūr (1932–78). ʿAbd al-Ḥakīm found inspiration in the popular heritage for several plays, including *Ḥasan wa-Naʿīmah* (Ḥasan and

Naʿīmah, 1960), *Shafīqah wa-Mitwallī* (Shafīqah and Mitwallī, 1961), and *Mawlid al-Malik Maʿrūf* (King Maʿrūf's Birthday, 1965). The first of these, concerning a country girl who is forced into prostitution and murdered by her brother for the sake of family honour, was a *cause célèbre* when during the 1970s it was presented in the ancient Ghūriyyah hostelry in Cairo under the direction of Laila Abou Seif. The theme of Ḥasan and Naʿīmah, also involving a murder but this time of the male lover, was also the subject of *Min ayn agīb nās?* (Where Will I Get the People From?, 1976), a verse play by Najīb Surūr, who was one of the most notable and complex participants in the Egyptian theatre scene during the 1960s and 1970s until his descent into the depression that contributed to his tragically early death. Surūr, a graduate of the Moscow Theatre School, directed many plays (including those of Nuʿmān ʿĀshūr), but his own contributions to the genre were steeped in the folkloric tradition of Egypt and crafted in a mellifluous colloquial poetry. These very qualities, coupled with the fact that in effect they constitute a series of tableaux, rendered them extremely difficult to stage, even at the hands of an experienced practitioner such as Karam Muṭāwiʿ.

The mention of Surūr here brings back into focus the issue of verse drama in Arabic. We noted above the early tendency of theatre directors to incorporate musical episodes into performances and the desire of early pioneers to move away from the apparent inevitability of this association in audience expectations. Aḥmad Shawqī's plays, full as they were of beautiful poetry, tended to follow this tendency. During the golden age of Egyptian drama that we have been exploring here, at least two writers, ʿAbd al-raḥmān al-Sharqāwī (1920–87) and Ṣalāḥ ʿAbd al-Ṣabūr (1931–81), succeeded in making contributions that both avoided the linkage with music and were successfully performed on stage. Of the two ʿAbd al-Ṣabūr was certainly the more accomplished, most especially in his remarkable play, *Maʾsāt al-Ḥallāj* (The Tragedy of al-Ḥallāj, 1965), which retells the true story of the famous mystic, al-Ḥallāj, crucified in AD 922 for uttering the phrase ʿAnā l-ḥaqqʾ (ʿI am the Truthʾ).

This survey of the Egyptian drama tradition in the decade or so before the 1967 War has only been able to touch on the most significant contributions and issues. Some idea of the richness of the theatre scene during this period can be gauged by considering the two years before 1967, in the latter of which I was in Cairo myself. In addition to the usual number of productions of plays by foreign writers, these two years witnessed stage performances of works by almost every dramatist whose works we have considered above. Once again, the political environment and the availability of personnel and resources were the envy of the Arab world as a whole. All of which makes it regrettable that the period since 1970 has been widely characterised by participants in every aspect of the complex organism that is a theatre tradition as being one of a continuing 'theatre crisis'. While some of the issues involved are clearly of a local nature, others reflect broader questions that will be discussed below.

RECENT TRENDS ELSEWHERE IN THE ARAB WORLD

Syria, Lebanon, and Palestine

Sharīf Khazandar, the prominent French-trained Syrian authority on the theatre, indulges in what seems like a little dramatic gesture of his own when he writes in 1967 that Syrian drama is only seven years of age. He has noted previously, as have we, that the theatre tradition has its beginnings in Syria in the nineteenth century, but he is suggesting that, with the departure of so much talent from the region in the latter half of the last century, dramatic activity resided primarily in the survival of the traditional popular genres (such as the shadow play). He and other critics see the real beginning as only occurring with the foundation of the National Theatre Troupe in 1958. The same sense of timing characterises discussions of the recent tradition of theatre in Lebanon, with the foundation of the National Theatre in 1960 and the emergence of a number of troupes during that decade, including those of Munīr Abū Dibs, Roger ʿAssāf, and the Raḥbānī brothers (who were much aided in performances of their operettas by the spectacularly beautiful voice of the world-famous singer, Fayrūz); it goes without saying that the impact of the Lebanese civil war which began in 1975 and gradually petered out at the conclusion of the 1980s had a dire effect on these efforts at reviving the theatre tradition. In the case of Lebanon, particular mention needs to be made of two important littérateurs who composed dramas that made significant contributions to the societal acceptability of the genre. Within the *émigré* (*mahjar*) environment of the United States, Mīkhāʾīl Nuʿaymah published *Al-Ābāʾ wa-al-banūn* (Fathers and Sons, 1916), a play set within the Christian Lebanese community that explores the complexities of corruption, arranged marriages, and true love. What is most remarkable about this play is its early search for a solution to the problems of dramatic language in Arabic, with characters from poorer classes using the colloquial dialect while others use the standard written form of the language. Nuʿaymah's own ambiguous feelings on the topic are clearly reflected in his perspicacious introduction to the play. Another contributor to the literary tradition of Lebanese drama is the renowned symbolist poet, Saʿīd ʿAql (b. 1912), who is clearly reflecting his well known concern with the Phoenician aspect of Lebanese nationalism in composing a verse drama on the theme of *Qadmūs* (1944), a tale culled from Greek myth about the quest of Cadmus to rescue his sister, Europa, who has been carried off by Zeus. Like the plays of Shawqī within the Egyptian theatrical tradition, this work contributes to the public awareness of drama as literature, but is memorable more for the musicality of its poetry than for its genuine dramatic qualities.

In the period immediately preceding the 1948 'disaster' – as the Palestinians term the war that followed the creation of the State of Israel, there were a large number of theatre troupes in Jerusalem. The dispersal of Palestinian intellectuals to other Arab countries served to enrich cultural life elsewhere, but their departure, when coupled with a particularly severe system of military censorship within Israel (and, after 1967, the Occupied Territories as well) rendered any notion of founding, let alone sustaining, a theatre tradition problematic in the extreme. In such circumstances, it is hardly surprising that the plays which Palestinian littérateurs composed tended to be contributions to the more literary and intellectual side of the dramatic tradition. Their works relied to a significant extent on the symbolic power of the re-enactment on stage of incidents of tyranny, cunning, and revolt culled from history: for example, *Thawrat al-zanj* (The Zanj Revolt) and *Shamsūn wa-Dalīlah* (Samson and Delilah) by Muʿīn Basīsū (1927–84), and *Qarqāsh* by Samīḥ al-Qāsim (b. 1939). However, one troupe that has confronted the realities of this fraught political and social situation in a fashion which is as creative as it is courageous is the Palestinian Al-Ḥakawātī troupe, founded in 1977 and taking its name from the function of that most traditional of public performers, the story-teller (*ḥakawātī*). Performing in theatres whenever the censorship authorities allow or else becoming itinerant players with performances in public squares and village meeting-places, the Ḥakawātī troupe gather together stories from a variety of sources, present and past (such as that of the great hero cavalier-poet, ʿAntarah), and turn them into solo or group performances that comment on the injustices of the present. One might perhaps characterise this as total communal theatre in that the drama itself can be seen as beginning with the act of announcing the place and time of the performance, whereby a car with loudspeaker tours the area issuing orders to the audience not to stay away in a fashion that parodies the parlance of the Israeli military authorities.

This same technique of taking drama to the people and indeed of creating 'plays' in the process of collecting and re-enacting stories was also adopted by Roger ʿAssāf in Lebanon during the protracted fighting of the Lebanese civil war. The vast disruption of communal life, particularly that of the Shīʿite communities in the south, provided a rich store of material for these presentations. Indeed, the very destruction caused by the war made performances of this type virtually the only feasible mode of dramatic presentation. In view of the relative newness of the modern drama tradition in both Lebanon and Syria, not to mention the shortage of theatres in which to mount productions, it is not surprising that such an unsettled political and social environment has not been conducive to the natural development of that aggregation of elements that is needed to promote a popular tradition of drama performance. However, one Syrian writer, Saʿdallāh Wannūs (1940–97), has managed to make a major contribution to the advancement of drama not only in his own country but also on a much broader scale. Playwright, director, drama critic and theorist, Wannūs succeeds in his plays in combining classical themes and modern techniques in order to create works that possess immediate contemporary relevance. The solutions that his plays have offered to the dilemmas associated with audience and language in the modern Arab-world context have not always made for successful productions, but they have undoubtedly been the most innovative contributions to Arabic drama in recent decades.

While Wannūs had written some short plays before 1967, it was *Ḥaflat samr min ajl al-khāmis min Ḥuzayrān* (Soirée for the fifth of June, 1968), a searing criticism of the attitudes of Arab society that were so cruelly exposed by the June War, that really brought him into the public eye. If Idrīs's *Farāfīr* had placed actors in the audience, Wannūs's 'happening' sets out to involve the entire audience in what can best be described as a corporate act of civil disobedience. Here the stage directions request that invitations be sent out to senior government officials and that the start of the performance be deliberately delayed so that the audience will be aggravated; to enhance that effect, actors placed in the audience are instructed to start whistling and making a fuss. The acting troupe proceeds to present the set of scenes that they have prepared for a play that is supposed to illustrate the official version of what happened during the June War. However, 'members of the audience' continually interrupt the action, coming up on stage to give their own personal accounts. As the reality of the defeat is underlined with increasing clarity, the 'officials' of the Ministry of the Interior who are sitting in the front row become more and more agitated. Eventually, the performance is stopped, the theatre is declared closed, and the entire audience is 'arrested' and escorted out. It is hardly surprising that this play, which is clearly a product of a tense period of self-examination within Arab society, was an instant *cause célèbre* when it was presented for a short time in 1968 before being banned or that in 1972 it was presented again with great success in Damascus. Above all, it marks the beginning of Wannūs's concern with some of the theoretical dimensions of modern drama, most especially the relationship between the actors in the play and the audience – a relationship that he is to explore during the 1970s in three notable plays and also in a series of prefaces and essays discussing what he terms '*masraḥ al-tasyīs*' (theatre of politicisation).

Wannūs's next play continues his pointed exploration of lessons to be learned from the 1967 defeat, but the message is incorporated within a more subtle and malleable framework that includes within it many areas of creative experiment in the process of transferring it to the stage. In an introduction to the play, *Maghāmarat ra᾽s al-Mamlūk Jābir* (The Adventure of the Mamlūk Jābir's Head, 1970), the author informs readers that the script is to be regarded as merely a blueprint for performance; the text should be translated into the colloquial dialect of whichever region is to be the location of performance, and the appropriate local music is to be incorporated within the intervals between scenes and acts. The actors are instructed to come out on to the stage and engage the audience in dialogue before the performance starts so as to establish a rapport. When such an atmosphere is felt to have been established, the play can start. Orchestrating the events of the play and the interaction between the actors serving as café audience and others playing parts in the inner story is, once again, the figure of the *ḥakawātī* (story-teller). This particular character, however, is not willing to entertain his listeners with tales of past Arab glories such as that of the Mamlūk Sultan Baybars who drove back the Mongols in the thirteenth century:

CUSTOMER 2: This time we'll get the story we want.
CUSTOMER 3: You mean, the saga of Baybars.
CUSTOMER 2: Of course, that's what I mean. We've been waiting for long enough!

CUSTOMER 1: You're dead right there! It's time for the Baybars saga.
CUSTOMER 3: What times those were!
CUSTOMER 1: Days of heroism and victories!
CUSTOMER 3: Days of security, days when people had real nobility and their way of life flourished.
CUSTOMER 2: We've been waiting for the Baybars saga for ages!
CUSTOMER 1: That's right, storyteller Mu'nis. Do you have the Baybars saga?
STORYTELLER (responding quietly as he drinks his tea): It's not the right time for the Baybars saga yet.
CUSTOMERS (all at once): What do you mean, it's not time yet?!
–We've been waiting since the end of last summer.
–Every time we ask for Baybars, you say it's not time yet.
–Tell us, for heaven's sake, when will it be time?
STORYTELLER: We have many tales before us before we can get to the Baybars saga.

Instead these café customers have to listen to (and see acted out before them) a gruesome tale of opportunism and treachery set during an unsettled period of the ʿAbbāsī caliphate when rival factions were engaged in a struggle for power. A Mamlūk (slave) is sent from Baghdad to Persia with a secret message inscribed on his head, requesting that the King send forces to help one side in the struggle. Unbeknown to the Mamlūk, the message also instructs the king to get rid of the messenger. At the moment when Jābir the Mamlūk imagines his mission to be complete, he is taken away to be executed. As the play concludes, the actors advance towards the audience; such is the reward, they announce, of all people who are prepared to go on saying 'anyone who marries our mother we call uncle'. This however is the central core of this play. Much of the impact comes from the discussions between the *hakawātī* and his audience concerning the content of the story and their desire to listen to something more cheerful. One might suggest that much of the message of the play lies in the manner in which the café audience reacts to what they see. For example, at the very moment when Jābir is to be executed, the following exchange takes place in the cafe:

CUSTOMER 1: God forbid! That's horrible! More tea, Muḥammad!
CUSTOMER 2: Yes, really ghastly! Make mine a cup of coffee.

With such a degree of detachment the actual audience (as opposed to the one on stage) is presumably left to wonder whether the moral of the story is really being understood by these café customers who are serving as symbols of their society's value system.

Both these plays were clearly a major challenge to the theatre tradition in the Arab world in the expectations that they placed on the audience itself. Comments on productions make it clear that the kind of interaction for which Wannūs was searching did not occur. In the words of one critic: 'These were essentially artificial devices which failed to establish an impromptu, warm or genuine dialogue between stage and audience'. In a typical gesture Wannūs proceeded to explore this dilemma further by composing another play that examines the issue of audience in the context of the experiences of Abū Khalīl al-Qabbānī, his nineteenth-century predecessor. *Sahrah maʿa Abī Khalīl al-Qabbānī* (An Evening with Abū Khalīl al-Qabbānī, 1972) takes the form of a play within a play: the outer play depicts al-Qabbānī in Ottoman Damascus in the 1880s struggling to produce a play in the face of conservative opposition, continually changing Ottoman regulations, and unruly audiences. The inner play consists of *Hārūn al-Rashīd maʿa Qūt al-qulūb wa-Ghānim ibn Ayyūb* (Hārūn al-Rashīd with Qūt al-Qulūb and Ghānim ibn Ayyūb), one of al-Qabbānī's works culled from the *Thousand and One Nights* collection concerning the caliph and the love story between his favourite slave-girl and her lover. In the introduction to the play, Wannūs again points to the fact that the audience is expected to react to what they see, but such interruptions are now inserted into the script itself, along with other distancing devices such as a town crier and even a prompter to help the actors when they fumble their lines.

If this play represents something of a retreat from the stark confrontations envisaged for performances of Wannūs's earlier plays, then his next work, *al-Malik huwa al-malik* (The King's the King, 1977), continues and refines the process. Once again, the inspiration comes from the *Thousand and One Nights*, this time the tale of 'Abū al-Ḥasan al-mughaffal' which had also provided Mārūn al-Naqqāsh with the theme for one of his plays in the nineteenth century. In Wannūs's version of the story, a king and his minister overhear a merchant (now named Abū ʿIzzah) wishing to find solutions to problems with his business and his shrewish wife. They decide to take the man back to the palace and make him king for a day. However, their plans for entertainment go sadly awry: no one, including the actual King's wife, appears to notice any difference, and Abū ʿIzzah himself takes to his new role as though 'to the palace born'. Within the framework of performance this inner story is given considerable contemporary symbolic resonance by the fact that the actors are divided up into two groups, each standing behind its leader: the King's group behind ʿUbayd, Abū ʿIzzah's behind Zāhid. The stage directions call for placards listing the events of each scene to be prominently displayed, and at one point the two leaders intone the following statement in unison:

The details may differ, but the essentials are the same. When any system is based on disguise and property ownership, the above principle is the primary one. (*Al-Malik huwa al-malik*, 1977, p. 100)

As if to emphasise their manipulative role, Shaykhs Shahbandar and Ṭāhā remain at the side of the stage during the scenes operating puppets.

We have devoted considerable attention to the plays of Wannūs here because his career in drama showed yet another Arab dramatist struggling to address the manifold issues confronting the genre – from the moment of creation to its realisation on stage. In confronting questions of language, of theatre semiotics, of acting technique, and of production through both his plays and critical writings, he fulfilled an invaluable role in the continuing process of developing an Arabic drama that is both lively and relevant. Once again, however, some combination of factors – political, bureaucratic, personal – combined to put an end to this interesting and controversial series of experiments. During the final decade of his life Wannūs created a number of new works which were performed on stage to wide acclaim but *al-Malik huwa al-malik* must be reckoned his last truly major contributions to Arabic drama. No other dramatist in Syria and Lebanon has thus far managed to match the comprehensive nature of Wannūs's contribution to the Arabic theatre tradition, but several other playwrights have written significant dramas. In Lebanon, mention should be made of Raymond Jabbārah (b. 1935) and ʿIṣām Maḥfūẓ (b. 1939), and, in Syria, Muḥammad al-Māghūṭ (b. 1934), Walīd Ikhlāṣī (b. 1935), and Mamdūḥ ʿAdwān (b. 1941).

The Maghrib: Tunisia, Algeria, Morocco

Of the countries that are included within the region known as the Maghrib it was Tunisia that had made the earliest gestures in the development of a drama tradition. From initial efforts that followed visits by Egyptian troupes in 1908 several theatre troupes were founded that performed regularly in the period before independence (1956). However, many of the plays presented were translations or adaptations of Western works, and further development in the areas of acting and production was hampered by a combination of factors, not the least of which was society's unfavourable attitude to women appearing on stage. These were just some of many features in the Tunisian drama tradition that were to change during the 1960s: a large number of plays were written and produced, an Arab Theatre Festival was established in 1964 – an event that has continued to be a major annual event in Arab drama, and there was much discussion concerning the nature and direction of the drama genre in the Arab world. One of the participants in such discussion was ʿIzz al-dīn al-Madanī (b. 1938), who by both his own output as a dramatist and his critical writings on the genre has made a major contribution to Tunisian and Arabic drama.

Al-Madanī has written a series of four plays that take as their theme popular revolution: in order of publication they are *Thawrat ṣāḥib al-ḥimār* (The Donkey-owner's Revolt, 1971), *Riḥlat al-Ḥallāj* (Al-Ḥallāj's Journey, 1973), *Dīwān al-Zanj* (The Zanj Collection, 1974), and *Mawlay al-Sulṭān al-Ḥasan al-Ḥafṣī* (Our Lord, Sultan al-Ḥasan the Ḥafṣī, 1977). The staging of the third of these works, set during the period of the Zanj slave revolt in Iraq in the latter half of the ninth century, conveys some idea of the author's experiments with dramatic form. The stage is virtually subdivided into three segments: the first is used to present the action of the play; in the second the 'author' comments on the nature of revolutions; and in the third extracts are read from documents contemporary with the events themselves, most famous of which is undoubtedly the famous poetic elegy of ibn al-Rūmī (mentioned above in ch. 4). In *al-Ghufrān* (Forgiveness, 1976), a further play that combines a classical theme with the exploration of the dimensions of modern drama, al-Madanī examines the career and thought of the great poet, Abū al-ʿAlāʾ al-Maʿarrī.

The annual drama festival and the continuing experiments of a number of younger dramatists, most especially those of the group formed in 1975 under the title 'al-Masraḥ al-jadīd' (modern theatre), make Tunisia a continuing focus of interest in the field of Arabic drama. In Algeria and Morocco, by contrast, the pace of development has been slower; the reasons involve a complex of issues, including those of language use and educational policy and not excluding, of course, the political dimensions of such a public cultural activity. While a number of Algerian writers have made contributions to popular drama in the colloquial dialect of the region – not least the renowned novelist, Kātib Yāsīn, the process of *taʿrīb*, arabising the cultural and educational systems in the country, is still under way. In Morocco two writers have played a central role in the fostering and expansion of a theatre tradition. Aḥmad Ṭayyib al-ʿIlj (b. 1928) emulated the earlier example of ʿUthmān Jalāl in Egypt by transferring to the Moroccan environment Molière's *Tartuffe* under the title, *Walī Allāh*, a work that was presented with great success in the Theatre Festival in Tunisia in 1968. Al-ʿIlj's colleague, al-Ṭayyib al-Ṣiddīqī (b. 1938), is a man of the theatre in every sense: playwright, producer, and actor. His play, *Dīwān Sīdī ʿAbd al-raḥmān al-Majdhūb* (The Collection of Sīdī ʿAbd al-raḥmān al-Majdhūb, 1966), tells the story of an itinerant poet, a role that he has often taken himself, while in *Maqāmāt Badīʿ al-zamān al-Hamadhānī* (The Maqāmāt of 'the Wonder of the Age' al-Hamadhānī, 1971) he explores in contemporary dramatic form the long appreciated potential of the picaresque episodes written ten centuries earlier by al-Hamadhānī (discussed in ch. 5).

Iraq and the Gulf States

While the theatre tradition in Iraq owes a good deal to the pioneering efforts of Ḥaqqī al-Shiblī who founded a theatre troupe in 1927, joined the famous Egyptian troupe of Fāṭimah Rushdī, and later studied drama in Paris, there can be little doubt that Yūsuf al-ʿĀnī (b. 1927) has been the predominant figure in Iraqi theatre during the modern period. In his concern for and involvement in every aspect of drama, he stands within the Iraqi tradition as the equivalent of Wannūs, al-Madanī, and al-Ṣiddīqī in theirs. Al-ʿĀnī invokes all the emotive power of the colloquial dialect of the region in *Anā ummak yā Shākir* (I'm your Mother, Shākir, 1955) to provide an accurate reflection in dramatic form of the period that preceded the bloody Iraqi revolution of 1958; the principal character, Umm Shākir, sees her children suffer and die in the struggle for liberation but insists on the rightness of the nationalist cause. *Al-Miftāḥ* (The Key, 1968) is a more accomplished piece of theatre. A popular song is introduced to invoke the tale of a young married couple, symbolically named Ḥayrān and Ḥayrānah (the masculine and feminine forms of the adjective meaning perplexed). They have determined not to become parents until they have discovered a fulfilling role in life; they are in quest of a key to a magical box, but at every turn they are thwarted in their efforts. As the play concludes, the two have to face a reality that they have studiously avoided, that the wife is pregnant and they have to confront the future realistically.

The level of official support and popular interest for theatre in the other nations of the Gulf region has, at least thus far, been considerably less than in the countries we have discussed above. With the expansion of educational and cultural opportunities the status of drama is changing, albeit slowly. An example of such a trend can be seen in Kuwait where initial gestures in the 1940s are now beginning to bear fruit in the plays of writers such as Ṣaqr al-Rashūd and ʿAbd al-ʿazīz Surayyiʿ.

CONCLUSION

In the Introduction to this chapter I discussed briefly the essence of drama, and especially the fact that it differed from the other genres being considered in this book in that its cultural standing within society is related not only to its place within the textual, literary tradition, but also – and perhaps more significantly – to its essential nature as performance. In that context it is as well for me to point to what is reasonably obvious: the above discussion of developments in modern Arabic drama is limited by the fact that it is itself based on materials available in textual form. While I am familiar with all the works discussed here as texts – through both the works themselves and critical writings about them, I have to admit to having seen only a very small sampling of them on stage, and then only in Egypt. While the writings of a Tawfīq al-Ḥakīm or Saʿdallāh Wannūs may provide a good deal of background to the theoretical issues involved in the performance of their oeuvre and, by extension, of Arabic drama in general, my only recourse in assessing the efficacy of the receptive aspect has been the writings of critics who attended performances of the play in question.

The pioneering work of Tawfīq al-Ḥakīm and his analogues in other regions of the Arab world has ensured that drama has now come to be regarded as a literary genre in its own right. The texts of plays by writers across the length and breadth of the Arab world are generally available, and in many areas these texts will include works written in the colloquial dialect. Journals devoted specifically to theatre affairs are published, more often than not under the aegis of the official cultural apparatus of the government, and in them critics will review the latest productions.

As the above surveys have shown clearly, it is in the complex area of stage performance that many of the thorniest problems connected with modern Arabic drama continue to lie. The issues involved have changed surprisingly little from those which confronted the genre at the outset. There is first the major problem of censorship. While certain countries in the region – specifically Egypt between 1956 and 1967 – seem to have permitted a good deal of freedom of expression within the theatrical medium, the general principle has been one of the closest governmental control over drama, as both text and performance. This covers not merely the conduct of the playwrights themselves, the acceptance of scripts, and the availability of theatres, but also the continuity of funding for academies of drama at which the younger generation can be trained in the skills of acting and production. When scripts have been rejected or continually blue-pencilled, when entire seasons or individual performances have been officially cancelled, and when new plays have been inadequately rehearsed or performed, the response of many dramatists has, not unnaturally, been disillusion and despair; the consequence has often been a resort to silence, another literary genre, or even exile.

Beyond these issues lies the much debated and continuing question of the nature of the desired theatre audience. The tradition of farce in the colloquial language that remains so popular today has been a part of the modern Arabic drama tradition from the outset and clearly traces its origins to earlier exemplars. Alongside it has developed a tradition of what is generally referred to as 'serious' drama, the popularity of which has rarely, if ever, rivalled that of the comic tradition. This is not to suggest, of course, that playwrights in certain countries have not been able to attract large audiences to dramas with a serious message to impart; I hope that the above sections have provided evidence enough of that. However, I would suggest that the most successful experiments in attracting a popular audience to such drama have been those that have endeavoured, in a variety of ways, to transcend the cultural and attitudinal boundaries set up by the two extremes of 'serious' and 'popular' drama and to fill part of the substantial space that lies in between the two: thus the plays of Alfred Faraj, for example, or of Saʿdallāh Wannūs.

Behind such attempts at categorising drama by anticipated audience (which have a built-in tendency to become self-fulfilling prophesies) lie, of course, the continuing discussions regarding the language of drama. It is now clear that a large number of highly accomplished Arab playwrights compose their contributions to drama in the colloquial dialect of their own region. If the myriad political and social factors involved in theatre production are working in their favour, they have a reasonable expectation of popular success. As we have shown in the sections above, every region of the Arab world can provide examples of dramatists who fit this category. However the linguistic boundaries of each colloquial dialect virtually guarantee that any such success will be a local one. Any aspiration that the playwright may have to broaden the audience to the pan-Arab level will involve a willingness to compromise on the question of language. Some experiments in this area have clearly been declared failures, mostly because they did not represent linguistic reality; thus, early attempts to vary language level according to class. But, between the efforts of al-Ḥakīm and Faraj at finding a median level of language and Wannūs's recommendation that his text is intended as a blueprint for a script in the local dialect, there is clearly plenty of room for continuing experiment. In an article on the future of the language of Arabic drama, the Lebanese playwright, ʿIṣām Maḥfūẓ, notes that people who insist on the use of the standard literary language in dramatic dialogue – out of some aspiration for Arab unity – are in fact contributing to its failure. He concludes that the most satisfactory way of reconciling the artistic needs of drama and the process of communication with an Arab audience is to take Wannūs's suggestion one step further: for the playwright to prepare a colloquial 'script' for performances in his own region and, at the time of the text's publication in book form, 'to convert the text directed at readers elsewhere in the Arab world into a simplified form of the literary language' (*Al-ʿArabī* 374 (Jan. 1990): 153). The fact that this question of language use in drama involves a complex of political, social, cultural, and religious factors guarantees that it will continue to be the subject of experiment, debate, and contumely into the foreseeable future.

Critical debates, discussions, experiments, these are all signs of an artistic milieu that is filled with creative energy. If the world of Arabic drama shows such signs today, then that is a tribute to the amazing resilience of practitioners of the theatre in the face of considerable odds. Many of the more political and social problems involved have already been discussed. However, recent decades have introduced a further factor which may be the most powerful of all: what in the West are known as the media. The tradition of Western drama is, of course, of considerable vintage and appears to be holding its own against the attractions of the cinema and, most especially television and multimedia technology. Even here, the prevalence of Lloyd Webber musicals in the theatres of London has been cause for concern to a number of drama critics, while on a more general level other commentators view with alarm the deleterious effects that the unchallenging demands of popular television drama are having on the ability of the theatre-going public to watch and listen with that attention and interpretive skill that are both regarded as prerequisites for any successful participation in the complexities of a live theatre performance (John Peter, 'A Hard Act to Follow', *The Times*, 2 Jan. 1994, Sec. 7: 27). Arabic drama on the other hand is much younger; as we have noted above, a modern performance tradition in certain countries is no more than twenty years of age. It is clearly an extremely difficult task for such nascent traditions to have to create *ab initio* a space for themselves within a cultural environment that is daily bombarded by modern media in the form of soap operas and films that can be watched in the home. It is here that the initiatives of the Ḥakawātī Troupe and of Roger ʿAssāf – taking drama to the people where they are – turn the necessity of an unsettled political situation into an experimental virtue. Perhaps the unkindest cut of all may be seen in Egypt, the primary exporter of films and soap operas in Arabic to the rest of the Arab world. For, not only are many Egyptians now complaining that the serials that they watch on television have lost their Egyptian authenticity in a quest for a larger market (and especially that of the Gulf), but also the large fees that these very media pay to actors mean that it is only what is termed the commercial theatre, predominantly consisting of domestic farces, that can afford to mount expensive productions. One should express the hope that the success of a play such as *Bi al-ʿArabī al-faṣīḥ* (In plain Arabic, 1992) by Lenīn al-Ramlī, a wittily accurate portrayal of the prejudices of the Arab world about itself which was performed by a group of young actors to tremendous popular acclaim, may serve to convince a younger generation of writers, actors, and directors of the continuing need for a drama tradition that will address itself to the pressing issues of the day.

As Yūsuf Idrīs observed, drama and the dramatic are to be witnessed everywhere in the Arab world. As certain productions take to the streets, the more experimental practitioners of the genre would seem to be going back to its indigenous cultural roots. Meanwhile, the institution of the theatre itself has become a part of the literary and cultural milieu of the Arab world, bringing with it from the West the large number of theoretical issues that impact upon the performance of drama and adding to them a further collection of questions that are intrinsic to the Arabic environment. With Arabic drama we witness a genre in a continuing process of adaptation and development, one that, by its very nature, must confront the political, social, and cultural problems of the day. In the Arab world that can be a dangerous role, but within that broad and variegated space the struggle for creative change is a continuing process.

CHAPTER 7

The critical tradition

'Criticism is reason applied to the imagination.' Francis Bacon

INTRODUCTION

In the previous three chapters I have surveyed the development of poetry, belles-lettres, and drama – the works of literature themselves. As I noted in the first chapter, on principles, any anthologising process such as this and indeed the very utilisation of the concept of genre as a means of differentiation and organisation involve acts of interpretation that are based on modes of evaluation; to wit, criticism. Having already had frequent recourse to the views of individual Arab critics regarding these genres, schools, and authors, I would now like to devote this chapter to a brief survey of the critical tradition in its own right.

The word 'criticism' (derived from the Greek word for 'judgement') initially involves the process of making an evaluative decision, but it has also come to incorporate within its semantic field the study of the modes of evaluation that result from the codification of that process into a system. Within the Western academic environment, the quest of much twentieth-century scholarship for an objectification of the principles of humanistic learning has led literary scholars to a close examination of the bases of our critical systems, something that has led in turn to the elaboration of literary theory as the investigation of the linguistic, philosophical, and hermeneutic processes that govern the making of critical decisions. Debate on what we might term the politics of the many issues that these investigations have raised has never been less than lively and often fractious; Dennis Donohue's book on the subject is aptly entitled *Ferocious Alphabets* (New York, 1981). While the import of some of these debates has been implicit in the organisation and discussions of previous chapters and will be in this one, I prefer to concentrate in my discussion of literary criticism in Arabic on the often close linkage between the literary texts themselves and the critical tradition that assessed them. That such a closeness exists can be illustrated by a representative listing of Arab writers who have made important contributions to both fields; a short list would include Abū Tammām, ibn al-Muʿtazz, ibn ʿAbd Rabbihi, ibn Rashīq, al-Sharīf al-Raḍī, ibn Shuhayd, Ḥāzim al-Qarṭājannī, Ṣafī al-dīn al-Ḥillī, Mīkhāʾīl Nuʿaymah, ʿAbbās Maḥmūd al-ʿAqqād, Yaḥyā Ḥaqqī, Nāzik al-Malāʾikah, Ṣalāḥ ʿAbd al-Ṣabūr, and Adūnīs.

The process of criticism, *qua* the evaluation of literary works, is evident in abundance in every period of Arabic literary history and can be traced back to the very beginnings. As we noted in ch. 4 above, the earliest accounts we possess of poets evaluating each other describe annual poetry fairs such as the famous one in the Arabian city of ʿUkāẓ. The evaluation procedures used at the most ancient of poetic competitions and jousts are replicated in parts of the Arab world today: the *zajal* tradition of Lebanon, for example, with its virtuosi poets (*zajjālūn*) touring the country and challenging local poets to an evening of improvised poetry, and the use of poetry competitions in Yemen as a means of resolving local disputes (see Steven Caton, *Peaks of Yemen I Summon*, 1990). On these various occasions and others like them a decision is made as to which poet has created the better poetry. While experts may be called upon to give their verdict, the audience as a whole will also participate vigorously in the evaluative process. They will voice their enthusiasms and evaluations in the manner of any other type of joust or competition; many is the poet whose pleasure I have witnessed as, in response to a yelled request from his audience, he has repeated a particularly admired line. Negative judgements will also be expressed, and a personal anecdote provides a useful illustration of the way in which even this becomes an opportunity for poetic creativity. As part of a festival held in Egypt in 1984, participants were invited to attend a poetry evening in Alexandria. I was fortunate enough to be seated in the audience among a group of poets: among the more prominent, as I recall, were Jabrā Ibrāhīm Jabrā and Aḥmad ʿAbd al-muʿṭī Ḥijāzī. At one point during the proceedings, an aged Alexandrian poet was helped up on to the stage. He launched into a tediously lengthy and bombastic ode in traditional form in which a soccer match between Egypt and the (then) Soviet Union became a symbol for negative reflections on Egyptian–Soviet relations. As the poet's stentorian delivery revealed one hackneyed image after another, it was not long before the poets around me decided to couch their evaluation of the poem in their own particular way; in hushed tones that were nevertheless clearly audible to those around them, they took turns in reacting instantaneously to the first half of each of the poet's lines by providing an irreverent and often ribald second half – all within the interval that it took for the poet on stage to recite his own version thereof. Here, one might suggest, the critical act has itself become a process of improvising poetry.

The public performance of poetry and other genres of literature has thus been intimately linked to the often equally public modes of their evaluation. The other aspect of criticism mentioned above, the systematisation of those modes of evaluation into a tradition of critical scholarship, was to be yet another development in the gradual process of collection, synthesis, and codification that was explored in our second chapter within the broader context of the Islamic sciences as a whole. The relationship between the process of passing judgements as practised in public fora of various kinds – briefly illustrated above – and the development of a system of critical learning was, in the Arabic context as elsewhere, often a contentious one. The Syro-Lebanese poet and critic, Adūnīs, sees this 'cart and horse' relationship as a confrontation between the 'static' and 'dynamic' (*al-Thābit wa-al-mutaḥawwil* (3 vols., Beirut, 1974 *et seq.*)), using these two poles as a means of exploring the tension that has existed between the prescriptive tendencies of the critical tradition and the desire of the creative writer to set the literary agenda rather than to follow it. It is to an assessment of the nature of that confrontation that this chapter is addressed.

FROM PHILOLOGY TO CRITICISM

The first works in Arabic that attempt to define and analyse poetry and its features date from the latter half of the ninth century. As is the case with all the literary genres that have been studied in previous chapters, the process of development that led up to the appearance of these works of systematisation can be traced back to the revelation of the Qur'ān to Muḥammad and the increasingly wide-scaled movement of intellectual exploration and cultural transformation that it instigated. The Qur'ān, it will be recalled, had announced that it was 'an Arabic Qur'ān'. The process of examining the meanings of words and the structuring of phrases and sentences in the newly recorded sacred text led philologists to collect and examine the largest extant archive of the language, the tradition of poetry that had been handed down from poet to bard (*rāwī*) for centuries. Certain collectors of poetry, Ḥammād al-Rāwiyah (d. 785) and Khalaf al-Aḥmar (d. 796), became proverbial for the amount of poetry they had memorised, and the results of their recording were turned into collections based on different organising principles: for example, the primary criterion for the most famous collection of poems, the *muʿallaqāt*, was that of length (they are often referred to as the long odes); by contrast, the *al-Mufaḍḍaliyyāt* collection, named after its compiler, al-Mufaḍḍal al-Ḍābbī (d. 786), was compiled as a teaching anthology of shorter poems.

The number of these early collections and the prestige they were accorded are a reflection of the fact that the earliest Arabic poetry had acquired canonical status; its lexicon became the basis for the beginnings of semantics and its grammatical structures were the model for correct usage; its discourse principles and the imagery that it used to create and portray a pre-Islamic vision, were a yardstick by which later critics of a conservative bent judged the 'naturalness' of Arabic poetry. The poetic corpus became the object of intensive study by scholars, no more so than at the two intellectual centres of al-Kūfah and al-Baṣrah in Iraq. As noted earlier, al-Khalīl ibn Aḥmad of al-Baṣrah (d. 781) began work on a dictionary (*Kitāb al-ʿAyn*), recorded a system of metrics, and wrote treatises on music, suggesting a linkage between poetry and music that was to find its finest expression the *Kitāb al-aghānī* of Abū al-faraj al-Iṣfahānī and in the lost work of the great singer and musician, Isḥāq al-Mawṣilī (d. 849). Within a discussion of criticism, however, al-Khalīl is most remembered for his contribution to the study of prosody (*ʿarūḍ*) whereby, to cite the import of his own words, he recorded the pulses of the lines of Arabic poetry as he heard them and organised them into a system. This description of al-Khalīl was to become a prescription at the hands of later critics, one that was to differentiate what was poetry from what was not till well into the twentieth century.

The goals of those who participated in this initial process of collecting and recording the poetry were, needless to say, maximal: to gather as large and representative a sample of the tradition as possible. Once the repertoire became available for analysis, the task of sifting and anthologising – and thus the earliest glimpses of activity that might be termed critical – began. Given the canonical status of the ancient poetry as a linguistic precedent to the Qur'ān, there was a priority for the production of useful referential materials, dictionaries, studies of grammar, and the like. However, the study of poetry soon expanded beyond the more practical need for information extrapolated from the recorded corpus to an examination of the poetry itself. Among the most famous members of the community of philologists who, in addition to studies on *ḥadīth* and grammar, devoted themselves to this particular task were Abū ʿAmr ibn al-ʿAlāʾ (d. 770), Abū ʿUbaydah (d. 825), and al-Aṣmaʿī (d. 831). It was their task to familiarise themselves with the work of the transmitters and recorders (like Khalaf al-Aḥmar), to consider the different versions of poems and – analogous to the process of *ḥadīth* scholarship described in ch. 2 – to check on the authenticity of the recording process. From such concerns with the validity of the corpus at their disposal, they moved on to the processes of analysis and classification. Abū ʿAmr ibn al-ʿAlāʾ, for example, subdivided the poetry into four major topic areas: boasting (*fakhr*), eulogy or panegyric (*madīḥ*), lampooning (*hijāʾ*), and love (*nasīb*). Abū ʿUbaydah, whose familiarity with the poetic tradition was proverbial (he was said by one contemporary to be 'a head stuffed full of learning'), wrote a work, *Majāz al-Qurʾān* (Figurative Language in the Qurʾān), which serves as an early example of what was to become a major strand in Arabic literary criticism, the relationship between the inimitable language of the Qurʾān and the varieties of literary language. The work of Abū ʿUbaydah and of the seemingly ubiquitous ibn Qutaybah (d. 889), whose *Kitāb taʾwīl mushkil al-Qurʾān* (Book of Interpretion of Problematic Usage in the Qurʾān) is a further study of the way in which the language of the Qurʾān is 'different', were to serve as important precedents to the later emergence of *iʿjāz al-Qurʾān* (the inimitable nature of the Qurʾān) as a focus of critical analysis – a topic to be discussed below. The later critic, ibn Rashīq (d. 1064), acknowledges that these pioneers, with their encyclopaedic knowledge of ancient poetry and the erudition that they transmitted to the next generation of scholars, were instrumental in establishing the pre-Islamic poetic corpus as a cultural and linguistic yardstick, the repository of the Arabs' most cherished cultural ideals – a status that, as we will shortly observe, was to play a part in many of the major controversies during the development of Arabic literary criticism.

It will be recalled that one of the most typical organising matrices in use during this particular phase in the development of the Islamic sciences was the 'class' (*ṭabaqah*). Al-Aṣmaʿī, himself the compiler of a collection of poetry known as *al-Aṣmaʿiyyāt*, composed a work under the title *Fuḥūlāt al-shuʿarāʾ* (Champion Poets, *fuḥūl* being the plural of the word for particularly valuable riding-animals) in which he categorises poets. Like his fellow philologists mentioned above however, al-Aṣmaʿī was a firm upholder of the ancient poetic tradition and its 'naturalness' as the norm for what was to be admired and emulated (that being yet another topic of critical debate, as we will see below). This quotation, for example, provides his prerequisites for the status of champion poet:

No poet will ever become a champion in the realm of poetry till he has performed the ancient poems of the Arabs, listened to accounts, learned topics, and allowed phrases to permeate his hearing. He must first learn prosody so that his speech may have balance, then grammar so that he may speak distinctly and accurately, then genealogies and great battles so that he can make use of them to recognise points of virtue and dishonour which he can then depict with praise or blame.

One of al-Aṣmaʿī's students, ibn Sallām al-Jumaḥī (d. 847), used the same concept of *fuḥūl* in his *Ṭabaqāt fuḥūl al-shuʿarāʾ* (Classes of Champion Poets). As with his teacher, no definition is provided of the features that delineate the excellence of such poets, but the champions that he selects are placed into separate categories, using such criteria as time (pre-Islamic and Islamic) and theme. While this mode of classification may have been primarily a reshuffling of material already existing in the work of his teacher and other predecessors, the work of ibn Sallām is often seen as marking a beginning to the development of literary criticism in Arabic since the principles that he adopted marked a process whereby the critical activity and its practitioners began to acquire a separate validity of their own.

As the above paragraphs have shown, the canonical status that was accorded pre-Islamic poetry and the relatively late emergence of a tradition of bellettristic prose (discussed in ch. 5) combined to make the poetic corpus the focus of the earliest contributions to literary criticism. The name of the great polymath, al-Jāḥiẓ (d. 869), merits inclusion in this context, as in so many others. Firstly, there is his famous collection, *Kitāb al-ḥayawān* (Book of Animals), a collection of poetry and anecdote that also included a number of observations on poets and poetry and a most perceptive section on the impossibility of translating poetry. However, it is in an anthology of both poetry and prose entitled *Kitāb al-bayān wa-al-tabyīn* (Book on Clarity and Eloquence), as well as in a number of shorter treatises, that he expands the framework of critical discussion by making the base of his observations the question of *balāghah* (eloquence) and the unique properties of the Arabic language – an opinion that once again looks to the Qurʾān as its yardstick and justification. In *Kitāb al-bayān* al-Jāḥiẓ's discussion sets the groundwork for a number of debates that are to preoccupy his successors: the relative roles of form (*lafẓ*) and meaning (*maʿnā*), the different attributes of poetry and prose, and the question of coherence within a single composition. The balance between poetry and belles-lettres was also taken up by al-Mubarrad of al-Baṣrah (d. 898), the compiler of another famous literary anthology, *al-Kāmil* (The Complete). In a short treatise written in response to a question regarding the superiority of one or the other type of composition, he also addresses the question in terms of eloquence, suggesting that both require three elements: the full rendering of the meaning involved; the selection of the appropriate kind of expression; and a pleasing composition. Moving beyond these basics, however, he still awards the palm to poetry on the grounds that, as versified (*manẓūm*) discourse, it also involves the complexities of metre and rhyme.

The broad interests of ibn Qutaybah led him to delve into a large number of different intellectual spheres – the education of bureaucrats, for example, and the difficulties of language in the Qur'ān, and he is also much involved in these early efforts aimed at classifying poets and poetry and developing analytical criteria. His *Kitāb al-shiʿr wa-al-shuʿarāʾ* (Book on Poetry and Poets) is yet another large, analytical anthology, the title of which announces its intention of discussing poetry *per se* as well as its practitioners. The work itself is prefaced with an introduction that offers some important new principles: that poetry should not be judged by its time period but on its own merits – in other words, more ancient poetry was not automatically to be judged superior to modern poetry; that poetry being written for performance in ninth-century Baghdad was not obliged to replicate the imagery of the sixth-century desert ode, however revered the latter's canonical status; and, most famously of all, that 'some people of learning' maintained that the *qaṣīdah* had an internal structural logic of its own, one that gave the performance of such poems a function similar to a communal rite. Continuing the discussion regarding the naturalness of the poetic composition, ibn Qutaybah details the characteristics of yet another pair of opposites prevalent in Arabic literary criticism: naturalness (*ṭabʿ*), a quality of innate talent, and artifice (*ṣanʿah*), the exercise of craft, something that he associates with the process of revising poetic compositions (he mentions the poets, Zuhayr ibn Abī Sulmā and al-Ḥuṭay'ah in this category). Ibn Qutaybah then divides poetry into four categories, making use of the form/content dichotomy noted above in connection with the writings of al-Jāḥiẓ: thus, there can be good meanings expressed using good form (words), good meanings using bad form, and so on.

Viewed in retrospect, the works of writers such as ibn Sallām and ibn Qutaybah cannot be regarded as literary criticism, as the modern Egyptian critic, Muḥammad Mandūr (d. 1965) points out in his important study of classical criticism, *Al-Naqd al-manhajī ʿinda al-ʿArab* (Methodical Criticism Among the Arabs, 1948). They do however serve as important transitional figures; their primary goal is to compile data on poets – the topics of their poems and the occasions on which they were delivered, but the schemata that they develop lay the groundwork for the more critically focused works of their successors. The same holds true of Thaʿlab (d. 904), the grammarian of al-Kūfah, to whom is attributed a work entitled *Qawāʿid al-shiʿr* (The Rules of Poetry). *Qawāʿid* is a term still used in language textbooks to indicate the section devoted to grammar rules, and the organising principles of this work underline a point that we noted above, namely the linkage at this early stage between the study of grammar and poetry. The discussion focuses on four types of poetic discourse: imperative, prohibition, statement, and interrogative, but Thaʿlab moves beyond the purely grammatical to elaborate on the topic areas of poetry identified by Abū ʿAmr and to devise some categories for the analysis of poetic tropes that would appear to have been the basis of later works on the subject. Indeed, one of Thaʿlab's students is ibn al-Muʿtazz (d. 908), the renowned poet and caliph for one day, who is credited, along with Qudāmah ibn Jaʿfar (d. 948), with establishing the basis for the emergence of a school of poetics in Arabic.

MAJOR CRITICAL DEBATES

Ibn Qutaybah's seemingly modest suggestion that the poetry of modern poets could be as meritorious as that of the ancients was a gesture of compromise in an era marked by fractious debate and confrontation. The transfer of the caliphal capital from Damascus to Baghdad in the mid-eighth century was symbolic of a shift to a more culturally diverse community, one that moved away both physically and mentally from the venues and ideals of the Arabian peninsula. Baghdad rapidly became not only the locus of an elaborate court system and the vast bureaucracy that went with it but also a glittering cultural centre that thrived on the patronage that the court provided and came to rival the intellectual prestige of the twin cities of al-Kūfah and al-Baṣrah.

The poets of the period provide evidence of some of the tensions that were aroused within such an intellectual environment. In opening a *khamriyyah* (discussed in ch. 4), Abū Nuwās (d. 814) scoffs at the conventions of the traditional ode:

> Some poor wretch turned aside to question a camp-ground; my purpose
> in turning aside was to ask for the local pub.
> May God never dry the eyes of people who cry over rocks nor soothe the
> agony of those who yearn for tent-pegs!
> "Have you made mention of the grounds of the Banū Asad?" they asked.
> Tell me, for heaven's sake, who are the Banū Asad,
> and Tamīm, Qays, and their ilk? In God's view, those Bedouin are
> nothing.

while the tensions that developed between the cultures of the Arab Muslims and those of the new converts are well captured in the words of the poet, Bashshār ibn Burd (d. 784) that were already cited as part of our discussion of the controversy in ch. 2. Within the realms of theology, the religious scholars (*ʿulamāʾ*) who had been producing a vast library of studies on the Qurʾān and other sources of doctrine were confronting some of the dilemmas that emerged from their research; among them were questions regarding predestination and the non-created nature of the Qurʾān. A direct confrontation on some of the issues involved was initiated when the Caliph, al-Maʾmūn (one of the sons of Hārūn al-Rashīd), interposed an element of human reason into the discussion by adopting the concerns of the *Muʿtazilah* as official doctrine: if the Qurʾān was uncreated, it was asked, then was every copy of it likewise uncreated; if God was all-powerful and everything was predestined, how could a deity that preordained evil be a good God? Into this environment of debate between old and new, faith and reason, Arab and non-Arab Muslims, al-Maʾmūn also introduced an intensified focus on Hellenistic learning through the foundation of the House of Wisdom (*Bayt al-ḥikmah*) as a research library where the repertoire of works from the heritage of Greek learning that had been translated into Arabic were available for consultation. While the courses of influence are never as easy to trace as some might assume (and have assumed), it seems clear that the availability of these translated texts played a role in framing the nature and course of these debates.

It is within this intellectual environment (that can have been nothing less than lively) that the creations of Arab poets who have been designated modernist (*muḥdath*) must be placed. Bashshār, Abū Nuwās, and Muslim ibn al-Walīd (d. 823) are the names most frequently cited as the originators in this move to break away from the normative expectations regarding poetry, and especially its language, that had been established as part of the process of philological canonisation noted above. Al-Jāḥiẓ himself appears to have been the first to apply the term *badīʿ* (new, novel – from the verbal root that also provides the word for heresy, *bidʿah*) to describe their approach to poetic language. However, it was to be ibn al-Muʿtazz who managed to reflect the debates of the era by analysing the phenomenon in detail.

Ibn al-Muʿtazz and Qudāmah ibn Jaʿfar.

The very title of ibn al-Muʿtazz's work, *Kitāb al-badīʿ* (Book on *badīʿ*–translatable perhaps as figurative language) announces an approach that will focus on one aspect of the use of a particular level of language in literary texts; it thus can be seen as marking a beginning of what we might term an Arabic poetics. He identifies five elements of *badīʿ*: metaphor (*istiʿārah*), paronomasia (*tajnīs*–the use in the same line of a similar word or verbal root with two different meanings), antithesis (*ṭibāq* – for example, black and white, sword and pen), *radd al-aʿjāz* (internal repetition within the line), and lastly the most problematic category: *al-madhhab al-kalāmī* which, some modern scholars specialising in Arabic criticism maintain, is best rendered as 'the replication of the speculative discourse of theology' (*kalām*). To these five principal categories of trope ibn al-Muʿtazz adds twelve examples of what he terms 'discourse embellishments' (*maḥāsin al-kalām*). By identifying and analysing these poetic devices, ibn al-Muʿtazz moves beyond ibn Qutaybah's expressed concern with the need to consider the qualities of contemporary poetry along with that of the older tradition and engages the modern in its own right; as an extension of this concern we can point to his compilation, *Ṭabaqāt al-shuʿarāʾ* (Classes of Poets), in which he not only restricts his listing of accounts of poets (*akhbār*) to modernists (*muḥdathūn*) but also suggests that it is not only the ancient poets who can be considered as 'naturally gifted' (*maṭbūʿ*). However, in spite of these extremely important aspects of ibn al-Muʿtazz's work – most particularly the way in which his analysis moves from the level of grammar and theme towards a consideration of how poetic discourse functions, we need to return to the general intellectual environment in order to place the impact of his contributions into context. As we noted above, the element of *badīʿ* and some of its features had already been identified and discussed by previous writers such as al-Jāḥiẓ and Thaʿlab, and indeed the phenomenon had become associated with certain poets, including Muslim ibn al-Walīd and Bashshār ibn Burd. However, it was the poet, Abū Tammām (d. 845), who was to carry the potentialities of this new concern with poetic ornamentation to a higher level of complexity; as Iḥsān ʿAbbās notes somewhat ruefully in his study of the Arabic critical tradition, the poetry of Abū Tammām alone was to become one of the major instigators of critical writing in the tenth century. It is indeed Abū Tammām whose poetry is most often cited in ibn al-Muʿtazz's *Kitāb al-badīʿ*, mostly with disapproval. We can illustrate the nature of the latter's concerns by citing two lines of poetry, one by Abū Tammām himself, the other by his illustrious successor, al-Mutanabbī. One of Abū Tammām's most famous odes, a eulogy composed on the occasion of the victory against the Byzantines at the Battle of Amoreum in Anatolia, opens with the following line:

> The sword conveys truer tidings than books; its cutting edge separates the serious from the flippant.

Here we find antitheses between 'sword' and 'book', and 'serious' and 'frivolous'; the Arabic also provides two instances of paronomasia, the one partial between 'edge' and 'seriousness' (*ḥadd, jidd*), the other complete between 'edge' and 'dividing line' (*ḥadd, ḥadd*). Al-Mutanabbī's line is the second in his ode celebrating yet another battle against the Byzantines and is clearly inspired by Abū Tammām's:

> In the eyes of the puny, puny deeds seem important; in the eyes of the important, important deeds seem puny.

This line shows not only parallelism of structure between the two halves of the line, but examples of both antithesis and paronomasia crafted into a memorably gnomic statement. Both lines clearly illustrate the increased emphasis that the application of the principles of *badīʿ* was placing on the use of poetic devices and an elaboration of language, and it is this trend, as exemplified by Abū Tammām, that results in ibn al-Muʿtazz's clearly expressed unease. He invokes citations from the texts of the Qurʾān, *ḥadīth*, and the early poets in order to demonstrate that the phenomenon termed *badīʿ* (with the literal meaning of 'new') is in fact not new; what is different and, in ibn al-Muʿtazz's opinion, of questionable desirability is the extent to which modernist poets and one in particular – Abū Tammām – are using its repertoire of devices in their poetry. Seen in such a light, ibn al-Muʿtazz's work seems to fulfil a Janus-like function: on the one hand it can be viewed as the base from which much future critical writing would develop; on the other, it is a call for moderation that underlines the historical precedents of *badīʿ* rather than its radical extremes.

The works of ibn al-Muʿtazz are significant not only for the modes of organisation and analysis that they present but also because they underline an important aspect of the nature of the debate over the ancients and modern(ists) that is to colour future developments in criticism. For, while ibn al-Muʿtazz's compendium of modernist poets does address itself specifically to the poetry of his contemporaries, the *Kitāb al-badīʿ* seems to reflect a more comprehensive, if conservative, view of the situation. Its clear implication is that any debate regarding the merits of ancient and modern poets could never be an either/or situation; the establishment of such a dichotomy did not imply the possibility of a process of change that would lead to one replacing the other. The ancient poetry was and would always remain a canonical point of reference, an aesthetic yardstick. In the light of such a realisation, it would become the principal task of critics who set out to evaluate the poetry of their own time to integrate an appreciation of its virtues into the tradition that already existed. The tensions that inevitably arose regarding this issue were to be a major feature of critical writing in the eleventh and twelfth centuries and are seen at their most intense in the critical focus on the poetry of Abū Tammām and al-Mutanabbī which will be discussed below.

The other famous figure in criticism during this period was Qudāmah ibn Jaʿfar (d. 948). He was clearly aware of ibn al-Muʿtazz's studies, in that he composed not only a work on the poetry of Abū Tammām but also a retort to ibn al-Muʿtazz. However, in *Naqd al-shiʿr* (Poetic Criticism) Qudāmah seems determined to plot his own separate course, in that he sets out to describe the craft of poetry and to provide a manual for its description and evaluation; as he candidly observes, 'So far I have not discovered a single work of poetic criticism that distinguishes good from bad poetry'. He then proceeds to provide a definition of poetry: 'discourse (the word *kalām* implies speech) that is metred, rhymed, and conveys meaning'. This terse definition of what constitutes poetry (and by implication what does not) is to serve as a prescriptive yardstick, to be invoked by students of Arabic poetry for many centuries. In the assessment of the poetic craft, Qudāmah provides a schema through which judgements can be made. Four categories are involved: words, meaning, metre, and rhyme. They can be combined in eight different ways to provide a basis for the evaluation of good and bad poetry; thus, a poem in which the combined categories are all good is thus a very good poem, but, as weak points emerge in one or more category, so does the poem fit into a descending scale towards 'badness'.

Qudāmah's adoption of such a logically systematic mode of analysis has led some scholars to see in his work the natural product of a familiarity with the translations of Greek learning that, as was noted above, were becoming increasingly available. However, while the logical patterns of organisation characteristic of that tradition may perhaps be reflected in the modes adopted in *Naqd al-shiʿr*, Qudāmah's text does not reveal an awareness of the specific ideas or terminology of the most obvious source on the subject, namely Aristotle; such influences emerge more clearly in the works of other critics to be mentioned below.

A cluster of dichotomies

The works of ibn al-Muʿtazz and Qudāmah ibn Jaʿfar usher in an era in which the system of Arabic criticism and its theoretical underpinnings are elaborated in a number of ways. Several factors combine to make the process somewhat diffuse. Firstly there is the obvious factor of distance; for, while many of the critics whose works we will be examining wrote and taught in the cities under the immediate control of the ʿAbbāsī caliph in Baghdad, ibn Rashīq al-Qayrawānī (d. *c.* 1065), for example, was writing in Tunisia; at a still later stage Ḥāzim al-Qarṭājannī (d. 1285) hails, as his name implies, from Cartagena in Spain. Bearing in mind the methods of recording and transmitting materials that were available at this time, we should regard the extent to which a writer like ibn Rashīq is aware of developments elsewhere as a tribute to the efficacy of the modes of communication and education that did exist. Another factor is clearly the cultural environment within which critics were operating. Disagreements over doctrinal matters between Sunnīs and Shīʿīs (and between other religious groups) and on cultural values between Arabs and non-Arab converts are a continuing backdrop to intellectual debates, and to those we can also add issues of sectarian and even personal rivalries. Thus, while we may perhaps regard the silence of Qudāmah ibn Jaʿfar about ibn al-Muʿtazz's *Kitāb al-badīʿ* as an assertion of intellectual independence, the same can hardly be said concerning the fate of the large repertoire of compilations and critical works by ibn Abī Ṭāhir Ṭayfūr (d. 894), to all appearances a major, if controversial, cultural figure of his age, whose role remains, for reasons unknown, tantalisingly unappreciated.

The basic framework adopted by the majority of critics continues to revolve around questions concerning the nature of poetry, its themes, tropes, and language, and the evaluation of its practitioners and their works. Many of the rubrics under which these critical issues are explored consist of a series of dichotomies, a number of them adopted by earlier scholars, that reflect not only the priorities and methods of textual exegesis and commentary (*tafsīr*) out of which they emerge but also the tensions aroused by changes in taste and the relationship to the cherished tradition of the earliest period of Arabic literature. There is firstly much discussion of the relative priority to be assigned to form and content (*lafẓ* and *maʿnā*, words and meaning); the very process of differentiating these two entities and considering their relative 'merits', coupled to the enormous antipathies expressed regarding certain poets such as Abū Tammām and al-Mutanabbī, leads to the development of an elaborate literature on plagiarism. Secondly, the community's fervent belief in the 'truth' of its canonical texts and the process of checking their authenticity is combined with the Qurʾān's expressed disapproval of the statements of poets to produce some rigorous comparisons between the veracity of the poetic message and that of other categories of text. This results in the incorporation into many critical works of a discussion of the role of truth and lies in poetry. The tenor of the debate can be illustrated by one of its most often quoted opinions, that 'the most poetic poetry is that which lies the most' (*ashʿar al-shiʿr akdhabuhu*), a view almost completely echoed by Touchstone in Act III of Shakespeare's *As You Like It* when he responds to Audrey's inquiry about poetry: 'No, truly, the truest poetry is the most feigning'. In our discussion of ibn Qutaybah above we have already encountered the third pair of terms, 'naturalness' and 'artifice, craft' (*ṭabʿ* and *ṣanʿah*, or, in adjectival form, *maṭbūʿ* and *maṣnūʿ*), attributes the discussion of which intensified, needless to say, as the *badīʿ* poets began to craft – in written form, perhaps – their complex creations.

The continuing focus on the desired characteristics of poetry is exemplified by *ʿIyar al-shiʿr* (The Yardstick of Poetry) of ibn Ṭabāṭabā (d. 934), a work that neatly mirrors some of the tensions mentioned above. For, while his emphasis on meaning as a separable entity and his distaste for all but the most transparent of metaphors link his views firmly to those of earlier critics, his concern with units of composition beyond the single line marks a new trend. Indeed, in his discussion of the element of cohesion within segments of the poem he makes particular use of the qualities of the (prose) epistle (*risālah*) – its concision, awareness of beginnings and endings, and purity of language (*faṣāḥah*) – as 'yardsticks' in poetic construction. Here we find ourselves presented with evidence of the role that the emerging tradition of *adab* and its repertoire of manuals on epistolography were beginning to play within the domain of criticism. The balance of critical attention continues to favour the study of poets and their works as opposed to bellettristic prose and its exponents – something that the twentieth-century Egyptian critic, Ṭāhā Ḥusayn, attributes to a more universal instinct in human societies that gives precedence to the imagination (represented by poetry) over the intellect (expressed in prose), but the early contributions of al-Mubarrad and al-Jāḥiẓ (noted above) to a discussion of the nature of eloquence and a comparison of poetry and prose serve as precedents to a series of manuals and catalogue works – to be discussed later in this chapter – that place the discussion of the qualities of 'the two arts' into a broader framework.

Poets in the balance

Iḥsān ʿAbbās notes that three 'forces' are responsible for the use of much critical ink during the eleventh century: Abū Tammām, Aristotle, and al-Mutanabbī. We will consider the role of Greek ideas in a separate section below, but we first turn to a consideration of the large number of studies that were devoted to two of Arabic's most famous poets. The process of developing modes of comparative analysis by which they were to be judged is, not unnaturally, the occasion for several notable advances in critical method.

The first work of this type that we will discuss is *Kitāb al-muwāzanah bayn al-Ṭāʾiyayn* (The Book of weighing the two Ṭāʿī Poets Abû Tammām and al-Buḥturī in the Balance) by Abū al-qāsim al-Āmidī (d. 987). Al-Āmidī announces at the outset that, without expressing a preference for either of the two poets, he intends to consider the merits of their odes using a variety of criteria. Before he actually does so, however, he provides a long survey of comments on different aspects of the poetic art – metre, prosody, meaning, *badīʿ*, plagiarism, and so on. When the actual comparison section is finally reached, we find not only that the scope of the analysis is limited to small groups of lines, but also that the deck is somewhat stacked. Al-Āmidī adopts the basic structure of the *qaṣīdah* as outlined by ibn Qutaybah and goes through the thematic segments of the poem – the deserted encampment, the departure, love sentiments (*ghazal*), and so on, concentrating in particular on opening lines in order to illustrate the ways in which al-Buḥturī's poetry is more in line with the norms of the classical tradition (for which he uses the term *ʿamûd al-shiʿr*) than is Abū Tammām's. He accuses Abū Tammām of over-indulgence in obscure imagery and suggests that the poet's admirers are lacking in good taste. For al-Āmidī, of course, the bases of that taste were firmly rooted in what he saw as the natural poetry of the ancient poets, and his critical stance thus emerges as a conservative one. However, once again we need to consider the critical tradition in the broader context of textual studies in which clarity of expression was firmly established as a *desideratum*. What al-Āmidī desires is comprehensibility, metaphors that reveal their points of similarity in appropriate ways, and in such a context al-Buḥturī, a student of Abū Tammām, was never in danger of 'losing'. Even so, the somewhat biased nature of al-Āmidī's comparative method should not obscure the extent of his achievement. By focusing his attention exclusively on specific poets and developing a system for the evaluation of actual segments of poems, he provides the critical enterprise with a greater methodological rigour. As Muḥammad Mandūr notes, the fact that his own utilisation of the system reveals some predetermined attitudes does not diminish the significance of what he achieved.

The critical furore created by Abū Tammām's complex imagery was but a prelude to the one that developed around the career and work of his pre-eminent successor, al-Mutanabbīi. The title of a second comparative work, *Kitāb al-wasāṭah bayn al-Mutanabbī wa-khuṣūmihi* (Book of Mediation Between al-Mutanabbī and His Antagonists) by ʿAlī al-Jurjānī (d. 1002), reflects the fact that al-Mutanabbī's highly developed sense of his own importance (that we noted in ch. 4, on poetry) was quite sufficient to attract enemies, quite apart from the consequences of more literary debates concerning the merits of his poetic output. This al-Jurjānī was himself a judge (*qāḍī*), and he is thus usually known as al-Qāḍī al-Jurjānī in order to distinguish him from ʿAbd al-qāhir al-Jurjānī, the eminent critic whose works we will consider below. The qualities of a judge were clearly demanded to bring an element of impartiality to the fierce and continuing debate over al-Mutanabbī's poetry which had already been the subject of a number of minutely detailed, not to say finicky, studies and personal attacks that focused on his alleged plagiarisms, such as *al-Risālah al-mūḍiḥah fī dhikr sariqāt Abī al-ṭayyib al-Mutanabbī wa-sāqiṭ shiʿrihi* (The Explicit Epistle Describing the Plagiarisms and Faulty Poetry of Abū al-ṭayyib al-Mutanabbī) by al-Ḥātimī (d. 998) and *al-Risālah fī al-kashf ʿan masāwī al-Mutanabbī* (Epistle revealing the shortcomings of al-Mutanabbī) by al-Ṣāḥib ibn ʿAbbād

(d. 995) whom we encountered as a contributor to the tradition of bellettristic prose in ch. 5. Al-Qāḍī al-Jurjānī establishes some fresh terms of reference from the outset by remarking that poets from all periods have included inferior lines in their poems, but critics have chosen to attack such faults in modernist poetry while excusing it in more ancient examples. What is needed, he suggests, is for poets to write in a manner that is 'natural' for their age. In such a context naturalness (*ṭabʿ*) ceases to be a quality exclusively confined to early poetry; indeed, it is the primary fault of Abū Tammām that he did not adhere to the facets of his own age but instead tried to graft his modernist imagery on to poems that strived to imitate the ancients. Like al-Āmidī, al-Qāḍī al-Jurjānī prefaces his 'mediating' section with examples of poetic devices, including three of ibn al-Muʿtazz's five – metaphor, paronomasia, and antithesis – thus indicating perhaps an early realisation of the problematic nature of the other two. After a section in which he examines the properties of al-Mutanabbī's poetry, he turns to a mammoth survey of plagiarism (which he dubs 'an ancient disease'), identifying false accusation made against al-Buḥturī, Abū Nuwās, and Abū Tammām, before devoting some two hundred pages to a line-by-line analysis of al-Mutanabbī's various sins in this regard. Al-Qāḍī al-Jurjānī ends with an analysis of the points on which al-Mutanabbī has been attacked and a defence of him. Once again, he points out that the faults that critics have identified in his poetry – his propensity for hyperbole, for example – exist in abundance in the work of earlier poets. Thus, he returns at the conclusion of this 'judiciously' balanced work to the major point with which he commenced: the Arabic poetic tradition is a continuum, and the issues involved in evaluating the products of different periods need to be viewed in context.

With al-Mutanabbī the topic of plagiarism had become a major growth industry, and so here is probably an appropriate place to pause for a brief consideration of the topic. Quite apart from the personal animosities that surrounded the lives of both poets with controversy, this close focus on the topic of plagiarism can be viewed as yet another product of not only the tensions arising from the process of transfer from a culture that relied on oral communication to one that stored its information in written form but also a literary côterie that set great store by the preservation of a classical corpus and chose to illustrate its superiority by identifying the ways in which modern poets borrowed from it. The principles of plagiarism-analysis were firmly grounded im the twin notions of word (*lafẓ*) and meaning (*maʿnā*) mentioned above: a precis of them is provided by Abū Hilāl al-ʿAskarī whose manual on poetry and prose will be discussed below:

I've heard it said that anyone who adopts a concept word for word is a [full-scale] plagiarist; anyone who takes part of one is [designated] an inserter; and anyone who takes one and adorns it with words that are better than the original is more worthy than his predecessor.

The final category refers to the process known as *muʿāraḍah* whereby a poet would gain kudos by consciously adopting a line by a predecessor and improving on it. It was, of course, part of the critical debate over al-Mutanabbī to determine whether some of his memorably gnomic lines of poetry unjustly rode on the shoulders of his predecessors.

Al-Āmidī and al-Qāḍī al-Jurjānī made major contributions to the field of poetic criticism, but at the same time both clearly express an anxiety about change; not so much the process itself as the pace and direction of the modernist poets. Both alluded to a set of principles, termed *ʿamūd al-shiʿr*, which served as locus for the classical ideals in which they both believed. Those ideals were elaborated by al-Marzūqī (d. 1030) as part of his commentary on the *al-Ḥamāsah* (Collection of Poetry on Chivalry) of Abū Tammām. We are given a glimpse of al-Marzūqī's predilections when he expresses a clear preference for the clarity of prose writing over the complexity and potential obscurity of poetry. He then sets out to explore the elements that make poetry good and, more specifically, to identify the particular characteristics that have made the early poetic corpus into a model of naturalness. Within the context of the twin pairs of word-meaning and truth-falsehood he notes that there are both extremes and means. Poetry can be utterly truthful or untruthful, but al-Marzūqī identifies a middle position between those two through a slight adjustment in the wording of the formula we noted above: the best poetry is the most moderate (*aḥsan al-shiʿr aqṣaduhu*). He then elaborates on his preference in a listing of the elements of *ʿamūd al-shiʿr*. Poetry, he says, should possess nobility and soundness of meaning; polished and appropriate wording; apposite description; and closeness of resemblance in simile (none of those far-fetched examples of Abū Tammām). These categories had already been identified by al-Qāḍī al-Jurjānī, and to them al-Marzūqī appends: tight cohesion of segments and pleasant metre; appropriateness of similarity in the two elements of a metaphor; and suitable choice of wording in accordance with the demands of rhyme. These criteria, needless to say, serve to canonise the normative function of ancient poetry as the classical model of naturalness (*ṭab*ʿ); they form the yardstick against which the contemporary swings of modernist poets between naturalness and craft are to be evaluated.

The Qurʾān as miracle: different discourse

The challenge to record, codify, and understand the Qurʾān, as we have noted above, presented the Muslim community with a clear set of research priorities in the fields of lexicography, philology, and grammar. Early works in these fields became the tools through which the community of scholars developed a hermeneutic tradition; the exegesis (*tafsīr*) of the Qurʾān required the development of rigorous modes of textual analysis and commentary that were to have a profound effect on the critical tradition. As part of this process, scholars such as Abū ʿUbaydah and ibn Qutaybah identified those elements of the sacred text that showed aspects of difference or difficulty. Abū ʿUbaydah explores *majāz*, defined by the nineteenth-century writer, Ḥusayn al-Marṣafī (d. 1890) as

> a process whereby a comment leaves its basic meaning behind and takes on another appropriate sense that you wish to use and which the addressee will understand.

However, from these concerns with interpreting the Qurʾān and its discourse features scholars moved on to another topic, one that finds its origins in the text itself when, in response to a challenge to produce a miracle, Muḥammad is inspired to retort that the Qurʾān itself is miraculous. This revelation is the origin of a school of critical writing that moves the debate on the Qurʾān beyond the early processes of relating it to its linguistic environment (and especially its literary precedents) to one that sets out to prove *iʿjāz al-qurʾān*, that the Qurʾān is the supreme example of Arabic discourse, different from and superior to the literary genres composed by humans.

In a short treatise entitled *al-Nukat fī iʿjāz al-Qurʾān* (Comments on the Miraculous Nature of the Qurʾān) the Muʿtazilī grammarian al-Rummānī (d. 994), makes *iʿjāz* the highest of three categories of *balāghah*. Examining ten different tropes (including simile and metaphor), he notes that only the Qurʾān has features that place it alone into the highest category. The title of al-Khaṭṭābī's (d. 988) work on this same topic, *Bayān iʿjāz al-Qurʾān*, neatly encapsulates the focus of al-Rummānī's argument, and to it the former adds sections on words and meanings and an important gesture whereby the two are fused into the concept of 'arrangement' (*naẓm*), which is to be brought to its finest elaboration in the work of ʿAbd al-qāhir al-Jurjānī. However, the staunchest of these early proponents of *iʿjāz al-Qurʾān* is al-Bāqillānī (d. 1013) who in a work of that title launches himself undaunted into a proof of the Qurʾān's superiority through a comparison of its discourse with that of two prominent poets, one ancient – Imru al-Qays, the other contemporary – al-Buḥturī. Imru al-Qays's famous *muʿallaqah* is shown not only to lack cohesion but also to contain some tasteless and morally offensive passages; furthermore his use of a large number of place names is found otiose to the purposes of the poem. The structure and contents of al-Buḥturī's ode are found to be likewise deficient. According to al-Bāqillānī's premises, the Qurʾān does indeed prove superior; the 'apples and oranges' comparative method that he adopts makes it a relatively easy task to dismiss his work as a central contribution to the development of a critical system. However, what makes al-Bāqillānī's diatribe significant in a broader perspective is that he chooses to demonstrate the superiority of the Qurʾān in terms of the linkages that bind its surahs together and of the coherence of its discourse as a whole. In emphasising these qualities as *desiderata*, he can be seen to be amplifying on the example of ibn Ṭabāṭabā (discussed above) in moving the analytical exercise beyond a focus on the smallest units (in poetry, the individual line) to larger semantic and structural segments.

ʿAbd al-qāhir al-Jurjānī

The critic who made a major contribution to the analysis of *iʿjāz al-Qurʾān* is one whose name has already been mentioned, ʿAbd al-qāhir al-Jurjānī (d. 1079), without doubt the major figure in Arabic literary criticism and one whose contributions to the history of criticism in general deserve a much wider recognition. His two great works are *Dalāʾil al-iʿjāz* (Features of *Iʿjāz*) and *Asrār al-balāghah* (The Secrets of Eloquence). While each acquired an enormous reputation in its own right, al-Jurjānī's repute was most firmly preserved and transmitted through a series of works that summarised his theories: *Nihāyat al-ījāz fī dirāyat al-iʿjāz* (The high point of concision concerning the study of *iʿjāz*) by Fakhr al-dīn al-Rāzī (d. 1209); *Miftāḥ al-ʿulūm* (Key to the sciences) by al-Sakkākī (d. 1229); and *Takhlīṣ al-miftāḥ* (Summary of the key of the sciences) by al-Qazwīnī (d. 1338).

Al-Jurjānī was a grammarian, and the contents of *Dalāʾil al-iʿjāz* reveal that aspect of his expertise through a detailed analysis of those elements of syntax (tense, negation, and connection, for example) and stylistics (word order, use of tropes) that contribute to the qualities of *faṣāhah* (proper usage of Arabic) and *balāghah* (eloquence). However, when he moves to the notion of *iʿjāz* itself, he takes his syntactic analysis beyond the level of the word and sentence into a discussion of the function of meaning, to the point of conjunction between linguistic analysis and the aesthetic dimension of literary criticism that has been the focus of much modern research. Language, he writes, conveys meaning through the way in which words are organised into contextualised sets of semantic relationships, a notion for which he adopts the term 'the arrangement of discourse' (*naẓm al-kalām*), *naẓm* being a term used earlier by al-Jāḥiẓ and al-Khaṭṭābī. The individual word cannot have a value of its own; it is merely a tool through which meaning is conveyed. As a consequence, the dichotomy, much belaboured by earlier critics, between word (*lafẓ*) and meaning (*maʿnā*), is deemed to be a false one. Furthermore, since language operates in this fashion, figurative language and imagery need to be viewed as another mode of conveying meaning and to be incorporated within the same analytical process. Such a mode requires that we consider not merely the meaning but 'the meaning of the meaning' (*maʿnā al-maʿnā*); thus, when, for example, the poet speaks in context about 'stars of guidance', the listener needs to move beyond the surface meaning of the words in order to appreciate that it is religious scholars who are being described. Al-Jurjānī uses this analytical framework to illustrate the miraculous nature of the Qurʾān, citing passages that show the blending together of words and concepts into a cohesive discourse that is unique and inimitable. Other types of writing, poetry and prose, are assessed on the same terms; for example, he reserves his disapproval for excessively elaborate and artificial rhyming prose (*sajʿ*) and paronomasia (*tajnīs*) – citing Abū Tammām – precisely because they destroy the necessary harmony between word and meaning by giving emphasis to the former over the latter.

In his second major work, *Asrār al-balāghah*, al-Jurjānī addresses himself to the poetic image (*ṣūrah*) and its functions. Having established that imagery should not be treated as a decorative addendum to poetic discourse but rather as a different mode for the expression of meaning through language, he proceeds to analyse the paths through which it is conceived and received. He categorises images in terms of similarity (metaphor and simile) and contiguity (allusion and devices involving substitution such as synecdoche – for example, that the notion found in

Arabic, as in English, of 'giving someone a hand' implies doing someone a favour). Al-Jurjānī devotes the bulk of his attention to the categories of similarity, simile (*tashbīh*) and metaphor (*istiʿārah*). He identifies two types of meaning, one that resorts to the intellect (*ʿaqlī*), the other to the imagination (*takhyīlī*); each has several sub-categories. The first consists of what is considered rationally justifiable and objective, linkages that appear to be verifiable; many examples of this type, as al-Jurjānī notes, are to be found in the texts of *ḥadīth* and the Qurʾān itself as well as in poetry and oratory. The second type involves what is not truthful; it is not intended to be deliberately false however, but is simply unverifiable – a notion that finds a later echo in Sir Philip Sidney's (d. 1586) 'An Apology for Poetry': 'The poet nothing affirmeth and therefore never lieth.' That Abū Tammām's poetry provides one of the examples for the discussion is hardly surprising:

> Do not discount the possibility of a generous man being penniless; the flood is always at war with lofty places.

The links between generosity and loftiness, the flow of wealth and water, are shown to create a 'truth' of their own that is not intended to be based on the world of the verifiable. Here al-Jurjānī is setting out to resolve yet another of the dichotomies addressed above, that of truth and falsehood, suggesting that the criteria of veracity and its presumed moral superiority do not apply in all contexts, but rather the artist's conception of the most appropriate expression and the listener's appreciation of it. Kamal Abu Deeb, one of al-Jurjānī's most sophisticated contemporary analysts, notes that, in spite of the objective stance that is implicit in this analysis of similarity, al-Jurjānī nevertheless reflects the important place of the Qurʾān in his thinking and in Islamic culture as a whole by confining the limits in the discovery of similarities to what is already known; it may be the function of the poet to reveal what is hidden, but that is the extent of discretion.

Those twentieth-century scholars who have specialised in the achievements of the heritage of Arabic literary criticism have come to marvel at the sophistication of the ideas set forth by al-Jurjānī. His writings seem to represent such a high point that, with the exception of Ḥāzim al-Qarṭājannī to be considered shortly, his successors contented themselves with the compilation of summaries of his principal ideas. Muḥammad Mandūr, Kamal Abu Deeb, and Aziz al-Azmeh, among many other modern writers, have written eloquently about the extraordinary contemporary relevance of what he wrote. Al-Azmeh describes al-Jurjānī's achievement as 'one of the most sustained, refined, rigorous, and durable attempts to construct a theory of the production of meaning in discourse and of discourse analysis in any language and at any time'.

The integration of critical thought brought about by al-Jurjānī's principle of 'arrangement' (*naẓm*) was to have a profound effect on the way in which his successors studied the Qur'ān. One such was al-Zamakhsharī (d. 1143), who wrote a study of the Qur'ān, *al-Kashshāf ʿan ḥaqāʾiq al-tanzīl wa-ʿuyūn al-aqāwīl fī wujūh al-taʾwīl* (The discoverer of the verities of revelation and crucial sayings regarding aspects of interpretation), the lengthy title of which illustrates not only the continuing fascination with the rhyming proclivities of *sajʿ* but also the author's desire to combine in a single work aspects of syntactic analysis and the textual details of philology with the stylistics of al-Jurjānī's treatment of *iʿjāz*. The linkages between what had previously been viewed as antagonistic approaches are yet more evident in the works of the Egyptian scholar, ibn Abī al-Iṣbaʿ (d. 1256): in *Badīʿ al-Qurʾān* (The *Badīʿ* in the Qur'ān) and *Taḥrīr al-taḥbīr fī ṣināʿat al-shiʿr wa-al-nathr wa-bayān iʿjāz al-Qurʾān* (Refined Composition Concerning the Craft of Poetry, Prose, and the Clarity of The Miraculous Nature of the Qur'ān) in which aspects of syntax, stylistics, and poetics are analysed with citations from the Qur'ān. Indeed the issues surrounding ibn al-Muʿtazz's problematic fifth trope, *al-madhhab al-kalāmī*, are openly addressed in a section specifically devoted to it: 'Ibn al-Muʿtazz had claimed', ibn Abī al-Iṣbaʿ notes, 'that [the trope] does not exist in the text of the Qur'ān, whereas it is stuffed full [*maḥshuw*] of it'. These studies of the Qur'ānic disciplines (*ʿulūm al-Qurʾān*) are continued in the works of ibn Qayyim al-Jawziyyah (d. 1350) and al-Zarkashī (d. 1392) in a huge compilation entitled *al-Burhān* (The proof). Al-Suyuṭī (d. 1505) contributes to this, as to many other, fields with the less than modestly titled *al-Itqān fī ʿulūm al-Qurʾān* (The perfection [The last word, perhaps] on the Qur'ānic Disciplines), subdivided into eighty subsections (*anwāʿ*) that cover the text's revelation, subdivisions, recitation, grammar, and style.

The study of the stylistic and structural properties of the Qur'ān continued along similar lines into the modern period. The encounter between the traditional approaches to the study of the text, especially those founded on the principles of *iʿjāz al-Qurʾān*, and the critical methods that Arab scholars acquired through a European education almost inevitably led to confrontations that engendered some of the most famous controversies in the intellectual life of the region during the early decades of the twentieth century. In 1925, for example, Ṭāhā Ḥusayn wrote a study of the earliest period of Arabic literature, *Fī al-shiʿr al-jāhilī* (On pre-islamic poetry) – to be examined below – in which he suggested that certain stories in the Qur'ān appear to be fables. In 1995, another Egyptian scholar, Naṣr Ḥāmid Abū Zayd, who in his *Naqd al-khaṭāb al-dīnī* (Critique of Religious Discourse, 1992) attempts to apply contemporary modes of critical analysis to religious discourse, was declared divorced from his wife since his ideas had shown him to be a 'heretic'. It would appear that, even though al-Jurjānī's great work of synthesis and analysis had fused the early dichotomies of the critical tradition into a system of *naẓm* that could address texts as repositories of language and its different uses and though his successors had proceeded to explore and elucidate many of the implications of his theories, the sensitivities of doctrinal debate have continued to impinge upon the critical endeavour.

THE CONTRIBUTION OF GREEK THOUGHT

Recent scholarship on the Middle East has tended to take a relatively cautious approach to the tracing of influences that occur when cultures meet and coalesce. The Arabic literary tradition provides many examples of this phenomenon, as the courts and cultural centres of the widespread Islamic dominions brought littérateurs and scholars into contact with the culture and learning of regions as distant as Europe and China. One such instance involves an assessment of the precise nature and extent of the role of Greek thought in the development of Arabic literary criticism. Indeed, the debate is not confined to more recent times. The hardly disguised aggravation displayed by Ḍiyā' al-dīn ibn al-Athīr (d. 1239), whose work will be examined below, suggests that the subject was able to provoke strong feelings. Not only does he maintain that poets like Abū Tammām and al-Mutanabbī had no recourse to the works of Greek scholars, but suggests that his own work on the Arabic tradition – composed, he says, without recourse to Greek sources – is a sufficient proof of the minimal influence of the Greek tradition. This position is, no doubt, somewhat extreme when we bear in mind the cosmopolitan atmosphere of Baghdad during the heyday of the ʿAbbāsī caliphate (ninth and tenth centuries) and the research activities fostered by the Baghdad library, *Bayt al-Ḥikmah* (House of Wisdom), yet it is clearly the case that those aspects of Greek learning that did make their way into Arabic literary discourse as a result of cultural contacts and translation were assimilated into a critical tradition, the basic parameters of which had already been firmly established within the context of the early priorities of the Muslim community and especially of the hermeneutics of the Qurʾān. That said, Iḥsān ʿAbbās is clearly correct in making Aristotle himself one of the three 'forces' to whose impetus the bulk of Arabic critical activity in the tenth century can be attributed; indeed many of the scholars whose contributions will now be discussed were themselves philosophers, and their works on literary topics need to be viewed within a broader framework than that of poetic criticism alone.

The great philosopher, al-Fārābī (d. 950), contemporary of the poet al-Mutanabbī at the court of Sayf al-dawlah al-Ḥamdānī at Aleppo and dubbed 'the second teacher' (*al-muʿallim al-thānī* – Aristotle being the first), composed a *Risālah fī qawānīn ṣinaʿat al-shuʿarāʾ* (Epistle on the canons of the poets' craft) in which he attempted a synthesis of the principles gleaned from a reading of the far from satisfactory Arabic early translation of Aristotle's *Poetics* with the poetic tradition of the Arabs. Having identified five types of discourse, ranging from a demonstrably true form appreciated by the philosophers to one that is palpably false (that of the poets) – a schema that is an interesting mirror of the five categories of permissibility in Islamic law, from required to forbidden, he then proceeds to place poets into three types: those who possess a natural gift and thus do not need to resort to craft (*ṣinaʿah*), those who set out to master craft, and those who do neither and are to be considered incompetent. What is interesting about al-Fārābī's presentation of aspects of the poet's craft in this way is that, having used Aristotle's mode of categorisation to present his system, he then shows a clear preference for the more conservative tendencies of the Arab tradition of his day by stressing the virtues of naturalness over those of craft.

Ibn Sīnā (d. 1037), the renowned physician-philosopher – known in Europe as Avicenna – who, as we noted in ch. 5, wrote a philosophical allegory entitled *Ḥayy ibn Yaqẓān*, discussed the nature and role of poetry in several of his works, including his major philosophical treatise, *al-Shifāʾ* (The healing), and a commentary on Aristotle's *Poetics* entitled *Fann al-shiʿr* (The art of poetry). Al-Fārābī had earlier invoked the concept of *takhyīl* (invoking the imaginary) as a feature of poetic mimesis (*muḥākah*), but it was ibn Sīnā who, as part of a less conservative approach, set out to explore in greater detail the implications of the Aristotelian categories within the context of Arabic poetics. He noted that poetry, besides its more obvious features of rhyme and metre, can be defined by the way in which it invokes the imagination. Thus the analysis of poetry should not concern itself with issues of morality or a semblance of reality, but with the process of utilising imitation (*muḥākah*) as a means of arousing a sense of delight, a sensation that produces in the listener a feeling of harmony and assent with what is being expressed. Adopting the oft-stated notion that the principal topics of Arabic poetry are praise and its opposite, ibn Sīnā suggests that mimesis falls similarly into two categories aimed at portraying things as either beautiful (*taḥsīn*) or ugly (*taqbīḥ*). He also acknowledges that Greek poets often strove for a further kind of mimesis, one whose purpose was entirely neutral; he thus allows for the possibility of three goals within his system.

Another Arab philosopher whose name was renowned in Christian Europe was ibn Rushd (d. 1198) – known as Averroes, who served as physician and judge in Spain and Morocco. One of the most famous interpreters of Aristotle's corpus, he wrote several commentaries, including one on the *Poetics* entitled *Takhlīṣ kitāb Arisṭūṭalīs fī al-shiʿr* (A Summary of Aristotle's *Poetics*). He makes clear at the outset that the purpose of his 'summary' is not to discuss Aristotle's views as a whole, but only those that can be extrapolated into general principles and thus applied to the tradition of Arabic poetry. In setting himself those goals, he finds himself, needless to say, addressing many of the issues that had confronted Abū Bishr Mattā ibn Yūnus (d. 940), the work's first translator, what Walter Benjamin termed a work's 'translatability': that the search for equivalents of certain technical terms is rarely precise (the notion, for example, that the Arabic word for 'eulogy, panegyric' (*madīḥ*) conveys the sense of the Greek concept of tragedy). Like ibn Sīnā, ibn Rushd views poetry as being the invoker of the imagination, its principal topics being praise and invective (reflecting man's proclivity for either virtue or vice). Bearing in mind ibn Rushd's seemingly practical purpose of integrating Aristotle's ideas on poetry into the Arabic tradition for the benefit of poets and critics alike, it is somewhat curious, indeed saddening, to note that, at least in this field, his labours seem to have had a minimal effect, even in the Western domains of Islam where he himself lived and worked. Indeed, the writings of another prominent Andalusian and one of Arabic's most notable literary critics, Ḥāzim al-Qarṭajannī (d. 1285), who was born a mere thirteen years after ibn Rushd's death, show no awareness of his writings on criticism but rather owe an acknowledged debt to the writings of ibn Sīnā.

Ḥāzim of Cartagena (al-Qarṭajannī) was a well-known poet. However, his famous and mostly successful attempt at making a synthesis of the Aristotelian and Arabic traditions of poetics, *Minhāj al-bulaghā' wa-sirāj al-udabā'* (Course for the Eloquent and Beacon for the Literate), is not only singularly short of poetic examples but composed in a style and structure that are of considerable complexity, not least because of his proclivity for classification. As the title indicates, al-Qarṭajannī regards his focus as being literary discourse, combining thereby rhetoric (*balāghah*) – with its task of persuasion (*iqnā'*) – and poetry – aimed at invoking the imaginary (*takhyīl*). The work is subdivided into four major sections, beginning with an analysis of two categories very familiar to Arabic literary criticism, words (*alfāẓ*) and meanings (*ma'ānī*), and then proceeding to two other sections that discuss combinations of the first two: *naẓm* (the joining of words) and *uslūb* (of meanings). However, in spite of this organised sequence of topics, al-Qarṭajannī's system does not quite hold together; for, as the Egyptian critic, Shukrī 'Ayyād (cited by van Gelder) observes, al-Qarṭajannī makes use of the concept of *naẓm* (already elaborated by 'Abd al-qāhir al-Jurjānī) to transcend the boundaries of syntax and the single line in order to broach larger units of poetry, the section and even the poem as a whole. Al-Qarṭajannī's definition of poetry itself invokes the by now time-honoured words of Qudāmah ibn Ja'far, 'discourse that is metred and rhymed', but the impact of some of the critical investigations of the intervening period and of al-Qarṭajannī's own understandings of the Arabic and Greek traditions is clear from what is added to the basic statement: 'and whose purpose is to invoke in the soul a like or dislike for what poetry intends should be liked or disliked'. Poetry's purpose of *takhyīl* is achieved, he writes, through a combination of factors; one of the most important is mimesis (*muḥākah*), which at its best arouses in the listener a sense of wonderment at its extraordinary qualities and therefrom of pleasure. This discussion of modes and degrees of similarity leads into a painstaking investigation of the notions of truth and falsehood within the context of poetry, the categories of each, and the ways in which their use can be justified within the context of the poet's choice of theme(s) (*gharaḍ*, pl. *aghrāḍ*).

This impressive attempt to present a systematic study of the creative and receptive processes of poetry and the structure(s) of the Arabic *qaṣīdah* appears to have become a victim of place and circumstance. Those aspects of al-Qarṭajannī's work that are now considered most significant within the development of Arabic literary criticism were ignored by his successors; some modern historians of the critical tradition have even had occasion to invoke a wistful 'if only...' However, as noted elsewhere in this chapter, the primary focus of critical attention remained the increasingly elaborate and exhaustive analyses of the devices of *badīʿ* and of the elements that contributed to eloquent usage *balāghah* (with the Qurʾān's *iʿjāz* as its supreme model).

COMPILATIONS OF CRITICAL OPINION

Alongside the more particular trends in criticism that we have investigated above there are also a number of works that endeavour to keep score, as it were, on the critical tradition, mostly reflecting the views expressed in the works of others but in some cases making contributions of their own. The organising principles of these works vary, but the primary goal is summative. The case of poetic tropes provides a ready example. The *Kitāb al-badīʿ* of ibn al-Muʿtazz had, it will be recalled, identified five tropes and fifteen so-called embellishments. A section of *Kitāb al-ṣināʿatayn: al-kitābah wa-al-shiʿr* (The Book on the Two Arts: (prose) writing and poetry) by Abū Hilāl al-ʿAskarī (d. *c.* 1009), analysed more than thirty, and by the time of al-Suyūṭī (d. 1505) the figure had topped two hundred. One is reminded here of Roman Jakobson's thought: 'Is it then possible to limit the range of poetic devices? Not in the least; the history of art attests to their constant mutability'. (Roman Jakobson, *Language in Literature*, Cambridge, Mass. 1987, p. 369.)

In the case of al-ʿAskarī we are definitely dealing with a summary of the works of others, a kind of handbook on the craft of writing. It needs to be admitted that, while certain authorities from the past are cited by name, many others (including most notably ibn Ṭabāṭabā) remain unacknowledged. Al-ʿAskarī's goal is to describe and codify the elements of *balāghah* (correct usage, good style), and thus another direct link is established to the goals and methods of exegesis (*tafsīr*), jurisprudence (*fiqh*), and grammar (*naḥw*). Good and bad *balāghah* is explained in terms of correctness of usage based on logic (one would not say, for example, 'I saw him tomorrow') and of grammar (nor would one say, 'I Zayd saw yesterday'); the question of the probity of false statements (such as 'I carried a camel') is also raised. His examination of good writing involves detailed catalogues of literary genres and concepts, of types of expression, and of plagiarism (from which we have cited a passage above). There is an interesting discussion of parallelism and rhyming prose (*sajʿ*) in the context of Qurʾānic discourse which leads into the lengthy section of *badīʿ* and its, now, thirty-five subcategories (including such figures as hyperbole). This how-to-do-it manual ends with a section on appropriate beginnings and endings.

Another critical compilation is ibn Rashīq's (d. *c.* 1065) *al-ʿUmdah fī maḥāsin al-shiʿr wa-adabihi wa-naqdihi* (The Pillar Regarding Poetry's Embellishments, Proper Usage, and Criticism); in a short aside, it is interesting to note the way in which the word *adab* is used here in the context of poetry to describe the normative values of the tradition. As ibn Rashīq's title implies, the focus is mostly on poetry, but he is concerned with the quality (*faḍl*) of both poetic and prose writing; in that quest his work may show somewhat less organisation than that of al-ʿAskarī but considerably more critical insight. Thus, in addition to sections devoted to the more traditional subdivisions that we have discussed above, ibn Rashīq devotes some attention to the social context of poetry and its practitioners – the tribal context of the earlier poets, for example, and the role of patronage. In two areas in particular he seems concerned to provide a counterbalance to the conservative instincts of previous critics. In the context of his discussion of the role of hyperbole, he notes that poetry is the kind of discourse that is specifically intended to make untruth into something beautiful and adjusts the older statement noted above regarding poetry and truth into 'the most poetic person is someone whose untruthfulness is extolled and whose inferior work is derided'. In the ongoing debate over 'naturalness' and 'craft' he suggests that the dichotomy is a false one and that there is no necessary linkage between the latter notion, with its linkages to the modernist poets, and the quality that had become attached to it, namely 'artificiality' (*takalluf*). Like the works of his predecessors, ibn Rashīq's survey of the elements of poetry brings together within a single, undifferentiated format information of a wide variety: the principles of metre and rhyme, structural elements (beginnings and endings), characteristics of eloquence, poetic tropes (continuing the numerical expansion yet further), and genres (eulogy, elegy, lampoon). He also appends a fascinating selection from the accounts of the great battle days (*ayyām al-ʿarab*) of the pre-Islamic era. The extent to which *al-ʿUmdah* becomes a frequently quoted source regarding the Arabic poetic tradition is a tribute not only to the thoroughness with which he sets out to reflect the work of his predecessors (yet again, not always traceable to their actual source) but also to his attempts to find a more critically sophisticated middle-ground between the series of dichotomies that we discussed above.

If al-ʿAskarī and ibn Rashīq express a predilection for poetry in their discussion of 'the two arts', then with *Al-Mathal al-sā'ir fī adab al-kātib wa-al-shā'ir* (The Current Ideal For the Literary Discipline of the Secretary and Poet) by Ḍiyā' al-dīn ibn al-Athīr (d. 1239), we appear to encounter a tilt in the other direction. Since ibn al-Athīr (one member in a prominent family of writers) was himself a well-known prose writer (as we noted in ch. 5), this balance clearly reflects his personal proclivities although one must assume that it also reflects the increasing significance of prose writing and its criticism and of practitioners of both. Ibn al-Athīr's aim, he tells his readers, is to explore the nature of clear expression (*bayān*) in both poetry and prose; in describing his overall purpose he expresses his admiration for two previous writers in particular, al-Āmidī and ibn Sinān al-Khafājī (d. 1073), the author of an earlier work entitled *Sirr al-faṣāḥah* (The Secret of Proper Discourse). Ibn al-Athīr then embarks upon a truly massive exploration of every conceivable aspect of his topic, all expressed in the forthright tone of a senior administrator accustomed by dint of his elevated status to having his statements and opinions accepted. The practical goals of this manual are immediately apparent. The syntax of the sentence is explored from the simple to the more complex; the advantages of memorising the texts of the Qur'ān and *ḥadīth* are pointed out; the basic features of poetry – metre and rhyme – are discussed as well as the (still increasing) number of tropes; and different skills associated with the scribal profession – types of beginning and ending, suitable rebuttal techniques, and methods of précis – are discussed and illustrated. There is a lengthy and profusely exemplified section on plagiarism which subdivides the phenomenon into its different degrees of acceptability. While in most of these fields ibn al-Athīr is gathering into a huge compilation the views and attitudes of his predecessors, there is one in which he does appear to offer something unusual, namely an attempt to formulate the basic framework for a poetics of rhyming prose (*saj'*).

Al-Mathal al-sā'ir became a widely cited sourcework. It is, no doubt, a reflection of the authority that it came to command and of the fractious cultural relations between different courts of the times and indeed different administrators within those courts that ibn al-Athīr's work was the target of retorts: one by ibn Abī Ḥadīd (d. 1257), entitled *al-Falak al-dā'ir 'alā al-Mathal al-sā'ir* (The Cosmos Revolving Around *al-Mathal al-sā'ir*) is a section-by-section – blow-by-blow, perhaps – rebuttal of ibn al-Athīr's work, based on the model of 'He said this...' and 'I Say this...' Similarly critical and somewhat more literary in focus is *Nuṣrat al-thā'ir 'alā al-Mathal al-sā'ir* (Support for one who objects to *al-Mathal al-sāʾir*) by the prolific *adīb*, Ṣalāḥ al-dīn al-Ṣafadī (d. *c.* 1263), himself the son of a prominent Mamlūk *amīr*. However, while ibn al-Athīr's discourse manual seems to have been widely known, the great historian, ibn Khaldûn (d. 1406), expresses a clear preference for ibn Rashīq's *al-ʿUmdah* in the section of his *Muqaddimah* that deals with poetry. Ibn Khaldūn introduces a fresh element into his compilation of materials by including within his frame of reference examples of literary genres that had remained outside the purview of previous critics, including not only segments of popular narrative but also the Andalusian strophic poetry that had been the subject of an earlier study, *Dār al-ṭirāz* (The house of embroidery), by the Egyptian critic, ibn Sanāʾ al-Mulk (d. 1210). With such apparent innovations in mind, it comes as something of a surprise to note quite how conservative ibn Khaldūn's opinions about poetry actually are: in spite of the integrative work of ʿAbd al-qāhir al-Jurjānī outlined above, ibn Khaldūn emphasises form over meaning and indeed the concentration on the line of poetry as the major unit of analysis; it is perhaps all encapsulated in his injunction to those in quest of a definition of poetry, that 'they follow the style of the Arabs'.

The tendency of these compilers of large critical collections to reflect the more conservative aspects of the tradition is amply reflected in the writings of the Egyptian writer, Jamāl al-dīn al-Suyūṭī (d. 1505), whose *al-Muzhir fī ʿulūm al-lughah wa-anwāʿihā* (The Luminous Work Concerning the Language Sciences and Their Categories) might well be described as 'the last word' on the Arabic language and its ancillary sciences (including the literary). If ibn al-Athīr had gone back to the basic sentence in *al-Mathal al-sāʾir*, al-Suyūṭī goes one better by beginning at the level of the phoneme, working outwards through the entire morphology of the language, and including sections on those who communicate through it, the non-native speakers who have learned it and even the colloquial usages to be encountered in its different social registers. When al-Suyūṭī eventually considers the art of writing, it is in a thoroughly derivative fashion, recording comments on all the major transmitters and language analysts (al-Khalīl, al-Aṣmaʿī, al-Mubarrad, and Thaʿlab, for example) and, like ibn Khaldūn, relying heavily on ibn Rashīq's *al-ʿUmdah* in his estimates of poets and poetry.

These manuals and compilations, which conveniently brought together a wealth of information from a number of sources and venues, provided the most available source for Arab scholars in the nineteenth century who, in the light of cultural developments that were affecting the Middle East region, set themselves to re-examine the Arabic literary heritage. One such figure was the Egyptian, Ḥusayn al-Marṣafī (d. 1890), who converted his lectures at the *Dār al-ʿulūm* (House of Sciences) into a book entitled *al-Wasīlah al-adabiyyah ilā al-ʿulūm al-ʿArabiyyah* (The Literary Way to the Arabic Sciences, 1872–75). Taking large segments from al-ʿAskarī's *Kitāb al-ṣinaʿatayn*, he follows his predecessors in beginning with a definition of the concept of *bayān* and then proceeding to the analysis of words (*lafẓ*), morphology, and syntax. A second volume investigates the figurative level of language (*majāz*), the syntactic features of the sentence, then includes a large section on the categories of *badīʿ* before finishing with sections on poetic metres and rhyme (the last incorporating a discussion of the rhyme schemes of both *muwashshaḥ* and *zajal*). Al-Marṣafī's work is thus a genuine piece of neo-classicism, a nineteenth-century capstone gesture that recreates for a new generation of Egyptian students the tradition of Arabic criticism as reflected in the great collections that we have just described. In spite of the work's essentially retrospective qualities however, we need to recall that it was al-Marṣafī for whom Ṭāhā Ḥusayn (d. 1973), one of the greatest figures in twentieth-century Arabic criticism – to be discussed below, expressed enormous respect; it was to al-Marṣafī that his precocious pupil regularly reported on the foibles and defective pedagogy of his teachers at al-Azhar. Ṭāhā Ḥusayn is in many ways one of the symbols of the profound changes that were to have a major impact on the direction and nature of Arabic literary criticism. The pedagogical manual of his revered teacher thus serves as a fitting symbol of the turbulent era of cultural change during which it was composed.

CONTACTS WITH THE WEST AND THE TENSIONS OF CHANGE

The aesthetic principles espoused by the system of criticism that has just been described, with selections of the theories and opinions of its famous individual contributors gathered together in widely used compilations, were to serve as a strong conservative bastion against the incursion of new ideas of Western provenance that reached the Arab world during the nineteenth and early twentieth centuries. The tensions aroused by such confrontations are well illustrated by controversies that would regularly erupt in the press, that new and rapidly spreading mode of communication. One such episode in Egypt may serve as an example in that it involved some of the most important littérateurs of the time.

In 1898, Aḥmad Shawqī (d. 1932), the Egyptian court poet, published his collected poems (*Dīwān*) and prefaced them with a statement of his views about poetry. Looking at the classical tradition of Arabic poetry, he says, all he found were bombastic *qaṣīdahs* by the ancients and others imitating them. It was only when he turned to Europe and encountered Lamartine and La Fontaine that his ideas on poetry were truly formed. Such a statement could not and did not go unchallenged; it was taken up in a famous series of articles by Muḥammad al-Muwayliḥī (d. 1930), the renowned author of *Ḥadīth ʿĪsā ibn Hishām* discussed in ch. 5. His criticism begins by noting that in the past poets like Abū Tammām were subjected to exacting criticism; the practice, he suggests, should be continued. Shawqī is then criticised for his poor choice of poets as exemplars of the classical tradition, but above all for his failure to realise that the composition of poetry consists of that time-honoured pair, words and meanings (*alfāẓ* and *maʿānī*), and must thus inevitably involve a resort to the Arabic language and its poetic tradition. It is, no doubt, a reflection of the politics of the time that al-Muwayliḥī published no more than five of these articles, but the debate that he had started was continued in the Egyptian press by others, including another famous poet, Ḥāfiẓ Ibrāhīm (d. 1932). These critical remarks and the line by line, indeed word by word, analyses of some of Shawqī's poems, place al-Muwayliḥī firmly within the classical tradition of criticism as updated in the work of al-Marṣafī, thus providing us with a convenient turn-of-the-century point from which to assess the process of change that has occurred in Arabic literary criticism during the twentieth century.

One of the modern poets mentioned with admiration by Shawqī in his Introduction is Khalīl Muṭrān (d. 1949). This poet who emigrated to Egypt from Lebanon also wrote an introduction to his collected poems in 1908 in which he too declares his disappointment with the classical tradition, both the poetry itself and criticism of it – a further reflection, one might suggest, of the emphasis accorded certain aspects of the critical heritage over others in the processes of compilation and transmission. Muṭrān goes on to announce that he intends to forge his own poetic path in the modern world, untrammelled by metre or rhyme, and to concern himself with the unity of the poem. While the agenda of this brief statement (*bayān mūjaz*) have been considered by some critics as a pre-romantic gesture, we need to note also that its call for change finds little reflection in Muṭrān's poetry.

In fact it was the poets and critics of the next generation who mounted a challenge to the conservative values of the neo-classical poets and critics and brought the principles of romanticism to full flower; that this movement should come to prominence in a period in which pan-Arab and local nationalist sentiments were being vociferously expressed is, of course, no accident. In these critical endeavours, as in the literary genres that we have surveyed in previous chapters, much use was to be made of the growing library of translated works, a process that began in the nineteenth century and has expanded during the twentieth as the availability of books and journals has increased. This process has tended to be based mostly on the individual choice of the translator and has thus been somewhat haphazard (as has the translation movement in the opposite direction, it needs to be added); the Palestinian writer-critic Jabrā Ibrāhīm Jabrā characterised it as a 'series of chain explosions'. Even so, it has had the considerable benefit of introducing many of the major works of Western criticism into the modern Arabic cultural milieu.

The language competence that has been required in order to undertake this translation process is yet another reflection of the large number of Arab students who had studied in Western institutions and who returned with both enhanced foreign language skills and new approaches to the study of literary texts. These skills inevitably led to an increase of the extent to which those interested in the study of literature made use of critical writings in European languages. We learn, for example, that, when Najīb Maḥfūẓ decided early in his writing career to undertake a systematic survey of world literature, he turned to John Drinkwater's *The Outline of Literature*; the 'Dīwān School', whose impact we are about to consider, was much influenced by readings of Palgrave's collection of romantic poetry, *The Golden Treasury*. An interesting by-product of these modes of cultural transfer is that, in criticism as in creative writing, the influence of particular European literary traditions and their educational systems – and especially those of Britain and France – make themselves felt. To cite as examples two writers who contribute to both the creative and critical spheres, the Anglo-American influence on Jabrā, who wrote his first novel in English and translated part of Sir James Frazer's classic, *The Golden Bough* into Arabic, is as evident as the French on Adūnīs who has lectured at the Collège de France.

Arabic romantic poetry found its more radical early voice among the distant emigrant communities of the United States (*al-mahjar, the émigrés*), but the formulation of the critical principles of romanticism was most prominently elaborated in the Arab world itself by three Egyptian writers: Ibrāhīm ʿAbd al-qādir al-Māzinī (d. 1949), ʿAbbās Maḥmūd al-ʿAqqād (d. 1964), and ʿAbd al-raḥmān Shukrī (d. 1958). As early as 1909, al-ʿAqqad and Shukrī met and discovered that they were both much influenced not only by the English lyrical poetry of Byron, Shelley, and others, but also by the critical school of Hazlitt, Carlyle, Lamb, and Matthew Arnold. These predilections were further strengthened for Shukrī – the finest poet of the trio – when he spent three years studying at Sheffield University in England. Following his return in 1912, al-ʿAqqād and Shukrī combined with al-Māzinī to form a powerful new critical force. All three writers penned a number of articles in which they called for an end to the traditional artifice and rhetoric of poetry and sought instead a greater emphasis on poetic unity and the role of the individual poet (and thus an end to patronised verse forms), and on the centrality of emotion and the subjective in creating poetry. In citing these principles to advocate a new approach to poetry, these critics were, needless to say, mounting a direct assault on the bastion of neo-classical poetry as personified in Egypt by the work of such illustrious poets as Aḥmad Shawqī and Ḥāfiẓ Ibrāhīm. Their attacks reached an acme in a two-volume publication that appeared in 1921 under the title *al-Dīwān*. While al-Māzinī used the occasion to savage the sentimental and somewhat pompous prose musings of Muṣṭafā Luṭfī al-Manfalūṭī (d. 1924), al-ʿAqqād took on a relatively easy target – one of Shawqī's sonorous occasional odes (an elegy of the nationalist hero, Muṣṭafā Kāmil). Rearranging the lines with minimal effect, he showed in pedantic detail that the poem is 'a disjointed collection of verses with only rhyme and metre as a unifying factor' (*al-Dīwān* II, 1921, p. 45). By the time *al-Dīwān* was published, this trio of Egyptian poet-critics influenced by the English romantics had torn itself apart through internal dissension: in 1916 Shukrī had accused al-Māzinī of plagiarising English poets in some of his poems, and this led to unpleasant exchanges that culminated in a violent attack by al-Māzinī on his former friend, Shukrī, in *al-Dīwān* in which the latter was said to be suffering from delusions. With all this contumely in mind, it is particularly unfortunate that this group of critics, originally termed the 'English group', is now generally known as the Dīwān School. In fact, al-Māzinī came to recognise that his talents lay elsewhere and concentrated on fictional writing. Al-ʿAqqād however continued to make contributions to both poetry and criticism; opinion is virtually unanimous in stating that he had a far more significant role in the latter than the former. He was in every sense a 'man of ideas', and for several generations of Egyptians his works served as an introduction to Western writings on not only poetry and poetics, but also philosophy, religion, and natural science. Among his more interesting, if dated, contributions to criticism were a series of studies in which he examined the 'personalities' of several prominent classical poets – al-Mutanabbī, ibn al-Rūmī, and Abū Nuwās, for example – and the impact of physical and mental attributes on their writing. Later in his career al-ʿAqqād, the perennial polemicist, found himself upholding a set of aesthetic principles that were clearly in confrontation with the rapidly changing cultural values of his homeland and the Arab world in general. Already in the 1940s we encounter a case of 'the biter bit' when one of his own poems was subjected to the very same treatment he had meted out to Shawqī's poem in *al-Dīwān*, and in the next decade Aḥmad ʿAbd al-muʿṭī Ḥijāzī (b. 1935), one of the most prominent modern Egyptian poets, delivered a stinging retort to al-ʿAqqād for the latter's decision to send all submissions to a poetry festival in Damascus that were not metrical and rhymed to the prose panel:

> You who have something to say on every topic, whereas
> you are barely competent in any of them,
> to you I address this lampoon...
> In our age you live as a guest, and yet you abuse us.
> We are the ones who chant to its pulse
> and afford the days what they demand,
> whereas with you history has lost its sense of purpose...

One could hardly wish for a more graphic illustration of Jabrā's series of 'chain-explosions' referred to above.

The work of al-ʿAqqād and his colleagues served a crucial role in the development of modern Arabic poetry by weakening the ties that bound it to the classical tradition and thereby opening up the field to new ideas and directions. The path that they helped to establish in the Arab world itself (through their criticism more than their poetry, as we suggested above) found itself exemplified by the poetry of their predominantly Syro-Lebanese colleagues in the Americas. It is indeed a sign of al-ʿAqqād's important position as a critic that he was asked by Mīkhāʾīl Nuʿaymah (d. 1988), the most prominent critic of the *mahjar* school, to write the introduction to his own significant contribution to the early development of modern Arabic literary criticism, *al-Ghurbāl* (The Sieve), which appeared in 1923. Like *al-Dīwān*, *al-Ghurbāl* was a summary of ideas that had been developing in the author's mind for several years, but it differs from the Egyptian work in its detached and less polemical tone. It too seeks to rid Arabic poetry of its preoccupation with the decorative and to liberate the Arabic language itself so that it can explore new structures and images; the chapter in which these issues are discussed is entitled 'the croaking of frogs'. The spirit of romanticism is clearly reflected in Nuʿaymah's complaint that in the Arab world the poet tends to speak with the tongue and not the heart; the poet, he suggests, needs to be someone who 'feels' (the literal meaning of *shāʿir*, 'poet'), and it should be the role of poetry to convey an emotion from the soul of the poet to that of the listener. Nuʿaymah also has some interesting comments on the role of the critic. As the title of his volume suggests, it is the critic's function to sift, but to sift writings rather than writers. A severe problem faced by Arabic literature in his time, he notes, is the lack of competent critics.

Turning now to a consideration of what might be dubbed the French school, we can begin with that young Egyptian student, Muḥammad Ḥusayn Haykal (d. 1956), who, as was noted in ch. 5, returned from his period of study in France with the text of a novel, *Zaynab*. In addition to that important contribution to Arabic fiction, Haykal also came home with a firm grasp of French critical principles and a desire to apply them to his own literary heritage. Under the initial tutelage of Aḥmad Luṭfī al-Sayyid (d. 1963), an Egyptian journalist and intellectual who, through his positions as editor of the newspaper, *al-Jarīdah*, and university educator, was to serve as mentor to a whole generation of young Egyptian writers, Haykal caught the nationalist mood of the times by supporting the notion of an Egyptian literature (and other national literatures) that would reflect the spirit of each nation. The Egyptian example would permit its writers to exploit the continuity of its cultural history from Pharaonic times to the present, the former being much in the public eye following the discovery of Tutankhamun's tomb in 1922. Haykal also acknowledges a direct debt to Hippolyte Taine (d. 1893) in advocating the need for an objective, scientific critical method, based on the study of works of art as a product of their social and temporal environment. Later in his career Haykal became more involved in journalism and politics; in his writings he moved away from the presentation of Western civilisation and its accomplishments to more traditional Islamic themes. The banner of literary criticism was carried forward by his contemporary, Ṭāhā Ḥusayn (d. 1973), without question one of the most significant figures in the whole of modern Arabic literature.

Blind from the age of two, Ṭāhā Ḥusayn initially received a thoroughly traditional Islamic education which provided him with a complete grounding in the classics of Arabo-Islamic culture. As part of that process, he attended al-Azhar mosque-university in Cairo where, in addition to lectures on the traditional topics of higher religious education, he came under the influence of Ḥusayn al-Marṣafī (whose *al-Wasīlah al-adabiyyah* was noted above) and other more progressive pedagogues. With their encouragement, Ṭāhā Ḥusayn moved across the city and began studies at the new secular university (now the University of Cairo). The courses on history and literature were a revelation to him, and he was soon recognised by his mentors (including, yet again, Aḥmad Luṭfī al-Sayyid) as a brilliant prospect; by 1914 he had completed a doctoral degree with a thesis on the blind poet, Abū al-ʿAlāʾ al-Maʿarrī. He was sent to France for further study and, having completed a second doctoral thesis on ibn Khaldūn, returned to Egypt in 1919. Like other scholars who had returned from Europe, he was eager to apply to the Arabic literary heritage some of the objective principles that he had studied in France. In order to illustrate these ideas, he selected a topic that could hardly have been more controversial: his renowned work, *Fī al-shiʿr al-jāhilī* (On pre-Islamic poetry, 1926), examines the texts of the Qurʾān itself and pre-Islamic poetry, its linguistic precursor and thus a primary canonical source for Arabic. Clearly announcing his intention to study the texts involved according to scientific principles and without preconceptions, he concludes not only that the Qurʾān contains narratives that are fables but also that portions of the corpus of pre-Islamic poetry appear to date from the Islamic period and thus to be fake. This attack by a Western-educated Muslim son of Egypt on the sanctity of the Qurʾān itself and the poetic tradition that preceded it aroused a firestorm of controversy, as a result of which the book had to be withdrawn; it was reissued in revised form as *Fī al-adab al-jāhilī* (On pre-Islamic literature, 1927), with the offending section on the Qurʾān removed, but the other parts expanded. It needs to be pointed out that this furore over the 'authenticity' of the earliest stages in the Arabic poetic tradition (and the simultaneous argument on the same topic put forward by A. J. Arberry) antedate the pioneering research of Parry and Lord regarding the nature of oral-performance practice. However, even though such theories have cast new light on the nature of authenticity within such a tradition and have thus rendered the arguments surrounding Ṭāhā Ḥusayn's work invalid, they do not diminish the significance of this episode as a turning-point in the intellectual life of the Arab world in the twentieth century. For the student generation of Egypt at the time – and Najīb Maḥfūẓ was one of them – the sheer drama of the episode and the new stance towards the study of literary texts that it represented were to have a major impact on the future direction of literature studies.

This incident and its consequences made Ṭāhā Ḥusayn the *bête-noire* of the establishment and hero of the younger generation. He now proceeded to use his prominent position in the cultural life of his country as a platform through which to educate an entire generation about the treasures of the Arabic literary heritage. He may have described his methodological aim as being to introduce 'scientific' criteria into the evaluation of literary texts, but there remained a strong element of subjectivity in his judgements. However, the breadth of his erudition and the critical acumen with which he addressed the literary tradition guaranteed that his contributions to the development of modern criticism would be of major significance. Following his studies of al-Maʿarrī and ibn Khaldūn, he addressed himself to a number of classical figures in both poetry and prose; his weekly talks on radio devoted to prominent figures and genres in Arabic literary history were gathered together into volumes under the title *Ḥadīth al-arbaʿāʾ* (Wednesday Talk, 1926 *et seq.*). From the classical period, topics include the *muʿallaqah* poets, the *ghazal*, a series of chapters on the clash between the ancients and modernists that we have discussed above, and perceptive analyses of the work of individual poets such as Bashshār ibn Burd. In the third collection, he considers some contributions to modern literature, and here his critical comments assume a tone more redolent of a schoolmaster's function. Those who receive his plaudits, such as Tawfīq al-Ḥakīm for his pioneering efforts in drama, find their reputations enhanced thereby. However, Ṭāhā Ḥusayn is ever the guardian of the sanctity of the Arabic language, and in this area few authors escape unscathed; when the young Yūsuf Idrīs (d. 1991) published his second collection of short stories, *Jumhūriyyat Farḥāt* (Farḥāt's Republic, 1956), Ṭāhā Ḥusayn's preface upbraided the author for using the language of the street.

This question of language use provides a link to another significant aspect of Ṭāhā Ḥusayn's career. In 1938 he published a broad-scaled assessment of Egypt's cultural status, *Mustaqbal al-thaqāfah fī Miṣr* (The Future of Culture in Egypt), in which he suggested that, in order to become part of the modern world, Egypt should stress its more Mediterranean aspect and use the virtues of European culture–cultural, societal, and political – as models for emulation. However, while advocating such a posture, he remains in this work and indeed for the rest of his life a stalwart defender of the written Arabic language as the basis of literary culture and deplores the notion that the colloquial language might become an appropriate medium for literary creativity, declaring that the spoken language of the populace is nothing but a corrupt version of the written. Ṭāhā Ḥusayn himself insisted on speaking the written form of the language on all occasions; during what I had planned to be an interview with him at his home in 1967, I soon found that I was the one under interrogation as my carefully acquired competence in the colloquial dialect of Cairo was systematically corrected. My delight at meeting this famous figure and gleaning so much information from him was tempered by a certain chagrin at the inquisition which it entailed; my feelings however were considerably alleviated when one week later I watched him mete out the very same treatment to a hapless television interviewer.

During the course of his long career as a teacher Ṭāhā Ḥusayn trained many illustrious students. We have already encountered Suhayr al-Qalamāwī in the context of studies on the *Thousand and One Nights*; another was Muḥammad Mandūr (d. 1965). In discussing above the earlier periods of literary criticism we have already noted some of Mandūr's comments; they come from his doctoral thesis, later published as *al-Naqd al-manhajī ʿinda al-ʿArab* (Systematic Criticism Among the Arabs, 1948), a work that, in tracing the predominant trends in classical criticism, decries the influence of Qudāmah ibn Jaʿfar while assigning al-Āmidī and his *al-Muwāzanah* a key role in the development of 'systematic criticism'. Upon his return from a period of study in Paris that was interrupted by the Second World War, Mandūr began to write articles for the cultural magazine, *al-Thaqāfah*; many of those that were clustered around particular topics were gathered together in a very influential book, *Fī al-mīzān al-jadīd* (In the New Balance, 1944). Mandūr here acknowledges the influence on his thinking of the renowned French literary historian, Gustave Lanson (d. 1934), who had been one of Ṭāhā Ḥusayn's teachers; a selection of his writings had been translated into Arabic by Mandūr. The collection contains significant sections on the work of the playwright Tawfīq al-Ḥakīm, a renewed look at the critics of the earlier period and especially ʿAbd al-qāhir al-Jurjānī, and a segment on metrics, but the one that attracted the most critical attention discusses what he terms 'whispered poetry' (*al-shiʿr al-mahmūs*). Here Mandūr examines the various schools of romantic poetry, including the Mahjar school as exemplified by the famous poem '*Akhī*' (My Brother) by Mīkhā'īl Nu'aymah, discussed in ch. 4; he extols its more muted qualities as opposed to the loud, rhetorical tones of traditional poetry as revived by the neo-classical poets. In addition to writing these important studies of early and modern criticism, Mandūr had become closely involved in the political life of his country during the turbulent period that led up to the 1952 Revolution and thereafter; for that reason it is not surprising that he should adopt the more *engagé* attitude that emerges from his later writings. This change takes its most explicit form in *Qaḍāyā jadīdah fī adabinā al-ḥadīth* (New Issues in Our Modern Literature, 1958), where once again his title suggests the thought of a critical mind that is constantly aware of what is new and transforming. Mandūr's career and the extent to which he was prepared to see the need to change his critical approaches seems to reflect the forces of change that have had such a major impact on the Arabic literary tradition since the Second World War. Thus, while a prominent figure like al-'Aqqād seemed unwilling to make any compromises with those forces as they emerged during the post-Revolution period, Mandūr espoused the goals of commitment that were to be the rallying-cry of writers in the 1950s and beyond. While his political and academic career may have had their share of disappointments, he was a much revered figure; it is surely a tribute to his status in Egyptian cultural life that his persona, sporting a large hat, is present as a member of the incorporated 'audience' in Yūsuf Idrīs's experimental play, *Al-Farāfīr* (The Farfūrs), staged just one year before Mandūr's death in 1965.

Among these major figures who developed a critical base for modern Arabic literature studies, mention should also be made of a Lebanese writer who actually was a schoolmaster, Mārūn 'Abbūd (d. 1962). While the developments that we have just described in the Egyptian context and the polemics surrounding them preoccupied much of the attention of the intellectual community in the Arab world, 'Abbūd maintained a watchful eye on the literary output of his own and other countries in the region. He is the author of one of the relatively few histories of the Arabic literary tradition written in Arabic; organised along dynastic lines, it includes an unusually large coverage of the 'medieval' period and indeed of the modern where emphasis is on Syro-Lebanon (including the American school) but Shawqī and al-Manfalūṭī are also given brief recognition. It finishes with an interesting section on criticism itself, showing very clearly 'Abbūd's practical and pedagogical intent. To interpret a text, he says, you need to know not only about the author and his works but also details of the social environment. With this knowledge at hand, the text can be read and its particular features can be identified. With such a common-sense approach, with a remarkable tolerance for change and experiment, and, above all, with a healthy dislike of pomposity and posturing, ʿAbbūd provided his students and the Arab world at large with a whole series of collected pieces of literary criticism with such colourful titles as *ʿAlā al-miḥakk* (On the Touchstone, 1946) and *Dimaqs wa-urjuwan* (Silk and Scarlet, 1952). When roused, he was capable of a withering sarcasm, as when al-ʿAqqād published a poetry collection, *ʿĀbir sabīl* (Passer-by, 1937), aimed at introducing a common touch by addressing mundane topics. The truly inspired poet, ʿAbbūd says, does not need to state credos or indulge in such stunts; al-ʿAqqād is nothing more than a child playing with butterflies, and the sheer size of his output makes him the Arab equivalent of the Ford Motor Company.

The bulk of critical attention among these central figures in the development of modern Arabic criticism was devoted to poetry, the genre that had predominated during the pre-modern period and retained its central position within the culture well into the twentieth century. Among the pioneers in the analysis of prose genres from the earlier period was yet another Egyptian returnee from study in Paris, Zakī Mubārak, who managed to accrue enough doctoral degrees to insist on being referred to as Drs. While he seems to have regarded the publication of critical attacks on Ṭāhā Ḥusayn as something akin to an avocation, he is most remembered for his pioneering study, *La prose arabe au IVe siècle de l'Hégire (Xe siècle)* (Paris, 1931), originally his Paris thesis and later published in Arabic, in which he analyses the works of many of the more famous exponents of *adab* discussed above in ch. 5, including al-Tanūkhī, al-Thaʿālibī, and al-Hamadhānī. In the study of modern prose the situation was also gradually changing: the new genres of fiction were steadily gaining in popularity and, at some undefined point in the post-independence period, were to become the most popular form of literary expression.

THE AFTERMATH OF INDEPENDENCE: COMMITMENT AND BEYOND

As we noted in ch. 2, the decade of the 1950s was one during which many Arab states achieved the independence for which they had long struggled. The period immediately preceding this transforming decade – one that witnessed the political and social consequences of the end of the Second World War, had been particularly fractious; the confrontation between colonisers and colonised had intensified, often erupting into riots and assassinations. However, the advent of independence – a process in which politically disparate opposition groups had united their efforts – did not work in the interests of all those who had opposed the *anciens régimes*. While certain members of the older cultural élite tended to become politically marginalised (for example, at the time of the Egyptian Revolution, Ṭāhā Ḥusayn himself was serving as Minister of Education), a new generation set itself to develop a significant role for literature and its evaluation within the context of the new political and social realities. The rallying-cry of the era was 'literature with a purpose' (*al-adab al-hādif*), gathered around the concept of commitment (*iltizām*). While much inspiration was drawn at the time from Sartre's 'Qu'est que la littérature?' (1947) and its notion of *engagement*, the inspiration for the movement can be traced back to an earlier period. The ideas of socialism, introduced into the Arab world by such pioneers as Shiblī Shumayyil (d. 1917) and Faraḥ Anṭūn (d. 1922), had been developed in the writings of Salāmah Mūsā (d. 1947), a Coptic intellectual who laid great stress in his autobiography on the role that the English Fabians and writers like Ibsen and Nietzsche had played in his own education and who aroused the ire of conservative scholars by suggesting that much of the heritage of Arabic literature consisted of writings for the élite that were of little relevance to the needs of the Arab world in his generation. Through his role as both mentor and publisher, Mūsā was a major influence on an entire generation of younger writers, including Najīb Maḥfūẓ and Lewis ʿAwaḍ (d. 1994?), a critic of major importance. ʿAwaḍ's translation of Shelley's *Prometheus Unbound* was published in 1947; in the introduction he suggests that the English poet's romanticism is in fact an expression of middle-class reaction against the values of the aristocracy. In an iconoclastic manifesto that accompanies his poetry collection, *Plutoland*, published in the same year, he opens with the disarming statement that, while poetry itself is not dead, Arabic poetry is. These were just some among many expressions in the Arab world of a rapidly changing critical scenario that reflected a much broader political and social discontent. In periodicals and books, a number of intellectuals introduced Marxist notions regarding the function of literature and the littérateur in society: in Lebanon Raʾīf al-Khūrī and Ḥusayn Muruwwah (d. 1987), and in Syria ʿUmar al-Fākhūrī, who, besides editing a journal, *al-Ṭalīʿah* (The Vanguard), published a work under the title *al-Adīb fī al-sūq* (The Littérateur in the Market, 1944).

A major turning-point in this process of transformation occurs in

January 1953, with the appearance of the first issue of *al-Ādāb*, the Beirut monthly edited by Suhayl Idrīs, which announced the principles of commitment as its guiding criteria and has served in the intervening period as a major advocate and reflector of change in Arabic literature. The 1950s were, as noted above and elsewhere, a period of *élan* and optimism in the Arab world, and for the newly installed régimes in many countries the commitment of its creative writers to the support of causes espoused by the government was regarded as a matter of course. A new generation of creative writers took to this task with relish, and a number of 'realistic' works in a variety of genres, many of them establishing new levels of technical excellence, began to appear. When the causes to be addressed included the dire fate of the Palestinian people following the disastrous war of 1948 and the plight of peasantry working the land and of the poor in the inner cities, such principles could and did lead to the appearance of works in poetry and prose that were not only significant weapons in the hands of those who would bring about change but also valuable additions to the literary tradition. However, the results of such orchestrated sets of expectations, conveyed by officialdom with varying degrees of subtlety, were not always of enduring merit, and, as a publication such as the *Index of Censorship* reveals in depressing detail, the consequences of a creative writer's failure or unwillingness to 'toe the official line' could often be severe; if imprisonment or execution were not the sentence, then the remaining options were either silence or exile.

This enthusiastic advocacy of *engagé* literature by the critics noted above and others led, not surprisingly, to some notable debates that pitted the younger generation against the guardians of the traditional heritage. In 1955, two Egyptian critics, ʿAbd al-ʿaẓīm Anīs and Maḥmūd Amīn al-ʿĀlim, published *Fī al-thaqāfah al-Miṣriyyah* (On Egyptian Culture) in which they encapsulated many of the arguments that had been debated in a newspaper-article joust with, among others, Ṭāhā Ḥusayn and al-ʿAqqād. Literature, they suggested, could no longer adopt an 'ivory-tower' attitude and indulge in the detached effusions of romantic (and especially symbolist) poets or the lengthy philosophical contemplations of al-Ḥakīm's plays. For Anīs and al-ʿĀlim, and indeed for other critics like Khūrī and Ḥusayn Muruwwah, the littérateur was under an obligation to write for a general public. When we bear in mind the critical views of Ṭāhā Ḥusayn noted above, it is no surprise that he should react strongly to these ideas; indeed in 1955 he participated in a formal debate on the topic in Beirut with Raʾīf al-Khūrī. He did so by suggesting that, when literature concerns itself so directly with the material, it loses its precious attribute as nourishment for the spiritual side of humanity. Views such as these, however, did not find a wide audience among a post-revolutionary generation that was being fed on a continuing diet of optimistic propaganda; whence the shattering blow to the Arab consciousness that followed yet another defeat, that of 1967 – the so-called *naksah* (setback).

The nature and pace of the changes represented by these debates inevitably had a significant effect on the relationship between creative writing and criticism. To cite just one illustration, two Iraqi poets, Badr Shākir al-Sayyāb (d. 1956) and Nāzik al-Malā'ikah (b. 1923) simultaneously but separately composed poems in 1947 that challenged the long-standing criteria of Qudāmah ibn Jaʿfar regarding the metre and rhyme of Arabic poetry. When al-Malā'ikah's poem was published in the collection, *Shaẓāyā wa-ramād* (Splinters and Ashes, 1949), she prefaced it with an explanation that, by making adjustments to the requirement of al-Khalīl's system, she was liberating the poet from the shackles of tradition, a view that she later elaborated in her book, *Qaḍāyā al-shiʿr al-muʿāṣir* (Problems of Contemporary Poetry, 1962). While indeed these poems did represent a radical shift away from the prescriptive dictates of the classical tradition of criticism, giving the Arabic poem a completely new look on the page and inevitably arousing the opposition of conservative critics, the floodgates of innovation and change that had been opened by this and other gestures were not content with the prospect of replacing one set of rules with another. The process of freeing verse from the confines of tradition proceeded to expand the domain and aesthetic of poetry, not least through the advent of the prose poem. When Adūnīs, Arabic's most radical contemporary poet, announces that the purpose of poetry is to change the meanings of words and that the content of each individual poem will determine afresh what its structure will be, he is, among other things, confirming the end to any notion of prescriptive criticism.

CONCLUSION

As is the case with the literary genres examined in previous chapters, developments in modern Arabic literary criticism constitute a process of blending whereby an awareness of Western ideas (and particularly those associated with disciplines such as linguistics, folklore, and psychology) has interacted with a re-examination of the heritage of the past. Translations of Western writings on semiotics, structuralism, and narratology, for example, have led to the appearance of a number of critical and theoretical works in Arabic that not only confront the principles of the Arabic literary canon (in the realms of prosodic analysis and popular narrative, for example), but also suggest entirely new ways of looking at literary genres from a variety of periods within the literary heritage. In addition to works that have appeared in book form, the principal avenue through which these new ideas have been fostered has been the pages of a number of distinguished literary journals; a short list, in addition to the already mentioned *al-Ādāb*, would include *Alif*, *al-Aqlām*, *Fuṣūl*, *al-Fikr*, *Mawāqif*, and *al-Mawqif al-adabī*.

The principles of linguistics provide a basis for the work of many contemporary Arabic critics, an apt reflection of the situation in the West; among several possible exemplars we would list Salāḥ Fadl, Kamāl Abū Dīb, and Maurice Abū Nādir. For other interpreters of modern Arabic literature, the theoretical underpinnings are less specific: ʿIzz al-din Ismāʿīl, Muḥammad Bannīs, and Jābir ʿUṣfūr with poetry; Laḥmadāni Ḥamīd, Ṣabrī Ḥāfiẓ, and ʿAbd al-fattāh Kilito with prose. As critic, Adūnīs has endeavoured to take in the entire literary tradition in a sweeping survey, most notably in *al-Thābit wa-al-mutaḥawwil* (The Static and Dynamic) but also in other, more recent, works. From the perspective of a contemporary Arab writer who is a student of cultural traditions and the way they change, he insists that the past cannot be treated as a fixed entity forever frozen in time, but must be reinterpreted in accordance with the ideologies and methods, and therefrom with the insights, of the present. It is in the very act of (re-)discovering the essence of that past, he suggests, that the Arab writer will become aware of the nature of the 'modern'.

Guide to further reading

2 THE CONTEXTS OF THE LITERARY TRADITION

The works cited below are intended as a representative sample, selected for their comprehensive approach.

al-Azmeh, Aziz, *Arabic Thought and Islamic Societies*, London: Croom Helm, 1986.

Arabic literature to the end of the Umayyad Period, Cambridge History of Arabic Literature, vol. 1. Cambridge: Cambridge University Press, 1983.

Badran, Margot and Cooke, Miriam (eds.) *Opening the Gates: A Century of Arab Feminist Writing*, London: Virago Press, 1990.

Barakat, Halim, *The Arab World: Society, Culture, and State*, Berkeley: University of California Press, 1993.

Bosworth, C. E., *The Islamic Dynasties*, Islamic Surveys, no. 5, Edinburgh: Edinburgh University Press, 1967.

Boullata, Issa, J., *Trends and Issues in Contemporary Arabic Thought*, Albany, New York: State University of New York Press, 1990.

Caton, Steven C., *Peaks of Yemen I Summon: Poetry as Cultural Practice in a North Yemeni tribe*, Berkeley: University of California Press, 1990.

Endress, Gerhard, *An Introduction to Islam*, trans. Carole Hillenbrand, New York: Columbia University Press, 1988.

Eph'al, Israel, *The Ancient Arabs: Nomads on the Borders of the Fertile Crescent 9th–5th Centuries B.C.*, Leiden: E. J. Brill, 1982.

Hourani, Albert, *History of the Arab Peoples*, New York: Warner Books, 1991.

Lapidus, Ira, *A History of Islamic Societies*, Cambridge: Cambridge University Press, 1988.

Laroui, Abdallah, *The Crisis of the Arab Intellectual*, trans. Diarmid Cammell, Berkeley, California: University of California Press, 1976.

Makdisi, George, *the Rise of Colleges*, Edinburgh: Edinburgh University Press, 1981.

Makdisi, George, *The Rise of Humanism*, Edinburgh: Edinburgh University Press, 1990.

Rosenthal, Franz, *Knowledge Triumphant*, Leiden: E. J. Brill, 1970.

Rosenthal, Franz, *A History of Muslim Historiography*, Leiden: E. J. Brill, 1968.

Schacht, Joseph and Bosworth, C. Edmund (eds.), *The Legacy of Islam*, Oxford: Clarendon Press, 1974.

Watt, Montgomery, *Islamic Philosophy and Theology*, Islamic Surveys, no. 1, Edinburgh: Edinburgh University Press, 1962, 1964.

3 THE QUR'ĀN: SACRED TEXT AND CULTURAL YARDSTICK

Even if listings are restricted mostly to works in English, the number of publications devoted to the Qur'ān that might be included here is enormous. The works that are listed are those that are pertinent to a literary approach to the text of the Qur'ān.

ENGLISH VERSIONS OF THE QUR'ĀN (A SELECTION)

Arberry, A. J., *Thr Koran Interpreted*, London: George Allen & Unwin, 1955; New York: Macmillan, 1986.

The Koran, trans. N. J. Dawood, London: Penguin Classics, 1956.

STUDIES ON THE QUR'ĀN

Bellamy, James, 'The Mysterious Letters of the Koran: Old Abbreviations of the *Basmalah*', *Journal of the American Oriental Society*, vol. 93 (1973): 267–85.

Burton, J., *The Collection of the Qur'ān*, Cambridge: Cambridge University Press, 1977.

Gätje, Helmut (ed.), *Grundriss der Arabischen Philologie: II Literaturwissenschaft*, Wiesbaden: Reichert Verlag, 1987, pp. 96–135.

Graham, William A., *Beyond the Written Word: Oral Aspects of Scripture in the History of Religion*, Cambridge: Cambridge University Press, 1987.

Hawting, G. R., and Shareef, Abdul-Kader A. (eds.), *Approaches to the Qur'ān*, London: Routledge, 1993.

Heinrichs, Wolfhart (ed.), *Neues Handbuch der Literaturwissenschaft: Orientalisches Mittelalter*, Wiesbaden: AULA-Verlag, 1990, pp. 166–85.

Jeffrey, Arthur, *The Foreign Vocabulary of the Qur'*ān, Baroda: Oriental Institute, 1938.

Martin, Richard (ed.), *Approaches to Islam in Religious Studies*, Tucson, Arizona: University of Arizona Press, 1985.

Mir, Mustansir, 'Humor in the Qur'*ān, Muslim World*, vol. 81, nos. 3–4 (Jul.–Oct. 1991): 179–93.

Mir, Mustansir, 'The Qur'ān as literature', *Religion and Literature*, vol. 20, no. 1 (Spring 1988): 49–64.

Mir, Mustansir, 'The Qur'ānic Story of Joseph: Plot, Themes, and Characters', *Muslim World*, vol. 76, no. 1 (Jan. 1986): 1–15.

Nelson, Kristina, *The Art of Reciting the Qur'ān*, Austin: University of Texas Press, 1985.

Neuwirth, Angelica, *Studien zur Komposition der mekkanischen Suren*, Berlin: Walter de Gruyter, 1981.

Rippon, Andrew (ed.), *Approaches to the History of the Interpretation of the Qur'ān*, Oxford: Clarendon Press, 1988.

Sells, Michael, 'Sound, Spirit, and Gender in *Sūrat al-Qadr*', *Journal of the American Oriental Society*, vol. III, no. 2 (Apr.–Jun. 1991): 239–59.

Sells, Michael, 'Sound and meaning in *Sūrat al-Qāriʿa*', *Arabica* XL (1993): 403–30.

Stewart, Devin, 'Sajʿ in the Qur'ān: Prosody and Structure', *Journal of Arabic Literature*, vol. 21, part 2 (Sept. 1990): 101–39.

Wansbrough, J., *Qur'ān Studies: Sources and Methods of Scriptural Interpretation*, Oxford: Oxford University Press, 1977.

Watt, W. Montgomery, *Bell's Introduction to the Qur'ān*, Islamic Surveys no. 8, Edinburgh: Edinburgh University Press, 1970.

4 POETRY

ANTHOLOGIES IN TRANSLATION AND EDITIONS

Beeston, A. F. L. (ed.), *Selections from the Poetry of Bashshar*, Cambridge: Cambridge University Press, 1977.

Clouston, W. A., *Arabian Poetry for English Readers*, London: Darf Publishers, 1986.

Jayyusi, Salma Khadra (ed.), *Modern Arabic Poetry: An Anthology*, New York: Columbia University Press, 1987.

Jones, Alan (ed.), *Early Arabic Poetry*, vol. II: *Marāthī and Ṣuʿluk Poems*, Reading: Ithaca Press, 1992.

Nicholson, Reynold A., *Translations of Eastern Poetry and Prose*, Cambridge: Cambridge University Press, 1922.

Sells, Michael A., *Desert Tracings*, Middletown: Wesleyan University Press, 1989.

STUDIES

ʿ*Abbasid Belles-Lettres*, Cambridge History of Arabic Literature, vol. II, Cambridge: Cambridge University Press, 1990, esp. chs. 9–19.

Abu-Lughod, Lila, *Veiled Sentiments: Honor and Poetry in a Bedouin Society*, Berkeley: University of California Press, 1986.

Adonis, *An Introduction to Arab Poetics*, trans. Catherine Cobham, London: Saqi Books, 1990.

Arabic Literature to the end of the Umayyad Period, Cambridge History of Arabic Literature, vol. I, Cambridge: Cambridge University Press, 1983, esp. chs. 2, 18, 20, and 21.

Badawi, M. M., *A Critical Introduction to Modern Arabic Poetry*, Cambridge: Cambridge University Press, 1975.

Badawi, M. M. (ed.), *Modern Arabic Literature*, The Cambridge History of Arabic

Literature, Cambridge: Cambridge University Press, 1993, esp. chs. 1, 2, 3, 4, and 14.
Bailey, Clinton, *Bedouin Poetry from Sinai and the Negev*, Oxford: Clarendon Press, 1991.
Bannīs, Muḥammad, *Al-Shiʿr al-ʿArabī al-ḥadīth: bunyatuhu wa- ibdālātihā*, 4 vols., Casablanca: Dār Tubqāl, 1989–91.
Bencheikh, Jamaleddine, *Poétique arabe*, Paris: Editions Anthropos, 1975.
Caton, Steven C., *Peaks of Yemen I Summon: Poetry as Cultural Practice in a North Yemeni Tribe*, Berkeley: University of California Press, 1990.
Gätje, Helmut (ed.), *Grundriss der Arabischen Philologie: II Literaturwissenschaft*, Wiesbaden: Reichert Verlag, 1987, pp. 7–95.
Hamori, Andras, *On the Art of Medieval Arabic Literature*, Princeton: Princeton University Press, 1974.
Heinrichs, Wolfhart (ed.), *Neues Handbuch der Literaturwissenschaft: Orientalisches Mittelalter*, Wiesbaden: AULA-Verlag, 1990, pp. 142–165, 216–41, 284–300, 409–22, 440–64, 482–523.
Homerin, Th. Emil, *From Arab Poet to Muslim Saint: Ibn al-Farid, His Verse, and His Shrine*, Columbia: University of South Carolina Press, 1994.
Jayyusi, Salma Khadra, *Trends and Movements in Modern Arabic Poetry*, 2 vols., Leiden: E. J. Brill, 1977.
Kheir Beik, Kamal, *Le mouvement moderniste de la poésie arabe contemporaine*, Paris: Publications Orientalistes de France, 1978.
Kurpershoek, P. M., *Oral Poetry and Narratives from Central Arabia*, 3 vols., Leiden: E. J. Brill, 1994–96.
Meisami, Julie S., *Medieval Persian Court Poetry*, Princeton: Princeton University Press, 1987.
Moreh, S., *Modern Arabic Poetry 1800–1970*, Leiden: E. J. Brill, 1976.
Schimmel, Annemarie, *As Through a Veil: Mystical Poetry in Islam*, New York: Columbia University Press, 1982.
Sowayan, Saad A., *Nabati Poetry*, Berkeley: University of California Press, 1985.
Sperl, Stefan, *Mannerism in Arabic Poetry*, Cambridge: Cambridge University Press, 1989.
Sperl, Stefan and Shackle, Christopher (eds.), *Qasidah Poetry in Islamic Asia and Africa*, vol. I: *Classical Traditions and Modern Meanings*; vol. II: *Eulogy's Bounty, Meaning's Abundance: An Anthology*, Leiden: E. J. Brill, 1996.
Stetkevych, Jaroslav, *The Zephyrs of Najd: the Poetics of Nostalgia in the Classical Arabic nasib*, Chicago: University of Chicago Press, 1993.
Stetkevych, Suzanne P., *Abū Tammām and the Poetics of the ʿAbbāsid Age*, Leiden: E. J. Brill, 1991.
Stetkevych, Suzanne P., *The Mute Immortals Speak: Pre-Islamic Poetry and the Poetics of Ritual*, Ithaca: Cornell University Press, 1993.
Stetkevych, Suzanne P. (ed.), *Reorientations/Arabic and Persian Poetry*, Bloomington: Indiana University Press, 1994.
Zwettler, Michael, *The Oral Tradition of Classical Arabic Poetry*, Columbus: Ohio State University Press, 1978.

5 BELLETTRISTIC PROSE AND NARRATIVE

TRANSLATIONS

The Arabian Nights, trans. Husain Haddawy, New York: W. W. Norton & Co., 1990.

Arabic Short Stories, trans. Denys Johnson-Davies, Berkeley: University of California Press, 1994.

Badran, Margot and Cooke, Miriam (eds.), *Opening the Gates: a Century of Arab Feminist Writing*, London: Virago Press, 1990.

The Book of the Thousand Nights and a Night, trans. R. F. Burton, 10 vols., Benares, 1885.

Dunn, Ross E., *The Adventures of Ibn Baṭṭūṭa, a Muslim Traveler of the 14th Century*, Berkeley, California: University of California Press, 1989.

Guillaume, A., *The Life of Muhammad. A Translation of Ibn Isḥāq's Sīrat Rasūl Allāh*, London: Oxford University Press, 1955.

al-Hamadhānī, Badīʿ al-zamān, *The Maqāmāt of Badīʿ al-zamān al-Hamadhānī*, trans. W. J. Prenderghast, London: Curzon Press, 1973.

al-Ḥarīrī, al-Qāsim, *Makamat or Rhetorical Anecdotes of al-Hariri of Basra*, trans. Theodore Preston, London: W. H. Allen & Co., 1850 (reprint: Gregg International Publishers, 1971).

Ibn Shuhayd, *Treatise of Familiar Spirits and Demons*, trans. James T. Monroe, Berkeley: University of California Press, 1971.

Kassem, Ceza and Hashem, Malak (eds.), *Flights of Fantasy: Arabic Short Stories*, Cairo: Elias Modern Publishing House, 1985.

The Laṭāʾif al-maʿārif of Thaʿālibī, trans. C. E. Bosworth, Edinburgh: Edinburgh University Press, 1968.

Lewis, Bernard (ed.), *Islam from the Prophet Muhammad to the Capture of Constantinople*, 2 vols., New York: Harper and Row, 1974.

Lichtenstadter, Ilse, *Introduction to Classical Arabic Literature*, New York: Twayne Publishers, 1974.

Manzalaoui, Mahmoud (ed.), *Arabic Writing Today: the Short Story*, Cairo: American Research Center in Egypt, 1968.

Les Mille et Une Nuit [sic], trans. Antoine Galland, Paris, 1726.

Modern Arabic Short Stories, trans. Denys Johnson-Davies, Oxford: Oxford University Press, 1967.

Al-Qushayrī, *Principles of Sufism*, trans. B. R. von Schlegell, Berkeley: Mizan Press, 1990.

Al-Ṭabarī, *The History of al-Tabari*, 40 vols., Albany: State University of New York Press.

The Thousand and One Nights, trans. E. W. Lane, 3 vols., London, 1877.

STUDIES

ʿ*Abbasid Belles-Lettres*, Cambridge History of Arabic Literature vol. II, Cambridge: Cambridge University Press, 1990, esp. chs. 1–8.

Allen, Roger, *The Arabic Novel: an Historical and Critical Introduction*, 2nd edn, Syracuse: Syracuse University Press, 1995.

Allen, Roger, *Modern Arabic Literature*, Library of Literary Criticism Series, New York: Ungar, 1987.

Arabic Literature to the end of the Umayyad Period, Cambridge History of Arabic Literature, vol. 1, Cambridge: Cambridge University Press, 1983, esp. chs. 3, 4, 5, 10, 11, 13, 15, 16, 17 and 19.

Badawi, M. M. (ed.), *Modern Arabic Literature*. The Cambridge History of Arabic Literature, Cambridge: Cambridge University Press, 1993, esp. chs. 1, 5, 6, 7, 8, and 11.

Bencheikh, Jamal Eddine, *Les Mille et Une Nuits ou la Parole Prisonnière*, Paris: Gallimard, 1988.

Blachère, Régis, *Histoire de la littérature arabe des origines à la fin du XVe siècle de J-C*, vol. 3, Paris: Adrien-Maisonneuve, 1966, esp. part three, ch. 5 and 6.

Bosworth, C. Edmund, *The Mediaeval Islamic Underworld*, Leiden: E. J. Brill, 1976.

Bürgel, J. C., 'Repetitive Structures in Early Arabic Prose,' *Critical Pilgrimages: Studies in the Arabic Literary Tradition [Literature East and West]* ed. Fedwa Malti-Douglas, Texas: Department of Oriental and African Languages and Literatures, 1989: 49–64.

Gätje, Helmut (ed.), *Grundriss der arabischen Philologie* Band II: Literaturwissenschaft, Wiesbaden: Reichert Verlag, 1987, pp. 208–63.

Gerhardt, Mia, *The Art of Storytelling*, Leiden: E J. Brill, 1963.

Ghazoul, Ferial, *The Arabian Nights: a Structural Analysis*, Cairo: Associated Institution for the Study and Presentation of Arab Cultural Values, 1980.

Hafez, Sabry, *The Genesis of Arabic Narrative Discourse; a Study in the Sociology of Modern Arabic Literature*, London: Saqi Books, 1993.

Heinrichs, Wolfhart (ed.), *Neues Handbuch der Literatur-Wissenschaft*, Band 5: Orientalisches Mittelalter, Wiesbaden: AULA-Verlag, 1990, esp. pp. 326–45.

'Ḥikāya' in *Encyclopedia of Islam*, 2nd edn, Leiden: E. J. Brill, 1954, *et seq.*

Irwin, Robert, *The Arabian Nights: a Companion*, London: Penguin Books, 1995.

Khalidi, Tarif, *Arabic Historical Thought in the Classical Period*, Cambridge University Press, 1994.

Kilito, Abdelfattah, *L'auteur et ses doubles: essai sur la culture arabe classique*, Paris: Editions du Seuil, 1985.

Kilito, Abdelfattah, *L'oeil et l'aiguille*, Paris: Editions La Decouverte, 1992.

Kraemer, Joel L., *Humanism in the Renaissance of Islam*, Leiden: E. J. Brill, 1986.

Leder, Stefan and Kilpatrick, Hilary, 'Classical Arabic Prose Literature: a Researcher's Sketch Map', *Journal of Arabic Literature*, vol. 23, Part 1 (March 1992): 2–26.

Lyons, M. C., *The Arabic Epic: Heroic and Oral Story-Telling*, 3 vols., Cambridge: Cambridge University Press, 1995.

Makdisi, George, *The Rise of Humanism in Classical Islam and the Christian West*, Edinburgh: Edinburgh University Press, 1990.

Malti-Douglas, Fedwa, *Structures of Avarice: the Bukhalaʾ in Medieval Arabic Literature*, Leiden: E. J. Brill, 1985.

al-Maqdisī, Anīs, *Taṭawwur al-asālīb al-nathriyyah fī al-adab al-ʿArabī* (The Development of Prose Styles in Arabic Literature), Beirut: Dār al-ʿilm li-al-malāyīn, 1968.

Monroe, James T., *The Art of Badīʿ al-Zamān al-Hamadhānī as Picaresque Narrative*, Beirut: American University of Beirut, 1983.

Mubarak, Zaki, *La prose arabe au IVe siècle de l'Hégire (Xe siècle)*, Paris: Maisonneuve, 1931.

Pellat, Charles (ed.), *The Life and Works of Jāḥiẓ* trans. D. M. Hawke, Berkeley: University of California Press, 1969.

Pinault, David, *Story-telling Techniques in the Arabian Nights*, Leiden: E. J. Brill, 1992.

Religion, Learning and Science in the ʿAbbasid Period, Cambridge History of Arabic Literature, vol. III. Cambridge: Cambridge University Press, 1991, esp. chs. 5, 6, 11, 12, 13, and 17.

Rosenthal, *A History of Muslim Historiography*, Leiden: E. J. Brill, 1968.

Slyomovics, Susan, *The Merchant of Art: an Egyptian Hilai Oral Epic Poet in Performance*, Berkeley: University of California Press, 1987.

6 DRAMA

TRANSLATIONS

Anthologies

Arabic Writing Today: the Drama ed. Mahmoud Manzalaoui, Cairo: American Research Center in Egypt, 1977.

Mahmoud Taymour, 'The Court Rules'; Tewfiq al-Hakim, 'Song of Death' and 'The Sultan's Dilemma'; Mahmoud Diyab, 'The Storm'; Shawky Abdel-Hakim, 'Hassan and Naima'; Youssef Idris, Flipflap and His Master [*al-Farafir*]; Farouk Khorshid, 'The Wines of Babylon'; Mikhail Roman, 'The Newcomer'; Mohamed Maghout, 'The Hunchback Sparrow'.

Egyptian One-act Plays trans. Denys Johnson-Davies, London: Heinemann, and Washington: Three Continents Press, 1981.

Farid Kamil, 'The Interrogation'; Alfred Farag, 'The Trap'; Abdel-Moneim Selim, 'Marital Bliss'; Ali Salem, 'The Wheat Well'; Tewfiq al-Hakim, 'The Donkey Market'.

Modern Egyptian Drama, ed. Farouk Abdel Wahab, Minneapolis and Chicago, 1974.

Tawfiq al-Hakim, 'The Sultan's Dilemma'; Mikhail Roman, 'The New Arrival'; Rashad Rushdy, 'A Journey Outside the Wall'; 'Yusuf Idris, 'The Farfoors'.

Modern Arabic Drama, ed. Salma al-Jayyusi and Roger Allen, Indiana: Indiana University Press, 1995.

ʿIsam Mahfouz, 'The China Tree'; Mamdouh Udwan, 'That's Life'; Saʿdallah Wannus, 'The King is the King'; Walid al-Ikhlasi, 'The Path'; ʿIzz al-din al-Madani, 'The Zanj Revolution'; the Balalin Troupe, 'Darkness'; ʿAbd al-ʿAziz al-Surayyiʿ, 'The Bird Has Flown'; Yusuf al-ʿAni, 'The Key'; Salah ʿAbd al-Sabur, 'Night Traveller'; Alfred Farag, 'Ali Janah al-Tabrizi and His Servant Quffa'; ʿAli Salim, 'The Comedy of Oedipus, or You're the One who Killed the Beast'; Mahmoud Diyab, 'Strangers Don't Drink Coffee'.

INDIVIDUAL WRITERS

ʿAbd al-Sabur, Salah, *Murder in Baghdad* [Ma'sāt al-Ḥallāj] trans. Khalil I. Semaan, Leiden: E. J. Brill, 1972.

ʿAbd al-Sabur, Salah, *Night Traveller*, trans. M. M. Enani, Cairo: General Egyptian Book organization, 1980.

ʿAbd al-Sabur, Salah, *Now the King is Dead...*, trans. Nehad Selaiha, Cairo: General Egyptian Book Organization, 1986.

al-Hakim, Tawfiq, 'The Donkey Market', trans. Denys Johnson-Davies, in *Egyptian One-Act Plays*, Arab Authors Series 18. London: Heinemann, 1981, 101–118.

al-Hakim, Tawfiq, 'The Donkey Market', trans. Roger Allen, *Arab World* October–February 1971–72, 20–28. reprinted in *Small Planet*, New York: Harcourt Brace Jovanovich, 1975, 70–81.

al-Hakim, Tawfiq, *Fate of a Cockroach and Other Plays*, trans. Denys Johnson-Davies, Arab Authors Series 1. London: Heinemann, 1973. 'Fate of a Cockroach', 'The Song of Death', 'The Sultan's Dilemma', 'Not a Thing out of Place'.

al-Hakim, Tawfiq, *Plays, Prefaces and Postscripts of Tawfiq al-Ḥakīm*, trans. W. M. Hutchins, Washington: Three Continents Press, 1981.

al-Hakim, Tawfiq, 'The Wisdom of Solomon', 'King Oedipus', 'Shahrazad', 'Princess Sunshine', 'Angel's Prayer'.

al-Hakim, Tawfiq, *The Tree Climber*, trans. Denys Johnson-Davies, Arab Authors Series 17. London: Heinemann, 1980.

SOURCES

Allen, Roger, 'Egyptian Drama after the Revolution', *Edebiyat*, vol. 4, no. 1 (1979): 97–134.

Allen, Roger, 'Drama and Audience: the case of Arabic theater', *Theater Three*, no. 6 (Spring 1989): 7–20.

Badawi, M. M., *Early Arabic Drama*, Cambridge: Cambridge University Press, 1988.

Badawi, M. M., *Modern Arabic Drama in Egypt*, Cambridge: Cambridge University Press, 1988.

Badawi, M. M. (ed.), *Modern Arabic Literature*, Cambridge History of Arabic

Literature, Cambridge: Cambridge University Press, 1993.

Fontaine, Jean, *Aspects de la littérature tunisienne (1975–83)*, Tunis: RASM, 1985.

Gadtjè, Helmut (ed.), *Grundriss der arabischen Philologie*, Band II: Literaturwissenschaft, Wiesbaden: Reichert Verlag, 1987, pp. 244–48.

Al-Khozai, Mohamed A., *The Development of Early Arabic drama 1847–1900*, London: Longmans, 1984.

Landau, Jacob M., *Studies in the Arab Theater and Cinema*, Philadelphia: University of Pennsylvania Press, 1958.

Moosa, Matti, *The Origins of Modern Arabic Fiction*, Washington: Three Continents Press, 1983.

Moreh, Shmuel, *Live Theatre and Dramatic Literature in the Medieval Arabic World*, Edinburgh: Edinburgh University Press, 1992.

al-Rāʿī, ʿAlī, *Al-Masraḥ fī al-waṭan al-ʿarabī*, Kuwait: ʿAlam al-maʿrifah, 1980.

Slyomovics, Susan, '"To Put One's Finger in the Bleeding Wound": Palestinian Theatre under Israeli Censorship', *The Drama Review*, vol. 35, no. 2 (Summer 1991): 18–38.

Tomiche, Nada (ed.), *Le théâtre arabe*, Louvain: UNESCO, 1969.

SPECIFIC AUTHORS

Allen, Roger, 'Arabic Drama in Theory and Practice: the writings of Saʿdallāh Wannūs', *Journal of Arabic Literature*, 15 (1984): 94–113.

de Moor, C. M. (ed.), *Un oiseau en cage*, Amsterdam: Rodopi, 1991.

Fontaine, Jean, *Mort-resurrection: une lecture de Tawfīq al-Ḥakīm*, Tunis: Editions Bouslama, 1978.

Long, Richard, *Tawfīq al-Ḥakīm playwright of Egypt*, London: Ithaca Press, 1979.

Reid, Donald M., *The Odyssey of Farah Anṭūn*, Minneapolis & Chicago: Bibliotheca Islamica, 1975.

Starkey, Paul, *From the Ivory Tower: a critical study of Tawfīq al-Ḥakīm*, London: Ithaca Press, 1987.

7 THE CRITICAL TRADITION

ʿAbbās, Iḥsān, *Tārīkh al-naqd al-adabī ʿinda al-ʿArab* [History of Literary Criticism Among the Arabs], Beirut: Dār al-thaqāfah, 1971.

Abbasid Belles-Lettres, Cambridge History of Arabic Literature, vol. II, Cambridge: Cambridge University Press, 1990, chs. 20 and 21.

Abu Deeb, Kamal, *Al-Jurjānī's Theory of Poetic Imagery*, Warminster: Aris & Phillips, 1979.

Adonis, *An Introduction to Arab Poetics*, trans. Catherine Cobham, London: Saqi Books, 1985.

Ajami, Mansour, *The Alchemy of Glory*, Washington: Three Continents Press, 1988.

Ajami, Mansour, *The Neckveins of Winter*, Leiden: E. J. Brill, 1984.

Allen, Roger, *Modern Arabic Literature*, Library of Literary Criticism Series, New York: Ungar Publishing Company, 1987.

Badawi, M. M. (ed.), *Modern Arabic Literature*, Cambridge History of Arabic Literature, Cambridge: Cambridge University Press, 1993, ch. 12.

Bonebakker, Seeger A., 'Aspects of the History of Literary Rhetoric and Poetics in Arabic Literature', *Viator*, vol. I (1970): 75–95.

Bonebakker, Seeger A., 'Poets and Critics in the Third Century A.H.', in *Logic in Classical Arabic Culture.*

Brugman, J., *An Introduction to the History of Modern Arabic Literature in Egypt*, Leiden: E. J. Brill, 1984.

Cantarino, Vicente, *Arabic Poetics in the Golden Age*, Leiden: E. J. Brill, 1975.

Gätje, Helmut (ed.), *Grundriss der arabischen Philologie* Band II: Literaturwissenschaft, Wiesbaden: Reichert Verlag, 1987, pp. 177–207.

Heinrichs, Wolfhart and Allen, Roger, 'Arabic Poetics', in *The New Princeton Encyclopedia of Poetry & Poetics*, Princeton: Princeton University Press, 1993.

Religion, Learning and Science in the ʿAbbasid Period, Cambridge History of Arabic Literature, vol. III, Cambridge: Cambridge University Press, 1991, esp. chs. 4, 8, 22, and 23.

Semah, David, *Four Egyptian Literary Critics*, Leiden: E. J. Brill, 1974.

Stetkevych, Suzanne, *Abū Tammām & the Poetics of the ʿAbbasid Age*, Leiden: E. J. Brill, 1991.

van Gelder, G. J. H., *Beyond the Line: Classical Arabic Literary Critics on the Coherence and Unity of the Poem*, Leiden: E. J. Brill, 1982.

Index

NOTE

The majority of technical terms in this index are listed under their Arabic names, with cross-references to their English equivalents (as far as they exist).